DEVELOPMENTAL PSYCHOLOGY

Studies in Human Development

THE DORSEY SERIES IN PSYCHOLOGY

EDITOR HOWARD F. HUNT *Columbia University*

BARNETTE (ed.) *Readings in Psychological Tests and Measurements* rev. ed.

BENNIS, SCHEIN, STEELE, & BERLEW (eds.) *Interpersonal Dynamics: Essays and Readings on Human Interaction* rev. ed.

COURTS *Psychological Statistics: An Introduction*

DENNY & RATNER *Comparative Psychology: Research in Animal Behavior* rev. ed.

DESLAURIERS & CARLSON *Your Child Is Asleep: Early Infantile Autism*

DEUTSCH & DEUTSCH *Physiological Psychology*

FISKE & MADDI *Functions of Varied Experience*

FITZGERALD & MCKINNEY *Developmental Psychology: Studies in Human Development*

FLEISHMAN (ed.) *Studies in Personnel and Industrial Psychology* rev. ed.

FREEDMAN (ed.) *The Neuropsychology of Spatially Oriented Behavior*

HAMMER & KAPLAN *The Practice of Psychotherapy with Children*

HENDRY *Conditioned Reinforcement*

KLEINMUNTZ *Personality Measurement: An Introduction*

KOLSTOE *Introduction to Statistics for the Behavioral Sciences*

LIEBERT & SPIEGLER *Personality: An Introduction to Theory and Research*

MADDI *Personality Theories: A Comparative Analysis*

MARKEL *Psycholinguistics: An Introduction to the Study of Speech and Personality*

ROZEBOOM *Foundations of the Theory of Prediction*

VON FIEANDT *The World of Perception*

DEVELOPMENTAL PSYCHOLOGY

STUDIES IN HUMAN DEVELOPMENT

Edited by

HIRAM E. FITZGERALD, Ph.D.
Assistant Professor of Psychology

and

JOHN PAUL McKINNEY, Ph.D.
Associate Professor of Psychology

Both of Michigan State University

1970 | THE DORSEY PRESS, Homewood, Illinois
IRWIN-DORSEY LIMITED, Georgetown, Ontario

First Printing, May, 1970

Library of Congress Catalog Card No. 73–118192

Printed in the United States of America

To Dolores and Madeleine

PREFACE

SEEMINGLY, the explicit purpose of collected readings is to counter the decreasing availability of original resource materials caused by exploding student enrollments in our colleges and universities. The effects of this student population explosion are nowhere more severely felt than by libraries which attempt to serve the scholarly requirements of the university community. Unfortunately, libraries no longer can financially nor logistically provide sufficient copies of scientific and professional journals so necessary for adequate student exposure to original scientific writing, and it would be a foolhardy educator who would expect students to purchase personal copies of each journal that contained a required reading. We believe the edited readings included in this text, as well as other collected readings, serve the very practical function of making primary resource material directly available to the student.

It is not possible to find in any one book of readings a comprehensive and systematic treatment of a particular discipline. Admittedly, this book is no exception. This book was designed for use as a basic or supplementary text for undergraduate students interested in, and concerned about, human development. The book is organized into five major sections: (1) Theoretical orientations to human development, (2) Prenatal development, (3) Infancy and early childhood, (4) Middle childhood, and (5) Adolescence. Thus, the text is suitable for courses which attempt to cover human development from conception through adolescence. On the other hand, one of our goals was to provide a book sufficiently versatile for use in courses concerning more restricted periods of development. We believe we have approached that versatility, and to that end suggest the following combinations of readings as appropriate for age-specific courses in human development:

Infancy and Early Childhood: Chapters 1, 2, 3, 4, 5, 6, 7, 8, 9, 10, 11, 12, 13, 14, 15, 16, 17.

Middle Childhood: Chapters 1, 2, 3, 4, 5, 18, 19, 20, 21, 22, 23, 24, 25, 26, 27, 28, 29.

Adolescence: Chapters 1, 2, 3, 4, 5, 30, 31, 32, 33, 34, 35, 36, 37, 38, 39.

The student is strongly encouraged to make extensive use of the workbook which accompanies the text. In it he will find helpful suggestions for discussion questions and term papers, as well as exercises for self-testing the mastery of the material.

We are indebted to the following publishers and gratefully acknowledge their permission to reprint or quote materials from the following sources:

Academic Press (*Journal of Experimental Child Psychology, Advances in Child Development and Behavior*: Lipsitt and Reese); American Association for the Advancement of Science (*Science*); American Medical Association (*Journal of the American Medical Association*); American Psychological Association (*American Psychologist, Journal of Abnormal and Social Psychology, Journal of Personality and Social Psychology, Psychological Review*); American Orthopsychiatric Association (*American Journal of Orthopsychiatry*); American Sociological Society (*American Sociological Review*); The Journal Press (*Journal of Genetic Psychology*); Merrill-Palmer Institute (*Merrill-Palmer Quarterly of Behavior and Development*); National Association for the Education of Young Children (*Young Children*); New York Academy of Science (*Annuals of the New York Academy of Science*); The William Alanson White Psychiatric Foundation, Inc. (*Psychiatry*); Psychology Press, Inc. (*Psychology in the Schools*); Society for Research in Child Development (*Child Development, Monographs of the Society for Research in Child Development*); TRANS-action Inc. (*Trans*-action); and W. W. Norton Co. (*Identity, Youth and Crisis:* Erikson). In each case the original source of the article and copyright is cited on the title page of each article.

We would like to express our thanks to Charles Brainerd, M. Peter Scontrino, Margaret Connolly, and Stephen W. Porges for their assistance. We would like to extend a special note of appreciation to Miss Joyce Pennington for the considerable time and energy she expended assisting us in the preparation of this book.

Finally, we are grateful to all the authors who so kindly consented to allow us to reprint their articles.

April, 1970

HIRAM E. FITZGERALD
JOHN PAUL MCKINNEY

CONTENTS

PART I

Theoretical Orientations to Human Development

INTRODUCTION

THE HISTORY of psychology abounds with theoretical explications of the laws, constructs, and principles advanced to account for the behavior of organisms. This proliferation of theory oftentimes serves to confuse the beginning student in as much as he seldom has any referent with which to assess the relative merits of each theory. To add to the confusion, theorists have been inconsistent in their use of the term "theory." For example, Marx (1963) draws a distinction among four different uses of the term "theory." One use of the term refers to the conceptual process of science as contrasted with its empirical or observational aspects, while another use of the term essentially equates theory with the term "hypothesis." Other theorists have effectively equated theory with the concept of system (e.g., functionalism, behaviorism), while a fourth use refers to theory as a means for summarizing and providing order to empirical data.

The primary purpose of scientific theory is to facilitate explanation of an accumulated set of phenomena. Nevertheless, theory can meaningfully function to serve more than just the explanation of empirical phenomena. According to Marx (1963), theory serves a dual function: on the one hand, to stimulate and direct empirical research; and on the other hand, to integrate accumulated knowledge with the intent of deriving empirical laws. Knowing the functions theory serves and knowing a variety of ways in which theory has been defined, we can now go about the task of establishing criteria for evaluating the usefulness of theories for explaining behavior.

Allport (1955), considering the problem of evaluative criteria for assessing theories, outlines six factors for such assessment. The first factor concerns the extent to which the theory is in agreement with the empirical facts on which it is based. If the empirical input to the theory is inconsistent with the postulates and hypotheses generated by the theory, there is every reason to suspect the theory's utility. The second factor refers to the generality of the theory, i.e., the completeness of the theory and the potential the theory has for encompassing phenomena which may initially be outside its scope. The degree of parsimony (i.e., the fewer the laws the more sound the theory) which characterizes the theory is the third factor to be considered. The principle of parsimony cannot be too heavily underscored, for it is just this principle which serves to thwart the proliferation of insufficiently empirically supported theoretical propositions (Marx, 1963). The fourth factor alludes to the extent to which operationism is an important characteristic of the theory. Operationism refers to the philosophy of science which underlies scientific psychology. Simply put, the concept of operationism refers to specification by definition of the operations used to identify a particular concept under investigation. As Bridgman (1928) originally stated the principle, "The concept is synonymous with the corresponding set of operations." Stevens (1939) reaffirms a critical aspect of science by suggesting that only those propositions which are based upon operations which are public and replicable should be accepted into the cumulative body of science. Note that operationism excludes no single area of psychology. As Stevens remarks, "Operationism does not deny images, for example, but asks: What is the operational definition of the term 'image'?" (Stevens, 1939). The fifth factor useful for evaluating theories is the internal consistency of the theory. If the theory is replete with contradictions, surely criticism leveled from those who adhere to alternative viewpoints will be rampant. The final factor refers to the ability of the theory to adequately explain behavior. In other words, the test of a good theory is the extent to which it makes some sense out of an assorted collection of phenomena. And by *explanation* here, Allport means "a description in terms that are more general than those with which we started." (Allport, 1963).

In Chapter 1, Professor Spiker of the University of Iowa considers a number of issues which have been at the forefront of theoretical argument for some time in developmental psychology. Moreover, he dismisses several of these issues as irrelevant for an effective concept of development. Specifically, Spiker considers irrelevant for understanding the concept of development traditional preferences for particular theoretical orientations and research methods to the exclusion of alternatives and preferences among developmental psychologists for applied research.

In Chapter 2, Professor Bijou of the University of Illinois discusses the meaning of the empirical concept of reinforcement. The aim of Bijou's approach is to study the interaction between environmental stimulus events and organismic responses in order to extend and develop more parsimonious empirical laws of behavior. According to Bijou's argument, reinforcement holds only for psychological interaction that varies in strength in accordance with antecedent stimulus action (i.e., it holds only for operants). Note carefully Bijou's distinction between operant and respondent behaviors: the former referring to interactions which vary in strength as a result of antecedent stimulus action, while the latter class of behaviors refers to interactions which vary as a result of consequent stimulus action.

Moving from Bijou's Skinnerian learning theory approach to child development, we encounter in Chapter 3 an alternative point of view. In Chapter 3 Professor Kagan of Harvard University draws our attention to the need for more relativistic definitions of some of the traditional psychological constructs related to human development. By relativistics Kagan refers to definitions in which situational as well as state variables are incorporated into the definition. Kagan suggests that it is time for psychologists to redirect their energies from a search for absolute stimulus characteristics of reinforcement to a search for the antecedents of attentional processes.

Still another orientation to development is provided in Chapter 4 by Professor Erik Erikson of Harvard University. Professor Erikson draws our attention to the importance of conceptualizing the developmental process as one which is not solely restricted to the period of infancy and early childhood. Indeed, the organism at a number of significant points in its life may be faced with crises which may have a profound effect on the remainder of his development. Operating from the epigenetic principle which has its origins in the growth of the organism *in utero,* Erikson theorizes that personality develops "according to steps predetermined in the human organism's readiness to be driven toward, to be aware of, and to interact with a widening radius of significant individuals and institutions."

In Chapter 5, Ruth Benedict, the distinguished cultural anthropologist, draws our attention to cultural continuities and discontinuities which exert an influence on the organism's development throughout the life cycle. Discontinuous conditioning refers to the training, habit formation, and selective reinforcement of behaviors which are age dependent, while continuity refers to those cultures where the child is taught nothing that it must later unlearn as it advances to adulthood.

REFERENCES

Allport, F. H. *Theories of perception and the concept of structure.* New York: Wiley, 1955.

Bridgman, P. W. *The logic of modern physics.* New York: Macmillan, 1928.

Marx, M. H. The general nature of theory construction. In M. H. Marx (Ed.). *Theories in contemporary psychology.* New York: Macmillan, 1963. Pp. 4–46.

Stevens, S. S. Psychology and the science of science. *Psychological Bulletin,* 1939, *36,* 221–263.

1
THE CONCEPT OF DEVELOPMENT: RELEVANT AND IRRELEVANT ISSUES*

CHARLES C. SPIKER

RELEVANT ISSUES FOR THE CONCEPT OF DEVELOPMENT

THE FIRST relevant issue is concerned with the meaning of the term "development." We must agree on a preliminary definition of the concept before we can sensibly discuss it. The second relevant issue is concerned with the nature of developmental laws and explanations of them. We need to agree on what it is that the developmental psychologist is trying to do—what kinds of laws he is seeking and how he is trying to explain the laws that he finds. Let us begin with a discussion of what seems to be a fruitful definition of the term "development."

The Meaning of Development

In evaluating the utility and logical status of a scientific concept, it is invariably helpful to review some of the empirical phenomena that the concept is supposed to name and to help organize. Let us examine, for a moment, some of the grosser, empirical facts associated with the concept of "development." One does not need to be a scientifically trained observer to note that there are some differences between newborn infants and adult humans. Many of the differences are obvious and incontrovertible. Furthermore, even the layman will discover, in the normal course of living, that most newborn infants eventually become adults and that in this process the originally observed differences disappear. Since the differences disappear, there must have been changes, either gradual, sudden, or both.

The concept of "development" has been used to name those changes in behavior that normally occur with an increase in the chronological age of the

---

* Previously published in H. W. Stevenson (Ed.), *Concept of Development. Monographs of the Society for Research in Child Development.* 1966, *31* (5), 40–54. Reprinted with permission from the author and the Society for Research in Child Development.

child. Thus, we speak of *developmental changes* in behavior. Used in this way, "developmental" is completely synonymous with "ontogenetic." I do not see how anyone could deny that there are such changes in behavior and that the concept, so used, has utility. The term "development," used in this way, is no more or less abstract or theoretical than the terms "behavior" or "chronological age."

I strongly urge that we restrict our usage of "development" to this meaning, at least for the present time. Such a definition is entirely consistent with historical usage and with much of current practice. The early students of child behavior began to study developmental changes in behavior. Although they did not explicitly delineate their goals, it is clear from their work that they wished to tabulate some of the more interesting changes in behavior, increase the precision of our common-sense knowledge of these changes, and provide a satisfactory explanation of why the changes occurred. Thus, common sense knew that most children first sit up alone, then crawl, then stand, then walk, and, finally, run. The scientific observer could discover what percentage of children actually follow this sequence and the mean ages at which each of the several stages occur. Common sense knew that children *do* learn new tasks and that older children learn more complicated tasks than do younger children; the scientific observers could analyze the skills required by the tasks, the skills possessed by the children of different ages, and they could specify in advance what tasks will be learned at what ages. Common sense attributed the developmental changes to an increase in chronological age or to "growing older"; students of child behavior sought explanations in physiological changes, in experience, and in genetically determined characters.

Developmental Laws and Their Explanations

The second genuine issue pertaining to development is concerned with the nature of the empirical laws sought and the kinds of explanations of these laws that are offered. Let us look briefly at two common prototypes of developmental laws, such as are found in biology. One class of such laws specifies a sequence of states or stages that occur in a definite order. Thus, the egg-caterpillar-cocoon-butterfly sequence is a special instance of the general sequence, embryo-larva-pupa-imago. This type of developmental law may or may not specify the exact chronological age at which the various stages occur. Many of the developmental laws of Freud or of Piaget are examples of such laws in psychology. The sitting-crawling-standing-walking-running sequence, mentioned earlier, is also an example. Another type of developmental law is much more specific with respect to chronological age. The weight, volume, or height of a plant as a function of the time since it was planted in standard environmental conditions exemplifies such a law in botany. The number of different phonemic sounds typically produced by an infant at different ages between birth and 30 months exemplifies this type of law in child psychology.

Most child psychologists are clear about the nature of developmental laws. There does not seem to be any issue here. Rather, the controversy is concerned with preferred explanations for these laws. The controversy is an old one; it has manifested itself in several different guises: nature-nurture, IQ constancy, heredity-environment, and maturation-learning.

Let us examine this controversy. The point at issue in this argument, in all its guises, seems to be that some students wish to emphasize the role of genetic factors—some would speak of organismic factors—in explaining developmental changes in behavior, whereas others wish to emphasize the role of factors operating after fertilization. The word *emphasize* is chosen advisedly. No child psychologist believes that there is anything one can do to an infant monkey to make a human adult out of it. Similarly, no one believes that the genetic resources of the human infant will have further opportunity to unfold if the environment does not provide it with sufficient food. Genetic and environmental factors both play a role in producing the developmental changes that occur. Recognizing this fact, one may well wonder what is left to disagree about. Hydrogen and oxygen combine to form water. Which is more important in the formation of water—hydrogen because twice as much is needed, or oxygen because it is so potent that only half as much will suffice?

It is undoubtedly correct to say that the question is no longer whether both genetic and environmental factors are relevant to developmental changes in behavior. It is probably also correct that the question is no longer which set of factors plays the more important role. The question that remains is one pertaining to research strategy: Should we first investigate the role of genetic factors in development, can we investigate fruitfully nongenetic factors alone, or must we try to study simultaneously the two sets of factors? I should like to say immediately that we cannot answer such questions from the comfort of an armchair. With such questions, the role of wisdom largely ends with a recognition of the various alternatives. The subsequent choice will either be recorded by historians as brilliant insight or not recorded at all. No amount of contemporary drumbeating for one or another of the strategies will modify the degree of empirical success that it eventually enjoys.

Despite an unwillingness to make a prediction about the ultimate utility of that strategy that emphasizes the immediate study of genetic factors, I would like to make three comments that seem pertinent: *First,* some writers use the term "development" to refer to biological, possibly genetically determined, processes that presumably underlie and are correlated with the observed changes in behavior that accompany increase in chronological age. *This usage seems unwarranted* for several reasons. For one thing, it robs us of a unique, convenient term for the empirical phenomena we have already discussed. For another, it prejudges the issue with respect to what are the correct explanations for the empirical phenomena. It also promotes a confusion between the empirical phenomena and potential explanations of them. Finally, the usage does not concur well with an incontrovertible fact about the field, viz., a great deal of interesting research that was designed to discover developmental laws was *not* designed to tease out the roles of genetic, physiological, or organismic factors.

The *second* comment concerns the use of chronological age as a criterion for classifying a research project as *developmental. If developmental changes in behavior is understood to refer to changes that occur with increases in chronological age, then any experiment that shows that a given behavior does or does not change with chronological age makes some contribution to our knowledge of such changes.* It does not follow, however, that the investigator is necessarily interested in developmental psychology, although he probably is. He may have included the age factor only to increase the precision of his experiment—as a leveling factor.

If an investigation does not contain groups of children of different ages, it is not immediately apparent whether it contributes to our understanding of developmental laws of behavior. It is not apparent, either, whether the investigator is interested in developmental psychology, because it is possible to conduct research that is designed to explain developmental changes in behavior without varying chronological age. For example, an investigator may already know that the rate of instrumental conditioning varies as chronological age increases; he may attempt to find out why the rate changes by studying those variables that affect or determine the rate of conditioning in 5-year-old children. His attempt to discover some of the variables that determine the rate of learning in 5-year-olds may prove to be an extremely fruitful way of discovering why most 2-year-olds do not normally learn such a task at all and, possibly, how to arrange conditions so that they *do* learn. In his choice of 5-year-olds for intensive study, the experimenter is pursuing one of those hunches that ultimately makes the difference between research that is sterile and research that demonstrates the perspicacity of the investigator.

The *third* comment concerns the demonstrated fruitfulness of studying genetic or organismic factors. Many of the loudest drumbeaters for the importance of immediate investigation of genetic factors in development do not provide us with very convincing demonstrations of how such investigation is to be carried out. Their reasoning seems to run in this way: Since the sex of the child is determined at fertilization, at least so far as we know, the sex of the child is a genetic factor. If there are behavioral differences between boys and girls, and if these differences cannot be reasonably accounted for by environmental factors, then a genetic factor has produced them. Similarly, since we know that behavior patterns change with increase in chronological age, and since there must be corresponding changes in the physiological constitution of the child, then one way to get at the genetic factor or factors is to study behavior as a function of chronological age. Analogous reasoning leads to the conclusion that mental age is equally important in understanding the underlying genetic determinants of developmental changes in behavior. Although I do not follow the reasoning, I do understand the main assertion: Chronological age, mental age, and sex of child are important variables to study. Who wants to argue with that?

IRRELEVANT ISSUES FOR THE CONCEPT OF DEVELOPMENT

So far we have been discussing issues that are relevant to the notion of development. Let us now examine some that have been alleged to be so relevant that they have even been included in some definitions of the concept. There are three classes of such issues, all of which are irrelevant to the concept as we have developed it thus far. The first pertains to the kind of theory that one may prefer, the second, to a predilection for method, and the third, to a preference for research problems of an "applied" versus a "theoretical" character. It seems important for us to take some time to separate these issues from those that genuinely pertain to developmental psychology. Arguments about theory, method, and applicability are as old as our modern scientific frame of reference. To try to characterize developmental psychology in terms of such problems is misleading to the student unfamiliar with the history of science in general, and psychology in particular, and it muddies the water even for those who are reasonably familiar with the recent and more remote past.

Preferences for Theory

There have been several recent attempts to contrast the "truly developmental approach" with that advocated by "behavior theorists." The behavior theorist, it is said, believes that one set of laws suffices for all organisms; the developmentalist does not. The behavior theorist emphasizes the importance of formal, analytic terms; the developmentalist does not. The behavior theorist prefers the hypothetico-deductive method; the developmentalist prefers a developmental conceptualization. The behavior theorist avoids the use of purposive concepts; the developmentalist thinks in terms of purposes and ends. The behavior theorist deals with concepts referring to peripheral phenomena; the developmentalist prefers concepts naming central events. The behavior theorist emphasizes the study of learning; the developmentalist emphasizes the importance of perception.

The position to be presented here is that most of these claims reflect a preference for certain kinds of theoretical schema and that such preferences are not unique to developmental psychology and have little or nothing to do with the concept of development. In order to develop this thesis coherently, let us first review the purpose of theory in science.

The function of theory in science is to permit explanation. Scientific explanation takes the same form as does common-sense explanation. We show how a statement describing the phenomenon to be explained follows logically from other statements that we already believe to be true. Scientific theories can be described, in a somewhat oversimplified way, as logical arguments. (The term "hypothetico-deductive" has been used to refer to those cases in which we are not very confident of the truth of our premises; there is nothing else very special about the hypothetico-deductive method.) Theories in science are ordinarily constructed with greater logical rigor than common sense ordinarily provides. For example, scientists make greater use of mathematical deduction, and their systems of sentential and functional logic are more explicit, than is the case for nonscientists. Moreover, the rules governing the definition and use of scientific terms are more explicit and more rigorously followed than are the rules the layman ordinarily applies. Descriptions of scientific theory by the philosophers of science consist largely of technical elaboration on what we have just said. Most of the elaboration, however, is designed to show that scientific explanation is not fundamentally different from the kind of explanation that the intelligent layman proposes dozens of times each day.

Most of what passes for scientific theory in psychology, both general and developmental, is only schema for theories. A schema for a theory is a theory under construction; it is not a logically coherent, finished structure. Certainly, a theoretical schema cannot be proved satisfactory or unsatisfactory with a crucial experiment. In fact, we know already that it is unsatisfactory since it is only a schema. We can recognize a given formulation as a schema rather than a theory by several features among which are the appearance of parameters that cannot be measured but must be estimated from empirical data, terms that are not unequivocally defined, functional relations that are only implied but not explicitly specified, and an indeterminate scope.

Except for that provided by scientific theory, there is no other kind of explanation used in science. To state, therefore, that one does not like a logically systematized organization of laws and principles is to state that one is not interested in providing explanations for the empirical phenomena that one observes. This statement does not imply, however, that we cannot have definite, sensible preferences for one type of theoretical schema as compared to others. There are important, significant differences among theoretical schemata in psychology. The differences between the typical stimulus-response schema, whether of the Hullian or probability stripe, and the various phenomenological schemata are critical. The major difference in this case is in the character of the basic concepts and, therefore, is related to a difference in philosophies of science. The differences between the typical Hullian schema and the probability schemata of recent vintage are also significant. The basic concepts in the Hullian schema refer to subject variables: drive, habit, inhibition, anticipatory responses, etc. The basic concepts in the probability schemata are parameters to be estimated: alpha, beta, gamma, etc. Differences of this kind are important enough to govern sensibly choices among theoretical schemata. Too often, however, it seems that the choice is made on the basis of superficial differences. We may prefer the sound of the word "habit" to "sign-gestalt-expectation," but this is hardly a sensible basis for choosing Hull's schema over that of Tolman. (For one thing, we would soon discover that we are also expected to use the Hullian expression "momentary effective super-threshold reaction potential," which may reverse our preference.) Choice among schemata also seems to be determined by whether or not mathematical or quasi-mathematical statements appear in the schemata. A choice on this basis seems as irrelevant as the even more frequent choice based on personal preferences for the persons who are proponents of the schema.

Preferences for specific schemata, and occasional senseless bases for such preferences, are not unique to psychologists concerned with discovering developmental laws. The only special question the developmental psychologist needs to ask is whether a given schema permits the introduction of individual-difference variables. If the schema does allow for such variables, then the developmental psychologist has a means of identifying his 4-year-olds, 5-year-olds, and 6-year-olds in terms of such a schema. In the last section of this paper, I will argue that all major behavior theories permit or provide for the introduction of such variables.

Now let us analyze four or five of the theoretical considerations that have been alleged to be of special concern to the developmental psychologist: First, it has been said that the behavior theorist thinks that one set of laws will suffice for both rats and men. In one sense, this may be true; in another sense, it is misleading. I suspect, without knowing, that many behavior theorists hope that a single, integrated theory will eventually be developed that will account for the behavior of many, if not all, types of organisms—in much the same way that the theory of mechanics explains both rectilinear and circular motion. But I know of no behavior theorist who believes that rats are as articulate as preschool children. None believes, so far as I know, that what the preschool child says, either to himself or to others, has no effect on his behavior. Therefore, without knowing for sure, I feel confident in concluding that behavior theorists do not expect exactly the same laws in their theory, with exactly the same range of values for the parameters, to be applicable to the prediction, understanding, and explanation of both child and rat behavior.

A second allegation is that the behavior theorist eschews purpose and purposive concepts, whereas the child psychologist needs such concepts. We should note, however, that there is as much need to refer to the rat's purpose in turning right to obtain food as to refer to the child's purpose in crying to elicit sympathy. Behavior theories, in general, do not contain purposive terms as *basic* terms, but they must deal with the empirical phenomena, and *defined* terms such as "drive," "reinforcement," "goal," "expectation," and "anticipatory goal responses" have been introduced in an attempt to account for these phenomena. The behavior theorist's reservation about the term "purpose" does not have to do with purpose *in* nature but purpose *of* nature. That organisms behave purposefully is an incontrovertible fact. That nature behaves purposefully is a religious dictum. The purposeful behavior of organisms does not contradict the scientist's hope for behavioral determinism.

A third claim is that the developmentalist must have a schema that allows for the introduction of terms that refer to "central processes" and not merely to "peripheral processes." The justification for this proclamation is hard to understand. We do not yet know what parts of the nervous system are involved in a great many of the behavioral phenomena that we observe. Physiological psychologists are working diligently to shed light on some of these questions. Personally, I wish them success. In the meantime, I shall endeavor to provide them with significant behavioral laws that they can subsequently attempt to relate to physiological or neurophysiological processes.

In the same context with the central-peripheral discussion, it is sometimes asserted that the developmental psychologist must be particularly careful to choose a theory that includes full treatment of perception as opposed to mere learning and conditioning. The implication is that perception is a centrally located phenomenon, whereas conditioning and learning are peripheral. It is true that theoretical schemata of the Hullian variety have not been prone to emphasize, all in a bunch and all in one place, the classical problems of perception. Whether such schemata can handle the classical problems in new ways is an empirical question that remains to be decided. It is certainly not yet clear that they *cannot* handle these problems. In the meantime, research on perception-like problems continues, much of it conducted by adherents to schemata like the Hullian.

Of one thing I am sure: If a developmental psychologist, or any other kind of psychologist, finds the neurophysiological correlates of either conditioning or perception in either the central or peripheral nervous system, he will find behavior theorists stumbling over each other in their attempts to incorporate his results into their theoretical schemata. Until such time, we do not have much to fuss about.

With regard to theoretical preference, the present thesis is that the developmental psychologist has no special problems as long as his theoretical schema allows for the inclusion of individual-difference variables. Since all explanatory formulations with which he is likely to become concerned are only schemata, he has the possibility of modifying them in such a way that developmental laws can be readily stated. Whether or not he wishes to utilize a schema that emphasizes the role of logic and mathematics, of physiological or neurophysiological variables, of perception or learning, of purposive concepts that are basic or purposive concepts that are defined with reference to other basic concepts—all these questions he has in common with psychologists in other areas. It would be unfortunate if we began to think of these problems as peculiarly developmental in nature.

Preferences for Method

The second major issue that is irrelevant to the concept of development is concerned with attempts to characterize developmental psychology in terms of methodological necessities. For example, developmental psychology has been distinguished from child psychology in terms of a preference for controlled observations as opposed to experimental observations. The historical preference for the experimental method in science, wherever it can be used, is undeniable. Nevertheless, we know that certain scientific disciplines (astronomy) have managed rather well without benefit of man-made experimentation. It is difficult to see what special problems the developmental psychologist has that would make one or the other of these two methods peculiarly appropriate. To be sure, he cannot vary chronological age within a child from one moment to another. This is no more than an extreme example, however, of the situation that also exists with respect to hunger, thirst, and body weight in the laboratory rat. The experimenter must wait in either case. Yet the psychologist has managed to perform laboratory experiments on motivation with rats. The developmental psychologist cannot vary chronological age with all other variables held constant. But then who wants to? Who believes that an increase in chronological age would have any effect on subsequent behavior if the organism were frozen, let us say, so that all its physiological processes ceased and it did not interact in any way with its environment? Our immediate answer to this rhetorical question reflects our belief that chronological age will not appear in our advanced theories as a basic variable. Chronological age is merely a measure of the time that provides a medium in which other processes can occur. The developmental psychologist cannot reverse chronological age, either by manipulation or by waiting; in this respect, he shares a problem with the physicist who also cannot reverse time, but has managed fruitful experimentation for several centuries.

It is certainly true that some scientists make a fetish of certain aspects of methodology, that some allow the tail to wag the dog. Some developmental psychologists have studied trivial variables because they could measure them, while they ignored important ones because they could not. Some developmental psychologists also design elaborate experiments to test hypotheses that common, even uncontrolled, observations could verify or disconfirm. It is important to realize, however, that our judgments of what is important or trivial, of what is easy to confirm or disconfirm, are often determined by the results of the very studies we are evaluating. It is surprising to the scientist how often it happens that what common sense thinks it knows so well cannot be established as true under carefully controlled conditions.

As a final comment on method, let us note that "methodological" and "logical" are not synonyms. Good methodological practice is not always a logical matter. It is, in truth, usually an empirical matter. Effective methodology is largely determined by what works. Often it is the case that if we were wise enough, or clairvoyant enough, to determine good methodology a priori, we would have no need for the methodology; we could intuit the knowledge that the method is to subserve.

Preferences for Application

The final irrelevant issue is concerned with an attitude found among some developmental psychologists that seems to reflect a preference for the conduct of applied research. For many years, students of developmental changes in behavior have committed themselves rather heavily to problems with considerable social significance: thumb-sucking, nail-biting, masturbation, stealing, lying, honesty, buttoning, shoe-tying, aggression, dependency, juvenile delinquency, etc. During the early years of developmental investigations, the potential fruitfulness of a problem seems to have been determined more by its social significance than by its potential contribution to a science of behavior. During the past 15 to 20 years, there has been an increasing conviction that developmental studies can play an important role in the construction of a general theory of human behavior. Research problems have been increasingly concerned with such variables as magnitude of reinforcement, drive, stimulus similarity, social reinforcement, cessation of reinforcement, stimulus preferences, and the like. In short, students of child behavior have found research interests very similar to those of students of infrahuman and adult human behavior.

Developmental psychology finds itself in the same situation as does general psychology: Some research workers are more interested in the immediately applied, practical types of problems, some are more interested in research problems that promise contributions to the development of theory, and some are interested in both types of questions. There is no more justification in reserving the term "developmental" for one type of investigation or activity than for the other. There appear to be quite a number of persons who find it difficult to conceive of developmental psychology as anything other than a clinically oriented discipline. Be this as it may, I do not believe that one's view on this matter has anything to do with the definition of the concept of development. Whether one is seeking to find or is using them, developmental laws remain what they are.

The preference for application is reflected by the injection of an old Gestalt phrase into some discussions of the concept of development. Sometimes we are still admonished to "study our children whole." It is said that only if we have a theory, a schema, an approach, or a viewpoint that will permit us to study the child as a whole can we possibly succeed in contributing anything to developmental psychology. I have great difficulty in understanding this principle. Since I have never heard of a child psychologist who seriously advocated vivisection of his subjects, there is no urgency in considering the literal meaning of this phrase. Frankly, I have never met anyone who could insist with a straight face that he studied his organisms whole. To be sure, some psychologists look at bigger chunks of the child than do others. But everyone looks at chunks. To be able to look at the whole would require all the knowledge we do not yet have. Even the most avid promoters of the person-as-a-whole approach are forced to deal with manageable chunks when they conduct research. They consider the chronological age of the child, the sex of the child, the educational level of the parents, the socio-economic background, the school grade, the IQ or MA, etc. But one never has any difficulty in finding *known relevant variables* that are not mentioned and, therefore, presumably not studied or controlled. Let us put this tired old saw to rest, once and for all; there are all too many first-year graduate students who try seriously to apply it.

There is another myth about research that is conducted with children; it is probably related in some way to the person-as-a-whole issue. It is said that some investigators are interested in children only as potential subjects; some investigators consider children only as *convenient* subjects. These investigators, it is said, are not interested in the child qua child and, therefore, are not concerned with development. We have already stated the issue that is really pertinent here: viz., that it is possible to study developmental changes in behavior without using chronological age in a particular series of experiments, and that some investigators may include the age variable solely to increase the precision of their experiments. What is incredible is that anyone could seriously maintain that the child, particularly the preschool-age child, is a *convenient* experimental subject. The experience of most investigators has been that as one moves down the age range from college sophomore to the infant, experimental difficulties increase. Many developmental psychologists are quite frustrated, I am sure, by the fact that the very young child seems to be the only type of subject that manifests certain behavioral phenomena that we must study if we are to achieve an understanding of human behavior. It would be far easier to experiment with the older child or the adult, if he would oblige us by behaving like the younger child—consistently. My hat will always come off to the successful experimenter with the preschool-age child. I will always mentally bow low to the successful experimenter with the infant. It is probable that many investigators avoid applying the experimental method to children simply because it is often extremely difficult to apply. But where necessity commands virtue, we have no need for moral and ethical principles.

COGNITIVE DEVELOPMENT

My discussion so far has been explicitly concerned with a general concept of development and with some issues, both relevant and irrelevant, that pertain to the concept. In the space that remains, I will discuss the concept in relation to cognitive aspects of behavior. That so little will be said on the specific application is not entirely because of space restrictions. From my viewpoint, most of the real problems or pseudoproblems have to do with the general concept. In attempting to solve the problems associated with the general concept, we deal with some problems associated with specific applications.

I am not going to try to define either "cognition" or "learning." *Cognition* is a chapter-heading word, like the terms "intellectual development" or "motor skill." A reasoned definition of *cognition* would take far more space than has been allotted to the entire discussion. The term "learning" has different meanings within different theoretical churches, and only atheistic eclectics seem to understand the word when they talk to each other; the price they pay in triviality, however, is often very high. For my purposes, I will try to get by without highly specific definitions of these terms. We must remember, however, that some important issues can be resolved only if we specify more precise meanings.

The student of the development of cognitive behavior and learning is concerned with the cognitive behavior of children that changes with age. He is also concerned with any processes or variables that he finds associated with changes in such behavior. Concerning these processes, I should like to make three statements immediately: First, we should certainly expect to find that there are physiological and anatomical accompaniments of cognitive behavioral changes, which accompaniments are largely independent of the organism's experience. Restating this less precisely but perhaps more intelligibly, we should expect that physiological maturation rather than learning accounts for some of the developmental changes in cognitive behavior. Rate of conditioning in infants, for example, may turn out to be a phenomenon requiring a maturational explanation. Second, we should expect to find changes in cognitive behavior that are largely independent of the physiological changes that are themselves not dependent on experience. Stated less precisely again, we should expect to find developmental changes in cognitive behavior that cannot be attributed to physiological maturation. We can be fairly sure of this point from current research on short-term learning. Finally, we should not be surprised if we find that an interaction between variables of experience and physiological factors is necessary to explain some, perhaps most, developmental changes in cognitive behavior. We should not be surprised if any of these three statements turns out to be true since each statement is an empirical one; logic cannot settle the issue a priori.

There is always some embarrassment in making statements like these because it is difficult to see how any reasonable scientific psychologist could question their plausibility. Yet, it seems that periodically some people need to hear their colleagues assert a conviction of their plausibility; perhaps I am one of these people.

Developmental Laws and Current Theoretical Schemata

Let us turn once again to the introduction of individual-difference variables into our theoretical schemata. Certain developmental psychologists have asked how a developmental psychologist could possibly be interested in using a theoretical schema like the Hullian. "Where does the organism enter into the theory?" they ask. The answer is, "Just about any place you wish to put it. The theory is only a schema; change it to fit your facts."

Hull suggested certain places in the theory where organisms or individual-difference variables might be located. Let us look at these for a moment. Habit growth in classical conditioning, according to Hull, is an exponential function of the number of conditioning trials, i.e., $\mathbf{H} = (\mathbf{1} - \mathbf{10}^{-\mathbf{i}N})$, where H is habit, N is number of conditioning trials, and **i** is an *individual-difference variable* that must be empirically estimated at present.

One might choose to follow Hull's suggestion and try to determine the manner in which the **i**-parameter varies in children with chronological age. Or, one might choose to consider that the **i**-parameter is a composite of several variables; for example, it might be a function of chronological age, the particular response system involved, the sensory modality stimulated, etc. In this case, the **i**-parameter would itself become the dependent variable in a functional relation, with at least one of its determinants a developmental variable.

One might also take a more drastic step. We might find it more useful to assume that the habit-trial relation is best stated so that it differs more markedly for children of different ages. Thus, we could hypothesize that habit is an exponential function of conditioning trials until the child begins to verbalize names for the conditioning stimuli, but is a logarithmic, linear, or any other function thereafter.

Nearly all the basic postulates in the Hullian 1943 theoretical schema contain at least one such parameter. There is a parameter in the generalization principle, the principle of reward magnitude, the principle relating length of the CS-UCS interval to habit asymptote, and several others. There seems to be no more reason to ask where the organism fits into Hull's schema than to ask where the body fits in the law of falling bodies. One almost suspects that the problem is not so much to find a place for developmental variables, but to find a place for psychologists who have misgivings about theoretical schemata with certain kinds of words, reasonably rigorous logic, abstract symbols, and statements formulated in a quasi-mathematical language.

There is still another class of reasonably articulate theoretical schema that offers special promise for the developmental psychologist. Here I refer to the recently developed probability or mathematical models. Nearly all these schemata contain several parameters that must be estimated from data at the present time and, for this reason, are especially promising in comparative studies of children. Although the scope of any one of such theories is ordinarily far more restricted than is the classical Hullian schema, the variety of phenomena to which they apply, as a group, offers a considerable range of choice to developmental psychologists who are concerned with the study of children's learning of relatively simple tasks. Comparisons in the learning of children of different ages are possible through the comparison of fitted or estimated parameters, as well as through modification of basic assumptions in the theories. For example, recent research indicates that young children do not show the negative recency effect or "gambler's fallacy" that is characteristic of adults in probability situations. To obtain theoretical schemata that can handle both the positive and negative recency effects probably requires modification of the basic assumptions of the theories, not merely the estimation of different parameters.

Because I have discussed at some length the use of theoretical schemata in the conduct of developmental research, it does not follow that I think significant research on the concept of development can be conducted only within the framework of a particular theoretical schema. It is not necessary for one to choose a particular schema in which to conduct all his research. Sometimes it is possible to work within a framework consisting of assumptions that are common to each of several different theoretical schemata. For example, there are several versions of current **S-R** theory that have reference to mediating responses, and are therefore promising to the student of children's language development. Significant work in this field has been conducted with children for more than two decades and scarcely needs any advertisement at the present time. Judging from recent publications, unpublished manuscripts that are circulating, and notices of federal research grants, research on the child's language development continues at an accelerated pace.

Finally, it is important to realize that it is possible to conduct valuable research on development without having great concern for any theoretical schema. It is possible to discover, even without theoretical aid, developmental laws about language, problem solving, discrimination, reading, number ability, reasoning, and many other forms of cognitive functioning. There are no a priori rules to instruct us when the knowledge in a given area is ready to be organized into a theory. Different scholars in a field should be expected to have honest differences of opinion about the fruitfulness of an attempt to organize what is known. We can recognize that this is so and still encourage investigators to work toward the discovery of developmental laws, even though, for whatever reason, they have little or no theoretical inclination. Atheoretical investigators have no special obligation to defend the fruitfulness of their work. Certainly, they need not pretend that the commonsense formulations within which they work *are* theoretical.

Laws are the heart and lungs of all science. If we have enough of them, and if they are the right ones, we can organize them into theories. But laws are laws—without them, we know nothing of any generality.

CONCLUDING REMARKS

I have suggested that the term "development" be used to refer to those changes in behavior that accompany increasing chronological age. I have indicated that the task of students of developmental changes in behavior is to discover developmental laws and, when possible, to organize them into a theoretical system. I have considered, and rejected as of no special relevance to the concept of development, certain issues that are of concern to all students of behavior: the desirability of purposive concepts, the relative importance of central and peripheral concepts, the relative importance of perception and learning, the feasibility of experimentation versus controlled observation, the complexity of phenomena studied, and social significance of problems.

The discussion has led to the conclusion that developmental psychology has no special kinds of problems. The successful resolution of controversies in science presupposes an identification of those problems that can be solved by the application of logic and of those that require empirical observations. Many of the problems pertaining to the concept of development are of our own making. We attempt to solve by logic alone issues that call for research. Thus, we frequently make pronouncements on the *necessity* for certain kinds of methods, the *necessity* for the use of theory or theories of certain types, the *necessity* to study certain kinds of research problems, the *necessity* for observing interactions of variables, the *necessity* for studying phenomena of certain degrees of complexity, and so on. I, for one, do not know who wills this necessity. Systematic observation, careful and explicit definition, rigorous application of logic—these are the necessities.

2
AN EMPIRICAL CONCEPT OF REINFORCEMENT AND A FUNCTIONAL ANALYSIS OF CHILD BEHAVIOR*

SIDNEY W. BIJOU

THE MEANING of an empirical concept of reinforcement for a theory of child development cannot be appreciated in isolation. Reinforcement is not thought of as a kind of learning theory (such as reinforcement learning theory) or as a miniature behavior theory. It is viewed as a significant statement concerning the temporal relationships between certain classes of stimuli and responses; therefore, this discussion is preambled with an outline of a theory of development that involves an empirical concept of reinforcement (9).

A CONTEXT FOR AN EMPIRICAL CONCEPT OF REINFORCEMENT

Data of psychological development are viewed as progressive changes in behavior (i.e., as differentiations and increases in complexity) that evolve from interactions with the environments of development. The phrase "environments of development" refers to *stimulus events*. Stimulus events include circumstances that *have* interacted with the developing organism (historical) as well as those that *are* interacting with it. Stimulus events may be described by their functional properties *and* by their physical properties. For example, a tone may be characterized by changes in electrical impulses on an oscilloscope and, at the same time, by specific changes in the behavior of an organism. With respect to its relationship with behavior, the onset of the tone may be correlated with an orienting reflex, with a response that has

* From the *Journal of Genetic Psychology,* 1964, *104,* 215–225. Reprinted with permission from the author and the American Psychological Association.

This paper, with some modification, was delivered at a symposium on reinforcement effects, Society for Research in Child Development, Pennsylvania State University, March 16, 1961.

been reinforced in the past, or with an increase in strength of a response that preceded it (as observed in the future occurrences of responses of the same class). Thus, the tone may be described by one or by several functional characteristics; it may also be described by its physical dimensions, such as wavelength, amplitude, and composition.

Many stimulus events influence the strength of specific stimulus-response relationships. Such stimulus events are *setting events* or setting factors.

> Such setting factors as the hungry or satiated condition of the organism, its age, hygienic or toxic condition, as well as the presence or absence of certain environing objects clearly influence the occurrence or non-occurrence of interbehavior or facilitate the occurrence of the activities in question in varying degrees (20, p. 95).

Consider the example of hunger or, better still, the deprivation of food as a setting event in the eating behavior of a 10-year-old boy. The training that the boy receives relative to food and to members of the family around the table is in part a function of food deprivation for about four-and-a-half hours prior to coming to the table. Fasting for four-and-one-half hours between meals is a setting event that plays a role in the learning supervised by the boy's parents. When this setting event is changed, the boy's behavior is altered. If we were to observe the boy's eating behavior under conditions of a setting event of only one hour since he last ate, we would be likely to say that his table manners were "poor" or that he exhibited low frequencies of "approved" behaviors and high frequencies of other kinds of behavior. (He spends most of his time "playing with his food.") If we were to watch him under conditions of a setting event of seven hours of food deprivation, we would also be likely to say that his table behaviors were "poor," or that he exhibited low frequencies of "good" behaviors and high frequencies of still other kinds of behavior. (He "devours his food.")

We turn now to an empirical concept of the child as a psychological organism. The developing child may be considered equivalent to a constellation of stimulus and response events. Stimulus events inside the organism are viewed as part of the environments of development and are analyzed in the same manner as external stimuli. No new assumptions are invoked. Because of the frequent inaccessibility of internal stimuli, adherence to an objective conception of them poses special, but not insurmountable, problems for a natural science approach.

The response aspect of the child is analyzed in terms of its physical and functional properties. From the point of view of physical analysis, responses are described by space-time dimensions, such as latency, frequency, and amplitude. From a functional vantage point, responses are described by their relationships to stimuli. To say that a stimulus has a stimulus function is to say that it interacts with a psychological response, a response that involves the organism as a unified system. The response in the interaction is said to have a response function.

Psychological interactions may be divided into two categories on the basis of temporal relationships. One group consists of interactions that vary in strength in accordance with antecedent stimulus action; the other group consists of interactions that vary in accordance with consequent stimulus action. Skinner (34) refers to the first group as respondents; to the second, as operants. Such a classification may be used advantageously to analyze the continual interactions between the developing child and environmental changes divided into stages. An analysis of development in terms of operant and respondent interactions throughout all developmental phases would be in contrast to approaches that view development as changes in motor, linguistic, intellectual, emotional, and social patterns of behavior. The difficulty with schemes of the latter sort is that they are based on shifting and overlapping criteria (physical, social, physiological, etc.), some of which are objectively defined and some of which are not. Furthermore, the specific stimulus functions that are involved (the environmental situations to which they are related) are ignored or minimized.

The other aspects of the systematic and empirical theory of development concern the strengthening and weakening of stimulus-response relationships, interrelationships between operant and respondent processes, generalization and discrimination, differentiation, chaining, conflict, and self-control.

The aim of the approach is to observe, analyze, and interpret interactions between environmental events and responses so as to extend and refine empirical laws. Accomplishments to date have contributed to an objective theory of development and have provided some principles for educational and child-rearing practices.

AN EMPIRICAL CONCEPT OF REINFORCEMENT

So much for a theoretical frame of reference. We now turn to a discussion of an empirical concept of reinforcement within the context given. At the outset, it should be noted that the concept of reinforcement (empirical and other) is believed to hold only for operant interactions. The concept may be stated as follows:

> [A certain class of behavior is strengthened by certain classes of consequent stimulus events.] The only way to tell whether or not a given event is reinforcing to a given organism under given conditions is to make a direct test. We observe the frequency of a selected response (operant level) then make an event contingent upon it and observe any change in frequency. If there is a change, we classify the event as reinforcing to the organism under the existing conditions (35, p. 73).

One may ask, "Why does a stimulus with reinforcing properties strengthen such behavior?" Some points of view seek an answer in terms of biological or biochemical inferences and data (the reductionistic approaches); some, in terms of hypothetical variables (usually some variation on a drive-reduction notion); still others, in terms of consequent feeling-states. A natural science approach avoids these kinds of attempts at explanation. It accepts the fact of reinforcement. It accepts the fact that a class of objectively defined responses is strengthened by consequent environmental events. It accepts the fact that such events are of two sorts: one sort strengthens on presentation; the other, on withdrawal. Environmental events in the first group are called *positive reinforcers* to emphasize the adding operation; environmental events in the second group are called *negative reinforcers* to emphasize the subtracting operation. A detailed account of the empirical concept of reinforcement involves the procedures for weakening operant behavior (19, 21, 34, 35).

Instead of searching for the correlates of operant strengthening in the neighboring branches of science or of constructing "explanatory interval variables," the empirical approach emphasizes the need for systematic information on the empirical relations between reinforcing stimuli and operants. For example, many investigators are exploring the range of reinforcing stimuli applicable to the young infant (primary reinforcers), the time of the initial appearance of certain operants, the processes and circumstances under which neutral stimuli take on reinforcing functions (acquired reinforcers), and the patterns of interactional contacts between reinforcers and responses (schedules). One of the major tasks in an experimental analysis of child behavior and behavior development is the discovery of stimuli that have positive or negative reinforcing properties for children at different stage levels, and a delineation of their parameters together with their relevant setting events.

In passing, it should be noted that the empirical concept of reinforcement is similar to Hilgard's "neutral definition" of reinforcement (18). There is a difference, however. Hilgard's conception applies to responses that acquire their functions through consequent stimulation (operants) *as well as* through antecedent stimulus action (respondents). Here, the empirical concept of reinforcement does not apply to respondent behavior. It is true that under proper circumstances, operants, as well as respondents, correlate with antecedent stimulation, but these functional relationships are established through different histories. Because each class of interactions has a different history and the stimuli and responses that are involved have different functions, separate analysis is indicated. In the interest of clarity, it is suggested that the empirical concept of reinforcement be restricted to interactions controlled by consequent stimulation and that, as suggested by MacCorquadale (27), Schlosberg (33), and Skinner (34), a different term be applied to interactions controlled by antecedent stimulation.

EXAMPLES OF RESEARCH WITH CHILDREN

During the past four years, examples of research with children from the point of view of an empirical concept of reinforcement have become more available. Some investigations, as they must in initiating an experimental approach, have been devoted to exploration of the physical features, methods, procedures, and techniques appropriate for the laboratory study of children of all ages. Thus, Bijou (5, 6) and Baer (3) have worked on a methodology for normal preschool children. Bijou was concerned with general laboratory techniques; Baer was concerned with specific procedures for analysis of verbal-social stimuli that involved an animated, talking puppet. Long, Hammack, May, and Campbell (23) and Long (22), have concentrated on laboratory methods for preschool children and, particularly, for middle-childhood children. Ellis, Barnett, and Pryer (12) and Orlando, Bijou, Tyler, and Marshall (31) have explored methods appropriate to retarded children in a residential school, and Ferster and DeMyer (13) have made intensive investigations on procedures appropriate for young autistic children in a hospital setting.

Another group of studies, and a rather large group, has been devoted to the specification of reinforcing stimuli for neonates, infants, preschool children, and older children, as well as to the patterns of behavior that are associated with the basic schedules of reinforcement. In a way, this area of inquiry is continuous with methodological investigations because such information is essential to the planning and execution of all studies. In striving to produce reliable relationships, these studies make explicit the reinforcers in operation and the schedule with which they are presented or withdrawn. Some investigators have taken leads from studies on infrahuman subjects; other investigators have explored new contingencies. For example, Bijou (7) has studied the presentation of positive reinforcers by comparing continuous and intermittent schedules on preschool children. Long (22) has studied fixed ratios, fixed intervals, and variable intervals. Ellis, Barnett, and Pryer (12) and Orlando and Bijou (30) have studied basic intermittent schedules with retarded children. Ferster and DeMyer (13) have studied intermittent schedules with autistic children. Examples of studies on the loss of positive reinforcers (withdrawal of short intervals of cartoon movies) include those by Baer (2, 3) on escape and avoidance behavior in normal preschool children, and by Marshall (28) on institutionalized retarded subjects.

A third group of investigations has been concerned with the response functions of normal and deviant children of varying ages. For example, Brackbill (11) wondered whether the smiling behavior of six-month-old babies has operant properties. Rheingold, Gewirtz, and Ross (32) asked a similar question about the vocalization of infants. The provocative findings from both of these investigations open the way for a host of new studies. In the same vein, Flanagan, Goldiamond, and Azrin (14, 15) sought to learn whether stuttering can be conditioned according to operant principles. Their encouraging results have new implications for this recalcitrant problem area.

A fourth group of studies has been devoted to setting events; i.e., to circumstances that influence the relationships in a specific psychological interaction. Included in this group are studies by Gewirtz and Baer (16) on the effects of satiation and deprivation of social stimulation on a task reinforced by social stimuli, and by Lovaas (24) on the influence of exposure to symbolic aggression on aggressive behavior in normal preschool children.

A fifth group of investigations centers around problems of discriminative stimuli (stimulus control, cues, perceptual stimuli). Studies on the acquisition and stability of multiple schedules by Bijou (8) on normal children and by Bijou and Orlando (10) on retarded children are of this nature. The influence of verbal behavior on other verbal behavior and on nonverbal behavior, as studied by Lovaas (24, 25), are also pertinent. The laboratory study by Azrin and Lindsley (1) on cooperative behavior also falls in this category. In this last-named study, the cue for the behavior of the "follower" was an objectively defined response by the "leader."

There are several clearly apparent trends in the work of investigators who are following a natural science theory of development that embodies an empirical concept of reinforcement. They may be mentioned briefly. First, the work of such investigators shows a strong interest in adding to an empirical theory of development rather than in testing deductions from a formal theory. Second, there is a preference for laboratory-experimental studies. Third, there is a tendency to study individual children intensively and to seek control of variables through laboratory procedures rather than through psychometric procedures. Experimental design by laboratory control is not indigenous to this approach but is attractive, since many investigators believe that individual analysis is an ultimate objective of a behavioral science. One correlate of this practice is the preference for a standard laboratory situation for all studies, using variations of stimulus or response functions pertinent to the particular study. A second preference is for analysis in free operant situations (rather than under restricted operant conditions as is exemplified in the WGTA) because free operant situations allow for greater control and provide more detailed and continuous information.

SUMMARY

The empirical concept of reinforcement as related to child development has been discussed in the context of a theory from a natural science point of view. The position states that the data of psychological development are progressive changes in behavior (differentiation and increases in complexity) that evolve from interactions with the environment of development. The environments of development consist of stimulus events and of setting events. Stimulus events are stimuli that are described by physical and functional procedures; setting events are operations that affect specific stimulus-response interactions. The developing child is said to be a series of stimulus and response events. The stimulus aspects of the child (internal stimuli) are analyzed in the same way as those in the external environment.

The response aspect is also described by its physical properties (frequency, amplitude, latency, etc.) and by its functional properties (whether they are controlled by stimuli that precede or follow them). The former are called respondents, reflexes, or involuntary responses. The latter are designated as operants, instrumental or voluntary responses.

The empirical concept of reinforcement applies only to operant behavior. It states that operant behavior is strengthened by certain consequent stimulus events. Some stimuli strengthen on presentation; some, on withdrawal. The only way to find out whether a stimulus is neutral (no strengthening value), positive (strengthens on presentation), or negative (strengthens on withdrawal) is by empirical test. Research along this line seeks not to "explain" reinforcement with organismic data or with intervening variables, but seeks to delineate the empirical relationships between reinforcing conditions and changes in operant strength.

Samples of research have been grouped into five categories. The first group is devoted to the development of a methodology; the second, to an analysis of the effects of schedules of reinforcing stimuli; the third, to a study of response functions; the fourth, to an investigation of some setting events; the fifth, to discriminative or perceptual stimuli. Some of the predominant characteristics of the work in this area have been pointed out. These include an emphasis on empirical theory building and a preference for laboratory analysis, individual control, and free operant methods.

REFERENCES

1. Azrin, N. H., & Lindsley, O. R. The reinforcement of cooperation between children. *J. Abn. & Soc. Psychol.,* 1956, **52,** 100–102.
2. Baer, D. M. Escape and avoidance response of pre-school children, to two schedules of reinforcement withdrawal. *J. Exper. Anal. Behav.,* 1960, **3,** 155–160.
3. Baer, D. M. Effects of withdrawal of positive reinforcement on an extinguishing response in your children. *Child Devel.,* 1961, **32,** 67–74.
4. Baer, D. M. A technique of social reinforcement for the study of child behavior: Behavior avoiding reinforcement withdrawal. *Child Devel.,* 1962, **33,** 847–858.
5. Bijou, S. W. A systematic approach to an experimental analysis of young children. *Child Devel.,* 1955, **26,** 161–168.
6. Bijou, S. W. Methodology for an experimental analysis of child behavior. *Psychol. Rep.,* 1957, **3,** 243–250.
7. Bijou, S. W. Patterns of reinforcement and resistance to extinction in young children. *Child Devel.,* 1957, **28,** 47–54.
8. Bijou, S. W. Discrimination performance as a baseline for individual analysis of young children. *Child Devel.,* 1961, **32,** 163–170.
9. Bijou, S. W., & Baer, D. M. Child development: A systematic and empirical theory. New York: Appleton-Century-Crofts, 1961.

10. BIJOU, S. W., & ORLANDO, R. Rapid development of multiple-schedule performance with retarded children. *J. Exper. Anal. Behav.,* 1961, **4,** 7–16.
11. BRACKBILL, Y. Extinction of the smiling response in infants as a function of reinforcement schedule. *Child Devel.,* 1958, **29,** 115–124.
12. ELLIS, N. R., BARNETT, C. D., & PRYER, M. W. Operant behavior in mental defectives: Exploratory studies. *J. Exper. Anal. Behav.,* 1960, **3,** 63–69.
13. FERSTER, C. B., & DEMYER, M. K. The development of performances in autistic children in an automatically controlled environment. *J. Chronic Dis.,* 1961, **13,** 312–345.
14. FLANAGAN, B., GOLDIAMOND, I., & AZRIN, N. Operant stuttering: The control of stuttering through response contingent consequences. *J. Exper. Anal. Behav.,* 1958, **2,** 173–178.
15. FLANAGAN, B., GOLDIAMOND, I., & AZRIN, N. Instatement of stuttering in normally fluent individuals through operant procedures. *Science,* 1959, **130,** 979–981.
16. GEWIRTZ, J. L., & BAER, D. M. Deprivation and satiation of social reinforcers as drive conditions. *J. Abn. & Soc. Psychol.,* 1958, **56,** 165–172.
17. GILBERT, T. F. Fundamental dimensional properties of the operant. *Psychol. Rev.,* 1958, **65,** 272–282.
18. HILGARD, E. R. Theories of Learning (2d ed.) New York: Appleton-Century-Crofts, 1956.
19. HOLLAND, J. G., & SKINNER, B. F. The Analysis of behavior. New York: McGraw-Hill, 1961.
20. KANTOR, J. R. Interbehavioral psychology (rev. ed.) Bloomington, Ind.: Principia, 1959.
21. KELLER, F. S., & SCHOENFELD, W. N. Principles of psychology. New York: Appleton-Century-Crofts, 1950.
22. LONG, E. R. The use of operant conditioning techniques in children. In S. Fisher (Ed.), *Child Research in Psychopharmacology.* Springfield, Ill.: Charles C. Thomas, 1959.
23. LONG, E. R., HAMMACK, J. T., MAY, F., & CAMPBELL, B. J. Intermittent reinforcement of operant behavior in children. *J. Exper. Anal. Behav.,* 1958, **1,** 315–339.
24. LOVAAS, O. I. Effects of exposure to symbolic aggression on aggressive behavior. *Child Devel.,* 1961, **32,** 37–44.
25. LOVAAS, O. I. Interaction between verbal and non-verbal behavior. *Child Devel.,* 1961, **32,** 329–336.
26. LOVAAS, O. I. Cue properties of words: The control of operant responding by rate and content of verbal operants. *Child Devel.,* 1964, **35,** 245–256.
27. MACCORQUADALE, K. Learning. *Ann. Rev. Psychol.,* 1955, **6,** 29–62.
28. MARSHALL, D. A. The effects of withdrawal of a positive reinforcer on an extinguishing response in developmentally retarded children. Unpublished Master's thesis, University of Washington, Seattle, 1961.
29. MOWRER, O. H. On the dual nature of learning: A reinterpretation of "conditioning" and "problem-solving." *Harvard Educ. Rev.,* 1947, **17,** 102–148.
30. ORLANDO, R., & BIJOU, S. W. Single and multiple schedules of reinforcement in developmentally retarded children. *J. Exper. Anal. Behav.,* 1960, **3,** 339–348.

31. Orlando, R., Bijou, S. W., Tyler, R. M., & Marshall, D. A. A laboratory for the experimental analysis of developmentally retarded children. *Psychol. Rep.*, 1960, **7**, 261–267.
32. Rheingold, H. L., Gewirtz, J. L., & Ross, H. W. Social conditioning of vocalizations in the infant. *J. Comp. & Physiol. Psychol.*, 1959, **52**, 68–73.
33. Schlosberg, H. The relationship between success and the laws of conditioning. *Psychol. Rev.*, 1937, **44**, 379–394.
34. Skinner, B. F. The Behavior of Organisms. New York: Appleton-Century-Crofts, 1938.
35. Skinner, B. F. Science and Human Behavior. New York: Macmillan, 1953.

3
ON THE NEED FOR RELATIVISM*

JEROME KAGAN

THE PSYCHOLOGY of the first half of this century was absolutistic, outer directed, and intolerant of ambiguity. When a college student carries this unholy trio of traits he is called authoritarian, and such has been the temperament of the behavioral sciences. But the era of authoritarian psychology may be nearing its dotage, and the decades ahead may nurture a discipline that is relativistic, oriented to internal processes, and accepting of the idea that behavior is necessarily ambiguous.

Like her elder sisters, psychology began her dialogue with nature using a vocabulary of absolutes. Stimulus, response, rejection, affection, emotion, reward, and punishment were labels for classes of phenomena that were believed to have a fixed reality. We believed we could write a definition of these constructs that would fix them permanently and allow us to know them unequivocally at any time in any place.

Less than 75 years ago biology began to drift from the contraints of an absolute view of events and processes when she acknowledged that the fate of a small slice of ectodermal tissue depended on whether it was placed near the area of the eye or the toe. Acceptance of the simple notion that whether an object moves or not depends on where you are standing is a little over a half century old in a science that has 5 centuries of formalization. With physics as the referent in time, one might expect a relativistic attitude to influence psychology by the latter part of the century. But philosophical upheavals in one science catalyze change in other disciplines and one can see signs of budding relativism in the intellectual foundations of the social sciences.

The basic theme of this paper turns on the need for more relativistic definitions of selected theoretical constructs. "Relativistic" refers to a definition in which context and the state of the individual are part of the defining statement. Relativism does not preclude the development of operational

* From the *American Psychologist,* 1967, *22,* 131–142. Reprinted with permission from the author and the American Psychological Association.

Preparation of this paper was supported in part by research Grant MH-8792 from the National Institute of Mental Health, United States Public Health Service. This paper is an abridged version of a lecture presented at the Educational Testing Service, Princeton, New Jersey, January 1966.

definitions, but makes that task more difficult. Nineteenth-century physics viewed mass as an absolute value; twentieth-century physics made the definition of mass relative to the speed of light. Similarly, some of psychology's popular constructs have to be defined in relation to the state and belief structure of the organism, rather than in terms of an invariant set of external events. Closely related to this need is the suggestion that some of the energy devoted to a search for absolute, stimulus characteristics of reinforcement be redirected to a search for the determinants of attention in the individual.

It is neither possible nor wise to assign responsibility to one person or event for major changes in conceptual posture, but Helson's recent book on adaptation-level theory (Helson, 1964), Schachter's (Schachter & Singer, 1962) hypothesis concerning the cognitive basis of affects, and Hernández-Peón's demonstration of the neurophysiological bases of selective attention (Hernández-Peón, Scherrer, & Jouvet, 1956) are contemporary stimulants for a relativistic view of psychological phenomena.

Three messages are implicit in the work of these men.

1. If a stimulus is to be regarded as an event to which a subject responds or is likely to respond then it is impossible to describe a stimulus without describing simultaneously the expectancy, and preparation of the organism for that stimulus. Effective stimuli must be distinct from the person's original adaptation level. Contrast and distinctiveness, which are relative, are part and parcel of the definition of a stimulus.

2. The failure of one individual to respond to an event that is an effective stimulus for a second individual is not always the result of central selection after all the information is in, but can be due to various forms of peripheral inhibition. Some stimuli within inches of the face do not ever reach the interpretive cortex and, therefore, do not exist psychologically.

3. Man reacts less to the objective quality of external stimuli than he does to categorizations of those stimuli.

These new generalizations strip the phrase "physical stimulus" of much of its power and certainty, and transfer the scepter of control—in man, at least—to cognitive interpretations. *Contrast, cognitively interpreted, becomes an important key to understanding the incentives for human behavior.* Since contrast depends so intimately on context and expectancy, it must be defined relativistically.

The issue of relativism can be discussed in many contexts. Many existing constructs are already defined in terms of contextual relations. The concept of authority only has meaning if there are fiefs to rule. The role of father has no meaning without a child. The concept of noun, verb, or adjective is defined by context—by the relation of the word to other constituents. We shall consider in some detail the ways in which a relativistic orientation touches two other issues in psychology: the learning of self-descriptive statements (the hoary idea of the self-concept), and, even more fundamentally, some of the mechanisms that define the learning process.

THE CONCEPT OF THE SELF

The development and establishment of a self-concept is often framed in absolute terms. The classic form of the statement assumes that direct social reinforcements and identification models have fixed, invariant effects on the child. Praise and love from valued caretakers are assumed to lead the child to develop positive self-evaluations; whereas, criticism and rejection presumably cause self-derogatory beliefs. The presumed cause-effect sequences imply that there is a something—a definable set of behaviors—that can be labeled social rejection, and that the essence of these rejecting acts leads to invariant changes in the self-concept of the child. Let us examine the concept of rejection under higher magnification.

The concept of rejection—peer or parental—has been biased toward an absolute definition. Witness the enormous degree of commonality in conceptualization of this concept by investigators who have studied a mother's behavior with her child (Baldwin, Kalhorn, & Breese, 1945; Becker, 1964; Kagan & Moss, 1962; Schaefer, 1959; Schaefer & Bayley, 1963; Sears, Maccoby, & Levin, 1957). These investigators typically decide that harsh physical punishment and absence of social contact or physical affection are the essential indexes of an attitude called maternal rejection. It would be close to impossible for an American rater to categorize a mother as high on both harsh beating of her child and on a loving attitude. A conventionally trained psychologist observing a mother who did not talk to her child for 5 hours would probably view the mother as rejecting. This may be a high form of provincialism. Alfred Baldwin reports that in the rural areas of northern Norway, where homes are 5 to 10 miles apart, and the population constant for generations, one often sees maternal behaviors which an American observer would regard as pathognomonically rejecting in an American mother. The Norwegian mother sees her 4-year-old sitting in the doorway blocking the passage to the next room. She does not ask him to move, but bends down, silently picks him up and moves him away before she passes into the next room. Our middle-class observer would be tempted to view this indifference as a sign of dislike. However, most mothers in this Arctic outpost behave this way and the children do not behave the way rejected children should by our current theoretical propositions.

An uneducated Negro mother from North Carolina typically slaps her 4-year-old across the face when he does not come to the table on time. The intensity of the mother's act tempts our observer to conclude that the mother hates, or at best, does not like her child. However, during a half-hour conversation the mother says she loves her child and wants to guarantee that he does not grow up to be a bad boy or a delinquent. And she believes firmly that physical punishment is the most effective way to socialize him. Now her behavior seems to be issued in the service of affection rather than hate.

Determination of whether a parent is rejecting or not cannot be answered by focusing primarily on the behaviors of the parents. Rejection is not a fixed, invariant quality of behavior qua behavior. Like pleasure, pain, or beauty, rejection is in the mind of the rejectee. It is a belief held by the child; not an action by a parent.

We must acknowledge, first, a discontinuity in the meaning of an acceptance-rejection dimension before drawing further implications. We must distinguish between the child prior to 30 or 36 months of age, before he symbolically evaluates the actions of others, and the child thereafter.

We require, first, a concept to deal with the child's belief of his value in the eyes of others. The child of 4 or 5 years is conceptually mature enough to have recognized that certain resources parents possess are difficult for the child to obtain. He views these resources as sacrifices and interprets their receipt as signs that the parents value him. The child constructs a tote board of the differential value of parental gifts—be they psychological or material. The value of the gift depends on its scarcity. A $10.00 toy from a busy executive father is not a valued resource; the same toy from a father out of work is much valued. The value depends on the child's personal weightings. This position would lead to solopsism were it not for the fact that most parents are essentially narcissistic and do not readily give the child long periods of uninterrupted companionship. Thus, most children place high premium on this act. Similarly, parents are generally reluctant to proffer unusually expensive gifts to children, and this act acquires value for most youngsters. Finally, the child learns from the public media that physical affection means positive evaluation and he is persuaded to assign premium worth to this set of acts. There is, therefore, some uniformity across children in a culture in the evaluation of parental acts. But the anchor point lies within the child, not with the particular parental behaviors.

This definition of acceptance or rejection is not appropriate during the opening years. The 1-year-old does not place differential symbolic worth on varied parental acts, and their psychological significance derives from the overt responses they elicit and strengthen. A heavy dose of vocalization and smiling to an infant is traditionally regarded as indicative of maternal affection and acceptance. This bias exists because we have accepted the myth that "affection" is the essential nutrient that produces socially adjusted children, adolescents, and adults. The bias maintains itself because we observe a positive association between degree of parental smiling and laughing to the infant and prosocial behavior in the child during the early years. The responses of smiling, laughing, and approaching people are learned in the opening months of life on the basis of standard conditioning principles. This conclusion is supported by the work of Rheingold and Gewirtz (1959) and Brackbill (1958). However, phenotypically similar behaviors in a 10- or 20-year-old may have a different set of antecedents. The argument that different definitions of rejection-acceptance must be written for the pre- and postsymbolic child gains persuasive power from the fact that there are no data indicating that degree of prosocial behavior in the child is stable from 6 months to 16 years. Indeed, the longitudinal material from the Fels Research Institute study of behavior stability (Kagan & Moss, 1962) showed no evidence of any relation between joy or anxiety in the presence of adults during the first 2–3 years of life and phenotypically similar behaviors at 6, 12, or 24 years of age. The child behaviors that are presumed, by theory, to be the consequences of low or high parental rejection do not show stability from infancy through adolescence. This may be because the childhood responses, though phenotypically similar to the adult acts, may be acquired and maintained through different experiences at different periods.

It seems reasonable to suggest, therefore, that different theoretical words are necessary for the following three classes of phenomena: (*a*) an attitude on the part of the parent, (*b*) the quality and frequency of acts of parental care and social stimulation directed toward the infant, and (*c*) a child's assessment of his value in the eyes of another. All three classes are currently viewed as of the same cloth. The latter meaning of "rejection" (i.e., a belief held by a child) is obviously relativistic for it grows out of different experiences in different children.

SELF-DESCRIPTIVE LABELS

Let us probe further into the ideas surrounding the learning of self-evaluation statements, beyond the belief, "I am not valued." The notion of a self-concept has a long and spotted history and although it has masqueraded by many names in different theoretical costumes, its intrinsic meaning has changed only a little. A child presumably learns self-descriptive statements whose contents touch the salient attributes of the culture. The mechanisms classically invoked to explain how these attributes are learned have stressed the invariant effects of direct social reinforcement and identification. The girl who is told she is attractive, annoying, or inventive, comes to believe these appellations and to apply these qualifiers to herself. We have assumed that the laws governing the learning of self-descriptive labels resemble the learning of other verbal habits with frequency and contiguity of events being the shapers of the habit. Identification as a source of self-labels involves a different mechanism, but retains an absolutistic frame of reference. The child assumes that he shares attributes with particular models. If the model is viewed as subject to violent rages, the child concludes that he, too, shares this tendency.

Theory and data persuade us to retain some faith in these propositions. But relativistic factors also seem to sculpt the acquisition of self-descriptive labels, for the child evaluates himself on many psychological dimensions by inferring his rank order from a delineated reference group. The 10-year-old does not have absolute measuring rods to help him decide how bright, handsome, or likeable he is. He naturally and spontaneously uses his immediate peer group as the reference for these evaluations. An immediate corollary of this statement is that the child's evaluation is dependent upon the size and psychological quality of the reference group, and cannot be defined absolutely. Specifically, the larger the peer group, the less likely a child will conclude he is high in the rank order, the less likely he will decide he is unusually smart, handsome, or capable of leadership. Consider two boys with IQs of 130 and similar intellectual profiles. One lives in a small town, the other in a large city. It is likely that the former child will be the most competent in his peer group while the latter is likely to regard himself as fifth or sixth best. This difference in perceived rank order has obvious action consequences since we acknowledge that expectancies govern behavior. In sum, aspects of the self-descriptive process appear to develop in relativistic soil.

LEARNING AND ATTENTION

A second issue that touches relativistic definitions deals with a shift from external definitions of reinforcement—that is, reward or pleasure—to definitions that are based more directly on internal processes involving the concept of attention. Failure to understand the nature of learning is one of the major intellectual frustrations for many psychologists. The query, "What is learning?" has the same profound ring as the question, "What is a gene?" had a decade ago. Our biological colleagues have recently had a major insight while psychology is still searching. The murky question, "What is learning?" usually reduces to an attempt to discover the laws relating stimuli, pain, and pleasure, on the one hand, with habit acquisition and performance, on the other. Pain, pleasure, and reinforcement, are usually defined in terms of events that are external to the organism and have an invariant flavor. Miller (1951) suggested that reinforcement was isomorphic with stimulus reduction; Leuba (1955) argued for an optimal level of stimulation, but both implied that there was a level that could be specified and measured. We should like to argue first that sources of pleasure and, therefore of reinforcement, are often relative, and second, that the essence of learning is more dependent on attentional involvement by the learner than on specific qualities of particular external events.

The joint ideas that man is a pleasure seeker and that one can designate specific forms of stimulation as sources of pleasure are central postulates in every man's theory of behavior. Yet we find confusion when we seek a definition of pleasure. The fact that man begins life with a small core set of capacities for experience that he wishes to repeat cannot be disputed. This is a pragmatic view of pleasure and we can add a dash of phenomenology to bolster the intuitive validity of this point of view. A sweet taste and a light touch in selected places are usually pleasant. Recently, we have added an important new source of pleasure. It is better to say we have rediscovered a source of pleasure, for Herbert Spencer was a nineteenth-century progenitor of the idea that *change in stimulation* is a source of pleasure for rats, cats, monkeys, or men. But, change is short-lived. quickly digested, and transformed to monotony. Popping up in front of an infant and saying peek-a-boo is pleasant for a 3-month-old infant for about 15 minutes, for a 10-month-old infant for 3 minutes and for a 30-month-old child, a few seconds. This pleasant experience, like most events that elicit their repetition a few times before dying, is usually conceptualized as a change in stimulation. The source of the pleasure is sought in the environment. Why should change in external stimulation be pleasant? The understanding of pleasure and reinforcement in man is difficult enough without having to worry about infrahuman considerations. Let us restrict the argument to the human. The human is a cognitive creature who is attempting to put structure or create schema for incoming stimulation. *A schema is a representation of an external pattern;* much as an artist's illustration is a representation of an event. A schema for a visual pattern is a partial and somewhat distorted version of what the photograph would be. Consider the usefulness of the following hypothesis:

The creation of a schema for an event is one major source of pleasure. When one can predict an event perfectly, the schema is formed. As long as prediction is not perfect the schema is not yet formed. The peek-a-boo game works for 15 minutes with a 12-week-old for it takes him that long to be able to predict the event—the "peek-a-boo." Charlesworth (1965) has demonstrated the reinforcing value of "uncertainty" in an experiment in which the peek-a-boo face appeared either in the same locus every trial, alternated between two loci, or appeared randomly in one of two loci. The children persisted in searching for the face for a much longer time under the random condition than under the other two conditions. The random presentation was reinforcing for a longer period of time, not because it possessed a more optimum level of external stimulation than the other reinforcement schedules, but because it took longer for the child to create a schema for the random presentation and the process of creating a schema is a source of pleasure.

Consider another sign of pleasure beside persistence in issuing a particular response. Display of a smile or laugh is a good index of pleasure. Indeed, Tomkins' (1962) scheme for affect demands that pleasure be experienced if these responses appear. Consider two studies that bear on the relation between pleasure and the creation of schema. In our laboratory during the last 2 years, we have seen the same infants at 4, 8, and 13 months of age and have shown them a variety of visual patterns representative of human faces and human forms. In one episode, the 4-month-old infants are shown achromatic slides of a photograph of a regular male face, a schematic outline of a male face, and two disarranged, disordered faces. The frequency of occurrence of smiling to the photograph of the regular face is over *twice* the frequency observed to the regular schematic face—although looking time is identical—and over *four times* the frequency shown to the disordered faces. In another, more realistic episode, the 4-month-old infants see a regular, flesh-colored sculptured face in three dimensions and a distorted version of that face in which the eyes, nose, and mouth are rearranged. At 4 months of age the occurrence of smiling to the regular face is over three times the frequency displayed to the distorted version, but looking time is identical. There are two interpretations of this difference (Kagan, Henker, Hen-Tov, Levine, & Lewis, 1966). One explanation argues that the mother's face has become a secondary reward; the regular face stands for pleasure because it has been associated with care and affection from the mother. As a result, it elicits more smiles. An alternative interpretation is that the smile response has become conditioned to the human face via reciprocal contact between mother and infant. A third interpretation, not necessarily exclusive of these, is that the smile can be elicited when the infant matches stimulus to schema —when he has an "aha" reaction; when he makes a cognitive discovery. The 4-month-old infant is cognitively close to establishing a relatively firm schema of a human face. When a regular representation of a face is presented to him there is a short period during which the stimulus is assimilated to the schema and then after several seconds, a smile may occur. The smile is released following the perceptual recognition of the face, and reflects the assimilation of the stimulus to the infant's schema—a small, but significant act of creation. This hypothesis is supported by the fact that the typical latency between the onset of looking at the regular face (in the 4-month-old) and the onset of smiling is about 3 to 5 seconds. The smile usually does not occur immediately but only after the infant has studied the stimulus. If one sees this phenomenon live, it is difficult to avoid the conclusion that the smile is released following an act of perceptual recognition.

Additional data on these and other children at 8 months of age support this idea. At 8 months, frequency of smiling to both the regular and distorted faces is *reduced dramatically,* indicating that smiling does not covary with the reward value of the face. The face presumably has acquired more reward value by 8 months than it had at 4 months. However, the face is now a much firmer schema and recognition of it is immediate. There is no effortful act of recognition necessary for most infants. As a result, smiling is less likely to occur. Although smiling is much less frequent at 8 than 4 months to all faces, the frequency of smiling to the distorted face now *equals* the frequency displayed to the regular face. We interpret this to mean that the distorted face is sufficiently similar to the child's schema of a regular face that it can be recognized as such.

The pattern of occurrence of cardiac deceleration to the regular and distorted three-dimensional faces furnishes the strongest support for this argument. A cardiac deceleration of about 8 to 10 beats often accompanies attention to selected incoming visual stimuli in adults, school-age children, and infants. Moreover, the deceleration tends to be maximal when the stimuli are not overly familiar or completely novel, but are of intermediate familiarity. One hypothesis maintains that a large deceleration is most likely to occur when an act of perceptual recognition occurs, when the organism has a congitive surprise. Let us assume that there is one trial for which this type of reaction occurs with maximal magnitude. If one examines the one stimulus presentation (out of a total of 16 trials) that produces the largest cardiac deceleration, a lawful change occurs between 4 and 8 months of age. At 4 months of age more of the infants showed their largest deceleration to the regular face (45% of the group: $n = 52$) than to the scrambled (34%), no eyes (11%), or blank faces (10%). At 8 months, the majority of the infants ($n = 52$) showed their largest deceleration to the scrambled face (50% to scrambled versus 21% to regular face). This difference is interpreted to mean that the scrambled face now assumes a similar position on the assimilation continuum that the regular face did 16 weeks earlier.

At 13 months of age these infants are shown six three-dimensional representations of a male human form and a free form matched for area, coloration, and texture with the human form. The stimuli include a faithful representation of a regular man, that same man with his head placed between his legs, the same man with all limbs and head collaged in an unusual and scrambled pattern, the man's body with a mule's head, and the mule's head on the man's body, the man's body with three identical heads, and a free form. The distribution of smiles to these stimuli is leptokurtic, with over 70% of all the smiles occurring to the animal head on the human body and the three-headed man, forms that were moderate transformations of the regular man, and stimuli that required active assimilation. The free form and the scrambled man rarely elicited smiles from these infants. These stimuli are too difficult to assimilate to the schema of a human form possessed by a 13-month-old infant. It is interesting to note that the regular human form sometimes elicited the verbal response "daddy" or a hand waving from the child. These instrumental social reactions typically did not occur to the transformations. The occurrence of cardiac deceleration to these patterns agrees with this hypothesis. At 13 months of age, the man with his head between his legs, the man with the animal head, or the three-headed man, each elicited the largest cardiac decelerations more frequently than the regular man, the scrambled man, or the free form ($p < .05$ for each comparison). Thus, large cardiac decelerations and smiles were most likely to occur to stimuli that seemed to require tiny, quiet cognitive discoveries—miniaturized versions of Archimedes' "Eureka."

It appears that the act of matching stimulus to schema when the match is close but not yet perfect is a dynamic event. Stimuli that deviate a critical amount from the child's schema for a pattern are capable of eliciting an active process of recognition, and this process behaves as if it were a source of pleasure. Stimuli that are easily assimilable or too difficult to assimilate do not elicit these reactions.

A recent study by Edward Zigler adds important support to the notion that the smile indicates the pleasure of an assimilation. Children in Grades 2, 3, 4, and 5 looked at cartoons that required little or no reading. The children were asked to explain the cartoon while an observer coded the spontaneous occurrence of laughing and smiling while the children were studying the cartoons. It should come as no surprise that verbal comprehension of the cartoons increased in a linear fashion with age. But laughing and smiling increased through Grade 4 and then declined markedly among the fifth-grade children. The fifth graders understood the cartoons too well. There was no gap between stimulus and schema and no smiling. Sixteen-week-old infants and 8-year-old children smile spontaneously at events that seem to have one thing in common—the event is a partial match to an existing schema and an active process of recognitory assimilation must occur.

The fact that a moderate amount of mismatch between event and schema is one source of pleasure demands the conclusion that it is not always possible to say that a specific event will always be a source of pleasure. The organism's state and structure must be in the equation. This conclusion parallels the current interest in complexity and information uncertainty. The psychologist with an information-theory prejudice classifies a stimulus as uncertain and often assumes that he does not have to be too concerned with the attributes of the viewer. This error of the absolute resembles the nineteenth-century error in physics and biology. This is not a titillating or pedantic, philosophical issue. Psychology rests on a motive-reinforcement foundation which regards pleasure and pain as pivotal ideas in the grand theory. These constructs have tended to generate absolute definitions. We have been obsessed with finding a fixed and invariant characterization of pleasure, pain, and reinforcement. Melzack & Wall (1965) point out that although the empirical data do not support the notion of a fixed place in the brain that mediates pain, many scientists resist shedding this comfortable idea. Olds' (1958, 1962) discovery of brain reinforcing areas has generated excitement because many of us want to believe that pleasure has a fixed and absolute locus. The suspicious element in this discovery of pleasure spots is that there is no habituation of responses maintained by electrical stimulation to hypothalamic or septal nuclei, and minimal resistance to extinction of habits acquired via this event. Yet, every source of pleasure known to phenomenal man does satiate—for awhile or forever—and habits that lead to pleasant events do persist for a while after the pleasure is gone. These observations are troubling and additional inquiry is necessary if we are to decide whether these cells are indeed the bed where pleasure lies.

We are convinced that contiguity alone does not always lead to learning. Something must ordinarily be added to contiguity in order to produce a new bond. Psychology has chosen to call this extra added mysterious something reinforcement, much like 18th-century chemists chose to label their unknown substance phlogiston. If one examines the variety of external events that go by the name of reinforcement it soon becomes clear that this word is infamously inexact. A shock to an animal's paw is a reinforcement, a verbal chastisement is a reinforcement, an examiner's smile is a reinforcement, a pellet of food is a reinforcement, and a sigh indicating tension reduction after watching a killer caught in a Hitchcock movie is a reinforcement. These events have little, if any, phenotypic similarity. What then, do they have in common? For if they have nothing in common it is misleading to call them by the same name. Learning theorists have acknowledged their failure to supply an independent a priori definition of reinforcement and the definition they use is purely pragmatic. A reinforcement is anything that helps learning. And so, we ask: What has to be added to contiguity in order to obtain learning? A good candidate for the missing ingredient is the phrase "attentional involvement." Let us consider again the events called reinforcements: a shock, food, a smile, each of these acts to attract the attention of the organism to some agent or object. They capture the organism's attention and maybe that is why they facilitate learning. Consider the idea that what makes an event reinforcing is the fact that it (*a*) elicits the organism's attention to the feedback from the response he has just made and to the mosaic of stimuli in the learning situation and (*b*) acts as an incentive for a subsequent response. The latter quality is what ties the word "reinforcement" to the concepts of motivation and need, but much learning occurs without the obvious presence of motives or needs. Ask any satiated adult to attend carefully and remember the bond syzygy-aardvark. It is likely that learning will occur in one trial. It is not unreasonable to argue that a critical component of events that have historically been called reinforcement is their ability to attract the organism's attention. They have been distinctive cues in a context; they have been events discrepant from the individual's adaptation level. If attention is acknowledged as critical in new mental acquisitions it is appropriate to ask if attention is also bedded in relativistic soil. The answer appears to be "Yes." The dramatic experiments of Hernández-Peón and his colleagues (1956) are persuasive in indicating that attention investment may not be distributed to many channels at once. One has to know the state of the organism. Knowledge of the organism's distribution of attention in a learning situation may clarify many controversial theoretical polemics that range from imprinting in chickens to emotion in college undergraduates. For example, comparative psychologists quarrel about which set of external conditions allow imprinting to occur with maximal effect. Some say the decoy should move; others argue that the young chick should move; still others urge that the decoy be brightly colored (e.g., Bateson, 1964a, 1964b; Hess, 1959; Klopfer, 1965; Thompson & Dubanoski, 1964). The quarrel centers around the use of phenotypically different observable conditions. Perhaps all these suggestions are valid. Moving the decoy, or active following by the infant chick, or a distinctively colored decoy all maximize the organism's level of attention to the decoy. The genotypic event may remain the same across all of these manipulations.

A similar interpretation can be imposed on Held's (1965) recent hypothesis concerning the development of space and pattern perception. Held controlled the visual experience of pairs of kittens. The only exposure to light was limited to a few hours a day when one kitten was placed in a gondola and moved around by an active, free kitten in an arena whose walls were painted in vertical stripes. After 30 hours of such experience each kitten was tested. The free kitten showed appropriate visual reactions. It blinked when an object approached; it put up its paws to avoid collision when carried near to a surface; it avoided the deep side of a visual cliff. The passive passenger kitten did not show these normal reactions. Why? Held, focusing on the obvious external variable of activity versus no activity, concludes that the sensory feedback accompanying movement is necessary to develop visual-motor control. This conclusion rests on the assumption that the passive kitten sitting in the gondola was attending to the stripes on the wall as intently as the free walking kitten. This assumption may be gratuitous. If the passive kitten were staring blankly—as many human infants do—then one would not expect these animals to develop normal perceptual structures. This interpretation may not be better, but it has a different flavor than the one suggested by Held.

A final example of the central role of attention is seen in Aronfreed's (1964, 1965) recent work on the learning of self-critical comments. Aronfreed states that the learning of a self-critical comment proceeds best if the child is first punished and then hears a social agent speak the self-critical statement. He interprets this result in drive reduction language. However, suppose one asks which sequence is most likely to maximize a child's attention to the adult's comment—Punish first and then speak to the child? Or speak first and then punish? The former sequence should be more effective. The punishment is a violation of what the child expects from a strange adult and recruits the child's attention to the adult. The child is primed to listen to the self-critical commendation and thus more likely to learn it.

Distinctiveness of Cues

The above examples suggest that the organism's distribution of attention is a critical process that should guide our search for the bases of many diverse phenomena. One of the critical bases for recruitment of attention pivots on the idea of distinctiveness of the signal. Jakobson and Halle (1956) argue that the chronology of acquisition of phonemes proceeds according to a principle of distinctive elements. Distinctive elements capture the child's attention and give direction to the order of learning.

The importance of *relative distinctiveness of cues* finds an interesting illustration in the concept of affect. The concept of emotion has lived through three distinct eras in modern times. The pre-Jamesian assumed the sequence was: stimulus event—cognition—visceral response. James interchanged events two and three and said that the visceral afferent feedback occurred before the cognition. But Cannon quieted Jamesian ideas until Schachter's ingenious studies and catching explanations suggested that the individual experiences a puzzling set of visceral afferent sensations and integrates them cognitively. The language integration of visceral feelings, cognition, and context is an affect. This imaginative suggestion may be maximally valid for Western adults but perhaps minimally appropriate for children because of a developmental change in the relative distinctiveness of visceral cues.

Let us share a small set of assumptions before we proceed with the argument. Aside from pain and its surrogates, the major psychological elicitors of unpleasant visceral afferent sensations are violations of expectancies (uncertainty); anticipation of receiving or losing a desired goal; anticipation of seeing or losing a nurturant person; blocking of goal attainment; and anticipation of harm to the integrity of the body. Each of these event situations becomes conditioned to visceral afferent feedback early in life. These events—or conditioned stimuli—are salient and maximally distinctive for children and affect words are attached to the events, not primarily to the visceral afferent sensations. Thus, the 6-year-old says he is mad because mother did not let him watch television; he says he is sad because the cat died; he says he is happy because he just received a prized toy. Affect words are labels for a set of external events. With development, individuals—with the help of social institutions—learn to protect themselves against most of the unpleasant sources of visceral afferent feedback—against the apocalyptic horsemen of uncertainty, loss of nurturance, goal blocking, and bodily harm. Moreover, they erect defenses against recognizing these events. They defend against recognition that they are confused, rejected, unable to attain a goal, or afraid. Thus, when events occur that are, in fact, representations of these situations, the events are not salient or distinctive and are not labeled. However, the conditioned visceral afferent sensations do occur, as they always have in the past. In the adult, the visceral afferent sensations become more distinctive or salient; whereas, for the child, the external events were salient and distinctive. The adult provides us with the situation Schachter and his colleagues have described. The adult often has visceral afferent sensations but cannot decide why he has them or what they mean. So he scans and searches the immediate past and context and decides that he is happy, sad, alienated, uncommitted, or in love. The essence of this argument is that for the child the external event is more distinctive than the visceral afferent sensations and the affect word is applied to external events. In the adult, the visceral afferent sensations are relatively more distinctive and the affect words are more often applied to them.

The personality differences ascribed to children in different ordinal positions are the result, in part, of differences in relative distinctiveness of social agents. For the firstborn, the adult is the distinctive stimulus to whom to attend; for the second born the older sibling has distinctive value and competes for the attention of the younger child. Only children lie alone for long periods of uninterrupted play. A parent who enters the room and speaks to the infant is necessarily a distinctive stimulus. For a fifth born whose four older siblings continually poke, fuss, and vocalize into the crib, the caretaking adult, is, of necessity, less distinctive and, as a result, less attention will be paid to the adult. The importance of distinctiveness with respect to adaptation level engages the heated controversy surrounding the role of stimulus enrichment with infants and young children from deprived milieux. The pouring on of visual, auditory, and tactile stimulation willy-nilly should be less effective than a single distinctive stimulus presented in a context of quiet so it will be discrepant from the infant's adaptation level. If one takes this hypothesis seriously, a palpable change in enrichment strategies is implied. The theme of this change involves a shifting from a concern with increasing absolute level of stimulation to focusing on distinctiveness of stimulation. Culturally disadvantaged children are not deprived of stimulation; they are deprived of distinctive stimulation.

The early learning of sex role standards and the dramatic concern of school children with sex differences and their own sex role identity becomes reasonable when one considers that the differences between the sexes are highly distinctive. Voice, size, posture, dress, and usual locus of behavior are distinctive attributes that focus the child's attention on them.

One of the reasons why the relation between tutor and learner is important is that some tutors elicit greater attention than others. They are more distinctive. Those of us who contend that learning will be facilitated if the child is identified with or wants to identify with a tutor believe that one of the bases for the facilitation is the greater attention that is directed at a model with whom the child wishes to identify. A recent experiment touches on this issue.

The hypothesis can be simply stated. An individual will attend more closely to an initial stranger with whom he feels he shares attributes than to a stranger with whom he feels he does not share attributes, other things equal. The former model is more distinctive, for a typical adult ordinarily feels he does not share basic personality traits with most of the strangers that he meets. The subjects in this study were 56 Radcliffe freshmen and sophomores preselected for the following pair of traits. One group, the academics, were rated by four judges—all roommates—as being intensely involved in studies much more than they were in dating, clubs, or social activities. The second group, the social types, were rated as being much more involved in dating and social activities than they were in courses or grades. No subject was admitted into the study unless all four judges agreed that she fit one of these groups.

Each subject was seen individually by a Radcliffe senior, and told that each was participating in a study of creativity. The subject was told that Radcliffe seniors had written poems and that two of the poets were selected by the Harvard faculty as being the best candidates. The faculty could not decide which girl was the more creative and the student was going to be asked to judge the creativity of each of two poems that the girls had written. The subjects were told that creativity is independent of IQ for bright people and they were told that since the faculty knew the personality traits of the girls, the student would be given that information also. The experimenter then described one of the poets as an academic grind and the other as a social activist. Each subject listened to two different girls recite two different poems on a tape. Order of presentation and voice of the reader were counterbalanced in an appropriate design. After the two poems were read the subject was asked for a verbatim recall of each poem, asked to judge its creativity, and finally, asked which girl she felt most similar to. Incidentally, over 95% of the subjects said they felt more similar to the model that they indeed matched in reality. Results supported the original hypothesis. Recall was best when a girl listened to a communicator with whom she shared personality traits. The academic subjects recalled more of the poem when it was read by the academic model than by the social model; whereas, the social subjects recalled more of the poem when it was read by the social model than the academic model. This study indicates that an individual will pay more attention to a model who possesses similar personality attributes, than to one who is not similar to the subject. Distinctiveness of tutor is enhanced by a perceived relation between learner and tutor.

Myths and superstitions are established around the kinds of experimental manipulations teachers or psychologists should perform in order to maximize the probability that learning will occur. When one focuses on the kind of manipulation—providing a model, giving a reinforcement, labeling the situation, punishing without delay—there is a strong push to establish superstitions about how behavioral change is produced. Recipes are written and adopted. If one believes, on the other hand, that a critical level of attention to incoming information is the essential variable, then one is free to mix up manipulations, to keep the recipe open, as long as one centers the subject's attention on the new material.

The most speculative prediction from this general argument is that behavioral therapy techniques will work for some symptoms—for about 20 years. A violation of an expectancy is a distinctive stimulus that attracts attention. The use of operant shaping techniques to alleviate phobias is a dramatic violation of an expectancy for both child and adult, and attention is magnetized and focussed on the therapeutic agent and his paraphernalia. As a result, learning is facilitated. But each day's use of this strategy may bring its demise closer. In time, a large segment of the populace will have adapted to this event; it will be a surprise no more and its attention getting and therapeutic value will be attenuated. Much of the power of psychoanalytic techniques began to wane when the therapist's secrets became public knowledge. If therapy is accomplished by teaching new responses, and if the learning of new responses is most likely to occur when attention to the teacher is maximal, it is safe to expect that we may need a new strategy of teaching patients new tricks by about 1984.

Let us weave the threads closer in an attempt at final closure. The psychology of the first half of this century was the product of a defensively sudden rupture from philosophy to natural science. The young discipline needed roots, and like a child, attached itself to an absolute description of nature, much as a 5-year-old clings to an absolute conception of morality. We now approach the latency years and can afford to relax and learn something from developments in our sister sciences. The message implicit in the recent work in psychology, biology, and physics contains a directive to abandon absolutism in selected theoretical areas. Conceptual ideas for mental processes must be invented, and this task demands a relativistic orientation. Learning is one of the central problems in psychology and understanding of the mechanisms of learning requires elucidation and measurement of the concept of attention. Existing data indicate that attention is under the control of distinctive stimuli and distinctiveness depends intimately on adaptation level of subject and context, and cannot be designated in absolute terms.

These comments are not to be regarded as a plea to return to undisciplined philosophical introspection. Psychology does possess some beginning clues as to how it might begin to measure elusive, relative concepts like "attention." Autonomic variables such as cardiac and respiratory rate appear to be useful indexes, and careful studies of subtle motor discharge patterns may provide initial operational bases for this construct.

Neurophysiologists have been conceptualizing their data in terms of attention distribution for several years, and they are uncovering some unusually provocative phenomena. For example, amplitude of evoked potentials from the association areas of the cortex are beginning to be regarded as a partial index of attention. Thompson and Shaw (1965) recorded evoked potentials from the association area of the cat's cortex—the middle suprasylvian gyrus—to a click, a light, or a shock to the forepaw. After they established base level response to each of these "standard" stimuli, the investigators presented these standard stimuli when the cat was active or when novel stimuli were introduced. The novel events were a rat in a bell jar, an air jet, or a growling sound. The results were unequivocal. Any one of these novel stimuli or activity by the cat produced reduced cortical evoked responses to the click, light, or shock. The authors suggest that the "amplitude of the evoked responses are inversely proportional to attention to a particular event [p. 338]." Psychology is beginning to develop promising strategies of measurement for the murky concept of attention and should begin to focus its theorizing and burgeoning measurement technology on variables having to do with the state of the organism, not just the quality of the external stimulus. The latter events can be currently objectified with greater elegance, but the former events seem to be of more significance. Mannheim once chastised the social sciences for seeming to be obsessed with studying what they could measure without error, rather than measuring what they thought to be important with the highest precision possible. It is threatening to abandon the security of the doctrine of absolutism of the stimulus event. Such a reorientation demands new measurement procedures, novel strategies of inquiry, and a greater tolerance for ambiguity. But let us direct our inquiry to where the pot of gold seems to shimmer and not fear to venture out from cozy laboratories where well-practiced habits have persuaded us to rationalize a faith in absolute monarchy.

REFERENCES

Aronfreed, J. The origin of self criticism. *Psychological Review,* 1964, **71,** 193–218.

Aronfreed, J. Internalized behavioral suppression and the timing of social punishment. *Journal of Personality and Social Psychology,* 1965, **1,** 3–16.

Baldwin, A. L., Kalhorn, J., & Breese, F. H. Patterns of parent behavior. *Psychological Monographs,* 1945, **58**(3, Whole No. 268).

Bateson, P. P. G. Changes in chicks' responses to novel moving objects over the sensitive period for imprinting. *Animal Behavior,* 1964, **12,** 479–489. (a)

Bateson, P. P. G. Relation between conspicuousness of stimuli and their effectiveness in the imprinting situation. *Journal of Comparative and Physiological Psychology,* 1964, **58,** 407–411. (b)

Becker, W. C. Consequences of different kinds of parental discipline. In M. L. Hoffman & L. W. Hoffman (Eds.), *Review of child development research.* Vol. 1. New York: Russell Sage Foundation, 1964. Pp. 169–208.

Brackbill, Y. Extinction of the smiling response in infants as a function of reinforcement schedule. *Child Development,* 1958, **29,** 115–124.

Charlesworth, W. R. Persistence of orienting and attending behavior in young infants as a function of stimulus uncertainty. Paper read at Society for Research in Child Development, Minneapolis, March 1965.

Held, R. Plasticity in sensory motor systems. *Scientific American,* 1965, **213**(5), 84–94.

Helson, H. *Adaptation level theory: An experimental and systematic approach to behavior.* New York: Harper & Row, 1964.

Hernández-Peón, R., Scherrer, H., & Jouvet, M. Modification of electrical activity in cochlear nucleus during attention in unanesthetized cats. *Science,* 1956, **123,** 331–332.

Hess, E. H. Two conditions limiting critical age for imprinting. *Journal of Comparative and Physiological Psychology,* 1959, **52,** 515–518.

Jakobson, R., & Halle, M. *Fundamentals of language.* The Hague: Mouton, 1956.

Kagan, J., Henker, B. A., Hen-Tov, A., Levine, J., & Lewis, M. Infants' differential reactions to familiar and distorted faces. *Child Development,* 1966, **37,** 519–532.

Kagan, J., & Moss, H. A. *Birth to maturity.* New York: Wiley, 1962.

Klopfer, P. H. Imprinting: A reassessment. *Science,* 1965, **147,** 302–303.

Leuba, C. Toward some integration of learning theories: The concept of optimal stimulation. *Psychological Reports,* 1955, **1,** 27–33.

Melzack, R., & Wall, P. D. Pain mechanisms: A new theory. *Science,* 1965, **150,** 971–979.

Miller, N. E. Learnable drives and rewards. In S. S. Stevens (Ed.), *Handbook of experimental psychology.* New York: Wiley, 1951. 435–472.

Olds, J. Self stimulation of the brain. *Science,* 1958, **127,** 315–324.

Olds, J. Hypothalamic substrates of reward. *Physiological Review,* 1962, **42,** 554–604.

Rheingold, H., Gewirtz, J. L., & Ross, H. Social conditioning of vocalizations in the infant. *Journal of Comparative and Physiological Psychology,* 1959, **52,** 68–73.

Schachter, S., & Singer, J. E. Cognitive, social and physiological determinants of emotional states. *Psychological Review,* 1962, **69,** 379–399.

Schaefer, E. S. A circumflex model for maternal behavior. *Journal of Abnormal and Social Psychology,* 1959, **59,** 226–235.

Schaefer, E. S. & Bayley, N. Maternal behavior, child behavior and their intercorrelations from infancy through adolescence. *Monographs of the Society for Research in Child Development,* 1963, **28,** No. 87.

Sears, R. R., Maccoby, E. E., & Levin, H. *Patterns of child rearing.* Row Peterson, 1957.

Thompson, R. F., & Shaw, J. A. Behavioral correlates of evoked activity recorded from association areas of the cerebral cortex. *Journal of Comparative and Physiological Psychology,* 1965, **60,** 329–339.

Thompson, W. R., & Dubanoski, R. A. Imprinting and the law of effort. *Animal Behavior,* 1964, **12,** 213–218.

Tomkins, S. S. *Affect imagery consciousness.* Vol. 1. *The positive affects.* New York: Springer, 1962.

4
THE LIFE CYCLE: EPIGENESIS OF IDENTITY*

ERIK H. ERIKSON

Among the indispensable coordinates of identity is that of the life cycle, for we assume that not until adolescence does the individual develop the prerequisites in physiological growth, mental maturation, and social responsibility to experience and pass through the crisis of identity. We may, in fact, speak of the identity crisis as the psychosocial aspect of adolescing. Nor could this stage be passed without identity having found a form which will decisively determine later life.

Let us, once more, start out from Freud's far-reaching discovery that neurotic conflict is not very different in content from the "normative" conflicts which every child must live through in his childhood, and the residues of which every adult carries with him in the recesses of his personality. For man, in order to remain psychologically alive, constantly re-resolves these conflicts just as his body unceasingly combats the encroachment of physical deterioration. However, since I cannot accept the conclusion that just to be alive, or not to be sick, means to be healthy, or, as I would prefer to say in matters of personality, *vital,* I must have recourse to a few concepts which are not part of the official terminology of my field.

I shall present human growth from the point of view of the conflicts, inner and outer, which the vital personality weathers, re-emerging from each crisis with an increased sense of inner unity, with an increase of good judgment, and an increase in the capacity "to do well" according to his own standards and to the standards of those who are significant to him. The use of the words "to do well" of course points up the whole question of cultural relativity. Those who are significant to a man may think he is doing well when he "does some good" or when he "does well" in the sense of acquiring possessions; when he is doing well in the sense of learning new skills and new knowledge or when he is not much more than just getting along; when he learns to conform all around or to rebel significantly; when he is merely free from neurotic symptoms or manages to contain within his vitality all manner of profound conflict.

* From *Identity, youth and crisis*. New York: W. W. Norton & Company, Inc., 1968, Pp. 91–141. Reprinted with permission from the author and W. W. Norton & Co., Inc.

There are many formulations of what constitutes a "healthy" personality in an adult. But if we take up only one—in this case, Marie Jahoda's definition, according to which a healthy personality *actively masters* his environment, shows a certain *unity of personality,* and is able to *perceive* the world and himself *correctly*—it is clear that all of these criteria are relative to the child's cognitive and social development. In fact, we may say that childhood is defined by their initial absence and by their gradual development in complex steps of increasing differentiation. How, then, does a vital personality grow or, as it were, accrue from the successive stages of the increasing capacity to adapt to life's necessities—with some vital enthusiasm to spare?

Whenever we try to understand growth, it is well to remember the *epigenetic principle* which is derived from the growth of organisms *in utero.* Somewhat generalized, this principle states that anything that grows has a ground plan, and that out of this ground plan the parts arise, each part having its time of special ascendancy, until all parts have arisen to form a functioning whole. This, obviously, is true for fetal development where each part of the organism has its critical time of ascendance or danger of defect. At birth the baby leaves the chemical exchange of the womb for the social exchange system of his society, where his gradually increasing capacities meet the opportunities and limitations of his culture. How the maturing organism continues to unfold, not by developing new organs but by means of a prescribed sequence of locomotor, sensory, and social capacities, is described in the child-development literature. As pointed out, psychoanalysis has given us an understanding of the more idiosyncratic experiences, and especially the inner conflicts, which constitute the manner in which an individual becomes a distinct personality. But here, too, it is important to realize that in the sequence of his most personal experiences the healthy child, given a reasonable amount of proper guidance, can be trusted to obey inner laws of development, laws which create a succession of potentialities for significant interaction with those persons who tend and respond to him and those institutions which are ready for him. While such interaction varies from culture to culture, it must remain within "the proper rate and the proper sequence" which governs all epigenesis. Personality, therefore, can be said to develop according to steps predetermined in the human organism's readiness to be driven toward, to be aware of, and to interact with a widening radius of significant individuals and institutions.

It is for this reason that, in the presentation of stages in the development of the personality, we employ an epigenetic diagram analogous to the one employed in *Childhood and Society* for an analysis of Freud's psychosexual stages. It is, in fact, an implicit purpose of this presentation to bridge the theory of infantile sexuality (without repeating it here in detail) and our knowledge of the child's physical and social growth.

[In the diagram which follows] the double-lined squares signify both a sequence of stages and a gradual development of component parts; in other words, the diagram formalizes a progression through time of a differentiation of parts. This indicates (1) that each item of the vital personality to be discussed is systematically related to all others, and that they all depend on the proper development in the proper sequence of each item; and (2) that each item exists in some form before "its" decisive and critical time normally arrives.

If I say, for example, that a sense of basic trust is the first component of mental vitality to develop in life, a sense of autonomous will the second, and a sense of initiative the third, the diagram expresses a number of fundamental relations that exist among the three components, as well as a few fundamental facts for each.

VIII								INTEGRITY vs. DESPAIR
VII							GENERATIVITY vs. STAGNATION	
VI						INTIMACY vs. ISOLATION		
V	Temporal Perspective vs. Time Confusion	Self-Certainty vs. Self-Consciousness	Role Experimentation vs. Role Fixation	Apprenticeship vs. Work Paralysis	IDENTITY vs. IDENTITY CONFUSION	Sexual Polarization vs. Bisexual Confusion	Leader- and Followership vs. Authority Confusion	Ideological Commitment vs. Confusion of Values
IV				INDUSTRY vs. INFERIORITY	Task Identification vs. Sence of Futility			
III			INITIATIVE vs. GUILT		Anticipation of Roles vs. Role Inhibition			
II		AUTONOMY vs. SHAME, DOUBT			Will to Be Oneself vs. Self-Doubt			
I	TRUST vs. MISTRUST				Mutual Recognition vs. Autistic Isolation			
	1	2	3	4	5	6	7	8

Each comes to its ascendance, meets its crisis, and finds its lasting solution in ways to be described here, toward the end of the stages mentioned. All of them exist in the beginning in some form, although we do not make a point of this fact, and we shall not confuse things by calling these components different names at earlier or later stages. A baby may show something like "autonomy" from the beginning, for example, in the particular way in which he angrily tries to wriggle his hand free when tightly held. However, under normal conditions, it is not until the second year that he begins to experience the whole critical alternative between being an autonomous creature and being a dependent one, and it is not until then that he is ready for a specifically new encounter with his environment. The environment, in turn, now feels called upon to convey to him its particular ideas and concepts of autonomy in ways decisively contributing to his personal character, his relative efficiency, and the strength of his vitality.

It is this encounter, together with the resulting crisis, which is to be described for each stage. Each stage becomes a crisis because incipient growth and awareness in a new part function go together with a shift in instinctual energy and yet also cause a specific vulnerability in that part. One of the most difficult questions to decide, therefore, is whether or not a child at a given stage is weak or strong. Perhaps it would be best to say that he is always vulnerable in some respects and completely oblivious and insensitive in others, but that at the same time he is unbelievably persistent in the same respects in which he is vulnerable. It must be added that the baby's weakness gives him power; out of his very dependence and weakness he makes signs to which his environment, if it is guided well by a responsiveness combining "instinctive" and traditional patterns, is peculiarly sensitive. A baby's presence exerts a consistent and persistent domination over the outer and inner lives of every member of a household. Because these members must reorient themselves to accommodate his presence, they must also grow as individuals and as a group. It is as true to say that babies control and bring up their families as it is to say the converse. A family can bring up a baby only by being brought up by him. His growth consists of a series of challenges to them to serve his newly developing potentialities for social interaction.

Each successive step, then, is a potential crisis because of a radical change in perspective. Crisis is used here in a developmental sense to connote not a threat of catastrophe, but a turning point, a crucial period of increased vulnerability and heightened potential, and therefore, the ontogenetic source of generational strength and maladjustment. The most radical change of all, from intrauterine to extrauterine life, comes at the very beginning of life. But in postnatal existence, too, such radical adjustments of perspective as lying relaxed, sitting firmly, and running fast must all be accomplished in their own good time. With them, the interpersonal perspective also changes rapidly and often radically, as is testified by the proximity in time of such opposites as "not letting mother out of sight" and "wanting to be independent." Thus, different capacities use different opportunities to become full-grown components of the ever-new configuration that is the growing personality.

1. INFANCY AND THE MUTUALITY OF RECOGNITION

For the most fundamental prerequisite of mental vitality, I have already nominated a *sense of basic trust,* which is a pervasive attitude toward oneself and the world derived from the experiences of the first year of life. By "trust"

I mean an essential trustfulness of others as well as a fundamental sense of one's own trustworthiness.

In describing a development of a series of alternative basic attitudes, including identity, we take recourse to the term "a sense of." It must be immediately obvious, however, that such "senses" as a sense of health or vitality, or a sense of the lack of either, pervades the surface and the depth, including what we experience as consciousness or what remains barely conscious or is altogether unconscious. As a conscious experience, trust is accessible to introspection. But it is also a way of behaving, observable by others; and it is, finally, an inner state verifiable only by testing and psychoanalytic interpretation. All three of these dimensions are to be inferred when we loosely speak of "a sense of."

As is usual in psychoanalysis, we learned first of the "basic" nature of trust from adult psychopathology. In adults a radical impairment of basic trust and a prevalence of *basic mistrust* is expressed in a particular form of severe estrangement which characterizes individuals who withdraw into themselves when at odds with themselves and with others. Such withdrawal is most strikingly displayed by individuals who regress into psychotic states in which they sometimes close up, refusing food and comfort and becoming oblivious to companionship. What is most radically missing in them can be seen from the fact that as we attempt to assist them with psychotherapy, we must try to "reach" them with the specific intent of convincing them that they can trust us to trust them and that they can trust themselves.

Familiarity with such radical regressions as well as with the deepest and most infantile propensities in our not-so-sick patients has taught us to regard basic trust as the cornerstone of a vital personality. Let us see what justifies our placing the crisis and the ascendancy of this component at the beginning of life.

As the newborn infant is separated from his symbiosis with the mother's body, his inborn and more or less co-ordinated ability to take in by mouth meets the mother's more or less co-ordinated ability and intention to feed him and to welcome him. At this point he lives through, and loves with, his mouth, and the mother lives through, and loves with, her breasts or whatever parts of her countenance and body convey eagerness to provide what he needs.

For the mother this is a late and complicated accomplishment, highly dependent on her development as a woman, on her unconscious attitude toward the child, on the way she has lived through pregnancy and delivery, on her and her community's attitude toward the act of nursing and caring—and on the response of the newborn. To him the mouth is the focus of a general first approach to life—the incorporative approach. In psychoanalysis this stage is usually referred to as the oral stage. Yet it is clear that in addition to the overwhelming need for food, a baby is, or soon becomes, receptive in many other respects. As he is willing and able to suck on appropriate objects and to swallow whatever appropriate fluids they emit, he is soon also willing and able to "take in" with his eyes whatever enters his visual field. His senses, too, seem to "take in" what feels good. In this sense, then, one can speak of an *incorporative stage,* in which he is, relatively speaking, receptive to what he is being offered. Yet babies are sensitive and vulnerable too. In order to insure that their first experiences in this world will not only keep them alive but will also help them to co-ordinate their sensitive breathing and their metabolic and circulatory rhythms, we must see to it that we deliver to their senses stimuli as well as food in the proper intensity and at the right time; otherwise their willingness to accept may change radically into diffuse defense or into lethargy.

Now, while it is quite clear what must happen to keep a baby alive—the minimum supply necessary—and what must not happen, lest he be physically damaged or chronically upset—the maximum of early frustration tolerable—there is a certain leeway in regard to what *may* happen, and different cultures make extensive use of the prerogatives to decide what they consider workable and insist upon calling necessary. Some people think that a baby, lest he scratch his own eyes out, must necessarily be swaddled completely for most of the day and throughout the greater part of the first year, and that he should be rocked or fed whenever he whimpers. Others think that he should feel the freedom of his kicking limbs as early as possible, but also that, as a matter of course, he should be forced to cry "please" for his meals until he literally gets blue in the face. All of this, more or less consciously, seems related to the culture's general aim and system. I have known some old American Indians who bitterly decried the way in which we once let our small babies cry because we believed that it would "make their lungs strong." No wonder, these Indians said, that the white man, after such an initial reception, seems to be so intent on getting to "heaven." But the same Indians spoke proudly of the way their infants, breast fed into the second year, became blue in the face with fury when they were thumped on the head for "biting" their mother's nipples; here the Indians, in turn, believed that it would "make good hunters of them."

There is, then, some intrinsic wisdom, some unconscious planning, and much superstition in the seemingly arbitrary varieties of child training. But there is also a logic—however instinctive and prescientific—in the assumption that what is "good for the child," what *may* happen to him, depends on what he is supposed to become and where.

At any rate, it is already in his earliest encounters that the human infant meets up with the principal modalities of his culture. The simplest and the earliest modality is *to get,* not in the sense of "go and get" but in that of receiving and accepting what is given. This is easy when it works and yet any disturbance shows how complicated the process really is. The groping and unstable newborn's organism learns this modality only as he learns to regulate his readiness to "get" with the methods of a mother who, in turn, will permit him to co-ordinate his means of getting as she develops and co-ordinates her means of giving. But in thus getting what is given, and in learning to get somebody to do for him what he wishes to have done, the baby also develops the necessary groundwork "to get to be" the giver—that is, to identify with her and eventually to become a giving person.

In some especially sensitive individuals, or in individuals whose early frustration was never compensated for, a weakness in such early mutual regulation can be at the root of a disturbance in their relationship to the world in general, and especially to significant people. But, of course, there are ways of maintaining mutuality through the satiation of other than oral receptors: the baby's pleasure in being held, warmed, smiled at, talked to, rocked, and so forth. Besides such "horizontal" compensation (compensation during the same stage of development) there are many "longitudinal" compensations in life which emerge from later stages of the life cycle.

During the "second oral" stage the capacities to pursue and take pleasure in a more active and more directed incorporative approach ripen. Teeth develop and with them the pleasure of biting on hard things, biting through things, and biting off things. This active-incorporative mode characterizes a variety of other activities, as did the first incorporative mode. The eyes, first seemingly passive in accepting impressions as they come along, have now learned to focus on, isolate, and "grasp" objects from the vaguer background and follow them. The organs of hearing similarly have learned to discern significant sounds, localize them, and guide appropriate changes in position, such as lifting and turning the head or lifting and turning the upper body. The arms have learned to reach out determinedly and the hands to grasp firmly. We are, then, more interested in the overall configuration of developing approaches to the world than we are in the first appearance of isolated abilities which are so well documented in the child-development literature. One can think of a stage as the time when a given capacity first appears (or appears in testable form) or as that period when a number of related items are so well established and integrated that the next step in development can safely be initiated.

During the second stage, interpersonal patterns are established which are united in the social modality of *taking* and *holding on* to things—things which are more or less freely offered and given and things which have more or less a tendency to slip away. As the baby learns to change positions, to roll over, and very gradually to establish himself on the throne of his sedentary kingdom, he must perfect the mechanisms of grasping, appropriating, and holding as well as chewing all that is within his reach.

The crisis of the second oral stage is difficult to assess and more difficult to verify. It seems to consist of the coincidence in time of three developments: (1) a more "violent" drive to incorporate, appropriate, and observe more actively, a tension associated with the discomfort of "teething" and other changes in the oral machinery; (2) the infant's increasing awareness of himself as a distinct person; and (3) the mother's gradual turning away from the baby toward pursuits which she had given up during late pregnancy and postnatal care. These pursuits include her full return to conjugal intimacy and perhaps to a new pregnancy.

Where breast feeding lasts into the biting stage, and, generally speaking, this has been the rule, it is now necessary to learn how to continue sucking without biting, so that the mother will not withdraw the nipple in pain or anger. Our clinical work indicates that this stage in the individual's early history provides him with some sense of basic loss, leaving the general impression that once upon a time one's unity with a maternal matrix was destroyed. Weaning, therefore, should not mean sudden loss of both the breast and the mother's reassuring presence, unless, of course, other women can be depended upon to sound and feel much like the mother. A drastic loss of accustomed mother love without proper substitution at this time can lead, under otherwise aggravating conditions, to acute infantile depression or to a mild but chronic state of mourning which may give a depressive undertone to the remainder of one's life. But even under more favorable circumstances, this stage seems to introduce into the psychic life a sense of division and a dim but universal nostalgia for a lost paradise.

It is against the combination of these impressions of having been deprived, of having been divided, and of having been abandoned, all of which leave a residue of basic mistrust, that basic trust must establish and maintain itself.

What we here call "trust" coincides with what Therese Benedek has called "confidence." If I prefer the word "trust," it is because there is more naïveté and more mutuality in it: an infant can be said to be trusting, but it would be assuming too much to say that he has confidence. The general state of trust, furthermore, implies not only that one has learned to rely on the sameness and continuity of the outer providers but also that one may trust oneself and the capacity of one's own organs to cope with urges; that one is able to consider oneself trustworthy enough so that the providers will not need to be on guard or to leave.

In the psychiatric literature we find frequent references to an "oral character," which is an emphasis on traits representative of the unsolved conflicts of this stage. Wherever oral pessimism becomes dominant and exclusive, infantile fears such as that of "being left empty" or simply of "being left," and also of being "starved of stimulation," can be discerned in the depressive forms of "being empty" and of "being no good." Such fears, in turn, can give orality that particular avaricious quality which in psychoanalysis is called oral sadism, that is, a cruel need to get and to take in ways harmful to others or to oneself. But there is an optimistic oral character, too, one who has learned to make giving and receiving the most important thing in life. And there is "orality" as a normal substratum in all individuals, a lasting residuum of this first period of dependency on powerful providers. It normally expresses itself in our dependencies and nostalgias, and in our all too hopeful and all too hopeless states. The integration of the oral stage with all the following ones results, in adulthood, in a combination of faith and realism.

The pathology and irrationality of oral trends depend entirely on the degree to which they are integrated with the rest of the personality and the degree to which they fit into the general cultural pattern and use approved interpersonal techniques for their expression.

Here, as elsewhere, we must therefore consider as a topic for discussion the expression of infantile urges in cultural patterns which one may or may not consider a pathological deviation in the total economic or moral system of a culture or nation. One could speak, for example, of the invigorating belief in "chance," that traditional prerogative of American trust in one's own resourcefulness and in Fate's store of good intentions. This belief, at times, can be seen to degenerate in large-scale gambling, or in "taking chances" in the form of an arbitrary and often suicidal provocation of Fate or in the insistence that one has not only the right to an equal chance, but also the privilege of being preferred over all other "investors." In a similar way, all the pleasant reassurances which can be derived, especially in company, from old and new taste sensations, inhaling and sipping, munching and swallowing and digesting can turn into mass addictions neither expressive of nor conducive to the kind of basic trust we have in mind. Here we are obviously touching on phenomena calling for an epidemiological approach to the problem of the more or less malignant elaboration of infantile modalities in cultural excesses, as well as in mild forms of addiction, self-delusion, and avaricious appropriation, which are expressive of a certain weakness in oral reassurance.

It must be said, however, that the amount of trust derived from earliest infantile experience does not seem to depend on absolute quantities of food or demonstrations of love, but rather on the quality of the maternal relationship. Mothers create a sense of trust in their children by that kind of administration which in its quality combines sensitive care of the baby's individual needs and a firm sense of personal trustworthiness within the trusted framework of their community's life style. This forms the very basis in the child for a component of the sense of identity which will later combine a sense of being "all right," of being oneself, and of becoming what other people trust one will become. Parents must not only have certain ways of guiding by prohibition and permission, they must also be able to represent to the child a deep, almost somatic conviction that there is a meaning in what they are doing. In this sense a traditional system of child care can be said to be a factor making for trust, even where certain items of that tradition, taken singly, may seem arbitrary or unnecessarily cruel—or lenient. Here much depends on whether such items are inflicted on the child by the parent in the firm traditional belief that this is the only way to do things or whether the parent misuses his administration of the baby and the child in order to work off anger, alleviate fear, or win an argument, either with the child himself or with somebody else—mother-in-law, doctor, or priest.

In times of change—and what other times are there, in our memory?—one generation differs so much from another that items of tradition often become disturbances. Conflicts between mother's ways and one's own self-made style, conflicts between the expert's advice and mother's ways, and conflicts between the expert's authority and one's own style may disturb a young mother's trust in herself. Furthermore, all the mass transformations in American life (immigration, migration, and Americanization; industrialization, urbanization, mechanization, and others) are apt to disturb young mothers in those tasks which are so simple yet so far-reaching. No wonder, then, that the first section of the first chapter of Benjamin Spock's book is entitled "Trust Yourself."

In a discussion of development, it is unavoidable that one must begin with the beginning. This is unfortunate because we know so little of the earliest and deepest strata of the human mind. But I would claim that we have now touched upon the major directions from which any of the emerging components of human vitality can be studied—from the beginning of life to the identity crisis and beyond. We will not be able to be equally expansive in regard to the other stages, although this chapter as a whole should complete an "inventory" such as we have now outlined for the first stage of life. In addition to the measurable aspects of growth, our implicit scheme should cover: (1) The *expanding libidinal needs* of the developing being and, with them, new possibilities of satisfaction, of frustration, and of "sublimation." (2) *The widening social radius,* i.e., the number and kinds of people to whom he can respond meaningfully on the basis of (3) his ever more highly differentiated *capacities.* (4) The *developmental crisis* evoked by the necessity to manage new encounters within a given time allowance. (5) A new *sense of estrangement* awakened along with the awareness of new dependences and new familiarities (e.g., in early infancy, the sense of abandonment). (6) A specifically new *psychosocial strength* (here a favorable ratio of trust over mistrust) which is a foundation for all future strengths.

This is a forbidding array of items and is too demanding for what is our immediate task, namely, a descriptive account of the early experiences which facilitate or endanger the future identity.

What would we consider to be the earliest and most undifferentiated "sense of identity"? I would suggest that it arises out of the encounter of maternal person and small infant, an encounter which is one of mutual trustworthiness and mutual recognition. This, in all its infantile simplicity, is the first experience of what in later reoccurances in love and admiration can only be called a sense of "hallowed presence," the need for which remains basic in man. Its absence or impairment can dangerously limit the capacity to feel "identical" when adolescent growth makes it incumbent on the person to abandon his childhood and to trust adulthood and, with it, the search for self-chosen loves and incentives.

At this point, I must add to the list already given one further dimension, the seventh—namely, the contribution of each stage to one major human endeavor which in adulthood takes over the guardianship of the particular strength originating in this stage and the ritual appeasement of its particular estrangement.

Each successive stage and crisis has a special relation to one of the basic institutionalized endeavors of man for the simple reason that the human life cycle and human institutions have evolved together. The relation between them is twofold: each generation brings to these institutions the remnants of infantile needs and youthful fervor and receives from them—as long as they, indeed, manage to maintain their institutional vitality—a specific reinforcement of childlike vitality. If I name religion as the institution which throughout man's history has striven to verify basic trust, I disavow any intention to call religion as such childish or religious behavior as such regressive, although it is obvious that large-scale infantilization is not foreign to the practice and the intent of organized religion. As we overcome our universal amnesia for the frightening aspects of childhood, we may well also acknowledge gratefully the fact that, in principle, the glory of childhood also survives in adult life. Trust, then, becomes the capacity for *faith*—a vital need for which man must find some institutional confirmation. Religion, it seems, is the oldest and has been the most lasting institution to serve the ritual restoration of a sense of trust in the form of faith while offering a tangible formula for a sense of evil against which it promises to arm and defend man. Childlike strength as well as a potential for infantilization are suggested in the fact that all religious practice includes periodic childlike surrender to the Power that creates and re-creates, dispensing earthly fortune as well as spiritual well-being; the demonstration of smallness and dependence by reduced posture and humble gesture; the confession in prayer and song of misdeeds, misthoughts, and evil intentions and the fervent appeal for inner reunification by divine guidance. At best, all of this is highly stylized and thus becomes suprapersonal; individual trust becomes a common faith, individual mistrust a commonly formulated evil, while the individual's plea for restoration becomes part of the ritual practice of many and a sign of trustworthiness in the community.

When religion loses its actual power of presence, then, it would seem, an age must find other forms of joint reverence for life which derive vitality from a shared world image. For only a reasonably coherent world provides the faith which is transmitted by the mothers to the infants in a way conducive to the vital strength of *hope,* that is, the enduring predisposition to believe in the attainability of primal wishes in spite of the anarchic urges and rages of dependency. The shortest formulation of the identity gain of earliest childhood may well be: I am what hope I have and give.

2. EARLY CHILDHOOD AND THE WILL TO BE ONESELF

Psychoanalysis has enriched the vocabulary with the word "anality" to designate the particular pleasureableness and willfulness which are often attached to the eliminative organs in early childhood. The whole procedure of evacuating the bowels and the bladder is, of course, enhanced from the beginning by a premium of satisfaction over a major job "well done." At first this premium must make up for quite frequent discomfort and tension suffered as the bowels learn to do their daily work. Two developments gradually give anal experiences the necessary "volume": the arrival of better-formed stool and the general coordination of the muscle system which permits the development of voluntary release as well as of retention. This new dimension of approach to things, however, is not restricted to the sphincters. A general ability, indeed, a violent need, develops to alternate withholding and expelling at will and, in general, to keep tightly and to throw away willfully whatever is held.

The over-all significance of this second stage of early childhood lies in the rapid gains in muscular maturation, in verbalization, and in discrimination and the consequent ability—and doubly felt inability—to co-ordinate a number of highly conflicting action patterns characterized by the tendencies of *"holding on"* and *"letting go."* In this and in many other ways, the still highly dependent child begins to experience his *autonomous will.* At this time sinister forces are leashed and unleashed, especially in the guerilla warfare of unequal wills, for the child is often unequal to his own violent will and parent and child are often unequal to one another.

As far as anality proper is concerned, everything depends on whether the cultural environment wants to make something of it. There are primitive and agrarian cultures where the parents ignore anal behavior and leave it to the older children to lead the toddler out to the bushes so that his compliance in this matter may coincide with his wish to imitate the bigger ones. Our Western civilization (as well as others—for example, Japan), and especially certain classes within it, have chosen to take the matter more seriously. It is here that the machine age has provided the ideal of a mechanically trained, faultlessly functioning, and always clean, punctual, and deodorized body. In addition, it has been more or less superstitiously assumed that early and rigorous training is absolutely necessary for the kind of personality which will function efficiently in a mechanized world in which time is money. Thus a child becomes a machine which must be set and tuned even as before it was an animal which must be broken—while, in fact, will power can develop only by steps. At any rate our clinical work suggests that the neurotics of our time include the *compulsive type,* who is stingy, retentive, and meticulous in matters of affection, time, and money as well as in the management of his bowels. Also, bowel and bladder training has become the most obviously disturbing item of child training in wide circles of our society.

What, then, makes the anal problem potentially important and difficult?

The anal zone lends itself more than any other to the expression of stubborn insistence on conflicting impulses because, for one thing, it is the model zone for two contradictory modes which must become alternating, namely, retention and elimination. Furthermore, the sphincters are only part of the muscle system with its general ambiguity of rigidity and relaxation, of flexion and extension. This whole stage, then, becomes a *battle for autonomy.* For as he gets ready to stand on his feet more firmly, the infant also learns to delineate his world as "I" and "you," and "me" and "mine." Every mother knows how astonishingly pliable a child may be at this stage, if and when he has made the decision that he wants to do what he is supposed to do. It is impossible, however, to find a reliable formula for making him want to do just that. Every mother knows how lovingly a child at this stage will snuggle close to her and how ruthlessly he will suddenly try to push her away. At the same time the child is apt both to hoard things and to discard them, to cling to treasured objects and to throw them out of the windows of houses and vehicles. All of these seemingly contradictory tendencies, then, we include under the formula of the *retentive-eliminative modes.* All basic modalities, in fact, lend themselves to both hostile and benign expectations and attitudes. Thus, "to hold" can become a destructive and cruel retaining or restraining, and it can become a pattern of care: "to have and to hold." To "let go," too, can turn into an inimical letting loose of destructive forces, or it can become a relaxed "to let pass" and "to let be." Culturally speaking, these modalities are neither good nor bad; their value depends on how they are built into the patterns of affirmation and rejection demanded in the culture.

The matter of mutual regulation between adult and child now faces its severest test. If outer control by too rigid or too early training persists in robbing the child of his attempt gradually to control his bowels and other functions willingly and by his free choice, he will again be faced with a double rebellion and a double defeat. Powerless against his own anal instinctuality and sometimes afraid of his own bowel movements and powerless outside, he will be forced to seek satisfaction and control either by regression or by fake progression. In other words, he will return to an earlier, oral control; that is, he will suck his thumb and become doubly demanding; or he will become hostile and willful, often using his feces (as he will later the corresponding dirty words) as aggressive ammunition; or he will pretend an autonomy and an ability to do without anybody's help which he has by no means really gained.

This stage, therefore, becomes decisive for the ratio between loving good will and hateful self-insistence, between co-operation and willfulness, and between self-expression and compulsive self-restraint or meek compliance. A sense of self-control without loss of self-esteem is the ontogenetic source of a sense of *free will*. From an unavoidable sense of loss of self-control and of parental overcontrol comes a lasting propensity for *doubt* and *shame*.

For the growth of autonomy a firmly developed early trust is necessary. The infant must have come to be sure that his faith in himself and in the world will not be jeopardized by the violent wish to have his choice, to appropriate demandingly, and to eliminate stubbornly. Only parental firmness can protect him against the consequences of his as yet untrained discrimination and circumspection. But his environment must also back him up in his wish to "stand on his own feet," while also protecting him against the now newly emerging pair of estrangements, namely, that sense of having exposed himself prematurely and foolishly which we call shame or that secondary mistrust, that "double take," which we call doubt—doubt in himself and doubt in the firmness and perspicacity of his trainers.

Shame is an infantile emotion insufficiently studied because in our civilization it is so early and easily absorbed by guilt. Shame supposes that one is completely exposed and conscious of being looked at—in a word, self-conscious. One is visible and not ready to be visible; that is why in dreams of shame we are stared at in a condition of incomplete dress, in night attire, "with one's pants down." Shame is early expressed in an impulse to bury one's face or to sink, right then and there, into the ground. This potentiality is abundantly utilized in the educational method of "shaming" used so exclusively by some primitive peoples, where it supplants the often more destructive sense of guilt to be discussed later. The destructiveness of shaming is balanced in some civilizations by devices for "saving face." Shaming exploits the increased sense of being small, which paradoxically develops as the child stands up and as his awareness permits him to note the relative measures of size and power.

Too much shaming does not result in a sense of propriety but in a secret determination to try to get away with things when unseen, if, indeed, it does not result in deliberate shamelessness. There is an impressive American ballad in which a murderer to be hanged on the gallows before the eyes of the community, instead of feeling mortally afraid or totally shamed, begins to berate the onlookers, ending every salvo of defiance with the words, "God damn your eyes." Many a small child, when shamed beyond endurance, may be in a mood (although not in possession of either the courage or the words) to express defiance in similar terms. What I mean by this sinister reference is that there is a limit to a child's and an adult's individual endurance in the face of demands which force him to consider himself, his body, his needs, and his wishes as evil and dirty, and to believe in the infallibility of those who pass such judgment. Occasionally, he may turn things around, become secretly oblivious to the opinion of others, and consider as evil only the fact that they exist: his chance will come when they are gone or when he can leave them.

The psychiatric danger of this stage is, as it is at all other stages, the potential aggravation of the normative estrangement to the point where it will cause neurotic or psychotic tendencies. The sensitive child may turn all his urge to discriminate against himself and thus develop a *precocious conscience.* Instead of willfully appropriating things in order to test them by repetitive play, he will become obsessed by his own repetitiveness and will want to have everything "just so," and only in a given sequence and tempo. By such infantile obsessiveness and procrastination, or by becoming a stickler for ritualistic repetitions, the child then learns to gain power over his parents in areas where he could not find large-scale mutual regulation with them. Such hollow victory, then, is the infantile model for an adult compulsion neurosis.

In adolescence, for example, a compulsive person may attempt to free himself with maneuvers expressing the wish to "get away with" things and yet find himself unable to get away even with the wish. For while such a young person learns evasion from others, his precocious conscience does not let him really get away with anything, and he goes through his identity crisis habitually ashamed, apologetic, and afraid to be seen; or else, in an "overcompensatory" manner, he evinces a defiant kind of autonomy which may find sanction and ritual in the shameless defiance of gangs.

Doubt is the brother of shame. Whereas shame is dependent on the consciousness of being upright and exposed, doubt has much to do with a consciousness of having a front and a back—and especially a "behind." For this reverse area of the body, with its aggressive and libidinal focus in the sphincters and buttocks, cannot be seen by the child, and yet it can be dominated by the will of others. The "behind" is the small being's dark continent, an area of the body which can be magically dominated and effectively invaded by those who would attack one's power of autonomy and who would designate as evil those products of the bowels which were felt to be all right when they were being passed. This basic sense of doubt in whatever one has left behind is the model for the habitual "double take" or other later and more verbal forms of compulsive doubting. It finds its adult expression in paranoiac fears concerning hidden persecutors and secret persecutions threatening from behind (and from within the behind). Again, in adolescence, this may be expressed in a transitory total self-doubt, a feeling that all that is now "behind" in time—the childhood family as well as the earlier manifestations of one's personality—simply do not add up to the prerequisites for a new beginning. All of this may then be denied in a willful display of dirtiness and messiness, with all the implications of "dirty" swearing at the world and at oneself.

As was the case with the "oral" personality, the compulsive or "anal" personality has its normal aspects and its abnormal exaggerations. If eventually integrated with compensatory traits, some *impulsiveness* releases expression even as some *compulsiveness* is useful in matters in which order, punctuality, and cleanliness are of the essence. The question is always whether we remain the masters of the modalities by which things become more manageable or whether the rules master the ruler.

It takes stamina as well as flexibility to train a child's will so as to help him to overcome too much willfulness, develop some "good will," and (while learning to obey in some essential ways) maintain an autonomous sense of free will. As far as psychoanalysis is concerned, it has focused primarily on excessively early toilet training and on unreasonable shaming as causes of the child's estrangement from his own body. It has attempted at least to formulate what should *not* be done to children, and there are, of course, any number of avoidances which can be learned from the study of the life cycle. Many such formulations, however, are apt to arouse superstitious inhibitions in those who are inclined to make anxious rules out of vague warnings. We are gradually learning what exactly not to do to what kind of children at what age; but then we must still learn what to do, spontaneously and joyfully. The expert, to quote Frank Fremont-Smith, can only "set the frame of reference within which choice is permissible and desirable." In the last analysis, as comparative studies in child training have convinced us, the kind and degree of a sense of autonomy which parents are able to grant their small children depends on the dignity and sense of personal independence they derive from their own lives. We have already suggested that the infant's sense of trust is a reflection of parental faith; similarly, the sense of autonomy is a reflection of the parents' dignity as autonomous beings. For no matter what we do in detail, the child will primarily feel what it is we live by as loving, co-operative, and firm beings, and what makes us hateful, anxious, and divided in ourselves.

What social institution, then, guards the lasting gains of the second stage of life? Man's basic need for a delineation of his autonomy seems to have an institutional safeguard in the principle of *law and order,* which in everyday life as well as in the courts of law apportions to each his privileges and his limitations, his obligations and his rights. Only a sense of rightfully delimited autonomy in the parents fosters a handling of the small individual which expresses a suprapersonal indignation rather than an arbitrary righteousness. It is important to dwell on this point because much of the lasting sense of doubt, and of the indignity of punishment and restriction common to many children, is a consequence of the parents' frustrations in marriage, in work, and in citizenship. Where large numbers of people have been prepared in childhood to expect from life a high degree of personal autonomy, pride, and opportunity, and then in later life find themselves ruled by impersonal organizations and machineries too intricate to understand, the result may be deep chronic disappointment that makes them unwilling to grant each other —or their children—a measure of autonomy. They may be possessed, instead, by irrational fears of losing what is left of their autonomy or of being sabotaged, restricted, and constricted in their free will by anonymous enemies and at the same time, paradoxically enough, of not being controlled enough, of not being *told* what to do.

We have, again at length, characterized the struggles and triumphs of a childhood stage. In what way does this stage contribute to the identity crisis, either by supporting the formation of identity or by contributing a particular kind of estrangement to its confusion? The stage of autonomy, of course, deserves particular attention, for in it is played out the first emancipation, namely, from the mother. There are clinical reasons to believe that the adolescent turning away from the whole childhood milieu in many ways repeats this first emancipation. For this reason the most rebellious youths can also regress partially (and sometimes wholly) to a demanding and plaintive search for a guidance which their cynical independence seems to disavow. Apart from such "clinical" evidence, however, the over-all contribution to an eventual identity formation is the very courage to be an independent individual who can choose and guide his own future.

We said that the earliest stage leaves a residue in the growing being which, on many hierarchic levels and especially in the individual's sense of identity, will echo something of the conviction "I am what hope I have and give." The analogous residue of the stage of autonomy appears to be "I am what I can will freely."

3. CHILDHOOD AND THE ANTICIPATION OF ROLES

Being firmly convinced that he is a person on his own, the child must now find out what kind of a person he may become. He is, of course, deeply and exclusively "identified" with his parents, who most of the time appear to him to be powerful and beautiful, although often quite unreasonable, disagreeable, and even dangerous. Three developments support this stage, while also serving to bring about its crisis: (1) the child learns to move around more freely and more violently and therefore establishes a wider and, to him, unlimited radius of goals; (2) his sense of language becomes perfected to the point where he understands and can ask incessantly about innumerable things, often hearing just enough to misunderstand them thoroughly; and (3) both language and locomotion permit him to expand his imagination to so many roles that he cannot avoid frightening himself with what he himself has dreamed and thought up. Nevertheless, out of all this he must emerge with a *sense of initiative* as a basis for a realistic sense of ambition and purpose.

What, then, are the criteria for an unbroken sense of initiative? The criteria for the development of all the "senses" discussed here are the same: a crisis beset with some new estrangement is resolved in such a way that the child suddenly seems to be "more himself," more loving, more relaxed, and brighter in his judgment—in other words, vital in a new way. Most of all, he seems to be more activated and activating; he is in the free possession of a certain surplus of energy which permits him to forget many failures rather quickly and to approach new areas that seem desirable, even if they also seem dangerous, with undiminished zest and some increased sense of direction.

We are now approaching the end of the third year, when walking is getting to be a thing of ease, of vigor. The books tell us that a child can walk much before this, but walking and running become an item in his sphere of mastery when gravity is felt to be within, when he can forget that he is doing the walking and instead find out what he can do with it. Only then do his legs become part of him instead of being an ambulatory appendix. Only then will he find out with advantage what he now *may* do, along with what he *can* do, and now he is ready to visualize himself as being as big as the perambulating grownups. He begins to make comparisons and is apt to develop untiring curiosity about differences in size and kind in general, and about sexual and age differences in particular. He tries to comprehend possible future roles or, at any rate, to understand what roles are worth imagining. More immediately, he can now associate with those of his own age. Under the guidance of older children or special women guardians, he gradually enters into the infantile politics of nursery school, street corner, and barnyard. His learning now is eminently intrusive and vigorous; it leads away from his own limitations and into future possibilities.

The *intrusive mode,* dominating much of the behavior of this stage, characterizes a variety of configurationally "similar" activities and fantasies. These include (1) the intrusion into space by vigorous locomotion; (2) the intrusion into the unknown by consuming curiosity; (3) the intrusion into other people's ears and minds by the aggressive voice; (4) the intrusion upon or into other bodies by physical attack; (5) and, often most frighteningly, the thought of the phallus intruding the female body.

This, therefore, is called the *phallic stage* in the theory of infantile sexuality. It is the stage of infantile curiosity, of genital excitability, and of a varying preoccupation and overconcern with sexual matters, such as the apparent loss of the penis in girls. This "genitality" is, of course, rudimentary, a mere promise of things to come; often it is not even particularly noticeable. If not specifically provoked into precocious manifestation by especially seductive practices or by pointed prohibitions and threats of "cutting it off" or special customs such as sex play in groups of children, it is apt to lead to no more than a series of peculiarly fascinating experiences which soon become frightening and pointless enough to be repressed. This leads to the ascendancy of that human specialty which Freud called the "latency" period, that is, the long delay separating infantile sexuality (which in animals merges into maturity) and physical sexual maturation. It is accompanied by the recognition of the fact that in spite of all efforts to imagine oneself as being, in principle, as capable as mother and father, not even in the distant future is one ever going to be father in sexual relationship to mother, or mother in sexual relationship to father. The very deep emotional consequences of this insight and the magic fears associated with it make up what Freud has called the Oedipus complex. It is based on the logic of development which decrees that boys attach their first genital affection to the maternal adults who have otherwise given comfort to their bodies and that they develop their first sexual rivalry against the persons who are the sexual owners of those maternal persons. The little girl, in turn, becomes attached to her father and other important men and jealous of her mother, a development which may cause her much anxiety, for it seems to block her retreat to that self-same mother, while it makes her mother's disapproval much more magically dangerous because it is secretly "deserved."

Girls often undergo a sobering change at this stage, because they observe sooner or later that although their locomotor, mental, and social intrusiveness is as vigorous as that of the boys', thus permitting them to become perfectly good tomboys, they lack one item, the penis, and, with it, important prerogatives in most cultures and classes. While the boy has this visible, erectable, and comprehensible organ to which he can attach dreams of adult bigness, the girl's clitoris only poorly sustains dreams of sexual equality, and she does not even have breasts as analogously tangible tokens of her future. The idea of her eventual *inception* of the intruding phallus is as yet too frightening, and her maternal drives are relegated to play fantasy or baby tending. On the other hand, where mothers dominate households the boy can develop a sense of inadequacy because he learns at this stage that while he can do well outside in play and work, he will never boss the house, his mother, or his older sisters. His mother and sisters may, in fact, get even with him for their doubts in themselves by making him feel that a boy is really a somewhat repulsive creature.

Where the necessities of economic life and the simplicity of its social plan make the male and female roles and their specific powers and rewards comprehensible, these early misgivings about sexual differences are, of course, more easily integrated into the culture's design for the differentiation of sexual roles. Both girl and boy are, therefore, extraordinarily appreciative of any convincing promise of the fact that someday they will be as good as mother or father—perhaps better; and they are grateful for sexual enlightenment, a little at a time and patiently repeated at intervals.

The ambulatory stage, that of play and infantile genitality, adds to the inventory of basic social modalities in both sexes that of "making," first in the childlike sense of "being on the make." There are no simpler, stronger words to match basic social modalities than those of Basic English. The words suggest enjoyment of competition, insistence on goal, pleasure of conquest. In the boy the emphasis remains on "making" by head-on attack; in the girl it may turn to "catching" either by aggressive snatching or by making herself attractive and endearing. The child thus develops the prerequisites for masculine or feminine initiative and, above all, some sexual self-images which will become essential ingredients in the positive and negative aspects of his future identity. On the way, however, the vastly increased imagination and, as it were, the intoxication of increased locomotor powers lead to secret fantasies of gigantic and terrifying proportions. A deep *sense of guilt* is awakened—a strange sense, for it seems forever to imply that the individual has committed crimes and deeds that were, after all, not only not committed but would have been biologically quite impossible. While the struggle for autonomy at its worst had concentrated on keeping rivals out, and was therefore more an expression of *jealous rage* most often directed against encroachments by younger siblings, initiative brings with it *anticipatory rivalry* with those who were there first and who may therefore occupy with their superior equipment the field toward which one's initiative is at first directed. Jealousy and rivalry, those often embittered and yet essentially futile attempts at demarcating a sphere of unquestioned privilege, now come to a climax in a final contest for a favored position with one of the parents: the inevitable and necessary failure leads to guilt and anxiety. The child indulges in fantasies of being a giant or a tiger, but in his dreams he runs in terror for dear life. This, then, is the stage of fear for life and limb, of the *"castration complex"*—the intensified fear of losing, or on the part of the girl the conviction that she has lost, the male genital as punishment for secret fantasies and deeds.

The great governor of initiative is *conscience*. The child, we said, now not only feels afraid of being found out, but he also hears the "inner voice" of self-observation, self-guidance, and self-punishment, which divides him radically within himself: a new and powerful estrangement. This is the ontogenetic cornerstone of morality. But from the point of view of human vitality, we must point out that if this great achievement is overburdened by all too eager adults, it can be bad for the spirit and for morality itself. For the conscience of the child can be primitive, cruel, and uncompromising, as may be observed in instances where children learn to constrict themselves to the point of over-all inhibition; where they develop an obedience more literal than the one the parent wishes to exact; or where they develop deep regressions and lasting resentments because the parents themselves do not seem to live up to the conscience which they have fostered in the child. One of the deepest conflicts in life is caused by hate for a parent who served initially as the model and the executor of the conscience, but who was later found trying to "get away with" the very transgressions which the child could no longer tolerate in himself. Thus the child comes to feel that the whole matter is not one of universal goodness but of arbitrary power. The suspiciousness and evasiveness which is added to the all-or-nothing quality of the superego makes moralistic man a great potential danger to himself and to his fellow men. Morality can become synonymous with vindictiveness and with the suppression of others.

All of this may seem strange to readers who have not suspected the potential powerhouse of destructive drives which can be aroused and temporarily buried at this stage, only to contribute later to the inner arsenal of a destructiveness so ready to be used when opportunity provokes it. By using the words "potential," "provoke," and "opportunity," I mean to emphasize that there is little in these inner developments which cannot be harnessed to constructive and peaceful initiative if we learn to understand the conflicts and anxieties of childhood and the importance of childhood for mankind. But if we should choose to overlook or belittle the phenomena of childhood, along with the best and the worst of our childhood dreams, we shall have failed to recognize one of the eternal sources of human anxiety and strife. For again, the pathological consequences of this stage may not show until much later, when conflicts over initiative may find expression in *hysterical denial* or in a *self-restriction* which keeps an individual from living up to his inner capacities or to the powers of his imagination and feeling, if not in relative sexual impotence or frigidity. All of this, in turn, may be "over-compensated" in a great show of tireless initiative, in a quality of "go-at-itiveness" at any cost. Many adults feel that their worth as people consists entirely in what they are "going at" in the future and not in what they are in the present. The strain consequently developed in their bodies, which are always "on the go," with the engine racing even at moments of rest, is a powerful contribution to the much-discussed psychosomatic diseases of our time. It is as if the culture had made a man overadvertise himself and so identify with his own advertisement that only disease can designate the limit.

A comparative view of child training, however, suggests a fact most important for identity development, namely, that adults by their own example and by the stories they tell of the big life and of what to them is the great past, offer children of this age an eagerly absorbed *ethos of action* in the form of ideal types and techniques fascinating enough to replace the heroes of picture book and fairy tale. For this reason also the play age relies on the existence of some form of basic family, which teaches the child by patient example where play ends and irreversible purpose begins and where "don'ts" are superseded by sanctioned avenues of vigorous action. For the children now look for new identifications which seem to promise a field of initiative with less of the conflict and guilt which attach to the hopeless rivalry of the home. Also, in connection with comprehensible games and work activities, a companionship may develop between father and son, and between mother and daughter, an experience of essential equality in worth, in spite of the inequality in developmental schedule. Such companionship is a lasting treasure not only for parent and child, but for the community, as it is a counterforce to those hidden hatreds based on differences in mere size or age.

Only thus are guilt feelings integrated in a strong but not severe conscience, only thus is language certified as a shared actuality. The "Oedipal" stage thus eventually results not only in a moral sense constricting the horizon of the permissible; it also sets the direction toward the possible and the tangible which attaches infantile dreams to the varied goals of technology and culture.

We may now see what induced Freud to place the Oedipus complex at the core of man's conflicted existence, and this not only according to psychiatric evidence but also to the testimony of great fiction, drama, and history. For the fact that man began as a playing child leaves a residue of play-acting and role playing even in what he considers his highest purposes. These he projects on the glorified past as well as on a larger and always more perfect historical future; these he will dramatize in the ceremonial present with uniformed players in ritual arrangements which sanction aggressive initiative even as they assuage guilt by submission to a higher authority.

Among the group psychological consequences of the initiative stage, then, there is also a latent and often rageful readiness in the best and the most industrious to follow any leader who can make goals of conquest seem both impersonal and glorious enough to excite an intrinsically phallic enthusiasm in men (and a compliance in women) and thus to relieve their irrational guilt. It is obvious, then, that man's aggressive ideals are to a large extent anchored in the stage of initiative, a fact of importance for the conflict of identity formation—and confusion.

The indispensable contribution of the initiative stage to later identity development, then, obviously is that of freeing the child's initiative and sense of purpose for adult tasks which promise (but cannot guarantee) a fulfillment of one's range of capacities. This is prepared in the firmly established, steadily growing conviction, undaunted by guilt, that "I am what I can imagine I will be." It is equally obvious, however, that a widespread disappointment of this conviction by a discrepancy between infantile ideals and adolescent reality can only lead to an unleashing of the guilt-and-violence cycle so characteristic of man and yet so dangerous to his very existence.

4. SCHOOL AGE AND TASK IDENTIFICATION

Such is the wisdom of the ground plan that at no time is the child more ready to learn quickly and avidly, to become big in the sense of sharing obligation, discipline, and performance than at the end of the period of expansive imagination. He is also eager to make things together, to share in constructing and planning, instead of trying to coerce other children or provoke restriction. Children now also attach themselves to teachers and the parents of other children, and they want to watch and imitate people representing occupations which they can grasp—firemen and policemen, gardeners, plumbers, and garbage men. If they are lucky they live at least part of their lives near barnyards or on safe streets around busy people and around many other children of all ages so that they can observe and participate as their capacities and their initiative grow in tentative spurts. But when they reach school age, children in all cultures receive some systematic instruction, although it is by no means always in the kind of school which literate people must organize around teachers who have learned how to teach literacy. In preliterate people much is learned from adults who become teachers by acclamation rather than by appointment, and much is learned from older children, but the knowledge gained is related to the basic skills of simple technologies which can be understood the moment the child gets ready to handle the utensils, the tools, and the weapons (or facsimiles thereof) used by the big people. He enters the technology of his tribe very gradually but also very directly. More literate people, with more specialized careers, must prepare the child by teaching him things which first of all make him literate. He is then given the widest possible basic education for the greatest number of possible careers. The greater the specialization, the more indistinct the goal of initiative becomes, the more complicated the social reality, and the vaguer the father's and mother's role in it. Between childhood and adulthood, then, our children go to school, and school skill seems to many to be a world all by itself, with its own goals and limitations, its achievements and disappointments.

At nursery-school age, playfulness reaches into the world shared with others. At first these others are treated as things; they are inspected, run into, or forced to "be horsie." Such learning is necessary in order to discover what potential play content can be admitted only to fantasy or only to play by and with oneself; what content can be successfully represented only in the world of toys and small things; and what content can be shared with others and even forced upon them. It is not restricted to the technical mastery of toys and things, but also includes an infantile way of mastering social experience by experimenting, planning, and sharing.

While all children at times need to be left alone in solitary play or, later, in the company of books and radio, motion pictures and television, and while all children need their hours and days of make-believe in games, they all, sooner or later, become dissatisfied and disgruntled without a sense of being able to make things and make them well and even perfectly: it is this that I have called the *sense of industry*. Without this, even the best-entertained child soon acts exploited. It is as if he knows and his society knows that now that he is psychologically already a rudimentary parent, he must begin to be something of a worker and potential provider before becoming a biological parent. With the oncoming latency period, then, the advancing child forgets, or rather quietly "sublimates"—that is, applies to concrete pursuits and approved goals—the drives which have made him dream and play. He now learns to win recognition by producing things. He develops perseverance and adjusts himself to the inorganic laws of the tool world and can become an eager and absorbed unit of a productive situation.

The danger at this stage is the development of an estrangement from himself and from his tasks—the well-known *sense of inferiority*. This may be caused by an insufficient solution of the preceding conflict: the child may still want his mommy more than knowledge; he may still prefer to be the baby at home rather than the big child in school; he still compares himself with his father, and the comparison arouses a sense of guilt as well as a sense of inferiority. Family life may not have prepared him for school life, or school life may fail to sustain the promises of earlier stages in that nothing that he has learned to do well so far seems to count with his fellows or his teacher. And then again, he may be potentially able to excel in ways which are dormant and which, if not evoked now, may develop late or never.

It is at this point that wider society becomes significant to the child by admitting him to roles preparatory to the actuality of technology and economy. Where he finds out immediately, however, that the color of his skin or the background of his parents rather than his wish and will to learn are the factors that decide his worth as a pupil or apprentice, the human propensity for feeling unworthy may be fatefully aggravated as a determinant of character development.

Good teachers who feel trusted and respected by the community know how to alternate play and work, games and study. They know how to recognize special efforts, how to encourage special gifts. They also know how to give a child time and how to handle those children to whom school, for a while, is not important and is considered something to endure rather than enjoy, or even the child to whom, for a while, other children are much more important than the teacher. But good parents also feel a need to make their children trust their teachers, and therefore to have teachers who can be trusted. For nothing less is at stake than the development and maintenance in children of a positive identification with those who know things and know how to do things. Again and again in interviews with especially gifted and inspired people, one is told spontaneously and with a special glow that *one* teacher can be credited with having kindled the flame of hidden talent. Against this stands the overwhelming evidence of vast neglect.

The fact that the majority of teachers in our elementary schools are women must be considered here in passing, because it can lead to a conflict with the nonintellectual boy's masculine identification, as if knowledge were feminine, action masculine. Bernard Shaw's statement that those who can, do, while those who cannot, teach, still has frequent validity for both parents and children. The selection and training of teachers, then, is vital for the avoidance of the dangers which can befall the individual at this stage. The development of a sense of inferiority, the feeling that one will never be "any good," is a danger which can be minimized by a teacher who knows how to emphasize what a child *can* do and who recognizes a psychiatric problem when she sees one. Obviously, here lies the best opportunity for preventing the particular identity confusion which goes back to incapacity or a flagrant lack of opportunity to learn. On the other hand, the child's budding sense of identity can remain prematurely fixed on being nothing but a good little worker or a good little helper, which may by no means be all he might become. Finally, there is the danger, probably the most common one, that throughout the long years of going to school a child will never acquire the enjoyment of work and pride in doing at least one kind of thing really well.

Regarding the period of a developing sense of industry, I have referred to outer and inner hindrances in the use of new capacities but not to aggravations of new human drives, nor to submerged rages resulting from their frustration. This stage differs from the earlier ones in that it is not a swing from an inner upheaval to a new mastery. Freud calls it the latency stage because violent drives are normally dormant. But it is only a lull before the storm of puberty, when all the earlier drives re-emerge in new combinations.

On the other hand, this is socially a most decisive stage. Since industry involves doing things beside and with others, a first sense of division of labor and of differential opportunity—that is, a sense of the *technological ethos* of a culture—develops at this time. Therefore, the configurations of culture and the manipulations basic to the *prevailing technology* must reach meaningfully into school life, supporting in every child a feeling of competence—that is, the free exercise of dexterity and intelligence in the completion of serious tasks unimpaired by an infantile sense of inferiority. This is the lasting basis for co-operative participation in productive adult life.

Two poles in American grammar school education may serve to illustrate the contribution of the school age to the problem of identity. There is the traditional extreme of making early school life an extension of grim adulthood by emphasizing self-restraint and a strict sense of duty in doing what one is told to do, as opposed to the modern extreme of making it an extension of the natural tendency in childhood to find out by playing, to learn what one must do by doing what one likes to do. Both methods work for some children in some ways, but impose on others a special adjustment. The first trend, if carried to the extreme, exploits a tendency on the part of the preschool and grammar school child to become entirely dependent on prescribed duties. He thus may learn much that is absolutely necessary and he may develop an unshakable sense of duty. But he may never unlearn an unnecessary and costly self-restraint with which he may later make his own life and other people's lives miserable, and in fact spoil, in turn, his own children's natural desire to learn and to work. The second trend, when carried to an extreme, leads not only to the well-known popular objection that children do not learn anything any more but also to such feelings in children as those expressed in the by now famous question of a metropolitan child: "Teacher, *must* we do today what we *want* to do?" Nothing could better express the fact that children at this age do like to be mildly but firmly coerced into the adventure of finding out that one can learn to accomplish things which one would never have thought of by oneself, things which owe their attractiveness to the very fact that they are not the product of play and fantasy but the product of reality, practicality, and logic; things which thus provide a token sense of participation in the real world of adults. Between these extremes we have the many schools which have no styles at all except grim attendance to the fact that school must be. Social inequality and backwardness of method still create a hazardous gap between many children and the technology which needs them not only so that they may serve technological aims, but, more imperatively, so that technology may serve humanity.

But there is another danger to identity development. If the overly conforming child accepts work as the only criterion of worthwhileness, sacrificing imagination and playfulness too readily, he may become ready to submit to what Marx called "craft-idiocy," i.e., become a slave of his technology and of its dominant role typology. Here we are already in the midst of identity problems, for with the establishment of a firm initial relationship to the world of skills and tools and to those who teach and share them, and with the advent of puberty, childhood proper comes to an end. And since man is not only the learning but also the teaching and above all the working animal, the immediate contribution of the school age to a sense of identity can be expressed in the words "I am what I can learn to make work." It is immediately obvious that for the vast majority of men, in all times, this has been not only the beginning but also the limitation of their identity; or better: the majority of men have always consolidated their identity needs around their technical and occupational capacities, leaving it to special groups (special by birth, by choice or election, and by giftedness) to establish and preserve those "higher" institutions without which man's daily work has always seemed an inadequate self-expression, if not a mere grind or even a kind of curse. It may be for that very reason that the identity problem in our time becomes both psychiatrically and historically relevant. For as man can leave some of the grind and curse to machines, he can visualize a greater freedom of identity for a larger segment of mankind.

5. ADOLESCENCE

As technological advances put more and more time between early school life and the young person's final access to specialized work, the stage of adolescing becomes an even more marked and conscious period and, as it has always been in some cultures in some periods, almost a way of life between childhood and adulthood. Thus in the later school years young people, beset with the physiological revolution of their genital maturation and the uncertainty of the adult roles ahead, seem much concerned with faddish attempts at establishing an adolescent subculture with what looks like a final rather than a transitory or, in fact, initial identity formation. They are sometimes morbidly, often curiously, preoccupied with what they appear to be in the eyes of others as compared with what they feel they are, and with the question of how to connect the roles and skills cultivated earlier with the ideal prototypes of the day. In their search for a new sense of continuity and sameness, which must now include sexual maturity, some adolescents have to come to grips again with crises of earlier years before they can install lasting idols and ideals as guardians of a final identity. They need, above all, a moratorium for the integration of the identity elements ascribed in the foregoing to the childhood stages: only that now a larger unit, vague in its outline and yet immediate in its demands, replaces the childhood milieu—"society." A review of these elements is also a list of adolescent problems.

If the earliest stage bequeathed to the identity crisis an important need for trust in oneself and in others, then clearly the adolescent looks most fervently for men and ideas to have *faith* in, which also means men and ideas in whose service it would seem worth while to prove oneself trustworthy. At the same time, however, the adolescent fears a foolish, all too trusting commitment, and will, paradoxically, express his need for faith in loud and cynical mistrust.

If the second stage established the necessity of being defined by what one can *will* freely, then the adolescent now looks for an opportunity to decide with free assent on one of the available or unavoidable avenues of duty and service, and at the same time is mortally afraid of being forced into activities in which he would feel exposed to ridicule or self-doubt. This, too, can lead to a paradox, namely, that he would rather act shamelessly in the eyes of his elders, out of free choice, than be forced into activities which would be shameful in his own eyes or in those of his peers.

If an unlimited *imagination* as to what one *might* become is the heritage of the play age, then the adolescent's willingness to put his trust in those peers and leading, or misleading, elders who will give imaginative, if not illusory, scope to his aspirations is only too obvious. By the same token, he objects violently to all "pedantic" limitations on his self-images and will be ready to settle by loud accusation all his guiltiness over the excessiveness of his ambition.

Finally, if the desire to make something work, and to make it work well, is the gain of the school age, then the choice of an occupation assumes a significance beyond the question of remuneration and status. It is for this reason that some adolescents prefer not to work at all for a while rather than be forced into an otherwise promising career which would offer success without the satisfaction of functioning with unique excellence.

In any given period in history, then, that part of youth will have the most affirmatively exciting time of it which finds itself in the wave of a technological, economic, or ideological trend seemingly promising all that youthful vitality could ask for.

Adolescence, therefore, is least "stormy" in that segment of youth which is gifted and well trained in the pursuit of expanding technological trends, and thus able to identify with new roles of competency and invention and to accept a more implicit ideological outlook. Where this is not given, the adolescent mind becomes a more explicitly ideological one, by which we mean one searching for some inspiring unification of tradition or anticipated techniques, ideas, and ideals. And, indeed, it is the ideological potential of a society which speaks most clearly to the adolescent who is so eager to be affirmed by peers, to be confirmed by teachers, and to be inspired by worth-while "ways of life." On the other hand, should a young person feel that the environment tries to deprive him too radically of all the forms of expression which permit him to develop and integrate the next step, he may resist with the wild strength encountered in animals who are suddenly forced to defend their lives. For, indeed, in the social jungle of human existence there is no feeling of being alive without a sense of identity.

Having come this far, I would like to give one example (and I consider it representative in structure) of the individual way in which a young person, given some leeway, may utilize a traditional way of life for dealing with a remnant of negative identity. I had known Jill before her puberty, when she was rather obese and showed many "oral" traits of voracity and dependency while she also was a tomboy and bitterly envious of her brothers and in rivalry with them. But she was intelligent and always had an air about her (as did her mother) which seemed to promise that things would turn out all right. And, indeed, she straightened out and up, became very attractive, an easy leader in any group, and, to many, a model of young girlhood. As a clinician, I watched and wondered what she would do with that voraciousness and with the rivalry which she had displayed earlier. Could it be that such things are simply absorbed in fortuitous growth?

Then one autumn in her late teens, Jill did not return to college from the ranch out West where she had spent the summer. She had asked her parents to let her stay. Simply out of liberality and confidence, they granted her this moratorium and returned East.

That winter Jill specialized in taking care of newborn colts, and would get up at any time during a winter night to bottle feed the most needy animals. Having apparently acquired a certain satisfaction within herself, as well as astonished recognition from the cowboys, she returned home and reassumed her place. I felt that she had found and hung on to an opportunity to do actively and for others what she had always yearned to have done for her, as she had once demonstrated by overeating: she had learned to feed needy young mouths. But she did so in a context which, in turning passive into active, also turned a former symptom into a social act.

One might say that she turned "maternal" but it was a maternalism such as cowboys must and do display; and, of course, she did it all in jeans. This brought recognition "from man to man" as well as from man to woman, and beyond that the confirmation of her optimism, that is, her feeling that something could be done that felt like her, was useful and worth while, and was in line with an ideological trend where it still made immediate practical sense.

Such self-chosen "therapies" depend, of course, on the leeway given in the right spirit at the right time, and this depends on a great variety of circumstances. I intend to publish similar fragments from the lives of children in greater detail at some future date; let this example stand for the countless observations in everyday life, where the resourcefulness of young people proves itself when the conditions are right.

The estrangement of this stage is *identity confusion.* For the moment, we will accept Biff's formulation in Arthur Miller's *Death of a Salesman:* "I just can't take hold, Mom, I can't take hold of some kind of a life." Where such a dilemma is based on a strong previous doubt of one's ethnic and sexual identity, or where role confusion joins a hopelessness of long standing, delinquent and "borderline" psychotic episodes are not uncommon. Youth after youth, bewildered by the incapacity to assume a role forced on him by the inexorable standardization of American adolescence, runs away in one form or another, dropping out of school, leaving jobs, staying out all night, or withdrawing into bizarre and inaccessible moods. Once "delinquent," his greatest need and often his only salvation is the refusal on the part of older friends, advisers, and judiciary personnel to type him further by pat diagnoses and social judgments which ignore the special dynamic conditions of adolescence. It is here, as we shall see in greater detail, that the concept of identity confusion is of practical clinical value, for if they are diagnosed and treated correctly, seemingly psychotic and criminal incidents do not have the same fatal significance which they may have at other ages.

In general it is the inability to settle on an occupational identity which most disturbs young people. To keep themselves together they temporarily overidentify with the heroes of cliques and crowds to the point of an apparently complete loss of individuality. Yet in this stage not even "falling in love" is entirely, or even primarily, a sexual matter. To a considerable extent adolescent love is an attempt to arrive at a definition of one's identity by projecting one's diffused self-image on another and by seeing it thus reflected and gradually clarified. This is why so much of young love is conversation. On the other hand, clarification can also be sought by destructive means. Young people can become remarkably clannish, intolerant, and cruel in their exclusion of others who are "different," in skin color or cultural background, in tastes and gifts, and often in entirely petty aspects of dress and gesture arbitrarily selected as the signs of an in-grouper or out-grouper. It is important to understand in principle (which does not mean to condone in all of its manifestations) that such intolerance may be, for a while, a necessary defense against a sense of identity loss. This is unavoidable at a time of life when the body changes its proportions radically, when genital puberty floods body and imagination with all manner of impulses, when intimacy with the other sex approaches and is, on occasion, forced on the young person, and when the immediate future confronts one with too many conflicting possibilities and choices. Adolescents not only help one another temporarily through such discomfort by forming cliques and stereotyping themselves, their ideals, and their enemies; they also insistently test each other's capacity for sustaining loyalties in the midst of inevitable conflicts of values.

The readiness for such testing helps to explain . . . the appeal of simple and cruel totalitarian doctrines among the youth of such countries and classes as have lost or are losing their group identities—feudal, agrarian, tribal, or national. The democracies are faced with the job of winning these grim youths by convincingly demonstrating to them—by living it—that a democratic identity can be strong and yet tolerant, judicious and still determined. But industrial democracy poses special problems in that it insists on self-made identities ready to grasp many chances and ready to adjust to the changing necessities of booms and busts, of peace and war, of migration and determined sedentary life. Democracy, therefore, must present its adolescents with ideals which can be shared by young people of many backgrounds, and which emphasize autonomy in the form of independence and initiative in the form of constructive work. These promises, however, are not easy to fulfill in increasingly complex and centralized systems of industrial, economic, and political organization, systems which increasingly neglect the "self-made" ideology still flaunted in oratory. This is hard on many young Americans because their whole upbringing has made the development of a self-reliant personality dependent on a certain degree of choice, a sustained hope for an individual chance, and a firm commitment to the freedom of self-realization.

We are speaking here not merely of high privileges and lofty ideals but of psychological necessities. For the social institution which is the guardian of identity *is* what we have called *ideology*. One may see in ideology also the imagery of an aristocracy in its widest possible sense, which connotes that within a defined world image and a given course of history the best people will come to rule and rule will develop the best in people. In order not to become cynically or apathetically lost, young people must somehow be able to convince themselves that those who succeed in their anticipated adult world thereby shoulder the obligation of being best. For it is through their ideology that social systems enter into the fiber of the next generation and attempt to absorb into their lifeblood the rejuvenative power of youth. Adolescence is thus a vital regenerator in the process of social evolution, for youth can offer its loyalties and energies both to the conservation of that which continues to feel true and to the revolutionary correction of that which has lost its regenerative significance.

We can study the identity crisis also in the lives of creative individuals who could resolve it for themselves only by offering to their contemporaries a new model of resolution such as that expressed in works of art or in original deeds, and who furthermore are eager to tell us all about it in diaries, letters, and self-representations. And even as the neuroses of a given period reflect the ever-present inner chaos of man's existence in a new way, the creative crises point to the period's unique solutions.

. . . But there is a third manifestation of the remnants of infantilism and adolescence in man: it is the pooling of the individual crises in transitory upheavals amounting to collective "hysterias." Where there are voluble leaders their creative crises and the latent crises of their followers can be at least studied with the help of our assumptions—and of their writings. More elusive are spontaneous group developments not attributable to a leader. And it will, at any rate, not be helpful to call mass irrationalities by clinical names. It would be impossible to diagnose clinically how much hysteria is present in a young nun participating in an epidemic of convulsive spells or how much perverse "sadism" in a young Nazi commanded to participate in massive parades or in mass killings. So we can point only most tentatively to certain similarities between individual crises and group behavior in order to indicate that in a given period of history they are in an obscure contact with each other.

But before we submerge ourselves in the clinical and biographic evidence for what we call identity confusion, we will take a look beyond the identity crisis. The words "beyond identity," of course, could be understood in two ways, both essential for the problem. They could mean that there is more to man's core than identity, that there is in fact in each individual an "I," an observing center of awareness and of volition, which can transcend and must survive the *psychosocial identity* which is our concern in this book. In some ways, as we will see, a sometimes precocious self-transcendence seems to be felt strongly in a transient manner in youth, as if a pure identity had to be kept free from psychosocial encroachment. And yet no man (except a man aflame and dying like Keats, who could speak of identity in words which secured him immediate fame) can transcend himself in youth. We will speak later of the transcendence of identity. In the following "beyond identity" means life after adolescence and the uses of identity and, indeed, the return of some forms of identity crisis in the later stages of the life cycle.

6. BEYOND IDENTITY

The first of these is the crisis of *intimacy.* It is only when identity formation is well on its way that true intimacy—which is really a counter-pointing as well as a fusing of identities—is possible. Sexual intimacy is only part of what I have in mind, for it is obvious that sexual intimacies often precede the capacity to develop a true and mutual psychosocial intimacy with another person, be it in friendship, in erotic encounters, or in joint inspiration. The youth who is not sure of his identity shies away from interpersonal intimacy or throws himself into acts of intimacy which are "promiscuous" without true fusion or real self-abandon.

Where a youth does not accomplish such intimate relationships with others—and, I would add, with his own inner resources—in late adolescence or early adulthood, he may settle for highly stereotyped interpersonal relations and come to retain a deep *sense of isolation.* If the times favor an impersonal kind of interpersonal pattern, a man can go far, very far, in life and yet harbor a severe character problem doubly painful because he will never feel really himself, although everyone says he is "somebody."

The counterpart of intimacy is *distantiation:* the readiness to repudiate, isolate, and, if necessary, destroy those forces and people whose essence seems dangerous to one's own. Thus, the lasting consequence of the need for distantiation is the readiness to fortify one's territory of intimacy and solidarity and to view all outsiders with a fanatic "overvaluation of small differences" between the familiar and the foreign. Such prejudices can be utilized and exploited in politics and in war and secure the loyal self-sacrifice and the readiness to kill from the strongest and the best. A remnant of adolescent danger is to be found where intimate, competitive, and combative relations are experienced with and against the selfsame people. But as the areas of adult responsibility are gradually delineated, as the competitive encounter, the erotic bond, and merciless enmity are differentiated from each other, they eventually become subject to that *ethical sense* which is the mark of the adult and which takes over from the ideological conviction of adolescence and the moralism of childhood.

Freud was once asked what he thought a normal person should be able to do well. The questioner probably expected a complicated, "deep" answer. But Freud simply said, *"Lieben und arbeiten"* ("to love and to work"). It pays to ponder on this simple formula; it grows deeper as you think about it. For when Freud said "love," he meant the generosity of intimacy as well as genital love; when he said love and work, he meant a general work productiveness which would not preoccupy the individual to the extent that he might lose his right or capacity to be a sexual and a loving being.

Psychoanalysis has emphasized *genitality* as one of the developmental conditions for full maturity. Genitality consists in the capacity to develop orgastic potency which is more than the discharge of sex products in the sense of Kinsey's "outlets." It combines the ripening of intimate sexual mutuality with full genital sensitivity and with a capacity for discharge of tension from the whole body. This is a rather concrete way of saying something about a process which we really do not yet quite understand. But the experience of the climactic mutuality of orgasm clearly provides a supreme example of the mutual regulation of complicated patterns and in some way appeases the hostilities and the potential rages caused by the daily evidence of the oppositeness of male and female, of fact and fancy, of love and hate, of work and play. Such experience makes sexuality less obsessive and sadistic control of the partner superfluous.

Before such genital maturity is reached, much of sexual life is of the self-seeking, identity-hungry kind; each partner is really trying only to reach himself. Or it remains a kind of genital combat in which each tries to defeat the other. All this remains as part of adult sexuality, but it is gradually absorbed as the differences between the sexes become a full polarization within a joint life style. For the previously established vital strengths have helped to make the two sexes first become similar in consciousness, language, and ethics in order to then permit them to be maturely different.

Man, in addition to erotic attraction, has developed a selectivity of "love" which serves the need for a new and shared identity. If the estrangement typical for this stage is *isolation,* that is, the incapacity to take chances with one's identity by sharing true intimacy, such inhibition is often reinforced by a fear of the outcome of intimacy: offspring—and care. Love as mutual devotion, however, overcomes the antagonisms inherent in sexual and functional polarization, and is the vital strength of young adulthood. It is the guardian of that elusive and yet all-pervasive power of cultural and personal style which binds into a "way of life" the affiliations of competition and co-operation, production and procreation.

If we should continue the game of "I am" formulations "beyond identity" we should have to change the tune. For now the increment of identity is based on the formula "*We* are what we love."

Evolution has made man a teaching as well as a learning animal, for dependency and maturity are reciprocal: mature man needs to be needed, and maturity is guided by the nature of that which must be cared for. *Generativity,* then, is primarily the concern for establishing and guiding the next generation. There are of course, people who, from misfortune or because of special and genuine gifts in other directions, do not apply this drive to offspring of their own, but to other forms of altruistic concern and creativity which many absorb their kind of parental drive. And indeed, the concept of generativity is meant to include productivity and creativity, neither of which, however, can replace it as designations of a crisis in development. For the ability to lose oneself in the meeting of bodies and minds leads to a gradual expansion of ego-interests and to a libidinal investment in that which is being generated. Where such enrichment fails altogether, regression to an obsessive need for pseudointimacy takes place, often with a pervading *sense of stagnation,* boredom, and interpersonal impoverishment. Individuals, then, often begin to indulge themselves as if they were their own—or one another's—one and only child; and where conditions favor it, early invalidism, physical or psychological, becomes the vehicle of self-concern. On the other hand, the mere fact of having or even wanting children does not "achieve" generativity. Some young parents suffer, it seems, from a retardation in the ability to develop true care. The reasons are often to be found in early childhood impressions; in faulty identifications with parents; in excessive self-love based on a too strenuously self-made personality; and in the lack of some faith, some "belief in the species," which would make a child appear to be a welcome trust. The very nature of generativity, however, suggests that its most circumscribed pathology must now be sought in the next generation, that is, in the form of those unavoidable estrangements which we have listed for childhood and youth and which may appear in aggravated form as a result of a generative failure on the part of the parents.

As to the institutions which reinforce generativity and safeguard it, one can only say that *all* institutions by their very nature codify the ethics of generative succession. Generativity is itself a driving power in human organization. And the stages of childhood and adulthood are a system of generation and regeneration to which institutions such as shared households and divided labor strive to give continuity. Thus the basic strengths enumerated here and the essentials of an organized human community have evolved together as an attempt to establish a set of proven methods and a fund of traditional reassurance which enables each generation to meet the needs of the next in relative independence from personal differences and changing conditions.

In the aging person who has taken care of things and people and has adapted himself to the triumphs and disappointments of being, by necessity, the originator of others and the generator of things and ideas—only in him the fruit of the seven stages gradually ripens. I know no better word for it than *integrity*. Lacking a clear definition, I shall point to a few attributes of this stage of mind. It is the ego's accrued assurance of its proclivity for order and meaning—an emotional integration faithful to the image-bearers of the past and ready to take, and eventually to renounce, leadership in the present. It is the acceptance of one's one and only life cycle and of the people who have become significant to it as something that had to be and that, by necessity, permitted of no substitutions. It thus means a new and different love of one's parents, free of the wish that they should have been different, and an acceptance of the fact that one's life is one's own responsibility. It is a sense of comradeship with men and women of distant times and of different pursuits who have created orders and objects and sayings conveying human dignity and love. Although aware of the relativity of all the various life styles which have given meaning to human striving, the possessor of integrity is ready to defend the dignity of his own life style against all physical and economic threats. For he knows that an individual life is the accidental coincidence of but one life cycle with but one segment of history, and that for him all human integrity stands and falls with the one style of integrity of which he partakes.

Clinical and anthropological evidence suggest that the lack or loss of this accrued ego integration is signified by *disgust* and by *despair:* fate is not accepted as the frame of life, death not as its finite boundary. Despair expresses the feeling that time is short, too short for the attempt to start another life and to try out alternate roads to integrity. Such a despair is often hidden behind a show of disgust, a misanthropy, or a chronic contemptuous displeasure with particular institutions and particular people—a disgust and a displeasure which, where not allied with the vision of a superior life, only signify the individual's contempt of himself.

A meaningful old age, then, preceding a possible terminal senility, serves the need for that integrated heritage which gives indispensable perspective to the life cycle. Strength here takes the form of that detached yet active concern with life bounded by death, which we call *wisdom* in its many connotations from ripened "wits" to accumulated knowledge, mature judgment, and inclusive understanding. Not that each man can evolve wisdom for himself. For most, a living *tradition* provides the essence of it. But the end of the cycle also evokes "ultimate concerns" for what chance man may have to transcend the limitations of his identity and his often tragic or bitterly tragicomic engagement in his one and only life cycle within the sequence of generations. Yet great philosophical and religious systems dealing with ultimate individuation seem to have remained responsibly related to the cultures and civilizations of their times. Seeking transcendence by renunciation, they yet remain ethically concerned with the "maintenance of the world." By the same token, a civilization can be measured by the meaning which it gives to the full cycle of life, for such meaning, or the lack of it, cannot fail to reach into the beginnings of the next generation, and thus into the chances of others to meet ultimate questions with some clarity and strength.

To WHATEVER abyss ultimate concerns may lead individual men, man as a psychosocial creature will face, toward the end of his life, a new edition of an identity crisis which we may state in the words "I am what survives of me." From the stages of life, then, such dispositions as faith, will power, purposefulness, competence, fidelity, love, care, wisdom—all criteria of vital individual strength—also flow into the life of institutions. Without them, institutions wilt; but without the spirit of institutions pervading the patterns of care and love, instruction and training, no strength could emerge from the sequence of generations.

Psychosocial strength, we conclude, depends on a total process which regulates individual life cycles, the sequence of generations, and the structure of society simultaneously: for all three have evolved together.

5
CONTINUITIES AND DISCONTINUITIES IN CULTURAL CONDITIONING*

RUTH BENEDICT

ALL CULTURES must deal in one way or another with the cycle of growth from infancy to adulthood. Nature has posed the situation dramatically: on the one hand, the new born baby, physiologically vulnerable, unable to fend for itself, or to participate of its own initiative in the life of the group, and, on the other, the adult man or woman. Every man who rounds out his human potentialities must have been a son first and a father later and the two roles are physiologically in great contrast; he must first have been dependent upon others for his very existence and later he must provide such security for others. This discontinuity in the life cycle is a fact of nature and is inescapable. Facts of nature, however, in any discussion of human problems, are ordinarily read off not at their bare minimal but surrounded by all the local accretions of behavior to which the student of human affairs has become accustomed in his own culture. For that reason it is illuminating to examine comparative material from other societies in order to get a wider perspective on our own special accretions. The anthropologist's role is not to question the facts of nature, but to insist upon the interposition of a middle term between "nature" and "human behavior"; his role is to analyse that term, to document local man-made doctorings of nature and to insist that these doctorings should not be read off in any one culture as nature itself. Although it is a fact of nature that the child becomes a man, the way in which this transition is effected varies from one society to another, and no one of these particular cultural bridges should be regarded as the "natural" path to maturity.

From a comparative point of view our culture goes to great extremes in emphasizing contrasts between the child and the adult. The child is sexless, the adult estimates his virility by his sexual activities; the child must be protected from the ugly facts of life, the adult must meet them without psychic catastrophe; the child must obey, the adult must command this obedience. These are all dogmas of our culture, dogmas which, in spite of the

* From *Psychiatry*, 1938, *1*, 161–167. Reprinted with permission from the Ruth Benedict Estate and the William Alanson White Psychiatric Foundation, Inc.

facts of nature, other cultures commonly do not share. In spite of the physiological contrasts between child and adult, these are cultural accretions.

It will make the point clearer if we consider one habit in our own culture in regard to which there is not this discontinuity of conditioning. With the greatest clarity of purpose and economy of training, we achieve our goal of conditioning everyone to eat three meals a day. The baby's training in regular food periods begins at birth and no crying of the child and no inconvenience to the mother is allowed to interfere. We gauge the child's physiological make-up and at first allow it food oftener than adults, but, because our goal is firmly set and our training consistent, before the child is two years old it has achieved the adult schedule. From the point of view of other cultures this is as startling as the fact of three-year-old babies perfectly at home in deep water is to us. Modesty is another sphere in which our child training is consistent and economical; we waste no time in clothing the baby and, in contrast to many societies where the child runs naked till it is ceremonially given its skirt or its pubic sheath at adolescence, the child's training fits it precisely for adult conventions.

In neither of these aspects of behavior is there need for an individual in our culture to embark before puberty, at puberty or at some later date upon a course of action which all his previous training has tabued. He is spared the unsureness inevitable in such a transition.

The illustration I have chosen may appear trivial, but in larger and more important aspects of behavior, our methods are obviously different. Because of the great variety of child training in different families in our society, I might illustrate continuity of conditioning from individual life histories in our culture, but even these, from a comparative point of view, stop far short of consistency and I shall therefore confine myself to describing arrangements in other cultures in which training, which with us is idiosyncratic, is accepted and traditional and does not therefore involve the same possibility of conflict. I shall choose childhood rather than infant and nursing situations not because the latter do not vary strikingly in different cultures but because they are nevertheless more circumscribed by the baby's physiological needs than is its later training. Childhood situations provide an excellent field in which to illustrate the range of cultural adjustments which are possible within a universally given, but not so drastic, set of physiological facts.

The major discontinuity in the life cycle is of course that the child who is at one point a son must later be a father. These roles in our society are strongly differentiated; a good son is tractable, and does not assume adult responsibilities; a good father provides for his children and should not allow his authority to be flouted. In addition the child must be sexless so far as his family is concerned, whereas the father's sexual role is primary in the family. The individual in one role must revise his behavior from almost all points of view when he assumes the second role.

I shall select for discussion three such contrasts that occur in our culture between the individual's role as child and as father: 1. responsible—non-responsible status role, 2. dominance—submission, 3. contrasted sexual role. It is largely upon our cultural commitments to these three contrasts that the discontinuity in the life cycle of an individual in our culture depends.

RESPONSIBLE—NON-RESPONSIBLE STATUS ROLE

The techniques adopted by societies which achieve continuity during the life cycle in this sphere in no way differ from those we employ in our uniform conditioning to three meals a day. They are merely applied to other areas of life. We think of the child as wanting to play and the adult as having to work, but in many societies the mother takes the baby daily in her shawl or carrying net to the garden or to gather roots, and adult labor is seen even in infancy from the pleasant security of its position in close contact with its mother. When the child can run about it accompanies its parents still, doing tasks which are essential and yet suited to its powers, and this dichotomy between work and play is not different from that [which] its parents recognize, namely, the distinction between the busy day and the free evening. The tasks it is asked to perform are graded to its powers and its elders wait quietly by, not offering to do the task in the child's place. Everyone who is familiar with such societies has been struck by the contrast with our child training. Dr. Ruth Underhill tells me of sitting with a group of Papago elders in Arizona when the man of the house turned to his little three-year-old granddaughter and asked her to close the door. The door was heavy and hard to shut. The child tried, but it did not move. Several times the grandfather repeated, "Yes, close the door." No one jumped to the child's assistance. No one took the responsibility away from her. On the other hand there was no impatience, for after all the child was small. They sat gravely waiting till the child succeeded and her grandfather gravely thanked her. It was assumed that the task would not be asked of her unless she could perform it, and having been asked the responsibility was hers alone just as if she were a grown woman.

The essential point of such child training is that the child is from infancy continuously conditioned to responsible social participation while at the same time the tasks that are expected of it are adapted to its capacity. The contrast with our society is very great. A child does not make any labor contribution to our industrial society except as it competes with an adult; its work is not measured against its own strength and skill but against high-geared industrial requirements. Even when we praise a child's achievement in the home we are outraged if such praise is interpreted as being of the same order as praise of adults. The child is praised because the parent feels well disposed, regardless of whether the task is well done by adult standards, and the child acquires no sensible standard by which to measure its achievement. The gravity of a Cheyenne Indian family ceremoniously making a feast out of the little boy's first snowbird is at the furthest remove from our behavior. At birth the little boy was presented with a toy bow, and from the time he could run about serviceable bows suited to his stature were specially made for him by the man of the family. Animals and birds were taught him in a graded series beginning with those most easily taken, and as he brought in his first of each species his family duly made a feast of it, accepting his contribution as gravely as the buffalo his father brought. When he finally killed a buffalo, it was only the final step of his childhood conditioning, not a new adult role with which his childhood experience had been at variance.

The Canadian Ojibwa show clearly what results can be achieved. This tribe gains its livelihood by winter trapping and the small family of father, mother and children live during the long winter alone on their great frozen hunting grounds. The boy accompanies his father and brings in his catch to his sister as his father does to his mother; the girl prepares the meat and skins for him just as his mother does for her husband. By the time the boy is 12, he may have set his own line of traps on a hunting territory of his own and return to his parent's house only once in several months—still bringing the meat and skins to his sister. The young child is taught consistently that it has only itself to rely upon in life, and this is as true in the dealings it will have with the supernatural as in the business of getting a livelihood. This attitude he will accept as a successful adult just as he accepted it as a child.[1]

DOMINANCE—SUBMISSION

Dominance-submission is the most striking of those categories of behavior where like does not respond to like but where one type of behavior stimulates the opposite response. It is one of the most prominent ways in which behavior is patterned in our culture. When it obtains between classes, it may be nourished by continuous experience; the difficulty in its use between children and adults lies in the fact that an individual conditioned to one set of behavior in childhood must adopt the opposite as an adult. Its opposite is a pattern of approximately identical reciprocal behavior, and societies which rely upon continuous conditioning characteristically invoke this pattern. In some primitive cultures the very terminology of address between father and son, and more commonly, between grandchild and grandson or uncle and nephew, reflects this attitude. In such kinship terminologies one reciprocal expresses each of these relationships so that son and father, for instance, exchange the same term with one another, just as we exchange the same term with a cousin. The child later will exchange it with his son. "Father—son," therefore, is a continuous relationship he enjoys throughout life. The same continuity, backed up by verbal reciprocity, occurs far oftener in the

[1] Landes, Ruth, *The Ojibwa Woman,* Part 1, Youth—Columbia University Contributions to Anthropology, Volume XXXI.

grandchild-grandson relationship or that of mother's brother-sister's son. When these are "joking" relationships, as they often are, travellers report wonderingly upon the liberties and pretensions of tiny toddlers in their dealings with these family elders. In place of our dogma of respect to elders such societies employ in these cases a reciprocity as nearly identical as may be. The teasing and practical joking the grandfather visits upon his grandchild, the grandchild returns in like coin; he would be led to believe that he failed in propriety if he did not give like for like. If the sister's son has right of access without leave to his mother's brother's possessions, the mother's brother has such rights also to the child's possessions. They share reciprocal privileges and obligations which in our society can develop only between age mates.

From the point of view of our present discussion, such kinship conventions allow the child to put in practice from infancy the same forms of behavior which it will rely upon as an adult; behavior is not polarized into a general requirement of submission for the child and dominance for the adult.

It is clear from the techniques described above by which the child is conditioned to a responsible status role that these depend chiefly upon arousing in the child the desire to share responsibility in adult life. To achieve this little stress is laid upon obedience but much stress upon approval and praise. Punishment is very commonly regarded as quite outside the realm of possibility, and natives in many parts of the world have drawn the conclusion from our usual disciplinary methods that white parents do not love their children. If the child is not required to be submissive, however, many occasions for punishment melt away; a variety of situations which call for it do not occur. Many American Indian tribes are especially explicit in rejecting the ideal of a child's submissive or obedient behavior. Prince Maximilian von Wied who visited the Crow Indians over a hundred years ago describes a father's boasting about his young son's intractibility even when it was the father himself who was flouted; "He will be a man," his father said. He would have been baffled at the idea that his child should show behavior which would obviously make him appear a poor creature in the eyes of his fellows if he used it as an adult. Dr. George Devereaux tells me of a special case of such an attitude among the Mohave at the present time. The child's mother was white and protested to its father that he must take action when the child disobeyed and struck him. "But why?" the father said, "he is little. He cannot possibly injure me." He did not know of any dichotomy according to which an adult expects obedience and a child must accord it. If his child had been docile he would simply have judged that it would become a docile adult—an eventuality of which he would not have approved.

Child training which brings about the same result is common also in other areas of life than that of reciprocal kinship obligations between child and adult. There is a tendency in our culture to regard every situation as having in it the seeds of a dominance-submission relationship. Even where dominance-submission is patently irrelevant we read in the dichotomy, assuming that in every situation there must be one person dominating another. On the other hand some cultures, even when the situation calls for leadership, do not see it in terms of dominance-submission. To do justice to this attitude it would be necessary to describe their political and especially their economic arrangements, for such an attitude to persist must certainly be supported by economic mechanisms that are congruent with it. But it must also be supported by—or what comes to the same thing, express itself in—child training and familial situations.

CONTRASTED SEXUAL ROLE

Continuity of conditioning in training the child to assume responsibility and to behave no more submissively than adults is quite possible in terms of the child's physiological endowment if his participation is suited to his strength. Because of the late development of the child's reproductive organs continuity of conditioning in sex experience presents a difficult problem. So far as their belief that the child is anything but a sexless being is concerned, they are probably more nearly right than we are with an opposite dogma. But the great break is presented by the universally sterile unions before puberty and the presumably fertile ones after maturation. This physiological fact no amount of cultural manipulation can minimize or alter, and societies therefore which stress continuous conditioning most strongly sometimes do not expect children to be interested in sex experience until they have matured physically. This is striking among American Indian tribes like the Dakota; adults observe great privacy in sex acts and in no way stimulate children's sexual activity. There need be no discontinuity, in the sense in which I have used the term, in such a program if the child is taught nothing it does not have to unlearn later. In such cultures adults view children's experimentation as in no way wicked or dangerous but merely as innocuous play which can have no serious consequences. In some societies such play is minimal and the children manifest little interest in it. But the same attitude may be taken by adults in societies where such play is encouraged and forms a major activity among small children. This is true among most of the Melanesian cultures of Southeast New Guinea; adults go as far as to laugh off sexual affairs within the prohibited class if the children are not mature, saying that since they cannot marry there can be no harm done.

It is this physiological fact of the difference between children's sterile unions and adults' presumably fertile sex relations which must be kept in mind in order to understand the different mores which almost always govern sex expression in children and in adults in the same culture. A great many cultures with preadolescent sexual license require marital fidelity and a great many which value pre-marital virginity in either male or female arrange their marital life with great license. Continuity in sex experience is complicated by factors which it was unnecessary to consider in the problems previously discussed. The essential problem is not whether or not the child's sexuality is consistently exploited—for even where such exploitation is favored in the majority of cases the child must seriously modify his behavior at puberty or at marriage. Continuity in sex expression means rather that the child is taught nothing it must unlearn later. If the cultural emphasis is upon sexual pleasure the child who is continuously conditioned will be encouraged to experiment freely and pleasurably, as among the Marquesans;[2] if emphasis is upon reproduction, as among the Zuni of New Mexico, childish sex proclivities will not be exploited, for the only important use which sex is thought to serve in his culture is not yet possible to him. The important contrast with our child training is that although a Zuni child is impressed with the wickedness of premature sex experimentation he does not run the risk as in our culture of associating this wickedness with sex itself rather than with sex at his age. The adult in our culture has often failed to unlearn the wickedness or the dangerousness of sex, a lesson which was impressed upon him strongly in his most formative years.

DISCONTINUITY IN CONDITIONING

Even from this very summary statement of continuous conditioning the economy of such mores is evident. In spite of the obvious advantages, however, there are difficulties in its way. Many primitive societies expect as different behavior from an individual as child and as adult as we do, and such discontinuity involves a presumption of strain.

Many societies of this type however minimize strain by the techniques they employ, and some techniques are more successful than others in ensuring the individual's functioning without conflict. It is from this point of view that age-grade societies reveal their fundamental significance. Age-graded cultures characteristically demand different behavior of the individual at different times of his life and persons of a like age-grade are grouped into a society whose activities are all oriented toward the behavior desired at that age. Individuals "graduate" publicly and with honor from one of these groups to another. Where age society members are enjoined to loyalty and mutual support, and are drawn not only from the local group but from the whole tribe as among the Arapaho, or even from other tribes as among the Wagawaga of Southeast New Guinea, such an institution has many advantages in eliminating conflicts among local groups and fostering intra-tribal peace. This seems to be also a factor in the tribal military solidarity of the similarly organized Masai of East Africa. The point that is of chief interest

---

[2] Ralph Linton, class notes on the Marquesans.

for our present discussion, however, is that by this means an individual who at any time takes on a new set of duties and virtues is supported not only by a solid phalanx of age mates but by the traditional prestige of the organized "secret" society into which he has now graduated. Fortified in this way, individuals in such cultures often swing between remarkable extremes of opposite behavior without apparent psychic threat. For example, the great majority exhibit prideful and non-conflicted behavior at each stage in the life cycle even when a prime of life devoted to passionate and aggressive head hunting must be followed by a later life dedicated to ritual and to mild and peaceable civic virtues.

Our chief interest here, however, is in discontinuity which primarily affects the child. In many primitive societies such discontinuity has been fostered not because of economic or political necessity or because such discontinuity provides for a socially valuable division of labor, but because of some conceptual dogma. The most striking of these are the Australian and Papuan cultures where the ceremony of the "Making of Man" flourishes. In such societies it is believed that men and women have opposite and conflicting powers, and male children, who are of undefined status, must be initiated into the male role. In Central Australia the boy child is of the woman's side and women are tabu in the final adult stages of tribal ritual. The elaborate and protracted initiation ceremonies of the Arunta therefore snatch the boy from the mother, dramatize his gradual repudiation of her. In a final ceremony he is reborn as a man out of the men's ceremonial "baby pouch." The men's ceremonies are ritual statements of a masculine solidarity, carried out by fondling one another's *churingas,* the material symbol of each man's life, and by letting out over one another blood drawn from their veins. After this warm bond among men has been established through the ceremonies, the boy joins the men in the men's house and participates in tribal rites.[3] The enjoined discontinuity has been tribally bridged.

West of the Fly River in southern New Guinea there is a striking development of this Making of Men cult which involves a childhood period of passive homosexuality. Among the Keraki[4] it is thought that no boy can grow to full stature without playing the role for some years. Men slightly older take the active role, and the older man is a jealous partner. The life cycle of the Keraki Indians includes, therefore, in succession, passive homosexuality, active homosexuality and heterosexuality. The Keraki believe that pregnancy will result from post-pubertal passive homosexuality and see evidences of such practices in any fat man whom, even as an old man, they may kill or drive out of the tribe because of their fear. The ceremony that is of interest in connection with the present discussion takes place at the end of

---

[3] Spencer, B., and Gillen, F. J., *The Arunta;* N.Y., Macmillan, 1927 (2 vols.). Róheim, Géza, Psycho-Analysis of Primitive Cultural Types. *Internat. J. Psychoanal.* (1932) 13:1–224—in particular, Chapter III, on the Aranda, The Children of the Desert.

[4] Williams, Francis E., *Papuans of the Trans-Fly;* Oxford, 1936.

the period of passive homosexuality. This ceremony consists in burning out the possibility of pregnancy from the boy by pouring lye down his throat, after which he has no further protection if he gives way to the practice. There is no technique for ending active homosexuality, but this is not explicitly tabu for older men; heterosexuality and children however are highly valued. Unlike the neighboring Marindanim who share their homosexual practices, Keraki husband and wife share the same house and work together in the gardens.

I have chosen illustrations of discontinuous conditioning where it is not too much to say that the cultural institutions furnish adequate support to the individual as he progresses from role to role or interdicts the previous behavior in a summary fashion. The contrast with arrangements in our culture is very striking, and against this background of social arrangements in other cultures the adolescent period of *Sturm und Drang* with which we are so familiar becomes intelligible in terms of our discontinuous cultural institutions and dogmas rather than in terms of physiological necessity. It is even more pertinent to consider these comparative facts in relation to maladjusted persons in our culture who are said to be fixated at one or another pre-adult level. It is clear that, if we were to look at our social arrangements as an outsider, we should infer directly from our family institutions and habits of child training that many individuals would not "put off childish things"; we should have to say that our adult activity demands traits that are interdicted in children, and that far from redoubling efforts to help children bridge this gap, adults in our culture put all the blame on the child when he fails to manifest spontaneously the new behavior or, overstepping the mark, manifests it with untoward belligerence. It is not surprising that in such a society many individuals fear to use behavior which has up to that time been under a ban and trust instead, though at great psychic cost, to attitudes that have been exercised with approval during their formative years. Insofar as we invoke a physiological scheme to account for these neurotic adjustments we are led to overlook the possibility of developing social institutions which would lessen the social cost we now pay; instead we elaborate a set of dogmas which prove inapplicable under other social conditions.

PART II

The Origins of Human Development

INTRODUCTION

Today it is common knowledge that fertilization occurs when an ovum, contributed by the female, is penetrated by a sperm, contributed by the male. Historically, the union of sperm and ovum in the process of conception was not known. Though the ancient Greeks were aware that intercourse was related to the production of offspring, they were not aware of the ovum's role in this creation. As a matter of fact, neither were they aware that semen contained spermatazoa. The male was thought to implant the seed of life in the female, who in turn served only as a reservoir of nourishment from which the developing fetus could draw what it required for successful growth. It was not until the 17th century that a Dutch scientist, De Graaf, discovered that the female human produced an ovum. Similarly, and shortly after De Graaf's discovery, another Dutch scientist, Van Leeuwenhoek, discovered that sperm cells abounded in male semen. Nevertheless, the prevailing theory of fertilization differed little from that of the Greeks. It was not until the 19th century that union of ovum and sperm was found to be essential for the creation of a new organism.

One of the more interesting aspects of human sexuality is the extent to which nature has worked to provide optimal conditions for sperm and ovum to unite. For example, ovulation (release of the ovum from the ovary into the Fallopian tube) occurs at relatively predictable times during the course of each menstrual cycle. The time from release of the ovum to its descent into the Fallopian tube is roughly six hours. Spermatazoa have been conveniently provided a life time of from 24 to 36 hours. Thus, impregnation could occur even if intercourse should precede ovulation. In addition, nature has provided nearly insurmountable odds against the ovum's chances of escaping fertilization. The ovum is the largest cell in the human body, roughly $1/175$ inch in diameter (Corner, 1944). To seek out this large target, from 200 million to 500 million sperm are released with any one ejaculation of seminal fluid. The number of sperm cells released is a function of the amount of seminal fluid released. This amount ranges from 2.5 to 5 cubic centimeters (cc), with approximately 100 million sperm cells per cc., several hundred of which cross the cervical barrier. Thus, pitted against a single ovum are an abundance of spermatazoa, only one of which must penetrate the ovum to complete fertilization. If fertilization does occur, the ovum continues its three- to four-day journey down the Fallopian tube to eventually become embedded in the uterine wall. Thus, the conceptus begins its comfortable parasitic dependence on the mother. To further assure that the developing conceptus is secure and well protected in the uterine environment, it is surrounded by protective fluid and the amniotic sac. Barring any untoward environmental event, approximately 280 days after fertilization a new thriving infant emerges to begin its struggle for development. If fertilization fails to occur, most of the uterine lining is discharged, along with blood, into the vagina—a process known as menstruation.

Stages of prenatal development. The nine calendar months comprising normal gestation is typically divided into three stages. During the first stage, *the period of the ovum,* the fertilized ovum makes its descent down the Fallopian tube and enters the uterus. The major developmental event of this period is implantation in the uterine wall and this occurs approximately 24 hours after entrance into the uterus. Having become embedded in the lining of the uterus, the zygote—as the fertilized ovum is now called—is now secure in the uterine environment and the conditions necessary for placental growth and umbilical attachment to the fetus are now met.

The second stage of prenatal development, *the period of the embryo,* is characterized by the continued differentiation of the zygote into three major layers: the ectoderm, the mesoderm, and the endoderm. From the ectoderm will eventually emerge the nervous system, skin and skin glands, hair and nails. From the mesoderm come the musculature, skeleton, circulatory and excretory systems and from the endoderm emerge the lining of the gastrointestinal tract, Eustachian tubes, trachia, bronchia and vital organs and glands. In addition to the differentiation of the zygote into three layers, the period of the embryo marks the time when the placenta develops as well as the umbilical attachment between placenta and embryo. The critical feature of this period then is the organization of the major growth processes. It is during this period that environmental intrusions into the developmental process can effect severe and permanent damage to the organism.

The third stage of prenatal development, roughly three months to birth, is marked by the continued growth and development of the basic organized systems. Growth during this period follows clearly defined laws of developmental direction: cephalocaudal—from head to foot, and proximodistal—from central to peripheral. Also contained within this period is a critical point in the fetus' development: the period of viability. The period of viability refers to that point in time, generally taken to be 28 weeks, when the fetus if born has a reasonable chance of survival. Though the period of viability is generally defined as 28 weeks gestational life, Makeyeva (1959) suggests on the basis of his study of thousands of infants in Moscow lying-in hospitals that time alone is not a sufficient criterion. He places the additional restrictions of over 1000 grams birth weight and at least 35 centimeters length as necessary for a good prognosis of survival. We will have occasion to see that Makeyeva's suggestions that birth weight and length be considered along with number of gestational weeks find ample support in studies of prematurely born infants. In any event, by 28 weeks prenatal development all major systems have developed and the remaining three months seem to be devoted to continued strengthening of the fetus in preparation for its emergence into an environment decidedly different from its prenatal environment.

Nature has indeed provided a safe and nurturant environment for the growing fetus. Nevertheless, man and nature have provided a number of environmental agents which can have a most distressing effect on the rapidly organizing and growing fetus. To what extent does the maternal environment protect the fetus from these untoward environmental agents? To what extent has fetal development been prearranged through the contributions of heredity? Arguments concerning whether heredity or environmental factors are more significant influential factors in the development of the human organism have been waged throughout the history of scientific psychology. Geneticists, theologians, philosophers, mothers, grandparents, and nearly everyone else have detailed the relative contributions of heredity and environment in human development. As a little test, ask your roommate, girlfriend or boyfriend to recount some of the tales they have been told concerning the effect environmental experiences can have on the fetus. Unfortunately, the heredity-environment controversy is not dead. Nevertheless, recent theory and research have emerged which hold forth promise for discovering how heredity and environment contribute to our knowledge of behavior.

The heredity-environment issue. Environmentalism has had a stormy history in psychology. Having its philosophical origins in the work of the British empiricists and the associationists, environmentalism attracted considerable numbers of psychologists including: Pavlov, Titchener, Watson, Tolman, Skinner, Lashley, Hull, Spence—a most impressive listing of psychologists. If one also considers the experimental methodology and psychological theory generated by these psychologists and others, the contribution of environmentalism becomes even more impressive.

If one considers the early exponents of environmentalism, John Watson was perhaps the most concerned with human behavior from a developmental viewpoint. Watson's publication of his book on care of infants and children marked the first attempt to extrapolate the results of experimental research to child rearing practices (Watson, 1928). The central theme of Watson's behaviorism was that the infant could be molded and shaped by effective control of the reinforcement contingencies of the environment. Rejecting the notion of individual differences and denying the existence of consciousness, Watson saw parental environmental control as the avenue for effective child rearing. Nevertheless, as one recent author has suggested, the extent of Watson's influence on developmental psychology is subject to debate. "Watson's extreme environmentalism may have inflamed the heredity-environment controversy, but was not a novel position. It was concluded that Watson had no direct influence on the widespread interest that developmental psychologists have had (and continue to have) in mental development" (Love, 1969, p. 15). Indeed Watson's advice on child rearing practices and his experimental research with infants (Watson & Rayner, 1920) were not the only fuel feeding the heredity-environment controversy. There was also research and theory from the heredity side of the controversy stoking the fire.

The heredity-environment controversy simply put, was and continues to be an argument concerning the relative contribution of nature (heredity) and nurture (environment) to the behavior of organisms. Nativism, another term for the heredity argument, had its philosophical origins in the work of Descartes and Kant. Their general theorizing was translated by the Gestaltists into a theoretical foundation for perceptual development.

Simultaneous with the emergence of environmentalism, Darwinian evolutionary theory was acquiring advocates among psychologists. Interestingly, it was Darwin's cousin, Sir Francis Galton the distinguished psychologist-psychometrician, who was significantly influential in extrapolating from evolutionary theory principles applicable to the study of psychological phenomena. Galton, on the basis of his extensive studies of the inheritance of mental ability, advocated selective mating as the effective method for eliminating undesirable and contaminating subnormal mental ability. Galton was not alone in advocating selective mating. Calvin Hall (1938), considering a broader spectrum of behavior, suggested that controlled breeding was man's most effective alternative for eliminating feeblemindedness, insanity, and psychopathic behavior.

As the heredity-environment controversy raged and the pages of heated debate massed, it was becoming increasingly clear that resolution of the argument was impossible. The times were ripe for a refreshingly new approach to the entire issue.

Suggesting that the appropriate question was not *what* is contributed by heredity and *what* is contributed by environment, but rather *how* the two interact, Professor Anne Anastasi of Fordham University provided a way out of the heredity-environment controversy. As you read Chapter 6 by Professor Anastasi and Chapter 7 by Professor McClearn, note particularly their arguments to support the contention that indeed heredity and environment interact and contribute jointly, but perhaps not always equally, to all behavior. Given that the task now is to discover the how of heredity-environment interaction, how does the researcher go about seeking answers to the question, "How?" Professor Anastasi suggests seven methodological procedures appropriate for investigating "the etiological mechanism whereby any given hereditary or environmental condition ultimately leads to a behavioral characteristic."

One of the tenets of contemporary behavioral genetics is that each individual is a unique organism. The only exception to this is monozygotic (identical) twins. Genotypically the organism is unique. Nevertheless, as we all know, the uniqueness of the organism extends beyond its genetic characteristics. This becomes readily obvious when one considers the phenotypic uniqueness of each of the individuals we contact in our daily activities. Phenotype refers to the observable characteristics of the individual which in turn result from the genotype in interaction with the environment, while genotype refers to the inferred genetic makeup of each individual. In Chapter 7 Professor McClearn of the University of Colorado discusses in detail the current status of behavioral genetics. Picking up from Anastasi's article posing the question, "How?" behavioral genetics provides one disciplinary approach to the study of heredity-environment interaction. Professor McClearn draws attention to the theoretical perspective which behavioral genetics brings to bear on our understanding of behavior. Notice that the notion of heritability assumes a specialized definition referring to the extent to which phenotypic characteristics are reliable indices to the genotype. In addition, note that behavioral genetics puts the question of how into a working formula: phenotypic variance equals genotypic variance plus the environment. Such a definition dictates an interactionist point of view.

Prenatal Environmental Influences on Development

Recall that one of the questions raised in the beginning of this discussion referred to factors which can set limiting conditions for development even before the organism's birth and subsequent interaction with postnatal environment. Professor McClearn's discussion of behavioral genetics reviews a number of these factors, particularly those which occur during the period of the ovum. For example, Down's syndrome (Mongoloidism) is a direct result of improper chromosonal division with Down's babies being characterized by an excessive number of chromosomes. In addition to chromosonal aberrations, there are a variety of environmental agents which can place severe restrictions on the fetus' opportunities for normal development.

Nutrition. Nearly all of us are aware of the importance of nutrition in our personal lives. In addition, we have probably all seen examples of children, whether in Biafra, rural or inner city America, or countless other parts of the world, where children suffer appallingly from severe lack of food. Indeed, Borgstrom's (1969) depressing review of the problem of hunger facing the exploding population of the world promises an unfortunate increase in nutritional difficulty for countless millions of people unless drastic remedial steps are immediately taken. It should not be surprising that nutritional inadequacy has profound adverse effects on the developing fetus. Indeed, Mellanby (1933) underscoring the importance of good nutrition, suggests that nutrition may be the most important of all the environmental factors that can influence fetal growth.

Hurlock (1964) draws a distinction between two kinds of nutritional deficit: qualitative and quantitative hunger. Qualitative hunger refers to malnutrition caused by inadequate supplies of the necessary vitamins essential for normal growth and development, and represents the more serious type of nutritional deficit. Quantitative hunger refers to insufficient quantities of food, but with the possibility that minimally adequate vitamin and nutritional requirements are met. Inadequate diet has been found to be associated with premature birth (Antonov, 1947) as well as the length and weight of the newborn (Antonov, 1947; Smith, 1946). Other investigators have pointed out the untoward effect of protein deficiency on fetal development (Sontag & Wines, 1947). In one study, for those mothers rated as having good diets, significantly more infants were rated as excellent or good than were infants whose mothers had inadequate diets (Burke, Harding & Stuart, 1943).

In Chapter 8, Dr. Hepner of the University of Missouri Medical School poignantly underscores the profound and potentially damaging effects of inadequate diet during the fetal period. On the basis on his review, Dr. Hepner recommends that the starting point for establishing nutritional adequacy is best placed prior to the conception of the new organism. If the Soviet obstetrical emphasis on prevention and prophylaxis (Makeyeva, 1959) has any merit, and indeed there is every reason to believe that it does, Hepner's suggestion is well taken. In general, nutritional deficiencies have been associated with mental deficiency, nervous instability, cerebral palsy, birth weight loss and decreased length, rickets, general physical weakness. In addition, chronic malnutrition resulting from poverty or war conditions, appears to be associated with premature birth, stillbirth, and abnormal bone formation.

Infectious disease. Infectious diseases are potentially extremely damaging to fetal development. This is particularly true during the first two stages of pregnancy, the periods of ovum and embryo, when the organism is critically receptive to untoward environmental interruptions in its normal development. We have all likely heard at some time or other that German measles (rubella) is to be avoided particularly during the first months of pregnancy. Such advice is not to be lightly dismissed. It has been estimated that hundreds of infants born in the state of Michigan during a recent outbreak of rubella were severely marked for life. For example, one of the highest incidences of hydrocephalism was recorded during that outbreak. Other infectious diseases known to produce untoward effects on the fetus include the venereal diseases—syphilis and gonorrhea—and poliomyeletis. Infectious diseases have been associated with high incidence of stillbirth, miscarriage, blindness, mental deficiency, deafness, microcephaly, and deaf-mutism—indeed, a particularly displeasing and unnerving list of difficulties.

Blood incompatibility. Requiring that prospective married couples receive blood tests is not without purpose. Considering the detrimental effects of infectious diseases, uncovering the presence of venereal infection and its subsequent eradication is far more advantageous to the individual and to future offspring of that individual than any embarrassment one might temporarily suffer. Neurological degeneration is not temporary! In addition to identifying blood type and presence of infection, blood tests can alert parents and obstetricians to potential blood difficulties that might require special prenatal and postnatal care. Rh factors have been found to be associated with miscarriage, abortion, stillbirth, and subnormal intelligence (Gerver & Day, 1950).

Drugs. With the increasing use of drugs in our culture, increasing attention should be directed to the potential harmful effects these drugs may have on fetal development. The thalidomide tragedy of recent years is all too painful an example of the wrong way to discover the harmful effects of drugs. Considering the suffering and emotional distress in both parent and child caused by this particular drug, it seems well worthwhile advising caution in the combining of drugs with conception.

Narcotics have been found to cross the placenta readily. Taussig (1962) found barbiturates to be associated with fetal difficulties. Moreover, a variety of agents used as anesthetics and analgesics have been found to readily cross the placenta and it is not uncommon to observe tranquil newborns in the newborn nursery. (Bowes, 1970, has recently published a comprehensive review of the effects of anesthetics and analgesics used during labor and delivery.) Studies of the untoward effects of mind-expanding drugs on fetal development have been inconclusive in showing any detrimental effects.

It should not be surprising today that nicotine, being an extremely toxic drug, may be detrimental to the fetus. Sontag and Richards as long ago as 1938 reported that smoking was associated with increase in fetal heart rate. Prematurity has been related to smoking during pregnancy (Simpson, 1949), the heaviest smokers having produced the highest incidence of prematurely born infants. Ashley Montagu (1959) has theorized that increasingly common cardiac and circulatory disorders among adults may be related to smoking during pregnancy. Indeed, it is well known that males are less viable organisms than females and the increase in cardiac involvement among middle age males may be a reflection of further loss in viability. Nevertheless, although such speculating may be fun, there is altogether insufficient research on the multitude of chemical agents ingested by pregnant women to pose strong conclusive statements. A safe conclusion might be that with few exceptions, drugs in whatever form they are ingested probably do not assist positively the fetus' development and more likely have potentially adverse effects. This is particularly true during the early stages of pregnancy.

Mother's age. The optimal biological age range for child bearing is roughly from 20 to 29 years of age (Scott, 1968). The largest percentage of fetal difficulties as a function of mother's age occur in women over forty years of age when they conceive. For example, there is a higher incidence of Down's babies born among women over forty. If there is any relation between mother's age and the declining adequacy of her reproductive system or conversely mother's age and immaturity of her reproductive system, one might expect to find higher incidences of fetal distress as a result of decreased reproductive system capability.

Radiation. Mankind is, of course, concerned about the reality of potential self-destruction by atomic holocaust. Nevertheless, a holocaust of deathly radiation is not necessary for radiation to produce adverse effects on fetal development. In many cases women with cancer or pelvic tumors require treatments, usually with radium radiation. Small amounts of such treatments have not been found to have adverse effects; nevertheless, large dosages are to be avoided. Unfortunately, there is no clear definition of what might be a large or small dose for any one individual. In general, the earlier in pregnancy that radiation is experienced in the form of X-ray or otherwise, the greater the potential damage to the fetus. In one study, one-third of a group of infants whose mothers received therapeutic radiation during pregnancy, manifested mental or physical abnormalities which were not attributable to any source but the treatments (Ellis, Brown, Tisdall, Moyle, & Bell, 1942).

Several studies conducted in the cities of Hiroshima and Nagasaki point out the horrendous effects of such radiation. Neel related radiation to stillbirth, abortion, malformation, and low birth weight (Neel, 1953). Yamazaki, Wright and Wright (1954) studied mothers who were within 2000 meters of the hypocenter of the nuclear blast in Nagasaki and found radiation was related to fetal death, neonatal and infant death, mental retardation, and retardation in height and weight.

Emotional state of the mother. In as much as there are no direct neural connections between mother and fetus it may seem an unlikely suggestion that mother's emotional state can affect fetal and subsequent behavior. Nevertheless, emotionality of mother has been related to fetal behavior and to the infant's subsequent behavior. Ferreira (1965) suggests on the basis of an extensive literature review that a reappraisal of mother's emotionality and its effects on the fetus is in order.

Ottinger and Simmons (1964) administered the IPAT anxiety scale to pregnant women each trimester of pregnancy. Mother's anxiety scores were related to behavior of infants during the neonatal period. Recording body activity and crying at two, three, and four postnatal days of age, these investigators found a positive relationship between anxiety scores during pregnancy and amount of neonatal crying. Moss and Robson (1968) investigating attitudes in primiparous mothers (those having their first born infants) toward their expected child found that mother's attitudes were significantly correlated with female infant's visual fixation times at 3 months postnatal age. The effect was not obtained with male infants.

Rabin (1965, 1968) suggests in some preliminary studies, that motivation for parenthood may set the tone for future parent-child relations long before the child is even conceived and eventually exposed to daily child-rearing routines. Other investigators have found that women who were dissatisfied with their social status and otherwise emotionally unstable, were less happy with their pregnancies, more anxious, and more emotionally maladjusted in general during pregnancy (Davids & Rosengren, 1962). The effects of prolonged anxiety, upset, and unhappiness with pregnancy have been found to be associated with hyperactivity, irritability, crying, feeding difficulties, and sleeping problems (Sontag, 1944). Moreover, Lakin (1957) reports that mothers of colic infants were characterized as more tense and anxious during their pregnancies than were mothers of noncolic infants. Interestingly, considering Rabin's findings concerning motivation for parenthood, Lakin reports that mothers of colic infants also felt more inadequate about their ability to care for the coming baby.

Bear in mind that there are no direct neural connections between mother and fetus. How then does mother's emotionality come to exert an influence on the behavior of the fetus? The answer lies not in central nervous system innervation but in autonomic nervous system innervation. Emotional outbursts and chronic states of anxiety and hypertension have a profound effect on the autonomic nervous system, which in turn activates a constant outpouring of hormones into the blood stream of the mother. Despite the fact that no blood is directly exchanged between fetus and mother, considerable amounts of these autonomically released chemicals readily cross the placenta and expose the fetus to abnormal hormonal imbalance.

Summary. It is obvious that an extraordinary number of events can markedly affect the course of normal fetal development. Nutrition, disease, blood incompatibility, drugs, mother's age, radiation, and mother's emotional state have all been found to be all too effective environmental disruptors of the normal course of development.

Premature Birth

Of all the topics associated with fetal development premature birth is probably the one that receives the least attention in the introductory course in human development. The implications of premature birth for later development demand more extensive consideration.

The typical notion of prematurity is that the infant is born sometime before normal gestation length is reached. However, this definition, though in part correct, does not alone account for the discouraging prognosis of prematurely born infants. The World Health Organization, recognizing that length of gestation was an inadequate single index of prematurity, established a definition based on both birth weight and gestation length. A premature infant was defined as one whose birth weight was less than 2500 grams (5½ lbs.) and whose length of gestation was less than 37 weeks (WHO, 1950). More recently, the World Health Organization has recommended that the definition of prematurity refer specifically to low birth weight (WHO, 1961). (Thirty-seven weeks is based on the scaling of gestational length into 10 equal lunar months of 28 days each. Using nine calendar months as gestation length, the critical time would be roughly 34 weeks.) Thus, combining a specified birth weight with gestational length it was thought that these criteria would account for most infants who should be identified as premature. Nevertheless, as Drillien points out in her exhaustive longitudinal study of prematurely born infants, the definition fails to take into account a host of interacting factors including: geographical and sexual differences, birth order, social status, age of mother, multiple births, and the adequacy of prenatal care (Drillien, 1964). Drillien found in her longitudinal study, over a five-year period, that physical development, health, and mental development were all associated with low birth weight. Incidence of all problems in the preschool years increased when maternal care was unsatisfactory. Moreover, premature children of overanxious, rigid, or indulgent mothers were more likely to have feeding, sleeping and/or toilet problems.

Drillien's study provides an excellent illustration of one methodological procedure used to study the effects of prematurity, i.e., the anterospective longitudinal method. With this method the investigator chooses a sample of infants who are characterized by a specific condition which is the object of study. Then an appropriate matched control group is selected, presumably devoid of the condition of interest and both groups are followed longitudinally to assess the incidence of the condition of interest. Thus, with premature birth as the condition of interest, one would select a group of prematurely born infants and match them with a group of term infants. During the longitudinal study one could administer a variety of tests and examinations to determine the presence of differences between the groups. Interestingly enough, despite the difficulties associated with longitudinal research, there are a number of prodigious longitudinal investigations still in progress investigating this important aspect of human development.

In general, prematurity, as defined by gestation length and low birth weight, has been found to be associated with (*a*) intellectual deficiencies (Knobloch, Rider, Harper & Pasamanick, 1956; Wiener, Rider, Oppel, Fischer & Harper, 1965), (*b*) perceptual-motor disabilities (Wiener, et al.,

1965), (*c*) brain injury (Graham, Pennoyer, Caldwell, Greenway & Hartman, 1957; Lubchenco, Horner, Reed, Hix, Metcalf, Cohig, Elliott, & Bourg, 1963), (*d*) immature speech (Wiener et al., 1965), (*e*) toxemia of pregnancy (Braine, Heimer, Wortis & Freeman, 1966), (*f*) cerebral palsy (Deaver, 1952; Greenspan & Deaver, 1953; Ingram & Russell, 1961), (*g*) visual defects (Lubchenco et al., 1963), and (*h*) difficulty with abstract reasoning (Wiener et al., 1965). Moreover, these effects seem to hold up even when investigators control for the effects of race, maternal attitudes, maternal practices, and social class (Wiener et al., 1965).

On the basis on their extensive studies of prematurity, Knobloch and her associates conclude that the most reasonable course of action for resolution of the problems of prematurely born infants lies in the area of prevention. Such a conclusion is not unique to investigators in this country. Makeyeva (1959) in his extensive analysis of maternal and infant diseases emphasizes the prophylactic techniques used so extensively in obstetrical practice in the Soviet Union. For example, for the prophylaxis of toxemia, Makeyeva recommends a variety of hygienic procedures to be observed throughout the course of pregnancy. These procedures include: avoidance of excessive intake of liquids and food, limitation of salt intake, restriction of manual and mental work, good ventilation and sufficient sleep, adequate time out of doors, and loose and comfortable dress. Indeed, most mothers-to-be would likely relish such a regimen.

It is, of course, fortunate that not all premature infants are subject to the devastating conditions described above. Nevertheless, the incidence of premature infants who do suffer untoward effects of being born too soon is sufficiently great to warrant continued research on adequate preventative and prophylactic techniques useful for assisting the premature infant to normal development. For the interested reader, more extensive reviews of the effects of premature birth can be found in Harper and Wiener (1965) and in Wiener (1962).

Fetal Behavior

Having discussed the many discouraging events which can produce adverse effects on fetal and subsequent development, it is perhaps appropriate that the concluding chapter in this unit considers the behavior capabilities of the normal fetus. A related question concerns the significance of fetal behavior for the organism's later behavior.

It is well known that the fetus moves about in the protective uterine environment. Nearly every pregnant woman can attest to these movements. Squirms, stretches, pushes, kicks, jerks, and rhythmic movements have all been identified as characteristic fetal movements (Newberry, 1941). Research conducted at the Fels Research Institute by Professor Lester Sontag and his associates has been concerned with extensive investigation of fetal behavior, particularly with reference to fetal and subsequent normal development. In the concluding chapter of this unit Professor Sontag reviews in detail the results of 35 years of longitudinal investigation of the effects of fetal behavior. Bearing in mind that it was not until the 19th century that even the knowledge of fertilization was completely understood, the work of Sontag and his associates is a remarkable testament to man's persistent desire to understand his own development.

REFERENCES

ANTONOV, A. N. Children born during the siege of Leningrad in 1942. *Journal of Pediatrics,* 1947, *30,* 250–259.

BORGSTROM, G. The realities of hunger. *Format,* Department of Information Services, Michigan State University, 1969, *4,* 10–13.

BOWES, W. A., JR. Effect of maternal medications on the fetus and newborn. In H. E. Fitzgerald & Y. Brackbill (Eds.). *Design and method in infant research.* Chicago: University of Chicago Press, 1970 (in press).

BRAINE, M. D. S., HEIMER, C. G., WORTIS, H., & FREEDMAN, A. M. Factors associated with impairment of the early development of prematures. *Monographs of the Society for Research in Child Development,* 1966, *31,* Serial No. 106.

BURKE, B. S., HARDING, V. V., & STUART, H. C. Nutrition studies during pregnancy, relation of protein content of mother's diet during pregnancy to birth weight, length and condition of infant at birth. *Journal of Pediatrics,* 1943, *23,* 506–515.

CORNER, G. W. *Ourselves unborn: an embryologist's essay on man.* New Haven: Yale University Press, 1944.

DAVIDS, A., & ROSENGREN, W. R. Social stability and psychological adjustment during pregnancy. *Psychosomatic Medicine,* 1962, *24,* 579–583.

DEAVER, G. C. Etiological factors in cerebral palsy. *Bulletin of the New York Academy of Medicine.* 1952, *28,* 532–536.

DRILLIEN, C. M. *The growth and development of the prematurely born infant.* Edinburgh: E. & S. Livingstone, Ltd., 1964.

EBBS, J. H., BROWN, A., TISDALL, F. F., MOYLE, W. J., & BELL, M. The influence of improved prenatal nutrition upon the infant. *Canadian Medical Association Journal,* 1942, 6–8.

FERREIRA, A. J. Emotional factors in prenatal environment. *Journal of Nervous and Mental Disease,* 1965, *141,* 108–118.

GERVER, J. M., & DAY, R. Intelligence quotients of children who have recovered from erythroblastosis fetalis. *Journal of Pediatrics,* 1950, *36,* 342–349.

GRAHAM, F. K., PENNOYER, M. M., CALDWELL, B. M., GREENMAN, M., & HARTMANN, A. F. Relationship between clinical status and behavior test performance in a newborn group with histories suggesting anoxia. *Journal of Pediatrics,* 1957, *50,* 177–189.

GREENSPAN, L., & DEAVER, G. C. The clinical approach to the etiology of cerebral palsy. *Archives of Physical Medicine.* 1953, *34,* 478–485.

Hall, C. S. The inheritance of emotionality. *Sigma Xi Quarterly,* 1938, *26,* 17–27.

Harper, P. A., & Wiener, G. Sequelae of low birth weight. *Annual Review of Medicine,* 1965, *16,* 405–420.

Hirsch, J., & Ksander, G. *Behavior-genetic analysis.* Dubuque, Iowa: Wm. C. Brown, 1969.

Hurlock, E. B. *Child development.* 4th ed. New York: McGraw-Hill, 1964.

Ingram, T. T. S., & Russell, E. M. The reproductive histories of mothers of patients suffering from congenital diplegia. *Archives of Diseases of Childhood.* 1961, *36,* 34–41.

Knobloch, H., Rider, R., Harper, P., & Pasamanick, B. Neuropsychiatric sequelae of prematurity. *Journal of the American Medical Association,* 1956, *161,* 581–585.

Lakin, M. Personality factors in mothers of excessively crying (colicky) infants. *Monographs of the Society for Research in Child Development.* 1957, *22,* No. 1.

Love, J. M. The influence of behaviorism in child psychology. Paper presented at the annual meeting of the Southeastern Psychological Association. Symposium on, 'Historical conceptions of mental development.' New Orleans, 1969.

Lubchenco, L. O., Horner, F. A., Reed, L. H., Hix, I. E., Jr., Metcalf, D., Cohig, R., Elliott, H. C., & Bourg, M. Sequelae of premature birth. *American Journal of Diseases of Children.* 1963, *106,* 101–115.

Makeyeva, O. *Prevention of maternal and infant diseases.* Foreign Languages Publishing House, Moscow, 1959.

Mellanby, E. Nutrition and child bearing. *Lancet,* 1933, *1,* 131.

Montagu, A. *Human heredity.* New York: Harcourt, Brace & World, 1959.

Moss, H. A., & Robson, K. S. Maternal influences in early social visual behavior. *Child Development.* 1968, *39,* 401–408.

Neel, J. A. The effect of exposure to the atomic bombs on pregnancy termination in Hiroshima and Nagasaki: preliminary report. *Science,* 1953, *118,* 537–541.

Ottinger, D. R., & Simmons, J. E. Behavior of human neonates and prenatal maternal anxiety. *Psychological Reports,* 1964, *14,* 391–394.

Rabin, A. I. Motivation for parenthood. *Journal of Projective Techniques & Personality Assessment.* 1965, *29,* 405–411.

Rabin, A. I., & Greene, R. J. Assessing motivation for parenthood. *The Journal of Psychology,* 1968, *69,* 39–46.

Scott, J. P. *Early experience and the organization of behavior.* Belmont, Calif.: Wadsworth, Brooks/Cole, 1968.

Simpson, G. G. *The meaning of evolution.* New Haven: Yale University Press, 1949.

Sontag, L. W. Some psychosomatic aspects of childhood. *Nervous Child.* 1946, *5,* 296–304.

Sontag, L. W., & Wallace, R. F. The effect of cigarette smoking during pregnancy upon the fetal heart rate. *American Journal of Obstetrics and Gynecology,* 1935, *29,* 77–83.

Sontag, L. W., & Richards, T. W. Studies in fetal behavior, I. Fetal heart rate as a behavioral indicator. *Monographs of the Society for Research in Child Development,* 1938, *3,* No. 4.

Sontag, L. W., & Wines, J. Relation of mothers' diet to status of their infants at birth and in infancy. *American Journal of Obstetrics and Gynecology,* 1947, *54,* 994–1003.

Taussig, H. B. The thalidomide syndrome. *Scientific American,* 1962, *207,* 29–35.

Watson, J. B. *Psychological care of infant and child.* New York: Norton, 1928.

Watson, J. B., & Rayner, R. Conditioned emotional reactions. *Journal of Experimental Psychology,* 1920, *3,* 1–14.

World Health Organization. Expert group on Prematurity. (Final Report). *World Health Organization* technical report series, 1950, No. 27.

World Heath Organization. Public health aspects of low birth weight. Third report of the expert committee on maternal and child health. *World Health Organization.* Technical report series, 1961, No. 217.

Wiener, G. Psychological correlates of premature birth: a review. *Journal of Nervous and Mental Diseases.* 1962, *134,* 129.

Wiener, G., Rider, R. V., Oppel, W. C., Fischer, L. K., & Harper, P. A. Correlates of low birth weight: psychological status at six to seven years of age. *Pediatrics,* 1965, *35,* 434–444.

Yamazaki, J. N., Wright, S. W., & Wright, P. M. Outcome of pregnancy in women exposed to atomic bomb in Nagasaki. *American Journal of the Diseases of Children.* 1954, *87,* 448–463.

6

HEREDITY, ENVIRONMENT, AND THE QUESTION "HOW?"*

ANNE ANASTASI

TWO OR THREE decades ago, the so-called heredity-environment question was the center of lively controversy. Today, on the other hand, many psychologists look upon it as a dead issue. It is now generally conceded that both hereditary and environmental factors enter into all behavior. The reacting organism is a product of its genes and its past environment, while present environment provides the immediate stimulus for current behavior. To be sure, it can be argued that, although a given trait may result from the combined influence of hereditary and environmental factors, a specific difference in this trait between individuals or between groups may be traceable to either hereditary or environmental factors alone. The design of most traditional investigations undertaken to identify such factors, however, has been such as to yield inconclusive answers. The same set of data has frequently led to opposite conclusions in the hands of psychologists with different orientations.

Nor have efforts to determine the proportional contribution of hereditary and environmental factors to observed individual differences in given traits met with any greater success. Apart from difficulties in controlling conditions, such investigations have usually been based upon the implicit assumption that hereditary and environmental factors combine in an additive fashion. Both geneticists and psychologists have repeatedly demonstrated, however, that a more tenable hypothesis is that of interaction (13, 19, 25, 36). In other words, the nature and extent of the influence of each type of factor depend upon the contribution of the other. Thus the proportional contribution of heredity to the variance of a given trait, rather than being a constant, will vary under different environmental conditions. Similarly, under different hereditary conditions, the relative contribution of environment will differ. Studies designed to estimate the proportional contribution of heredity

* From *Psychological Review*, 1958, *65*, 197–208. Reprinted with permission from the author and the American Psychological Association.

Address of the President, Division of General Psychology, American Psychological Association, September 4, 1957.

and environment, however, have rarely included measures of such interaction. The only possible conclusion from such research would thus seem to be that both heredity and environment contribute to all behavior traits and that the extent of their respective contributions cannot be specified for any trait. Small wonder that some psychologists regard the heredity-environment question as unworthy of further consideration!

But is this really all we can find out about the operation of heredity and environment in the etiology of behavior? Perhaps we have simply been asking the wrong questions. The traditional questions about heredity and environment may be intrinsically unanswerable. Psychologists began by asking *which* type of factor, hereditary or environmental, is responsible for individual differences in a given trait. Later, they tried to discover *how much* of the variance was attributable to heredity and how much to environment. It is the primary contention of this paper that a more fruitful approach is to be found in the question *"How?"* There is still much to be learned about the specific *modus operandi* of hereditary and environmental factors in the development of behavioral differences. And there are several current lines of research which offer promising techniques for answering the question "How?"

VARIETY OF INTERACTION MECHANISMS

Hereditary factors. If we examine some of the specific ways in which hereditary factors may influence behavior, we cannot fail but be impressed by their wide diversity. At one extreme, we find such conditions as phenylpyruvic amentia and amaurotic idiocy. In these cases, certain essential physical prerequisites for normal intellectual development are lacking as a result of hereditary metabolic disorders.

. . .

A somewhat different situation is illustrated by hereditary deafness, which may lead to intellectual retardation through interference with normal social interaction, language development, and schooling. In such a case, however, the hereditary handicap can be offset by appropriate adaptations of training procedures.

. . .

A third example is provided by inherited susceptibility to certain physical diseases, with consequent protracted ill health. If environmental conditions are such that illness does in fact develop, a number of different behavioral effects may follow. Intellectually, the individual may be handicapped by his inability to attend school regularly. On the other hand, depending upon age of onset, home conditions, parental status, and similar factors, poor health may have the effect of concentrating the individual's energies upon intellectual pursuits. The curtailment of participation in athletics and social functions may serve to strengthen interest in reading and other sedentary activities.

. . .

Finally, heredity may influence behavior through the mechanism of social stereotypes. A wide variety of inherited physical characteristics have served as the visible cues for identifying such stereotypes. These cues thus lead to behavioral restrictions or opportunities and—at a more subtle level—to social attitudes and expectancies. The individual's own self concept tends gradually to reflect such expectancies. All of these influences eventually leave their mark upon his abilities and inabilities, his emotional reactions, goals, ambitions, and outlook on life.

The geneticist Dobzhansky illustrates this type of mechanism by means of a dramatic hypothetical situation. He points out that, if there were a culture in which the carriers of blood group AB were considered aristocrats and those of blood group O laborers, then the blood-group genes would become important hereditary determiners of behavior (**10**, p. **147**). Obviously the association between blood group and behavior would be specific to that culture. But such specificity is an essential property of the causal mechanism under consideration.

More realistic examples are not hard to find. The most familiar instances occur in connection with constitutional types, sex, and race. Sex and skin pigmentation obviously depend upon heredity. General body build is strongly influenced by hereditary components, although also susceptible to environmental modification. That all these physical characteristics may exert a pronounced effect upon behavior within a given culture is well known. It is equally apparent, of course, that in different cultures the behavioral correlates of such hereditary physical traits may be quite unlike. A specific physical cue may be completely unrelated to individual differences in psychological traits in one culture, while closely correlated with them in another. Or it may be associated with totally dissimilar behavior characteristics in two different cultures.

It might be objected that some of the illustrations which have been cited do not properly exemplify the operation of hereditary mechanisms in behavior development, since hereditary factors enter only indirectly into the behavior in question. Closer examination, however, shows this distinction to be untenable. First it may be noted that the influence of heredity upon behavior is always indirect. No psychological trait is ever inherited as such. All we can ever say directly from behavioral observations is that a given trait shows evidence of being influenced by certain "inheritable unknowns." This merely defines a problem for genetic research; it does not provide a causal explanation. Unlike the blood groups, which are close to the level of primary gene products, psychological traits are related to genes by highly indirect and devious routes. Even the mental deficiency associated with phenylketonuria is several steps removed from the chemically defective genes that represent its hereditary basis. Moreover, hereditary influences cannot be dichotomized into the more direct and the less direct. Rather do they represent a whole "continuum of indirectness," along which are found all degrees of remoteness of causal links. The examples already cited illustrate a few of the points on this continuum.

It should be noted that as we proceed along the continuum of indirectness, the range of variation of possible outcomes of hereditary factors expands rapidly. At each step in the causal chain, there is fresh opportunity for interaction with other hereditary factors as well as with environmental factors. And since each interaction in turn determines the direction of subsequent interactions, there is an ever-widening network of possible outcomes. If we visualize a simple sequential grid with only two alternatives at each point, it is obvious that there are two possible outcomes in the one-stage situation, four outcomes at the second stage, eight at the third, and so on in geometric progression. The actual situation is undoubtedly much more complex, since there will usually be more than two alternatives at any one point.

In the case of the blood groups, the relation to specific genes is so close that no other concomitant hereditary or environmental conditions can alter the outcome. If the organism survives at all, it will have the blood group determined by its genes. Among psychological traits, on the other hand, some variation in outcome is always possible as a result of concurrent circumstances. Even in cases of phenylketonuria, intellectual development will exhibit some relationship with the type of care and training available to the individual.

. . .

Parenthetically, it may be noted that geneticists have sometimes used the term "norm of reaction" to designate the range of variation of possible outcomes of gene properties (cf. **11**, p. **161**). Thus heredity sets the "norm" or limits within which environmental differences determine the eventual outcome. In the case of some traits, such as blood groups or eye color, this norm is much narrower than in the case of other traits. Owing to the rather different psychological connotations of both the words "norm" and "reaction," however, it seems less confusing to speak of the "range of variation" in this context.

. . .

Environmental factors: organic. Turning now to an analysis of the role of environmental factors in behavior, we find the same etiological mechanisms which were observed in the case of hereditary factors. First, however, we must differentiate between two classes of environmental influences: (*a*) those producing organic effects which may in turn influence behavior and (*b*) those serving as direct stimuli for psychological reactions. The former may be illustrated by food intake or by exposure to bacterial infection; the latter, by tribal initiation ceremonies or by a course in algebra. There are no completely satisfactory names by which to designate these two classes of influences. In an earlier paper by Anastasi and Foley (3), the terms "structural" and "functional" were employed. However, "organic" and "behavioral" have the advantage of greater familiarity in this context and may be less open to misinterpretation. Accordingly, these terms will be used in the present paper.

Like hereditary factors, environmental influences of an organic nature can also be ordered along a continuum of indirectness with regard to their relation to behavior. This continuum closely parallels that of hereditary factors. One end is typified by such conditions as mental deficiency resulting from cerebral birth injury or from prenatal nutritional inadequacies. A more indirect etiological mechanism is illustrated by severe motor disorder—as in certain cases of cerebral palsy—*without* accompanying injury to higher neurological centers. In such instances, intellectual retardation may occur as an indirect result of the motor handicap, through the curtailment of educational and social activities. Obviously this causal mechanism corresponds closely to that of hereditary deafness cited earlier in the paper.

Finally, we may consider an environmental parallel to the previously discussed social stereotypes which were mediated by hereditary physical cues. Let us suppose that a young woman with mousy brown hair becomes transformed into a dazzling golden blonde through environmental techniques currently available in our culture. It is highly probable that this metamorphosis will alter, not only the reactions of her associates toward her, but also her own self concept and subsequent behavior. The effects could range all the way from a rise in social poise to a drop in clerical accuracy!

. . .

Environmental factors: behavioral. The second major class of environmental factors—the behavioral as contrasted to the organic—are by definition direct influences. The immediate effect of such environmental factors is always a behavioral change. To be sure, some of the initial behavioral effects may themselves indirectly affect the individual's later behavior. But this relationship can perhaps be best conceptualized in terms of breadth and permanence of effects. Thus it could be said that we are now dealing, not with a continuum of indirectness, as in the case of hereditary and organic-environmental factors, but rather with a continuum of breadth.

Social class membership may serve as an illustration of a relatively broad, pervasive, and enduring environmental factor. Its influence upon behavior development may operate through many channels. Thus social level may determine the range and nature of intellectual stimulation provided by home and community through books, music, art, play activities, and the like. Even more far-reaching may be the effects upon interests and motivation, as illustrated by the desire to perform abstract intellectual tasks, to surpass others in competitive situations, to succeed in school, or to gain social approval. Emotional and social traits may likewise be influenced by the nature of interpersonal relations characterizing homes at different socio-economic levels. Somewhat more restricted in scope than social class, although still exerting a relatively broad influence, is amount of formal schooling which the individual is able to obtain.

A factor which may be wide or narrow in its effects, depending upon concomitant circumstances, is language handicap. Thus the bilingualism of an adult who moves to a foreign country with inadequate mastery of the new language represents a relatively limited handicap which can be readily overcome in most cases. At most, the difficulty is one of communication. On the other hand, some kinds of bilingualism in childhood may exert a retarding influence upon intellectual development and may under certain conditions affect personality development adversely (2, 4, 8). A common pattern in the homes of immigrants is that the child speaks one language at home and another in school, so that his knowledge of each language is limited to certain types of situations. Inadequate facility with the language of the school interferes with the acquisition of basic concepts, intellectual skills, and information. The frustration engendered by scholastic difficulties may in turn lead to discouragement and general dislike of school. . . . In the case of certain groups, moreover, the child's foreign language background may be perceived by himself and his associates as a symbol of minority group status and may thereby augment any emotional maladjustment arising from such status (30).

A highly restricted environmental influence is to be found in the opportunity to acquire specific items of information occurring in a particular intelligence test. The fact that such opportunities may vary with culture, social class, or individual experiential background is at the basis of the test user's concern with the problem of coaching and with "culture-free" or "culture-fair" tests (cf. 1, 2). If the advantage or disadvantage which such experiential differences confer upon certain individuals is strictly confined to performance on the given test, it will obviously reduce the validity of the test and should be eliminated.

. . .

METHODOLOGICAL APPROACHES

The examples considered so far should suffice to highlight the wide variety of ways in which hereditary and environmental factors may interact in the course of behavior development. There is clearly a need for identifying explicitly the etiological mechanism whereby any given hereditary or environmental condition ultimately leads to a behavioral characteristic—in other words, the "how" of heredity and environment. Accordingly, we may now take a quick look at some promising methodological approaches to the question "how."

Within the past decade, an increasing number of studies have been designed to trace the connection between specific factors in the hereditary backgrounds or in the reactional biographies of individuals and their observed behavioral characteristics. There has been a definite shift away from the predominantly descriptive and correlational approach of the earlier decades toward more deliberate attempts to verify explanatory hypotheses. Similarly, the cataloguing of group differences in psychological traits has been giving way gradually to research on *changes* in group characteristics following altered conditions.

Among recent methodological developments, we have chosen seven as being particularly relevant to the analysis of etiological mechanisms. The first represents an extension of selective breeding investigations to permit the identification of specific hereditary conditions underlying the observed behavioral differences. When early selective breeding investigations such as those of Tryon (32) on rats indicated that "maze learning ability" was inherited, we were still a long way from knowing what was actually being transmitted by the genes. It was obviously not "maze learning ability" as such. Twenty—or even ten—years ago, some psychologists would have suggested that it was probably general intelligence. And a few might even have drawn a parallel with the inheritance of human intelligence.

But today investigators have been asking: Just what makes one group of rats learn mazes more quickly than the other? Is it differences in motivation, emotionality, speed of running, general activity level? If so, are these behavioral characteristics in turn dependent upon group differences in glandular development, body weight, brain size, biochemical factors, or some other organic conditions? A number of recent and ongoing investigations indicate that attempts are being made to trace, at least part of the way, the steps whereby certain chemical properties of the genes may ultimately lead to specified behavior characteristics.

• • •

Evidence of current interest in the specific hereditary factors which influence behavior is to be found in an extensive research program in progress at the Jackson Memorial Laboratory, under the direction of Scott and Fuller (27). In general, the project is concerned with the behavioral characteristics of various breeds and cross-breeds of dogs. Analyses of some of the data gathered to date again suggest that "differences in performance are produced by differences in emotional, motivational, and peripheral processes, and that genetically caused differences in central processes may be either slight or non-existent" (26, p. 225). In other parts of the same project, breed differences in physiological characteristics, which may in turn be related to behavioral differences, have been established.

A second line of attack is the exploration of possible relationships between behavioral characteristics and physiological variables which may in turn be traceable to hereditary factors. Research on EEG, autonomic balance, metabolic processes, and biochemical factors illustrates this approach. A lucid demonstration of the process of tracing a psychological condition to genetic factors is provided by the identification and subsequent investigation of phenylpyruvic amentia. In this case, the causal chain from defective gene, through metabolic disorder and consequent cerebral malfunctioning, to feeblemindedness and other overt symptoms can be described step by step (cf. **28**; **29**, pp. 389–391). Also relevant are the recent researches on neurological and biochemical correlates of schizophrenia (**7**). Owing to inadequate methodological controls, however, most of the findings of the latter studies must be regarded as tentative (**16**).

Prenatal environmental factors provide a third avenue of fruitful investigation. Especially noteworthy is the recent work of Pasamanick and his associates (**24**), which demonstrated a tie-up between socioeconomic level, complications of pregnancy and parturition, and psychological disorders of the offspring. In a series of studies on large samples of whites and Negroes in Baltimore, these investigators showed that various prenatal and paranatal disorders are significantly related to the occurrence of mental defect and psychiatric disorders in the child. An important source of such irregularities in the process of childbearing and birth is to be found in deficiencies of maternal diet and in other conditions associated with low socioeconomic status. An analysis of the data did in fact reveal a much higher frequency of all such medical complications in lower than in higher socioeconomic levels, and a higher frequency among Negroes than among whites.

Direct evidence of the influence of prenatal nutritional factors upon subsequent intellectual development is to be found in a recent, well controlled experiment by Harrell et al. (**14**). The subjects were pregnant women in low-income groups, whose normal diets were generally quite deficient. A dietary supplement was administered to some of these women during pregnancy and lactation, while an equated control group received placebos. When tested at the ages of three and four years, the offspring of the experimental group obtained a significantly higher mean IQ than did the offspring of the controls.

Mention should also be made of animal experiments on the effects of such factors as prenatal radiation and neonatal asphyxia upon cerebral anomalies as well as upon subsequent behavior development. These experimental studies merge imperceptibly into the fourth approach to be considered, namely, the investigation of the influence of early experience upon the eventual behavioral characteristics of animals. Research in this area has been accumulating at a rapid rate. In 1954, Beach and Jaynes (**6**) surveyed this literature for the *Psychological Bulletin,* listing over 130 references. Several new studies have appeared since that date (e.g., **12**, **18**, **21**, **22**, **27**). The variety of factors covered ranges from the type and quantity of available food to the extent of contact with human culture. A large number of experiments have been concerned with various forms of sensory deprivation and with diminished opportunities for motor exercise. Effects have been observed in many kinds of animals and in almost all aspects of behavior, including perceptual responses, motor activity, learning, emotionality, and social reactions.

In their review, Beach and Jaynes pointed out that research in this area has been stimulated by at least four distinct theoretical interests. Some studies were motivated by the traditional concern with the relative contribution of maturation and learning to behavior development. Others were designed in an effort to test certain psychoanalytic theories regarding infantile experiences, as illustrated by studies which limited the feeding responses of young animals. A third relevant influence is to be found in the work of the European biologist Lorenz (20) on early social stimulation of birds, and in particular on the special type of learning for which the term "imprinting" has been coined. A relatively large number of recent studies have centered around Hebb's (15) theory regarding the importance of early perceptual experiences upon subsequent performance in learning situations. All this research represents a rapidly growing and promising attack on the *modus operandi* of specific environmental factors.

The human counterpart of these animal studies may be found in the comparative investigation of child-rearing practices in different cultures and subcultures. This represents the fifth approach in our list. An outstanding example of such a study is that by Whiting and Child (34), published in 1953. Utilizing data on 75 primitive societies from the Cross-Cultural Files of the Yale Institute of Human Relations, these investigators set out to test a number of hypotheses regarding the relationships between child-rearing practices and personality development. This analysis was followed up by field observations in five cultures, the results of which have not yet been reported (cf. 33).

Within our own culture, similar surveys have been concerned with the diverse psychological environments provided by different social classes (9). Of particular interest are the study by Williams and Scott (35) on the association between socioeconomic level, permissiveness, and motor development among Negro children, and the exploratory research by Milner (23) on the relationship between reading readiness in first-grade children and patterns of parent-child interaction. Milner found that upon school entrance the lower-class child seems to lack chiefly two advantages enjoyed by the middle-class child. The first is described as "a warm positive family atmosphere or adult-relationship pattern which is more and more being recognized as a motivational prerequisite of any kind of adult-controlled learning." The lower-class children in Milner's study perceived adults as predominantly hostile. The second advantage is an extensive opportunity to interact verbally with adults in the family. The latter point is illustrated by parental attitudes toward mealtime conversation, lower-class parents tending to inhibit and discourage such conversation, while middle-class parents encourage it.

Most traditional studies on child-rearing practices have been designed in terms of a psychoanalytic orientation. There is need for more data pertaining to other types of hypotheses. Findings such as those of Milner on opportunities for verbalization and the resulting effects upon reading readiness represent a step in this direction. Another possible source of future data is the application of the intensive observational techniques of psychological ecology developed by Barker and Wright (5) to widely diverse socioeconomic groups.

A sixth major approach involves research on somatopsychological relationships. To date, little direct information is available on the precise operation of this class of factors in psychological development. The multiplicity of ways in which physical traits—whether hereditary or environmental in origin—may influence behavior thus offers a relatively unexplored field for futue study.

The seventh and final approach to be considered represents an adaptation of traditional twin studies. From the standpoint of the question "How?" there is need for closer coordination between the usual data on twin resemblance and observations of the family interactions of twins. Available data already suggest, for example, that closeness of contact and extent of environmental similarity are greater in the case of monozygotic than in the case of dizygotic twins (cf. 2). Information on the social reactions of twins toward each other and the specialization of roles is likewise of interest (2). Especially useful would be longitudinal studies of twins, beginning in early infancy and following the subjects through school age. The operation of differential environmental pressures, the development of specialized roles, and other environmental influences could thus be more clearly identified and correlated with intellectual and personality changes in the growing twins.

Parenthetically, I should like to add a remark about the traditional applications of the twin method, in which persons in different degrees of hereditary and environmental relationships to each other are simply compared for behavioral similarity. In these studies, attention has been focused principally upon the amount of resemblance of monozygotic as contrasted to dizygotic twins. Yet such a comparison is particularly difficult to interpret because of the many subtle differences in the environmental situations of the two types of twins. A more fruitful comparison would seem to be that between dizygotic twins and siblings, for whom the hereditary similarity is known to be the same.

. . .

SUMMARY

The heredity-environment problem is still very much alive. Its viability is assured by the gradual replacement of the questions, "Which one?" and "How much?" by the more basic and appropriate question, "How?" Hereditary influences—as well as environmental factors of an organic nature—vary along a "continuum of indirectness." The more indirect their connection with behavior, the wider will be the range of variation of possible outcomes. One extreme of the continuum of indirectness may be illustrated by brain damage leading to mental deficiency; the other extreme, by physical characteristics associated with social stereotypes. Examples of factors falling at intermediate points include deafness, physical diseases, and motor disorders. Those environmental factors which act directly upon behavior can be ordered along a continuum of breadth or permanence of effect, as exemplified by social class membership, amount of formal schooling, language handicap, and familiarity with specific test items.

Several current lines of research offer promising techniques for exploring the *modus operandi* of hereditary and environmental factors. Outstanding among them are investigations of: (*a*) hereditary conditions which underlie behavioral differences between selectively bred groups of animals; (*b*) relations between physiological variables and individual differences in behavior, especially in the case of pathological deviations; (*c*) role of prenatal physiological factors in behavior development; (*d*) influence of early experience upon eventual behavioral characteristics; (*e*) cultural differences in child-rearing practices in relation to intellectual and emotional development; (*f*) mechanisms of somatopsychological relationships; and (*g*) psychological development of twins from infancy to maturity, together with observations of their social environment. Such approaches are extremely varied with regard to subjects employed, nature of psychological functions studied, and specific experimental procedures followed. But it is just such heterogeneity of methodology that is demanded by the wide diversity of ways in which hereditary and environmental factors interact in behavior development.

REFERENCES

1. Anastasi, Anne. *Psychological testing.* New York: Macmillan, 1954.
2. Anastasi, Anne. *Differential psychology.* (3rd ed.) New York: Macmillan, 1958.
3. Anastasi, Anne, & Foley, J. P., Jr. A proposed reorientation in the heredity-environment controversy. *Psychol. Rev.,* 1948, **55,** 239–249.
4. Arsenian, S. Bilingualism in the post-war world. *Psychol. Bull.,* 1945, **42,** 65–86.
5. Barker, R. G., & Wright, H. F. *Midwest and its children: The psychological ecology of an American town.* Evanston, Ill.: Row, Peterson, 1955.
6. Beach, F. A., & Jaynes, J. Effects of early experience upon the behavior of animals. *Psychol. Bull.,* 1954, **51,** 239–263.
7. Brackbill, G. A. Studies of brain dysfunction in schizophrenia. *Psychol. Bull.,* 1956, **53,** 210–226.
8. Darcy, Natalie T. A review of the literature on the effects of bilingualism upon the measurement of intelligence. *J. genet. Psychol.,* 1953, **82,** 21–57.
9. Davis, A., & Havighurst, R. J. Social class and color differences in child rearing. *Amer. sociol. Rev.,* 1946, **11,** 698–710.

10. Dobzhansky, T. The genetic nature of differences among men. In S. Persons (Ed.), *Evolutionary thought in America.* New Haven: Yale Univer. Press, 1950. Pp. 86–155.
11. Dobzhansky, T. Heredity, environment, and evolution. *Science,* 1950, **111,** 161–166.
12. Forgus, R. H. The effect of early perceptual learning on the behavioral organization of adult rats. *J. comp. physiol. Psychol.,* 1954, **47,** 331–336.
13. Haldane, J. B. S. *Heredity and politics.* New York: Norton, 1938.
14. Harrell, Ruth F., Woodyard, Ella, & Gates, A. I. *The effect of mothers' diets on the intelligence of the offspring.* New York: Bur. Publ., Teach. Coll., Columbia Univer., 1955.
15. Hebb, D. O. *The organization of behavior.* New York: Wiley, 1949.
16. Horwitt, M. K. Fact and artifact in the biology of schizophrenia. *Science,* 1956, **124,** 429–430.
17. Kallmann, F. J. *Heredity in health and mental disorder; Principles of psychiatric genetics in the light of comparative twin studies.* New York: Norton, 1953.
18. King, J. A., & Gurney, Nancy L. Effect of early social experience on adult aggressive behavior in C57BL10 mice. *J. comp. physiol. Psychol.,* 1954, **47,** 326–330.
19. Loevinger, Jane. On the proportional contributions of differences in nature and in nurture to differences in intelligence. *Psychol. Bull.,* 1943, **40,** 725–756.
20. Lorenz, K. Der Kumpan in der Umwelt des Vogels. Der Artgenosse als auslösendes Moment sozialer Verhaltungsweisen. *J. Orn., Lpz.,* 1935, **83,** 137–213; 289–413.
21. Luchins, A. S., & Forgus, R. H. The effect of differential postweaning environment on the rigidity of an animal's behavior. *J. genet. Psychol.,* 1955, **86,** 51–58.
22. Melzack, R. The genesis of emotional behavior: An experimental study of the dog. *J. comp. physiol. Psychol.,* 1954, **47,** 166–168.
23. Milner, Esther A. A study of the relationships between reading readiness in grade one school children and patterns of parent-child interaction. *Child Develpm.,* 1951, **22,** 95–112.
24. Pasamanick, B., Knobloch, Hilda, & Lilienfeld, A. M. Socioeconomic status and some precursors of neuropsychiatric disorder. *Amer. J. Orthopsychiat.,* 1956, **26,** 594–601.
25. Schwesinger, Gladys C. *Heredity and environment.* New York: Macmillan, 1933.
26. Scott, J. P., & Charles, Margaret S. Some problems of heredity and social behavior. *J. gen. Psychol.,* 1953, **48,** 209–230.
27. Scott, J. P., & Fuller, J. L. Research on genetics and social behavior at the Roscoe B. Jackson Memorial Laboratory, 1946–1951—A progress report. *J. Hered.,* 1951, **42,** 191–197.
28. Snyder, L. H. The genetic approach to human individuality. *Sci. Mon., N.Y.,* 1949, **68,** 165–171.
29. Snyder, L. H., & David, P. R. *The principles of heredity.* (5th ed.) Boston: Heath, 1957.

30. Spoerl, Dorothy T. Bilinguality and emotional adjustment. *J. abnorm. soc. Psychol.*, 1943, **38**, 37–57.

31. Thompson, W. R., & Melzack, R. Early environment. *Sci. Amer.*, 1956, **194** (1), 38–42.

32. Tryon, R. C. Genetic differences in maze-learning ability in rats. *Yearb. nat. Soc. Stud. Educ.*, 1940, **39**, Part I, 111–119.

33. Whiting, J. W. M., et al. *Field guide for a study of socialization in five societies.* Cambridge, Mass.: Harvard Univer., 1954 (mimeo.).

34. Whiting, J. W. M., & Child, I. L. *Child training and personality: A cross-cultural study.* New Haven: Yale Univer. Press, 1953.

35. Williams, Judith R., & Scott, R. B. Growth and development of Negro infants: IV. Motor development and its relationship to child rearing practices in two groups of Negro infants. *Child Develpm.*, 1953, **24**, 103–121.

36. Woodworth, R. S. Heredity and environment: A critical survey of recently published material on twins and foster children. *Soc. Sci. Res. Coun. Bull.*, 1941, No. 47.

7
BEHAVIORAL GENETICS: AN OVERVIEW*

GERALD E. McCLEARN

THE INHERITANCE of "mental" traits was discussed by Darwin and was the central focus of Galton's inquiries. In the early years of this century, the work of Pearson and others seemed to demonstrate that behavioral properties were inherited in the same manner as were physical traits, and prospects for advances in understanding of behavioral inheritance appeared to be very good indeed. Then came Behaviorism and the futile nature-nurture controversy. The old natural and easy relationship between psychology and biology was sundered, and the dogma was established that, however much heredity might determine physical and physiological characteristics, behavioral characteristics were immune and subject only to environmental influence.

This attitude came to be emotionally charged, and, as a consequence, behavioral scientists in the past several decades not only did not encounter genetics during their training, they typically acquired a feeling of estrangement toward that subject matter. The enormous recent advances in genetics have therefore had but a limited impact upon psychology in general.

There has been, however, increasing activity in the interdisciplinary field of behavioral genetics, and there is now compelling evidence concerning the influence of heredity on a wide variety of traits in a wide variety of organisms. These findings are of relevance to all psychologists, and one of the purposes of this paper is to provide examples of the types of evidence that have been adduced. An equally important purpose is to describe the general theoretical perspectives which genetical research can bring upon a problem, behavioral or otherwise.

In the space available, it has been necessary to simplify and condense, but never, I hope, to the jeopardy of the general argument. Readers interested in

---

* From the *Merrill-Palmer Quarterly,* 1968, *14,* 8–24. Reprinted with permission from the author and the Merrill-Palmer Institute.

Presented at The Merrill-Palmer Institute Conference on Research and Teaching of Infant Development, February 9–11, 1967, directed by Irving E. Sigel, chairman of research. The conference was financially supported in part by the National Institute of Child Health and Human Development.

more extensive literature reviews might consult the papers listed in "review references" in the bibliography. More detailed accounts of genetic theory may be found in any number of recent texts. Specific applications of various genetic models, techniques and procedures to behavioral genetics are discussed in Hirsch (1967).

SIMPLE GENETIC SYSTEMS

The conceptually simplest genetic system is one in which a single gene has a large effect upon the trait under consideration. A formal description of such a system of inheritance is quite simple. A given gene can exist in two or more alternative forms, called *alleles*. Each individual has two of a given gene, one having been contributed by each parent. Different combinations of the alleles give different outcomes. For example, consider the letter A to represent one allele of a gene, and A' to represent another allele. Three combinations are possible: AA, $A'A$, and $A'A'$. If the *phenotype,* which is the observed or measured characteristic, for AA is the same as for AA', it is said that A is dominant, and that A' is recessive. Various degrees of dominance and recessiveness are possible, with AA' yielding a phenotypic value somewhere between or even outside the range of AA and of $A'A'$. If AA' is exactly intermediate between AA and $A'A'$, the situation is described as additive.

A number of examples could be cited in which single genes have an important influence upon a behavioral characteristic. One of the best known is that of phenylketonuria in man. The dominant allele of this gene may be symbolized by P and the recessive allele by p. Both PP and Pp individuals are within the normal range of intelligence, but pp individuals suffer from mental retardation. Several other conditions of mental defect have been ascribed to single genes. Certain circumscribed conditions of sensory deficit have also been demonstrated to have a single gene basis. Ability to taste phenylthiocarbamide is an example of such a condition. Individuals who have two of the recessive alleles (these individuals being described as *homozygous* for the recessive allele) cannot taste the substance. People who are *homozygous* for the dominant allele find the substance to be bitter, as do those who are *heterozygous* (having one of each allele).

. . .

CYTOGENETICS

Physically, the genes are located on small thread-like bodies called chromosomes, which are found within the nucleus of all body cells. For present purposes, the chromosomes may be regarded as linear arrays of many genes each. The chromosomes occur as paired structures, with one chromosome of each pair having come from the mother, and the other from the father. The number of chromosomes is quite constant from cell to cell with an organism, and from individual to individual within a species, although the number varies substantially from species to species. In human beings, there are 23 pairs of chromosomes; in mice there are 20 pairs; in the crayfish there are 100 pairs; and in Drosophila only 4, for example. A large part of the original research work relating genes to chromosomes was performed with fruit flies, where in certain tissues the chromosomes are unusually large and easy to see. Research on chromosomes in mammals has been much more difficult, but the development of new techniques has recently made possible much more refined research on mammalian tissues in general and on human tissues specifically. There has been an exciting burst of activity in this area, and a number of findings relating chromosomal anomalies to behavioral characteristics have been described.

Ordinarily, in the process of development of sperm and eggs, a very precise mechanism guarantees that each egg or sperm will contain one of each of the pairs of chromosomes characteristic of the species. Thus, when fertilization occurs, the joining of the nuclei of the two germ cells gives rise to a single cell with the normal chromosomal complement. However, it occasionally happens that a mistake occurs, which results in a sperm or an egg containing either both members of a pair instead of only one, or containing no representative at all of a given pair. When such a germ cell is involved in fertilization, the resulting organism will possess three instead of two of one pair (which condition is called *trisomy*) or only one instead of two chromosomes (which condition is called *monosomy*). Trisomy of many of the chromosomes appears to be lethal. In some cases, the organism survives, but is affected by a number of abnormalities. One of these latter conditions is monogolism, more frequently known today as Down's syndrome. The chromosomes of man are classifiable according to size and certain other characteristics and a standard nomenclature has been established. The chromosome identified as number 21 has been found to be present in triplicate in many cases of Down's syndrome, and the condition is therefore also widely known as trisomy 21. It has become apparent that it is not necessary for all of chromosome number 21 to be present in triplicate for the multiple defects including mental retardation to occur; in certain cases only part of the third chromosome number 21 is present. (See Polani et al., 1960).

In most cases, the individual members of the chromosome pairs appear to be equal, in the sense that each contains genetic information comparable to that contained on the other. In the case of sex chromosomes, however, this is not so. In man, as well as in many other organisms, females have two equivalent chromosomes, called the *X* chromosomes, while males have one *X* and a small *Y* chromosome. It seems that much of the genetic material carried on the *X* chromosome is not represented by corresponding material on the *Y*. The *Y* chromosome in mammals, however, does contain male-determining genetic information of some kind. As is true of the other, non-sex, chromosomes (called the *autosomes*) the distribution of sex chromosomes is usually quite precise, giving rise to *XX* daughters and *XY* sons through the generations.

However, mistakes also occur occasionally with respect to the sex chromosomes. A clinical condition involving incomplete sexual development in ostensible males, called Klinefelter's syndrome, has been shown in many cases to involve the presence of two *X* chromosomes in addition to a *Y* chromosome. In addition to the symptoms of retarded sexual development, there are behavioral concomitants in a generally reduced intelligence level. Another condition of retarded sexual development, in this case of ostensible females, is Turner's syndrome. In many Turner's patients, it has been found that there are only 45 instead of the normal number of 46 (23 pairs) of chromosomes. Detailed analysis has revealed that only one sex chromosome, an *X*, is present. A very specific type of cognitive defect appears to occur in these *XO* females. Money (1966) has discussed a number of observations which suggest that Turner's syndrome patients are grossly defective with respect to spatial abilities, although verbal I.Q. measures may fall within the normal range. A more recently reported condition is the *XYY* male. Jacobs, et al. (1965) found seven out of a population of 203 male inmates of a maximum security hospital to have an *XYY* constitution. This incidence is greatly in excess of that in the non-institutionalized population. They seemed to be characterizable as tall, aggressive, and mentally subnormal. Price and Whatmore (1967) have since compared the behavior of *XYY* individuals with *XY* ("normal") males in the same hospital. The aggression of the *XYY* individuals appears to be more directed to property than persons, and disturbed behavior was manifested earlier in the *XYY* than in the *XY* patients.

QUANTITATIVE GENETICS

The basic rules governing the transmission of genetic elements were worked out with reference to dichotomous, qualitative traits. After the generality of these rules had been demonstrated for many traits and in many organisms, efforts were made to apply them to continuously varying, quantitatively distributed characteristics. The analytical models that have been developed in this context assume that there are a number of different genes that exert influence upon the trait, with the individual effect of any particular gene being relatively small. The effect of the individual gene cannot therefore be followed by examination of progency of various mating types, as in "Mendelian" traits. Instead, the effect of all of the genes, working in concert, must be assessed by statistical measures. There are several important ideas and terms that pertain to the analysis and interpretation of quantitative inheritance. The total system is sometimes described as a multiple-factor system, but a more frequently employed term is *polygenic*. As mentioned above, the basic notion of a polygenic system is that a number of genes each have an effect on the same character. A related term is *pleiotropy,* which is used to describe situations in which a given single gene has an effect upon several phenotypic characters. An example of this has already been presented, in that the albino gene in the mouse has behavioral effects in addition to the obvious effect upon coat color.

Perhaps the central concept of quantitative genetics is that of *heritability*. In a very general sense, heritability is the extent to which the phenotype is a reliable guide to the genotype. Phenotype has been defined as that which is measured. Genotype is the genetic makeup respecting all of the genes relevant to the particular character in question. One reason for a lack of one-to-one correspondence between genotype and phenotype is the phenomenon of dominance, where different genotypes (one homozygous for the dominant allele, the other heterozygous) give rise to the same phenotypic result. Another major source of discrepancy between genotype and phenotype is the effect of environment. Figure 1 is a pictorial representation of some of these ideas. This figure shows two normal distributions with representative individuals within each. An individual is represented by two connected symbols; one, a circle, represents the phenotypic value; the other, a triangle, represents the genotypic value. The latter is not directly measurable, of course, although estimates can be attempted by various procedures. One way of conceptualizing the genotypic value is to consider it to be the mean of the phenotypic values that would result if the given individual could be indefinitely replicated and reared under all of the environmental conditions to which the population is exposed. It may be seen that in the top distribution, phenotypic and genotypic values are quite close together. In the bottom distribution, however, the average discrepancy between phenotypic and genotypic values is relatively high. In the top distribution, therefore, the heritability of the character in question is higher and the phenotypic value of an individual is a far more reliable index of the individual's genotypic value than in the bottom distribution.

It is worth repeated emphasis that consideration of environmental sources of variance form an integral part of any discussion of quantitative genetics. During the old nature-nurture controversy, the question was frequently asked: Is a given trait due to heredity or environment? This dichotomous implication is easily seen to be faulty. With our modern perspective, we may inquire as to the relative proportions of phenotypic variance attributable to genetic differences among the individuals in the population and the proportion due to differences in their environments. In a somewhat simplified form, we may state that the phenotypic variance is equal to the genotypic variance plus the environmental variance:

$$V_P = V_G + V_E$$

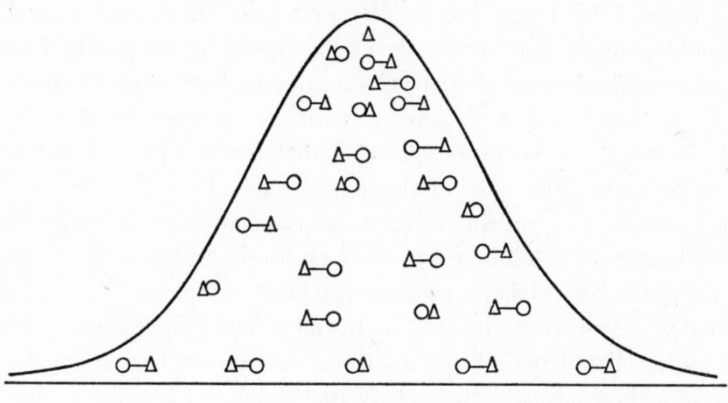

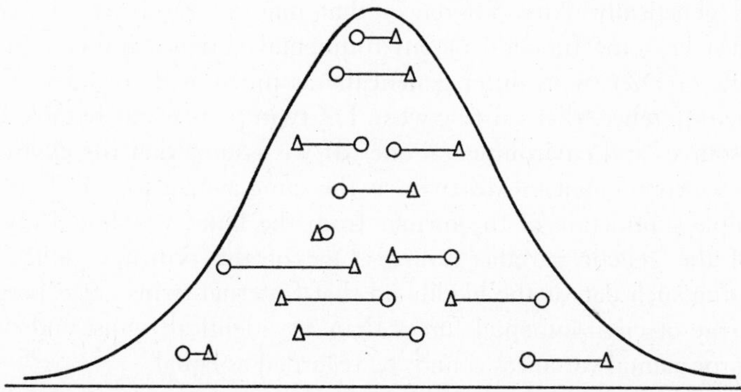

Two normal distributions with representative individuals within each one. Each set of connected symbols represents an individual—the circle standing for a *phenotypic* value (a characteristic as observed or measured), the triangle for a *genotypic* value (the individual's actual genetic makeup relevant to that characteristic). As can be seen, the two values are quite close together for all of the individuals in the top distribution, in contrast to those in the bottom one. In the top distribution, therefore, the heritability of the particular characteristic is higher, and the phenotypic value of an individual a more reliable index of his genotypic value.

However, as we have already seen, certain types of genetic interactions (e.g., dominance) contribute to a lack of one-to-one correspondence between genotype and phenotype. Without rigorous derivations (for which the interested reader should consult Falconer, 1960), it can be appreciated that the covariance among relatives of different degrees could be converted to statistical form which permits the estimation of heritability. The examination of such resemblances among relatives has indeed been widely used in human behavioral genetics. They were, in fact, an important source of data in the nature-nurture controversy and a brief review of some of the difficulties of interpretation is therefore in order. It is a common finding that the parent-offspring correlation for intelligence tests is around 0.5, which is of the same general magnitude as the correlation found for traits of bodily dimension and so on. Rather smaller correlations have been typically found for measures of personality. These values are rather complicated to interpret (see McClearn, 1962a) and one of the principal difficulties is in the confounding of genotype and environment. It should be intuitively reasonable, from the above discussion, that it is necessary to have unambiguous assessments of environmental and genetic variance sources. If these are confounded, interpretation becomes very difficult indeed. Just such confounding appears to be rather the rule in the case of socially valued human traits. Those individuals who, on the average, are contributing the greater number of alleles for superior intelligence to their children, are most likely contributing also the environmental supports for intellectual attainment.

Another widely used technique in human behavioral genetics is that of studying twins. Problems similar to those encountered in correlational research present themselves in twin-study methodology. The basic logic of the twin technique is quite simple. Identical (monozygotic or MZ) twins are identical genetically. Any differences that may appear between MZ twin pairs must be some function of environmental variance sources. Fraternal (dizygotic or DZ) twins differ genetically as much as do ordinary siblings. Thus the differences that exist between DZ twin pairs is attributable both to genetic sources and environmental ones. If we assume that the environmental variance component in MZ twins is the same as that for DZ twins, then by a simple subtraction of the former from the latter we should obtain an index of the genetic variance source. One of the principle difficulties in interpreting such data is the likelihood that fraternal twins are exposed to a wider array of environmental forces than are identical twins, and that the two environmental variances cannot be regarded as equal.

In spite of all this and other difficulties of interpretation, the twin-study approach has been quite useful in behavioral genetics research. As in the case of data from correlations among relatives, the twin-study data suggest that the heritability of intellectual traits, as a class, is higher than that of personality traits, as a class. Recent research has emphasized finer grained analyses of the intellectual domain, with the interesting result that different varieties of intellectual function appear to have different proportions of genetic determination (Vandenberg, 1965). Various considerations of quantitative inheritance have suggested differential evolutionary significance of some of these intellectual sub-units in man's evolutionary history (Roberts, 1967).

The preceding comments concerning difficulties in the interpretation of human data should not be construed as a criticism of current research or a discouragement to further research. The implication rather is that conclusions from such human data must be interpreted with circumspection. Many traits are capable of study only in man. If man's conditions of social existence are such as to confound the available techniques, then the techniques must be used as best they can, with the interpretation always being made in the total context of information about heredity in general, and specifically including the data obtained on behavioral genetics in animals, where control procedures can circumvent many of the difficulties of human research.

Studies of the resemblance of relatives in animals is, of course, possible, and indeed is much less subject to the confounding of environmental and genetic variables that occurs in research on man. Likewise, the basic twin-study paradigm could be applied to animal species in which twinning occurs. In point of fact, however, the techniques most frequently used in the study of quantitative aspects of animal behavioral genetics have been two which are not possible in human research. The first of these techniques is the use of highly inbred strains. The mating of relatives in consecutive generations leads to a reduction in heterozygosity. In some cases, for instance sib mating, there is an asymptomatic approach to a condition of homozygosity for all genes in a strain thus derived (with certain complications not necessary for the current discussion). That is to say, every animal of a single strain in which each generation is derived from a single sibling mating pair will be homozygous in like allelic state for practically all genes. There is, therefore, no (or very little) genetic variability within such a strain, and the exhibited phenotypic variance must be attributable to environmental sources. If different inbred strains, reared in the same environment, exhibit different behavioral characteristics, these differences must be attributable to genetic differences between the strains. A comparison of various inbred strains on a particular behavioral characteristic is therefore a good indicator of the existence of genetic influence on a behavioral trait.

Many such strain differences have been described with respect to such behavioral characters as learning ability, activity level, sexual behavior, alcohol preference, and aggressiveness (see McClearn, 1962a). A particularly interesting type of strain difference, and one that has important implications for methodology in animal research generally, is that in which strains respond differentially to the application of an independent variable. An example of this type of outcome is that of the effects of administration of alcohol fumes upon activity level of mice (McClearn, 1962b). Some strains of animals have activity increased as a consequence of forced inhalation of alcohol vapor; some strains are unaffected; and some strains have their activity level decreased by the identical treatment.

The establishment of strain differences is only an indicator of genetic determination, and more detailed analysis of the inheritance requires the comparison of means and variances of the inbred strains and of generations derived from them. The F_1 generation, that is to say the offspring of the mating of animals of two inbred strains, is also uniform genetically, although these F_1 animals will be heterozygous for all genes which were homozygous in different allelic states in the parent strains. Phenotypic variance in the F_1 populations, therefore, like phenotypic variation of the inbred strains, must be attributable to environmental sources. The F_2 generation is obtained by mating F_1 animals with other F_1 animals. This generation is genetically heterogenous, and this fact permits the comparison of the variance in F_1's to the variance of the F_2 and other generations in which both environmental and genetic variance exists. This comparison can yield a type of heritability estimate. Fuller and Thompson (1960), for example, studied activity in descendant populations from two strains of mice and found that 60% of the variance of the F_2, under the existing environmental conditions, was due to genetic variability within the group.

The other principally used mating technique in animal behavioral genetics has been selective breeding. In selective breeding, subjects with extreme manifestation of the trait in question are mated together with the objective of shifting the population mean. In practical efforts—such as those directed toward increase in milk production in cattle, or egg size in chickens, for example—this selective breeding is usually carried out only in the more desirable direction of the trait. In laboratory research, however, it is cutomary (indeed for proper analysis, essential) to breed in both directions. The rate of differentiation of the high and low selected lines is dependent upon the heritability of the trait. This can be appreciated by referring again to Figure 1. In the upper distribution, selection of an animal with an extreme score will provide an animal with an extreme genotype. In the lower distribution, an animal with an extreme phenotype may be genotypically quite ordinary or average. Since none of the effects of environment can be transmitted to the next generation, only the genotypic value is of importance in determining the changes in population mean as a consequence of selective breeding. Thus traits of high heritability provide a more rapid divergence of strains selected bidirectionally and traits of low heritability show slower progress.

Successful selective breeding has been accomplished for a variety of behavioral traits. The classic example, of course, is that of Tryon (1940) who selectively bred rats for maze "brightness" and maze "dullness" in a 17-unit multiple T-maze. Other workers (see McClearn, 1962a) have selectively bred for learning in rats, activity in rats, aggressiveness in mice, geotaxis in fruit flies, mating speed in fruit flies, and other characteristics. Not only do these successful breeding programs reveal retrospectively that there was genetic contribution to the variability of the trait in the foundation population from which selection was begun, they also provide research animals with different values of the behavioral trait of interest. These animals therefore make excellent subjects for research on correlated characters and especially on physiological mechanisms. An excellent example of such procedures is the history of research on Tryon's bright and dull rats which have been investigated for the association of their performance differentials with motivational factors (Searle, 1949), specific "hypotheses" preferences (Krechvesky, 1933), brain size (Silverman et al., 1940), and enzyme differences (Rosenzweig et al., 1960).

PHYSIOLOGICAL AND BIOCHEMICAL GENETICS

The past fifteen years has witnessed an explosion of knowledge concerning the mechanisms through which the genes express themselves, and the whole new field of molecular biology has emerged. The chemical nature of the gene is now quite clearly understood. The fundamental component of the hereditary material is deoxyribonucleic acid (DNA). The molecule of DNA has a double helical structure. This may be visualized as two strands of phosphate and deoxyribose sugar groups wrapped around each other, but held a fixed distance apart by pairs of bases on the interior of the helix. The space limitations of the molecular structure are such that the four bases involved are always paired in a certain way: adenine pairs with thymine; guanine pairs with cytosine. The doubled nature of this molecule and the pairing restrictions on the bases give it the capacity of self-duplication. This property is of course a requisite of the hereditary material, since the basic genetic information available in the fertilized egg must be duplicated many times over in the development of a multicellular organism. Essentially, what appears to happen is that the two helices unwind, and each carries with it one base of each base pair. The composition of the cell nucleus, in which this takes place, is rich in unattached bases. These attach themselves to the single bases that are in turn attached to the helix. Because of the strict rules governing which base may pair with which other base, the newly formed pairs are exact duplicates of the original. The process also involves duplication of the phosphate and deoxyribose sugar strands.

The DNA is, of course, located in the nucleus of cells. However, it is known that much of the vital work of the cells takes place in the cytoplasm. In some fashion, therefore, the information that is contained in the DNA molecule must be transmitted to the cytoplasm. This is accomplished by another nucleic acid, in this case single-stranded, called ribonucleic acid (RNA). By a process similar to that involved in DNA replication, an RNA molecule is transcribed on the DNA molecule, so that the sequences of bases in the DNA determines the sequence of bases in RNA. (In RNA, uracil substitutes for thymine.) The RNA molecule then goes into the cytoplasm, where it is involved in protein synthesis. The genetic "information" is coded by the sequence of bases and the code has been shown to consist of three letter "words." Each succeeding triplet of bases specifies an amino acid. For example, three uracils in a row (UUU) specifies phenylalanine; AUG (adenine, uracil, guanine) specifies glutamic acid. These amino acids join and ultimately form proteins. Of particular interest are the proteins that act as enzymes. These act as catalysts and are vital to the operation of the organism. The reactions that are the very basis of behavior and indeed, of life itself, could not take place in their absence.

A particularly cogent example relating gene to enzyme to behavioral consequence is that of phenylketonuria. As we have seen earlier, the evidence is clear that phenylketonuria arises from the homozygous recessive state of a particular gene. Phenylketonurics are deficient with respect to the enzyme, phenylalanine hydroxylase. With this deficiency, the metabolism of phenylalanine is stopped or greatly reduced, and there is an accumulation of phenylalanine and a number of related metabolic products. Some of these are evidently toxic to the developing nervous system, and lead to mental retardation if the individual is untreated. Fortunately, knowledge of the metabolic difficulty has given rise to a rational therapy. With special diets lacking phenylalanine, it is possible to keep the biochemical status of phenylketonuric patients within normal bounds, and there appears to be substantial improvement in mental status if the treatment is begun early enough. To the latter end, many states now require the testing of all newborn infants.

A number of other defects of amino acid metabolism with mental retardation have now been identified, and research is proceeding rapidly on problems of identification and therapy. A review of these and other conditions of mental retardation is given by Anderson (1964).

In research on animals, one of the most thorough attempts to trace the biochemical route from gene to behavior has been the work of Rosenzweig and co-workers (1964). Descendants of the selectively bred Tryon "bright" and "dull" rats have been found to differ in brain levels of acetylcholinesterase and acetylcholine. These results, combined with data from other strains selectively bred for the level of enzyme activity, suggest that the ratio of these two substances is correlated with learning ability.

. . .

DEVELOPMENTAL GENETICS

An area of genetical research especially pertinent is that which deals with the role of genes in developmental processes.

Occasionally, confusion arises between the concepts of "hereditary" and "congenital." Consideration of the inheritance of adult traits that do not appear in the newborn should make clear, however, that not all genes are "turned on" at birth or at conception. A specific example is provided by the condition, Huntington's Chorea, which is due to the presence of a dominant allele of the particular gene involved. The average age of onset of the condition is about 35 years. Other characters, such as blood groups, do seem fixed at birth. Still others, for example, hemoglobin type, change systematically with age. Presumably, genes that are part of polygenic systems have differing times of onset, as well.

In addition to these temporal considerations, there are many interesting aspects of spatial differences in gene functioning. A key biological problem, in fact, concerns the way in which a single cell, the fertilized egg, can differentiate into a complex multicellular organism, each cell of which presumably carries the same set of genetic information. Part of this differentiation can probably be accounted for in terms of initial lack of homogeneity of the egg cytoplasm, with resulting nonequivalence of the cytoplasm in various descendant cell lines.

The operon model of gene action (Jacob and Monod, 1961) has provided suggestions as to how genes themselves may be "turned on" or "turned off" in developmental sequences. Although the basic data have been obtained from micro-organisms, it seems a reasonable working hypothesis that similar mechanisms occur in higher organisms (Ursprung, 1965). The model postulates different types of gene: regulator genes and structural genes. The latter type is what we have previously been discussing simply as "genes," the function of which is to produce a type of RNA that will in turn produce enzymes. A structural gene has an "operator" adjacent to it. The operator is apparently the critical starting point for the molecular copying involved in transcribing RNA from DNA. A regulator gene, which need not be physically adjacent to operator or the structural gene, produces a repressor substance which attaches to operator and thus prevents RNA transcription.

An "inducer" introduced into the cell, for example, by diffusion from adjacent cells, or from the external environment, combines with repressor, which then cannot occupy the strategic site on operator. RNA transcription and enzyme production can begin. The gene has been "turned on." If one of the metabolic products of the reactions initiated by the enzyme happens to be the inducer, or a similar molecule, it effectively keeps the system locked on. A similar mechanism can turn off or lock off a gene that is initially on.

The complexity of interactions between different genes, where the product of one might intervene in the controlling system of another, is easy to imagine. For such situations, the type of model described by Waddington (1957) might be required. It is possible to imagine, for example, that a given genotype fixes the developmental "trajectory"; that environmental forces act to move development from this path, and that the lability of the system depends upon the extent to which feedback information causes compensatory readjustment in trajectory.

It is probably correct to say that behavioral geneticists have only begun to apply developmental genetic considerations to analyses of the development of behavioral patterns. Yet sufficient has been accomplished to indicate the high promise of this approach. Descriptively, there are several examples of timed action such as that provided by Huntington's Chorea. An example taken from the mouse research literature is that of audiogenic seizure susceptibility. Many strains of animals are resistant to audiogenic seizures. In one of the most thoroughly investigated susceptible strains, there is a very sharply peaked distribution of sensitivity, with the peak occurring at 21 days (Schlesinger et al., 1966). A rather different example is provided by another strain of mice, which shows a moderate preference for alcohol until about 9 weeks of age, at which time there is an abrupt decline in alcohol preference (Kakihana and McClearn, 1963). Other strains that are non-preferring as adults do not show this developmental function.

Another type of research that is relevant involves experimental intervention of some sort in early life, with an examination of the differential responsiveness to the treatment by different genotypes of animals. Lindzey and his co-workers (1963), for example, have investigated strain differences in the effect of handling and of auditory stimuli presented during infancy on learning performance and tests of temperament in the adults. Weir and DeFries (1964), and DeFries (1964), investigated strain differences in the effect of prenatal stress on behavior of the offspring. In all of these studies significant strain differences have been identified, indicating that the effect of environmental variables in influencing a developmental sequence is strongly dependent upon the genotype of the organism to which the environmental treatment is offered.

SUMMARY

To summarize, the evidence implicating heredity in the determination of behavior is compelling. Some behavioral traits are affected by single genes. In other cases, abnormalities are attributable to the presence of many extra genes in the form of a surplus chromosome. Many, perhaps most, traits are determined by a number of genes acting in concert with environmental forces. The routes by which the genes affect behavior are under investigation, and gene-enzyme-behavior relationships are beginning to emerge. The potential for genetic control of behavioral development is suggested by yet other research.

In brief, the rules of behavioral inheritance appear to be no different from the rules of inheritance of other traits. We might reasonably expect no less a return, therefore, from the application of a genetic perspective in studying behavior than that which has rewarded similar efforts elsewhere in the biological sciences.

REFERENCES

Review References

Anderson, V. E. Genetics in mental retardation. In H. A. Stevens & R. Heber (Eds.), *Mental retardation*. Chicago: Univer. Chicago Press, 1964. Pp. 348–394.

Böök, J. A. Some mechanisms of chromosome variations and their relation to human malformations. *Eugenics Rev.,* 1964, **56,** 151–157.

Broadhurst, P. L. Applications of biometrical genetics to the inheritance of behaviour. In H. J. Eysenck (Ed.), *Experiments in Personality*. New York: Humanities Press, 1960. Pp. 3–102.

Erlenmeyer-Kimling, L. & Jarvik, L. F. Genetics and intelligence: a review. *Science,* 1963, **142,** 1477–1479.

Fuller, J. L. Genetics and individual differences. In R. H. Waters, D. A. Rethlingshafer, & W. E. Caldwell (Eds.), *Principles of comparative psychology*. New York: McGraw-Hill, 1960. Pp. 325–354.

Fuller, J. L. & Thompson, W. R. *Behavior genetics*. New York: Wiley, 1960.

Hirsch, J. Individual differences in behavior and their genetic basis. In E. L. Bliss (Ed.), *Roots of behavior*. New York: Harper, 1962. Pp. 3–23.

Kallmann, F. J. (Ed.). *Expanding goals of genetics in psychiatry*. New York: Grune & Stratton, 1962.

Lejeune, J. The 21-trisomy—current stage of chromosomal research. In A. G. Steinberg & A. G. Gearn (Eds.), *Progress in medical genetics*. New York: Grune & Stratton, 1964. Pp. 144–177.

McClearn, G. E. & Meredith, W. M. Behavioral genetics. In P. R. Farnsworth (Ed.), *Annual review of psychology*, 1966, **17**, 515–550.

Penrose, L. S. *The biology of mental defect*. (Rev. ed.). New York: Grune & Stratton, 1963.

Shields, J. *Monozygotic twins*. London: Oxford Univer. Press, 1962.

Wimer, R. E. & Fuller, J. L. Patterns of behavior. In E. L. Green (Ed.), *Biology of the laboratory mouse*. (2d ed.). New York: McGraw-Hill, 1966. Pp. 629–653.

General References

Bastock, Margaret. A gene mutation which changes a behavior pattern. *Evolution*, 1956, **10**, 421–439.

DeFries, J. C. Prenatal maternal stress in mice; differential effects on behavior. *J. Hered.*, 1964, **55**, 289–295.

Falconer, D. S. *Introduction to quantitative genetics*. Edinburgh and London: Oliver & Boyd, 1960.

Hirsch, J. (Ed.). *Behavior-genetic analysis*. New York: McGraw-Hill, 1967.

Jacob, F. & Monod, J. On the regulation of gene activity. *Cold Spring Harb. Symp. on Quant. Biol.*, 1961, **26**, 193–209.

Jacobs, Patricia, Brunton, Muriel, Melville, Marie M., Brittain, R. P. & McClemont, W. F. Aggressive behaviour, mental sub-normality and the XYY male. *Nature*, 1965, **208**, 1351–1352.

Kakihana, Ryoko & McClearn, G. E. Development of alcohol preference in BALB/c mice. *Nature*, 1963, **199**, 511–512.

Krechevsky, I. Hereditary nature of "hypotheses." *J. comp. Psychol.*, 1933, **16**, 99–116.

Lindzey, G., Winston, H. D. & Manosevitz, M. Early experience, genotype, and temperament in *Mus musculus*. *J. comp. physiol. Psychol.*, 1963, **56**, 622–629.

McClearn, G. E. The inheritance of behavior. In L. J. Postman (Ed.), *Psychology in the making*. New York: Knopf, 1962. (a)

McClearn, G. E. Genetic differences in the effect of alcohol upon behavior of mice. In J. D. J. Havard (Ed.), *Proceedings of the third international conference on alcohol and road traffic*. London: British Medical Association, 1962. (b)

Money, J. Cognitive defects in Turner's syndrome. *Second invitational conference on human behavior genetics*. Louisville, 1966.

Polani, P. E., Briggs, J. H., Ford, C. E., Clarke, C. M. & Berg, J. M. A mongoloid girl with 46 chromosomes. *Lancet*, 1960, **1**, 721–724.

Price, W. H. & Whatmore, P. B. Criminal behaviour and the XYY male. *Nature*, 1967, 5078, 815.

ROBERTS, R. C. Some evolutionary implications of behavior. *Canad. J. genet. Cytol.,* 1967, **9,** 419–435.

ROSENZWEIG, M. R. Effect of heredity and environment on brain chemistry, brain anatomy, and learning ability in the rat. Symposium on Physiological Determinants of Behavior: Implications for Mental Retardation. *Kan. Stud. Educ.,* 1964, **14,** 3–34.

SCHLESINGER, K., ELSTON, R. C. & BOGGAN, W. The genetics of sound induced seizure in inbred mice. *Genetics,* 1966, **54,** 95–103.

SEARLE, L. V. The organization of hereditary maze-brightness and maze-dullness. *Genet. Psychol. Monogr.,* 1949, **39,** 279–325.

SILVERMAN, W., SHAPIRO, F. & HERON, W. T. Brain weight and maze-learning in rats. *J. comp. Psychol.,* 1940, **30,** 279–282.

TRYON, R. C. Genetic differences in maze-learning ability in rats. *Yearb. nat. Soc. Stud. Educ.,* 1940, **39,** Part I, 111–119.

URSPRUNG, H. Genes and development. In R. L. DeHaan & H. Ursprung (Eds.), *Organogenesis.* New York: Holt, Rinehart & Winston, 1965.

VANDENBERG, S. G. Multivariate analysis of twin differences. In S. G. Vandenberg (Ed.), *Methods and goals in human behavior genetics.* New York: Academic Press, 1965.

WADDINGTON, C. H. *The strategy of the genes.* New York: Macmillan, 1957.

WEIR, M. W. & DEFRIES, J. C. Prenatal maternal influence on behavior in mice: evidence of a genetic basis. *J. comp. physiol. Psychol.,* 1964, **58,** 412–417.

8

MATERNAL NUTRITION AND THE FETUS*

RAY HEPNER

HUMAN LOSSES in the newborn period are now the third leading medical cause of death in the United States, and these statistics exclude stillbirth, miscarriage, and surviving damaged children. When prematurity, stillbirth, and the great tragedy, the surviving damaged child, are considered, together with unnecessary maternal illness and morbidity or death of liveborn children, we find ourselves faced with an immensely complex, yet perfectly interrelated, problem. No doubt exists about the role of nutrition in the problem, but solid evidence to support this belief has been singularly difficult to marshal. This presentation offers, first, some of the difficulties in studying the problem; second, the results of some studies of the past; and, third, some incompletely developed, yet fundamental concepts.

It is axiomatic that fetal problems are the best index to obstetric practice. This index may be as confined as the neonatal death rate alone, or, and perhaps more properly, it may be as broad as the entire gamut of reproductive problems. This gamut ranges from sterility, pregnancy and labor complications, miscarriage, premature and immature birth, stillbirth, and malformation to a functional abnormality that may become manifest well beyond the newborn period in the form of convulsions, defects of intellect, and neuromuscular disturbances.[1]† These latter defects are known to the laity as epilepsy, feeblemindedness, and cerebral palsy, and, by the most conservative estimates, persons so affected make up at least 1% of our population today. Every indication is that this proportion will increase if the present production and survival rates of these children prevail.

Many studies have shown that nutrition plays a part in reproductive problems. Observations of war starvation in pregnancy,[2–5] of nutrition surveys in pregnancy,[6–8] of patients admitted to sterility and other special clinics, and of controlled animal investigations affirm this part.[9] A sufficient degree of starvation will cause sterility and amenorrhea that will not respond to adequate caloric intake until sufficient protein is provided. Attempts to

* From the *Journal of the American Medical Association.* 1958, *168,* 1774–1777. Reprinted with permission from the author and The American Medical Association.

† See References on page 139.

reduce stillbirth, premature birth, malformations, and neonatal death in special prenatal clinics are impressive when one sees how much can be done to help the individual mothers of each group in which a nutritional deficit is demonstrated. For instance, the sterile mother can be helped to conceive; the habitual aborter can be helped to carry a child to viability; the repeated bearer of stillborn infants can be helped to have a living child.

Even with these known and measurable accomplishments, there is little change in the total statistical results in each hospital. The failure of statistics to improve may well be due to the use of an improper base line, one that is chased from one category to the next. To compare the incidence of premature birth with total viable births fails entirely to recognize those women who have conceived who did not conceive before, those who have carried a fetus to viability who could not before, and those who carried their fetuses to term who never did before. Our statistical base line might better be placed on a level with the reproductive group as a whole than compared with the final result, which, after all, is a goal to be achieved and not the point at which to begin. For a baby to be born alive at term and go home with its mother is not enough. Real success must be measured by achievement of the potential to become a contributing member of society.

Children handicapped by convulsions, neuromuscular problems, or a mental deficiency are born commonly to mothers with reproductive histories of sterility, miscarriage, stillbirth, pregnancy complications, premature or immature birth, and malformation. The prevailing view has been that this relationship is based on genetic fault.[10] Good evidence is available now which shows that inadequate nutrition can produce defects of function as well as of structure.[11,12] Nutritional deficiencies may be related to any of the entire gamut of reproductive problems.

GENERAL FACTORS INFLUENCING REPRODUCTION

Apparently unrelated agents may produce injuries similar to those produced by a nutritional deficit. Trace elements, as well as major minerals, insulin, some infectious diseases, various corticoids, hypoxia, hyperoxia, vitamin excesses and deficiencies, and genetic faults can influence the reproductive spectrum. Repeated demonstrations both in man and in controlled animal experiments have shown that identical, or nearly identical, abnormalities may result from entirely different agents. A classic example in humans is found in the microcephalia of genetic fault and pelvic x-irradiation. In animals, the demonstration of identical bony defects in rats injured by riboflavin deficiency, x-irradiation, or inbreeding serves admirably for illustration.[13] Although different injurious agents may operate finally through similar pathways, the initiating agent remains different. Even so, the contributions of adequate nutritive stores may protect the organism against a considerable onslaught.

NUTRITIONAL FACTORS INFLUENCING REPRODUCTION

The concepts of timing, severity, type, and duration of nutritional deficit are of major import, since these factors often determine what part of the reproductive gamut is to be affected. In humans, acute starvation with protein depletion over a short period has been proved to be associated with a decrease in conception rate, and sterility with amenorrhea is produced over a longer starvation period. If acute depletion begins after conception, the babies are small. However, only inconclusive evidence of an increased incidence of malformation could be found in a previously well-nourished population.[2] Some evidence of increased reproductive problems can be found in several studies of humans living on chronically poor diets, particularly when the stress of continued growth and the depletion of repeated pregnancy are added burdens.[6] These patients run the gamut of reproductive problems. On the basis of insufficient amounts and variety of good quality foods, these diets were assessed as poor, even though sufficient (and often more than sufficient) calories were provided. The frequency of obesity in the patients of these studies suggested the aphorism "overfed and undernourished," and the offspring of these women, when compared with controls, suffered as well.

In several animals, vitamin A deficiency is associated with sterility, abortion, malformation, stillbirth, or small young, depending on the duration, severity, and timing of the deficiency.[14] In rats, similar effects have been produced by deficiencies of pure thiamine, riboflavin, pyridoxine, or pantothenic acid without protein deficiency.[15]

RESULTS OF PAST STUDIES

More than one third of lethal human malformations involve the nervous system. However, many anomalies of the nervous system are compatible with life. Brain function is often seriously disturbed, with little or no demonstrable structural abnormality. For many years speculation has been forwarded that agents known to produce structural alteration with related defects of function might, in smaller doses, produce defects of function without histological abnormality.

In 1951 Whitely, O'Dell, and Hogan[11] demonstrated that folic acid deficiency in pregnant rats could disturb the ability of the offspring to learn a standard maze, even though brain structure was apparently normal. More recently, doses of x-irradiation, smaller than necessary to produce anomalies of the nervous system of fetal rats, have produced similar results. Again, different agents have been proved able to produce a similar defect, but this defect is one of function rather than of structure.

The recent study of Harrell, Woodyard, and Gates[12] is of special interest for two reasons. The first is that their assay of results was based on significant differences in intellectual performance of human offspring, a function that might be damaged even in the absence of a gross anatomic abnormality. Second, the dietary supplements used were thiamine, riboflavin, niacinamide, and iron—factors almost invariably missing from poor diets, particularly those poor in protein. This experiment, then, might tend to separate the effects of poor diet from the effects of the trace materials found in good foods. Unfortunately, no data are available about other differences in results in the two groups. Furthermore, supplementation was offered late in pregnancy, and only the latter parts of gestation could be affected. Even so, this approach, if verified, may have some practicality, in that food fortification is easier than changing the dietary habits of an entire population, although the latter method is unquestionably superior.

INTERRELATIONSHIP OF FACTORS AFFECTING THE FETUS

The interdependence of the many agents known to affect the embryo and fetus is more apparent as investigation continues. Our knowledge of antagonism, competition, and interrelationships of drugs, hormones, chromosomal determinants, enzymes, trace elements, amino acids, and vitamins is broadening rapidly. The assurance of balance in dietary supplementation by high quality foods is great, whereas the principal assurance of supplementation by single factors is that imbalance is to be expected.

INTERRELATIONSHIP OF NUTRITIVE FACTORS

Long ago it was said that no professor's hemispheres could supply adequate nutrition to the infant as well as the mother's own mammary hemispheres. Perhaps this remark is the clinician's way of saying that the demands of growth reveal rapidly almost any defect of nutrition. Although the pregnant woman ingests foods not only to maintain herself but to store some elements and support the growth of her uterus, placenta, membranes, and baby, it is the baby who, once out of the uterus, has the greatest demands and serves as the best example. Although artificial feeding of human infants is safe today, and the results are comparable with natural feeding, the history of difficulties in preparation of safe, adequate substitutes for natural feeding is punctuated by difficulties with anemia, digestibility, increased susceptibility to rickets and to infections, chloride acidosis, hyperphosphatemia, tetany, and pyridoxine deficiency. Debate on the various constituents of artificial feedings continues. No doubt exists about the value of controversy backed by careful observation of controlled studies. Our need is for properly developed and properly challenged evidence. In the entire field of nutrition, good evidence, at least so far, is slow to unfold and not easy to interpret. The principal lessons to be learned by surveying the mass of new information on interrelationships of nutritive factors are a humble respect for nutritive balance in foods and a healthy skepticism of indiscriminate administration of single supplements.

DIETARY PROBLEMS IN THE UNITED STATES

Although our food consumption as a nation statistically proves us to have the best fed population on earth, and although surveys of nutrition in pregnancy in the United States are commonly negative because of an insufficient number of ill-nourished mothers, some segments of our childbearing population take borderline or lesser amounts of high quality foods. The incidence of abnormalities in the reproductive gamut of these people has been increased; however, some studies[16] indicate that it may be reducible by dietary supplementation. At least four barriers to easing the problem exist: eating habits passed from generation to generation; high cost of some commonly recommended, good quality foods; social pressures from companions; and ineffective lay education. Several studies have shown that, even with marked improvement of economic status, poor dietary habits tend to persist.[17] It is true that some commonly recommended, high quality foods, particularly animal protein, are more expensive; however, a casual stroll through a grocery store can be reassuring. A quart of whole milk costs about the same as a carton of six small bottles of carbonated beverage, and dry skim milk is still less expensive. The same weight of standard brands of peanut butter versus jelly or jam sells for the same price. Perhaps some of the social pressures on the prematernal group compound the problem. The popularity of the soft drink—chips-candy bar luncheon and snack and the current demands of clothing styles for extreme slenderness can wreak nutritional havoc on the prematernal teen-ager, who is pressed on the one hand by growth needs and on the other by the demands of pregnancy. Some realistic competition could be given the pop-and-chips regimen by milk dispensers; fruit, sandwich, and low-priced nut dispensers could compete with candy bar, chewing gum, and chips machines. These competitive devices exist and are occasionally observed in commercial use on the American scene. An effective program of lay education could make the battle of the commercial machines at least self-supporting and, even better, begin to break some poor patterns of eating at home. A more effective program of lay education is needed. Skilled personnel trained to break the inertia of the problem need to be found, and medical school programs must, because of the place of the physician in society, lead this nurture of the prophylactic concepts of reproduction, growth and development, and health and environment.

ROLE OF PLACENTA IN FETAL PROBLEMS

Evidence of the effect of maternal nutrition on the fetus is often studied, but the connecting link between mother and fetus, the placenta, has had little attention. We examine the mother by indirection, the fetus as allowed, and leave the all-important conveyor in dim light. The placentas of women with renal disease, hypertension, diabetes, and true toxemia are often abnormal, and the fetuses of these pregnancies are known, by any criterion, to have problems. The role of the placenta in true toxemia of pregnancy still is debated, even as a possible cause, and the role of the placenta in the fetal problems of abnormal pregnancy has received little consideration. Therefore, it is not unexpected that scanty mention as been made of placental abnormalities in otherwise normal pregnancies producing abnormal fetuses. The concept that placental insufficiency is responsible for the syndrome of postmaturity has aroused interest.[18] Flexner and co-workers[19] reported marked differences in placental blood flow in various abnormal pregnancy states. Recent observations suggest that, because of intrauterine malnutrition, placental abnormalities per se may play a role in some instances of prematurity and immaturity.[20] It might seem justified to speculate that abnormalities of placental function may be of far greater significance than so far supposed.

PROBLEMS IN CLASSIFYING NEONATES

The newborn infant is judged by the crudest methods. Marked individual differences in so-called normal infants are found, and none but the grosser structural abnormalities, particularly the important ones of the cardiac, renal, and nervous systems, are identifiable during the neonatal period. Although weight is used as a standard reference point, it is a poor index whether used for maturity, growth, or body composition. The wide variability of total body water in the newborn infant has been demonstrated by Friis-Hansen[21] but no general agreement about the significance of this variability has been reached by clinicians. Little use has been made of normal growth curves for length in early life, even though serial measurement of length is a better index of true growth. In addition, the pitfalls of differing body composition are excluded. Good methods for estimating iron stores of the individual infant are lacking, and no safe, practical, and generally accepted means of estimating calcium stores or body protein mass in the newborn infant are available. Tedious individual studies of small numbers of infants have recorded large individual differences in retentions of these basic substances. These various differences serve to underline some of our inadequacies to judge the newborn infant, even under the best of circumstances. Pregnancy histories including incidence of anemia, toxemia, and premature births, age of mother, number of pregnancies, and defective dietary habits are useful for planning each infant's nutritional management, but they can only be used circuitously to judge the adequacy of the gestation by its product. Repeated examinations through the first years of life, with special attention to linear growth and the rapid development of the nervous system in all its functions, are needed before an accurate opinion of an infant can be made. However, this opinion fails to separate the intrauterine from the extrauterine factors. Practical methods and normal standards must be established to provide a meaningful classification of infants in the newborn period.

SUMMARY

Loss of human life in the newborn period is the third leading medical cause of death in the United States. The problems of reproduction—sterility and abortion, premature or immature birth and stillbirth, toxemia, labor problems, anemia in the mother during pregnancy and, in the first year, in the offspring, as well as malformations and neurological disorders of function—can be related and considered together.

Prematurity, immaturity, surviving malformed children, unnecessary maternal illness during pregnancy and puerperium (including failure of natural feeding) make a tremendous and, in large part, needless burden. Some neurological defects in children, the convulsive, mentally deficient, and so-called cerebral palsied, may be related to nutritional factors, and human and animal studies suggest that all defects enumerated here can arise from nutritional deficiencies. However, injurious agents other than nutritional deficiencies can produce reproductive problems indistinguishable from those of nutritional origin. The same deficit of nutrition may produce many different effects on the reproductive gamut, depending on timing, severity, and duration of the deficit.

No single element of nutrition holds the key. Balance of foodstuffs, with emphasis on high quality foods, would seem to be the preferred approach. Effective nutritional protection of the fetus begins long before conception and must continue throughout the childbearing period. Further investigation of the role of the placenta in the reproductive process seems in order, and better methods and normal standards for the evaluation of newborn infants are needed. A long-range educational problem about the value of nutritional protection is needed for the coming generation, in medical schools, and for the public at large. The nutritional approach to the problems of reproduction can be more effectively used, both in practice and in investigation.

REFERENCES

[1] Lilienfeld, A. M., and Pasamanick, B. Association of Maternal and Fetal Factors with Development of Epilepsy: Abnormalities in prenatal and paranatal periods. *J. A. M. A.* **155**:719–724 (June 19) 1954.

[2] Smith, C. A. Effect of wartime starvation in Holland upon pregnancy and its product. *Am. J. Obst. & Gynec.* **53**:599–608 (April) 1947. [3] Nowak, J. Häufigkeit der Missgeburten in den Nachkriegsjahren 1945–1949, *Zentralbl. Gynak.* **72**:1313–1328, 1950. [4] Aresin, N., and Sommer, K. H. Missbildungen und Umweltfaktoren, ibid. **72**:1329–1336, 1950. [5] Antonov, A. N. Children born during siege of Leningrad in 1942. *J. Pediat.* **30**:250–259 (March) 1947.

[6] Ebbs, J. H. Tisdall, F. F., and Scott, W. A. Influence of prenatal diet on mother and child. *J. Nutrition* 22:515–526 (Nov.) 1941. [7] Woodhill, J. M., Van Den Berg, A. S., Burke, B. S., and Stare, F. J. Nutrition studies of pregnant Australian women. *Am. J. Obst. & Gynec.* **70**:987–1009 (Nov.) 1955. [8] Burke, B. S. Nutrition during pregnancy: Review. *J. Am. Dietet. A.* **20**:735–741 (Dec.) 1944.

[9] Hogan, A. G. Nutrition. *Ann. Rev. Biochem.* 22:299–318, 1953.

[10] Malpas, P. J. Incidence of human malformations and significance of changes in maternal environment in their causation. *J. Obst. & Gynaec. Brit. Emp.* **44**:434–454 (June) 1937.

[11] Whitely, J. R.; O'Dell, B. L., and Hogan, A. G. Effect of diet on maze learning in second generation rats: Folic acid deficiency. *J. Nutrition* **45**:153–160 (Sept.) 1951. [12] Harrell, R. F.; Woodyard, E. R.; and Gates, A. I. Influence of vitamin supplementation of diets of pregnant and lactating women on intelligence of their offspring. *Metabolism* **5**:555–562 (Sept.) 1956.

[13] Warkany, J. Congenital malformations induced by maternal dietary deficiency: Experiments and their interpretation. *Harvey Lect.* (1952–1953) **48**:89–109, 1954.

[14] Wilson, J. G., and Barch, S. Fetal death and mal-development resulting from maternal vitamin A deficiency in rat. *Proc. Soc. Exper. Biol. & Med.* **72**: 687–693 (Dec.) 1949.

[15] Pfaltz, H., and Severinghaus, E. L. Effects of vitamin deficiencies on fertility, course of pregnancy, and embryonic development in rats. *Am. J. Obst & Gynec.* 72:265–276 (Aug.) 1956.

[16] Balfour, M. I. Supplementary feeding in pregnancy. *Lancet* **1**:208–211 (Feb. 12) 1944. References 3*a* and 6*b*.

[17] Ferguson, J. H., and Hinson, M. L. Importance of protein in maternal diets: and charity hospital survey. *J. Louisiana M. Soc.* **105**:18–21 (Jan.) 1953.

[18] Nesbitt, R. E. L., Jr. Prolongation of pregnancy: A review. *Obst. & Gynec. Surv.* **10**:311–362 (June) 1955. Clifford, S. H. Postmaturity—with placental dysfunction: Clinical syndrome and pathologic findings. *J. Pediat.* **44**:1–13 (Jan.) 1954.

[19] Flexner, L. B., and others. Permeability of human placenta to sodium in normal and abnormal pregnancies and supply of sodium to human fetus as determined with radioactive sodium. *Am. J. Obst. & Gynec.* **55**:469–480 (March) 1948.

[20] Hepner, R. Unpublished data.

[21] Friis-Hansen, B. Changes in body water compartments during growth. *Acta paediat.* (supp. 110) **46**:1–68. (Jan.) 1957.

9

IMPLICATIONS OF FETAL BEHAVIOR AND ENVIRONMENT FOR ADULT PERSONALITIES*

LESTER W. SONTAG

Until recently, most *in vivo* studies of the human fetus have been designed to assess through electrocardiographic tracings its state of viability and to predict its survival chances. However, a number of studies, both in laboratory animals and in human beings, have been designed to explore the vulnerability of the fetus to changes in his environment. Environmental changes which have been explored include changes in the mother's emotional state, the introduction of drugs and toxic substances, the use of sounds of different frequencies both on the fetus and as a matter of changing the maternal environment.

Ader and Conklin (1963) have demonstrated that pregnant rats fondled for 10 minutes a day during pregnancy produced offspring which at maturity were less "neurotic" than the offspring of continually caged mothers. Liberman (1963) has mimicked emotional stress in mice by the injection of hydrocortisone, epinephrine and norepinephrine and has produced "neurotic" mice. W. R. Thompson (1957) has demonstrated that the production by a conflictual situation of a neurosis in pregnant rats resulted in offspring which showed "neurotic" characteristics at adolescence. W. D. Thompson and Sontag (1956) have demonstrated that audiogenic seizures induced in pregnant white rats at the ninth and tenth day of pregnancy resulted in offspring which at adolescence exhibited a poorer pattern of maze learning than did controls. In most of these experiments, neurotic behavior was assessed by measurements of frequency of urination and defecation and by open field tests.

The remainder of my paper I shall devote to the work carried on at the Fels Research Institute for the Study of Human Development in the years from 1932 to the present. It was designed to explore the behavior of the

---

* From *Annuals of the New York Academy of Sciences*, 1966, *132*, 782–786. Reprinted with permission from the author and the New York Academy of Sciences.

This research was supported in part by Research Grant HD-00868 from the National Institutes of Health, United States Public Health Service.

human fetus, its developmental progress, individual differences, capabilities, perceptions and responses to stimuli in a normal situation during the last four months of pregnancy. It was designed also to measure certain characteristics of fetal behavior and the environment, as represented by the mother, and its relationship to postnatal behavior and even adolescent and adult behavior, although the extended life span of human beings makes the latter objective an exotic and almost impossibly ambitious one.

FETAL MOVEMENT

Our original work on fetal movement was done on a group of 60 or so house subjects, or "living-in" subjects, and 200 extramural subjects whose fetal activity was measured for a period of two hours a week. During this two-hour period each week, some 60 or 70 samples of heart rate in 10-beat segments were recorded. We started our fetal movement study with an apparatus consisting of four rubber bags sewed into a cloth container, each connected with a tambour and a recording drum. Over this group of rubber bags, which corresponded to the four quadrants of the abdomen, we placed a plaster of Paris cast which had been made especially for the subject and was replaced with a new one each week as the fetus grew. This system was then inflated with air to the pressure of a few millimeters of water. When a movement of the fetus occurred, air in one bag was subjected to increased pressure by a presenting elbow, knee, head or what not, with a corresponding decrease in pressure in another bag. This combination of four bags and four tambours permitted us to rule out the constantly present respiratory movements of the mother. After using this equipment for a time, we began simultaneously having the mother record, by a system of buttons which activated kymograph pens, the periods during which she felt activity. We found the correlation between the mother's recording and the mechanically recorded samples was well above 0.8. Because we wanted access to the abdomen at frequent intervals to make heart rate recordings, we, therefore, eventually discarded the mechanical recording device for fetal activity. We discovered early that there were three differential types of fetal activity: (1) the sharp kicking or punching movement of the extremities which increase steadily from six months to birth; (2) a squirming or writhing slow movement which is at its maximum frequency during the third to fourth month before birth and declines steadily from there on until birth; and (3) a sharp, convulsive movement which others have described as a fetal hiccup or spasm of the diaphragm. Such fetal hiccups occurred in 33 of 48 subjects.

As anyone who has ever concerned himself with the care of pregnant women knows, there is a tremendous individual difference in activity level between different fetuses. It occurs not only as the fetuses of one woman are compared with another, but from one fetus to another in succeeding pregnancies of the same woman. Women say, "This one is not going to be anything like little Mary. She hardly kicked at all. This one is kicking all the time." Such statements are literally almost true.

These differences in fetal activity level appear to be predictive of the degree of activity, restlessness and, sometimes, resistance to handling, etc. of the infants during the first year of life. Richards and Nelson (1938) have also found that the active fetuses are more advanced at six months than are the relatively inactive ones as measured by their performance on the Gesell tests. This increased motor development may possibly be the product of greater prenatal activity or it may be another expression of it at a later stage of development. There is also a small but significant correlation between the body type of the newborn infant as expressed as weight over length cubed and the level of activity as measured during the last two months of pregnancy. This finding seems reasonable since calories used in exercise will not be stored as fat.

SOUND

There has been no adequate exploration of the ability of the fetus to perceive sound, and the way it may react to various kinds of sound. In the 1920's a German investigator reported a number of cases of expectant mothers who complained that they could not go to symphony concerts because of the greatly intensified activity level of the babies they were carrying. Another reported a case of an expectant mother who found that the applause of the audience at the symphony caused such extreme fetal activity that it was painful. When a small block of wood is placed over the abdomen of a woman eight months pregnant and a doorbell clapper is permitted to strike at the rate of 120 vibrations per second, there is, in about 90 percent of cases, an immediate and convulsive response on the part of the fetus. The response is in the form of violent kicking and moving. There is also an increase in heart rate. This increased heart rate occurs even when, in a small percentage of cases, there is no movement response. This startle reflex is, we believe, the same response as is the Moro reflex after birth.

One of the early observations we have made seems particularly germane in terms of the animal experimental work which I have described earlier. It is, that severe maternal emotions, during the last trimester of pregnancy at least, do cause an immediate and profound increase in the activity level of the fetus. We were, as a matter of pure fortune, presented with several examples of this situation. In one instance a young woman carrying her first baby, which we had been studying weekly in terms of activity and heart rate level, took refuge at the Fels Institute building one evening because her husband had just suffered a psychotic break and was threatening to kill her. She was terrified, felt alone and did not know where to turn for help. She came into the Institute, and we gave her a bed and room for the night. When she complained after a few minutes conversation that the kicking of her fetus was so violent as to be painful, we proceeded to record the activity level. It was more than ten-fold what it had been in the weekly sessions prior to this incident. Another case came to our attention when a woman we had been studying, lost her husband in an automobile accident. Again, the violence of the activity and the frequency of movement of the fetus increased by a factor of more than ten. During the period of ten years, we managed to collect eight such dramatic incidents, all showing the same phenomena of extreme increase in fetal activity in response to grief, fear and anxiety. Children of such mothers (who suffered their emotional trauma late in pregnancy and not early) showed, of course, no congenital defect. In general, they were, however, irritable, hyperactive, tended to have frequent stools, and three of them had marked feeding problems.

FETAL HEART RATE

Every physician is aware, of course, that there are continuous variations in heart rate during rest in individuals of almost any age, although this variability does tend to decrease with extreme age. A part of this great fluctuation, or lability, is associated with respiration. It is the sinus arrhythmia of respiration. The remainder, however, is not. The degree of this variation from second to second seems to be characteristic of each individual. A boy who has a high lability score at age 6 will also have a high lability score at 16 or 26. Lacey and Lacey of our laboratories have studied such phenomena in a considerable number of children and adults. Lacey and coauthors have studied possible relationships between this physiological variable and certain personality variables. Using three-hour interviews as a basis for rating a variety of personality characteristics, they found that the level of dependency material was much greater in labiles than in stabiles. A sex difference was apparent in their material. Cardiac labile males were more reluctant to depend on love objects, and they had more conflict over dependency than did the stabiles. They were more compulsive, indecisive and introspective. We have no explanation, of course, for these relationships. That these physiological correlates do exist, however, is fascinating. They make the question of what part of the incorporation of life experiences is a matter of the experiences themselves and what part is determined by gene-determined, or prenatally acquired physiological characteristics.

This suggestion that there may be a physiological component of personality or behavior brings to the fore the question of whether this constitutional gene-determined characteristic is really gene-determined or whether it is the result of differences in fetal environment. Differences in cardiac lability may very well be an indicator of the differences in physiological operation which are accountable for a part of the differences in behavior patterns and personality of individuals.

The above findings have led us to become interested in whether large fluctuations in *fetal* heart rate are related to the degree of lability and stability of the heart rate of the *adult*. Unfortunately, the problem is a difficult one for many reasons. To have the same individual and the same data available on him during his eighth fetal month and his twentieth year presents problems. If, then, we compound these problems by the fact that the fetus is an uncooperative research subject and will not rest while we take his heart rate, the magnitude of the problem is obvious. We do have a few preliminary figures which are much more intriguing than conclusive. On 12 fetuses (which are now adults), we have 400 or more short samples of fetal heart rate although not necessarily at rest. By calculating the standard deviation of the heart rate for each fetus from these 10-beat samples, we arrive at a measure of its variability, a measure comparable to a considerable degree to the variability of heart rate measured on these individuals as adults. It is possible, therefore, to make some comparison of the variability of heart rate of these individuals as 8-month fetuses with the resting variability of their heart rates at age 20 years. The scatter diagram of the lability of heart rate of fetuses, plotted against the lability of the heart rate of the individuals as adults, is most interesting. There is a 5:5 and 1:1 distribution. Because the number of cases is so small, a rho of 52 significant at the 0.05 level of confidence is suggestive rather than conclusive in indicating that there is a tendency for cardiac labiles during fetal life to be cardiac labiles in adult life. On the basis of the correlation between physiological variables in the form of cardiac lability-stability and personality variables already described, we are interested, then, in seeing whether certain aspects of personality in adults may be predicted from a constitutional factor measurable during the fetal period.

Another individual difference in autonomic nervous system function is the degree of cardiac rate response to a stress situation. Lacey and Lacey (1958) have found that cardiac response to different kinds of stress in a given individual is comparable. One individual does vary, of course, tremendously from another, however, in the degree of response that he exhibits. Lacey and his coauthors have found that there are also personality correlates; in this instance, there are differences in cognitive style, or ways of thinking and perceiving between strong reactors and weak. In general, these strong and weak cardiac reactors exhibit differences in perception of affect. In picture test situations, the strong reactors tend to attribute emotion or feeling to the human figure and the situations which they are viewing. They also tend to exhibit much more imagination in what they see or what they describe. They project feeling and emotion into the pictures. The low reactors, in addition, show evidence of a much higher degree of emotional and behavioral control in all kinds of situations. They are less likely to act out their emotions than high reactors are.

Fetuses differ in their response to a stress situation. In the instance of the sound stress applied with a door knocker, there was a marked difference between fetuses both in degree of cardiac acceleration and movement. We are currently interested in and are studying the relationship of the magnitude of this response during the eighth and ninth fetal months to responses to stress situations many years after the individual has emerged into the world. I am not in the position to give you any data which I would consider significant at this time. Perhaps, it is worth while, however, to tell you what we are trying to do.

SUMMARY

I have described some variables in the fetus which can be measured without severely disturbing him or damaging him. I have called attention to certain responses the fetus makes to his maternal, or outside, environment. I have indicated that there are some prenatal predictors of early postnatal environment or behavior, and that there very possibly may be predictors of some behavior or personality at a much later age. These observations are necessarily different as is the methodology from that used in the animal experiments quoted, but both are designed to assess the effects of prenatal environment on the behavior of the offspring.

REFERENCES

Ader, R., & Conklin, P. Handling of pregnant rats: Effects on emotionality on their offspring. *Science,* 1963, *142,* 411–412.

Lacey, J. I., & Lacey, B. C. The relationship of resting autonomic activity to motor impulsivity. *Res. Pub. Assoc. Res. Nerv. Ment. Dis.,* 1958, *36,* 144–209.

Lacey, J. I., Kagan, J., Lacey, B. C., & Moss, H. A. The visceral level: Situational determinants and behavioral correlates of autonomic response patterns. In P. J. Knapp (Ed.). *Expression of the emotions in man.* New York: International Universities Press, 1962.

Lieberman, M. Early developmental stress and later behavior. *Science,* 1963, *141,* 824–825.

Richards, T. W. & Nelson, V. L. Studies in mental development II. Analysis of abilities tested at the age of six months by the Gesell Schedule. *Journal of Genetic Psychology,* 1938, *52,* 327–331.

Thompson, W. R. Influence of prenatal and maternal anxiety on emotionality in young rats. *Science,* 1957, *125,* 698–699.

Thompson, W. D., Jr., & Sontag, L. W. Behavioral effects in the offspring of rats subjected to audiogenic seizure during the gestational period. *Journal of comparative and physiological Psychology,* 1956, *49,* 454–456.

PART III

Infancy and Early Childhood

INTRODUCTION

BIRTH DESIGNATES the point at which the human organism is expelled from the protective and nourishing confines of the womb, embarks into a markedly different environment, and begins its progressive development toward adulthood. The infant, having survived prenatal existence and the potentially traumatic effects of the birth experience (e.g., maternal medications used during labor and delivery, anoxia, Caesarean section, breech presentation, etc.) will nevertheless continue to maintain for some time its condition of dependence on the mother. Moreover, the hazardous conditions facing the newly born infant are not simply restricted to those associated with the birth process. The type and quality of caretaking, the family constellation, and the cultural experiences to which the organism will be exposed throughout development will all have their effects on its development. As the infant progresses developmentally, he will be required to decrease the extent of his dependence on his adult caretakers. This progressive development from intrauterine biological dependence to infantile emotional attachment to adulthood is extraordinarily complex and at times a hazardous developmental process.

You will recall from the preceding unit that Watson's environmentalism served to place supreme responsibility for the organism's development in the hands of parents who were thought to be in complete control of the reinforcing properties of the early environment. Little attention was directed to the possibility that the infant might be directing some of the parent's behavior. In Chapter 10, Professor Kessen of Yale University questions the significance of past psychological theory for infant behavior. What impact has psychological theory had on the study of infancy? We previously noted Love's (1969) conclusion that Watson's influence on at least one aspect of development, mental development, was of little significance. Nevertheless, in as much as theory plays a major role in determining the kinds of questions researchers ask, the methods which they choose in order to investigate those questions, and the conclusions they draw, we can conclude that environmentalism did in fact exert an influence on the psychology of infancy. As Professor Kessen notes in Chapter 10:

> The model of the child which was drawn from Pavlov through Watson, and supported by the development of learning psychology in the United States, was of a recipient organism—a reactive one. . . . This remains technically a sound view, but the effect of it on the psychology of the infant was to diminish our appreciation of how complicated and subtle is the child. (p. 173)

In contrast to Watson's rejection of individual differences, contemporary infant theorists and researchers are devoting considerable energy and resource to the study of individual differences with concern for the predictive developmental significance of these differences.

Infant state. In common with many constructs used in psychology, "state" or "arousal level" has been defined in a variety of ways. Nevertheless, each of the definitions has in common reference to a momentary level of functioning which can be specified by both behavioral and physiological parameters. According to Brackbill and Fitzgerald (1969), ". . . *level of arousal* or *state* refer to the organisms' overall level of functioning at any given period of time on a continuum ranging from deep sleep to awake, alert, and active." (p. 174). Just as there have been advanced a variety of definitions of state, there have been a number of rating scales designed to assess these momentary levels of functioning. An example of such a rating scale for state is provided in Table 1. Note that this scale, as do others, provides for assessing both behavioral and physiological aspects of the various states of the infant.

It is important to emphasize that the definition of "state" refers to a *momentary* level of functioning and that both behavioral and physiological responses must be considered. Merely to observe and rate the general *activity* of one infant and contrast it with the *activity* of another infant may lead one to spurious conclusions. Gordon and Bell (1961) observed similar activity levels in infants with perinatal central nervous system complications and in infants lacking these complications. They conclude that it is necessary to guard against inappropriately generalizing the significance of infant activity, particularly when activity measures are obtained from infants in noncorresponding states. For example, Bell (1966) found that following an anthropometric examination, breast fed newborns were characterized by higher levels of arousal than were newborns who were bottle fed. Thus, if one were assessing state of the infant without prior knowledge of the type of feeding practice, one might be led to incorrect interpretations of the infant's behavior or performance. Knowing that infants' performance may be affected by the method of feeding would allow one to make appropriate corrections when

TABLE 1

A Scale for Rating State*

State Number	*State Name*	*Description*
1	Quiet sleep	The infant's whole body gives the appearance of general muscular relaxation. This is interrupted periodically, however, by brief startles of an apparently spontaneous nature. The infant's eyes are usually closed. Respiration is regular and is somewhat slower than in active sleep.
2	Active sleep	Characteristic of this stage are diffuse movements of relatively frequent occurrence. These movements may involve the whole body but are most typically seen in the extremities and in the muscles of the face in the form of twitches, grimaces, smiling, sucking, and the like. In addition, one can sometimes see conjugate movements of the eyeballs. (As in state 1, the eyelids are usually closed.) Respiration is considerably more irregular and is somewhat faster than in quiet sleep.
3	Drowsiness	During this stage the infant's motor behavior is often much like that of sleepy people riding subway trains: he relaxes more and more as he gradually falls asleep, then suddenly jerks awake. His eyelids flutter, and his eyes, when visible, have a glassy appearance. Respiration is more apt to be marked by regularity than irregularity.
4	Quiet awake	There is little gross motor activity, i.e., movements involving the whole body, although there may be some movements of the extremities and face. The baby's eyes are open and in Wolff's terms (1966) are characterized by a bright, shiny appearance. The major difference between this state and the other two waking states is that this is a *peaceful* state. Accordingly, the vocalizations that occur during this state are not of an "unhappy" variety. Respiration is relatively regular, though less regular than in quiet sleep.
5	Active awake	This state is marked by a considerable amount of gross motor activity. For example, as an infant becomes unhappy he may begin to writhe. Respiration is often quite irregular. Within the spectrum of vocalizations occurring during this period are those of the cranky, fussy variety.
6	Crying awake	The criteria for this state are the same as those for the preceding state except that in addition the infant is crying. (He may or may not be producing tears; most very young infants do not.) The lower limit of crying is defined as protesting of a definite, sustained nature.

* Brackbill & Fitzgerald (1969). Reprinted with permission from Academic Press.

analyzing the behavior in question. One early investigator on the basis of her studies, concluded that state was of such importance that it be taken into account in all infant research.

Pacification. What can be done to quiet the baby? This is a recurrent question in every household in which a young infant resides. Moreover, it is a question of pacifying the infant and the familiar hard rubber pacifier can be effectively used with many infants for this end. Nevertheless, many parents object to the use of a pacifier either on the grounds that the pacifier is difficult to keep clean, or merely because they dislike seeing their baby with a blue plastic circle covering its mouth. On the other hand, many babies will not accept a pacifier whether parents wish to use it or not. Thus, a question of practical as well as theoretical concern is: are there any other ways to pacify an infant? Rephrased, this question asks what techniques are available for reducing the level of arousal or state of the infant, from one of crying rage to one of quiet awake or quiet sleep. Moreover, since every mother knows that one effective way to pacify an infant is to pick him up, cuddle, rock, sing or play with him, an additional question is raised. Are there any ways to pacify an infant which do not require direct mother-infant interaction?

One very effective technique for quieting an infant is to swaddle him. In one study swaddling was shown to be an effective method for inducing sleep and reducing the frequency of startle responses (Lipton, Steinschneider & Richmond, 1965). Giacoman (1969) also observed reduced arousal when infants were swaddled. Nevertheless, poor swaddling may be worse than no swaddling at all. Wolff (1966) observed that badly swaddled infants were more irritable than were infants who were properly swaddled or infants who were not swaddled. However, providing rich exogenous stimulation (produced from outside the organism) in the form of tactile comfort is not the only way that one can pacify infants.

Sound and light have also been found to be effective stimuli for pacifying infants. In one recent study, Brackbill and her associates (Brackbill, Adams, Crowell & Gray, 1966) found lower heart rates and general motor activity, more stable respiration and heart rates, less crying, and more rapid onset of sleep when infants were exposed to any one of three auditory stimuli (a metronome beating at 72 beats per minute, a tape recording of a heart beating at 72 beats per minute, and a phonographic recording of lullabies). Athough there were no differences among the three types of auditory stimuli in their quieting effects, any one of them proved to be a more effective pacifier than a no sound condition. Since it is the case that tactile, thermal, visual, or auditory stimuli act to lower infant level of arousal, might one obtain even more dramatic and effective results if these stimulus modalities were used in combination. Indeed, just such cumulative effects have been reported (Brackbill, 1970; Brackbill & Fitzgerald, 1969). Brackbill (1970) exposed one-month-old infants to five different stimulatory conditions: no stimulation (defined as the absence of the experimental stimuli), and continuous stimulation in the auditory, visual, proprioceptive-tactile, and temperature modalities. The four stimulus modalities were presented to infants using a design that permitted the use of all combinations of the four. As expected, Brackbill found that the effect of continuous stimulation was to lower level of arousal. Moreover, the effect was cumulative across modalities, i.e., combinations of proprioceptive-tactile, visual, auditory and temperature stimuli lowered arousal more effectively than the combination of only three of the stimuli; combinations of three stimuli lowered arousal more effectively than did combinations of two, and so forth. When contrasting the effects of continuous stimulation on the state of the infant, it was found that the extreme ends of the state continuum (see Table 1) were most markedly affected by continuous stimulation; i.e., infants slept more and cried less when exposed to continuous sensory stimulation.

Returning to our original question, what techniques are available for quieting the infant independent of direct mother-infant interaction, there appear to be many if one considers the range of possible ways to provide continuous tactile, auditory or visual stimulation. Brackbill and Fitzgerald (1969) have previously detailed the advantages of using continuous stimulation when infants are irritable, colicky or ill. In each condition, the infant may be driven by such a demand for exogenous stimulation that failing to receive it, he resorts to excessive endogenous stimulation (produced from within the organism); his thrashing and crying not only serve to upset parents but prevent him from securing sufficient sleep so vital for combating the effects of virus infections, etc. Moreover, these authors point out the potential significance of continuous stimulation for the prematurely born infant whose very survival may rest on its ability to remain in a relatively quiescent state. Providing continuous stimulation to quiet one's infant during those times when parents' patience is worn thin, or when mothers are upset and anxious, can be no more dramatically pointed out than by the following:

> . . . techniques of pacification are important tools in the parental armamentarium of effective ways of coping with children. In view of their importance it is unfortunate that they are outside the ken of many parents. Helfer and Kempe estimate that there are at least 30,000 cases of battered children each year in the United States (Brackbill, 1969). In these cases the most frequently reported precipitating cause is the child's prolonged crying, which the parents are at a loss to deal with and can tolerate no longer. (Brackbill, 1970, p. 374).

How much easier for all concerned it would be to turn on the radio or lights than to beat the child into submission, or death.

Handling. Unless the young infant's bottle is propped up on a blanket or he is fed via some automated mechanical device, it is a truism that mother-infant interaction in the feeding situation is equally a case of mother-infant interaction involving every functional sensory modality of the infant. The infant is likely to receive as a result of being handled, a variety of stimulation including vestibular, auditory, visual, proprioceptive-tactile, thermal, and taste. Kessen and Mandler (1961) suggest that the pacifying properties of handling (rocking) may be related to the similarity between the periodicity of rocking (back and forth, back and forth, etc.) and the infants visceral rhythms. Advancing the hypothesis that infants have a need for kinesthetic stimulation, Kulka, Fry and Goldstein (1960) found that handling served to reduce the incidence of crying for which there was no discernable cause. Other investigators have suggested that handling is drive reducing (Gordon & Foss, 1966; Ourth & Brown, 1961) in as much as crying shows such marked reduction when the infant is handled. Casler (1965) suggests that extra tactile stimulation is beneficial to infants who are deprived of "normal" handling experiences. Institutionalized infants, given extra tactile stimulation, showed marked improvement on all subscales of the Gesell Developmental Schedules with the exception of the motor scale. In addition to providing rich sensory stimulation, handling has been shown to facilitate the infant's ability to visually scan and explore the environment (Korner & Grobstein, 1966). Infants who were placed on the shoulder opened their eyes, became quietly alert and scanned the environment.

Another issue raised by Professor Kessen in his overview of infant research concerns the reciprocal relations between caretaker and infant and the extent to which individual differences substantially increase the complexity of mother-infant interaction. Studies of mother-infant interaction during handling provide evidence that indeed individual characteristics of the infant are important considerations for early mother-child interaction.

Schaffer and Emerson in their 1964 monograph concerning the development of social attachments observed that not all infants seemed to prefer (require?) identical amounts of handling. They report a follow-up study investigating this observation (Schaffer & Emerson, 1964). Two groups of infants were identified: cuddlers and noncuddlers. A cuddler was identified as an infant who responded positively and consistently to maternal attempts to cuddle and who actively sought cuddling experiences. Noncuddlers were infants who actively resisted close physical contact. More interesting from the interaction viewpoint, was the identification of handling and nonhandling mothers, i.e., mothers who sought cuddling experiences with their infants versus mothers who made little attempt to engage their infants in close physical contact. They found that cuddlers who had nonhandling mothers more frequently sought contact experiences from other members of the family as well as persisting in their demands for contact from their mothers. On the other hand, handling mothers when rejected by their noncuddling infants seem to have easily adjusted their caretaking behaviors to the *infant's* style of life. More recently, Ball (1969) found that mothers of female cuddlers supplied handling in the form of petting and holding behaviors, while mothers who described their infants as noncuddlers evidence considerably less close physical contact experiences.

Thus, considering the pacifying effects of sensory stimulation and the suggested importance of handling (or nonhandling), it appears that infants do possess something akin to a need for stimulation which they seek to satisfy initially through care-soliciting behaviors. In any event, it seems clear that by reducing endogenous stimulation, the human infant is more responsive to exogenous stimulation and it is an interesting feature of nature that mother is the one who is chiefly responsible for providing endogenous reducing exogenous stimulation.

Learning. A third issue raised by Kessen concerns the age at which the infant begins to learn. Can the day to day changes in the infant's behavior be taken as evidence that learning is occurring? Perhaps, but attempting to partial out maturational and adaptive influences on the young infant's daily activities from those due to learning would be a difficult task. Are we then to conclude that all the previous discussion of the importance of sensory stimulation and mother-infant interaction has no long-term effect on the infant, i.e., is of no developmental signficance since learning has not occurred? If in fact the infant is primed through a species specific mechanism to be highly responsive to stimuli and if the effect of that stimulation is of adaptive significance for the infant, might it not be possible that in addition to being capable of receiving and reacting behaviorally and physiologically to sensory stimulation, the infant begins to piece things together at an age earlier than heretofore expected? Indeed such seems to be the case.

Studies of infant learning have used both classical and operant methodologies. Classical conditioning of a variety of infant behaviors has been demonstrated including conditioned eyeblinking (Lintz, Fitzgerald & Brackbill, 1967); pupillary reflex dilation and constriction (Fitzgerald, Lintz, Brackbill & Adams, 1967; Brackbill, Fitzgerald & Lintz, 1967), Babkin reflex (Kaye, 1965; Connolly & Stratton, 1969); sucking (Lipsitt, Kaye & Bosack, 1966; Abrahamson, Brackbill, Carpenter & Fitzgerald, 1970); and head turning (Papousek, 1961, 1967).

Similarly, operant procedures have been successfully used with head turning (Siqueland, 1968; Siqueland & Lipsitt, 1966); sucking rate (Stern & Jeffrey, 1965); smiling (Brackbill, 1958); fear responses (Watson & Raynor, 1920); vocalizations (Rheingold, Gewirtz & Ross, 1959; Weisberg, 1963); lever pressing (Weisberg, 1969); and tapping (Simmons, 1964).

Consequently, the critical question is not can the infant learn, but under what conditions can learning be demonstrated? On the other hand, Kessen's question concerning the age at which learning begins remains unanswered. Clearly the young infant is capable of meeting the requirements of laboratory demonstrations of learning at a very young age.

Recently, Siqueland (1969) has suggested that instrumental-operant procedures may be especially effective for studying the young infant's exploratory behavior. He proposes that operant tasks in which the infant has an opportunity to learn that his behavior can in fact induce changes in the environment may be particularly applicable to a broad class of infant behaviors, particularly those which are not as stimulus bound as are the reflexive behaviors of the infant.

One such operant procedure has been called "conjugate reinforcement." As Professors Rovee and Rovee point out in Chapter 11, conjugate reinforcement refers to a "continuously available reinforcing event, the intensity of which is a direct consequence of response rate. Thus, the more rapid responding produces a more intense reward." (Chapter 11, p. 176). In their study, Rovee and Rovee successfully demonstrate conjugate reinforcement of visual exploration in ten-week-old infants. Other investigators have been equally successful using conjugate reinforcement (Lipsitt, Pederson & DeLucia, 1966).

In response to the question, when does learning begin, some preliminary reports from Siqueland's laboratory (1969) suggest that learning may occur at dramatically early ages. He attempted to train prematurely born infants to keep their eyes open in order to receive and maintain one of two classes of stimulation—nonnutritive sucking and auditory feedback. By 5 to 15 days of age premature infants were influenced by the operant conditioning procedures. Recall that Korner and Grobstein (1966) showed that shouldering an infant during handling interactions increased the infant's visual scanning. Extrapolating from Siqueland's findings, it is interesting to speculate on the extent to which particular (and indeed if not all) mother-infant interactions facilitate the learning of early conditioned reactions which might assist the infant's exploration of the environment. Clearly, Professors Rovee and Rovee have shown that conditioned exploratory behavior is possible.

SOCIAL AND EMOTIONAL DEVELOPMENT

In Chapter 12, Professor Ricciuti of Cornell University, presents an extensive and thorough review of current theoretical and empirical concerns regarding infant social and emotional development. Moreover, Ricciuti points out that social and emotional development does not occur in a vacuum. It cannot be considered independent of all other contributing and ongoing developmental processes. Consider, for example, if an infant comes to fear a stranger, his fear response is based first of all on perceiving the stranger as strange (a perceptual-cognitive task), and then retreating to that caretaker whom he has come to identify as a source of comfort (a learning task). As Ricciuti remarks, "perceptual-cognitive and learning processes clearly play a major role in determining what social or emotional responses will be elicited, as well as how such responses will be expressed in behavior." (Chapter 12, p. 198). In addition to summarizing the contemporary status of research concerning the infant's social and emotional development, Ricciuti draws our attention to a variety of theories which seek to explain the motivational dynamics underlying what appear to be spontaneously motivated activities (e.g., play, exploration, curiosity, problem solving) which have troubled traditional psychological theories. Note that these are precisely the behaviors with which Siqueland and the Rovees are concerned. A point made by Kessen in Chapter 10 is that he envisions the emergence of a comparative psychology of infancy. His prognostication finds ample support in Ricciuti's review.

Since it is clear that mother and infant spend considerable time together, it does not seem unreasonable to expect that at some point in time the infant will come to recognize his mother as distinct from nonmother adults. An inference made in psychiatric literature is that the infant does not make such a discrimination between familiar mother and nonfamiliar stranger until the third quarter of the first year of life (Spitz, 1950; Spitz & Wolf, 1946). Nonetheless, information based on behavioral research suggests that recognition occurs at some point earlier in the first year.

As long ago as 1900, Preyer maintained that the infant formed connections by the sixth week of life between his mother's sounds and her face. Canestrini (1913) observed in the first few days of life, differences in behavior when infants attended to their mother's sounds compared to those emitted by strangers. LaRoche and Tcheng (1963), using smiling and laughing as response indicants, found discrimination of mother's voice from stranger's voice in three- and four-month-old infants. Schaffer and Emerson (1964) concluded that mother-stranger discrimination begins sometime during the first three months of life, since infants three months old were already responding differently to mothers compared to strangers as measured by smiling, vocalizations, visual following and/or quieting. Banks and Wolfson (1967), using as their definition of recognition differential responding to mothers compared to strangers, combined auditory and visual presence of mothers versus strangers and found cardiac deceleration to accompany the presence of the infant's mother but not the stranger. In addition, continued increase in heart rate occurred when the infant's mother departed, but not when the stranger left the view of the infant. These differences in cardiac activity were observed in infants as young as six weeks of age! The Banks and Wolfson study suggests the potential value of autonomically regulated responses for infant research involving visually presented stimuli of social significance, a value already discovered by investigators studying visual fixation preferences in young infants (e. g., Kagan, Henker, Hen-tov, Levine, & Lewis, 1966; Lewis, 1966).

Working with adult human *S*s, Hess and Polt (1960) tested the hypothesis that pupillary change could be used as a measure of interest or pleasure value of a visual stimulus. Male college students evidenced greater pupillary dilation while viewing pictures of women than when viewing pictures of men. The reverse was true of females; they had larger pupils while looking at pictures of men. Differences in the presumed interest or pleasure value of the various stimuli were discerned within as well as between sexes. Pupillary reactivity has also been used to study higher mental processes, differences in pupil size occurring during the solving of math problems (Hess & Polt, 1964). Hess, Seltzer, and Shlien (1965), studying heterosexual and homosexual male responses to artistic representations of the human figure found greater pupil dilation among the heterosexual males to pictures of women than to pictures of men. Four of ten homosexual men showed pupillary dilation to pictures of men. In the case of certain aversive stimuli, constriction has been found to characterize pupillary responsiveness, just as dilation characterizes response to interesting or pleasant pictures (Hess, 1965). In an interesting variation to pupillary research, Stass and Wellis (1967) studied the effect of pupil size on person preference in an actual social situation. Attempting to validate Hess's definition of pupillary dilation (i.e., an expression of interest), they found that men and women were attracted to those persons who appeared to be interested in them, i.e., operationally, those whose pupils were artificially dilated compared to those whose pupils were normal.

In Chapter 13 Fitzgerald reports his study which attempted to determine whether the autonomically regulated pupillary reflex could be used to investigate infants' reaction to social and nonsocial visual stimuli. Pupillary activity to five visual stimuli—the subject's mother's face, a female stranger's face, a 4-square checkerboard pattern, a 144-square checkerboard pattern, and a triangle—was studied in 1-, 2-, and 4-month-old infants. Fitzgerald found that differential responding to mother versus stranger occurred in the four-month-old group. Moreover, social stimuli elicited greater pupillary dilation than nonsocial stimuli in the youngest and oldest subjects. Thus, the use of autonomic responses is of potential significance for investigating the social and perhaps the emotional antecedents of more readily observable behaviors of older infants.

PERCEPTION AND COGNITION

One methodological procedure used to study infant visual perception requires the infant to fixate targets which might vary in complexity, novelty, and/or familiarity. In the visual fixation method as developed by Marsden (1903) the observer's task was to record the total amount of time the infant spent looking at a specified target. With this technique, fixation responses were found to appear very early in infant development.

Recently, three particular methods for assessing the infant's perceptual preferences have come into common use. In the first of these (Fantz, 1956), targets are exposed on the ceiling of a chamber while an observer records the infant's reactions through a peephole in the chamber ceiling. Lighting and contrast of the targets with respect to background illumination are adjusted so that tiny images of the targets are mirrored on the infant's cornea. Since the mirrored images are visible to the observer, the observed location of the image relative to the infant's pupil provides a criterion of fixation. The second innovation in the study of visual preferences was provided by Hershenson's (1964) cinematographic method. Using Fantz's technique of corneal reflection together with infrared photography, Hershenson obtains permanent recordings of fixation responses. With proper selection of film and lighting parameters, the image of the target reflected on the infant's cornea is photographed and then systematically measured relative to the pupil of the eye. The degree of overlap of the target on the pupil determines the degree of fixation. With this technique, Salapatek and Kessen (1966) studied visual scanning of triangles in eight-day-old infants. Among other things, they were able to accurately plot the directions of scanning from the photographic records. Horizontal scanning was easier than vertical scanning, although infants scanned in both directions.

The third approach is characterized by the use of multiple response measures for more accurate analysis of infant attentional responding. The advantage of this method is that it allows the infant greater physical mobility while at the same time provides a discrete response—head and eye movement —with which one can measure preferences for visual stimuli as well as other attentional processes in the infant. In addition to head and eye movements, directional heart rate change provides an additional measure of infant attention (Lewis, Myers, Kagan & Grossberg, 1963; Lewis, Kagan & Kalafat, 1966).

The increasing use of multiple response measurement in infant research has had its effect on infant perceptual research. The typical definition of fixation refers to the amount of time the infant fixates on a target. However, since different responses serve different neurophysiological systems, the possibility exists that a response from one modality may yield quite different results than a response from another modality. Indeed, cardiac deceleration and visual fixation have yielded different sorts of information. In addition to fixation measures, Kagan *et al.* (1966) obtain measures of smiling, vocalization, and heart rate in their work concerning infant attention and perception. Lewis *et al.* (1963) found that even though the infant may be judged to be fixating, he may not necessarily be actively attending to the target or actively scanning it. These authors believe that cardiac activity together with fixation measures might be a step in the direction of discovering measures sensitive to the intensity level of infant attention in addition to providing measures of preferential responding. For example, in the Kagan *et al.* (1966) study, there were no differences in fixation time to regular and rearranged human faces, but smiling and cardiac deceleration occurred more frequently to the regular face. Consequently, smiling, vocalizations, directional cardiac activity, fixation, and pupillary reflex activity form a quintet of interrelated response measures with which one can more accurately assess attentional, perceptual, and cognitive processes in the infant.

One of the persistent investigators of infant attentional, cognitive, and perceptual processes is Dr. Lewis of the Educational Testing Service. In Chapter 14 Lewis and his associate, Professor Goldberg of the University of Zambia, propose a theoretical model which attempts to relate perceptual-cognitive development to mother-infant interaction. We have already considered the importance of such interaction in the context of sensory stimulation and emotional development. Lewis and Goldberg take us one step further away from the view that the infant is solely a receiver of environmental input. Rather, one emphasis of their proposed model is that the infant comes to actively engage his environment and more importantly comes to expect a reasonable degree of consistency in that environment. As these authors state,

"The proposed model is a motivational construct developed by the infant through the mother-infant interaction. The construct is a generalized expectancy that his behavior (the infant's) has consequence in affecting his environment." (Chapter 14, p. 225). Note the possibilities of the conjugate reinforcement method for studying these expectancies. If conjugate reinforcement of exploratory responses is occuring during the mother-infant interaction, might this not be a useful procedure for investigating the early development of the expectancies referred to by Lewis and Goldberg?

LANGUAGE

The first vocalization emitted by the infant is most likely the birth cry. From that point on the infant begins that aspect of human development which clearly distinguishes the human organism from all lower species, i.e., the development of language. Nevertheless, there is some disagreement concerning the specific point in human development when true language learning begins. During the first few months of life the infant's vocalizations consist of explosive sounds generically classed as cooing. Following cooing, and emerging around three months of age, babbling characterizes infant vocalizations. Babbling refers to sounds that typically are consonant-vowel combinations, the most commonly noted by parents being *da* or *ma.* From babbling of single consonant-vowel sounds the infant progressively moves to stringing these consonant-vowel combinations together producing *da da* or *ma ma.* Note that in these stages of language development the infant vocalizes with no apparant meaning attached to his vocalization. Indeed *da da* can refer to the infant's father, the family dog, or to a mobile suspended over the infant's crib. Thus, neither cooing nor babbling appear to lead directly to linguistically based speech (Lenneberg, Rebelsky & Nichols, 1963). Indeed, many psycholinguists and linguists theorize that these early infant vocalizations bear no relation to subsequent understanding of language. Nevertheless, this does not mean that infant vocalizations cannot be modified through environmental manipulation (Rheingold, Gewirtz & Ross, 1959; Weisberg, 1963).

One recent study considered the effect of age, state, and maternal behavior on infant vocalizations (Jones & Moss, 1969). Infants were studied when they were 7–14 days old and again when they were 85–95 days old. These investigators found that the effect of the mother's presence on the infant's vocalizations was dependent on infant state. When in a passive awake state there were no differences in amount of vocalization during mother present and mother absent conditions. On the other hand, when infants were in an active awake state, vocalizations were suppressed when mother was present. In addition, the presence of mother was found to be related to the infant's overall activity level as well as vocalizations. Friedlander (1968) studied the effects of the identity of the speaker, the speakers voice inflection, and redundancy of the message, on infant's selection of the type of voice feedback it prefered to have as reinforcement. Three infants, ranging in age from 11 to 15 months, were able to select from pairs of voices or other sounds by manipulating an automated toy. Infants significantly preferred their mother's voice when given a choice between mother's voice and music. Moreover, infants were able to discriminate between mother's voice and that of a stranger. Routh (1969), using smiling, tsk sounds, and stroking of the infant's abdomen as reinforcers, successfully conditioned vocal response differentiation in two- to seven-month-old infants. One group of infants was reinforced for emitting consonant sounds, one group reinforced for emitting vowel sounds, and one group reinforced for any type of vocalization. Routh found that the consonant group produced greater increases in vocalized consonants than vowels, the vowel group evidencing substantial increases in vocalized vowels.

Consequently, there is little doubt that infant vocalizations can be affected by the reinforcement contingencies of the environment. But does that mean that language learning is being demonstrated? Or are these simply demonstrations of manipulation of maturationally regulated behaviors? Professor Lenneberg of Cornell University has devoted the major portion of his research career to the study of just these questions. What aspects of language are maturationally determined and what aspects are learned? In Chapter 15 Professor Lenneberg reviews a substantial body of research literature and advances some theoretical viewpoints concerning the development of language. Bear in mind as you read Chapter 15 that Lenneberg is not concerned with the origins of language as a species specific behavior nor is he concerned with questions such as when does the first word appear? Rather, his concern is with "the development of the child's knowledge of how the language works." Concerning the maturational-learning issue, Lenneberg is lead to the conclusion that neither approach is likely to be absolutely correct. Rather, in the long run both orientations must give way to a composite viewpoint which has as its chief focus the understanding of language development.

CULTURAL DEPRIVATION

In Chapter 16, Professor Bronfenbrenner, of Cornell University, discusses one of the most critical aspects of early development in contemporary American society: education and development of the culturally deprived child. Noting that the process of cultural deprivation begins with inadequate prenatal care and insufficient nutrition, Bronfenbrenner begins with the observation that the idea that ". . . such deficiencies (motivational, emotional, and behavioral) have an innate basis in race differences has been so thoroughly discredited," and seeks to delineate the specific cultural antecedents of poor school achievement among the culturally deprived. One variable that very early comes up for discussion by Bronfenbrenner is the significance of father absence for child development. Considerable attention in the psychological literature has been devoted to the effects of maternal deprivation with regard to adequate emotional and personality development, but little attention has been paid to the role of the father. Is there a corresponding phenomena, father deprivation, which plays a significant role in child development? Indeed Nash (1965) in his excellent review of the role of the father in contemporary psychological theory of development clearly indicates that the deleterious effects of father absence have been vastly underplayed in developmental theory. How extensive in duration must father absence be to have an effect on the child? Sutton-Smith, Rosenberg and Landy (1968) studied the effects of varying lengths of father absence compared to the effects of father presence on one measure of academic achievement, the American College Entrance Examination (ACE). They found father absence to have a marked depressive effect (lower ACE scores) throughout development. The greatest effects occurred when father was absent during the subject's early and middle childhood. In addition, they found that the presence of siblings was also a significant factor. Boys without brothers were more adversely affected than were boys who had brothers. Moreover, girls with younger brothers were more greatly affected by father absence than were other girls, while only girls were more adversely affected than were only boys. In another study (Landy, Rosenberg & Sutton-Smith, 1969), the effect of father absence during night-shift work was related to the quantitative performance on the ACE of 100 girls. Girls whose fathers worked night shifts when the girls were from 1 to 9 years of age performed significantly more poorly on the quantitative subtests of the ACE. Thus, even relatively brief periods of father absence provoke significantly depressive effects on various aspects of academic achievement. One can only speculate about the potential untoward effects on development of sustained and habitual father absence.

In Chapter 17 Professors Gray and Klaus of George Peabody College discuss an intervention program developed to assist young children suffering the effects of cultural deprivation to become more proficient in academic achievement skills. It is indeed encouraging that such programs as discussed by Gray and Klaus are providing avenues for escape for those children so unfortunate to be suffering cultural suppression at so early an age.

REFERENCES

Abrahamson, D., Brackbill, Y., Carpenter, R., & Fitzgerald, H. E. Interaction of stimulus and response in infant conditioning. *Psychosomatic Medicine,* in press.

Ball, B. C. Some relationships among infant preference for tactile stimulation, developmental level, and maternal behaviors. Paper presented at the meeting of the Southeastern Psychological Association, New Orleans, Feb. 27, 1969.

Banks, J. H. Jr., & Wolfson, J. H. Differential cardiac response of infants to mother and stranger. Paper read at the annual meeting of the Eastern Psychological Association, Philadelphia, Pa., 1967.

BELL, R. Q. Level of arousal in breast-fed and bottle-fed human newborns. *Psychosomatic Medicine,* 1966, *28,* 177–180.

BRACKBILL, Y. Extinction of the smiling response in infants as a function of reinforcement schedule. *Child Development,* 1958, *29,* 115–124.

BRACKBILL, Y. A national disgrace. *Contemporary Psychology,* 1969, *14,* 373–374.

BRACKBILL, Y. Cumulative effects of continuous stimulation on arousal level in infants. In H. E. Fitzgerald & Y. Brackbill (Eds.). *Design and method in infant research.* Chicago: University of Chicago Press, 1970, in press.

BRACKBILL, Y., ADAMS, G., CROWELL, D. H., & GRAY, M. L. Arousal level in neonates and preschool children under continuous auditory stimulation. *Journal of Experimental Child Psychology,* 1966, *4,* 178–188.

BRACKBILL, Y., & FITZGERALD, H. E. Development of the sensory analyzers during infancy. In L. P. Lipsitt & H. W. Reese (Eds.) *Advances in child development and behavior.* Vol. 4. New York: Academic Press, 1969, pp. 173–208.

BRACKBILL, Y., FITZGERALD, H. E., & LINTZ, L. M. A developmental study of classical conditioning. *Monographs of the Society for Research in Child Development,* 1967, *32,* Serial No. 116.

CANESTRINI, S. Über das Sinnesleben des Neugeborenen (nach Physiologischen Experimenten), (On the sensory life of the newborn according to physiological experiments). *Gesamtebiete Neurologie Psychiatrie,* 1913, *5,* 1–104.

CASLER, L. The effects of extra tactile stimulation on a group of institutionalized infants. *Genetic Psychology Monographs,* 1965, *71,* 137–175.

CONNOLLY, K., & STRATTON, P. An exploration of some parameters affecting classical conditioning in the neonate. *Child Development,* 1969, *40,* 431–441.

ESCALONA, S. The study of individual differences and the problem of state. *Journal of the American Academy of Child Psychiatry,* 1962, *1,* 11–37.

FANTZ, R. L. A method for studying early visual development. *Perceptual and Motor Skills,* 1956, *6,* 13–16.

FITZERALD, H. E., LINTZ, L. M., BRACKBILL, Y., & ADAMS, G. Time perception and conditioning an autonomic response in human infants. *Perceptual and Motor Skills,* 1967, *24,* 479–486.

FRIEDLANDER, B. A. The effect of speaker identity, voice inflection, vocabulary, and message redundancy on infants' selection of vocal reinforcement. *Journal of Experimental Child Psychology,* 1968, *6,* 443–459.

GIACOMEN, S. L. Hunger and motor restraint on arousal and visual attention in the infant.

GORDON, H. S., & BELL, R. Q. Activity in the human newborn. *Psychological Reports.* 1961, *9,* 103–116.

GORDON, T., & FOSS, B. M. The role of stimulation in the delay of onset of crying in the newborn infant. *Quarterly Journal of Experimental Psychology,* 1966, *18,* 79–81.

HERSHENSON, M. Visual discrimination in the human newborn. *Journal of Comparative and Physiological Psychology.* 1964, *58,* 270–276.

HESS, E. H. Attitude and pupil size. *Scientific American,* 1965, *212,* 46–54.

Hess, E. H., & Polt, J. M. Pupil size as related to interest value of visual stimuli. *Science,* 1960, *132,* 349–350.

Hess, E. H., & Polt, J. M. Pupil size in relation to mental activity during simple problem solving. *Science,* 1964, *143,* 1190–1192.

Hess, E. H., Seltzer, A. L., & Shlien, J. M. Pupil response of hetero- and homosexual males to pictures of men and women. *Journal of Abnormal Psychology,* 1965, *70,* 165–168.

Jones, S. J., & Moss, H. A. Age, state and maternal behavior associated with infant vocalizations. Paper presented at the meeting of the Society for Research in Child Development, Santa Monica, Calif., March, 1969.

Kagan, J., Henker, B., Hen-tov, A., Levine, J., & Lewis, M. Infants' differential reactions to familiar and distorted faces. *Child Development,* 1966, *37,* 519–532.

Kaye, H. The conditioned Babkin reflex in human newborns. *Psychonomic Science,* 1965, *2,* 287–288.

Kessen, W., & Mandler, G. Anxiety, pain and the inhibition of distress. *Psychological Review,* 1961, *68,* 396–404.

Korner, A. F., & Grobstein, R. Visual alertness as related to soothing in neonates: implications for maternal stimulation and early deprivation. *Child Development,* 1966, *37,* 867–876.

Kulka, A., Fry, C., & Goldstein, F. J. Kinesthetic needs in infancy. *American Journal of Orthopsychiatry,* 1960, *30,* 562–571.

Landy, F., Rosenberg, B. G., & Sutton-Smith, B. The effect of limited father absence on cognitive development. *Child Development,* 1969, *40,* 941–944.

LaRoche, J. E., & Tcheng, P. Le sourire du Nourisson (Smiling of the Infant). Louvain: Publications Universitaires, 1963.

Lenneberg, E. H., Rebelsky, F. G., & Nicholas, I. A. The vocalizations of infants born to deaf and hearing parents. *Human Development,* 1965, *8,* 23–27.

Lewis, M. The meaning of a response or why researchers in infant behavior should be Oriental Metaphysicians. *Merrill-Palmer Quarterly,* 1967, *13,* 7–18.

Lewis, M., Kagan, J., & Kalafat, J. Patterns of fixation in the young infant. *Child Development,* 1966, *37,* 331–341.

Lewis, M., Myers, W. J., Kagan, J., & Grossberg, R. Attention to visual patterns in infants. *American Psychologist,* 1963, *18,* 357. (Abstract).

Lintz, L. M., Fitzgerald, H. E., & Brackbill, Y. Conditioning the eyeblink response to sound in infants. *Psychonomic Science,* 1967, *7,* 405–406.

Lipsitt, L. P., Kaye, H., & Bosack, T. N. Enhancement of neonatal sucking through reinforcement. *Journal of Experimental Child Psychology,* 1966, *4,* 163–168.

Lipsitt, L. P., Pederson, L. J., & DeLucia, C. A. Conjugate reinforcement of operant responding in infants. *Psychonomic Science,* 1966, *4,* 67–68.

Lipton, E. L., Steinschneider, A., & Richmond, J. B. Swaddling, child care practice: Historical, cultural and experimental observations. *Pediatrics,* 1965, *35,* 521–567.

Love, J. M. The influence of Behaviorism in child Psychology. Paper presented at the annual meeting of the Southeastern Psychological Association, New

Orleans, 1969. Symposium on "Historical conceptions of mental development."

Marsden, R. A study of the early color sense. *Psychological Review,* 1903, *10,* 37–47.

Nash, J. The father in contemporary culture and current psychological literature. *Child Development,* 1965, *36,* 261–297.

Ourth, L., & Brown, K. B. Inadequate mothering and disturbance in the neonatal period. *Child Development,* 1961, *32,* 287–295.

Papousek, H. Conditioned head rotation reflexes in infants in the first months of life. *Acta Paediatrica,* 1961, *50,* 565–576.

Papousek, H. Conditioning during early postnatal development. In Y. Brackbill & G. G. Thompson (Eds.). *Behavior in Infancy and Early Childhood,* New York: Free Press, 1967.

Preyer, W. *Die Seele des Kindes.* 5th ed. Leipzig: Fernau, 1900.

Rheingold, H., Gewirtz, J. L., & Ross, H. W. Social conditioning of vocalization in the infant. *Journal of Comparative and Physiological Psychology,* 1959, *52,* 68–73.

Routh, D. K. Conditioning of vocal response differentiation in infants. *Developmental Psychology,* 1969, *1,* 219–226.

Salapatek, P., & Kessen, W. Visual scanning of triangles by the human newborn. *Journal of Experimental Child Psychology,* 1966, *3,* 155–167.

Schaffer, H. R., & Emerson, P. E. The development of social attachments in infancy. *Monographs of the Society for Research in Child Development,* 1964, *29,* No. 3 (*a*)

Schaffer, H. R., & Emerson, P. E. Patterns of response to physical contact in early human development. *Journal of Child Psychology and Psychiatry,* 1964, *5,* 1–13 (*b*)

Simmons, M. W. Operant discrimination learning in human infants. *Child Development,* 1964, *35,* 737–748.

Siqueland, E. R. Reinforcement patterns and extinction in human newborns. *Journal of Experimental Child Psychology,* 1968, *6,* 431–442.

Siqueland, E. R. The development of instrumental exploratory behavior during the first year of human life. Paper presented at meeting of the Society for Research in Child Development, Santa Monica, Calif., March., 1969.

Siqueland, E. R., & Lipsitt, L. P. Conditioned head-turning in human newborns. *Journal of Experimental Child Psychology.* 1966, *3,* 356–376.

Spitz, R. A. Anxiety in infancy: A study of its manifestation in the first year of life. *International Journal of Psycho-analysis,* 1950, *31,* 138–143.

Spitz, R. A., & Wolf, R. A. The smiling response: A contribution to the ontogenesis of social relations. *Genetic Psychology Monographs,* 1946, *34,* 57–125.

Stass, J. W., & Wellis, F. N. Eye contact, pupil dilation, and personal preference. *Psychonomic Science,* 1967, *7,* 375–376.

Stern, E. R., & Jeffrey, W. E. Operant conditioning of non-nutritive sucking in the neonate: Paper presented at meeting of the Society for Research in Child Development, Minneapolis, Minnesota, April, 1965.

Sutton-Smith, B., Rosenberg, B. G., & Landy, F. Father-absence effects in families of different sibling compositions. *Child Development,* 1968, *39,* 1213–1221.

Watson, J. B., & Rayner, R. Conditioned emotional reactions. *Journal of Experimental Psychology,* 1920, *3,* 1–14.

Weisberg, P. Social and non-social conditioning of infant vocalizations. *Child Development,* 1963, *34,* 377–388.

Weisberg, P. Operant procedures for the establishment of stimulus control in two-year-old infants. *Journal of Experimental Child Psychology,* 1969, *7,* 81–95.

Wolff, P. H. The causes, controls and organization of behavior in the neonate. *Psychological Issues.* New York: International Universities Press, 1966.

10
RESEARCH IN THE PSYCHOLOGICAL DEVELOPMENT OF INFANTS: AN OVERVIEW*

WILLIAM KESSEN

THE INFANT has not always been treated kindly by American psychologists. Although almost all theories—whether in the tradition of Watson, Freud, or Koffka—celebrate the importance of infant behavior, and claim that the baby is striking proof of the validity of their views, systematic empirical study of the child in his crucial first year has been an on-again, off-again affair. And for a number of reasons, not the least of which is the difficulty of seeing young children in the large numbers that we have at our command in studying the pre-school child or the adolescent. Once a child leaves the hospital after the lying-in period, he is not again easily available for research until he appears in nursery school. It may also be that the infant is so clearly one of us—in that he is human, and so clearly and incomprehensibly different, in that he is a baby—that we have, on occasion, escaped our frustration by constructing theoretical babies instead of observing real ones.

Happily, these disabilities no longer block research. There is evidence, and not only in the United States, that psychologists are studying the infant more closely than ever before. Merely to call the names of investigators and refer to some of their findings would consume many pages. This is not to say, by the way, that the theoretical or constructed child has disappeared. Far from it! Behind each empirical investigation, there is a model, and this model colors and sometimes dominates the interpretation that is given the empirical protocols.

I would like to be able to present a neat, clear (even if artificial) dichotomy or trichotomy of theoretical positions concerning infancy—I recall with some nostalgia our antique friend "maturation *versus* learning"—but the current situation in the psychological study of infancy does not accept such simple classification. It is only a modest exaggeration to say that a recitation of theoretical subtleties would approach the complexity of a recita-

* From the *Merrill-Palmer Quarterly,* 1963, *9,* 83–94. Reprinted with permission of the author and the Merrill-Palmer Institute.

tion of research findings. In the face of this kind of variety, I cannot hope to lay out a complete or even a fair summary of current research and thought about the behavior of the infant. Rather, I will present for your comment, review, and evaluation, a short set of propositions about babies and studies of babies; under each of these loose-jointed statements, we can examine a part of the research and speculation that has appeared over the last several years.

The first proposition or summary statement that I will propose is that *a comparative psychology of infancy can be anticipated.* Harlow's well-known work (1958) on affectional systems in the monkey, though incomplete, is as stimulating a body of research as has been done on animal development over the last decade. Less widely known, but of at least equal theoretical impact, are T. C. Schneirla's (1959) speculations about approach and avoidance and their relation to stimulus intensity. Hess (1959), among others, has presented data and commentary on the phenomena of imprinting. Seymour Levine (1957) has contributed a number of papers on the effect of infantile stress on later behavior. These names only begin a list of the researchers who are working on developmental problems with infra-human animals.

Two general comments are warranted here. The animal work which is now going on in developmental psychology is not "dry-as-dust" laboratory demonstration. Moreover, little of this work leads to procedures routinely applicable to children, in the way that some current studies of reinforcement are; nor is the current animal work aimed at elaboration of the obvious. The psychologists studying animal development are in advance of their colleagues in human developmental studies, not only in regard to novel empirical techniques, but more important, in their willingness to take an intellectual chance or risk a speculation. The second note to be appended to the work with animals is the classical one, namely, the possibility of experimental manipulation of more than a trivial sort. We have only seen the beginning of work with animals, and particularly with primates, that will permit us to examine experimentally propositions that would otherwise remain available only to limited observational examination. Studies of the relation of infant to parent, for example, can be investigated along all relevant dimensions only by the use of animals. This is not to say that once we have found the rhesus we can abandon the human being, but the thoughtfulness and energy of investigators currently working in animal research will have no small impact on current research in the psychology of development.

But let me put aside the allure of precision and control possible with animal work and confine the rest of my general propositions to those about human behavior.

The first proposition about children to be considered, and perhaps the most obvious, is that *infants are various*—young children are different from one another. I may see a straw man when I speak against the notion that human infants at birth, like well-made cigarettes, cannot be distinguished from one another; but there is still abroad in psychology—at least in the academical variety—the feeling that children at birth are, by and large, pretty much undifferentiated protoplasm or no more than merely randomly varying beings. Whatever the present state is of the pure, undifferentiated position in the sociology of knowledge, evidence is accumulating that parents and nurses were right all along—stable differences in behavior can be detected in the first days of life. Hammond (1957) has shown the stability of physical growth patterns. Richmond and his colleagues at Syracuse (1955) have reported psychophysiological stabilities in the newborn. Thomas, Chess, Birch, and Hertzig (1960), although they have published only preliminary reports, have stated that on nine variables—among them, reactivity and irritability—they have found stability in children followed longitudinally over a period of two years. There are some suggestions in Bell's work (1960), and there are some findings in our work on newborns at Yale (1961), which tend to support a strong generalization that stable individual differences in a large number of behaviors—sucking, general movement, reactivity—exist very early in life. Yet, impressive as it is, the work on the assessment of individual differences among human infants has not, like some of the animal work, been "built out" from novel observations and speculations. Rather, it has come largely from the essential and tedious work of constructing adequate response measures. These advances in technology or method are clear and welcome, but they leave open two larger questions about individual differences.

First, what is the long-range stability or relevance of these differences? It is good to know that the newborn shows stable differences in activity level from his colleague in the next crib, but the importance of this observation is markedly reduced if the difference does not show up in some form later. Among the investigators, other than the Birch group, who have done some interesting speculative work on this score, is the French psychologist Stambak (1956). She has segregated two groups of infants—hypertonic and hypotonic—and has discussed the relation of this tendency to be active or quiet to such important developmental changes as onset of walking. In addition, the Czech group (Papoušek, 1961) is investigating the stability of the infant's behavior during conditioning over the first six months of life. Such studies are provocative curtain-raisers on the intricate question of behavioral stability in infancy.

There is a second question about which we have very little evidence. How are these early behavioral variations related to variations in the environment? How do different combinations of infant and caretaker mesh together? We can tag babies as active or quiet; we can make this discrimination in the first five or ten days of life. We can suspect, too, that some mothers like active babies and some mothers like quiet babies. What do you get when you combine an active baby with a mother who wanted a quiet one or a quiet baby with a mother who wanted an active one? We have very little to go on here, not only because of the obvious technical difficulties of longitudinal studies of this kind, and not only because of the fluidity of our ideas about what is important in the home, but also because, until recently, we have not had reliable ways of describing the young child's environment. The technical advance in the methods of describing newborn behavior have not been matched by methods for describing the home. But here, again, there is promise. Schaefer, Bell, and Bayley (1959) have proposed a parent attitude scale. The important interview work of Sears *et al.* (1957) provides a framework for the description of parents' behavior. Rheingold (1960) has recently specified some of the dimensions of variation between home and institution. These papers point the way toward the time when a genuine analysis can be made of the interaction between mother and child. The word "genuine" reflects the hope that this analysis will not be a contaminated one; that we can make assessments of the status of the newborn, independent of observing the mother, and make assessment of the mother, independent of observing the child.

The next summary proposition that I want to suggest warrants detailed examination. I submit that *the young infant is not incompetent* or, by André-Thomas' (1954) catching phrase, "the neonate is not a neophyte."

We have passed the time, not so very long ago, when the newborn was considered to be sensorily bereft (*e.g.,* Preyer's contention that children are born deaf), but the notion of newborn incompetence persists. It has perhaps its strongest statement in the work of the psychoanalysts, especially Spitz (1959), who maintains the existence of a nondifferentiated phase in early life, where the newborn does not code inputs at all. In this view of the infant, by no means limited to psychoanalysts, both the baby's sensory capacities and his response capacities are held to be severely limited. The trend of recent research is clearly against this conception of the child. Research on newborn behavior over the last five years has invariably added to the newborn's list of abilities. Peiper (1956) in his encyclopedic treatment, André-Thomas (1954) and his colleagues in Paris, Madame Ste. Anne-Desgassies, and Prechtl (1958) are among the workers who have discussed the extended sensory and response range of the newborn in some detail. Gorman and his associates (1959) have recently found in a study of acuity that the newborn has visual resolving powers which are not markedly inferior to those of the older child. From the research available on the competence of the newborn, let me present three studies in some detail as illustrative and somewhat representative of this newer view of the newborn.

The first study, by Blauvelt (1960), deals with the precision of at least one response the newborn makes. Following up earlier work of Prechtl on head-turning, Blauvelt has studied the baby's response to a very simple stimulation, in which the experimenter moves her finger from the tragus of the baby's ear—the baby lying on its back in the crib—toward the baby's mouth and then away again in a flat elliptical course. It turns out that the baby tracks this movement by turning his head at a speed and to a position that will reduce the distance between his mouth and the stimulating finger. He tracks this movement without special tuition; it is, if you like, built-in. The infant can pick up approaching stimulation and reduce the distance to it very quickly; he can "find" the approaching breast or bottle. What is impressive about this response is the precision of it. This is not the response of a wild newborn, flailing around uselessly and without direction; this is an organism making a precise and exact tracking response. It is a limited skill, to be sure, and certainly not widely generalizable to other activities, but it illustrates the responding precision of some newborn.

The second study illustrative of newborn competence may be one of the most important empirical research products of the last decade in infancy work. Bronshtein, Antonova, Kamenetskaya, Luppova, and Sytova (1958) have described a technique for assessing the limits of sensory differentiation in the infant that promises a precision in psychophysical description that has heretofore been possible only for the much older child. Briefly, the procedure is this. You permit or induce the child to suck, and record his rhythmic response. If, during sucking, you sound a brief tone, say of 512 cycles/sec., the baby stops sucking. When the tone stops, the baby begins to suck again. To a second stimulation of the same tone, he will stop sucking. This sequence can be repeated four or five times for sounds and then when you sound your 512-cycle tone he goes on sucking without interruption. He has adapted to that sound. If, however, you now present a different tone, say one of 1,024 cycles, he will stop sucking. If he continues to suck on the application of the second stimulus, this is presumptive evidence that he cannot discriminate the two stimuli. If he does stop sucking on the second stimulus, if it "undoes the adaptation," then there is evidence that he can discriminate these two stimuli. If this technique is as sensitive as the Russians suggest, we will be able to find out more about the sensory capacities of the young infant than we can find out about the sensory capacities of young five- or six-year-olds. Bronshtein presents data to indicate that the infant makes clearly differential responses to variations in pitch, light intensity, and other stimulus changes. Lipsitt, at Brown, has adapted this technique to a study of olfactory stimulation and has found that not only is sucking inhibited and adapted in this fashion but so also is movement. Just as the Blauvelt study illustrates the possible response flexibility of the newborn, so the Bronshtein and Lipsett studies indicate the remarkable amount of stimulus coding the newborn is capable of. The world of the infant is not a vast confusing "blob."

Consider yet a third study. In our work at Yale (1963), we have found that if you put a nipple in a baby's mouth, he will stop general movement at once, and when you take it out he will start moving again. This effect appears in the absence of nutrient; the nipple does not supply food—it only provides an opportunity to suck. And, this inhibition of movement takes place in the fourth or third or second, or even first day of life. The child is able to deal with a complex and vitally important input—namely, nipple or sucking—by a very regular response. Nor, apparently, does he have to learn either how to suck or how to quiet. There is of course the argument that he learned the responses *in utero,* but we have hardly advanced beyond Hippocrates' statement of that argument 2,500 years ago.

These studies suggest that the newborn has far greater capacities for sensory discrimination than could have been guessed a decade ago, and though less impressive, the evidence is beginning to indicate that he has surprising response competencies as well. But the evidence for newborn resourcefulness poses a peculiar paradox. To put the question very bluntly, if the human newborn is so capable, why does he not learn more? If he is so capable, why is he so stupid? These questions form the bridge to my next general proposition, one which seems so insecure that I have phrased it in the form of yet another question.

There is early adaptation, but is there early learning? The conflict represented in this question can be expressed simply enough. On the one hand the behavior of baby seems to change over the first few days of life. There are many examples; let me cite just one.

Peiper maintains that there are three techniques of infantile sucking. One of them is the response that most mammals use to get milk out of a breast; it is a lapping response that involves pressing the nipple against the roof of the mouth with the tongue and squeezing milk out of it. Another one is to reduce pressure inside the mouth so as to pull the milk in by a discrepancy in pressure. This is the way most babies suck from bottles. And the third, fairly infrequent technique—confined to bottle-fed babies for obvious reasons—is to bite hard at the back of the nipple and squirt milk into the mouth. This variation is interesting because babies apparently come to use one of these different patterns very quickly. They learn, if "learn" is appropriate, the kind of sucking to use.

The difficulty with calling this kind of change "learning" arises from our failure to demonstrate early learning in a controlled setting. If the newborn is capable of this natural learning it should be possible for a psychologist to teach him something in a systematic learning study. And yet the evidence, controlled evidence for newborn learning, hardly exists. There is research by Marquis (1931), recently replicated in the USSR, showing that the baby adapts to a feeding rhythm, but the evidence does not support the conclusion that learning according to the usual theoretical models takes place in the period of early infancy. The Russians, with their strong demand for environmental control of behavior, have tried a large number of times to condition young infants. Sometimes they are successful; oftentimes they are not. Russian studies do not report conditioning in children under eight or nine days of age, and most conditioning studies indicate that it may take weeks or even months to condition an infant child in the Pavlovian mode (Dashkovskaya, 1953). How do we interpret this curious discrepancy between the fact that the human baby seems to adapt his sucking style and to his feeding routines on the one hand, and the difficulty that all investigators have had in demonstrating newborn learning on the other?

The following three options seem available to us: First, in spite of my statements about newborn competence, there may be genuine neurological incapacity in the newborn. There is no such thing as early learning, in the usual sense, because the child is not complete. A case for this position can be made. There are data on myelinization, on changes in pattern of EEG, on developments of vision and prehension, on the appearance of smiling—to take the most obvious case—all of which can be used to bolster the view that the young infant is a neurologically deficient organism. Under this reading, how do we account for the changes in behavior that do take place? Perhaps by maintaining that the caretaker becomes more competent. This would be a case of training the parent to adapt more effectively to the child rather than teaching the child to adapt to his environment. And to the data from Bronshtein and Lipsett on the ability of the young infant to make sensory discriminations, we would have to say, "True, infants can make sensory discriminations, but there is no associative coding; there is a deficiency in the hooking of links together."

The second answer, and the one I think that would be given by the learning analysts (Gewirtz, 1961), is that nobody has tackled the problem of early learning. In particular, holders of this position would maintain that the procedures of classical conditioning as used by the Russians are the wrong tactics. What we should do if we want to demonstrate early learning is to use instrumental techniques; that is, to make some effective reinforcement contingent on the occurrence of some response of the infant. For example, let the baby turn his head and then give him something to suck on. This is a testable proposition and it is being tested.

I would like to suggest a third possibility—an unpopular one. In brief, there may be experiential effects that are not learning. To put it another way, not all adaptation of the infant represents either classical conditioning or instrumental learning. I think it is inappropriate to maintain that all changes in behavior that can be related to the child's contact with the environment are the result of reinforcement contingencies. Of course, the instrumental learning position can be made to fit them, but it seems to me that such a forced fit results in theoretical vagueness and a weakening of the instrumental position.

Perhaps in pulling apart the problem of behavioral change in early infancy to exaggerate the variation among options, I have only shown that the resolution of the problem will require revisions in method, new knowledge of infantile neurophysiology, and a reworking of contemporary learning theory.

But consider now another interesting problem which illuminates some theoretical disagreements among students of infancy. Two theoretical positions have occupied this field—the psychoanalytic and the learning-theoretical. Justice can be done to neither in a summary presentation; Rapaport (1959) and Wolff (1960) present the psychoanalytic presuppositions in detail and with force; Gewirtz (1961) has prepared a closely reasoned argument for a learning analysis. Now, there is a new entrant into the field of theories of mother attachment. John Bowlby in a series of recent papers (1958) has borrowed from the investigators of instinct in animals, a notion that sounds very much like imprinting and has suggested that the child's responses of sucking, clinging, and following lead to mother-attachment. Just sucking, and just clinging, and just following on the part of the child, without obvious reinforcement or redistribution of cathexis, will result in a union between child and mother; much as the chick will imprint on a blinking light. Not only does Bowlby discuss what ties the child to his mother—namely, these three responses—but he also discusses what links the mother to the child. Not only does the child become attached to the mother because of sucking, clinging, and following, but the mother is drawn or attached—Bowlby does not use the word "imprinting"—to the child by the child's smiling and crying. Smiling and crying are held to be congenital or innate releases of maternal behavior.

It is difficult to evaluate this position and I am hard pressed to invent a satisfactory test for it. Perhaps we must call on animal research to work out the implications of Bowlby's assertions. But the main value of this new view will probably be the value of all theories of development—that they jog thinking, they make people run a study just to see what happens. Certainly Bowlby's ideas have had that effect. His own research with Robertson on separation (1952), the work done by Schaffer (1959) on hospitalization of young children, and an unpublished study by Ainsworth (1961) have demonstrated the provocative effect of these speculations. One of the achievements of the work done by Ainsworth, in Uganda, is that, instead of discussing mother attachment as a unitary notion, she has, in these longitudinal field observations of the child between four weeks of age and fourteen months, described some ten or twelve indexes of the child's attachment to the mother, and in this way has made possible a more subtle analysis of the relation than we have had heretofore.

It is interesting to note, as an adjunct to the problem of mother-attachment, that something very curious indeed seems to happen to children near the middle of the first year. Ambrose's (1961) results on smiling indicate that at 17–25 weeks, general social smiling begins to decay and the child begins to smile only at its caretakers. Schaffer's work indicates that children who are hospitalized before they are 28 weeks old, accept hospital routines and separation easily; children hospitalized after 28 weeks-of-age show striking symptom patterns of distress and refusal to accept normal hospital care. Ainsworth finds that almost all of her criteria of mother attachment begin to show transition in the period from 17 to 30 weeks, with much of the change occurring in the narrow band between 25 and 28 weeks. Somewhere in the middle of the first year, the child appears to shift from being attached to human beings at large to being attached to one, or two, or three human beings.

The Ainsworth study is comparable in its impact to Rheingold's (1956) study of caretaking in institutionalized infants—both of these studies represent the payoff for the theoretical positions underlying them. The psychology of infancy undoubtedly profits from being in a state of theoretical dis-equilibrium, and the diversity of ideas about the nature of the child's attachment to his mother will almost certainly be productive of important empirical advances.

Consider one last generalization about infancy. It is one where contention, compromise, and reciprocation among theoretical positions has already resulted in general agreement. *The infant is active, and the relation of infant and caretaker is reciprocal.*

It is on this issue that the psychologist's view of the child has changed most dramatically in recent years. The model of the child which was drawn from Pavlov through Watson, and supported by the development of learning psychology in the United States, was of a recipient organism—a reactive one. Behavior at any particular time is the function of the current stimulating environment. This remains technically a sound view, but the effect of it on the psychology of the infant was to diminish our appreciation of how complicated and subtle is the child.

Not only can the child be usefully seen as active, rather than merely as reactive, but it may also be useful to think of even the infant as a problem-solver. Certainly the child, like the adult, can be seen as encountering problems in his environment. At least from the age of six months, the child's behavior can be discussed in terms of discrepancy, goal-seeking, means to an end, and so on. One student of children has not deviated from this view of the active searching child. Piaget and his students have seen the child, especially the infant, as being in a constant exchange with the environment, meeting its demands, and what American investigators somehow forgot, making its own demands on that environment.

The shift in point-of-view—to set the antithesis sharply—has been from the child who is a passive receptacle, into which learning and maturation pour knowledge and skills and affects until he is full, to the child as a complex, competent organism who, by acting on the environment and being acted on in turn, develops more elaborated and balanced ways of dealing with discrepancy, conflict, and dis-equilibrium. This shift, I believe, is of incalculable implication and seems to have been accepted to some degree by almost all students of children. Bowlby emphasizes the control by the child in crying and smiling; psychoanalytic theory makes more space for autonomous ego functions; child psychologists dedicated to a learning analysis speak of the child as active; and I suspect Piaget thinks of how he knew it all the time. But this shift only sets the problem for the psychology of the infant; questions abound. What is a "problem" for the infant? What is an environmental discrepancy for the newborn, for the six-month old, for a walker? Do Piaget's speculations about assimilation, accommodation, and equilibration have more than a metaphorical value? Can child psychologists follow the lead of psychologists of cognition in adults, who use computer analogies? Can we build a theory of cognitive development without the use of terms like reinforcement, drive, or dissonance resolution?

Only one thing seems certain. We are better equipped, with attitude and technique, to make a systematic and meaningful analysis of infant behavior than ever before. The current psychology of infant behavior, by and large, is managing to steer skillfully between the Scylla of "Oh, Oh, look what the baby did!" and the Charybdis of "But the theory says thus and so." We are engaging in hot, theoretical debate, but more and more the debate refers back to the child—back to the theory-illuminated facts.

REFERENCES

AINSWORTH, M. D. The development of infant-child interaction among the Ganda. Paper read at Tavistock Study Group on Mother-Infant Interaction, London, 1961.

AMBROSE, J. A. The development of smiling response in early infancy. In Foss, B. M. (Ed.), *Determinants of infant behavior.* New York: Wiley, 1961.

ANDRÉ-THOMAS. Ontogénèse de la vie psychoaffective et de la douleur. *Encéphale,* 1954, **43,** 289–311.

BELL, R. Q. Relations between behavior manifestations in the human neonate. *Child Develpm.,* 1960, **31,** 463–477.

BLAUVELT, H. & MCKENNA, J. Capacity of the human newborn for mother-infant interaction. II. The temporal dimensions of a neonate response. *Psychiat. Res. Rep.,* 1960, **13,** 128–147.

BOWLBY, J. The nature of the child's tie to his mother. *Int. J. Psychoanal.,* 1958, **39,** 1–24.

BRONSHTEIN, A. I., ANTONOVA, T. G., KAMENETSKAYA, A. G., LUPPOVA, N. N. & SYTOVA, V. A. On the development of the functions of analyzers in infants and some animals at the early stage of ontogenesis. In *Problems of evolution of physiological functions.* OTS Report No. 50–61066. Translation obtainable from U.S. Dept. of Commerce. Moscow: Acad. Sci., 1958.

DASHKOVSKAYA, V. S. First conditioned reactions in newly born children in normal state and in certain pathological states. *Zh. vyssh. nervn. Deiatel.,* 1953, **3**(2), 247–259.

GEWIRTZ, J. L. A learning analysis of the effects of normal stimulation, privation, and deprivation on the acquisition of social motivation and attachment. In Foss, B. M. (Ed.), *Determinants of infant behavior.* New York: Wiley, 1961.

GORMAN, J. J., COGAN, D. G. & GELLIS, S. S. A device for testing visual acuity in infants. *Sight-Saving Rev.,* 1959, **29,** 80–84.

HAMMOND, W. H. The constancy of physical types as determined by factorial analysis. *Hum. Biol.*, 1957, **29**, 40–61.

HARLOW, H. F. The nature of love. *Amer. Psychologist,* 1958, **13**, 673–685.

HESS, E. H. Imprinting. *Science,* 1959, **130**, 133–141.

KESSEN, W. & LEUTZENDORFF, A. M. The effect of non-nutritive sucking on movement in the human newborn. *J. comp. Physiol. Psychol.*, 1963, in press.

KESSEN, W., WILLIAMS, E. J. & WILLIAMS, J. P. Selection and test of response measures in the study of the human newborn. *Child Develpm.*, 1961, **32**, 7–24.

LEVINE, S. Infantile experience and resistance to psychological stress. *Science,* 1957, **126**, 405.

MARQUIS, D. P. Can conditioned responses be established in the newborn infant? *J. genet. Psychol.*, 1931, **39**, 479–492.

PAPOUŠEK, H. A physiological view of early ontogenesis of so-called voluntary movements. In P. Sobotka (Ed.) *Functional and metabolic development of the central nervous system.* Prague: State Pedagogic Publ., 1961.

PEIPER, A. *Die Eigenart der Kindlichen Hirntätigkeit* (2nd Ed.). Leipzig: Thieme, 1956.

PRECHTL, H. F. R. The directed head turning response and allied movements of the human baby. *Behaviour,* 1958, **13**, 212–242.

RAPAPORT, D. The structure of psychoanalytic theory: A systematizing attempt. In Koch, S. (Ed.) *Psychology: a study of a science, vol. 3.* New York: McGraw-Hill, 1959.

RHEINGOLD, H. L. The modification of social responsiveness in institutional babies. *Monogr. Soc. Res. Child Develpm.*, 1956, **21**(2).

RHEINGOLD, H. L. The measurement of maternal care. *Child Develpm.*, 1960, **31**, 565–575.

RICHMOND, J. B. & LUSTMAN, S. L. Autonomic function in the neonate: I. Implications for psychosomatic theory. *Psychosom. Med.*, 1955, **17**, 269–275.

ROBERTSON, J. & BOWLBY, J. Responses of young children to separation from their mothers. *Courrier de la Centre Internationale de l'Enfance,* 1952, **2**, 131–142.

SCHAEFER, E. S., BELL, R. Q. & BAYLEY, N. Development of a maternal behavior research instrument. *J. genet. Psychol.*, 1959, **95**, 83–104.

SCHAFFER, H. R. & CALLENDER, W. M. Psychologic efforts of hospitalization in infancy. *Pediatrics,* 1959, **24**, 528–539.

SCHNEIRLA, T. R. An evolutionary and developmental theory of biphasic processes underlying approach and withdrawal. In M. R. Jones (Ed.), *Nebraska symposium on motivation: 1959.* Lincoln: Univer. of Nebraska Press, 1959.

SEARS, R. R., MACCOBY, E. F. & LEVIN, H. *Patterns of child rearing.* Evanston, Ill.: Row Peterson, 1957.

SPITZ, R. A. *A genetic field theory of ego formation; its implications for pathology.* New York: Internat. Univer. Press, 1959.

STAMBAK, M. Contribution à l'étude du développement moteur chez le nourrisson. *Enfance,* 1956, **9**(4), 49–59.

THOMAS, A., CHESS, S., BIRCH, H. & HERTZIG, M. E. A longitudinal study of primary reaction patterns in children. *Comprehensive Psychiat.*, 1960, **1**, 103–112.

WOLFF, P. H. *The developmental psychologies of Jean Piaget and psychoanalysis.* New York: Internat. Univer. Press, 1960.

11
CONJUGATE REINFORCEMENT OF INFANT EXPLORATORY BEHAVIOR*

CAROLYN KENT ROVEE
and
DAVID T. ROVEE

Over the first 4 months of life, human infants increasingly search and explore their visual environment, the feedback from which is undoubtedly responsible for much of their early and extensive learning (Fantz, 1967; White, 1967). The exploratory motive is well-documented for monkey young and is notable for its strength and persistence in spite of its unspecified biological correlates (Butler, 1953). Piaget (in Flavell, 1963) has defined 1–4 months as the period during which visually guided manual activities emerge. These permit the development during sensorimotor stage 3 of secondary circular reactions, which in turn permit the 4- to 8-month-old infant to alter his environment for its interest value. Similar behaviors have been described by White (1967). Rheingold and her co-workers (Rheingold, Stanley, and Cooley, 1962; Rheingold, Stanley, and Doyle, 1964) found that infants coinciding in age with Piaget's stage 3 are responsive to visual and auditory changes, increasing rate of sphere-touching when it is accompanied by such changes.

Conjugate reinforcement, a variation of free-operant conditioning introduced by Lindsley (1963), has recently been used successfully to demonstrate manipulative learning in year-old children (Lipsitt, Pederson, and DeLucia, 1966). This schedule of reinforcement provides a continuously available reinforcing event, the intensity of which is a direct consequence of response rate. Thus, more rapid responding produces a more intense reward value.

* From the *Journal of experimental Child Psychology,* 1969, *8,* 33–39. Reprinted with permission of the authors and Academic Press.

This research was supported in part by a grant from the Trenton State College Student Executive Board. We thank Lewis P. Lipsitt, Brown University Psychology Department, for his encouragement and critical comments, Carol Ann Kovalich, for assistance with data collection, Arthur Steinman, for programming assistance, and Drs. Charles and Bombet of Baton Rouge, La. for the services of their office in making subjects available.

Not only does the schedule sustain responding longer and at higher rates than the more typical episodic schedules, but it also permits a continuous record of the efficacy of a reinforcer sensitive to both organismic state changes and learning (Lindsley, 1963; Lipsitt *et al.,* 1966).

In the present study, every attempt was made to provide a reinforcing stimulus which would sustain the attention and behavior of the infants beyond the typical 8- to 10-minute operant test session. The finding of Hunt and Uzgiris (1964) that infants prefer familiar to nonfamiliar mobiles and the evidence that novel stimuli are often preferred to familiar stimuli (Cantor, 1963) suggested that attention might be maximized through a source of "relative" novelty (Berlyne, 1960). This refers to the changing or reorganization of the parts of a familiar stimulus into a "new" stimulus or stimulus pattern. The conjugate reinforcement procedure essentially provided a continuous sequence of "relatively" novel reinforcers, in that the degree or rate of responding produced successive and unique rearrangements of the initially familiar but nonresponsive mobile components.

METHOD

Subjects. Eighteen healthy and apparently normal infants, ranging in age from 9 to 12 weeks, were tested at the time of day reported by the mother to coincide with their normal activity or alert period. The experimental group (four males, two females) had a mean age of 72.5 days; and control *S*s (seven males, five females) averaged 73.4 days.

Apparatus. All *S*s were tested in their home cribs with an L-shaped mobile (Nursery Plastics, Inc.) which had been secured to the crib within the first two postnatal weeks. The main features of the mobile were 7 to 10 brightly colored wooden figures suspended on five plastic lines 10- to 12-inches directly above the infant's head. The rigidity of the metal mobile base and the crib weight minimized sway of the figures during normal crib activity. During testing, a soft, silk cord was looped about the left ankle and hooked without slack to the overhead suspension bar.

Procedure. Conjugate reinforcement was provided by means of the ankle cord, in that foot or leg movements directly initiated sway and movement in the mobile figures attached to the suspension bar. Although it was not possible to quantify stimulus parameters, it was apparent that the variety of figure movement increased directly with the force or rate of response. Very rapid responding produced auditory feedback from colliding wooden figures, such that *effectively* more intense responding produced a more intense reward.

Experimental *S*s received an initial 27-minute session, consisting of a 3-minute baseline period during which the operant level of left foot kicks was established, a 15-minute acquisition phase with conjugate reinforcement, and a 5-minute extinction period. Two minutes intervened between conditions to permit preparation for the succeeding phase. During this interval, *S*s were permitted to observe the mobile, but leg movement did not effect activity of the mobile, which remained passive throughout.

Control *S*s received identical conditions for the first and third segments of the procedure; however, during the acquisition segment, all were presented with moving figures continuously activated by the experimenter in a manner simulating the moving figures seen by experimental *S*s for the 15-minute period. Six of the controls received only noncontingent visual stimulation from the moving figures as described (no ankle cord), and six received noncontingent visual and somesthetic stimulation (cord attached).

A response was defined as a vertical or horizontal excursion of the left foot that returned in the same continuous motion in the direction of origin. Responses were recorded over continuous minutes of testing and out of the direct view of the infant. As a reliability check, a second observer recorded responses independently.

RESULTS

A Spearman rank correlation yielded an interobserver reliability coefficient of .946 ($p < .001$). A lower coefficient obtained over experimental *S*s only (.82; $p < .01$) probably reflects the difficulty in tabulating all responses when the foot was kicking at the very high rates which characterized conjugate reinforcement periods. This suggests that the response measures may represent conservative records of the reinforcing value of the mobile.

Figure 1 shows mean responses per minute for the experimental group (solid line) and control groups (broken lines). The means of the final 3 minutes of each condition were used in all *t* tests in order to maximize the opportunity for any effect of the experimental conditions to be demonstrated. All within-*S* comparisons were indexed by 5 *df;* all between-*S* comparisons, by 10 *df*. The difference between the conjugate reinforcement procedure and the identical but noncontingent visual-somesthetic control group was reliable ($p < .01$), although these groups did not differ significantly ($p > .05$) in baseline or extinction. The attachment of the ankle cord to the mobile did not reliably enhance activity relative to visual stimulation alone ($p > .05$), and neither control group changed from their initial operant levels in successive segments. Within the experimental group *per se,* final acquisition level differed from operant level and extinction ($p < .05$), but extinction did not differ from baseline performance ($p > .05$).

Four observations were recorded over an additional 17-minute test phase, these infants completing 46 minutes of continuous testing. The additional phase included a 10-minute re-acquisition and a 5-minute reextinction period, separated by a 2-minute pause (see Figure 2). Comparing mean response levels over the final 3 minutes of each phase as before (see Table 1), performance in each condition significantly differed from that in the preced-

FIGURE 1

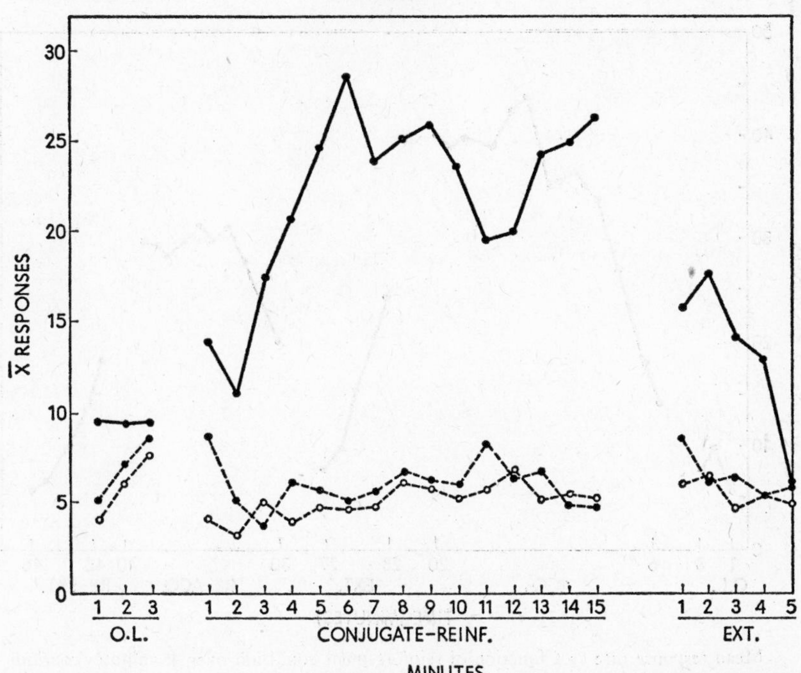

Rate of response as a function of reinforcement condition. Each *x*-axis point represents a successive minute of observation, approximately 2 minutes separating conditions. The solid line represents the experimental group (conjugate reinforcement); the dotted lines represent control groups (black circles = visual-somesthetic controls; white circles = visual only). Each curve represents six *S*s.

ing conditions with the exception that response levels in extinction did not differ from baseline performance.

Individual data indicated that all infants were clearly under operant

TABLE 1

Statistical Summary for Comparisons Between Five Test Conditions Shown in Figure 2 for 46-Minute Continuous Testing ($N = 4$)

Comparisons	*df*	*t*	*Type*	*Confidence Level*
Operant level X acquisition	3	4.000	One-tail	<.025
Operant level X extinction	3	2.718	Two-tail	>.05
Acquisition X extinction	3	3.365	One-tail	<.025
Extinction X re-acquisition	3	3.427	One-tail	<.025
Re-acquisition X re-extinction	3	2.935	One-tail	<.05
Re-acquisition X operant level	3	3.928	One-tail	<.025
Re-extinction X operant level	3	0.474	Two-tail	>.05

FIGURE 2

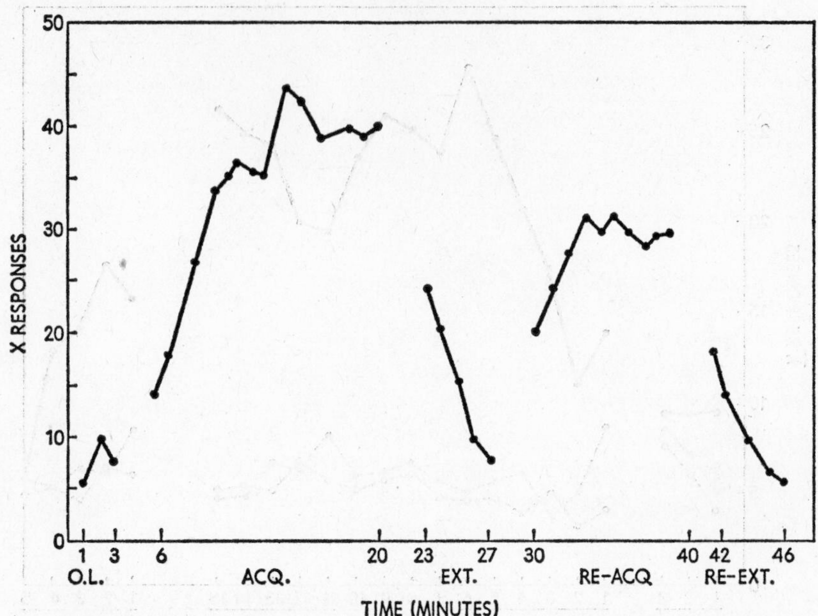

Mean response rate as a function of reinforcement condition over 46 minutes continuous testing. Note that the reinforcer continued to exert control over behavior even at minute 40, when the response rate was still about 2½ times the operant level ($N=4$).

control of the reinforcement contingencies. Within 3 minutes infants had doubled the initial response rate, and by 6 minutes of conjugate reinforcement, most had tripled it, both within single test sessions and over repeated sessions. Figure 2 indicates that the effect is clear and reproducible.

DISCUSSION

The use of the visual-somesthetic control group unequivocally demonstrates that the specific foot thrust represents true learning as a direct result of the contingency between the thrust and the mobile movement and does not reflect merely a state of general arousal produced by the moving target either singly or in combination with somesthetic feedback from the attached ankle cord. Note that using a foot kick rather than the hand-pulling or prehension response typically described in exploratory studies precludes possible visual obstruction of the reinforcer and evades the problem of clenched fists which characterize this stage of life.

As response intensity, reflected in response rate, increased, the intensity of the reward also increased in that more unique figure movements occurred more rapidly and, at high rates of response, auditory feedback from collisions of the moving figures became more and more prevalent. It may be presumed that the length of the session was achieved primarily through the "relative" novelty of the reinforcing stimulus over the duration of the conjugate condition. The potency of the reinforcing stimulus over such a relatively long time period is reminiscent of the rewarding effects of manipulation described for adult monkeys as a "curiosity drive" (Butler, 1954). The rapidity with which instrumental responses were established (see Figure 1) parallels that reported by Lipsitt *et al.* (1966) for older children and suggests that operant behavior might be effectively conditioned even more in advance of Piaget's stage 3 than has been shown.

The relation between environmental attention and infant learning has been noted in recent reviews (Fantz, 1967; White, 1967). Animal studies and adult human data (Held and Hein, 1963) have suggested that normal development of visually guided spatial perception and coordination depends on the opportunity to observe stimulus variation from self-produced movement. Deprivation studies of institution-reared infants retarded in this aspect of development have shown that simple placement of brightly colored objects in the visual field as early as 37 days of age enhances visual attention (White, 1967). If visual attention is prerequisite to obtaining environmental feedback, hence to learning, then the present study is notable for demonstrating a simple and direct way of achieving and sustaining such attention. Further, the stability of the behavior under the reinforcing contingency, as evidenced after 40 minutes of testing, suggests the usefulness of this technique for the systematic assessment of learning and sensory phenomena in very young infant.

REFERENCES

Berlyne, D. *Conflict, Arousal, and Curiosity.* p. 38. New York: McGraw-Hill, 1960.

Butler, R. A. Curiosity in monkeys. *Scientific American Offprint,* 1954 (Feb.), No. 426.

Butler, R. A. Discrimination learning by rhesus monkeys to visual exploration motivation. *Journal of Comparative and Physiological Psychology,* 1953, **46,** 95–98.

Cantor, G. N. Responses of infants and children to complex and novel stimulation. In L. P. Lipsitt and C. C. Spiker (Eds.), *Advances in Child Development and Behavior,* Vol. I, pp. 1–30. New York: Academic Press, 1963.

Fantz, R. L. Visual perception and experience in early infancy: A look at the hidden side of behavior development. In H. W. Stevenson, E. H. Hess, and H. L. Rheingold (Eds.), *Early Behavior.* Pp. 181–224. New York: Wiley, 1967.

Flavell, J. *The Developmental Psychology of Jean Piaget.* Pp. 85–109. Princeton, N.J.: Van Nostrand, 1963.

Held, R. M., and Hein, A. V. Movement-produced stimulation in the development of visually-guided behavior. *Journal of Comparative and Physiological Psychology,* 1963, **56,** 872–876.

Hunt, J. McV., and Uzgiris, I. C. Cathexis from recognitive familiarity: An exploratory study. Symposium paper presented at meetings of the American Psychological Association, Los Angeles, California, 1964. Pp. 1–15.

Lindsley, O. R. Experimental analysis of social reinforcement: Terms and methods. *American Journal of Orthopsychiatry,* 1963, **33,** 624–633.

Lipsitt, L. P., Pederson, L. J., and DeLucia, C. A. Conjugate reinforcement of operant responding in infants. *Psychonomic Science,* 1966, **4,** 67–68.

Rheingold, H. L., Stanley, W. C., and Cooley, J. Method for studying exploratory behavior in infants. *Science,* 1962, **136,** 1054–1055.

Rheingold, H. L., Stanley, W. C., and Doyle, G. Visual and auditory reinforcement of a manipulatory response in the young child. *Journal of Experimental Child Psychology,* 1964, **1,** 316–326.

White, B. L. An experimental approach to the effects of experience on early human behavior. In J. P. Hill (Ed.), *Minnesota Symposia on Child Psychology,* Vol. I, pp. 201–226. Minneapolis: University of Minnesota Press, 1967.

12

SOCIAL AND EMOTIONAL BEHAVIOR IN INFANCY: SOME DEVELOPMENTAL ISSUES AND PROBLEMS*

HENRY N. RICCIUTI

My major concern in the present discussion will not be to offer a broad summary of the principal literature dealing with social and emotional development in infancy. A number of excellent reviews and discussions of some of the most salient topics in this broad area have appeared within the past several years (e.g., Yarrow's review of the effects of maternal separation (1964), Bronfenbrenner's paper on early deprivation in mammals and man (1968), Rheingold's discussion of the development of social behavior in infancy (1966), etc.). Rather, my main purpose will be to point out and discuss what seem to me to be some important current research issues and areas of investigation which hold particular promise for advancing our understanding of the nature and development of social and emotional behavior in human infancy. At the same time, I would like to indicate both the historical contrast, as well as the continuity, between these contemporary research issues and those which represented some of the main concerns of earlier investigators in the field of child development. I shall therefore precede my discussion of current research emphases with a brief summary of the early descriptive studies of social and emotional behavior and development in infancy.

SOME DEFINITIONAL NOTES

Thus far I've used the terms "social" and "emotional" rather glibly, as though they were either closely related, or possibly even interchangeable.

* From *Merrill-Palmer Quarterly,* 1968, *14,* 82–100. Reprinted with permission from the author and the Merrill-Palmer Institute.

Presented at The Merrill-Palmer Institute Conference on Research and Teaching of Infant Development, February 9–11, 1967, directed by Irving E. Sigel, chairman of research. The conference was financially supported in part by the National Institute of Child Health and Human Development.

This usage of the two terms in close juxtaposition, which one finds quite commonly, reflects the fact that there is indeed a close relationship between social and emotional behavior. A great many significant social interactions in infancy involve important affective or emotional components; similarly, some of the most potent instigators of emotional responses are "social" stimuli, i.e. stimuli emitted by another person. On the other hand, if one regards social behavior, broadly considered, as any behavior that is evoked, maintained, and modified by the behavior of another person (Rheingold, 1966), obviously much social behavior is not associated with significant emotional responses; at the same time, important emotional responses are evoked by a wide range of non-social stimuli. In the present discussion, I shall be concerned with emotional behavior whether instigated by social or non-social stimuli; with respect to social behavior, however, my primary reference will be to social responses which typically have significant emotional or affective components associated with them.

The problem of defining the precise nature of what is meant by the "emotions" or "affects" has been a major concern of many philosophers, psychologists, and physiologists for a good many years. At this point in our discussion, it would be helpful to have at least a brief working definition of emotional behavior. I have found the following conceptualization, distilled from a variety of sources, to be particularly meaningful: we tend to regard a particular behavior as "emotional" when it represents an appreciable change from some typical "baseline," or characteristic level or mode of response, *and* where the behavioral change is accompanied by physiological or visceral changes and by a change in subjective or experiential state, generally along a pleasure-displeasure or hedonic continuum. Thus, we might say that an emotion typically has a behavioral or action component, a physiological or arousal component, and a subjective or hedonic component (Hamburg, 1963). This last component, that of subjective state or feeling, is obviously the most troublesome and controversial one conceptually, and as expected, it poses particular problems for us when we try to analyze the nature of emotions in infants. A final definitional note: while the terms "emotional" and "affective" are often used interchangeably, in common usage the latter usually implies some reference to the subjective component, whereas the former may not.

EARLY DESCRIPTIVE STUDIES OF SOCIAL AND EMOTIONAL BEHAVIOR IN INFANCY

Early studies of social and emotional behavior in infancy tended to be primarily descriptive in nature, and were addressed particularly to the question of what sorts of social and emotional responses were typically observable in children at successive age levels. The major historical change, as in many areas of study in child development, has been the transition from this descriptive focus to the contemporary emphasis on analytic studies, which are primarily concerned with understanding the nature of social and emotional behavior, and with the question of how particular patterns of developmental change come about. While it has become somewhat fashionable in recent years to speak rather disparagingly of studies which are primarily descriptive in nature, I would like to emphasize the very real importance of these early studies, which provided so many insightful observations and questions concerning social and emotional behavior, often foreshadowing a good deal of the content of contemporary research in the area.

Three major sources of data on social and emotional development are provided by these early studies in the field. First, there are the informal, but detailed qualitative observations and descriptions reported by such early investigators as Charles Darwin, whose classic treatise on "The expression of the emotions in man and animals," written nearly a hundred years ago (1873) is still an essential reference in the field; James Sully, writing in England in 1895, and Stern in Germany about 20 years later (1924), describing and speculating about the nature of young children's fear of strange, novel, or unusual objects; James Baldwin in America (1895), describing what he called "organic bashfulness" in the latter part of the first year of life, when the infant turned away from the stranger and toward the mother; and finally Karl and Charlotte Buhler in Austria, in the late 1920's and early thirties, describing the affective pleasure infants derive from simple motoric movements, and from mastery of simple motoric tasks (i.e., "function pleasure") (1930).

The second source of descriptive information on social and emotional behavior is provided by the systematic normative data collected in the development and standardization of the various infant tests, beginning with Buhler (1935) and Gesell (1928) in the twenties. While social and emotional responses represented only a small part of the total pool of items included in most of the early baby tests, we still depend very much on such data for descriptive information regarding the age of appearance of particular behaviors such as smiling and cooing in response to the adult face, showing displeasure at the removal of a toy, engaging in playful social imitation, etc. (e.g., Gesell, 1940; Griffiths, 1954).

The third major source of data is found in the relatively large number of systematic descriptive or quasi-experimental studies which began to appear mainly in the early and middle thirties. These investigations typically involved the collection of information concerning the age of appearance of a variety of specific emotional and social behaviors, based on observations or parental records and reports for fairly large samples of children. (For example, see Bridges, 1932; Blatz and Millichamp, 1935; Jersild and Holmes, 1935; Jones and Jones, 1928.)

Given this threefold body of literature, what is the general portrayal of the over-all course of social and emotional development in the first two years of life which emerges therefrom? First, with respect to the infant's changing social responsiveness, the general picture provided by these studies remains a fairly reliable one, although it is limited to rather gross developmental changes. Very briefly, clear-cut pleasureful social responses to other people do not appear until approximately the end of the second month, when any human face readily instigates smiling and other indications of positive affect. This indiscriminate positive social response to humans continues until approximately the 5th or 6th month, after which smiling at strangers seems to be considerably reduced. Moreover, toward the end of the first year there is a rather marked tendency for infants to respond to the approach of a stranger with considerable distress and anxiety. Simultaneously, affectional attachments to specific adults such as the parents become more marked and clearly delineated, and this trend continues into the second year, during the latter part of which one also sees increasing social and affectional interactions with other children. While the general pattern of development change just outlined seems reasonably well established, we sorely need more precise descriptions of these changes in social responsiveness and their variations, as well as systematic analyses of the various major influences which function as determinants of such changes. A concern with precisely these sorts of questions represents one of the major emphases of contemporary research in the field.

Turning next to a consideration of the somewhat more general problem of emotional behavior and development, it is probably fair to say that a good many of the specific issues and questions raised by early investigators in this field are still very much with us. Many of the early studies were concerned with such questions as what emotional responses, if any, are present in the neonate (Watson, 1917); at what points in subsequent development is it possible to identify specific emotions (or emotional behaviors, we would prefer to say nowadays); how are these expressed; what are the stimulus situations which evoke emotional responses of a particular sort; etc.

Again there are a few broad, empirical generalizations emerging from these studies which most people would probably regard as reasonably acceptable today. In the neonate, one can only differentiate between states of quiescence and undifferentiated excitement (according to Bridges, 1932), or between quiescence and a primitive sort of "unpleasure" (Spitz, 1950). By the end of the first month one can more readily distinguish between quiescence and what Bridges calls "distress" reactions, but it is not until the end of the 2nd or 3rd month that clear "pleasurable" responses are seen, chiefly in the smiling, increased vocalizations, and bodily activity constituting the positive social response to people. From this point on, with increasing development, more highly differentiated forms of positive as well as negative emotional behaviors occur. Just how distinct these are, and how one can best conceptualize, observe, and measure them are thorny problems that are very much in the forefront of our current thinking and research today (e.g., Escalona, 1963; Spitz, 1963; Tomkins, 1962, 1963; Wolff, 1966).

SOME CONTEMPORARY RESEARCH EMPHASES AND SIGNIFICANT AREAS OF INVESTIGATION

Having reviewed very briefly the general nature and major outcomes of the primarily descriptive earlier studies of social and emotional development in infancy, let us consider next two rather broad areas of contemporary research activity which appear to me to involve particularly promising lines of empirical as well as theoretical investigation.

One of the major emphases characterizing a large body of current research is a concern with more detailed analyses of the role of stimulus and situational determinants of social and emotional responses. This emphasis is particularly well represented in recent research on the development of attachment behavior in infants, and in research concerned with specifying the role of various stimulus cues as elicitors, and sometimes as reinforcers, of responses involved in adult-infant interaction. In both instances, we find a great deal of significant research currently being undertaken not only with humans, but with various species of infra-human mammals and birds as well.

Much of the recent and contemporary work aimed at specifying the processes involved in the development of the infant's attachment to familiar adults has been greatly influenced, if not stimulated, by Bowlby's theoretical writings on the nature of the mother-infant tie (1958) and the related problem of separation anxiety (1960). Bowlby suggested that certain innate response systems in the infant's repertoire play an important role in establishing the initial "tie" with the mother, since these responses are readily elicitable by appropriate stimuli and help to ensure proximity to and caretaking by mother. Included among such response systems are sucking, clinging, and visual or locomotor following behavior, as well as smiling and crying, the last two serving as particularly effective stimuli for eliciting social or caretaking responses from mother. The infant's first manifestations of protest and distress reactions on separation from mother are regarded as a form of "primary anxiety," associated with the persistent activation of such response systems as crying, clinging, and following under circumstances (i.e., isolation from mother) which prevent their normal termination (i.e., proximity to mother). Bowlby goes on to point out the importance of the connection between these separation reactions and the infant's fear or fright responses to stimuli instigating escape or freezing, such as sudden noise, strangeness, etc. Observations of infants of many species indicate that relatively intense fear reactions are terminated not by mere flight alone but by escape to a particular "haven of safety" (e.g., a home nest, another animal, or the mother). Thus, after the infant has developed specific attachments to adults, being frightened and at the same time separated from mother poses for the infant a situation where the terminating or distress-reducing situation both for the escape behaviors instigated by the fright stimulus, and for the crying, clinging, and following responses instigated by separation is essentially the same, i.e., closeness to mother. Circumstances such as these place the infant in a situation of "double exposure" to distress reactions which specifically require mother for their alleviation.

Several recent studies provide good illustrations of contemporary investigations in which problems of the sort just indicated are being investigated empirically under circumstances that permit one to examine rather closely some of the relevant stimulus and situational determinants of the behavior under investigation. Morgan and Ricciuti (1968) examined changes in infants' affective responses to a stranger during the period from 4 to 12 months, employing a laboratory situation in which a male and female stranger systematically approached the infant, who was sometimes on mother's lap, sometimes 4 feet away from her. Generally speaking, the younger the infants, the more positive the responses to the stranger, and it was not until the 12-month level that one could characterize the reactions as generally more negative than positive. Prior to 8 months of age, the infants were equally positive in their responses regardless of their proximity to mother. From that point on, however, closeness to mother began to play an increasingly important role, with the responses to the stranger being significantly less positive or more negative when the infant was separated from mother (as one would expect from Bowlby's theory). The younger infants responded more positively as the stranger initiated closer and more active social contact, whereas the opposite was true for the older infants. Finally, the female stranger elicited more positive and less negative reactions from the infants at all ages than the male stranger.

Another example of research concerned with specifying the role of particular situational variables may be found in an interesting series of experiments by Rheingold (1968) in which she examined the emotional and exploratory behavior of 9½-month-old infants in a strange laboratory room whose characteristics were systematically varied. Infants placed alone in the room when it was either empty, contained a few toys, or contained a strange young female about 6 feet away, showed a good deal of emotional distress and inhibited normal locomotor activity. In contrast to this group, babies who found their mothers present in the otherwise empty room produced non-distress vocalizations rather than crying, and explored the room freely. In short, Rheingold concludes, mother's presence seemed to neutralize the strangeness of the environment confronting the infant. There was some evidence, also, suggesting that the strange room was most distressing when it contained the unfamiliar person.

These findings, that proximity to mother attenuates the infants' negative responses to strange stimuli and supports positive emotional responses and exploratory behavior, are strikingly paralleled in recent animal studies, even when the "mother" happens to be a cloth-covered surrogate to which infant rhesus monkeys had become "attached" (Harlow, 1961), or a green styrofoam rectangle to which Peking ducklings had been imprinted (Stettner and Tilds, 1966). It seems quite clear that our understanding of the complex factors involved in the interplay between the infant's developing attachment to specific adults and the nature of his responses to separation and to fear-eliciting stimuli will be considerably facilitated as we continue to find ways of studying objectively the specific influence of various major determinants of the social and emotional behaviors involved.

Thus far we have been discussing recent analyses of stimulus and situational determinants of social and emotional responses at given points in development. There is obviously great need for a more complete understanding of how initial patterns of response are subsequently modified through experience and learning. This is particularly true in regard to the development of the complex, mutually adaptive response patterns involved in infant-adult attachment behavior. A number of investigators have been concerned with the role of specific stimuli as elicitors and reinforcers of some of the social and emotional responses involved in mother-infant interaction, within a learning framework. It has been shown, for example (Rheingold, Gewirtz, and Ross, 1959), that 3-month-old infants made increasingly frequent vocalizations to an adult when such vocalizations were immediately followed by the adult smiling broadly, making "tsk, tsk" sounds, and touching the infant lightly on the abdomen. When such "reinforcement" no longer followed the infants' vocalizations, their frequency decreased substantially.

The study just mentioned was concerned with the effects of adult reinforcement of infant vocalizations under controlled, experimental conditions. Can learning analyses of this sort be employed profitably in the study of naturally occurring infant-adult interaction? The recent work of Gewirtz and Gewirtz (1968) provides an excellent illustration of a research strategy aimed at facilitating learning analyses of infant-adult interaction occurring in "natural" settings. These investigators began by making detailed observational records of the sequential behaviors of infants and mothers (or other adult caretakers) in several different environments. Analysis of these records then permits them to define and compare the caretaking environments, in terms of the availability of specific stimuli of various sorts as potential elicitors and/or reinforcers of infant social responses (e.g., specific caretaking behaviors of adults, physical characteristics of the environment, etc.). Further analyses make it possible to determine the relative frequency of occurrence of various infant responses to particular adult behaviors, and vice versa. Some preliminary analyses indicate, for example, that the likelihood of an infant's vocalization being followed by an adult's smile varied from .21 to .42 for different adult-child pairs, whereas the likelihood that the infant's smile would elicit an adult smile was considerably greater, from .46 to .88. Further work, either under way or planned, is aimed at more refined evaluations of the degree to which various adult responses are made contingent upon particular infant behaviors, and at methods for handling longer sequential interaction "chains." Although complicated and time consuming, this approach holds great promise both for defining more precisely the salient features of the environment impinging on the infant, and for understanding how the infant and adults in his environment begin to modify one another's behavior.

The last problem just mentioned has been under investigation in a somewhat different manner in the earliest weeks of life by Sander and Julia (1966). By employing procedures which permit continuous 24-hour monitoring of the infant's motility, crying, periods of sleep and wakefulness, as well as various interventions by the nurse-caretaker, these investigators are able to examine relationships between the infants' rhythm patterns and the caretaker's interventions as these become modified over a period of weeks, in the direction of increasing or decreasing regulation and adaptation in the adult-infant interaction.

Turning from our discussion of research focused mainly on infant-adult interaction, I want to make brief reference to the increasing attention being directed to the problem of identifying the particular stimulus elements or cues which account for the apparent effectiveness of certain relatively complex stimulus configurations as elicitors of early social and emotional responses in infants, often of a presumably unlearned sort. (This line of approach has traditionally been employed to advantage by ethologists in their analysis of the stimulus determinants of behavior in various species of animals and birds—e.g., Hinde, 1966; Thorpe, 1963.) For example, it has long been known that one of the most potent elicitors of the smiling response in early infancy is the face of the human adult, particularly when it is animated by talking and smiling. In recent years, investigators have been trying to specify more precisely which particular cues in this stimulus configuration are primarily involved in instigating smiling behavior at various points in the infant's development, beginning with the first few weeks of life (Ahrens, 1954; Wolff, 1963, 1966).

Paralleling this line of inquiry is a concern with exploring the social or emotional response-eliciting characteristics of a rather broad range of stimuli in various modalities. Salzen (1963), for example, working with one infant, found that at 8 weeks of age relatively simple, non-human visual stimuli elicited smiling responses (e.g., a black-and-white cardboard oval, particularly when rotated slowly). By the 12th week such simple stimuli failed to elicit smiling, but "novel" combinations of visual and auditory cues, such as a rattle or clock, would do so. Wolff (1963) was readily able to elicit smiling as well as positive vocalizations in 4- to 5-week-old infants by placing the infant's hands in his own, and bouncing his hands together three times in rapid succession (as though playing "pat-a-cake"), while keeping his face out of sight of the infant. A particularly interesting recent investigation by Kistiakovskaia (1965) was concerned with determining the stimulus conditions which elicit and help to establish the "positive emotional complex of responses" in infants during the first weeks and months of life. Her interpretation placed particular emphasis upon the role of rather prolonged visual fixation of immobile target objects, and of convergence and divergence responses to an object being moved toward and away from the infant, as basic instigators of the earliest positive emotional responses of smiling, vocalization, and animated movements.

While the last several studies mentioned were directly concerned with stimulus determinants involved in the elicitation of smiling and other positive emotional responses, they can actually be regarded as part of several broader lines of currently active research dealing with the general problem of characteristics of incoming stimulation as they affect a variety of behavioral responses. It is to these lines of investigation that I would now like to turn.

The second broad area of contemporary research which I regard as having particularly promising implications for our understanding of the nature and role of emotional behavior in infancy is represented by studies dealing with the following set of discrete but related topics: (*a*) approach-withdrawal processes; (*b*) exploratory behavior, curiosity, and intrinsic motivation; and (*c*) arousal or activation, orienting and alerting responses. By way of introductory comment, let me say that I believe that studies of these problems, which are very much under investigation currently with both humans and animals, are extremely relevant for the study of affect and emotional behavior, even though many of the investigations have not been directly concerned with affect or emotion as such to begin with. What these studies have in common, despite often diverse initial aims, is a concern with the behavioral orientation of the infant (or animal) toward particular types of external stimulation, as well as a concern with explaining such orientation in terms of the nature of the stimulus information impinging upon the subject, and the manner in which such information is "processed" as a function of the previous experience or current state of the infant. Since we regard emotions or affects as having a physiological arousal or activation component, and a behavioral or action component which often takes the form of a heightened orientation toward or away from the salient object, the relevance of studies of the problems just mentioned should be obvious. At the same time, it seems to me that research on these very problems would often be enhanced by more direct efforts to isolate and study the affective or pleasure-displeasure components involved in the behavior being investigated.

Let me give you a few examples of some relevant issues and problems being considered in the general areas of research I have just mentioned.

Approach and withdrawal processes

While many of the previously discussed studies of infant-adult attachment dealt with approach and withdrawal responses of various types, I would like to speak here of research which reflects a more general concern with the nature of such processes. It is pretty generally agreed by many investigators that the response systems which mediate appropriate approach and withdrawal responses to stimuli of varying intensities (or qualities) are among the most fundamental, from the point of view of both phylogenetic and ontogenetic development. In attempting to integrate the results of many studies in this area into a broad theory of approach-withdrawal processes, Schneirla (1965) has argued that it is the intensity of stimulation which is crucial: a broad range of low stimulus intensities (or small changes in intensity) tend to instigate approach responses while a broad range of high stimulus intensities (or large intensity changes) produce withdrawal responses. Stimulus intensity is not definable entirely objectively, but it is rather a matter of "effective stimulus input," which is a function of such factors as the particular species involved, as well as age, previous experience, adaptation, etc. In the case of higher animals, intensity of stimulation is the crucial determinant early in life, while the qualitative features of different objects and stimuli become salient as a result of subsequent development and learning.

This point of view, of course, is directly opposed to the idea that animals (and human infants) are capable of manifesting approach or withdrawal responses to innately perceived qualitative features of stimuli (e.g., particular visual patterns or shapes). Schneirla has argued, for example, that the distress responses shown by ducklings to a moving hawk-shaped silhouette, and not to the same silhouette moving in the opposite direction (with the simulated appearance of a goose), can be explained in terms of differences in the magnitude of the changes in retinal stimulation produced, rather than by assuming an innate discrimination of the hawk from the goose configuration. A recent study (Green, Green, and Carr, 1966) provides some confirmatory evidence for ducklings responding selectively to the configurational properties of the hawk silhouette. Recent studies with human neonates, of course, also provide increasing evidence of preferential visual responses to shape and pattern (Fantz and Nevis, 1967).

There seems to be no doubt about the central importance of stimulus intensity and intensity change as one of the important determinants of approach and withdrawal responses (particularly the latter). At the same time, there is good evidence that qualitative or structural features of stimuli play a salient role even very early in development, both with humans and some lower species. One of the crucial problems which Schneirla was attempting to deal with and which most current investigators are still struggling with, is that of how best to conceptualize and define the relevant characteristics of "the stimulus," so that we can look for more meaningful relationships between the infant's approach and withdrawal behavior, or emotional responses, and the nature of the stimulation impinging upon him.

Exploratory Behavior, Curiosity, and Intrinsic Motivation

One of the people who has been very much concerned with defining characteristics of stimulation which instigate approach behaviors such as exploration and curiosity is Berlyne (1960, 1966). In searching for a motivational explanation of such behavior in rats as well as in human infants, Berlyne proposed that there are certain "collative" properties of stimuli which induce curiosity and specific exploratory (or information seeking) activity. These properties include such characteristics as novelty, surprisingness, incongruity, and complexity. They are referred to as "collative" properties since they require that the animal collate or compare information from different stimulus elements which appear in some sense to be discrepant or incompatible, either with other elements in the same stimulus or with previously perceived stimuli. According to Berlyne, it is this uncertainty or incompleteness of information which generates the state of discomfort he regards as perceptual curiosity, and the function of specific exploratory behavior is to provide the additional information needed to reduce this discomfort. (Note the persistent influence of drive reduction theory here!)

Berlyne has gone considerably farther than Schneirla in attempting to specify a number of clearly important qualitative characteristics of stimuli which appear to elicit approach behavior, and in providing a hypothesized explanation of such behavior in terms of its information-seeking function. On the other hand, the collative properties of stimuli are still extremely difficult to define and measure objectively, in part because they depend to some extent on the subject's previous experience with the stimuli. Another perplexing problem, which has been with us for a long time, is that some novel, surprising, or incongruous stimuli produce conflicting approach and withdrawal reactions, or clear escape and fear responses. Some examples of this are the human infant's fear responses to strangers toward the end of the first year of life, and the chimpanzee's marked fear reactions to cadavers or skulls of chimpanzees (Hebb, 1946).

This problem has been dealt with by a number of people, including Hunt (1965) who considers the issue in considerable depth as part of his recent detailed discussion of the role of "intrinsic motivation" in psychological development (i.e., motivation not dependent on primary drive reduction, but intrinsic to such "spontaneous" activities as play, exploration, problem solving, etc.). Hunt includes the collative stimulus properties proposed by Berlyne under his generic concept of "incongruity," which is a central part of his theory of intrinsic motivation and early development. In this broader context, incongruity represents a discrepancy between stimulus information impinging on the infant at any given time and some relevant standard of comparison, which may be either "external" to the subject, in terms of ongoing or concurrent stimulation, or "internal" in the sense of its being based upon the stored information or "schemata" resulting from previous experience. (See also Hunt, 1961, pp. 267–269.)

Hunt proposes that the notion of an "optimal level of incongruity," which has been suggested in various forms by other theorists as well, may be the best way to account for the broad range of responses we find to various novel, surprising, or strange stimuli. According to this model, stimuli representing optimal levels of incongruity would be generally attractive for the infant, and might be regarded as generating an "optimal" level of arousal or physiological activation. Stimuli constituting extreme degrees of incongruity would instigate withdrawal or escape responses, while stimulus conditions representing levels well below the optimal (e.g., conditions of minimal or unchanging stimulation) would elicit attempts to seek interaction with the environment providing higher levels of incongruity. Presumably the affective state or hedonic tone associated with optimal incongruity levels would be generally positive, while that associated with either of the extreme levels would be generally negative.

This "optimal level" model we have been discussing has seemed to many of us to be a basically reasonable and heuristically valuable one. On the other hand, it is extremely difficult to define levels of incongruity objectively in our specific research endeavors, and one has to guard against the tendency to base one's stimulus definitions, even in part, upon the nature of the infant's or animal's responses. As Hunt himself puts it, the concept of incongruity is "operationally slippery" (1965, p. 213). For example, Morgan and I found (1968) that while our infants began to respond less positively or more negatively to the strange experimenter as we moved from the 8-month to the 12-month level, they appeared increasingly to enjoy both a realistic and a grossly distorted mask of the human face which we presented at the end of a rod. How do we determine objectively whether the strange examiners or the masks were the most incongruous stimuli, representing the greater discrepancy from the infant's "schemata" of familiar faces or persons? There is also the problem, of course, of determining what other motivational or experiential factors might have been operating, in addition to incongruity as such. As we begin to find better solutions to specific questions like these, we ought to be able to gain a better understanding of the determinants of the infant's behavior, and to confirm, or elaborate on, the optimal level of incongruity notion.

Arousal or Activation; Orienting and Alerting Responses

Generally speaking the concepts of arousal or activation refer to such characteristics as excitation, alertness, or responsivity, which are manifested in a complex of physiological changes (e.g., in heart rate, respiration, electrical activity of the brain, muscle action potentials, etc.), as well as in such behavioral properties as activity level, motility patterns, postural responses, attentiveness to stimuli, etc. The question of the levels and patterns of arousal associated with various forms of approach and withdrawal reactions, exploratory behavior, and other intrinsically motivated behaviors, is obviously a very important one.

An increasing amount of systematic research attention is being directed to the general problems of arousal and activation in infants as well as animals, both in the context of the kinds of problems we've been discussing, as well as in other contexts (e.g., Duffy, 1962; Lynn, 1966). Much of the contemporary research in this area has been stimulated by the extensive Russian studies of the physiological and behavioral responses associated with the "orientation reaction" (when the animal responds to a stimulus with the mobilization of a complex of responses which appear to make him maximally alert to and prepared to deal with the stimulus). The differential response patterns associated with "defensive reactions," generated by too intense or too sudden stimuli, has also been under investigation. (See Lynn, 1966, for a summary of this Russian work.)

While there are many technical as well as conceptual problems involved in the securing and utilization of physiological measures as indices of arousal or activation, a good deal of hard and generally promising work is being done on the development and use of such measures, often in association with related behavioral indices. Changes in heart rate, respiration, or electrical skin potential, for example, are being employed as indices of degree of responsiveness or attention to both visual and auditory stimuli in neonates and in older infants (Brackbill et al., 1966; Graham and Clifton, 1966; Lewis et al., 1966; Stechler, Bradford and Levy, 1966; Steinschneider, Lipton, and Richmond, 1966).

There has also been a great deal of recent effort directed toward more precise assessment of the behaviorally observable arousal or activation characteristics of newborns and very young infants (sometimes referred to as the "state" variable), either as a relatively stable characteristic of the individual infant (Birns, 1965; Escalona, 1962), or as an important "baseline" condition which must be specified for any infant at the time when his responses to particular stimulation are being observed and evaluated (Escalona, 1965; Prechtl, 1965; Wolff, 1966).

In such studies of arousal in very young infants it seems pretty clear that we are often dealing with at least rudimentary precursors of emotional behavior. It is interesting to note, for example, that the highest level of behavioral arousal in these studies is usually judged by the presence of marked crying, agitation, and irritability, or what some of us might be quite willing to call a state of hedonically negative excitation. As a matter of fact, the general question of the aversiveness or attractiveness of different levels of arousal or activation is a very fundamental one which has concerned psychological theorists for a long time. Closely paralleling the notion of "optimal levels of incongruity," which we discussed earlier, is the point of view that much of the organism's behavior is directed toward obtaining or maintaining optimal levels of arousal or activation, since levels which are either too high or too low are aversive, and in some sense hedonically or affectively negative. (See Hunt, 1965, for a theoretical discussion of these issues.)

While the reduction of aversively high levels of arousal (or drive) has long been accepted as a prime motivational determinant of behavior, the notion that animals or humans will behave so as to increase their levels of arousal, incongruity, or stimulation, is a more recent arrival on the experimental scene. The precise circumstances under which such behavioral events will take place and why they take place, are questions that are far from being answered to everyone's satisfaction. For example, are some forms of exploratory behavior and simple problem solving activities engaged in by infants primarily because they are intrinsically pleasurable and perhaps generate an "optimal level of arousal" (as Buhler, 1930 or Hunt, 1965 might argue), or because they serve to reduce the discomfort of boredom drive or perceptual curiosity (as Berlyne might put the matter), or are both factors operative at different points in the ongoing behavior? Are some forms of perceptual or investigatory activity sustained because the organism is biologically and psychologically constructed to operate on incoming stimulus information until it is somehow meaningfully "processed" and assimilated with previously stored information (as Piaget, 1952 or Hunt, 1965 might put it), with the hedonic or affective state accompanying such activities often being essentially neither positive nor negative, though the infant may be operating at a relatively high level of arousal and alertness?

In the course of reviewing the impressive body of literature on approach and withdrawal processes, exploratory behavior, intrinsic motivation, and arousal or activation phenomena, it has seemed to me that some of the issues raised by research in these areas, including the specific questions I've just posed, might be approached more fruitfully if we attempted to specify more directly the hedonic, or pleasure-displeasure characteristics associated with the behaviors we are attempting to understand. Admittedly this is not always an easy task, particularly if we try to identify behavioral indicators of pleasure-displeasure (or affective tone) which are distinguishable from the responses we are utilizing as indicators of approach or withdrawal, and of arousal or activation, as I think needs to be done.

What are some of the alternatives to this approach? One alternative followed by some investigators, is to ignore the issue of hedonic qualities, on the grounds that these pleasure-displeasure components cannot be specified objectively anyway, although one might still be perfectly willing to employ expressive responses like the distress calls of pups or ducklings as objective indicators of avoidance reactions, and the smile of the infant as an indicator of approach behavior or attention. Other alternatives, shown in some of the theoretical discussions already cited, involve making a number of implicit assumptions about the qualities of aversiveness or attractiveness, pleasure or displeasure, which might be associated with various forms of approach and withdrawal behavior, and with various levels of arousal. Clearly, however, we'd be considerably better off if we had more direct measures of the pleasure-displeasure characteristics associated with these behaviors.

These are some of the reasons why, in our own current research on emotional behavior in the first year of life, we are directing some of our major efforts to the problem of identifying, hopefully by independent criteria, appropriate behavioral indicators of the three essential characteristics of the infant's responses which we've been discussing, namely: (1) the approach-withdrawal, or "directional" qualities of the behavior (distinguished as stimulus maintaining and enhancing, stimulus seeking, stimulus terminating and avoiding, much in the manner suggested by Schneirla, 1965 and Ambrose, 1963); (2) the arousal or activation characteristics (in terms of activity and motility increases or inhibition, intensity of responses, and eventually, selected physiological responses); and (3) the pleasure-displeasure, or hedonic qualities (as reflected in facial behavior, smiling, laughing, crying, other qualities of vocalizations and accompanying movements). Our hope is that if we can more adequately identify and assess these specific qualities of the infant's responses, we should be in a much better position to examine empirically the patterns of relationship among them, as components of what we regard as emotional behavior. At the same time, we ought to be able to arrive at more meaningful descriptions and analyses of the many ambiguous and conflictful or mixed reactions one observes so often in infants as they are confronted with such "incongruous" stimuli as unfamiliar or unexpected object movements or sounds, strange adults or strange environments, distortions of familiar stimuli, novel or "surprising" stimuli of various sorts, etc.

SUMMARY

In summary, my major purpose in this paper has been to point out and discuss some contemporary research issues and emphases which appear to me to be of particular significance in regard to the general problem of social and emotional behavior and development in infancy. I have tried to indicate very briefly the historical contrast, as well as the continuity, between these current research issues and some of the central concerns of early investigators in the field. One pervasive and important research emphasis has been a concern with more precise analyses of stimulus and situational determinants of social and emotional behavior, as shown in the many studies of infant attachment behavior in both humans and animals, and in analyses of the eliciting as well as the reinforcing effects of salient stimuli involved in infant-adult interaction.

Another set of very important issues is being investigated widely in connection with research on approach and withdrawal processes; exploratory behavior, curiosity and intrinsic motivation; and arousal or activation. These problem areas are particularly relevant to our concern with emotional behavior in infancy, since they deal essentially with the directional and the arousal characteristics of the infant's responses, both of which we regard as important components of emotional behavior. I have suggested that if we can combine our studies of these aspects of the infant's responses with better assessments of the pleasure-displeasure, or hedonic qualities involved in such behavior, our research efforts in this area should be considerably enhanced.

One of our main problems is still that of adequately conceptualizing the nature of emotional processes early in life, and the transformations undergone by these processes and their precursors during ontogenesis, beginning with birth. Some of the most perceptive discussions of these difficult issues may be found in the recent writing of Spitz (1963) and Wolff (1966, pp. 74–80). Concurrent with these conceptual problems are those we face in attempting to assess the most salient behavioral indicators of emotional responses in infants at different points in development. It seems to me that as we make further progress along these basic lines, investigations focussed on the influence of major "independent" variables on emotional and social development in infancy will be considerably more fruitful.

Finally, I think that it is probably obvious by now that we cannot adequately study social and emotional behavior in infancy independently of other basic psychological processes involved in the infant's behavior and development. Perceptual-cognitive and learning processes clearly play a major role in determining what social or emotional responses will be elicited by particular stimulus conditions, as well as how such responses will be expressed in behavior. Much of the contemporary research we've discussed has been very much concerned with just this sort of interaction. Conversely, social and emotional factors play a significant role in the development of perceptual-cognitive behavior and of various motivational systems. One of the significant features of the contemporary research scene is that many investigators are increasingly inclined to examine the role of the *various* psychological processes which may be involved in particular transactions of importance between the infant and his environment.

REFERENCES

Ahrens, R. Beitrag zur Entwicklung der Physiognomie und Mimikerkennens. *Zeit. fur exp. und ang. Psychol.,* 1954, 2, 414–454; 599–633.

Ambrose, J. A. The age of onset of ambivalence in early infancy: indications from the study of laughing. *J. Child Psychol. Psychiat.,* 1963, **4**, 167–187.

Baldwin, J. M. *Mental development in the child and in the race.* New York: Macmillan, 1895.

Berlyne, D. *Conflict, arousal and curiosity.* New York: McGraw-Hill, 1960.

BERLYNE, D. Curiosity and exploration. *Science,* 1966, **153,** 25–33.

BIRNS, BEVERLY. Individual differences in human neonates' responses to stimulation. *Child Develpm.,* 1965, **36,** 249–256.

BLATZ, W. E. & MILLICHAMP, D. A. The development of emotion in the infant. *Univer. Toronto Studies, Child Develpm. Series,* 1935, **4.**

BOWLBY, J. The nature of the child's tie to his mother. *Internat. J. Psychoanal.,* 1958, **39,** 350–373.

BOWLBY, J. Separation anxiety. *Internat. J. Psychoanal.,* 1960, **41,** 89–113.

BRACKBILL, YVONNE, ADAMS, GAIL, CROWELL, D. H., & GRAY, M. LIBBIE: Arousal level in neonates and preschool children under continuous auditory stimulation. *J. exp. Child Psychol.,* 1966, **4,** 178–188.

BRIDGES, K. M. B. Emotional development in early infancy. *Child Develpm.,* 1932, **3,** 324–341.

BRONFENBRENNER, U. Early deprivation: a cross-species analysis. In Grant Newton (Ed.), *Early experience and behavior.* Springfield, Ill.: Charles C. Thomas, 1968 (in press).

BUHLER, CHARLOTTE. *The first year of life.* New York: John Day, 1930.

BUHLER, CHARLOTTE & HETZER, H. *Testing children's development from birth to school age.* New York: Farrar & Rinehart, 1935.

BUHLER, K. *The mental development of the child.* New York: Harcourt Brace, 1930.

CATTELL, PSYCHE. *The measurement of intelligence of infants and young children.* New York: Psychological Corporation, 1940.

DARWIN, C. (1873). *The expression of the emotions in man and animals.* New York: Philosophical Library, 1955.

DUFFY, ELIZABETH. *Activation and behavior.* New York: Wiley, 1962.

ESCALONA, SIBYLLE K. The study of individual differences and the problem of state. *J. Child Psychiat.,* 1962, **1,** 11–37.

ESCALONA, SIBYLLE K. Some determinants of individual differences. *Trans. New York Acad Sci.,* 1965, **27,** 802–816.

ESCALONA, SIBYLLE K. Emotional development in the first year of life. In Milton J. E. Senn (Ed.), *Problems of infancy and childhood; transactions of the Sixth Conference, March 17 and 18, 1952.* New York: Josiah Macy, Jr. Foundation, 1953. Pp. 11–92.

FANTZ, R. L. & NEVIS, SONIA. Pattern preferences and perceptual-cognitive development in early infancy. *Merrill-Palmer Quart.,* 1967, **13,** 77–108.

GESELL, A. *Infancy and human growth.* New York: Macmillan, 1928.

GESELL, A., ET AL. *The first five years of life.* New York: Harper, 1940.

GEWIRTZ, HAVA B. & GEWIRTZ, J. L. Caretaking settings, background events, and behavior differences in four Israeli child-rearing environments: some preliminary trends. In B. M. Foss (Ed.), *Determinants of infant behavior: IV.* London: Methuen; New York: Wiley, 1968. (In press.)

GRAHAM, FRANCES K. & CLIFTON, RACHEL K. Heart rate change as a component of the orienting response. *Psychol. Bull.,* 1966, **65,** 305–320.

GREEN, MARSHA, GREEN, R., & CARR, W. J. The hawk-goose phenomenon: a replication and an extension. *Psychon. Sci.,* 1966, **4,** 185–186.

GRIFFITHS, R. *The abilities of babies.* London: Univer. of London Press, 1954.

HAMBURG, D. A. Emotions in the perspective of human evolution. In P. H.

Knapp (Ed.), *Expression of the emotions in man.* New York: Internat. Univer. Press, 1963. Pp. 300–317.

Harlow, H. F. The development of affectional patterns in infant monkeys. In B. M. Foss (Ed.), *Determinants of infant behavior: I.* London: Methuen; New York: Wiley, 1961. Pp. 75–97.

Hebb, D. O. On the nature of fear. *Psychol. Rev.*, 1946, **53**, 259–276.

Hinde, R. A. *Animal behavior.* New York: McGraw-Hill, 1966.

Hunt, J. McV. *Intelligence and experience.* New York: Ronald Press, 1961.

Hunt, J. McV. Intrinsic motivation and its role in psychological development. In David Levine (Ed.), *Nebraska symposium on motivation, 1965.* Lincoln: Univer. Nebraska Press, 1965. Pp. 189–282.

Jersild, A. T. & Holmes, F. B. *Children's fears.* (Child development monograph No. 20.) New York: Teachers College, Columbia Univer., 1935.

Jones, H. E. & Jones, Mary C. A study of fear. *Childhood Educ.*, 1928, **5**, 136–143.

Kistiakovskaia, M. I. Stimuli evoking positive emotions in infants in the first months of life. *Sov. Psychol. Psychiat.*, 1965, **3**, 39–48.

Lewis, M., Kagan, J., Campbell, Helen, & Kalafat, J. The cardiac response as a correlate of attention in infants. *Child Develpm.*, 1966, **37**, 63–72.

Lynn, R. *Attention, arousal, and the orientation reaction.* London: Pergamon Press, 1966.

Morgan, G. & Ricciuti, H. N. Infants' responses to strangers during the first year. In B. M. Foss (Ed.), *Determinants of infant behavior: IV.* London: Methuen; New York: Wiley, 1968 (in press).

Piaget, J. *The origins of intelligence in children.* New York: Internat. Univer. Press, 1952.

Prechtl, H. F. R. Problems of behavioral studies in the newborn infant. In D. S. Lehrman, R. A. Hinde, & E. Shaw (Eds.), *Advances in the study of behavior: I.* New York and London: Academic Press, 1965. Pp. 75–98.

Rheingold, Harriet L. The development of social behavior in the human infant. In H. W. Stevenson (Ed.), Concept of development: a report of a conference commemorating the fortieth anniversary of the Institute of Child Development, University of Minnesota. *Monogr. Soc. Res. Child Develpm.*, 1966, **31**, No. 5 (Serial No. 107). Pp. 1–17.

Rheingold, Harriet L. The effect of a strange environment on the behavior of infants. In B. M. Foss (Ed.), *Determinants of infant behavior: IV.* London: Methuen; New York: Wiley, 1968 (In press)

Rheingold, Harriet, Gewirtz, J. L., & Ross, Helen W. Social conditioning of vocalizations. *J. comp. physiol. Psychol.*, 1959, **52**, 68–73.

Salzen, E. Visual stimuli eliciting the smiling response in the human infant. *J. genet. Psychol.*, 1963, **102**, 51–54.

Sander, L. W. & Julia, H. Continuous interactional monitoring in the neonate. *Psychosom. Med.*, 1966, **28**, 822–835.

Schneirla, T. C. Aspects of stimulation and organization in approach/withdrawal processes underlying vertebrate behavioral development. In D. S. Lehrman, R. A. Hinde, & E. Shaw, (Eds.), *Advances in the study of behavior: I.* New York and London: Academic Press, 1965. Pp. 1–74.

Spitz, R. Anxiety in infancy. *Internat. J. Psychoanal.*, 1950, **31**, 138–143.

Spitz, R. A. Ontogenesis: the proleptic function of emotion. In P. H. Knapp (Ed.), *Expression of the emotions in man.* New York: Internat. Univer. Press, 1963. Pp. 36–64.

Stechler, G., Bradford, Susan, & Levy, H. Attention in the newborn: effect on motility and skin potential. *Science,* 1966, **151,** 1246–1248.

Steinschneider, A., Lipton, E. L., & Richmond, J. B. Auditory sensitivity in the infant: effect of intensity on cardiac and motor responsivity. *Child Develpm.,* 1966, **37,** 233–252.

Stern, W. *Psychology of early childhood.* New York: Holt, 1924.

Stettner, L. J. & Tilds, B. N. Effect of presence of an imprinted object on response of ducklings in an open field and when exposed to fear stimulus. *Psychon. Science,* 1966, **4,** 107–108.

Sully, J. *Studies of childhood.* New York: D. Appleton, 1895.

Thorpe, W: H. Learning and instinct in animals. London: Methuen, 1963.

Tomkins, S. S. *Affect, imagery, consciousness.* Vol. I. The positive affects. Vol. II. The negative affects. New York: Springer, 1962, 1963.

Watson, J. B. & Morgan, J. J. B. Emotional reactions and psychological experimentation. *Amer. J. Psychol.,* 1917, **28,** 163–174.

Wolff, P. H. The causes, controls, and organization of behavior in the neonate. *Psychol. Issues,* 1966, **5,** No. 17.

Wolff, P. H. Observations on the early development of smiling. In B. M. Foss (Ed.), *Determinants of infant behavior: II.* London: Methuen; New York: Wiley, 1963, 113–138.

Yarrow, L. J. Separation from parents during early childhood. In M. L. Hoffman and Lois Hoffman (Eds.), *Review of child development research: I.* New York: Russell Sage Found., 1964. Pp. 89–136.

13

AUTONOMIC PUPILLARY REFLEX ACTIVITY DURING EARLY INFANCY AND ITS RELATION TO SOCIAL AND NONSOCIAL VISUAL STIMULI*

HIRAM E. FITZGERALD

RESEARCH WITH adult human *S*s has demonstrated the usefulness of the autonomically regulated pupillary reflex as a measure of the affective value of visual stimuli (Hess, 1965; Hess and Polt, 1960, 1964; Hess, Seltzer, and Shlien, 1965). In these studies, pupillary constriction was found to characterize response to unpleasant visual stimuli, and pupillary dilation to characterize response to pleasant or interesting visual stimuli. Soviet investigators indicate that pupillary reflex dilation forms one component of the orienting reflex which results from change in stimulatory conditions, i.e., novelty (see Sokolov, 1963).

The infant's pupillary reflex is functional very early in postnatal life (Chaney and McGraw, 1932; Guernsey, 1925; Sherman and Sherman, 1925) and has been found to be a dependable measure for use in infant conditioning research (Brackbill, Fitzgerald, and Lintz, 1967; Brackbill, Lintz, and Fitzgerald, 1968; Fitzgerald, Lintz, Brackbill, and Adams, 1967), but has not been extensively investigated in situations other than those involving classical conditioning procedures.

The present study was designed first, therefore, to determine whether infants' preferences for visual stimuli, as measured by pupillary activity, parallel those preferences for visual stimuli (including both social and nonsocial stimulus-patterns) found when fixation is used as the response

* From *Journal of Experimental Child Psychology,* 1968, *6,* 470–482. Reprinted with permission from Academic Press.

Based on a doctoral dissertation submitted to the Faculty of the Graduate School of Arts and Sciences, University of Denver. The writer wishes to express his gratitude to Dr. Yvonne Brackbill for research direction, and to Drs. Kenneth B. Little, Sara A. Allen, and Janet E. Redfield for their help and direction. Grateful appreciation is extended to Dr. Lula Lubchenco and the Pediatric faculty of the University of Colorado Medical Center for their assistance in referral of subjects. This study was supported by USPHS grant MH-8297, NSF grant GB-4784, and the Department of Psychology, University of Denver.

measure. Fixation research has repeatedly suggested, over an age span of the first 6 months of life, that infants prefer stimuli with social value (i.e., human faces or schematic representations of human faces) to patterned, nonsocial stimuli (Fantz, 1958, 1963, 1965; Lewis, Meyers, Kagan, and Grossberg, 1963; Stechler, 1965; Watson, 1965; Thomas, 1965; McCall and Kagan, 1967). At the same time, recent evidence suggests that with at least one nonsocial patterned stimulus—a checkerboard pattern—there is a developmental change in preference during the first 4 months of life. Typically, these studies define complexity in terms of the number of checks contained in the pattern; the least complex checkerboard having the fewest squares. Using this definition, several investigators have shown that infants under 1 month of age prefer less complex checkerboard patterns (Ames and Silfen, 1965; Brennan, Ames, and Moore, 1966; Hershenson, 1964), while infants 4 months old prefer more complex checkerboard patterns (Ames and Silfen, 1965; Brennan *et al.,* 1966). Consequently, selection of stimuli for this study of pupillary activity was based on previously demonstrated stimulus-preferences found in studies of visual fixation.

The stimulus arrangements used in the present study consisted of two visual stimuli with social value (*S*'s mother's face and a female "stranger's" face), and three lacking in social value (a 4-square checkerboard pattern, a 144-square checkerboard pattern and a triangle, a nonsocial pattern found to elicit less preferential responding than checkerboards; Fantz, 1958). If infant pupillary activity is complementary to visual fixation and if pupillary dilation is a reliable index of preference or response to novelty, then (1) greater change in pupil size should accompany the presentation of face stimuli compared to nonsocial patterns, and (2) pupillary change among the nonsocial patterns should be comparable to the differences in fixation obtained by Ames and Silfen (1965), Brennan *et al.* (1966), and Hershenson (1964), i.e., a shift from preference for less complex checkerboards at younger ages to preference for more complex checkerboards at older ages. Finally, less pupillary activity should occur to the triangle due to its low preference value when compared to the other stimuli (Fantz, 1958).

The second purpose of the present study was to determine whether pupillary activity would provide an index of mother-stranger discrimination, i.e., differential responding to mother's face compared to stranger's face. Psychiatric literature suggests that the third quarter of the first year of life is the usual period during which the infant becomes capable of such a discrimination (e.g., Spitz and Wolf, 1946; Spitz, 1950). Behavioral research (Ainsworth, 1963; LaRoche and Tcheng, 1963; Schaffer and Emerson, 1964; Watson, 1965) suggests that differentiation of mother and stranger begins during the second quarter of the first year. Response measures in the latter studies have included smiling, crying, vocalizations, and/or laughing. Recently, Banks and Wolfson (1967), using a psychophysical measure of infant reactivity, cardiac rate, found evidence that differential responding to mothers compared to strangers occurred, surprisingly, as early as 6 weeks of age.

Presence of mother and stranger as well as vocalizations served as response-eliciting cues. If the developmental study of mother recognition and subsequent discrimination of mother and stranger is dependent on more sensitive autonomic measures, as Banks and Wolfson (1967) suggest, then it would seem reasonable to expect differences in pupillary activity—already established as a sensitive and reliable response measure for use in infant research—to reflect early perceptual discrimination of mother compared to stranger.

. . . .

METHOD

Subjects

The *S*s were 30 full-term, white, home-reared, clinically normal infants. There were 10 *S*s in each of three groups. The mean age of *S*s in the 1-month-old group (Group 1m) was 33 days ($SD = 1.9$ days), the mean age of *S*s in the 2-month-old group was 59.7 days ($SD = 5.2$ days), and the mean age of *S*s in the 4-month-old group (Group 4m) was 118.7 days ($SD = 5.0$ days). Of the 30 infants, 18 were male and 12 were female. Nineteen infants had blue eyes, eight had brown eyes, and three had gray eyes.

Nineteen infants were obtained through a newspaper article publicizing the research, and 11 infants were obtained through referrals from the Pediatric faculty of the University of Colorado Medical Center. All infants resided within the metropolitan area of Denver, Colorado.

Stimuli

Each *S*'s mother's face was photographed with a Pentax Hla 35 mm camera under constant-illumination conditions maintained by the use of fixed light meter settings. After the black and white films were processed, the mother's face was cut out of a 5 $\times$ 7 enlarged photograph and pasted on gray construction paper. The black and white reproduction of the unfamiliar adult female's face (hereafter referred to as the stranger's face) was obtained from a popular magazine, cut out, and mounted on the same type of construction paper. The checkerboard patterns and triangle were modified reproductions of patterns used in previous fixation research (Fantz, 1958, 1961; Hershenson, 1964); they were also mounted on gray construction paper. This same gray paper served as a homogeneous field and was presented during the intervals between stimulus presentation.

A Panasonic closed-circuit television camera, described in the apparatus section, was used to record stimuli on Panasonic video tape. Size of stimuli was controlled by adjusting the lens setting and the television camera-to-stimulus distance during the making of the tape. With the particular television apparatus used it was possible to fix the stimulus on the television monitor and measure its width and length immediately prior to recording it on the video tape. The checkerboards measured 7.5 × 7.5 inches; the faces were 7.5 × 5.5 inches, and the triangle measured 7.5 inches on each side.

When recording the stimuli on video tape and when presenting stimuli to *S*, differences in brightness of the stimuli were minimized by: (1) recording stimuli under constant environmental light conditions, (2) maintaining the video control on the tape recorder in a fixed position, (3) using a television camera which to a large extent automatically compensated for change in illumination within the field being recorded, (4) having as background for the test stimuli the same gray construction paper used during the intervals separating the social and nonsocial stimuli, (5) minimizing differences in brightness during the original selection of the stimuli, and (6) by maintaining constant brightness and contrast settings on the television monitor when presenting the stimuli to *S*.

Apparatus

Pupillary responses were recorded on Eastman HIR-430 infrared film with a Bolex H16 reflex camera, Kodak Cine Ektar 102mm *f*:2.7 lens, Bolex 25mm extension tubes, and a Wratten A25 red gelatin filter. The film speed was two frames per second with a 1/35-second exposure. The camera-to-*S* distance was 23 inches. The camera, located outside a ventilated soundproof booth, recorded a mirror image of *S*'s left pupil reflected through an opening in the wall of the booth. Above *S*'s left eye, and shielded from his view, was a small red pilot bulb which provided a photographic record of events. Two electronic timers regulated the on-off cycles of the pilot bulb. These cycles matched the exposure durations of the stimuli presented. An additional record of events, provided by a Grass Model-5 polygraph, was used to facilitate scoring of the films.

Two 25-watt red bulbs, 8 inches in front of *S*'s eyes and 3 inches above his line of vision, provided the light necessary for the infrared photography. The gelatin filter served to prevent light from the stimulus presentation apparatus from reaching the camera. Stimuli were presented via a Panasonic Model NV-7000 video-tape recorder and a Panasonic Model TR-120V television monitor encased in a dull-black housing located 10 inches in front of *S*'s face. A Panasonic Model WV-033P television camera and Cosmicar 25mm lens were used to record the stimuli on Panasonic NVR-71 video tape.

Procedure

Prior to the experiment, *S*'s mother's face was recorded on the video tape which already contained the other stimuli programmed into their respective presentation positions. Stimuli were programmed and presented in five random orders. Each experimental stimulus was presented for 20 seconds. Inter-stimulus intervals, during which the homogeneous gray field was presented, ranged from 10 to 30 seconds with a mean of 20.7 seconds.

After preparation of the video tape, *E* placed *S* in a commercial infant seat located inside the experimental booth and attached the pilot bulb over *S*'s left eyebrow with surgical tape. One *E,* who remained inside the booth, activated the tape recorder and held *S*'s head in position throughout the experiment. Another *E,* outside the booth, activated the camera and regulated the timer that controlled the stimulus exposure intervals. Infants were run while in the state commonly referred to as quiet-alert. If any deviation from this state occurred during the experiment, the session was terminated and the infant was tested at a later date.

The commercially processed films were projected on a Recordak viewer, Model 10, which provided 23× linear enlargement. The diameter of the pupil was measured to the nearest hundredth millimeter by data-reduction equipment composed of a Philbrick operational amplifier, Electro Instruments digital voltmeter, and a Clary digital printer. For analog-to-digital conversion of pupil diameters from projected-film records, the sensing element was a vernier caliper mechanically coupled to a 10-turn Helipot. Both zero point and the scale of the digital printout were selected by varying parameters of the operational amplifier. After adjusting the caliper to the diameter of the pupil, the scorer depressed a "record" button that triggered the data-reduction apparatus. This method of recording pupil diameter has the practical advantage of minimizing experimenter bias in that the scorer is never aware of the printed numerical values of his measurements. As previously reported (Fitzgerald *et al.,* 1967) interscorer reliability of measurement with this apparatus is high, ranging from .90 to .96 ($Md = .94$) for measurements to the nearest hundredth millimeter.

RESULTS AND DISCUSSION

Sex and Iris Color

One significant sex difference ($t = 2.46$) of 20 analyzed with individual t tests was dismissed as chance, since with 20 such comparisons the probability of obtaining a t of 2.46 is .67 (Ryan, 1959). Iris color differences were not statistically analyzed because (a) visual inspection of the data revealed no deviant means and (b) the proportion of *S*s with brown or gray iris color within groups was exceedingly small relative to those with blue eyes. Moreover, published research has shown iris color not to be an influential factor in infant pupillary research (Brackbill *et al.,* 1967).

. . . .

Social versus Nonsocial Patterns

If change in the size of the infant's pupil is a reliable index of responsiveness to visual stimuli, it should parallel the preferences for visual stimuli found when using the visual fixation method. Studies of visual fixation have consistently suggested that infants prefer human faces to nonsocial, geometrical patterns (e.g., Fantz, 1963; Lewis *et al.,* 1963; Stechler, 1965). Table 1 contains rank orders for change in pupil size, based on both the amount and direction of pupillary change for each stimulus presented. The stimulus eliciting the greatest pupillary constriction received a rank of 1, and the stimulus eliciting the greatest pupillary dilation received a rank of 5. Friedman's nonparametric analysis of variance by ranks (Siegel, 1956) indicated that change in pupil size for the five stimuli differed across the three age groups. Nevertheless, a face stimulus received the highest ranking in each of the three age-groups, suggesting that faces were more effective than nonsocial patterns for inducing pupillary activity, thus paralleling the relationship

TABLE 1

Rank Orders of Stimuli Based on Amount and Direction of Pupillary Change*

	Stimulus ranks†,‡				
			Checkerboards		
Group	*Mother*	*Stranger*	*4-square*	*144-square*	*Triangle*
1m	5 (+.04)	1.5 (−.04)	3 (−.02)	4 (+.03)	1.5 (−.04)
2m	5 (+.11)	3 (+.02)	1 (−.04)	2 (+.004)	4 (+.04)
4m	3 (−.02)	5 (+.11)	4 (+.05)	1.5 (−.04)	1.5 (−.04)

* The mean differences on which the ranks are based are shown in parentheses.

† The stimulus receiving the largest pupillary constriction was ranked 1, and rank 5 was assigned to the stimulus producing the largest pupillary dilation.

‡ $X_r^2 = 31.72$, $df = 4$, $p = <.001$.

between face stimuli and nonsocial patterned stimuli suggested in the visual fixation research.

Comparison of the amount of change in pupil size to social versus nonsocial patterns for each age group provided only partial support for the relationships suggested above. Difference scores were computed representing the amount of pupillary change that occurred to both faces combined, and were compared with similar difference scores for the nonsocial patterns. Tests for the significance of the difference between these correlated difference scores indicated that 1-month-old infants responded with significantly greater pupillary dilation to the face stimuli than to the nonsocial patterns ($t = 2.47$, $df = 8$, $p < .05$), as did the 4-month-old infants ($t = 4.35$, $df = 8$, $p < .01$). The difference between difference scores for the 2-month-old infants was nonsignificant ($t = 1.55$, $df = 8$). The differential responding to faces compared to nonsocial patterns which occurred in infants as young as 1 month suggests that infants begin to discriminate between social and nonsocial patterns in their environment very early in life.

Nonsocial Stimuli: Differences among Patterns

The second comparison with fixation research involved the developmental change in preference for checkerboard patterns (Ames and Silfen, 1965; Brennan *et al.,* 1966) and the low preference value of the triangle when compared to other designs (Fantz, 1958). Specifically, if pupillary activity and visual fixation are equivalent measures there should have been more pupillary change to the less complex checkerboard in Group 1m, and more change in pupil size to the more complex checkerboard pattern in Group 4m —complexity being defined as the number of squares contained in the pattern. In addition, greater pupillary activity should have accompanied the checkerboard patterns than the triangle. The statistical procedure used to

TABLE 2

Analysis of Variance of Pupillary Activity to Nonsocial Patterned Stimuli

Source	df	*MS*	*F*
Ages	2	2.13	<1
Stimuli	2	10.23	<1
Age × Stimuli	4	207.72	1.03
Error	81	200.99	
Total	89		

demonstrate the developmental change in checkerboard preferences has been analysis of variance (Ames and Silfen, 1965; Brennan *et al.,* 1966), and since in the present study pupillary activity to these stimuli is being compared to established fixation preferences, the same statistical procedure was used. The results of the analysis of variance were uniformly nonsignificant for the main effects of age and stimuli and for the age by stimulus interaction (Table 2). That is, there were no significant changes in pupil size to the three nonsocial patterns within or across age groups.

There are at least two interpretations for the failure to replicate fixation preferences. First, the preferences established in fixation-research may be in error. However, the frequent replication of these relationships with fixation as the response-measure would challenge this interpretation. The second interpretation is that the particular autonomic response used in the present study simply may not provide a sensitive measure of responsiveness to stimuli that presumably have little or no affective value for the infant, i.e., nonsocial patterns. Thus, the greater change in pupil size accompanying face stimuli in the present study may bear close relationship to the adult pupillary studies of Hess and his associates which show correspondence between the affective value of visual stimuli, and pupillary response to the stimuli.

Social Stimuli: Mother-Stranger Discrimination

The second question raised in the present study was whether infants as young as those in the present study would respond differently to their mother's face than to a stranger's face. For each of the three age groups, difference scores were computed representing the amount of pupillary change that occurred to mother's face, and were compared with similar difference scores for the stranger's face. Tests for the significance of the difference between these correlated difference scores indicated that only 4-month-old *S*s successfully discriminated between mother and stranger ($t = 2.39$, $df = 8$, $p < .05$); the comparisons for Groups 1m and 2m were not significant ($t = 1.55$, $df = 8$; $t = 1.93$, $df = 8$, respectively). This result for the 4-month group provides support for recent behavioral studies (Ainsworth, 1963; LaRoche and Tcheng, 1963; Schaffer and Emerson, 1964) in that the discrimination was successfully made by infants whose ages placed them in the second quarter of the first year of life. However, the fact that the stranger's face was the stimulus receiving greater pupillary dilation in Group 4m is contrary to both psychiatric and behavioral research, which typically suggests that discrimination has occurred only when the infant responds more positively to his mother than to a stranger. For example, infant smiling initially occurs indiscriminately to human faces, later declining or ceasing altogether to stranger's face, but remaining unchanged to familiar faces (Gewirtz, 1965). Thus greater pupillary response to the stranger's face may illustrate that the pupillary response is not only a measure of affectivity—i.e., reflecting the affective value of the human face for the infant—but also represents one component of the orienting reflex (see Sokolov, 1963). This latter interpretation might then suggest that for the 4-month-old infants in the present study, the stranger's face represented a change in stimulation sufficiently different from the mother's face to elicit the orienting reflex and subsequently cause the greater change in pupil size which accompanied the presentation of the stranger's face.

SUMMARY

One-month, 2-month, and 4-month-old home-reared infants were presented five visual stimuli—*S*'s mother's face, a female stranger's face, a 4-square checkerboard pattern, a 144-square checkerboard pattern, and a triangle—via a television video-tape system. Photographic recording of the infant's pupil showed that social stimuli elicited greater change in pupil size among 1- and 4-month-old infants. Four-month-old infants responded differently to mother than to stranger. Nonsocial patterns were not effective in producing differential changes in pupil diameter at any age studied.

REFERENCES

AINSWORTH, M. D. The development of infant-mother interaction among the Ganda. In B. M. Foss (Ed.), *Determinants of infant behavior II*. London: Methuen, 1963.

AMES, E. W., AND SILFEN, C. K. Methodological issues in the study of age differences in infant's attention to stimuli varying in movement and complexity. Paper presented at the biennial meeting of the Society for Research in Child Development, Minneapolis, Minn., 1965.

BANKS, J. H., JR., AND WOLFSON, J. H. Differential cardiac response of infants to mother and stranger. Paper read at the annual meeting of the Eastern Psychological Association, Philadelphia, Pa., 1967.

BRACKBILL, Y., FITZGERALD, H. E., AND LINTZ, L. M. A developmental study of classical conditioning. *Monographs of the society for research in child development,* 1967, **32,** Serial No. 116.

BRACKBILL, Y., LINTZ, L. M., AND FITZGERALD, H. E. Differences in the autonomic and somatic conditioning of infants. *Psychosomatic Medicine,* 1968, **30,** 193–201.

BRENNAN, W. M., AMES, E. W., AND MOORE, R. W. Age differences in infants attention to patterns of different complexities. *Science,* 1966, **151,** 354–366.

CHANEY, B. L., AND MCGRAW, M. B. Reflexes and other motor activities in newborn infants. *Bulletin of the neurological institute of New York,* 1932, **2,** 1–56.

FANTZ, R. L. Pattern vision in young infants. *Psychological Record,* 1958, **8,** 43–47.

FANTZ, R. L. Pattern vision in new-born infants. *Science,* 1963, **140,** 296–297.

FANTZ, R. L. Visual perception from birth as shown by pattern selectivity. *New York Academy of Science,* 1965, **118,** 793–814.

FITZGERALD, H. E., LINTZ, L. M., BRACKBILL, Y. B., AND ADAMS, G. Time perception and conditioning an autonomic response in human infants. *Perceptual and Motor Skills,* 1967, **24,** 479–486.

GEWIRTZ, J. L. The course of infant smiling in four-child-rearing environments in Israel. In B. M. Foss (Ed.), *Determinants of infant behavior III*. London, Methuen, 1965.

GUERNSEY, M. A quantitative study of the eye reflexes in infancy. *Psychological Bulletin,* 1929, **26,** 160–161.

HERSHENSON, M. Visual discrimination in the human newborn. *Journal of Comparative and Physiological Psychology,* 1964, **58,** 270–276.

HESS, E. H. Attitude and pupil size. *Scientific American,* 1965, **212,** 46–54.

HESS, E. H., AND POLT, J. M. Pupil size as related to interest value of visual stimuli. *Science,* 1960, **132,** 349–350.

HESS, E. H., AND POLT, J. M. Pupil size in relation to mental activity during simple problem-solving. *Science,* 1964, **143,** 1190–1192.

HESS, E. H., SELTZER, A. L., AND SHLIEN, J. M. Pupil response of hetero- and homosexual males to pictures of men and women. *Journal of Abnormal Psychology,* 1965, **70,** 165–168.

LaRoche, J. L., and Tcheng, F. *Le sourire du nourisson* (smiling of the infant). Publication Universitaires, Loutain, 1963.

Lewis, M., Meyers, W. J., Kagan, J., and Grossberg, R. Attention to visual patterns in infants. Paper presented at the annual meeting of the American Psychological Association, Philadelphia, Pa., 1963.

McCall, R. B., and Kagan, J. Attention in infants: effects of complexity, contour, perimeter, and familiarity. *Child Development,* 1967, **38,** 939–952.

Ryan, T. A. Multiple comparisons in psychological research. *Psychological Bulletin,* 1959, **56,** 26–47.

Schaffer, H. R., and Emerson, P. E. The development of social attachments in infancy. *Monographs of the society for research in child development,* 1964, **29,** No. 3.

Sherman, M., and Sherman, I. C. Sensori-motor response in infants. *Journal of Comparative Psychology,* 1925, **5,** 53–68.

Siegel, S. *Nonparametric statistics.* New York: McGraw-Hill, 1956.

Sokolov, Ye. N. *Perception and the conditioned reflex.* New York: Macmillan, 1963.

Spitz, R. A. Anxiety in infancy: a study of its manifestation in the first year of life. *International Journal of Psychoanalysis,* 1950, **31,** 138–143.

Spitz, R. A., and Wolf, K. M. The smiling response: a contribution to the ontogenesis of social relations. *Genetic Psychology Monographs,* 1946, **34,** 57–125.

Stechler, G. Attention and arousal: the infant. Paper presented at the biennial meeting of the Society for Research in Child Development. Minneapolis, Minn., 1965.

Thomas, H. An experimental study of infant visual fixation response. *Child Development,* 1966, **36,** 629–638.

Watson, J. S. Orientation-specific age changes in responsiveness to face stimulus in young infants. Paper presented at the biennial meeting of the Society for Research in Child Development, Minneapolis, Minn., 1965.

14
PERCEPTUAL-COGNITIVE DEVELOPMENT IN INFANCY: A GENERALIZED EXPECTANCY MODEL AS A FUNCTION OF THE MOTHER-INFANT INTERACTION*

MICHAEL LEWIS
and
SUSAN GOLDBERG

THE ROLE of the mother in infancy has long been considered important in the emotional development of the child. In recent years, with increased interest in cognitive development during infancy, there has been a corresponding increase in concern for the way in which the mother or caretaker might influence the infant's intellectual development.

The traditional view attributed intellectual ability largely to genetic factors. An individual had an innate capacity for intellectual development which was fixed and unfolded in a predetermined sequence as the infant matured. Since World War II, investigations of the effects of infantile experience have amassed sufficient evidence to demonstrate that at least some aspects of intellectual ability are learned, that is, influenced by experience (see Hunt, 1960; 1963). Thus, the mother or caretaker who is a primary source for a large part of early experience is potentially important for intellectual development. Although psychoanalytic theory was one of the major contributions to the notion of the importance of early experience, it generally assumed these influences to be primarily emotional (Freud,

* From *Merrill-Palmer Quarterly*, 1969, *15*, 81–100. Reprinted with permission from the authors and the Merrill-Palmer Institute.

Presented at The Merrill-Palmer Institute Conference on Research and Teaching of Infant Development, February 15–17, 1968, directed by Irving E. Sigel, chairman of research. The conference was financially supported in part by the National Institute of Child Health and Human Development. The research on which this paper is based was supported in part by Grants HD-00868, FR-00222, and FR-05537 from the National Institute of Mental Health, U.S. Public Health Service, to the Fels Research Institute where the research was conducted, and by the National Institute of Child Health and Human Development under Research Grant 1 PO1 HD01762, to the Educational Testing Service.

1905). The mother's love was seen to be essential to healthy emotional development. Extreme deprivation in early life might result in emotional problems which interfered with or prevented normal intellectual development. By and large, the capacity for intellectual development was, according to the psychoanalytic view, still fixed. Unsatisfactory emotional experiences could prevent free intellectual development, while adequate mothering provided the security in which innate capacity could reach its full potential.

It is now clear that some of the studies thought to demonstrate that maternal absence resulted in emotional starvation (e.g., Spitz, 1945; Dennis and Dennis, 1941) may be interpreted in another way. The mother is also a primary source of stimulation for the infant. What the infant lacks in her absence is not only emotional satisfaction, but stimulation as well. The developmental deterioration observed by Spitz and Dennis may well be attributed to this lack of stimulation rather than emotional impairment. Indeed, in a later paper, Dennis (1960) suggested that the source of severe retardation he observed in a Teheran orphanage was "homogeneity of stimulation."

More recently, the importance of the mother as a source of stimulation, as well as of emotional satisfaction, has been emphasized in a number of different approaches. Hunt (1963) for example, suggests that in the early months, the child is responsive primarily to changes in stimulation. Therefore, the extent to which the mother provides for frequent encounters with a wide variety of situations involving change in stimulation influences the infant's early learning. This applies both to the behavior of the mother and the total environment she provides. Thus, frequency and variation of stimulation are seen as the characteristics important in early development and the extent to which the mother provides this can depress or enhance the child's subsequent development.

Another view that is represented by Gewirtz (1966) and Watson (1966; 1967) is based on the role of the mother as a source of reinforcement. The infant will tend to repeat those behaviors which are reinforced within his memory span. Since the infant's memory span is judged to be relatively short (at three months, it is estimated to be about 5 seconds [Lewis, 1967; Watson, 1967]), reinforcements must follow behavior fairly quickly if he is to be aware of the contingencies involved. According to this view, the mother can encourage learning of desirable behaviors by contingent reinforcement of these behaviors when they occur.

A third approach also centers on the notion of contingency but maintains that contingency is important, not only because it shapes acquisition of specific behaviors, but because it enables the child to develop a motive which is the basis for all future learning. The main characteristic of this motive is the infant's belief that his actions affect his environment. In this case, the mother is important because it is the contingency between the infant's behavior and her responses that enables the infant to learn that his behavior does have consequences. The main differentiation between this view and the operant conditioning position is that the latter predicts only change in specifically reinforced behaviors while the former predicts change in behaviors not specifically reinforced.

It is this last approach with which the present paper is concerned. Data from the Fels Infant Study which support this view will be examined first, and subsequently, this view will be discussed in relation to research with older children as well as animal work which is consistent with this approach.

In order to observe the mother-child interaction and its effect in cognitive development, it is necessary to have some measure or continuum along which infants vary and which show changes indicative of cognitive development.

Recently, a model of schema development believed to represent a measure of cognitive capacity has been presented (Lewis, 1967; Lewis, Goldberg and Rausch, 1967). This schema development rests on the assumption that response decrement to a redundant signal does not necessarily depend on sensory fatigue or nerve accommodation.

It is believed that response decrement to a redundant signal is related to some more central process rather than a peripheral process such as organism or receptor fatigue. A neuronal model for explaining just such a response decrement has been offered by Sokolov (1963) who suggests that central processes, such as neuronal model acquisition (memory or storage of information), are involved in response decrement to repeated stimulation. He defines a neuronal model as an organization of neuronal cells in the cortex which retain and process such information as intensity, duration and quality of stimuli. Such a model is developed by the repetition of the same stimulus. In the process of model building, if the presented stimulus corresponds to the model, some type of negative feedback occurs, resulting in the decrease or absence of a response. However, if the presented stimulus does not correspond with the neuronal model or the model is not yet fully developed, central excitation takes place and an orienting reflex occurs. One might view model acquisition in the following way. Each presentation is compared to any memory trace or model created by the preceding presentations. Memory trace is reinforced or the model is made stronger by some process such as increasing the number of neuronal cells involved or by more permanent biochemical changes. Moreover, this postulated model and process of testing may involve many cells and their interaction or even possibly single cell memory.

In addition to Sokolov's work, there is a growing body of neurophysiological data demonstrating that central changes such as negative slow potential change in the human cortex take place as a function of the organism's building up of expectations (that is, the memory or model of some event) through repetitive stimulus presentation (Walter, 1964; Rebert, McAdam, Knott and Irwin, 1967; Walter, Cooper, Aldridge, McCallum and Winter,

1964). Moreover, visually evoked potentials are not solely determined by the physical qualities of the signal, but by such factors as reducing uncertainty, or the confirmation of an expectation (Sutton, Tueting, Zubin and John, 1967). These recent studies supply direct evidence for cortical changes as a function of the build-up of expectations or models.

This proposed model does not try to arrive at a final explanation of the mechanisms governing response decrement. It does, however, assume, as Sokolov does, that this process is related to some central mechanism such as memory or neuronal model acquisition. According to the theory, one way to measure the strength of the model is to observe whether the signal produces attentive behavior. As models (memory or schema) are built up, signals which match that model elicit little attention and lead to response decrement (we have called these stimuli "familiar"). Signals which do not match the model elicit attention and produce response recovery (we have called these stimuli "novel"). Finally, it appears that signals for which there is no model at all produce little attention. Thus, amount of response decrement is an important measure of model acquisition.

In the investigation of models, one can look at either experimentally produced models or models which the experimenter knows to have been developed or which are developing in the infant. Such models could include face schema (Lewis, 1965; Kagan et al., 1966) or conservation of substance (Piaget, 1954). Experimentally, models are produced by repeated presentation of a single signal. In the experimental production of models, the experimenter assumes the model is short-lived. The models which are built up over long periods of time are found in the environmental events of the organism or are determined by some basic maturational process. While the duration or strength of the models may be different, it is believed that the experimentally produced models are developed in the same manner and are governed by the same processes as the naturally developed ones, and therefore, it may be possible through experimental manipulation to gain some understanding of the infant's cognitive development.

Indeed, one might view the perceptual-cognitive development of the opening years of life as the maturation and alteration of these models, and it is believed that infant attention is in large part influenced by this process. This is not to overlook the importance of stimulus characteristics such as intensity, movement, contour and size which produce what William James (1890) has called "passive immediately sensorial attention." While these stimulus dimensions are important for attentive behavior, it would appear that model acquisition has more important significance for developmental inquiry.

Thus, the theoretical umbrella under which the experiments to be presented were conducted holds that amount of response decrement to a repeated signal is a measure of the speed of model acquisition and is associated with the efficiency of the model building system. The evidence to support this hypothesis consists of two parts. First, organism status variables usually considered to be predictors of efficient perceptual-cognitive capacity are found to be related to response decrement. These include age, state, extent of brain damage, and socioeconomic status. Second, the rate of response decrement to repeated stimulation was directly related to cognitive capacity as measured by tests of I.Q. and concept formation.

In a recent paper summarizing the work to date, we (Lewis, 1967) were able to show that there are age changes in response decrement to a repeated stimuli, such that within the first three years older infants show more rapid response decrement than younger ones.

Infants in the first three years of life were presented with a repeated visual signal lasting 30 seconds with a 30-second inter-trial interval. Four trials were presented and both fixation time as well as cardiac deceleration responses were observed.

The data from three experiments indicated that fixation time decreased over trials and that the degree of response decrement was directly related to age, the youngest infants showing the least response decrement. The cardiac response, specifically, the amount of cardiac deceleration—a measure found to be related to attention (Lewis et al., 1966; Lewis and Spaulding, 1967)—also showed a decrease over trials, the youngest infants again showing the least response decrement. To extend the generality of the results, other visual stimuli (such as different blinking light patterns and a configuration of curved lines) were presented to another sample. The results still indicated an age effect in amount of response decrement.

In a fourth experiment, the number of trials was extended from four to nine and the age effect was again significant. In older infants (1½–3 years), attention eventually approached an assymptote at some minimal level suggesting a well-formed model, but younger *Ss,* even after nine trials, were not able to acquire a satisfactory schema.

In all the experiments, the inter-trial interval was 30 seconds, which may be too long for a very young infant's memory span. If this is the case, each repeated trial represented a new event for the young infant. Few experiments varying the inter-trial interval have been performed using infants as *Ss*. Saayman, et al. (1964) produced response decrement in 3-month-olds by presenting one long trial of approximately 4 minutes. One could think of one long trial as having a 0-second inter-trial interval length. Bridger (1961), using neonates and various inter-trial intervals, could best elicit response decrement to a repeated loud tone when the inter-trial interval was less than 5 seconds. This result is supported by Bartoshuk's (1962) failure to find a difference between inter-trial intervals of 60, 30, and 15 seconds. Moreover, the data for adult *Ss* clearly indicated increased response decrement as a function of shortening the inter-trial interval (Geer, 1966). Using 12-week-old subjects, we have varied the inter-trial interval, using 0, 5, and 15 seconds. The data indicate that 12-week-old infants tend to habituate if the inter-trial interval is short enough; that is, on the order of 0–5 seconds, the inter-trial interval that Bridger found to be effective. While there are several alternative explanations for the data, age differences are best explained in terms of differential rates of model acquisition, with younger infants failing to build up models as rapidly as older ones.

Besides important age differences in response decrement, there are significant differences related to birth condition, another organism status variable known to affect cognitive capacity. Specifically, infants in regulatively poor condition at birth (as indicated by Apgar scores) showed significantly less response decrement than did *Ss* whose birth condition was rated as perfect. A similar result was found by Eisenberg, Coursin and Rupp (1966). Further evidence that physical trauma associated with central damage affects response decrement is reviewed by Thompson and Spencer (1966) and shows that animals with experimentally produced brain lesions failed to show response decrement. Psychic trauma can also affect response decrement as is demonstrated in a study by Israel (1966).

Amount of response decrement to visual stimuli in infants was found to be related to patterns of attention in free play. At 13 months, infants who habituated rapidly to the visual stimulus lost interest rapidly in individual toys and showed more toy changes than infants who showed little response decrement. Thus, amount of response decrement may be indicative of a more general individual response pattern which extends over various perceptual and cognitive areas.

Finally, both rate of response decrement and frequency of toy change were related to the socioeconomic status of the infant's family. Parents of relatively high socioeconomic level tended to have infants who showed rapid response decrement and frequent toy change, while low SES parents tended to have infants with little response decrement and few toy changes.

Up to this point in the discussion, the evidence presented indicates that response decrement is associated with those organism status variables usually considered to be predictors of efficient perceptual-cognitive capacity. Thus, older infants should have more capacity than younger ones, infants without brain damage more than damaged ones, etc. However, no evidence of a direct nature has been presented which would demonstrate that infants with greater response decrement to redundant signals perform better on some cognitive tasks than infants who show relatively less response decrement.

Two studies are now reported which show a direct relationship. For 40 infants seen at approximately one year, a full scale Stanford-Binet I.Q. score at 44 months of age was obtained. A positive and significant correlation between I.Q. score at 3½ years and rate of response decrement at one year was found (girls, $rho = .46$; boys, $rho = .50$, $p < .05$). This indicates that the greater the response decrement at a year, the higher the I.Q. at 3½ years.

In a second study, 20 *Ss* were seen at 3½ years and were given a concept formation task as well as a series of redundant visual signals. Comparing the response decrement to a visual signal with the total number of errors across six different concept tasks reveals a significant correlation ($rho = .37$, $p < .05$) such that *Ss* who show greater response decrement show greater concept attainment. Here then is clear evidence for the relation between response decrement and cognitive capacity.

In summary, response decrement to repeated signals was found to be related to a wide variety of organism status parameters: (1) age, (2) lesions, (3) mental disease, (4) birth condition, (5) other measures of satiation, (6) socioeconomic status. Moreover, response decrement was shown to be directly related to (7) measures of cognitive capacity such as I.Q. in the preschool child and (8) performance on a concept formation task.

The data to date, therefore, suggest that the use of response decrement as a measure of model acquisition, reflecting perceptual-cognitive development, may be a good index on which to judge the effect of maternal behavior on the infant's development.

METHOD

Subjects

Twenty *Ss* 12 weeks of age (± four days) were employed in order to test the effect of maternal behavior on the infants' development. Each *S* was brought to the Institute in the morning by his mother.

Apparatus

Two situations need be described. The first is the controlled naturalistic setting in which maternal and infant behavior was observed, and the second is the experimental situation in which response decrement data were obtained.

Controlled Naturalistic Setting

The observation of mother-infant interaction may be carried out either in the home or in the laboratory. Each method has some advantages and limitations. Observations carried out in the home permit both mother and infant to remain in familiar surroundings and carry on in their normal context. However, the "normal" setting will necessarily be different for each mother-infant pair and render any evaluation of individual differences difficult to compare. Not only is the home setting variable, but the activities and demands of other members of the family may actually interfere with the interactions with which the observer is concerned. Finally, the presence of the observer may lead to atypical behavior on the part of the mother or the infant. In one attempt to overcome this problem, Moss (1967) describes techniques for reducing the mother's self-consciousness. In this study, the observer spent several hours in the home on two occasions prior to each 8-hour observation. The mothers were told to pursue their normal routines and it was emphasized that the infant and not the mother was the subject of observation. Even under these conditions, it cannot be assumed that the presence of another adult had no effect on the mother's behavior. For example, in the Moss study, the correlation between infant irritability and maternal contact was .52 at three weeks of age. Given an irritable and crying baby, the mother is much more likely to hold him in the presence of another adult than when she is alone. In the presence of a relative stranger, this would be even more true. One might expect either a positive or no relationship between infant irritability and maternal contact. That is, if *S* is extremely irritable, the mother eventually may not respond to it at all. The presence of an observer might make a zero correlation positive and a low positive correlation high. Thus, the presence of an observer known to the mother makes the interpretation of any finding unclear.

Laboratory observations have the distinct advantage of enabling the experimenter to control the environment so that each observation is made under identical conditions and individual differences can be objectively evaluated. The mother and infant can be alone without the interference of other household events or the observer. On the other hand, the laboratory situation is artificial and places both mother and infant in an unfamiliar place which produces anxiety on the mother's part and therefore leads to different levels of interaction.

For our purposes, it was desirable to construct a controlled situation for observation in order to observe individual differences. At the same time, it was necessary to create as natural a setting as possible in order to elicit realistic interaction. A controlled, naturalistic setting was decided upon. This was done in the following way.

One hour prior to testing these infants, the mother and the infant were left alone in a room which was filled with an assortment of furniture, cribs and current popular magazines to read. The mother was informed that the equipment was warming up, given a cup of coffee if she wished, and was left alone. The baby was placed in a reclining infant seat in view of the mother. Finally, the magazines were pointed out and *E* left the room. These procedures were identical in every case and were designed to produce a controlled naturalistic setting. Two particular manipulations are to be noticed. One, the currency of the magazines (and therefore, their positive valance) was manipulated by changing the magazines regularly. This detail is an example of the attempt at controlled naturalistic observation. The second manipulation had to do with taking the baby from the mother. By doing this, we required each mother to make a discrete and measurable response in order to recover her infant, and, moreover, might have made it easier for the mother not to interact with the infant if she so desired. In this way, an attempt was made to produce a wider distribution in the mother's response to the infant.

Every 10 seconds, an observer unknown to the mother recorded the occurrence of various behaviors; e.g., whether the mother looked at, smiled, vocalized, held or touched the infant. Also recorded was whether or not the infant's eyes were open or closed, whether he moved, cried or vocalized. Moreover, each time the infant exhibited one of these behaviors, the observer recorded the nature of the maternal response, if any, and its latency. High inter-observer reliability was obtained for these behaviors (*rho* = .77 to .89).

Experimental Session

At the end of the observation period, the mother was interviewed. The duration of the interview varied depending on the state of the infant—if the infant was sleeping he was not awakened. No infant was tested until he was awake, alert, and not fussy. The experimenter then brought the mother and the infant to the experimental room. The infant was placed in a reclining seat and the mother sat to the rear and side of *S*. The infant and mother were completely enclosed and, except for several small observation windows, were surrounded by a uniform gray area. Immediately in front of *S* and approximately 18 inches from his head was the matrix panel on which the stimuli were presented. The matrix panel consisted of a plexiglass board containing six rows of six lights forming a 6 x 6 matrix which could be programmed to present any kind of temporal or spatial pattern. In this experiment, the stimulus was a single blinking light in the center of the panel. Each of the four trials consisted of this light blinking once every other second for 30 seconds. The inter-trial interval was 30 seconds.

During the testing session, the infant's attention to the stimulus was coded by two observers as follows. Each time *S* oriented his head and eyes toward the screen, each observer depressed a key marking the duration of that fixation on an event recorder. The interscorer reliability for total fixation was $r = .94$. Amount of response decrement was computed by subtracting the amount of time looking on Trial 4 from total fixation on Trial 1.

RESULTS

The correlations between response decrement and each of the maternal behaviors were computed. Data for one infant who could not be quieted for the matrix episode and two infants who slept for the entire observation period had to be omitted from the analysis. Response decrement was positively correlated with the amount of touching the mother exhibited (*rho* = .45, $p < .05$), amount of looking (*rho* = .65, $p < .01$), amount of holding (*rho* = .38, $p < .08$), and amount of smiling (*rho* = .26)—and negatively correlated with the amount of time the mother was reading ($rho = -.38$, $p < .08$). These correlations indicate that the more stimulation the mother provided the infant, the greater was the decrement to the repeated signal.

In order to explore the contingency relationship, the frequency of maternal response to each infant behavior was expressed as a percentage score. Thus, the percentage of time each mother responded to an infant behavior, independent of the number of times the behavior was emitted, was obtained. Crying and vocalizing were the only infant behaviors that occurred with sufficient frequency to compute correlations with response decrement. The correlation for percentage of maternal response to vocalization was $rho = .53$ ($p < .05$) and for response to crying was $rho = .44$ ($p < .05$). Thus, higher frequencies of maternal response were associated with greater response decrement.

A third approach to the contingency of the response data was to examine the *latency* of the mother's response to each infant behavior. Since the data were recorded in 10-second intervals, latencies of maternal responses could only be scored as occurring in the same 10-second period as the infant behavior or in a subsequent 10-second period. The maternal response was expressed as percentage of short latency responses independent of the amount of infant behavior. The correlations (*rho*) with response decrement were .33 for maternal latency to vocalization and .31 for latency to crying. Although neither of these correlations attains significance, both are in the predicted direction and may be considered suggestive of a relationship between maternal latency of response and response decrement. Infants whose mothers responded more rapidly to their behavior tended to be more efficient in processing repeated signal information. One refinement in data collection which would be essential in further study of this finding would be exact recording of latencies. If one considers the 3-month-old infant's memory span to be approximately 5 seconds, the present technique does not discriminate between maternal responses within that time period and responses with latencies as long as 10 seconds.

The data consistently indicate that there is a positive correlation between maternal response to infant behavior, such as vocalizing and crying, and the cognitive development of the infant as measured by response decrement. Furthermore, the correlations indicate that the latency of the maternal response and contingency of maternal response (i.e., not whether she stimulated the infant, but whether she stimulated after *S's* behavior) are important variables in these interactions.

DISCUSSION

Earlier, three theoretical systems were briefly presented to account for the dynamics of mother-infant interaction: (1) amount and variety of stimulation provided the infant by the mother, (2) reinforcement of behavior of the infant by the mother, and finally, (3) a contingency paradigm involving, not the learning of a particular behavior, but a generalized expectancy. This expectancy or motive was the infant's belief that his behavior could affect the environment.

It is clear that while varied stimulation level is important (Hunt, 1963), the amount of stimulation *per se* is not a sufficient condition. For example, the infant in an overcrowded slum with many other siblings would be receiving vast amounts of stimulation from a variety of sources. However, one would not view this type of varied stimulation situation as conducive to cognitive development because the stimulation is random in terms of its relationship to the infant. For example, there would be no contingency relationship between stimulation level and the level of alertness of the infant. Indeed, other data from the Fels Infant Study shows a negative correlation between attentiveness and number of siblings.

The reinforcement notion of Gewirtz has more validity in that it argues that the mother's role is that of reinforcer for sets of behavior she wishes to reward or punish. However, this view limits the development of the infant's response repertoire to those behaviors being reinforced. In the case of the present experiment, it would account for increases in smiling and crying behaviors, but not attentive ones. This position could clearly not account for the development of the vast amount and varied complexity of the infant's response repertoire. If, however, one concludes that the maternal reinforcement not only reinforces a specific response, but helps to create a generalized expectancy within the infant about his effectiveness in obtaining rewards or punishment in the world, the role of maternal reinforcement becomes clearer.

While the following discussion will stress the acquisition of this generalized expectation, it is to be noted that each of the other two aspects of the mother-infant interaction contributes to the development of the infant.

Perhaps the first body of work relating to the generalized expectancy of control of helplessness comes from the psychiatric literature. Adler's (Ansbacher and Ansbacher, 1956) concept of striving for superiority, which can be viewed as man's struggle to become more effective in controlling his personal world, and R. W. White's notion of competence (1959) are clearly relevant to this discussion. There are, however, more salient data to be found in the literature to suggest that this motive has important developmental consequences.

Provence and Lipton (1962) in their study of institutionalized infants provide information to support this motivational view. The authors showed that institutionalized infants differed from home-reared infants not in whether they exhibited a skill or when they reached a developmental stage, but whether they utilized the skill. For example, their data indicated that the institutionalized infant stood up in his crib at about the same age as the home-reared infant. That is, the maturational sequence was unfolding at the same rate for each of the groups, but the institutionalized infants showed no desire to practice the skill. It appeared to Provence and Lipton that these infants were not motivated to stand. Thus, it was the motive rather than the skill or structure that differentiated these groups. *It was not how much of the skill or structure that was important in differentiating the infants, rather it was the motivation to use the skill.* It is suggested that the basic quality of that lack of action was the infant's belief that his behavior could not affect the environment. With such a belief, it was little wonder that they gave up.

Most recently, Maier, Seligman and Solomon (in press), in experimenting with Pavlovian and instrumental conditioning paradigms, have come upon a phenomenon in the failure to learn which they have labeled helplessness. In their experimental paradigm, dogs first experienced unavoidable shock in a Pavlovian conditioning situation where shock was the US. After experiencing this situation, the animals were placed in an instrumental avoidance situation in which they had to learn to avoid shock by going from one area in a shuttle box to another. Maier, et al. found that after a minimum of unavoidable shock experience, the animals (67 percent) were unable to learn the instrumental behavior (leaving the area of the box) to avoid or even escape the shock. In searching for a reason for the failure of these animals to learn, the experimenters argue that the most parsimonious explanation involves the notion that the animals acquire expectations about the outcome of their acts. They postulate that in the Pavlovian conditioning situation, where shock is unavoidable, the animal learns that shock or rather the cessation of shock is independent of any response he makes. That is, Maier assumes the animal produces many different behaviors, some of which sometimes accidentally work (the shock goes off) and then do not. Thus, the animal learns not only is no behavior effective (that would be some type of learning), but even more important, it learns that the contingency between his action and outcome is zero. The animal has learned in the Pavlovian conditioning paradigm that no behavior he can produce will consistently affect the shock. He then generalizes this belief to other situations and so he sits in one compartment of the shuttle box and neither escapes nor avoids; that is, he sits there and "takes" the shock. Considering the intensity of shock used in these experiments, the lack of any attempt to escape or show superstitious behavior is indicative of the animal's helplessness. And the animal's helplessness is a result of his learning through noncontingency training that "nothing I do matters." Note that this phenomenon only occurs when unavoidable shock in a Pavlovian conditioning situation precedes the instrumental conditioning situation. Thus, it is clear that this learned motivational principle of helplessness is extremely important in determining subsequent behavior such as cognitive development or learning.

A third area of research relating to this generalized expectancy has been carried out under the press of Rotter's social learning theory (1954). In

Rotter's learning theory, the potential for any behavior to occur under a given situation is a function of the expectation that the given behavior will be effective in securing the available reinforcement, and the value of that reinforcement for the person. The generalized expectancy is that belief, generalized over many situations, that the individual's behavior will or will not be effective in producing the desired reinforcer (for a most recent presentation of his views, see Rotter, 1966). Internal control characterizes individuals who generally believe that their behavior can affect reinforcement—positive or negative—while external control refers to individuals who generally believe their behavior is not effective in producing reinforcement (Rotter, Seeman and Liverant, 1962). In a recent study (Katkovsky, Crandall and Good, 1967), parental antecedents of internal and external control expectancies were studied. The parental antecedents of general babying, protectivenesess, affection and approval are all significantly correlated with the development of the child's belief that he can affect his environment, that he can effect reinforcement by his action. From the observation of the mother-infant interaction, such behaviors as described above are usually associated with close physical contact and responsiveness, both characteristics which should enhance the consistent and short latencies reinforcement contingency characteristics discussed below.

Moreover, the relationship between belief in internal control and perceptual-cognitive and achievement behaviors is well documented. Crandall, Katkovsky and Preston (1962) found that intelligence test scores and reading and arithmetic performance were significantly related to an internal control belief. Recent studies (Cellura, 1963; Chance, 1965; Coleman et al., 1966) all found significant relationships between school performance and internality. McGhee and Crandall (in press) found perceived control predictive of performance in school as well as achievement test scores, and Crandall (personal communication) recently found a significant relationship between internality and performance on the Witkin Embedded Figures Test. Finally, investigations (see Lefcourt, 1966; Rotter, 1966; for two reviews) have demonstrated great individual differences among children and adults in this motive. SES data indicate that, in general, the lower SES groups show less internality than the higher SES groups. That is, lower-class children, often Negroes, demonstrate that they lack the belief that their actions can affect their environment (Franklin, 1963; Battle and Rotter, 1963; Lefcourt and Ladwig, 1965; Coleman et al., 1966). Moreover, that young children rather than older ones also show less internality (Crandall, Katkovsky and Crandall, 1965) suggests that *deprived* groups, in general, possess less of a belief that they can control their reinforcement.

Studies with children and adults all point to the position that the belief in control or conversely belief in helplessness in affecting one's environment is an important motive in subsequent perceptual-cognitive ability.

A GENERALIZED EXPECTANCY—A MOTIVATIONAL MODEL

The experimental data as well as the observational information collected by a wide variety of investigators demonstrate that helplessness or control is a learned motive and has important consequences for subsequent perceptual-cognitive development.

The proposed model is a motivational construct developed by the infant through the mother-infant interaction. The construct is a generalized expectancy that his behavior has consequence in affecting his environment. The learning of this motive is dependent upon *consistent* reinforcement with *short latencies* (that is, before the memory trace of the infant's act is gone). An example will serve to illustrate this construct.

The infant experiences some uncomfortable somatic sensation (call it hunger) to which he responds by crying. Assume that the mother, hearing the cry, goes to the infant, picks him up, and feeds him. If her behavior is consistent, it reinforces the event-action relation (namely, discomfort-cry) and develops within the infant a plan or expectation. It is difficult to imagine a perfect relationship where the mother always knows what to do and can always do it. Thus, the degree of her consistency will be an important variable with greater consistency resulting in a stronger motive. The plan or expectation built by the infant is produced in this manner: uncomfortable sensation →→ action →→ cessation of sensation. In other words, his cry or behavior was effective in relieving his pain. How much different is this from the experience of the infant who cries under the press of an uncomfortable somatic sensation and is not picked up and fed consistently or who cries and is not attended to because his mother, busy with other children, cannot reach him until several minutes after the onset of crying when he can no longer remember the event-action relationship. Or the institutionalized infant who, because of the institution's schedule cannot be held when he wants to be and is held when he does not want to be. In other words, although he may receive *equal amounts of stimulation,* these are noncontingent on his action and, thus, the principle of affecting his environment by his action is not learned well or is delayed. It is clear that all infants receive some degree of contingency experience. What is being discussed is the belief that the quantity of contingency experience is instrumental in developing the strength of this motive.

Moss (1967) suggests that in the early weeks of life, maternal behavior is controlled by the S-R conditions provided by the infant. As he gets older, "The mother, *if she behaved contingently* toward his signals, gradually acquires reinforcement value" (emphasis added). Moss views this point (where the infant's control of the mother declines and the mother's reinforcement value emerges) as the initial condition for social learning. We would extend this notion to say that the mother's acquisition of reinforcement value is only one indication that the infant has learned to expect environmental payoff and this is the basis for future learning. When the infant has acquired this expectation, he is potentially capable of instrumental behaviors *other than those already reinforced*. The behavior of the infant is increasingly intentional and motivated by the expectation of producing a desired result. Thus, the belief in control which emerges as a consequence of early contingency experience mediates subsequent S-R experiences. What is being suggested is that not only are S-R bonds being made for specific response patterns but that a motive (some type of cognitive process) mediating the production of subsequent responses is being developed. This motive "to behave" (which can include specific responses and/or general processes like exploration and attention) while dependent originally on reinforcement of specific behaviors, eventually becomes independent of these external reinforcements.

Finally, the operant conditioning approach which assumes that the initial behavior is emitted accidentally or at random does not adequately account for the rapidity with which new behaviors occur or the extent and complexity of the infant's behavioral repertoire. It is necessary to assume some internal state which motivates production of new behaviors. While this internal state is certainly in the service of a maturational sequence, it is suggested that it is also in the service of the motive to control based on the infant's expectation that he can effect change.

Initially, the mother serves as the major source of reinforcement of the S-R bonds and therefore, the source of this generalized expectancy. Given the basic development of this motive, the infant soon learns that he can obtain payoffs from the environment other than the mother. The generalized expectancy can then be facilitated by the environment as well as the mother. However, in the earliest months, it is primarily the mother who serves as the reinforcer. The mother, therefore, would appear to have two functions: one, initially to serve as the contingency producer (and creator of the expectancy) and two, to provide an environment which facilitates the infant's self-reinforcement, e.g., toys which can be reached for and touched, etc.

Several important dimensions of this motivational construct are the speed with which it can be formed and the duration and strength of the expectation. The Maier et al. data with animals and Provence and Lipton's data with institutionalized infants argue for the belief that the acquisition of the motive can occur within a relatively short time (in the Maier et al. experiments, it occurred within a relatively few trials). Both of these studies dealt with the acquisition of helplessness, and whether the same speed is involved in the acquisition of control is not yet known. If the acquisition of the expectancy of control is acquired as quickly as helplessness, the motive could easily be acquired in the opening months of life.

The duration and strength of this motive is a more complex issue. Again, referring to the Maier et al. data, the results indicated that not only is the motive learned in a few trials, but experiencing the unavoidable shock condition an additional time after the instrumental conditioning procedure renders the motive inextinguishable. The data indicate, therefore, that once well learned, the motive is not reversible. Whether this is true for infant and human development is not clear. It does seem possible, however, that the motive results in differential behavior patterns whose consequences would tend to reinforce the motive. Thus, whether the motive remains irreversible, or whether the behaviors as a consequence of the motive sustain the expectation, is not clear. There is some indication in the deprivation studies that the process is irreversible. However, whether this refers to the motive or the sets of behavior learned or not learned as a consequence of the motive is not clear.

The contingency relationship has been argued to be effective in producing a generalized expectancy of control or helplessness. Yet to be answered is how this learned expectation can affect perceptual-cognitive development and, specifically, response decrement to a redundant signal. The answer seems to be multiple. First, the lack of this expectation should reduce the infant's exploration of his environment; that is, if he cannot affect change or outcome, why pay attention to it? This lack of interest should prevent the infant from exploring his environment and enriching his set of experiences, expectations and schemata. Further, it is suggested that sensory processing not only involves orientation toward stimulation or exploring the environment, but a desire (an active process) to assimilate the information. In a visual exploration, this might be seen as the difference between an empty stare versus a taking in and processing—accompanied by cardiac deceleration. In both cases, the infant orients, but only in the latter is the information absorbed. There is evidence available, other than that presented above that the mother-infant interaction can affect the desire for novelty and familiarity (Rubenstein, 1967). Moreover, Watson's (1966) observation that contingency training increased attentive behavior and responses other than those reinforced is particularly relevant. Alternatively, without this expectancy, the infant is unlikely to rehearse developing skills and structures as they unfold in their developmental sequences. Thus, new skills are lost and additive funtions do not occur. Finally, Schaffer and Emerson (1968) have argued that stimulation levels can be considered to affect arousal level or alertness. This, in turn, will obviously affect attention toward environmental changes or consistency. While the exact nature of this generalized expectancy on response decrement is yet unclear, it is thought that infants with a relatively weaker expectancy should have less motive to process the signal and therefore take longer to build a model.

In conclusion then, what has been proposed is that the reinforcement of specific S-R bonds by the mother is effective in increasing the occurrence of that particular reinforced behavior; but more important, it develops within the infant the expectancy that his behavior can affect his environment. Given this expectancy, the infant is motivated to produce and utilize behaviors and skills not reinforced in his past experience. Thus, this motive can be thought to mediate the occurrence of new behavioral responses.

REFERENCES

Ansbacher, H. & Ansbacher, R. *The individual psychology of Alfred Adler.* New York: Basic Books, 1956.

Bartoshuk, A. K. Response decrement with repeated elicitation of human neonatal cardiac acceleration to sound. *J. comp. physiol. Psychol.,* 1962, **55,** 9–13.

Battle, E. S. & Rotter, J. B. Children's feelings of personal control as related to social class and ethnic group. *J. Pers.,* 1963, **3,** (4), 482–490.

Bridger, W. H. Sensory habituation and discrimination in the human neonate. *Amer. J. Psychiat.,* 1961, **117,** 991–996.

Cellura, A. R. Internality as a determinant of academic achievement in low SES adolescents. Unpublished manuscript, University of Rochester, 1963.

Chance, June E. Internal control of reinforcements and the school learning process. Paper presented at the meeting of Soc. Res. Child Develpm., Minneapolis, 1965.

Coleman, J. S., Campbell, E. Q., Hobson, C. J., McPortland, J., Mood, A. M., Weinfeld, F. D., & York, R. L. Equality of educational opportunity. Superintendent of Documents, Catalog No. FS 5.238: 38001, U.S. Government Printing Office, Washington, D.C. 1966.

Crandall, V. C., Katkovsky, W., & Crandall, V. J. Children's beliefs in their own control of reinforcements in intellectual-academic situations. *Child Develpm.,* 1965, **36,** 91–109.

Crandall, V. J., Katkovsky, W., & Preston, A. Motivational and ability determinants of young children's intellectual achievement behaviors. *Child Develpm.,* 1962, **33,** 643–661.

Dennis, W. Causes of retardation among institutional children: Iran. *J. genet. Psychol.,* 1960, **96,** 47–59.

Dennis, W. & Dennis, M. W. Infant development under conditions of restricted practice and minimum social stimulation. *Genet. Psychol. Monogr.,* 1941, **23,** 149–155.

Eisenberg, R. B., Coursin, D. B., & Rupp, N. R. Habituation to an acoustic pattern as an index of differences among human neonates. *J. Auditory Res.,* 1966, **6,** 239–248.

Franklin, R. D. Youth's expectancies about internal versus external control of reinforcement related to *N* variables. Unpublished doctoral dissertation, Purdue University, 1963.

Freud, S. *Three contributions to a theory of sex.* (1905) In A. A. Brill (Trans. & Ed.), *The basic writings of Sigmund Freud.* New York: Modern Library, 1938.

Geer, J. H. Effect of interstimulus intervals and rest period length upon habituation of the orienting response. *J. exp. Psychol.,* 1966, **72,** 617–619.

Gewirtz, J. L. On conceptualizing the functional environment: The roles of stimulation and change in stimulus conditions in effecting behavior outcomes. Unpublished manuscript, National Institute of Mental Health, 1966.

HUNT, J. McV. Experience and the development of motivation: some reinterpretations. *Child Develpm.,* 1960, **31,** 489–504.

HUNT, J. McV. The epigenesis of intrinsic motivation and the stimulation of early cognitive learning. Paper presented at Symposium on "Stimulation of Early Cognitive Learning," Amer. Psychol. Ass., Philadelphia, August, 1963.

ISRAEL, N. Individual differences in GSR orienting response and cognitive control. Unpublished manuscript, Research Center for Mental Health, New York University, 1966.

JAMES, W. *The principles of psychology.* New York: Henry Holt, 1890.

KAGAN, J., HENKER, B., HEN-TOV, A., LEVINE, J., & LEWIS, M. Infants' differential reactions to familiar and distorted faces. *Child Develpm.,* 1966, **37,** 519–532.

KATKOVSKY, W., CRANDALL, V. C., & GOOD, S. Parental antecedents of children's beliefs in internal-external control of reinforcement in intellectual achievement situations. *Child Develpm.,* 1967, **38,** 765–776.

LEFCOURT, H. M. Internal versus external control of reinforcement: a review. *Psychol. Bull.,* 1966, **65,** 206–220.

LEFCOURT, H. M & LADWIG, G. W. The American Negro—a problem in expectancies. *J. pers. soc. Psychol.,* 1965, **1,** 377–380.

LEWIS, M. Exploratory studies in the development of a face schema. Paper presented at Amer. Psychol. Ass. meeting, Symposium on "The Origin of Social Behavior," Chicago, 1965.

LEWIS, M. Infant attention: Response decrement as a measure of cognitive processes, or what's new, Baby Jane? Paper presented at the Soc. Res. Child Develpm. Meetings, Symposium on "The Role of Attention in Cognitive Development," New York, March, 1967.

LEWIS, M., GOLDBERG, S., & RAUSCH, M. Attention distribution as a function of novelty and familiarity. *Psychonom. Sci.,* 1967, **7,** 227–228.

LEWIS, M., KAGAN, J., CAMPBELL, H., & KALAFAT, J. The cardiac response as a correlate of attention in infants. *Child Develpm.,* 1966, **37,** 63–71.

LEWIS, M. & SPAULDING, S. J. Differential cardiac response to visual and auditory stimulation in the young child. *Psychophysiol.,* 1967, **3,** 229–237.

MAIER, S., SELIGMAN, M. E., & SOLOMON, R. L. Fear conditioning and learned helplessness. In R. Church & B. Campbell (Eds.), *Punishment and aversive behavior.* New York: Appleton-Century-Crofts, in press.

McGHEE, P. F. & CRANDALL, V. C. Beliefs in internal-external control of reinforcements and academic performance. *Child Develpm.,* in press.

MOSS, H. A. Sex, age and state as determinants of mother-infant interaction. *Merrill-Palmer Quart.,* 1967, **13,** 19–36.

PIAGET, J. *The construction of reality in the child.* (1937). New York: Basic Books (English translation by M. Cook), 1954.

PROVENCE, S. & LIPTON, R. C. *Infants in institutions.* New York: Internat. Univer. Press, 1962.

REBERT, C. S., McADAM, D. W. KNOTT, J. R., & IRWIN, D. A. Slow potential change in the human brain related to level of motivation. *J. comp. physiol. Psychol.,* 1967, **63,** 20–23.

ROTTER, J. B. *Social learning and clinical psychology.* Englewood Cliffs, N.J.: Prentice-Hall, 1954.

ROTTER, J. B. Generalized expectancies for internal versus external control of reinforcement. *Psychol. Monogr.,* 1966, **80,** No. 1 (Whole No. 609).

ROTTER, J. B., SEEMAN, M., & LIVERANT, S. Internal versus external control of reinforcement: A major variable in behavior theory. In N. F. Washburne (Ed.), *Decisions, values and groups,* Vol. 2. London: Pergamon Press, 1962.

RUBENSTEIN, J. Maternal attentiveness and subsequent exploratory behavior. *Child Develpm.,* 1967, **38,** 1089–1100.

SAAYMAN, G., AMES, E. W., & MOFFETT, A. Response to novelty as an indicator of visual discrimination in the human infant. *J. exp. child Develpm.,* 1964, **1,** 189–198.

SCHAFFER, H. R. & EMERSON, P. E. The effects of experimentally administered stimulation on developmental quotients of infants. *Brit. J. soc. clin. Psychol.,* 1968, **7,** 61–67.

SOKOLOV, YE. N. *Perception and the conditioned reflex.* New York: Macmillan Co. (S. W. Waydenfeld, Trans.), 1963.

SPITZ, R. A. Hospitalism: an inquiry into the genes of psychiatric conditions in early childhood. *Psychoanal. Stud. Child.,* 1945, **1,** 53–74.

SUTTON, S., TUETING, P., ZUBIN, J., & JOHN, E. R. Information delivery and the sensory evoked potential. *Science,* 1967, **155,** 1436–1439.

THOMPSON, R. F. & SPENCE, W. A. Habituation: a model phenomenon for the study of neuronal substrates of behavior. *Psychol. Rev.,* 1966, **173,** 16–43.

WALTER, W. G. The convergence and interaction of visual, auditory and tactual responses in human nonspecific cortex. In H. E. Whipple (Ed.), *Sensory evoked response in man. Ann. N.Y. Acad. Sci.,* 1964, **112,** 320–361.

WALTER, W. G., COOPER, R., ALDRIDGE, V. J., MCCALLUM, W. C., & WINTER, A. L. Contingent negative variation: an electric sign of sensorimotor association and expectancy in the human brain. *Nature,* 1964, **203,** 380–384.

WATSON, J. S. The development and generalization of contingency awareness in early infancy: some hypotheses. *Merrill-Palmer Quart.,* 1966, **12,** 123–135.

WATSON, J. S. Memory and "contingency analysis" in infant learning. *Merrill-Palmer Quart.,* 1967, **13,** 55–76.

WHITE, R. W. Motivation reconsidered: The concept of competence. *Psychol. Rev.,* 1959, **66,** 297–323.

15

ON EXPLAINING LANGUAGE*

ERIC H. LENNEBERG

MANY EXPLANATIONS have been offered for many aspects of language; there is little agreement, however, on how to explain various problems or even on what there is to be explained. Of course, explanations differ with the personal inclinations and interests of the investigator. My interests are in man as a biological species, and I believe that the study of language is relevant to these interests because *language has the following six characteristics. (i) It is a form of behavior present in all cultures of the world. (ii) In all cultures its onset is age correlated. (iii) There is only one acquisition strategy—it is the same for all babies everywhere in the world. (iv) It is based intrinsically upon the same formal operating characteristics whatever its outward form* (1). *(v) Throughout man's recorded history these operating characteristics have been constant. (vi) It is a form of behavior that may be impaired specifically by circumscribed brain lesions which may leave other mental and motor skills relatively unaffected.*

Any form of human behavior that has all of these six characteristics may likewise be assumed to have a rather specific biological foundation. This, of course, does not mean that language cannot be studied from different points of view; it can, for example, be investigated for its cultural or social variations, its capacity to reflect individual differences, or its applications. The purpose of this article, however, is to discuss the aspects of language to which biological concepts are applied most appropriately (2). Further, my concern is with the development of language in children—not with its origin in the species.

PREDICTABILITY OF LANGUAGE DEVELOPMENT

A little boy starts washing his hands before dinner no sooner than when his parents decide that training in cleanliness should begin. However, children begin to speak no sooner and no later than when they reach a given stage of physical maturation (Table 1). There are individual variations in

* From *Science,* 1969, *164,* 635–643. Reprinted with permission from the author and the American Association for the Advancement of Science.

development, particularly with respect to age correlation. It is interesting that language development correlates better with motor development than it does with chronological age. If we take these two variables (motor and language development) and make ordinal scales out of the stages shown in Table 1 and then use them for a correlation matrix, the result is a remarkably small degree of scatter. Since motor development is one of the most important indices of maturation, it is not unreasonable to propose that language development, too, is related to physical growth and development. This

TABLE 1

Correlation of Motor and Language Development (3, pp. 128–130)

Age (years)	*Motor Milestones*	*Language Milestones*
0.5	Sits using hands for support; unilateral reaching	Cooing sounds change to babbling by introduction of consonantal sounds
1	Stands; walks when held by one hand	Syllabic reduplication; signs of understanding some words; applies some sounds regularly to signify persons or objects, that is, the first words
1.5	Prehension and release fully developed; gait propulsive; creeps downstairs backward	Repertoire of 3 to 50 words not joined in phrases; trains of sounds and intonation patterns resembling discourse; good progress in understanding
2	Runs (with falls); walks stairs with one foot forward only	More than 50 words; two-word phrases most common; more interest in verbal communication; no more babbling
2.5	Jumps with both feet; stands on one foot for 1 second; builds tower of six cubes	Every day new words; utterances of three and more words; seems to understand almost everything said to him; still many grammatical deviations
3	Tiptoes 3 yards (2.7 meters); walks stairs with alternating feet; jumps 0.9 meter	Vocabulary of some 1000 words; about 80 percent intelligibility; grammar of utterances close approximation to colloquial adult; syntacic mistakes fewer in variety, systematic, predictable
4.5	Jumps over rope; hops on one foot; walks on line	Language well established; grammatical anomalies restricted either to unusual constructions or to the more literate aspects of discourse

impression is further corroborated by examination of retarded children. Here the age correlation is very poor, whereas the correlation between motor and language development continues to be high (*3*). Nevertheless, there is evidence that the statistical relation between motor and language development is not due to any immediate, causal relation; peripheral motor disabilities can occur that do not delay language acquisition.

Just as it is possible to correlate the variable language development with the variables chronological age or motor development, it is possible to relate it to the physical indications of brain maturation, such as the gross weight of the brain, neurodensity in the cerebral cortex, or the changing weight proportions of given substances in either gray or white matter. On almost all counts, language begins when such maturational indices have attained at least 65 percent of their mature values. (Inversely, language acquisition becomes more difficult when the physical maturation of the brain is complete.) These correlations do not prove causal connections, although they suggest some interesting questions for further research.

EFFECT OF CERTAIN VARIATIONS IN SOCIAL ENVIRONMENT

In most of the studies on this topic the language development of children in orphanages or socially deprived households has been compared with that of children in so-called normal, middle-class environments. Statistically significant differences are usually reported, which is sometimes taken as a demonstration that language development is contingent on specific language training. That certain aspects of the environment are absolutely essential for language development is undeniable, but it is important to distinguish between what the children actually do, and what they can do.

There is nothing particularly surprising or revealing in the demonstration that language deficits occur in children who hear no language, very little language, or only the discourse of uneducated persons. But what interests us is the underlying capacity for language. This is not a spurious question; for instance, some children have the capacity for language but do not use it, either because of peripheral handicaps such as congenital deafness or because of psychiatric disturbances such as childhood schizophrenia; other children may not speak because they do not have a sufficient capacity for language, on account of certain severely retarding diseases.

There is a simple technique for ascertaining the degree of development of the capacity for speech and language. Instead of assessing it by means of an inventory of the vocabulary, the grammatical complexity of the utterances, the clarity of pronunciation, and the like, and computing a score derived from several subtests of this kind, it is preferable to describe the children's ability in terms of a few broad and general developmental stages, such as those shown in Table 1. Tests which are essentially inventories of vocabulary and syntactic constructions are likely to reflect simply the deficiencies of the environment; they obscure the child's potentialities and capabilities.

I have used the schema described to compare the speech development of children in many different societies, some of them much more primitive than our own. In none of these studies could I find evidence of variation in developmental rate, despite the enormous differences in social environment.

I have also had an opportunity to study the effect of a dramatically different speech environment upon the development of vocalizations during the first 3 months of life (*4*). It is very common in our culture for congenitally deaf individuals to marry one another, creating households in which all vocal sounds are decidedly different from those normally heard and in which the sounds of babies cannot be attended to directly. Six deaf mothers and ten hearing mothers were asked, during their last month of pregnancy, to participate in our study. The babies were visited at home when they were no more than 10 days old and were seen biweekly thereafter for at least 3 months. Each visit consisted of 3 hours of observation and 24 hours of mechanical recording of all sounds made and heard by the baby. Data were analyzed quantitatively and qualitatively. Although the environment was quantitatively quite different in the experimental and the control groups, the frequency distributions of various baby noises did not differ significantly . . . Developmental histories of cooing noises are also remarkably alike in the two groups. The babies of deaf parents tend to fuss an equal amount, even though the hearing parents are much more likely to come to the child when it fusses. Thus the earliest development of human sounds appears to be relatively independent of the amount, nature, or timing of the sounds made by parents.

I have observed this type of child-rearing through later stages, as well. The hearing children of deaf parents eventually learn two languages and sound systems: those of their deaf parents and those of the rest of the community. In some instances, communication between children and parents is predominantly by gestures. In no case have I found any adverse effects upon the language development of standard English in these children. Although the mothers made sounds different from the children's, and although the children's vocalizations had no significant effect upon attaining what they wanted during early infancy, language in these children invariably began at the usual time and went through the same stages as is normally encountered.

Also of interest may be the following observations on fairly retarded children growing up in state institutions that are badly understaffed. During the day the children play in large, bare rooms, attended by only one person, often an older retardate who herself lacks a perfect command of language. The children's only entertainment is provided by a large television set, playing all day at full strength. Although most of these retarded children have only primitive beginnings of language, there are always some among them who manage, even under these extremely deprived circumstances, to pick up an amazing degree of language skill. Apparently they learn language partly through the television programs, whose level is often quite adequate for them!

From these instances we see that language capacity follows its own natural history. The child can avail himself of this capacity if the environment provides a minimum of stimulation and opportunity. His engagement in language activity can be limited by his environmental circumstances, but the underlying capacity is not easily arrested. Impoverished environments are not conducive to good language development, but good language development is not contingent on specific training measures (5); a wide variety of rather haphazard factors seems to be sufficient.

EFFECT OF VARIATIONS IN GENETIC BACKGROUND

Man is an unsatisfactory subject for the study of genetic influences; we cannot do breeding experiments on him and can use only statistical controls. Practically any evidence adduced is susceptible to a variety of interpretations. Nevertheless, there are indications that inheritance is at least partially responsible for deviations in verbal skills, as in the familial occurrence of a deficit termed congenital language disability (*2,* chapter 6). Studies, with complete pedigrees, have been published on the occurrence and distribution of stuttering, of hyperfluencies, of voice qualities, and of many other traits, which constitute supporting though not conclusive evidence that inheritance plays a role in language acquisition. In addition to such family studies, much research has been carried out on twins. Particularly notable are the studies of Luchsinger, who reported on the concordance of developmental histories and of many aspects of speech and language. Zygosity was established in these cases by serology. . . . Developmental data of this kind are, in my opinion, of greater relevance to our speculations on genetic background than are pedigrees.

The nonbiologist frequently and mistakenly thinks of genes as being directly responsible for one property or another; this leads him to the fallacy, especially when behavior is concerned, of dichotomizing everything as being dependent on either genes or environment. Genes act merely on intracellular biochemical processes, although these processes have indirect effects on events in the individual's developmental history. Many alterations in structure and function indirectly attributable to genes are more immediately the consequence of alterations in the schedule of developmental events. Therefore, the studies on twins are important in that they show that homozygotes reach milestones in language development at the same age, in contrast to heterozygotes, in whom divergences are relatively common. It is also interesting that the nature of the deviations—the symptoms, if you wish—are, in the vast majority, identical in homozygotes but not in heterozygotes.

Such evidence indicates that man's biological heritage endows him with sensitivities and propensities that lead to language development in children, who are spoken to (in contrast to chimpanzee infants, who do not automatically develop language—either receptive or productive—under identical treatment). The endowment has a genetic foundation, but this is not to say that there are "genes for language," or that the environment is of no importance.

ATTEMPTS TO MODIFY LANGUAGE DEVELOPMENT

Let us now consider children who have the capacity for language acquisition but fail to develop it for lack of exposure. This is the case with the congenitally deaf, who are allowed to grow up without either language or speech until school age, when suddenly language is brought to them in very unnatural ways. Before this time they may have half a dozen words they can utter, read, write, or finger-spell, but I have known of no profoundly deaf child (in New England, where my investigations were conducted) with whom one could communicate by use of the English language before school age.

When deaf children enter an oralist school, lipreading and speech become the major preoccupation of training. However, in most children these activities remain poor for many more years, and in some, throughout life. Their knowledge of language comes through learning to read and write. However, teachers in the oral tradition restrict expression in the graphic medium on the hypothesis that it interferes with lipreading and speech skills. Thus, exposure to language (*i*) comes much later in these children's lives than is normal, (*ii*) is dramatically reduced in quantity, (*iii*) is presented through a different medium and sensory modality, and (*iv*) is taught to the children rather as a second language is taught, instead of through the simple immersion into a sea of language that most children experience. The deaf children are immediately required to use grammatically correct sentences, and every mistake is discussed and explained to them.

The results of this procedure are interesting but not very encouraging from the educational point of view. During the early years of schooling, the children's spontaneous writings have a very unusual pattern; there is little evidence that the teachers' instruction in "how to compose correct sentences" is of any avail. Yet, careful analysis of their compositions shows that some subtleties of English syntax that are usually not part of the grammar taught in the school do make their appearance, sometimes quite early. There can be no question that the children do not simply imitate what they see; some of the teachings fall by the wayside, whereas a number of aspects of language are automatically absorbed from the written material given to the children.

There are other instances in which efforts are made to change a child's language skills by special training, as in the mildly retarded, for example. Many parents believe that their retarded child would function quite normally if somebody could just teach him to speak. At Children's Hospital in Boston I undertook a pilot study in which a speech therapist saw a small number of children with Downe's syndrome (mongolism) for several hours each week, in an effort to speed up language development. Later, two graduate students in linguistics investigated the children's phonetic skills and tried to assess the capacities of each child for clearer enunciation. Throughout these attempts, it was found that if a child had a small repertoire of single words, it was always possible to teach him yet another word, but if he was not joining these words spontaneously into phrases, there was nothing that could be done to induce him to do so. The articulatory skills were somewhat different. It was often possible to make a child who had always had slurred speech say a specific word more clearly. However, the moment the child returned to spontaneous utterances, he would fall back to the style that was usual for him. The most interesting results were obtained when the retarded children were required simply to repeat well-formed sentences. A child who had not developed to a stage in which he used certain grammatical rules spontaneously, who was still missing the syntactic foundations and prerequisites, could not be taught to repeat a sentence that was formed by such higher rules. This was true even in sentences of very few words. Similar observations have since been made on normal children (*6*), with uniformly similar results; normal children, too, can repeat correctly only that which is formed by rules they have already mastered. This is the best indication that language does not come about by simple imitation, but that the child abstracts regularities or relations from the language he hears, which he then applies to building up language for himself as an apparatus of principles.

WHAT SETS THE PACE OF LANGUAGE DEVELOPMENT?

There is a widespread belief that the development of language is dependent on the motor skills of the articulating organs. Some psychologists believe that species other than man fail to develop language only because of anatomical differences in their oral structures. However, we have evidence that this is not so.

It is important that we are clear about the essential nature of language. Since my interests are in language capacities, I am concerned with the development of the child's knowledge of how language works. This is not the same as the acquisition of "the first word." The best test for the presence and development of this knowledge is the manner in which discourse is understood. In most instances, it is true that there is a relation between speech and understanding, but this relation is not a necessary one (*7*).

By understanding, I mean something quite specific. In the realm of phonology, understanding involves a process that roughly corresponds to the linguists' phonematization (in contrast, for example, to a "pictographic" understanding: phonematization results in seeing similarities between speech sounds, whereas pictographic understanding would treat a word as an indivisible sound pattern). In the realm of semantics, understanding involves seeing the basis on which objects are categorized, thus enabling a child to name an object correctly that he has never seen before. (The child does not start out with a hypothesis that "table" is the proper name of a unique object or that it refers to all things that have four appendages.) In the realm of grammar, understanding involves the extraction of relations between word classes; an example is the understanding of predication. By application of these tests, it can be shown empirically that Aunt Pauline's favorite lapdog does not have a little language knowledge, but, in fact, fails the test of understanding on all counts.

A survey of children with a variety of handicaps shows that their grasp of how language works is intimately related to their general cognitive growth, which, in turn, is partly dependent on physical maturation and partly on opportunities to interact with a stimulus-rich environment. In many retarding diseases, for example, language development is predicted best by the rate of advancement in mental age (using tests of nonverbal intelligence). In an investigation of congenitally blind children (*8*), we are again finding that major milestones for language development are highly correlated with physical development. A naive conception of language development as an accumulation of associations between visual and auditory patterns would be hard put to explain this.

BRAIN CORRELATES

In adults, language functions take place predominantly in the left hemisphere. A number of cortical fields have been related to specific aspects of language. The details are still somewhat controversial and need not concern us here. It is certain, however, that precentral areas of the frontal lobe are principally involved in the production of language, whereas the postcentral parietal and superior temporal fields are involved in sensory functions. These cortical specializations are not present at birth, but become only gradually established during childhood, in a process very similar to that of embryological history; there is evidence of differentiation and regulation of function. In the adult, traumata causing large left-sided central cortical lesions carry a highly predictable prognosis; in 70 percent of all cases, aphasia occurs, and in about half of these, the condition is irreversible (I am basing these figures on our experience with penetrating head injuries incurred in war).

Comparable traumatic lesions in childhood have quite different consequences, the prognosis being directly related to the age at which the insult is incurred. Lesions of the left hemisphere in children under age 2 are no more injurious to future language development than are lesions of the right hemisphere. Children whose brain is traumatized after the onset of language but before the age of 4 usually have transient aphasias; language is quickly reestablished, however, if the right hemisphere remains intact. Often these children regain language by going through stages of language development similar to those of the 2-year-old, but they traverse each stage at greater speed. Lesions incurred before the very early teens also carry an excellent prognosis, permanent residues of symptoms being extremely rare.

The prognosis becomes rapidly worse for lesions that occur after this period; the young men who become casualties of war have symptoms virtually identical with those of stroke patients of advanced age. Experience with the surgical removal of an entire cerebral hemisphere closely parallels this picture. The basis for prognosticating operative success is, again, the age at which the disease has been contracted for which the operation is performed.

If a disturbance in the left hemisphere occurs early enough in life, the right hemisphere remains competent for language throughout life. Apparently this process is comparable to regulation, as we know it from morphogenesis. If the disease occurs after a certain critical period of life, namely, the early teens, this regulative capacity is lost and language is interfered with permanently. Thus the time at which the hemispherectomy is performed is less important than the time of the lesion.

CRITICAL AGE FOR LANGUAGE ACQUISITION

The most reasonable interpretation of this picture of recovery from aphasia in childhood is not that there is vicarious functioning, or taking over, by the right hemisphere because of need, but rather that language functions are not yet confined to the left hemisphere during early life. Apparently both hemispheres are involved at the beginning, and a specialization takes place later (which is the characteristic of differentiation), resulting in a kind of left-right polarization of functions. Therefore, the recovery from aphasia during preteen years may partly be regarded as a reinstatement of activities that had never been lost. There is evidence that children at this age are capable of developing language in the same natural way as do very young children. Not only do symptoms subside, but active language development continues to occur. Similarly, we see that healthy children have a quite different propensity for acquiring foreign languages before the early teens than after the late teens, the period in between being transitional. For the young adult, second-language learning is an academic exercise, and there is a vast variety in degree of proficiency. It rapidly becomes more and more difficult to overcome the accent and interfering influences of the mother tongue.

Neurological material strongly suggests that something happens in the brain during the early teens that changes the propensity for language acquisition. We do now know the factors involved, but it is interesting that the critical period coincides with the time at which the human brain attains its final state of maturity in terms of structure, function, and biochemistry (electroencephalographic patterns slightly lag behind, but become stabilized by about 16 years). Apparently the maturation of the brain marks the end of regulation and locks certain functions into place.

There is further evidence that corroborates the notion of a critical period for primary language acquisition, most importantly, the developmental histories of retarded children. It is dangerous to make sweeping generalizations about all retarded children, because so much depends on the specific disease that causes the retardation. But if we concentrate on diseases in which the pathological condition is essentially stationary, such as microcephaly vera or mongolism, it is possible to make fairly general predictions about language development. If the child's mental developmental age is 2 when he is 4 years old (that is, his I.Q. is 50), one may safely predict that some small progress will be made in language development. He will slowly move through the usual stages of infant language, although the rate of development will gradually slow down. In virtually all of these cases, language development comes to a complete standstill in the early teens, so that these individuals are arrested in primitive stages of language development that are perpetuated for the rest of their lives. Training and motivation are of little help.

Development in the congenitally deaf is also revealing. When they first enter school, their language acquisition is usually quite spectacular, considering the enormous odds against them. However, children who by their early teens have still not mastered all of the principles that underlie the production of sentences appear to encounter almost unsurmountable difficulties in perfecting verbal skills.

There is also evidence of the converse. Children who suddenly lose their hearing (usually a consequence of meningitis) show very different degrees of language skill, depending on whether the disease strikes before the onset of language or after. If it occurs before they are 18 months old, such children encounter difficulties with language development that are very much the same as those encountered by the congenitally deaf. Children who lose their hearing after they have acquired language, however, at age 3 to 4, have a different prospect. Their speech deteriorates rapidly; usually within weeks they stop using language, and so far it has proved impossible to maintain the skill by educational procedures [although new techniques developed in England and described by Fry (*9*) give promise of great improvement]. Many such children then live without language for a relatively long time, often 2 to 3 years, and when they enter the schools for the deaf, must be trained in the same way that other deaf children are trained. However, training is much more successful, and their language habits stand out dramatically against those of their less fortunate colleagues. There appears to be a direct relation between the length of time during which a child has been exposed to language and the proficiency seen at the time of retraining.

BIOLOGICAL APPROACH: DEFINING LANGUAGE FURTHER

Some investigators propose that language is an artifact—a tool that man has shaped for himself to serve a purpose. This assumption induces the view that language consists of many individual traits, each independent of the other. However, the panorama of observations presented above suggests a biological predisposition for the development of language that is anchored in the operating characteristics of the human brain (*10*). Man's cognitive apparatus apparently becomes a language receiver and transmitter, provided the growing organism is exposed to minimum and haphazard environmental events.

However, this assumption leads to a view different from that suggested by the artifact assumption. Instead of thinking of language as a collection of separate and mutually independent traits, one comes to see it as a profoundly integrated activity. Language is to be understood as an operation rather than a static product of the mind. Its modus operandi reflects that of human cognition, because language is an intimate part of cognition. Thus the biological view denies that language is the cause of cognition, or even its effect, since language is not an object (like a tool) that exists apart from a living human brain.

As biologists, we are interested in the operating principles of language because we hope that this will give us some clues about the operating principles of the human brain. We know there is just one species *Homo sapiens,* and it is therefore reasonable to assume that individuals who speak Turkish, English, or Basque (or who spoke Sanskrit some millennia ago) all have (or had) the same kind of brain, that is, a computer with the same operating principles and the same sensorium. Therefore, in a biological investigation one must try to disregard the differences between the languages of the world and to discover the general principles of operation that are common to all of them. This is not an easy matter; in fact, there are social scientists who doubt the existence of language universals. As students of language we cannot fail to be impressed with the enormous differences among languages. Yet every normal child learns the language to which he is exposed. Perhaps we are simply claiming that common denominators must exist; can we prove their existence? If we discovered a totally isolated tribe with a language unknown to any outsider, how could we find out whether this language is generated by a computer that has the same biological characteristics as do our brains, and how could we prove that it shares the universal features of all languages?

As a start, we could exchange children between our two cultures to discover whether the same language developmental history would occur in those exchanged. Our data would be gross developmental stages, correlated with the emergence of motor milestones. A bioassay of this kind (already performed many times, always with positive results) gives only part of the answer.

In theory, one may also adduce more rigorous proof of similarity among languages. The conception of language universals is difficult to grasp intuitively, because we find it so hard to translate from one language to another and because the grammars appear, on the surface, to be so different. But it is entirely possible that underneath the structural difference that makes it so difficult for the adult speaker to learn a second language (particularly one that is not a cognate of his own) there are significant formal identities.

Virtually every aspect of language is the expression of relations. This is true of phonology (as stressed by Roman Jakobson and his school), semantics, and syntax. For instance, in all languages of the world words label a set of relational principles instead of being labels of specific objects. Knowing a word is never a simple association between an object and an acoustic pattern, but the successful operation of those principles, or application of those rules, that lead to using the word "table" or "house" for objects never before encountered. The language universal in this instance is not the type of object that comes to have a word, nor the particular relations involved; the universal is the generality that words stand for relations instead of being unique names for one object.

Further, no language has ever been described that does not have a second order of relational principles, namely, principles in which relations are being related, that is, syntax in which relations between words are being specified. Once again, the universal is not a particular relation that occurs in all languages (though there are several such relations) but that all languages have relations of relations.

Mathematics may be used as a highly abstract form of description, not of scattered facts but of the dynamic interrelations—the operating principles—found in nature. Chomsky and his students have done this. Their aim has been to develop algorithms for specific languages, primarily English, that make explicit the series of computations that may account for the structure of sentences. The fact that these attempts have only been partially successful is irrelevant to the argument here. (Since every native speaker of English *can* tell a well-formed sentence from an ill-formed one, it is evident that some principles must exist; the question is merely whether the Chomskyites have discovered the correct ones.) The development of algorithms is only one province of mathematics, and in the eyes of many mathematicians a relatively limited one. There is a more exciting prospect; once we know something about the basic relational operating principles underlying a few languages, it should be possible to characterize formally the abstract system *language* as a whole. If our assumption of the existence of basic, structural language universals is correct, one ought to be able to adduce rigorous proof for the existence of homeomorphisms between any natural languages, that is, any of the systems characterized formally. If a category calculus were developed for this sort of thing, there would be one level of generality on which a common denominator could be found; this may be done trivially (for instance by using the product of all systems). However, our present knowledge of the relations, and the relations of relations, found in the languages so far investigated in depth encourages us to expect a significant solution.

ENVIRONMENT AND MATURATION

Everything in life, including behavior and language, is interaction of the individual with its milieu. But the milieu is not constant. The organism itself helps to shape it (this is true of cells and organs as much as of animals and man). Thus, the organism and its environment is a dynamic system and, phylogenetically, developed as such.

The development of language in the child may be elucidated by applying to it the conceptual framework of developmental biology. Maturation may be characterized as a sequence of states. At each state, the growing organism is capable of accepting some specific input; this it breaks down and resynthesizes in such a way that it makes itself develop into a new state. This new state makes the organism sensitive to new and different types of input, whose acceptance transforms it to yet a further state, which opens the way to still different input, and so on. This is called epigenesis. It is the story of embryological development observable in the formation of the body, as well as in certain aspects of behavior.

At various epigenetic states, the organism may be susceptible to more than one sort of input—it may be susceptible to two or more distinct kinds or even to an infinite variety of inputs, as long as they are within determined limits—and the developmental history varies with the nature of the input accepted. In other words, the organism, during development, comes to crossroads; if condition A is present, it goes one way; if condition B is present, it goes another. We speak of states here, but this is, of course, an abstraction. Every stage of maturation is unstable. It is prone to change into specific directions, but requires a trigger from the environment.

When language acquisition in the child is studied from the point of view of developmental biology, one makes an effort to describe developmental stages together with their tendencies for change and the conditions that bring about that change. I believe that the schema of physical maturation is applicable to the study of language development because children appear to be sensitive to successively different aspects of the language environment. The child first reacts only to intonation patterns. With continued exposure to these patterns as they occur in a given language, mechanisms develop that allow him to process the patterns, and in most instances to reproduce them (although the latter is not a necessary condition for further development). This changes him so that he reaches a new state, a new potential for language development. Now he becomes aware of certain articulatory aspects, can process them and possibly also reproduce them, and so on. A similar sequence of acceptance, synthesis, and state of new acceptance can be demonstrated on the level of semantics and syntax.

That the embryological concepts of differentiation, as well as of determination and regulation, are applicable to the brain processes associated with language development is best illustrated by the material discussed above under the headings "brain correlates" and "critical age for language acquisition." Furthermore, the correlation between language development and other maturational indices suggests that there are anatomical and physiological processes whose maturation sets the pace for both cognitive and language development; it is to these maturational processes that the concept differentiation refers. We often transfer the meaning of the word to the verbal behavior itself, which is not unreasonable, although, strictly speaking, it is the physical correlates only that differentiate.

PSEUDO-HOMOLOGIES AND NAIVE "EVOLUTIONIZING"

The relation between species is established on the basis of structural, physiological, biochemical, and often behavioral correspondences, called homologies. The identification of homologies frequently poses heuristic problems. Common sense may be very misleading in this matter. Unless there is cogent evidence that the correspondences noted are due to a common phylogenetic origin, one must entertain the possibility that resemblances are spurious (though perhaps due to convergence). In other words, not all criteria are equally reliable for the discovery of true homologies. The criteria must pass the following two tests if they are to reveal common biological origins. (*i*) They must be applicable to traits that have a demonstrable (or at least conceivable) genetic basis; and (*ii*) the traits to which they apply must not have a sporadic and seemingly random distribution over the taxa of the entire animal kingdom. Homologies cannot be established by relying on similarity that rests on a superficial inspection (a whale is not a fish); on logical rather than biological aspects (animals that move at 14 miles per hour are not necessarily related to one another); and on anthropocentric imputation of motives (a squirrel's hoarding of nuts may have nothing in common with man's provisions for his future).

Comparisons of language with animal communication that purport to throw light on the problem of its phylogenetic origins infringe on every one of these guidelines. Attempts to write generative grammars for the language of the bees in order to discover in what respect that language is similar to and different from man's language fail to pass test (*i*). Syntax does not have a genetic basis any more than do arithmetic or algebra; these are calculi used to describe relations. It may be that the activities or circumstances to which the calculi are applied are in some way related to genetically determined capacities. However, merely the fact that the calculus may or may not be applied obviously does not settle that issue.

The common practice of searching the entire animal kingdom for communication behavior that resembles man's in one aspect or another fails test (*ii*). The fact that some bird species and perhaps two or three cetaceans can make noises that sound like words, that some insects use discrete signals when they communicate, or that recombination of signals has been observed to occur in communication systems of a dozen totally unrelated species are not signs of a common phylogeny or genetically based relationship to language. Furthermore, the similarities noted between human language and animal communication all rest on superficial intuition. The resemblances that exist between human language and the language of the bees and the birds are spurious. The comparative criteria are usually logical (*12*) instead of biological; and the very idea that there must be a common denominator underlying all communication systems of animals and man is based on an anthropocentric imputation.

Everything in biology has a history, and so every communication system is the result of evolution. But traits or skills do not have an evolutionary history of their own, that is, a history that is independent of the history of the species. Contemporary species are discontinuous groups (except for those in the process of branching) with discontinuous communication behavior. Therefore, historical continuity need not lead to continuity between contemporary communication systems, many of which (including man's) constitute unique developments.

Another recent practice is to give speculative accounts of just how, why, and when human language developed. This is a somewhat futile undertaking. The knowledge that we have gained about the mechanisms of evolution does not enable us to give specific accounts of every event of the past. Paleontological evidence points to the nature of its fauna, flora, and climate. The precursors of modern man have left for us their bones, teeth, and primitive tools. None of these bears any necessary or assured relation to any type of communication system. Most speculations on the nature of the most primitive sounds, on the first discovery of their usefulness, on the reasons for the hypertrophy of the brain, or the consequences of a narrow pelvis are in vain. We can no longer reconstruct what the selection pressures were or in what order they came, because we know too little that is securely established by hard evidence about the ecological and social conditions of fossil man. Moreover, we do not even know what the targets of actual selection were. This is particularly troublesome because every genetic alteration brings about several changes at once, some of which must be quite incidental to the selective process.

SPECIES SPECIFICITIES AND COGNITIVE SPECIALIZATION

In the 19th century it was demonstrated that man is not in a category apart from that of animals. Today it seems to be necessary to defend the view (before many psychologists) that man is not identical with all other animals—in fact, that every animal species is unique, and that most of the commonalities that exist are, at best, homologies. It is frequently claimed that the principles of behavioral function are identical—in all vertebrates, for example—and that the differences between species are differences of magnitude, rather than quality. At other times, it is assumed that cognitive functions are alike in two species except that one of the two may have additionally acquired a capacity for a specific activity. I find fault with both views.

Since behavioral capacities (I prefer the term cognition) are the product of brain function, my point can well be illustrated by considering some aspects of brain evolution. Every mammalian species has an anatomically distinct brain. Homologies are common, but innovations can also be demonstrated. When man's brain is compared with the brain of other primates, extensive correspondences can be found, but there are major problems when it comes to the identification of homologies. Dramatic differences exist not only in size but also in details of the developmental histories; together with differences in cerebrocortical histology, topography, and extent, there are differences in subcortical fiber-connections, as pointed out by Geschwind (*13*) most recently and by others before him. The problem is, what do we make of the innovations? Is it possible that each innovation (usually an innovation is not a clear-cut anatomical entity) is like an independent component that is simply added to the components common to all the more old-fashioned brains? And if so, is it likely that the new component is simply adding a routine to the computational facilities already available? Both presumptions are naive. A brain is an integrated organ, and cognition results from the integrated operation of all its tissues and suborgans. Man's brain is not a chimpanzee's brain plus added "association facilities." Its functions have undergone reintegration at the same pace as its evolutionary developments.

The identical argument applies to cognitive functions. Cognition is not made up of isolated processes such as perception, storing, and retrieval. Animals do not all have an identical memory mechanism except that some have a larger storage capacity. As the structure of most proteins, the morophology of most cells, and the gross anatomy of most animals show certain species specificities (as do details of behavioral repertoires), so we may expect that cognition, too, in all of its aspects, has its species specificities. My assumption, therefore, is that man's cognition is not essentially that of every other primate with merely the addition of the capacity for language; instead, I propose that his entire cognitive function, of which his capacity for language is an integral part, is species-specific. I repeat once more that I make this assumption not because I think man is in a category all of his own, but because every animal species must be assumed to have cognitive specificities.

CONCLUSION

The human brain is a biochemical machine; it computes the relations expressed in sentences and their components. It has a print-out consisting of acoustic patterns that are capable of similar relational computation by machines of the same constitution using the same program. Linguists, biologists, and psychologists have all discussed certain aspects of the machine.

Linguists, particularly those developing generative grammar, aim at a formal description of the machine's behavior; they search mathematics for a calculus to describe it adequately. Different calculations are matched against the behavior to test their descriptive adequacy. This is an empirical procedure. The raw data are the way a speaker of a language understands collections of words or the relationships he sees. A totally adequate calculus has not yet been discovered. Once available, it will merely describe, in formal terms, the process of relational interpretation in the realm of verbal behavior. It will describe a set of operations; however, it will not make any claims of isomophism between the formal operations and the biological operations they describe.

Biologists try to understand the nature, growth, and function of the machine (the human brain) itself. They make little inroads here and there, and generally play catch-as-catch-can; everything about the machine interests them (including the descriptions furnished by linguists).

Traditionally, learning theory has been involved neither in a specific description of this particular machine's behavior nor in its physical constitution. Its concern has been with the use of the machine: What makes it go? Can one make it operate more or less often? What purposes does it serve?

Answers provided by each of these inquiries into language are not intrinsically antagonistic, as has often been claimed. It is only certain overgeneralizations that come into conflict. This is especially so when claims are made that any one of these approaches provides answers to all the questions that matter.

REFERENCES AND NOTES

1. E. H. Lenneberg, in *The Structure of Language, Readings in the Philosophy of Language,* J. A. Fodor and J. J. Katz, Eds. (Prentice-Hall, Englewood Cliffs, N.J., 1964).
2. For complete treatment, see E. H. Lenneberg, *Biological Foundations of Language* (Wiley, New York, 1967).
3. E. H. Lenneberg, I. A. Nichols, E. F. Rosenberger, in *Disorders of Communication* D. Rioch, Ed. (Research Publications of Association for Research in Nervous and Mental Disorders, New York, 1964), vol. 42.
4. E. H. Lenneberg, F. G. Rebelsky, I. A. Nichols, *Hum. Develop.* **8**, 23 (1965).
5. R. Brown, C. Cazden, U. Bellugi, in *The 1967 Minnesota Symposium on Child Psychology,* J. P. Hill, Ed. (Univ. of Minnesota Press, Minneapolis, in press).
6. D. Slobin, personal communication.
7. E. H. Lenneberg, *J. Abnorm. Soc. Psychol.* **65**, 419 (1962).
8. ———, S. Fraiberg, N. Stein, research in progress.
9. D. B. Fry, in *The Genesis of Language: A Psycholinguistic Approach,* F. Smith and G. A. Miller, Eds. (MIT Press, Cambridge, 1966).
10. For details, see E. H. Lenneberg, *Perception and Language,* in preparation.

11. N. Chomsky, "The formal nature of language" (in *2,* appendix A).
12. See, for instance, C. F. Hockett, in *Animal Communication,* W. E. Lanyon and W. N. Tavolga, Eds. (American Institute of Biological Sciences, Washington, D.C., 1960); and in *Sci. Amer.* **203,** 89 (1960).
13. N. Geschwind, *Brain* **88,** 237, 585 (1965).
14. I thank H. Levin and M. Seligman for comments and criticisms.

16
THE PSYCHOLOGICAL COSTS OF QUALITY AND EQUALITY IN EDUCATION*

URIE BRONFENBRENNER

THE COSTS of quality and equality in education—calculated, as they usually are, in dollars and cents—invariably turn out to be higher than expected. Not infrequently the public is unwilling to pay the price, and even when it does so, it is often with reluctance, pain, and resentment, toward both those who impose the payment and those who receive the benefits. The reasons for resistance are well known. Personal financial resources are slow to acquire, the demand invariably exceeds the supply, and what little we have is urgently needed to provide for ourselves and our families.

The sobering burden of this paper is to show that all these considerations apply with even greater force when the costs of quality and inequality are reckoned in psychological rather than economic terms. Here, too, the price turns out to be far higher than anticipated, but the available resources are even more limited, the needs of self and family more pressing, and the pain and resentment at having to pay the price far more acute. Yet, these costs will have to be met, for unless they are, no increase in school budget, however generous, no regrouping of pupils, however democratic, no new curriculum, however adapted to the child's environment, can bring either quality or equality in education to those who do not have them, or, as I hope to demonstrate, even for those who do.

To understand why this is so, we must come to terms with an unwelcome but nonetheless inexorable reality: whatever their origin, the most immediate, overwhelming, and stubborn obstacles to achieving quality and equality in education now lie as much in the character and way of life of the American Negro as in the indifference and hostility of the white community. The first part of this paper summarizes the bases for this assertion.

---

* From *Child Development*, 1967, *38*, 909–926. Reprinted with permission from the author and the Society for Research in Child Development.

This paper was presented at the Conference on Psychological Factors in Poverty held in Madison, Wisconsin, June 22–24, 1967.

THE PSYCHOLOGICAL CHARACTERISTICS OF THE NEGRO CHILD

Recognition in actual practice of the critical role played by psychological factors in the education of the Negro child begins with implementation of the 1954 Supreme Court decision that separate facilities are inherently unequal. Unfortunately, it all too often ends there. In many American communities the enlightened leadership, both Negro and white, and their supporters operate on the tacit assumption that once the Negro child finds himself in an integrated classroom with a qualified teacher and adequate materials, learning will take place, and with it the deficiencies of the American Negro, and the judgments of inferiority which they in part encourage, will be erased.

Regrettably, this is not the case. Neither the scars of slavery which the Negro child still bears nor the skills and self-confidence of his white companion rub off merely through contact in the same classroom. This is not to imply that integration is impotent as an instrument of change. On the contrary, it is a desperately necessary condition, but not a sufficient one. Objective equality of opportunity is not enough. The Negro child must also be able to profit from the educational situation in which he finds himself. This he cannot do if he lacks the background and motivation necessary for learning. And the evidence indicates that these essentials are often conspicuously absent.

Let us examine the data. Fortunately, most of the relevant facts are already brought together for us in Pettigrew's (1964) recent volume, *A Profile of the Negro American,* a masterful compendium and interpretation of the available research findings. We shall not concern ourselves here with the full array of facts which Pettigrew presents; they are eloquent testimony to the crippling psychological costs to the Negro of the inequality imposed upon him by slavery and its contemporary economic and social heritage. For our purposes, we select those findings that bear directly and indirectly on the educability of the Negro child of poverty.

The first of these is the sobering statistic that the longer such a child remains in school, even in integrated classrooms, the further behind he falls in relation to the norms for his age and grade. Such progressive retardation is reported not only for measures of academic achievement (Coleman, 1966; Deutsch, 1960; Kennedy, Van de Riet, & White, 1963) but also for scores on tests of general intelligence (Coleman, 1966; Deutsch & Brown, 1964; Kennedy et al., 1963; Pettigrew, 1964, chap. v). Moreover, the discrepanices between Negro and white children are not limited to poverty-stricken families. They are not only present across the socioeconomic spectrum but "the Negro-White differences increase at each higher SES level" (Deutsch & Brown, 1964, p. 27).

In analyzing the factors producing these results, investigators call attention to the inappropriateness of many test items to lower-class Negro culture.

But at the same time, they make clear that improvements in test construction will not change the fact of the Negro child's inferiority; he suffers from handicaps that are real and debilitating. For example, Deutsch (1960) cites evidence that, in comparison with white children from deprived socioeconomic backgrounds, lower-class Negro youngsters are especially retarded in reading and language skills. They also show a shorter attention span in any task which requires concentration and persistence. Deutsch's observations indicate that the failure in persistence reflects not only an inability to concentrate but also a lack of motivation and an attitude of futility in the face of difficulty. Thus he reports:

> Time after time, the experimental child would drop a problem posed by the teacher as soon as he met any difficulty in attempting to solve it. In questioning after, the child would typically respond "so what?" or "who cares" or "what does it matter?" In the control group [white children of "similar socio-economic level"], there was an obvious competitive spirit, with a verbalized anticipation of "reward" for a correct response. In general, this anticipation was only infrequently present in the experimental group and was not consistently or meaningfully reenforced by the teachers [Deutsch, 1960, p. 9].

Deutsch's observations are confirmed by a series of studies, cited by Pettigrew, showing that "lower class Negro children of school age typically 'give up the fight' and reveal unusually low need for achievement" (1964, pp. 30–31).

Not only does the Negro child feel powerless; he feels worthless as well. At the core of this sense of inferiority is the awareness of being black. From the age of 3 onward, Negro children begin to prefer white skin to black and to think of Negroes in general and themselves in particular as ugly, unwanted, and "bad." Results of the numerous studies of this phenomenon, summarized by Pettigrew (1964, chap. i), are epitomized in an example he cited of a small Negro boy who served as a subject in one of these investigations. "Asked if he were white or colored, he hung his head and hesitated. Then he murmured softly, 'I guess I'se kind o' colored' " (Pettigrew, 1964, p. 8).

It is this "mark of oppression" (Kardiner & Ovesey, 1951) which distinguishes the personality development of the Negro child from that of his white counterpart, especially in lower-class families. The psychological process and its consequences are summarized by the following excerpt from a more extended analysis by Ausubel.

> The Negro child . . . gradually becomes aware of the social significance of racial membership. . . . He perceives himself as an object of derision and disparagement, as socially rejected by the prestigeful elements of society, and as unworthy of succorance and affection. Having no compelling reasons for not accepting this officially sanctioned, negative evaluation of himself, he develops ingrained feelings of inferiority [Ausubel, 1958, p. 35].

It is all these intellectual, motivational, and emotional problems that the Negro child brings with him when he goes to school. The obstacles they place to the learning process are reflected in the marked contrast in classroom atmosphere reported by Deutsch (1960) in his study of schools in Negro and white lower-class neighborhoods. In the former setting, 50–80 percent of all classroom time was devoted to disciplinary and various essentially nonacademic tasks, whereas the corresponding percentage for the white control group was about 30.

What factors account for the special debilities and behavioral difficulties of Negro children? The thesis, still militantly upheld by some investigators (Garrett, 1960; 1961; 1962a; 1962b; McGurk, 1956; 1959; Shuey, 1958; Van den Haag, 1964), that such deficiencies have an innate basis in race differences, has been so thoroughly discredited (Anastasi, 1956; Chein, 1961; Pettigrew, 1964) that it needs no extended consideration here. We would call attention, however, to one additional fact which, if acknowledged, presents an interesting problem to those who seek to account for Negro inferiority in genetic terms. The intellectual, emotional, and social deficiencies observed in Negro children are considerably more pronounced in boys than in girls. Systematic data on this point are cited by Deutsch (1960). For instance, in his sample of Negro schoolchildren in grades 4–6, the proportion who scored below fourth-grade norms on the Stanford Achievement Test was 38 percent for girls and 68 percent for boys, the discrepancies being greatest on the reading subtest. No differences approaching this magnitude were found for the white controls. Similarly, in repeating digits forward or backward, Negro girls performed at about the same level as white controls, whereas Negro boys were markedly inferior to their white counterparts. Deutsch stresses the psychological significance of this difference in view of "the importance of attention for any academic learning and therefore the potential contribution of lowered attentivity to the achievement differences found" (Deutsch, 1960, p. 12). It is noteworthy that these sex differences in achievement are observed among Southern as well as Northern Negroes, are present at every socioeconomic level, and tend to increase with age (Kennedy et al., 1963, see especially Tables 68 and 69).

THE SOURCES OF INADEQUACY

Clearly any satisfactory explanation for the debilities of the Negro child must also account for the special ineptitude of the Negro male. Several lines of evidence are pertinent in this regard: the first is biological, the remainder social.

Organic Bases of Inadequacy

Though the Negro infant is not biologically inferior at the moment of conception, he often becomes so shortly thereafter. The inadequate nutrition and prenatal care received by millions of Negro mothers result in complications of pregnancy which take their toll in extraordinarily high rates of prematurity and congenital defect (Knobloch, Rider, Harper, & Pasamanick, 1956; Pasamanick & Knobloch, 1958; Pasamanick, Knobloch, & Lilienfeld, 1956). Many of these abnormalities entail neurological damage resulting in impaired intellectual function and behavioral disturbances, including hyperactivity, distractibility, and low attention span. Of particular relevance is the significant role played by paranatal and prenatal factors in the genesis of childhood reading disorders. In a retrospective comparison of hospital records, Kawi and Pasamanick (1959) found that instances of two or more complications of pregnancy were over nine times as frequent in the records of mothers whose children later exhibited severe reading difficulties as in a control population matched on social class and other relevant variables. Finally, it is a well established, though not thoroughly understood, fact that neurological disorders resulting from complications of pregnancy and birth are considerably more frequent for males than females. This differential rate has been identified as a major factor in contributing to the consistent sex differences observed in incidence of neuropsychiatric disorders and psychological disturbances in children (Kawi & Pasamanick, 1959, p. 19). Of special relevance in this connection is the statistic that "behavior disorders are two to three times more common in boys, reading disorders as much as eight or nine times" (Pasamanick & Knobloch, 1958, p. 7). These authors see in "reproductive casualty" and its sequelae a major factor contributing to school retardation in Negro children generally and Negro males in particular. Organic debilities, of course, result not only in intellectual dysfunction but also in discouragement. In this manner, they play a part in evoking the expectations of failure, the readiness to give up in the face of difficulty, and the low level of aspiration observed in Negro children, especially among boys.

The Impact of Paternal Absence

But even where organic factors do not set in motion the vicious circle of defeat and disinterest in achievement, social circumstances can be counted on to instigate and accelerate a similar downward spiral. A growing body of research evidence points to the debilitating effect on personality development in Negro children, particularly males, resulting from the high frequency of father absence in Negro families. The extent of such absence is eloquently reflected in census figures summarized by Pettigrew (1964).

Census data for 1960 illustrate the depth of this family disorganization among Negroes: over a third (34.3 per cent) of all non-white mothers with children under six years of age hold jobs as compared with less than a fifth (19.5 per cent) of white mothers with children under six; only three-fourths (74.9 per cent) of all non-white families have both the husband and the wife present in the household as compared with nine-tenths (89.2 per cent) of white families; and only two-thirds (66.3 per cent) of non-whites under eighteen years of age live with both of their parents as compared with nine-tenths (90.2 per cent) of such whites. . . .

The vast majority of incomplete Negro households is lacking the husband. Frazier estimated in 1950 that the male parent was missing in roughly 20 per cent of Negro households. In addition to divorce and separation, part of this phenomenon is due to a higher Negro male death rate. The percentage of widows among Negro women fifty-four years old or less is roughly twice that of white women [Pettigrew, 1964, pp. 16–17].

The consequence of this state of affairs for the personality development of the Negro child is indicated by several lines of investigations. First, a series of studies conducted in the United States (Bach, 1946; Barclay & Cosumano, 1967; Kuckenberg, 1963; Sears, 1951; Sears, Pintler, & Sears, 1946; Stolz, 1954) and in Norway (Grønseth, 1957; Lynn & Sawrey, 1959; Tiller, 1957; 1961) showed that father absence has far greater impact on sons than on daughters. The results, and their implications, are summarized by Pettigrew as follows:

. . . father-deprived boys are markedly more immature, submissive, dependent, and effeminate than other boys. . . . As they grow older, this passive behavior may continue, but more typically, it is vigorously overcompensated for by exaggerated masculinity. Juvenile gangs, white and Negro, classically act out this pseudomasculinity with leather jackets, harsh language, and physical "toughness" [Pettigrew, 1964, p. 18].

Consistent with this same line of evidence are the results of a substantial number of studies pointing to the importance of paternal absence and inadequacy in the genesis of delinquent behavior (Bacon, Child, & Barry, 1963; Bandura & Walters, 1959; Burton & Whiting, 1961; Glueck & Glueck, 1950; 1956; Miller, 1958; Rohrer & Edmonson, 1960; Scarpitti, Murray, Dinitz, & Reckless, 1960). In seeking an explanation for this relationship, several of the major investigators have concluded that the exaggerated toughness, aggressiveness, and cruelty of delinquent gangs reflect the desperate effort of males in lower-class culture to rebel against their early overprotective, feminizing environment and to find a masculine identity. For example, Miller analyzes the dynamics of the process in the following terms:

The genesis of the intense concern over "toughness" in lower class culture is probably related to the fact that a significant proportion of lower class males are reared in a predominantly female household, and lack a consistently present male figure with whom to identify and from whom to learn essential components of a "male" role. Since women serve as a primary object of identification during preadolescent years, the almost obsessive lower class concern with "masculinity" probably resembles a type of compulsive reaction-formation. . . . A positive overt evaluation of behavior defined as "effeminate" would be out of the question for a lower class male [Miller, 1958, p. 9].

The special relevance of this dynamic for public education is indicated in a similar conclusion drawn by Rohrer and Edmonson in their follow-up study of Negro youth in New Orleans. "The gang member rejects this femininity in every form, and he sees it in women and in effeminate men, in laws and morals and religion, in schools, and occupational striving" (Rohrer & Edmonson, 1960, p. 163).

Despite their desperate effort to prove the contrary, a latent femininity is nevertheless present in "fatherless" youngsters and results in a confused sex identity. Substantial support for this argument is found in the impressive number of studies, summarized by Pettigrew, which show that Negro men, especially those from lower-class homes, obtain high scores on indirect measures of femininity. Additional evidence points to father absence as a critical factor. In comparison with a control group from intact homes, Negroes whose fathers were absent during early childhood were far more likely to be either single or divorced; in addition, "they also felt more victimized, less in control of the environment, and more distrustful of others" (Pettigrew, 1964, p. 20).

Nor are the consequences of paternal absence limited to the emotional and social sphere. A series of investigations by Mischel (1958; 1961a; 1961b; 1961c) points to the crucial role of this same factor in the development of a capacity essential to achievement generally and academic achievement in particular—the ability to delay immediate gratification in order to obtain a later reward. The systematic investigation of this phenomenon was suggested to the investigator by anthropological reports alleging "a major personality difference" between Negro and East Indian groups on the island of Trinidad.

> This difference, as expressed by numerous informants, is that the Negroes are impulsive, indulge themselves, settle for next to nothing if they can get it right away, do not work or wait for bigger things in the future but, instead, prefer smaller gains immediately (Mischel, 1958, p. 57).

In a series of ingenious experiments (e.g., a child is offered a choice between a tiny candy bar now, and a larger bar in a week's time), Mischel (1958, 1961c) demonstrated that the preference for immediate gratification was a distinguishing characteristic observable in Negro children of 10 years of age and that the cultural difference could be attributed primarily, but not entirely, to the greater absence of the father among Negro families. In addition, the same investigator has shown that the desire for immediate gratification is associated with poorer accuracy in judging time, less achievement drive, lower levels of social responsibility, and a greater propensity toward delinquent behavior (Mischel, 1961a, 1961b).

The impact of paternal absence on actual school performance is reflected in Deutsch's (1960) finding that lower-class Negro children from broken homes were far more likely to score below grade level on tests of academic achievement than their classmates from intact families, and that the higher frequency of broken homes among Negro families accounted for most of the difference in achievement between the Negro and white samples. Moreover, children from intact families did better in school than those from broken homes, despite the fact that intact homes were more crowded, a circumstance which leads Deutsch to conclude that "*who* lives in the room is more important than *how many*" (Deutsch, 1960, p. 10). In a subsequent study, Deutsch and Brown (1964) have shown that a significant difference of about 8 points in IQ is specifically attributable to absence of the father from the home.

Finally, it is not only the absence of the Negro father that prevents the son from seeing the future realistically. Also relevant is the inferior position held by the adult Negro male in the economic world. In the matter of occupational choice, the Negro boy has few models to emulate that are actually within the realm of his possible achievement. This circumstance is reflected in a study of occupational aspirations among lower-class children (Deutsch, 1960, pp. 11–14). When asked what they wanted to be when they grew up, 25 per cent of the Negro boys named high-prestige professions, such as doctor or lawyer, etc.—goals completely beyond practical realization and hence reflecting idle wish fulfilment rather than an active achievement drive. In contrast, Negro girls were more realistic in scaling down their aspirations to occupations within their reach. Deutsch accounts for this difference in terms of the greater availability for the girls of an accepted role model both within the family and in the outside world.

The Impoverished Environment

We see, then, that both the high incidence of perinatal pathology and of paternal absence among lower-class Negroes have produced psychological deficits and disturbances in Negro children, particularly boys. But there are other early influences, equally baneful, which do not discriminate between the sexes. Among these is another product of poverty, the absence of an educationally stimulating environment during the preschool years. Studies of this phenomenon, summarized by Bloom, Davis, and Hess (1965), indicate that the lower-class Negro home is barren of objects (books, newspapers, pencils, paper, toys, games) and of coherent social interaction. For example, in a study of the "Social World of the Urban Slums," Keller (1963) reports that the children had little sustained contact with adults, few organized conversations, and little shared family activity. In the same vein, a comparison of Negro and white lower-class children (Deutsch, 1960) revealed that the former had fewer books in the home, got less help with their homework, took fewer trips beyond a 25-block radius from their home, ate less frequently with their parents, and spent less time with them on Sundays. Also, such verbal interaction with parents as did occur tended to be limited in complexity and completeness. For example, commands were likely to be one or several words rather than complete sentences and were typically given without explanation or elaboration.

Patterns of Child Rearing

An additional factor contributing to the inadequacies and problems of the Negro child is the alternately repressive and indulgent pattern of upbringing found in lower-class families in general (Bronfenbrenner, 1958) and Negro lower-class families in particular (Davis, 1941; Davis & Dollard, 1940; Davis & Havighurst, 1946; Frazier, 1957, Rohrer & Edmonson, 1960). Discipline is exercised principally by the mother, is focused on overt acts rather than motives or goals, and is mainly inhibitory in character; that is, the child is told *not* to do this or that, to keep quiet, not ask questions, stay out of trouble. The effect of such negative reinforcement is to discourage early initiative, curiosity, and exploration, as well as cooperative interaction with a guiding adult.

The Legacy of Slavery

It is noteworthy how many of the characteristics of the Negro family of today which are dysfunctional for modern society were functional for, or at least adaptive to, the conditions of bondage (Frazier, 1957). With the father constantly in risk of being sold to another owner, a matriarchal family structure became almost inevitable. But since the mother, too, had to work, it was necessary to keep the child from interfering by his activity, questions, or misbehavior. Moreover, as McClelland (1961) has pointed out, slavery is incompatible with and destructive of a high drive for achievement, since the rewards of the slave come not from initiative and independence but compliance. "Negro slaves should, therefore, have developed child-rearing practices calculated to produce obedience and responsibility not n-Achievement, and their descendents, while free, should still show the effects of such training in lower n-Achievement" (McClelland, 1961, pp. 376–377). In keeping with this prediction, Negro adolescents have the lowest scores in achievement motive among youth from six different ethnic groups in the United States (Rosen, 1959).

But the most important legacies of slavery were the conditions in which the American Negro found himself upon release from bondage—economic poverty and racial discrimination. The three together—slavery, poverty, and discrimination—lie at the root of the biological and social forces which produce widespread psychological debility and disturbance in the Negro child. From this perspective, it is the white man who is in the first instance primarily responsible for the inadequacies of the Negro and his way of life.

THE INTEGRATED CLASSROOM AND THE DISINTEGRATED CHILD

But allocation, or even acceptance, of responsibility for damage does not do away with the Negro child's deficiencies. Nor does placing him in an integrated classroom. On his arrival there he brings with him his full array of defects and disruptive behaviors. True, being able at least to sit with his white age mates may, under certain circumstances (Katz, 1964), bolster his self-esteem, provide him with more competent models to emulate, and significantly improve his academic performance (Coleman, 1966). But integration cannot repair a damaged brain, supply a father, equip a home with books, or alter a family's values, speech habits, and patterns of child rearing. Thus, in many cases, the Negro child in the integrated classroom is, and continues to be, intellectually retarded, unable to concentrate, unmotivated to learn; at first apathetic, but as he gets older, becoming resentful, rebellious, and delinquency-prone.

What is more, in the integrated classroom, all of these characteristics of the Negro child have their impact on his white companion. To begin with, unless countermeasures are introduced, they provide an objective basis and emotional provocation for devaluating and rejecting the Negro, thus reactivating and reinforcing the vicious circle of discrimination and defeat (Coles, 1963; Katz, 1964). But the white child is affected in other ways as well. Although the findings of the Coleman report (1966) indicate that middle-class white children do not suffer academically from attending the same schools as lower-class Negroes, the analysis was not carried out on a classroom basis, nor did it examine other aspects of behavior besides test performance.. As has been demonstrated both in field (Polansky, Lippitt, & Redl, 1954) and experimental (Bandura & Walters, 1963) studies, disintegrative and destructive behavior of peers is highly subject to contagion, against which contrasting values and practices of the family provide little immunity. In other words, the white child is likely to take on some of the aggressive and disruptive activities of his Negro classmates. Such developments are, of course, viewed with alarm by many white parents, who become understandably concerned about the consequences of integration for character development of their children. In short, in the integrated classroom, the problems of the Negro child become, at least in part, those of the white child as well. Thus, the costs of inequality to the Negro become the costs of equality to the white.

COUNTERMEASURES AND CONSEQUENCES

Nor do these costs end with the impact on the classroom of the inappropriate behavior of the Negro child. While the damage already done to the latter by the time he enters school cannot be undone completely, some counteractive measures can be taken within the school environment, or under its auspices, which may entail still further psychological problems for the white community. For example, to a limited but significant extent, a male teacher can serve some of the functions of the absent or inadequate father. The high incidence of fatherless families in the Negro lower class argues strongly for the involvement of many more men as teachers at the elementary level. The psychological costs here, to the extent that any exist, lie in the low prestige and consequent threat to self-esteem which elementary teaching still holds for men in American society. This threat may be alleviated in part by the special need for Negro men as primary teachers, and these are not so likely to resent the role. But they themselves may often be resented by the white community, not only on grounds of racial prejudice, but also on the basis of their teaching effectiveness. Only a small proportion of Negro teachers have been able to enjoy the same educational opportunities, from early childhood on, as were available to their white colleagues; and, for the reasons already outlined, it is the Negro male who is most likely to have been disadvantaged. For this reason, if Negro teachers—especially Negro men—are employed in the large numbers in which they are needed, there will be a drop in the general level of instruction, for these teachers will not have as good command of subject matter as their predecessors, and their speech will deviate from the white middle-class norm. Yet, despite these deficiencies, such persons can do much more for the education of the Negro child than the better-educated, more middle-class-acculturated white or Negro female who would otherwise be their teacher.

By exposing the Negro child to a male teacher of his own race is not enough. Given the absence of positive male figures in his out-of-school environment, the young Negro requires additional acquaintance with men, especially of his own race, who, by their example, demonstrate the possibility and attraction of masculine competence and constructive conduct in a variety of spheres. This need could be met through programs of after-school activities conducted by persons—both Negro and white—who possess such diverse skills and who have found a place in their community. The objective of such programs would be not so much to take the youngster off the streets (although they would have this effect if successful) as to involve him in patterns of interaction which can develop the basic skills, motives, and qualities necessary for a child to be able to profit from the classroom experience. In other words, these after-school activities are to be viewed as an essential part of the educational process, falling within the responsibility of those agencies charged with providing public instruction.

It should be stressed that the after-school program here invisioned is not offering pre-vocational training. Quite the contrary. The activities would be nontechnical in nature and would begin at levels accessible and attractive to the lower-class child—sports, games, selected movies, outings. In the beginning, such activities would have to be conducted by persons trained or experienced in recreational activities; but gradually other adults would participate in them; and the child would discover that one was a machinist, another worked in a bank, a third was a reporter on a newspaper, etc. The objective is to expose the child to and induce him to emulate models embodying the values, skills, and aspirations necessary for achievement in school and society.

There is no question that such programs would be difficult to develop and to administer, but there is some evidence that they are practicable. For example, in Soviet schools (Bronfenbrenner, 1962), members of the community are frequently invited to accompany and participate with children in after-school activities, hikes, expeditions, etc., with the explicit aim of exposing the youngster to intimate contact with adults who combine specialized knowledge or skill with sterling and attractive qualities of character (of course, from the Communist point of view). A related practice long employed in Soviet schools is the involvement of adolescents and pre-adolescents in activities with young children. Recently, similar utilization of this age group, under appropriate supervision, has been urged in our own country in connection with Project Headstart—the federally sponsored preschool program for children in economically deprived areas. An issue of the *Headstart Newsletter* (1965) points to the fact that high school students can, in certain respects, function more effectively than adults in working with young children: "Grown-ups, no matter how friendly and helpful, are in an important sense, in a world apart. Their abilities, skills, and standards are so clearly superior to those of the child as to appear beyond his grasp."

It is, of course, important that persons working in such programs, be they adults or teen-agers, not be restricted to one race; but the same consideration applies for the children as well. Unless white youngsters are also involved in after-school programs, the activity once again becomes identified as an operation for second-class, second-rate citizens. Nor is it sufficient if participation is limited to children—Negro and white—coming from deprived backgrounds. A growing body of research (summarized in Bronfenbrenner, 1962; Millsom, 1966) points to the conclusion that peers are at least as effective if not more potent than adults in their capacity to influence the behavior of the child. From this point of view, it is desirable that children from more favored environments also be included in after-school activities; and, if they are, they are of course exposed to the deleterious as well as constructive influences present in that situation.

The after-school program has other difficulties as well. Indeed, some of these difficulties are a direct function of the degree to which the program achieves its objectives. For, to the extent that the Negro child acquires the skills and values of his new companions, he becomes further removed from his own family. The conflict which such separation can arouse both within the family and within the child himself can undermine whatever progress has been made and lead ultimately to debilitating problems of self-identity. Regrettably, this phenomenon has not yet been investigated systematically by psychologists. The best available data and analyses of the Negro's identity crisis appear in the works of such gifted Negro writers as Richard Wright (1945) and James Baldwin (1962). Because of this danger, it is necessary that, insofar as possible, the child's parents become actively involved in their child's new activities and new world. To modify the pattern of life of parents is, of course, far more difficult than to influence their children, but some opportunities nevertheless exist. One approach is that being employed in Project Headstart (*Report of the Planning Committee,* 1965), where parents from low-income families participate as "paid volunteers" in a variety of tasks requiring little formal education or experience but, at the same time, involving close contact with professional workers as they interact with children. In this manner, some parents—or more realistically, some mothers—are exposed to new and different attitudes and methods in dealing with young children. The device employed in Project Headstart illustrates a general principle, the validity of which has been demonstrated in a substantial body of research in behavioral science generally and in the study of intergroup relations in particular, namely, that attitudes and behaviors are changed most readily when people work together in pursuit of a common goal to which they are committed (Sherif, 1958; Williams, 1947; 1964). And the goal of bettering life for children is one which most parents are willing to pursue.

If we apply the foregoing principle more generally to the role of parents in programs for disadvantaged children in school and out, we come to a conclusion that should properly give us pause; namely, the principle implies that parental involvement is necessary, not only on the part of underprivileged families, but of the privileged as well. It is only through nonantagonistic exposure to the different view and the different practice that the lower-class parent can come to tolerate, understand, and perhaps adopt the different way of dealing with his child employed by those charged with responsibility for his education. Accordingly, it becomes highly desirable for parents from more privileged circumstances—Negro as well as white—to become actively involved in programs concerned with the education of their children both in school and out.

We are asking a great deal. As we said at the outset of this paper, the psychological costs of quality and equality in education for *all* the children are high. They require a new conception of the scope of public education as extending beyond school walls and school hours. They call for a far greater involvement in education of parents and other members of the adult community. They may even require some sacrifice in academic advancement for children from advantaged families to make possible academic survival for children from disadvantaged families. In short, they demand heavy payment from the Haves in favor of the Have-nots, not just in money, but in the far harder coin of psychological security and status.

And if we who have are willing to pay, what is achieved? Whatever we pay cannot be enough. Those who receive payment will still feel cheated, and rightly so. One cannot repay to the children of slaves the present costs of ancient bondage.

It is the tragedy and irony of injustice that those who seek to right it gain as much if not more than those who have been wronged. Paradoxically, it is not the disadvantaged Negro alone who would benefit from equality in education, were we truly to achieve it. For the only way in which we can give the Negro child equality is to teach the white child how to treat him equally. This will not happen from mere physical association in the classroom. It will require the actual teaching and practice, in school and out, of the principles of human dignity to which our society is dedicated. It is a sobering fact that in Communist schools a deliberate effort is made to teach the child, through concrete experience, the values and behaviors most consistent with communist ideals (Bronfenbrenner, 1962; 1966). In American schools, training for action consistent with social responsibility and human dignity is at best an extracurricular activity. The belated recognition of our educational obligations to the child of poverty, white or black, offers us a chance to redress this weakness and to make democratic education not only a principle but a process.

REFERENCES

ANASTASI, ANNE. Intelligence and family size. *Psychological Bulletin,* 1956, **53,** 187–209.

AUSUBEL, D. P. Ego development among segregated Negro children. *Mental Hygiene,* 1958, **42,** 362–369.

BACH, G. R. Father-fantasies and father-typing in father-separated children. *Child Development,* 1946, **17,** 63–79.

BACON, M. K., CHILD, I. L., & BARRY, H., III. A cross-cultural study of correlates of crime. *Journal of abnormal and social Psychology,* 1963, **66,** 291–300.

BALDWIN, J. *Another country.* New York: Dial, 1962.

BANDURA, A., & WALTERS, R. H. *Adolescent aggression.* New York: Ronald, 1959.

BANDURA, A., & WALTERS, R. H. *Social learning and personality development.* New York: Holt, Rinehart & Winston, 1963.

BARCLAY, A., & COSUMANO, D. R. Father absence, cross-sex identity, and field dependent behavior in male adolescents. *Child Development,* 1967, **38,** 243–250.

BLOOM, B. S., DAVIS, A., & HESS, R. *Compensatory education for cultural deprivation.* New York: Holt, Rinehart & Winston, 1965.

BRONFENBRENNER, U. Socialization and social class through time and space. In E. Maccoby, T. M. Newcomb, & E. L. Hartley (Eds.), *Readings in social psychology.* New York: Holt, 1958. Pp. 400–425.

BRONFENBRENNER, U. Soviet methods of character education. *American Psychologist,* 1962, **17,** 550–564.

BRONFENBRENNER, U. Response to pressure from peers versus adults among Soviet and American school children. In *Social factors in the development of per-*

sonality. XVIII International Congress of Psychology, Symposium 35, 1966, Moscow. Pp. 7–18.

Burton, R. V., & Whiting, J. W. M. The absent father and cross-sex identity. *Merrill-Palmer Quarterly,* 1961, **7,** 85–95.

Chein, I. The roots of conspiracy, *SPSSI Newsletter,* December, 1961.

Coleman, J. S. *Equality of educational opportunity.* Washington: U.S. Office of Education, 1966.

Coles, R. *The desegregation of southern schools: a psychiatric study.* New York: Anti-Defamation League, 1963.

Davis, A. *Deep south.* Chicago: University of Chicago Press, 1941.

Davis, A., & Dollard, J. *Children of bondage.* Washington, D.C.: American Council on Education, 1940.

Davis, A., & Havighurst, R. J. Social class and color differences in child-rearing. *American sociological Review,* 1946, **11,** 698–710.

Deutsch, M. Minority group and class status as related to social and personality factors in scholastic achievement. *Monograph of the Society for applied Anthropology,* 1960, No. 2, 1–32.

Deutsch, M., & Brown, B. Social influences in Negro-white intelligence differences. *Journal of social Issues,* 1964, **20,** (2), 24–35.

Frazier, E. F. *The Negro in the United States.* New York: Macmillan, 1957.

Garrett, H. E. Klineberg's chapter on race and psychology: a review. *Mankind Quarterly,* 1960, **1,** 15–22.

Garrett, H. E. The equalitarian dogma. *Mankind Quarterly,* 1961, **1,** 253–257.

Garrett, H. E. Rejoinder by Garrett. *Newsletter of the Society for the Psychological Study of Social Issues,* May, 1962, 1–2. (a).

Garrett, H. E. The SPSSI and racial differences. *American Psychologist,* 1962, **17,** 260–263. (b).

Glueck, S., & Glueck, E. T. *Unraveling juvenile delinquency.* New York: Commonwealth Fund, 1950.

Glueck, S., & Glueck, E. T. *Physique and delinquency.* New York: Harper, 1956.

Grønseth, E. The impact of father absence in sailor families upon the personality structure and social adjustment of adult sailor sons. Part I. In N. Anderson (Ed.), *Studies of the family.* Vol. 2. Göttingen: Vandengoeck & Ruprecht, 1957. Pp. 97–114.

Headstart Newsletter. No. 2. Published by the Office of Economic Opportunity, July, 1965.

Kardiner, A., & Ovesey, L. *The mark of oppression.* New York: Norton, 1951.

Katz, I. Review of evidence relating to effects of desegregation on the intellectual performance of Negroes. *American Psychologist,* 1964, **19,** 381–399.

Kawi, A. A., & Pasamanick, B. Prenatal and parantal factors in the development of childhood reading disorders. *Monographs of the Society for Research in Child Development,* 1959, **24,** No. 4 (Serial No. 73).

Keller, S. The social world of the urban slum child: some early findings. *American Journal of Orthopsychiatry,* 1963, **33,** 823–831.

Kennedy, W. A., Van de Riet, V., & White, J. C., Jr. A normative sample of intelligence and achievement of Negro elementary school children in the Southeastern United States, *Monographs of the Society for Research in Child Development,* 1963, **28,** No. 6 (Serial No. 90).

KNOBLOCH, H., RIDER, R., HARPER, P., & PASAMANICK, B. Neural psychiatric sequelae of prematurity. *Journal of the American Medical Association,* 1956, **161,** 581–585.

KUCKENBERG, C. Effect of early father absence on scholastic aptitude. Unpublished doctoral dissertation, Harvard University, 1963.

LYNN, D. B., & SAWREY, W. L. The effects of father-absence on Norwegian boys and girls. *Journal of abnormal and social Psychology,* 1959, **59,** 258–262.

McCLELLAND, D. C. *The achieving society.* Princeton, N.J.: Van Nostrand, 1961.

McGURK, F. Psychological tests: a scientist's report on race differences. *United States News and world Report,* September 21, 1956, 92–96.

McGURK, F. Negro vs. white intelligence—an answer. *Harvard educational Review,* 1959, **29,** 54–62.

MILLER, W. B. Lower class culture as a generating milieu of gang delinquency. *Journal of social Issues,* 1958, **14,**(3), 5–19.

MILLSOM, C. *Conformity to peers versus adults in early adolescence.* Ph.D. Dissertation, submitted to the Graduate School of Cornell University, February, 1966.

MISCHEL, W. Preference for delayed reinforcement and experimental study of a cultural observation. *Journal of abnormal and social Psychology,* 1958, **56,** 57–61.

MISCHEL, W. Delay of gratification, need for achievement, and acquiescence in another culture. *Journal of abnormal and social Psychology,* 1961, **62,** 543–552. (b)

MISCHEL, W. Father-absence and delay of gratification: cross-cultural comparison. *Journal of abnormal and social Psychology,* 1961, **63,** 116–124. (c)

PASAMANICK, B., & KNOBLOCH, H. The contribution of some organic factors to school retardation in Negro children. *Journal of Negro Education,* 1958, **27,** 4–9.

PASAMANICK, B., KNOBLOCH, H., & LILIENFELD, A. M. Socionomic status and some precursors of neuropsychiatric disorder. *American Journal of Orthopsychiatrics,* 1956, **26,** 594–601.

PETTIGREW, T. F. *A profile of the Negro American.* Princeton, N.J.: Van Nostrand, 1964.

POLANSKY, N., LIPPITT, R., & REDL, F. An investigation of behavioral contagion in groups. In W. E. Martin & C. B. Stendler (Eds.), *Readings in child development.* New York: Harcourt Brace, 1954. Pp. 493–513.

Report of the planning committee. Project Head Start, Office of Economic Opportunity, 1965.

ROHRER, J. H., & EDMONSON, M. S. (Eds.) *The eighth generation.* New York: Harper, 1960.

ROSEN, B. C. Race, ethnicity, and the achievement syndrome. *American sociological Review,* 1959, **24,** 47–60.

SCARPITTI, F. R., MURRAY, E., DINITZ, S., & RECKLESS, W. C. The "good" boy in a high delinquency area: four years later. *American sociological Review,* 1960, **25,** 555–558.

SEARS, P. S. Doll play aggression in normal young children: influence of sex, age, sibling status, father's absence. *Psychological Monographs,* 1951, **65,** No. 6 (Whole No. 323).

SEARS, R. R., PINTLER, M. H., & SEARS, P. S. Effects of father-separation on preschool children's doll play aggression. *Child Development,* 1946, **17,** 219–243.

Sherif, M. Superordinate goals in the reduction of intergroup tensions. *American Journal of Sociology,* 1958, **53,** 349–356.

Shuey, A. *The testing of Negro intelligence.* Lynchburg, Va.: Bell, 1958.

Stolz, L. M. *Father relations of warborn children.* Palo Alto, Calif.: Stanford University Press, 1954.

Tiller, P. O. Father absence and personality development of children in sailor families: a preliminary research report. Part II. In N. Anderson (Ed.), *Studies of the family.* Vol. 2, Göttingen: Vandenhoeck & Reprecht, 1957. Pp. 115–137.

Tiller, P. O. *Father-separation and adolescence.* Oslo: Institute for Social Research, 1961. (Mimeographed)

Van den Haag, E. Negroes' intelligence and prejudice. *National Review,* December 1, 1964.

Williams, R. M., Jr. *The reduction of intergroup tensions.* Bull. **57.** New York: Social Science Research Council, 1947.

Williams, R. M., Jr. *Strangers next door.* Englewood Cliffs, N.J.: Prentice-Hall, 1964.

Wright, R. *Black boy.* New York: Harper & Row, 1945.

17
AN EXPERIMENTAL PRESCHOOL PROGRAM FOR CULTURALLY DEPRIVED CHILDREN*

SUSAN W. GRAY
and
RUPERT A. KLAUS

We should like to discuss some of the research in which we have been involved for the last 3 years, some of our interim findings, and some of the convictions that grow out of our work with the so-called Early-Training Project.

The research in question is an intervention project with young children. Its major purpose is to attempt to see whether it is possible, by specially planned techniques, to offset the progressive retardation in cognitive development and school achievement that characterizes the culturally deprived child as he passes through his years of schooling.

The general strategy of our research is based upon the fact that, short of a complete change of milieu for children in infancy, we have yet to demonstrate that it is possible to offset in any major way the progressive retardation that concerns us. And so, we have attempted to develop a research "package" based upon those variables that, on the basis of research on social class, cognitive development, and motivation, seem most likely to be related to the differences in school performance between middle-class and culturally deprived children. At the same time, we have attempted to do this within a framework it would be possible to employ on a widespread scale, should the project prove successful.

The Ss are 60 children in a city of 25,000 in the upper South, plus an additional group of 27 children in a nearby town who serve as a distal control group. These children were selected on the basis of father's or mother's occupation, education, housing conditions, and income. Parents' incomes at the beginning of the study were well below the present $3,000

* From *Child Development,* 1965, *36,* 885–898. Reprinted with permission of the authors and the Society for Research in Child Development.

This study is supported by Grant 5-R11-MH00765 from the National Institute of Mental Health.

cutting point for poverty; their occupations are unskilled or semiskilled, with some additional mothers on aid to dependent children; their educational level is eighth grade or below; their housing conditions are poor. Most of them have television sets, but no books or magazines, and little in the way of toys for the children. The median number of children is five; in nearly half of the homes there is no father present. The children were all born in 1958 and entered school in September, 1964. These children are Negro. At the time we began our study the schools of the city were segregated. Because of this it seemed wise to work with either Negro or white children. We had reason to believe that in the particular setting our chances of success were greater with the Negro children and therefore chose them.

The procedures we have used in our work with these youngsters grew out of the literature on differences in social class, in child-rearing practices, in motivational patterns, in language, and in perceptual and cognitive development. They were also influenced by our observations of, and speculations upon, the effects of the experiences our children were receiving within their homes.

One way we have attempted to structure these experiential differences is in terms of three stimulus-potential and five reinforcement dimensions that seem applicable in observing young children.

The possible stimulus dimensions we listed as these:

a. Gross amount of potential stimulus input.—Here we doubt that the culturally deprived child receives a lesser amount than the more privileged. An average of four noisy siblings in a small household would seem to guarantee this.

b. Number of different kinds of stimulus input.—Here it is probable that the culturally deprived child, particularly as he grows older, will find less variety in stimulation.

c. Figure and ground relations.—It is likely that the noisy, active home of the culturally deprived child is so full of conflicting stimuli that the child is unable to attend to those stimuli most relevant in terms of increased intellectual development. These homes, for example, are the ones where the television set booms from morning till night, no matter what else people are trying to do. The work of Hunt (1961) and Caldwell (1964) is representative of the approaches from which we derived these stimulus dimensions.

We are inclined to think, however, that cultural deprivation, at least as we have used the term, is more likely to arise from the particular patterns of interaction of children with others, and these we have grouped as reinforcement variables. There are five such dimensions which may be relevant.

1. Total amount of reinforcement.—Since adults, and specifically parents, will tend to be the major reinforcing agents for small children, the culturally deprived may receive a small gross amount of reinforcement. In the deprived homes the time and energy of the child-caring agent will tend to be directed toward subsistence activities. Terry Prothro (1963) has expressed this point well in saying that the culturally deprived mother spends her time *coping with* rather than *shaping* the behavior of the child.

2. *The source of reinforcement.*—The lack of adult reinforcing persons means not only that the culturally deprived child receives less reinforcement but also that what he does receive may occur in greater frequency from peers and siblings and from his own sensations—as the pleasure of gross motor activity in racing about, riding a tricycle, and the like.

3. *Amount of verbal reinforcement.*—From his position in the first two dimensions, it follows that the culturally deprived child will receive less verbal reinforcement. Even when the parent is the reinforcing agent, it is likely that there will be much less in the way of verbal responses, particularly of complex ones. In Bernstein's terms (1961) the parent will tend to use a restricted rather than an elaborated code.

4. *The direction of the reinforcement.*—In a home where the major concern is with coping rather than with shaping, not only may there be less reinforcement, but also reinforcement will be given for those behaviors that make coping easier. In a word, children will be rewarded for inhibitory rather than exploratory behavior. It is likely that most deprived children learn very young that the best way to stay out of trouble is to keep out from under foot and to be quiet. In such an environment, the "natural" curiosity of the child may wither for lack of encouragement. It is upon this dimension that Piaget's (1951) work may seem classbound.

5. *The focus of the reinforcement.*—Reinforcement may be diffuse—the "You're a bad girl" or "You're a fine boy" kind of generalized approval, or it may be focused precisely on the adequacy of the child's performance. The work of Zigler and Kanzer (1962) on verbal reinforcers and that of Bernstein (1961) on language codes would suggest that the diffuse type of verbal reinforcement may be more characteristic of the deprived than of the more privileged. Where reinforcement is diffuse, the child's attention is not directed toward the quality of the performance, nor is it possible for him to become self-reinforcing in terms of evaluating and improving his own performance.

From the standpoint of the three stimulus variables, we speculate that the children in our project came to us without having had contact with many of the objects and experiences commonplace to middle-class youngsters. In addition we suspect that these youngsters had lived in an environment that provided sufficient distraction in the way of extraneous stimuli that the children could not take advantage of what learning potential did exist in the home. An important aim of our intervention project was to provide an environment relatively rich in learning potential and structured in such a way that figure-ground relationships and predictable sequences could emerge.

In terms of the five reinforcement variables, we think it likely that the children such as those in our project at age 3 or 4 will have their behavior not too well under the control of adult verbal direction, that they will be highly responsive to adult reinforcement of a nonverbal sort (hugs, pats, being carried, and the like), and that they will tend to approach new situations by inhibiting behavior rather than by exploring. The problem in our study was to take advantage of the motivational patterns already built up and to move the children toward motivational patterns more in keeping with those likely to be associated with success in school.

The general programs and the actual day-by-day activities provided for children in the project centered around two classes of variables. The first of these was that of attitudes toward achievement. We were particularly concerned with achievement motivation, especially as it relates to the kinds of activities expected in school, with persistence, with ability to delay gratification, and with general interest in the use of typical school materials such as books, crayons, puzzles, and the like. These approaches grew out of research such as that of Rosen and Andrade (1959) and of Strodtbeck (1959) on achievement motivation, and of Mischel (1961) on delay of gratification. We attempted to translate these variables into certain operational procedures for the teachers and assistants who worked directly with the children. We were also interested in the parent's attitude toward achievement, particularly as it related to aspirations for their children and concern with the children's schooling in relation to these aspirations. Our work with parents has been carried on largely through a home visitor program in which a specially trained preschool teacher has met weekly with each mother and attempted to develop in her more awareness of the instrumental acts involved in her child's attaining these aspirations.

Our major class of variables has been that of aptitudes toward achievement. Here our concern has been with perceptual and cognitive development and with language. These are areas in which research workers such as Milner (1951), Leshan (1952), and Siller (1957) have found children from impoverished families to show deficits and which also appear closely related to school success in the early grades.

The general design of the study is given in Table 1. The first three treatment groups (T_1–T_3) were randomized from a pool of 60 children selected from homes that met our criteria of cultural deprivation in the main city in our study. The fourth group (T_4) consisted of 27 children from homes that met the same criteria but who lived in a similar small city 60 miles distant. This fourth group was included to check the possibility of diffusion effects, which seem possible in a small city where the subjects of the three treatment groups live in fairly close proximity.

The first treatment group has been through a training sequence which may be seen by reading down the table. It has consisted of three special summer-school experiences of 10 weeks each, plus weekly contacts over the remainder of the year with the home visitor. These contacts are continuing in the first grade. The second group has been in a similar program, except that it began a year later; this group has had two summer experiences and one winter of home visitor contacts prior to the first grade. The third group, the local control group, has received all tests but has not had other contacts with the project, except that, during the third summer, as public-relations measure we ran a two-hour play period for them once a week. The fourth, distal group has had no contacts except the regular series of pre- and post-tests.

Each of the two experimental groups had a specially trained head teacher and four teaching assistants who worked with groups of four to six children. The teaching staff was about equally divided as to sex and as to racial

TABLE 1

Layout of General Research Design

Treatments	T_1 *Three Summer Schools*	T_2 *Two Summer Schools*	T_3 *Local Controls*	T_4 *Distal Controls*
First winter (1961–62)	(Criterion development, curriculum planning, general tooling up)			
First Summer (1962)	Pretest Summer school Posttest	Pretest Posttest	Pretest Posttest	Pretest Posttest
Second winter (1962–63)	Home visitor contacts			
Second summer (1963)	Pretest Summer school Posttest	Pretest Summer school Posttest	Pretest Posttest	Pretest Posttest
Third winter (1963–64)	Home visitor contacts	Home visitor contacts		
Third summer (1964)	Pretest Summer school Posttest	Pretest Summer school Posttest	Pretest Posttest	Pretest Posttest
Fourth winter (1964–65)	Home visitor contacts Follow-up tests	Home visitor contacts Follow-up tests	Follow-up tests	Follow-up tests
Fifth winter (1965)	Follow-up tests	Follow-up tests	Follow-up tests	Follow-up tests

composition. The teaching assistants were either college students or trainees in a doctoral-school psychology program. The low ratio of children to adults had several major purposes. One was to change the motivational patterns of the children. With only four to six children to each adult, it was possible to reinforce children immediately for any desired behavior. It was also possible to individualize types of reinforcement and scheduling to fit a given child's level in the program. The adults also served as identification figures for the children, important particularly for the boys, who in general lacked appropriate achieving-role models in the home. The low ratio also made possible a large amount of verbal interaction between adult and child.

The teachers and assistants held work sessions each day in which daily lesson plans were worked out and experiences devised for the group and for individual children in accordance with the variables we were attempting to manipulate and in keeping with the current status of individual children. The materials and activities used in the summer sessions did not differ radically from those of a conventional nursery school and kindergarten. The difference lies rather in the way in which materials were used, the self-conscious attempt to focus on the experimental variables—for example, to promote achievement motivation, to stimulate language development, to encourage the child to order and classify the objects and events of his world.

An illustration of this approach might be given in our use of 1-inch colored cubes. We used these constantly. In terms of aptitudes variables, they were useful for learning numbers, for color naming, and recognition; they could be used for various position words: "Put the red block *on* the blue one"; "Put the green block *beside* the yellow one," and the like. Blocks could also be used in terms of the attitude variables. We encouraged the children to build the tallest towers they possibly could. In this way we tried to develop persistence toward a goal. We exclaimed over their successes in this activity; we called it to the attention of others, in an effort to get the children to take pride in their own performance and to internalize some standard of excellence. Blocks could obviously be used for more difficult constructions and for fairly complex designs in terms of colors.

As another illustration of our use of materials we might take that of wheel toys. Tricycles and the like were fairly important during the first summer when the children were 3½–4½. Wheel toys were highly attractive to the children; being allowed to ride was an effective kind of reinforcement. The tricycles also served well to encourage verbalization. It was easy to set up a situation in which the children could obtain a tricycle only by asking for it. Adults were at hand to see that the child obtained one only if he asked, and that when a child asked another child for a turn on the tricycle, the turn was forthcoming. "Taking turns" is also a way of learning to delay immediate gratification. Again, it was important to have adults there to see that gratification postponed was rewarded within a time limit tolerable for a given child. Later, during the second summer, tricycles were used in a miniature traffic situation where the children learned to respond appropriately to various traffic signs, and even to play traffic policeman. We had miniature traffic signals, through which the children would control the lights and command, with some success, obedience to traffic rules. Thus, tricycles were useful to stimulate verbal behavior, to teach delay of gratification, and, at a slightly older age, to develop an understanding of the meaning of symbols.

Books were of course our mainstay. We attempted to build up as wide a collection as possible of attractive picture books on subjects that would be appropriate to these children from the standpoint of their home experiences and their interests. We made considerable use of duplicate copies of certain books, so that children could learn to follow by pictures as a story was read to them. Looking at pictures promoted ability to discriminate forms and colors. Obviously books were of prime importance in terms of language development. It seemed to us in the first summer that the children with whom we were working could not pick up the meaning of a picture as adequately as middle-class children, probably more familiar with deriving meaning from two-dimensional surfaces. We read to the children several times each day; we encouraged the children to look at pictures as we read, to talk about what they were reading, to tell what would happen next in the

FIGURE 1

Binet MA Scores for Training (T_1 and T_2) and Control Groups (T_3 and T_4)

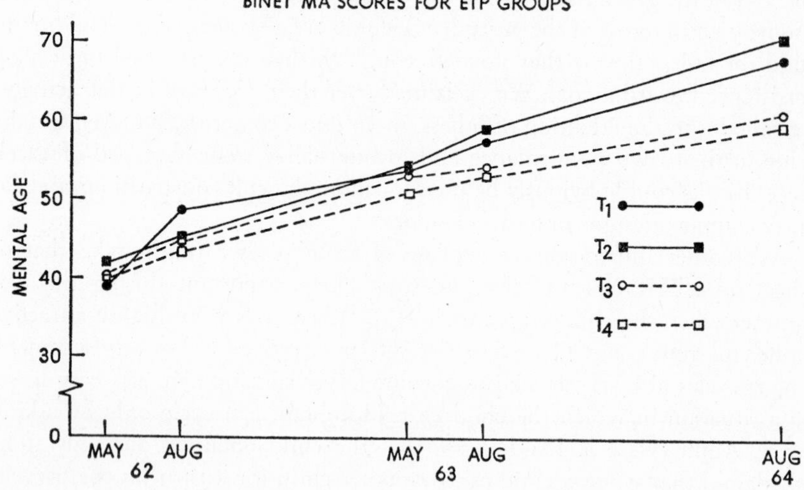

story, and, as time went on, to dramatize some of the familiar folk tales such as *Cinderella* or *Three Little Pigs*. Children were given small, inexpensive books as rewards for performance; the home visitor ran a small circulating library during the year.

At the beginning and end of each summer session, the children were tested on several instruments. The crucial tests of whether we have been able to offset progressive retardation must wait until the children have been in school for 2 or more years. Certain interim results on standardized tests of intelligence and language development, however, make us hopeful that we are on the right track insofar as improving school competence is concerned.

One of the interim measures used was the Stanford-Binet. Figure 1 shows the results of five successive testings upon the Binet for the four treatment groups. We did not give the Binet in May of 1964, but gave the WISC instead, as the children were rather well saturated with the Binet. This figure indicates that the two experimental groups (T_1 and T_2) are diverging from the two control groups (T_3 and T_4). The mean IQ of the first treatment group was 86 when we began our study. At the end of August 1964 it stood at 95, a modest gain, but one maintained over a period of 27 months. The second treatment group, with which we began a year later, had an original mean IQ of 91 and has shown a gain of 5 points. The two control groups have shown losses, the local one of 4 points, and the distal one of 6 points. This decrement is the more striking because of the probable slight elevation to be expected from repeated testing. Differences between the experimental and control groups are significant at the .05 level and beyond.

FIGURE 2

Hypothetical and Observed Binet MA Development for T_1 (training group) and T_4 (distal control group).

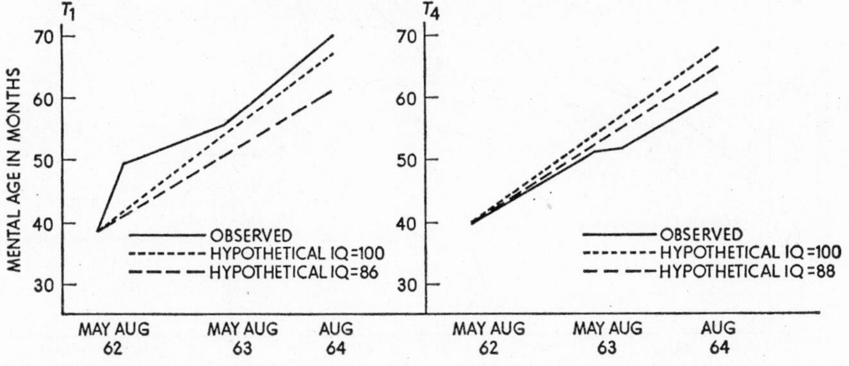

Figure 2 represents an attempt to trace hypothetical curves of intelligence development for the two most disparate groups, the first treatment group and the distal control group. This was done in an effort to throw some light upon the relation of our experimental treatments to progressive retardation. Each side of the figure shows three lines. The solid line represents the observed test results on the Binet for the two groups in terms of MA. The dashed line shows what might be predicted for a child who makes one month's gain in MA for each calendar month, that is, with IQ of 100. The dotted line shows what might be predicted on the basis of the first testing, with the assumption that an IQ represents the percentage of development to be expected, in this case 86 percent, since the initial IQ was 86 for T_4. For the experimental group it may be seen that the curve for the observed scores is elevated beyond either of the other two curves and that the observed curve parallels during the last few testings what might be predicted with an IQ of

100. If this relation continues, it looks as if we have offset the progressive retardation to be expected. In the other group shown on the figure (T_4) we would seem, so far, to have a clear case of progressive retardation, where observed scores are seen diverging even from what might be predicted on the basis of the initial IQ of 88. The difference between observed gain in MA and what might be predicted on the basis of the original IQ is 8 months in the positive direction for T_1; for T_4 it is 8 months in the negative direction. One should not take this 16-month's difference too seriously. It may, however, shed some light on the problem of progressive retardation.

Figure 3 shows the findings from the Peabody Picture Vocabulary Test,

FIGURE 3

Peabody Picture Vocabulary Test Raw Scores for Training (T_1 and T_2) and Control Groups (T_3 and T_4).

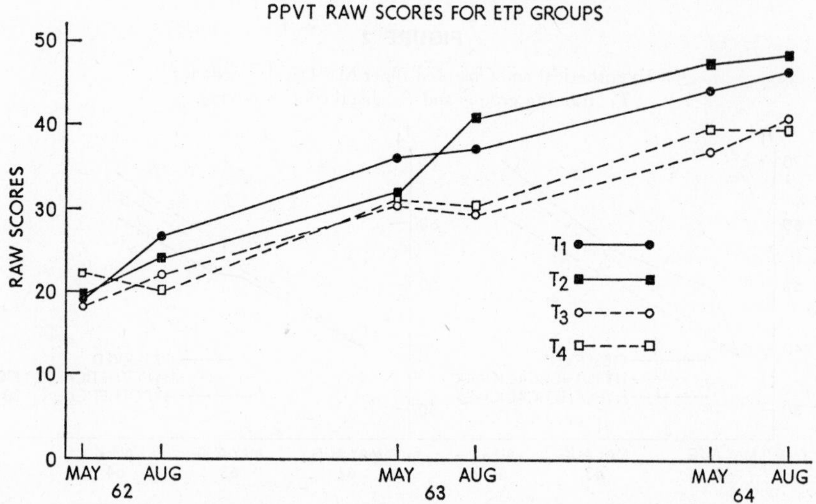

which was administered at each testing time, with alternation of Forms A and B. The findings in general are similar to those on the Binet, although here there is no tendency for the first treatment group to surpass the second. Differences between the experimental and control groups are significant at the .05 level.

The Illinois Test of Psycholinguistic Ability has been administered twice to the children. Figure 4 shows the results of the August, 1964, administration. For clarity in reading the figure, the two experimental groups and the two control groups have been combined. The perpendicular dotted line indicates the norm for that age. In general it may be seen that, even with the experimental groups, functioning is somewhat below the norm, although on three of the subtests the children are a little beyond expectancy. Experimental children are significantly (at the .05 level) superior to the control children on all subtests except that of motor encoding. An interesting aspect of the findings is the almost parallel nature of the two curves, the mean difference in the two being 8 months in language age.

The children of all four treatment groups are now in school; the time is approaching when it will be possible to evaluate possible differences in school performance. On an elaborate battery of preschool screening tests given to all children entering the first grade in our main city, the experimental children did conspicuously better than the controls and tend to approximate the

FIGURE 4

Illinois Test for Psycholinguistic Abilities Mean Language Ages for Training (T_1 and T_2) and Control Groups (T_3 and T_4), August, 1964.

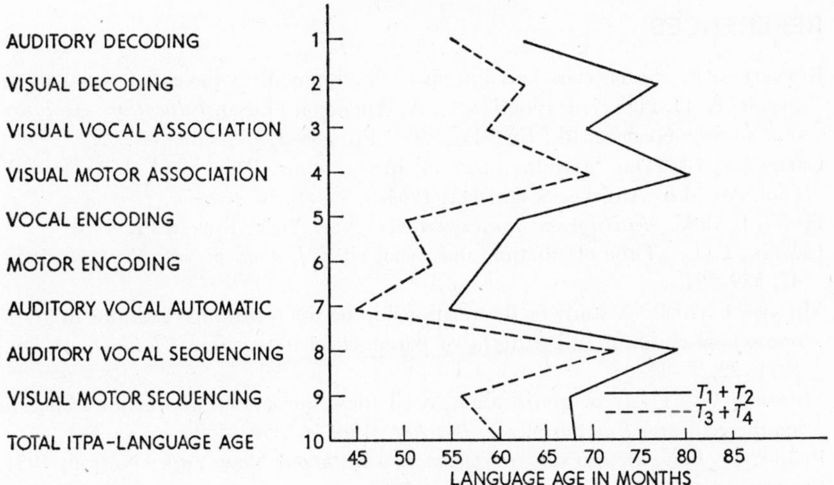

nondeprived children in the school. On reading-readiness tests they were again superior.

It is not until the children have been in school for several years, however, that we can know whether we have been able by this massive attack to offset the effect of a culturally deprived environment as it affects school performance. In the meantime, we are also engaged in collecting data that we hope will give us a clearer picture of our success—or lack of it—in manipulating those variables we have assumed, on the basis of previous research, to be related to school performance. Thus, we are attempting to measure achievement motivation, delay of gratification, some aspects of perceptual development and cognition, and language. In this way, if we are successful in altering appreciably the school performance of those children, we can look back at changes upon these measures for clues as to the most potent of our approaches in affecting school performance.

We are not so sanguine as to think that in the Early Training Project we have worked out a major solution for ameliorating the plight of the culturally deprived. We have planned, however, and are far along in carrying through a program that takes its cue from psychological research upon the development of motivation and intellect and that attempts to use this in the context of a program that is *developmental* rather than remedial. If our research project should prove successful we will have added some small amount to the store of knowledge sorely needed in order to cope with this major social problem for America, and indeed for the world—that of enabling children to develop the competencies and motivational patterns demanded by complex present-day society.

REFERENCES

Bernstein, B. Social class and linguistic development: a theory of social learning. In A. H. Halsey, J. Floud, & C. A. Anderson (Eds.), *Education, economy, and society*. Glencoe, Ill.: Free Pr., 1961. Pp. 288–314.

Caldwell, Bettye. Stimulus potential in the home. Paper read at Amer. Psychol. Ass., Los Angeles, September, 1964.

Hunt, J. McV. *Intelligence and experience*. New York: Ronald Pr., 1961.

Leshan, L. L. Time orientation and social class. *J. abnorm. soc. Psychol.,* 1952, **47**, 589–592.

Milner, Esther. A study of the relationship between reading readiness in grade one school children and patterns of parent-child interaction. *Child Developm.,* 1951, **22**, 95–112.

Mischel, W. Delay of gratification, need for achievement, and acquiescence in another culture. *J. abnorm. soc. Psychol.,* 1961, **62**, 543–552.

Piaget, J. *Play, dreams and imitation in childhood*. New York: Norton, 1951.

Prothro, T. Personal communication. 1963.

Rosen, B. C., & Andrade, R. B. The psychosocial origins of achievement motivation. *Sociometry,* 1959, **22**, 185–218.

Siller, J. Socio-economic status and conceptual thinking. *J. abnorm. soc. Psychol.,* 1957, **55**, 365–371.

Strodtbeck, F. L. Family interaction, values and achievement. In D. C. McCelland et al. (Eds.), *Talent and society*. Princeton, N.J.: Van Nostrand, 1959. Pp. 259–266.

Zigler, E., & Kanzer, P. The effectiveness of two classes of verbal reinforcers on the performance of middle and lower class children. *J. Pers.,* 1962, **30**, 157–163.

PART IV

Middle Childhood

INTRODUCTION

The period of "middle childhood" covers roughly the ages from five to twelve, that is, the elementary school years. The rapid growth of infancy having slowed down during the preschool years, the elementary school child is now growing at a much slower rate. This period of middle childhood lasts from the time the child ventures off to school as a kindergartener until he reaches that stage when he suddenly begins to grow more rapidly in preadolescence. In keeping with the slower development and the asexuality of this stage, Sigmund Freud termed this the "period of latency." "Towards the end of the fifth year this early period of sexual life (of the infant) normally comes to an end. It is succeeded by a period of more or less complete *latency,* during which ethical restraints are built up . . ." (Freud, 1959, v. 5, p. 120). According to Freud, it is during this period that the child develops inhibitions against the psychic urges which went unchecked during his infancy: "During the period of life which may be distinguished as the 'sexual latency period,' i.e., from the end of the fourth year to the first manifestations of puberty at about eleven, reaction formations, such as shame, disgust, and morality, are formed in the mental economy at the expense of the excitations proceeding from the erotogenic zones, and these reaction formations erect themselves as barriers against the later activity of the sexual instinct" (Freud, 1959, v. 2, p. 47). As to the basis of this moralization, Freud comments, "We may gain the impression that the erection of these dams in the civilized child is the work of education; and surely education contributes much to it. In reality, however, this development is organically determined and can occasionally be produced without the help of education." (Freud, 1938, p. 583).

Whether "latency" in the sense that Freud conceptualized it is an especially appropriate construct for distinguishing the middle childhood years is a debatable issue. Undoubtedly, it is a less relevant aspect of childhood today than it was in the Victorian Vienna which Freud knew when parental concern with inhibition was a more dominant force in child rearing and consequently in the development of personality. Professor Bronfenbrenner, of Cornell University, has observed that there have been distinct changes over the years in the way parents bring up their children (Bronfenbrenner, 1951). Commenting on data gathered over a 25 year period, Bronfenbrenner concludes:

> These secular trends may be summarized as follows: (*a*) greater permissiveness toward the child's spontaneous desires; (*b*) freer expression of affection; (*c*) increased reliance on indirect "psychological" techniques of discipline (such as reasoning or appeals to guilt) v. direct methods (such as physical punishment, scolding, or threats); (*d*) in consequence of the above shifts in the direction of what are predominantly middle-class values and techniques, a narrowing of the gap between social classes in their patterns of child rearing. (Bronfenbrenner, 1961, p. 74).

If indeed, parents have become more permissive and if the trend that Bronfenbrenner observed has continued into the present decade, the Freudian notion of latency would have less relevance in describing today's child than it would have in describing the inhibited child of the late 19th century. In addition, one can say that the term "latency" does not appear to do justice to the tremendous strides which the child makes in the cognitive area during these years when his physical growth has slowed.

If one were to characterize the period of middle childhood in terms of developmental tasks, one might call it the period of rapid academic growth. From the beginning of formal education at about age six, the learning of reading and mathematics is in full swing. The child, having begun to learn the basic skills of social relations and the perceptual skills needed for classroom performance, is busy grounding himself in those scholastic abilities which will be necessary for higher education. Another psychoanalyst, a modern ego psychologist, Erik Erikson, in his psychosocial theory of development, refers to this time as a period of resolving the antithesis of "industry v. inferiority." His description of this stage is worth careful study:

> The child must forget past hopes and wishes, while his exuberant imagination is tamed and harnessed to the laws of impersonal things—even the three R's. For before the child, psychologically already a rudimentary parent, can become a biological parent, he must begin to be a worker and a potential provider. With the oncoming latency period the normally advanced child, forgets, or rather sublimates, the necessity to "make" people by direct attack or to become papa and mama in a hurry; he now learns to win recognition by producing things. He has mastered the ambulatory field and the organ modes. He has experienced a sense of finality regarding the fact that there is no workable future within the womb of his family, and thus becomes ready to apply himself to the given skills and tasks,

which go far beyond the mere playful expression of his organ modes or the pleasure in the function of his limbs. He develops a sense of industry—i. e., he adjusts himself to the inorganic laws of the tool world. (Erikson, 1963, p. 258–259).

The distinction which Erikson makes between the motor and perceptual play of the younger child and the work of the schoolage child is an especially important distinction in modern American culture. It will be recalled that in an earlier chapter, Ruth Benedict, the cultural anthropologist, made the distinction between continuities and discontinuities in cultural conditioning. She used the work-play distinction as an example of a discontinuity which is prevalent in our conditioning of children which is not at all relevant, say, for the Ojibwa child whose play with bow and arrows gradually becomes his hunting and his responsibility to the family.

Academic work is one of the chief tasks of middle childhood, just as the corresponding cognitive growth is one of the major developmental changes. The psychologist best known for his classification of the developmental stages of cognition is the Swiss, Jean Piaget. Indeed, in Piaget's classification (Piaget, 1954), the years from six or seven to approximately eleven do correspond to a stage of cognitive development, namely the period of concrete operations. The child in this stage has largely overcome his egocentricity of language and thought and can now take the perceptual and cognitive point of view of another. Nor does he center on only one aspect of a situation but can consider several facets of a problem simultaneously. This decentering and socialization of thought allow for the objectivity which is essential to the learning of such subjects as mathematics and reading, for instance.

A corresponding development has occurred in the area of moral judgment. Unlike the younger child, whose moral judgment is characterized by the immutability of rules and adult constraint, the school age child recognizes that rules are based on cooperation and takes individual responsibility and intention into account in his moral judgment. This development of a sense of intentionality and a morality of autonomy rather than one of constraint may be as important in the development of academic skills as the cognitive growth which occurs during this period. (In reality, of course, these cannot be separated since the decentering which allows for objectivity in reasoning is the very basis of a subjective morality rather than one based on constraint.) Perhaps it is not too speculative to see a relationship between Piaget's observations on the development of autonomy in moral judgment and the development of another dimension, namely the internal locus of control as conceptualized by the American psychologist, Julian Rotter and his colleagues (Rotter, 1966; Lefcourt, 1966). According to Rotter's theory, an individual's behavior is a function of the likelihood of his obtaining reinforcement and the value of the reinforcement for the given individual. Rotter makes a distinction between those individuals who perceive their reinforcement as a function of their own behavior (internal control) and those who consider their reinforcements as the result of luck, chance, fate, or other external circumstances (external control). In a series of papers dealing with this dimension, Crandall and her associates (1965) demonstrate the relationship between internal control and academic achievement. In other words, one correlate of school achievement is the child's sense of his own responsibility for his behavior.

COGNITION AND INTELLIGENCE

Intelligence is one of the major dimensions used to describe individuals in a wide variety of contexts. One of the first requests that the teacher, parent, or doctor often makes concerning the child who is failing academically is for an assessment of his "mental level." However, the dimension has come under serious attack (e. g., Liverant, 1960) primarily because human ability is considered far too complex a phenomenon to be subsumed under a single factor. In a more recent paper, Chapter 18, Professor Sigel of Buffalo University levels another timely criticism, this time at the yardstick of intelligence tests as much as at the dimension itself. The thrust of Sigel's argument is that the intelligence test, as currently used, does not help us to understand the cognitive processes that the child uses in arriving at his answers. An underlying assumption seems to be that only one cognitive style is appropriate, or most appropriate. In an appeal for intelligence tests which consider cognitive style, Sigel remarks, "Resting with our current concepts will not help us understand the 'how' of intelligence." (Sigel, 1963, p. 55)

We are reminded of Piaget's concern with the same issue: understanding the 'how' of intelligence. In Chapter 19, Professor Tuddenham of the University of California, tells us that Piaget once worked in the laboratory of Alfred Binet, the well-known father of intelligence testing, but adds, "Certainly Piaget has relatively little in common with the Binet of the famous intelligence tests, because Piaget has never been much interested in mental testing or in individual differences." (Tuddenham, 1966, p. 209) Undoubtedly Piaget would agree wholeheartedly with Sigel's assessment of the role that intelligence tests have played (or rather have not played) in our understanding of cognitive development.

If Piaget has never been very interested in intelligence testing despite his years of work in Binet's laboratory, it was because he was more interested in the processes by which a child arrives at the right answer than he was in the answer itself. By focusing only on the answer, one might actually obscure these important processes which Piaget hoped to uncover. Closely related to the distinction between the processes of problem solving and the products, or right answers, is the distinction made by Professor Horn, of the University of Denver, between crystallized and fluid intelligence. As you will note in Chapter 20, by "fluid intelligence" Horn refers to a basic intellectual capacity which is independent of experience, whereas by "crystallized intelligence" he means the product of the combination of fluid intelligence and experience. This distinction offers a conceptual analysis which should go a long way towards answering questions dealing with the effect of early experience on the growth of intelligence.

Professor Tuddenham's paper includes an excellent introduction to Piaget's theory of cognitive development. The author first describes the man, Piaget, his scholarly background, and the development of his much used *method clinique*. It is important in this connection to draw attention to the difference between this Piagetian approach and the typical American experimental research with children. The close observation and intensive questioning of the *method clinique* has uncovered behavioral relations which have been ingeniously interpreted by Piaget in his theory of cognitive development. Piaget's theory has now generated a large volume of research, both in America and Europe, much of which employs the more classical experimental approaches. An excellent recent volume summarizing this research is *Logical Thinking in Children,* edited by Irving Sigel and Frank H. Hooper (1968).

Tuddenham concludes his review of Piaget with a brief description of the stages of cognitive development. Surely the development of concrete operations, about the age of six or seven, could serve as the landmark for the onset of "middle childhood." Now the child begins to "decenter," or consider an object from more than one perceptual perspective. He can make inferences about operations. Perhaps one could conceptualize the end of middle childhood or the onset of adolescence also in terms of cognitive growth. If so, the development of formal operational logic would appear to be the turning point.

LEARNING

The process of learning can be demonstrated in humans of all ages, from the prenatal child to the octogenarian as well as in other animal species, from the lowly planaria to the great apes. In many respects the process is similar in young and old, in man and animal. The learner, for example, must be able to act and to vary his response; he must be in a motivated state and the effects of his learning must be related to that state of motivation. The basic principles of learning seem to apply regardless of the task to be learned or the species of the learner. On the other hand, there are a number of ways in which the learning of the human differs from that of other animals and in which the learning of the young child differs from that of the adult. Kendler and Kendler (1959), for example, have provided a demonstration of differences in the learning processes of college students and young children. They have found differences in the way the two groups perform on discrimination learning tasks. When the conditions of the original learning situation have shifted, college students demonstrate that they have learned the discrimination in a way which would support a mediational interpretation of learning. Young children, as well as lower animals given similar tasks, appear to have learned in a way which supports a single-unit interpretation of learning. In other words, college students reveal that they have learned the dimension underlying their choice, while young children appear only to be responding to the characteristics of each individual stimulus and do not yet use mediational responses.

In Chapter 21 Professor Brackbill and her associates present another example of differences between the learning of animals and humans. Although the teaching machine is not a new invention, it gained its real popularity when its use appeared to have theoretical support in the learning theory of B. F. Skinner. Among other things it was noted that the teaching machine required active participation from the learner. In addition, it was argued that immediate feedback was not only possible but desirable. The idea of the effectiveness of immediate feedback, whether in terms of reinforcement or knowledge of results, had a venerable history, dating back at least to Thorndike (Hilgard, 1956). Thorndike's law of effect stated that the effect following a response was an important element in the learning situation. In its original form, the law of effect said that if the effect of a response were positive, it "stamped in" the right connections, and if the effect were negative, it "stamped out" the wrong response. The effectiveness of these after-effects was determined, in Thorndike's view, by their recency and specificity to the behavior which they followed.

It is this point of the immediacy of the after-effect, or reinforcement in more modern terms, which Brackbill and her colleagues question. They have demonstrated that while immediate feedback may be important in animal learning, it does not seem essential to human learning. In fact, it would seem to make retention poorer. Once again, it is probable that the language ability of human subjects makes it possible for mediating processes to operate over longer time periods and make a delay of feedback not only possible but, in some instances, preferable.

Brackbill *et al.* also clarify the distinction between two kinds of feedback. In the animal studies and in research with very young children, reinforcement by way of some tangible reward is usually given as feedback. With older children and with adults, knowledge of results is often sufficient. Commenting on this difference, the authors state, "If the learner comes to the learning situation with a 'built-in' motivation to learn, the experimenter need supply him only with knowledge of result." (Brackbill *et al.,* Chapter 21, p. 323).

This built-in motivation to learn is the topic of Chapter 22 by Professor Hunt of the University of Illinois. In an exciting reinterpretation of the whole notion of motivation, Hunt suggests that the earlier ideas of motivation as drive-reduction may be insufficient to account for the learning of many important behaviors. Play, curiosity, and exploration are all activities which seem to be engaged in more for the sake of the activity itself than for anything extrinsic to the activity. Related to Allport's (1937) concept of functional autonomy and to White's (1959) idea of competence, such an interpretation of motivation would appear important for explaining those behaviors which cannot be explained in traditional motivational terms.

In the final selection in the section on learning, Chapter 23 by Professor Deutsch of New York University, data are described which indicate that children of low socioeconomic status are deficient in the development of certain learning skills. Considering the importance of language in the development of other learning skills, this finding assumes critical importance.

SOCIALIZATION

Socialization refers to the process whereby a child, having acquired a status in a given group, either by ascription or achievement, learns the role behaviors appropriate to that status. He learns the values and expectations of the group and how to respond accordingly. For example, one important aspect of socialization is the development of appropriate sex role behavior. Even in their early play, boys and girls learn to differentiate themselves on the basis of sexual identity by the sorts of toys they choose, the games they prefer, and the amount of rough-and-tumble they engage in. The differential reinforcements which parents give to boys and girls in the way they hold, caress, and speak to their children even in infancy are undoubtedly instrumental in shaping sex appropriate behavior. Moreover, as we mentioned earlier, in the shaping of sex appropriate behavior the infant is not a passive participant and is, in fact, an active stimulant for parental handling practices. Later the toys which parents supply as well as the models which they themselves provide are additional factors in this important aspect of socialization.

In Chapter 24 Professors Barry, Bacon, and Child present evidence for "near-universal tendencies in the direction of difference between the socialization of boys and girls," although cultures differ with respect to the extent of this differentiation. The authors suggest two generalizations to explain cultural variation in this amount of differentiation by sex. One of these generalizations has to do with differences in the extent to which the economics of the various cultures are based on the strength and dominance of its males. A second generalization deals with the prevalence of large family groups in the culture. Sex differentiation is not as pronounced in those cultures which maintain small, relatively independent, nuclear families in which the husband and wife must often take on the duties of their partner from time to time.

In other words, while the universality of some sex differentiation in socialization suggests a biological trend, the cultural differences in the extent of this differentiation suggest the importance of the needs of the community in determining sex differences in socialization.

On the consequent side of this issue, one wonders what effect the emphasis on sex differences in socialization has on other aspects of the society. What influence, for example, might well-differentiated sex roles have on motivation for parenthood? In one study (Rabin, 1965) of American college students, it has been observed that for women the major motivation for parenthood lies in their perception of what is simply "natural" and to be expected for women. It would appear as though some of the respondents defined their womanhood in terms of their procreative function! Perhaps given a culture with less emphasis on sex role differentiation this motivation for parenthood would shift.

Aside from simply learning appropriate sex roles (although this is by no means a simple process), the whole process of learning to get along with others represents a major task for the school-age child. To respond according to the expectations of others, without losing one's sense of autonomy and independence is part of the process of becoming a socialized member of the community. In Chapter 25 Dr. Glen Heathers, of the Fels Research Institute, has examined the basis on which children develop a sense of dependence or independence. He suggests that they are learned needs and distinguishes between emotional and instrumental dependence, as well as independence. One important aspect of his analysis of the learning of dependence is the emphasis he places on the responses other people make to the child.

Another psychologist, well known for his studies of the development of dependence in children is Professor Hartup, of the University of Minnesota. In Chapter 26, Professor Hartup also emphasizes the role of the responses of other people in the development of both achievement and dependence. Far from contrasting dependence and independence, however, he sees them as two sides of the same coin and observes the important role that dependence plays in later social learning. In other words, he suggests that one ought not inhibit the development of dependence in the young child, but should even actively encourage it to some extent.

MORAL DEVELOPMENT

Whether the period of middle childhood is conceived of as a time of repression of basic urges, as in the Freudian notion of a "latency period," or is thought of as a period of rapid, active learning, nobody would question the fact that it is a period of intense socialization. One aspect of this socialization has to do with the development of moral judgment and moral behavior. The theoretical interpretations of this development are many and varied.

Freud (1959) thought of the superego as the basis of individual morality. He hypothesized that this system developed out of an identification with the same-sex parent, which resulted during the process of overcoming the Oedipus complex. Freud's idea of the superego is comprised of two components: an ego-ideal, which amounts to an internalization of parents' values, which rewards the child by making him feel proud of having done what is good; and a conscience, which amounts to an internalization of those negative parental values, which punishes the child by making him feel guilty for having done what is wrong. Supposedly, through identification with the parents the child internalizes their values until gradually they become his own.

The Freudian interpretation of moral development has been criticized on several grounds. In Chapter 27 Professor Winfred Hill, of Northwestern University, suggests that the psychoanalytic terms of identification, introjection, and internalization are too vague to account for the complex development of moral values. Indeed, as Stoke (1950) points out, even within psychoanalytic theory the term "identification" is fraught with difficulty. At times Freud used the term to mean behavioral similarity while at other times he used it to refer to a bond of affection. Hill has suggested replacing the Freudian terms with those of learning theory and has postulated that the learning of conscience proceeds in much the same way as any other learning. He suggests that researchers look for the stimulus conditions and reinforcers which are most efficient in facilitating the learning of moral values.

It would appear that the mediating processes described in the section on learning might be useful here as well. For example, the terms "guilt" and "pride" could be thought of as fractional anticipatory goal responses and the same principles which apply to the development of these responses could be examined in the realm of moral behavior.

The social learning interpretation of moral development (Bandura & Walters, 1963) places great emphasis on the role of the child's opportunity to observe the moral behavior of others. This observational learning is not new to developmental psychology (Miller & Dollard, 1941), but it has gained great impetus in the format presented by Bandura and Walters. These authors emphasize the role of the model in this observational learning—his age, sex, and relation to the child, as well as whether or not the child sees him as being reinforced for his behavior.

In Chapter 28, Bandura and McDonald present an experiment testing the principles of social learning. Their major finding is that moral judgments are influenced more by the observation of models than by direct reinforcement. In this study children observed adult models making either subjective or objective moral judgments about situations presented in a series of stories. This modeling influenced the later judgments of the children even in new story situations. The children learned not just specific behaviors, but a class of moral judgment responses. Piaget believed that the stages of moral judgment are sequential and invariant and that they are based on the growth of logical thinking in the child. The results of Bandura and McDonald suggest that this may not be so, but that, on the contrary, one may be able to shape the moral judgment of responses of children primarily through modeling.

The concluding chapter in this unit on middle childhood by Professor Bronfenbrenner represents another example of a cross-cultural comparison of socialization practices. Bronfenbrenner describes the role of the schools in the development of character in Soviet Russia and the emphasis that the Soviets place on the collective. This is in sharp contrast to the American practice in which the family is the main socializing force at least until adolescence. In the second half of his paper, Bronfenbrenner suggests a number of research strategies for examining the relative efficiency of the family v. the collective in the training of character.

REFERENCES

ALLPORT, G. W. *Personality: A psychological interpretation*. New York: Henry Holt, 1937.

BANDURA, A., & WALTERS, R. H. *Social learning and personality development*. New York: Holt, Rinehart & Winston, 1963.

BRONFENBRENNER, U. The changing American child—a speculative analysis. *Merrill-Palmer Quarterly*, 1961, *7*, 73–84.

CRANDALL, V. C., KATKOVSKY, W., & CRANDALL, V. J. Children's beliefs in their own control of reinforcements in intellectual-academic achievement situations. *Child Development*. 1965, *36*, 91–109.

ERIKSON, E. H. *Childhood and society*. 2d ed. New York: W. W. Norton, 1963.

FREUD, S. *The basic writings of Sigmund Freud*. III. A. A. Brill (Ed. & Trans.). New York: Random House, 1938, Ch. 2.

FREUD, S. *Collected papers*. E. Jones (Ed.). Vol. 2. New York: Basic Books, 1959, Ch. 4.

FREUD, S. *Collected papers*. E. Jones (Ed.). Vol. 5. New York: Basic Books, 1959, Ch. 11.

FREUD, S. *Collected papers*. E. Jones (Ed.). Vol. 3, New York: Basic Books, 1959.

HILGARD, E. R. *Theories of learning*. 2d ed. New York: Appleton-Century-Crofts, 1959.

KENDLER, T. S., & KENDLER, H. H. Reversal and nonreversal shifts in kindergarten children. *Journal of experimental Psychology*, 1959, *58*, 56–60.

LEFCOURT, H. M. Internal versus external control of reinforcement: A review. *Psychological Bulletin*, 1966, *65*, 206–220.

LIVERANT, S. Intelligence: A concept in need of re-examination. *Journal of consulting Psychology*. 1960, *24*, 101–110.

MILLER, N. E., & DOLLARD, J. *Social learning and imitation*. New Haven: Yale University Press, 1941.

PIAGET, J. *The construction of reality in the child*. New York: Basic Books, 1954.

RABIN, A. I. Motivation for parenthood. *Journal of projective techniques and personality assessment*. 1965, *29*, 405–411.

ROTTER, J. B. Generalized expectancies for internal versus external control of reinforcement. *Psychological Monographs*. 1966, No. 80.

Sigel, I. E., & Hooper, F. H. (Eds.). *Logical thinking in children.* New York: Holt, Rinehart & Winston, 1968.

Stoke, M. S. An inquiry into the concept of identification. *Journal of genetic Pschology,* 1950, *76,* 163–189.

White, R. W. Motivation reconsidered: The concept of competence. *Psychological Review,* 1959, *66,* 297–333.

Cognition and Intelligence

18

HOW INTELLIGENCE TESTS LIMIT UNDERSTANDING OF INTELLIGENCE*

IRVING E. SIGEL

THE PURPOSES of this paper are (*a*) to demonstrate how past and present use of intelligence tests continues to restrict our understanding of intellectual function, and (*b*) to propose alternatives to the current practice of test analyses. Raising these issues is not to deny the usefulness of intelligence tests —they do provide good bases of predicting academic and vocational success. The contention in this paper is that we are not taking advantage of all the information obtained on an intelligence test.

Intelligence tests usually provide a single summative score, expressed in the form of an IQ, MA, or equivalent. The total score represents the number of correct responses to a set of items of varied content. A unidimensional index is therefore implied in the single score. In reality, intelligence tests are multi-dimensional, not unidimensional, because the items represent a variety of areas of knowledge. The Stanford-Binet is a good illustration of the type of heterogeneous scale yielding a single index.

Test constructors, who are aware of the limitations of single score IQ, attempt to solve the problem by providing subtests, each of which is intended

* From *Merrill-Palmer Quarterly*, 1963, *9*, 39–56. Reprinted with permission of the author and The Merrill-Palmer Institute.

Read at 1962 Institute for School Psychologists, University of Wisconsin. Two studies reported are supported by: (*a*) "Cognitive Styles and Personality Dynamics," NIMH, M-2983; and (*b*) "Analysis of Errors on the Raven PM," Social Research Foundation.

Appreciation is extended to Dr. I. Torgoff, Micki Wolter, Helen Hanesian, Donna Harris, Paul Jarman, and Purna Subudhi for their contribution to the preparation of the materials for the paper. Dr. Martin Hoffman's editorial assistance is gratefully acknowledged.

to test particular aspects of intellectual ability. A score is obtained for each subtest. Comparisons of subtest scores enables the examiner to study intra-individual variability of performance. In this way, a more detailed and more sensitive assessment of intellectual ability is possible. An example of this type of test is the Wechsler Intelligence Scale of Children (WISC).

Mindful of these characteristics, let us now turn to a discussion of test limitations. A test response indicates "what" the subject can do, but provides no understanding of "how." To assess these underlying processes, it is necessary to make inferences from the subject's responses. A correct answer to an analogies item, for example, may be a function of particular learning, perceptual discrimination, syllogistic reasoning, or any combination of these. There is no way to judge, from the response itself, which of these processes was operating at the time the response was made.

Not only do we have to infer the underlying process, but also the respondent's repertoire of responses. Only one response is usually required and acceptable. Alternative responses other than those indicated by test manuals are not acceptable. The test constructor decides what is the best answer to items he selects as relevant. The psychometric procedures in test making are too well known to need discussion here. What is not sufficiently taken into account is that, for a number of items, alternative responses—although correct at times—are not considered "correct" or "good" or given equal credit, because of cultural conventions.

The most clear-cut illustrations can be found in verbal tests of analogies. For example, in the WISC similarities item, "How are a scissors and a copper pan alike?" the answer, "They are both household utensils," is given a score of one; the answer, "Both are metal," is given two credits. Both responses are class concepts. Yet, from Wechsler's framework, preference is given to a particular system. How does one decide which system is preferable?

The WISC is not the only test which can be looked at in this way. For example, Guilford (1959) employed some items to assess abilities to know classes of units. He asks the respondent to "pick one that does not belong" from the following: clam, tree, oven, and rose. Although Guilford does not provide the answer, perhaps assuming the item is simple enough for the psychologists reading the article, the correct answer probably is *oven*. The remaining three items—clam, tree, and rose—belong to a class of living things, but the same items could also be classified on the basis of function—clam, tree, and oven are related to the preparation of food, thus *rose* does not belong; and on the basis of location,—the *clam* may be picked as not belonging, because it lives in water and the other things belong on land. These would probably be wrong answers.

According to Guilford, Wechsler, and other test constructors, classes as units apparently must be organized on the basis of the common hierarchical logical taxonomy. It is a system by which particular characteristics are selected as the basis for a more extensive classification. The characteristics selected or "abstracted" are those "features which enable us to view that thing as an instance or example of indefinitely repeatable patterns or types of situations" (Cohen & Nagel, 1934, p. 371). The features are selected from among an almost infinite variety of properties. Thus, any attribution of similarity between two items (e.g. horse and cow, because they are animals) does not mean that because a horse is an animal it may not be something else. A particular type of class designation has been identified and valued as correct. Respondents deviating from this conception are "wrong" or "inferior." The conventional class logic is the preferred response.

A word here about "not sharing the conventional class system." The kinds of responses used as illustrations are not bizarre, but bear the reality of consensually agreed attributes of items. Respondents may not share conventional class systems because of different kinds of social and cultural experiences. But nonconventional responses may also reflect the *originality and the novel outlook of respondents*. Aware, as we are, of the obvious cultural and social differences, we still need to be more attentive to differences which emanate from creative thought. Our tests penalize all deviations, regardless of source.

One can disagree with the above contention, because of the assumption that one of the indices of intelligence is the ability to see things as organized in conventional classes of units. If one agrees with this point of view, then intelligence becomes, in part, synonymous with "conformity" in thinking or reasoning.

If this is true, then we are, in effect, saying that a characteristic of intelligence, as measured, is the ability to organize and to classify materials in a conventional way. Is such a notion really part of our conception of intelligence? If it is, should we not make this criterion articulate?

. . . .

A demonstration of how intelligence tests can be used to enlarge our view of intelligence involves discussion of three problems: (*a*) the relationship of cognitive style variables to performance on intelligence tests, (*b*) a model for qualitative analysis of verbal content, and (*c*) what can be learned from analysis of errors on IQ tests.

First, let us turn to a discussion of cognitive style. "Style" is used as an umbrella term, under which is subsumed a variety of cognitive behaviors (Sigel, 1961). It refers to "modes" an individual employs in perceiving, organizing, and labelling various dimensions of the environment.

Operationally, cognitive styles are apparent in everyday life. From a wide array of stimuli, an individual is provided with many alternatives from which to select a basis of organization and labelling. It is assumed that the characteristic selected—especially when little or no coercion is present—emanates from an acquired predisposition to be attentive to that particular type of cue. If given a number of glass tumblers, for example, some individuals will select color, size, quality, or function of the object materials as the most relevant cue by which to organize and subsequently label the stimuli. Since all cues are equally visible and, to a comparable sample of individuals, equally known, we need to explain the fact that different cues are selected and responded to as organizational bases.

Language provides the individual with a set of labels which refer to various aspects of the environment. These labels may refer to parts or to wholes, to attributes, or to the total. The acquisition of the labels is a function of the individual's socio-cultural experiences. The labels acquired enables him to identify and communicate about his environment.

Language, then, is a manifestation of cognitive style. The underlying reasoning is as follows: As an environmental complex, the world of the child or of the adult can be denoted in various terms (i.e., a glass is a drinking object, a cylindrical object, a three-dimensional round object, a useful object, something you use for drinking). Each of these descriptions or identifiers of the object "drinking glass" is accurate but only represents in language some of the attributes of the object under consideration. Many of these kinds of statements about a glass are known to most literate, verbal people. Chances are that if we reversed the procedure, gave a number of these descriptive statements about a glass to different people, and asked them to select the appropriate class term from a list of words among which was the word "glass," the agreement would be very high. In other words, the fact that individuals know a variety of ways of describing an item, does not necessarily enable prediction of how individuals will organize a set of items.

Previous research has demonstrated that individual differences in labelling behavior do exist (Kagan, Moss & Sigel, 1962). Children and adults, when faced with sorting and, consequently, labelling figures depicting humans and objects, employ labels which can be classified as descriptive, relational-contextual and categorical-inferential labels (Sigel, 1961).

Descriptive. This category includes labels which denote similarity based on manifest objective physical attributes. Subclasses have been identified as, (*a*) *descriptive part-whole,* labels denoting observable parts of the stimuli; for example, organizing a group of human figures as being similar because "they are all wearing hats" or because "they all have their right arm raised," and (*b*) *descriptive-global,* labels tending toward denoting the total manifest attributes of the stimuli; for example, identifying a group of uniformed figures as "they are all soldiers" or a group of male figures dressed in identifiable male clothing because "they are men."

Relational-contextual. This category includes labels denoting functional or thematic interdependence between two or more elements in an array. The interdependence is particular to that situation and not generalizable beyond the immediate. The meaning of each item in the grouping is defined in terms of its relation to other items in the grouping; for example, from an array of pictures, a horse and a stagecoach are selected because "a horse is used to pull a stagecoach," or, on a thematic basis a man with a cane who is wearing dark glasses and a young boy are selected because "the boy is helping the blind man to cross the street."

Categorical-inferential. These labels refer to inferred characteristics of the stimuli and each item in a grouping is representative of the total class or category label. Some subclasses of categorical-inferential are, (*a*) *functional,* where objects are grouped together on the basis of inferred use, (e.g., referring to a group of tools as "these are things to build with"), (*b*) *class-naming,* where a taxonomic class label is used (e.g., animals, tools, human beings), and (*c*) *attribute selection,* where only one particular attribute is inferred (e.g., "they are angry," or "they run by motors").

These styles of categorization are operating for the respondent whenever he is faced with the task of organization of items on the basis of similarity or belongingness. The assumption is that individuals have preferences for particular modes of categorization and these characteristic modes have stylistic properties. The tendency will be to classify on the basis of preferred modes whenever the stimuli allow such behavior to manifest itself.

In this framework, let us look at Wechsler's item, "How are a cat and mouse alike?" Since the task requires a perception of similarity, an individual inclined toward a descriptive part-whole approach may say, "They are alike because both have tails." A categorical-inferential response would be, "Both are animals." Note that these two kinds of responses are both correct, even by Wechsler standards. The descriptive part-whole response is, however, valued lower—it gets one point, while the latter response receives two.

. . . .

To this point, we have discussed how the current use of intelligence tests does limit our understanding of the nature of intellectual functioning because of the ways we test and handle test responses. Still before us is one question of whether it would be any better if we did provide for alternative responses, alternative scoring, or analytic procedures. What evidence is there to support the invocation of the concept of style as a significant variable? To this end, we shall discuss some current research.

Scott (1962) assessed the significance of styles of categorization as a predictor of acquisition of science concepts. He found that—for eleven-year-old boys and girls—the better the performance in a task to measure science concept achievement, the greater the use of categorical-inferential responses in sorting tasks. No significant correlation was found between the IQ test and the use of categorical-inferential labels, or between the IQ test and the science achievement test. In other words, the use of categorical-inferential labels on a sorting task was a better predictor of success in the science test than the IQ measure.[2]

Styles of categorization may be an important intellectual dimension to determine how intelligence operates. An individual's "style" dictates the cues he will use, but not necessarily determines the level on which he performs. The style of categorization sets the direction but not the level on which an individual's intelligence might function.

To illustrate further relationships between cognitive style and intelligence, let us turn to a current investigation of the age changes of styles of categorization among "high," "medium," and "low" text-anxious second and third grade boys and girls (Sigel, 1961). The aims of the study are to determine the relationship between styles of categorization and content to be categorized, as well as the relationship between styles of categorization and IQ, age, and test-anxiety level.

Styles of categorization were assessed by using three sorting tasks: (*a*) arrays of human figures all familiar to the child, (e.g., fireman, woman, boy), (*b*) object-animal figures, (e.g., items representing vehicles, animals, food), and (*c*) geometric forms varying in size and color, (e.g., circles, triangles, squares).

To illustrate, we analyzed the relationship between styles of categorization and performance on the Lorge-Thorndike Primary Form. The Lorge-Thorndike is a three-part, non-verbal intelligence test. We used two of the three parts. The subtests employed for the analysis were as follows: (*a*) a task requiring the child to identify one item out of four that does not belong, and (*b*) a task requiring the child to find those items, among four, that go together.

Because the child is required to discriminate in both tasks, and determine either an irrelevant item or find similar items, he thus has a requirement similar to that in the IQ test. Consequently, we assume that styles of categorization should be related to his performance on the Lorge-Thorndike.

For the high-anxious third grade boys and girls, the use of class-naming labels—a type of categorical-inferential categorization—was related significantly with the total IQ score. For these same children, the more select descriptive-global responses made, the less "able" they were in selecting the item that did not belong in a series of items. Thus, those children who organize material on the basis of global manifest characteristics made errors on tasks requiring perception of structural similarities. In other words, their performance on this test is related to the styles of categorization employed by these children. The success with which children perform on IQ tests is, to some measure, predictable from their styles of categorization. These findings,

[2] The IQ measure used was the Southend Test of Intelligence, London, England, George Harrup, publisher, 1953.

thus far limited to high test-anxious children, tend to support our contention that performance on an intelligence test measure *is* influenced by a style of categorization.

Another finding relevant to intelligence test performance is that a positive relationship exists between the frequency of use of descriptive part-whole responses and cautiousness. There is some indication that such a preference for categorization tends to call forth a reflective careful approach in making judgments. In fact, Kagan (1962) concludes that reflectiveness is associated with a preference for a descriptive part-whole approach. The concept of reflectiveness or cautiousness as used here can be considered a cognitive set, or approach, and certainly would be manifest in test performance.

How extensive the role of styles of categorization is for all the classes of items employed in intelligence tests is an open question. What can be said at this point is that there is enough evidence from a deductive-analytic basis, as well as an empirical one, to suggest that IQ test scores are influenced by the style of categorization of the individual. The larger task is to determine, with greater specificity, the degree to which such relationships exist, and whether particular styles facilitate or inhibit intellective responses.

. . . .

One last point on cognitive styles, although tangential, is of cardinal importance. In all our work on styles, a most consistent finding was the phenomena of "sex differences." Not only do boys and girls differ in their styles of categorization, but more important is that the psychological role played by particular styles differs for boys and girls. Personality correlates of styles of categorization differ for the sexes. We find, for example, that the descriptive part-whole approach relates positively with cautiousness for boys, but negatively for girls. The sex difference seems to be basic. Yet, in our intelligence test scores, we do not have separate norms for boys and girls. If we extrapolate from the research on style of categorization, it is reasonable to suppose that sex differences should show up in a host of intellectual operations.

Two kinds of evidence have now been presented to support the contention that intelligence tests, as now viewed, are restrictive. The suggestion has been made persistently that additional scoring systems are necessary in order to extract the meat from the responses, rather than our current approach which is so parsimonious that we lose perhaps more than we gain.

. . . .

Resting with our current concepts will not help us understand the "how" of intelligence. Using intelligence tests as we do, limiting our analysis to unsystematic analyses of responses, be they qualitative or quantitative, negates the relevance of other cognitive factors influencing IQ. It may well be that the reason IQ and creativity are not frequently related is just because we have used the IQ in a narrow restricted way. This is certainly an implication from the work of Getzels and Jackson (1962). If we broaden our use of IQ tests, we may be in a position to provide a significant test which would not only have broad predictive value, but enlarge our view of how intelligence operates.

In this way, we may avoid such curious contradictions that IQ and creativity are not related. Such findings are essentially artifacts of our test construction. The greater tests reflect theoretical conceptions, the greater our chance of clarifying many of the issues plaguing us.

REFERENCES

Cohen, M. R. & Nagel, E. *Logic and scientific method.* N.Y. Harcourt Brace and Co., 1934.

Getzels, J. & Jackson, P. *Creativity and intelligence.* New York: Wiley, 1962.

Guilford, J. P. Three faces of intellect. *Amer. Psychologist,* 1959, **14,** 569–579.

Kagan, J., Moss, H. A., & Sigel, I. E. The psychological significance of styles of conceptualization. In Wright, J. F. and Kagan, J. (Eds.) Proceedings of conference on cognitive processes. *Monogr., Soc. Res. Child Development,* 1962.

Scott, N. The relationship of inductive reasoning and cognitive styles and categorization behavior to science concept achievement in elementary school children. Unpubl. doctoral dissertation, Wayne State University, 1962.

Sigel, I. E. *Cognitive style and personality dynamics.* Interim progress report for National Institute of Mental Health, M-2983, 1961.

Wechsler, D. *Wechsler intelligence scale for children:* manual. New York: Psychological Corp., 1949.

19

JEAN PIAGET AND THE WORLD OF THE CHILD*

READ D. TUDDENHAM

IT IS DIFFICULT to characterize Piaget's work, for it is both deep and broad in scope. He has been in turn a biologist, psychologist, philosopher, and logician, and in all four fields he has made major contributions. He is currently Professor of Psychology at the University of Geneva and at the Sorbonne. He is coeditor of the *Archives de Psychologie* and of the *Revue Suisse de Psychologie.* He is Director of the Institut des Sciences de l'Éducation (successor to the Institut Jean Jacques Rousseau), founder of the Centre d'Epistemologie Génétique, and Director of the Bureau International de l'Éducation, an affiliate of the United Nations Educational, Scientific, and Cultural Organization, which entitles him to the black passport of diplomatic status. Widely traveled, he has been honored by many foreign universities and governments. He is a member of the French Légion d'Honneur and holds honorary doctorates from the Sorbonne, from Brussels, Brandeis, Harvard, and other universities.

Since his book, the *Language and Thought of the Child,* appeared in 1923, Piaget and his collaborators have published more than 20 full-length books and largely filled 30 bulky annual volumes of the *Archives de Psychologie;* in all, over 180 major studies covering thousands of pages, of which the barest fraction has been translated into English. I am acquainted with only a small part of this fantastic productivity, and considering the brief time at my disposal, it may be just as well that my knowledge of it is not encyclopedic. In any case you will understand why this morning's talk is scarcely a preface to an introduction to Piaget.

---

* From *American Psychologist,* 1966, *21,* 207–217. Reprinted with permission of the author and the American Psychological Association, Inc.

Public lecture given at Berkeley on May 23, 1964, as a part of the University of California fete celebrating the four hundredth anniversary of the founding of the University of Geneva.

The author wishes to acknowledge his indebtedness to earlier writers on Piaget, not all of whom could be mentioned in the lecture. However, special acknowledgment is owing to Flavell (1962) in connection with the biographical account, and to Wolff (1960) for portions of the summary of theory.

. . . .

Born in Neuchâtel in 1896, he published his first paper when he was 10 years old on an albino sparrow he found hopping in the public garden. His interest soon turned to molluscs. Before he was 21, he had published 20 papers on molluscs and related topics, and had been offered sight unseen the curatorship of molluscs at Geneva while still in secondary school. He took his baccalaureate at Neuchâtel in 1915 followed by his doctorate in 1918.

Throughout these early years he read widely in other fields—religion, philosophy, and psychology. He came thus to the view that biology should contribute to the solution of classical problems in epistemology, but realized that something was needed to bridge the two. In later years, his developmental psychology came to provide the link, culminating in his three-volume work of 1950 on genetic epistemology, unfortunately still untranslated.

After receiving his doctorate, his interests shifted more explicitly to psychology, and he left Neuchâtel to visit and study at various other centers, including Bleuler's psychiatric clinic and the Sorbonne. Binet had died in 1911, but in Paris, Piaget was given the opportunity by Simon, Binet's collaborator in the Simon-Binet tests, to work in Binet's old laboratory at a Paris grade school. The problem suggested was a standardization of Burt's reasoning tests on Paris school children. Although Piaget was not much interested in the psychometric aspects of the problem, he found himself fascinated by the processes whereby the child achieved his answers—and wrong answers were often more enlightening than right ones.

The psychiatric examining procedures learned at Bleuler's clinic were pressed into service to elucidate the child's reasoning, and came ultimately to constitute the *méthode clinique* by which much of Piaget's data have been collected. This method of intensive interrogation is common enough among psychiatrists, but it is likely to scandalize the American psychologist trained in the canons of objectivity and standardization of procedure, because it risks leading the child and putting words in his mouth. Yet in skillful hands, it yields subtle insights which our "measurement" approach precludes.

In view of his work in Binet's laboratory, it is interesting to trace Piaget's relation to the great French psychologist who had died when Piaget was in adolescence. Certainly Piaget has relatively little in common with the Binet of the famous intelligence tests, because Piaget has never been much interested in mental testing or in individual differences. But he has much in common with the Binet of earlier years, whose interests, like Piaget's, ranged over much of science. More specifically, he seems the direct heir of the Binet who wrote the famous volume, *The Psychology of Reasoning,* a book which anticipates Piaget in its concern with the subtle qualitative aspects of thought, and further anticipates him in the employment of the psychologist's own children as experimental subjects—a procedure which might be impractical in this country where statistically adequate samples of 40 or 50 are a desideratum for the simplest investigation!

In 1921 Piaget published four papers describing the results of his work with Burt's tests and other such problems. On the strength of them, Claparède, who was then the Professor of Psychology at Geneva, invited Piaget to the post of Director of Studies at the Institut Jean Jacques Rousseau, and Piaget accepted. Although at first he divided his time between Geneva and Neuchâtel, and until fairly recently spent part of each week at the Sorbonne, his work for the last 40 years has been largely identified with the University of Geneva.

In all the vast corpus of Piaget's work are there unifying trends or concerns which can serve to orient us in this brief survey? Apart from his zoological studies and a few mathematical papers on logic as such, the central preoccupation has been with epistemology—the fundamental problem of how we come to know our world. But this problem is approached, not via traditional philosophical speculation, but rather via scientific observation and experimentation, although sometimes of an unconventional kind. The subjects are infants, children, and adolescents, and the emphasis is always developmental.

Some of this work is on perception, and is concerned with discovering the laws of perceptual development and the differences between perceptual and cognitive functions. To this end, the Geneva workers have shown a persistent interest in optical illusions. For example, they have systematically altered various aspects of the stimulus configuration and measured the magnitude and direction of the observer's errors as a function of his age. These perception studies, over 40 in number, are more rigorous and quantitative than the studies on cognitive development, and substitute for the *méthode clinique* the traditional experimental approach.

In summary, Piaget finds a general tendency, though by no means a linear one, nor one found in all instances, whereby perceptual judgments grow more accurate with age. However, he regards perceptual development as essentially continuous, and he does not consider that the developmental stages, which are so important in his cognitive theory, exist in the perceptual domain. Indeed, he has repeatedly contrasted the perceptual versus the conceptual or inferential process even in the young child, and emphasized that the two functions follow very different paths in development. Wohlwill (1962) has suggested that Piaget's denial of stages in perception while affirming them for cognition stems not from the finding that ontogenetic change in perception is necessarily more gradual, but rather because the differences between successive perceptual achievements are only quantitative, whereas one can find structural criteria—that is to say the presence or absence of particular logical operations—to differentiate the stages of conceptual development.

Time precludes further discussion of the Geneva work on perception, though it constitutes a large and important body of data and interpretation for the perception psychologist. Let us turn instead to the more familiar studies concerned with reasoning and inference.

To throw Piaget's contributions into sharper focus, let us digress briefly to consider the epistemological problem, one of the great imponderables which have engaged men's attention at least since the golden age of Greek philosophy. Now philosophers often ask questions in ways which admit of no final answer. They thus get a great deal of mileage out of them, and the same controversies keep recurring, century after century. For our purpose we need go no further back than the views of the British associationists of the seventeenth and eighteenth centuries.

The epistemological problem has to do with the nature of reality and of our knowledge of it. It probably never occurs to the naive man in the street to question the objective reality and existence of the things of the physical world—tables, chairs, people, books, etc.—which we see all about us. So uncritical an attitude does not characterize philosophers, though different ones have taken opposite sides of the question, sides to which we give the general labels "empiricism" and "idealism."

John Locke (1947) was an empiricist. Writing near the end of the seventeenth century, he rejected the idealist doctrine offered by Descartes and tracing back through the scholastics to Plato, that the mind comes furnished a priori, with a considerable array of innate ideas. Instead he sponsored the view, then much less familiar than it is now, that *all* knowledge is derived from experience. In Book II of his great *Essay Concerning Human Understanding,* he writes,

> Let us then suppose the mind to be, as we say, white paper, void of all characters, without any ideas; how comes it to be furnished? Whence comes it by that vast store, which the busy and boundless fancy of man has painted on it with an almost endless variety? Whence has it all the materials of reason and knowledge? To this I answer one word, from experience: in that all our knowledge is founded, and from that ultimately derives itself [p. 26].

And again in Book IV,

> Since the mind in all its thoughts and reasonings hath no other immediate object but its own ideas, which it alone does or can contemplate, it is evident that our knowledge is only conversant about them [p. 252].

From this it would seem to follow that we cannot know of the existence of other people, or of the physical world; for these, if they exist, are not merely ideas. Each one of us, so far as knowledge is concerned, is shut up in himself and cut off from contact with the world.

Now Locke usually shrank back from drawing the implications of his theories when they seemed to run counter to his own common sense. George Berkeley, Bishop of Cloyne, is best known in California for our city of

Berkeley which was named for him, although he might not recognize his own name as we pronounce it. In philosophy, he was an immediate successor of Locke and set out to resolve Locke's inconsistencies. Boldly pushing Locke's views to their logical consequence, he found himself in the position of denying the very existence of matter, i.e., the external world, and affirming that only the mind is ultimately real. He asserted that material objects exist only through being perceived. Bertrand Russell (1945) puts the matter very clearly.

To the objection that, for example, a tree would cease to exist if no one was looking at it, he replied that God always perceives everything; if there were no God, what we take to be material objects would have a jerky life, suddenly leaping into being when we look at them; but as it is, owing to God's perceptions, trees, rocks, and stones have an existence as continuous as common sense supposes. This, in Berkeley's opinion, is a weighty argument for the existence of God [p. 647].

Berkeley's idealist view seems intuitively false to at least some philosophers, and to most people who are not philosophers, but it is hard to refute. Berkeley's finding himself in the idealist camp by merely seeking to embrace the implications of the empiricist position shows how slippery some of the central questions of philosophy can become when phrased in traditional forms. Obviously such questions as, "Is there an external reality?" or even merely, "What is knowledge?" can lead only to speculative controversy. If the epistemological problem is formulated in more restricted terms of *how* is knowledge acquired, rather than *what* is knowledge, it may become susceptible of scientific experimental attack.

Returning to Piaget, it is clear that his genius has lain in his resourcefulness in investigating the more manageable question, "How does knowledge develop and change?" As you can see, Piaget's epistemology is at once empirical—even experimental—and developmental in orientation. Leaving aside the question of whether the world is real, he has observed and recorded the activities of the child from earliest infancy to adolescence in acquiring the strategies for coping with it.

On the traditional epistemological issue, Piaget is hard to classify. Some have considered him an idealist, some an empiricist, and both sides can marshal quotations in support. Bärbel Inhelder (1962, p. 20) writes amusingly about this. It seems that after considerable contact in a seminar, Konrad Lorenz remarked, "All along I have thought that Piaget was one of those tiresome empiricists, and only now after studying his work on the genesis of the categories of thought, have I come to realize that he is not so far removed from Kant." On the other hand, some Russian colleagues who believed Piaget to be an idealist because he did not admit that knowledge of the external world is simply a reflection of the objects in it, posed to him the following leading question: "Do you think an object exists prior to any knowledge of it?" Piaget replied, "As a psychologist, I have no idea; I only know an object to the extent that I act upon it; I can affirm nothing about it prior to such an action." Then one of the Russians said, "For us an object is part of the world. Can *the external world* exist independently of and prior to our knowledge of it?" To this, Piaget replied, "The instruments of our knowledge form part of our organism, which in turn forms part of the external world." Later, Piaget overheard them talking and agreeing, "Piaget is *not* an idealist."

Perhaps the difficulty of locating Piaget unequivocally on the empiricist-idealist continuum illustrates a central problem for the student of his work. His ideas are highly original. The terms he has coined for his central theoretical constructs are not merely unfamiliar. They seem vigorously to resist translation into other people's conceptual categories. There is no help for it, if one would understand his theories, but to try to assimilate Piaget in his own terms.

. . . .

Let us turn first to Piaget's theory of cognitive development. Here a confusing situation arises for the English-speaking student. Piaget's five important books of the early 1920s were translated fairly promptly into English in the first flurry of interest in his work. These volumes—*Language and Thought of the Child, Judgment and Reasoning in the Child, The Child's Conception of Physical Causality,* and *The Moral Judgment of the Child*—are widely available. It is their contents—the famous inquiries about what makes clouds move, the origins of dreams, the basis of rules for games, and a host of other such topics—which come to mind for many people when Piaget is mentioned.

Now these works were gradually superseded in Piaget's theoretical formulations, but the point has not been sufficiently appreciated. In this country, there was a decline of interest in Piaget during what Koch (1959) has called the "Age of Theory" in American psychology—roughly from the early '30s to the end of the war—a tough-minded period dominated by the rules of "hypothetico-deduction" and "operational definition" and animated by belief in the imminence of a precisely quantitative behavior theory. Piaget's work was not easily reconciled with the fashions of the period, and little was translated. Now the tide has turned, and at least a portion of Piaget's recent work is available in English, not to mention several excellent "explanations" of him by Wolff (1960), Wohlwill (1960), Hunt (1961), and especially Flavell's comprehensive volume of 1963. However, the essential continuity of development of Piaget's ideas is obscured by the discontinuity of translation. So different are the recent works from the old ones, that to read them one must master a new vocabulary and a new theoretical formulation, and this time the task is made more difficult by the heavy emphasis upon propositions of symbolic logic to explicate the developmental stages of reasoning.

To the early Piaget belonged the painstaking compilation of the forms of verbal expression according to age level from 3 years to 10 years: the demonstration that children's "explanations" of phenomena pass through *stages*, from early animistic, through magical and artificialist forms, to rational thought, and that at each level, the child constructs a systematic "cosmology" according to the modes of reasoning available to him at that stage. The empirical bases for these findings were the children's verbalizations as elicited by the *méthode clinique,* with its inherent risks of misinterpretation of what the child is trying to express. Piaget was severely and perhaps unjustly criticized on this account, for he was sharply aware of the problem. As he put it (1929),

> It is so hard not to talk too much when questioning a child, especially for a pedagogue! It is so hard not to suggest! And above all, it is so hard to find the middle course between systematization due to preconceived ideas, and incoherence due to the absence of any directing hypothesis! . . . In short, it is no simple task, and the material it yields needs to be subjected to the strictest criticism [p. 8].

In retrospect, Piaget (1952a) recognizes that his method in those years was much too exclusively verbal.

> I well knew that thought proceeds from action, but believed then that language directly reflects the act, and that to understand the logic of the child one has to look for it in the domain of verbal interactions. It was only by studying the patterns of intelligent behavior of *the first two years* that I learned that for a complete understanding of the genesis of intellectual operations, manipulation and experience with objects had first to be considered [p. 247].

As Piaget notes, the shift from reliance on verbalization to observation and experiment is most important for genetic epistemology because it permits one to study infants as well as the later stages of growth, and by more or less comparable methods.

The cognitive theory starts from the central postulate that motor action is the source from which mental operations emerge. The *action* of the organism is central to the acquisitions of the operations (i.e., ideas, or strategies), which we acquire for coping with the world. In the Hegelian dialectical form which his lectures often assume, Piaget contrasts his emphasis upon the active interplay of organism and environment, both with the environmentalist view in which experience or conditioning is impressed upon a passive organism, and with the nativist view that intellectual capabilities exist preformed and merely unfold in the course of development.

Motor action is *adaptive,* and so are the cognitive activities which more and more replace overt motor behavior. Piaget's biological orientation is seen in his assertion that intelligence is an adaptation, and only one aspect of biological adaptation. Intelligence is an organizing activity which extends the biological organization. With respect to intelligence, a subject to which Piaget has given much attention, it should be noted that his interest is in the typical, not in the range of variation. For him, the word "intelligence" lacks the mental-testing connotations with which it is usually invested in English, and corresponds rather to "intellect" or to intellectual activity or adaptation.

> Life is a continuous creation of increasingly complex forms, and a progressive balancing of these forms with the environment [Piaget, 1952b, p. 3].
>
> Intellectual adaptation is the progressive differentiation and integration of inborn reflex mechanisms under the impact of experience. The differentiation of inborn reflex structures and their functions give rise to the mental operations by which man conceives of objects, space, time, and causality, and of the logical relationships which constitute the basis of scientific thought [Wolff, 1960, p. 9].

Another central postulate is that intellectual operations acquired by interaction between organism and environment are acquired in a *lawful sequence*. It should be emphasized again that Piaget's concern is with elucidating the sequence, *not* with establishing exact age norms for its stages. It should also be noted that Piaget has set out to write the ontogenetic history of cognition—*not* a complete account of personality development. What lies outside the cognitive domain is rigorously excluded.

The innate equipment consists of reflexes present at birth. A few reflexes, e.g., yawning or sneezing, are relatively fixed and unmodifiable by experience, though some, like the Babinski, change with maturation. The majority of reflexes, for example, grasping, *require* stimulation for their stabilization, are modified as a result of experience, and constitute the basic behavioral units from which more complex forms of behavior emerge. Most important, the feedback from the activation of a reflex alters all subsequent performance of that reflex. Thus, behavior is simultaneously determined by: first, the inborn structure; second, past activations, i.e., experience; and third, the particular present situation.

Now corresponding to each innate reflex there is assumed to exist in the mind a reflex *schema,* which will not become a stable structure unless repeatedly activated by external stimulation. The concept of schema is difficult. It is described as a flexible mental structure, the primary unit of mental organization. It is too invested with motor connotations to translate as "idea"; and being initially innate, it can hardly be a memory trace. Yet it covers both, and when fully developed bears some resemblance to Tolman's sign Gestalt.

When a reflex responds to a suitable external stimulus, the total sensory perception *and* motor activity are incorporated into the schema of that reflex, and change it; so that when the reflex is again stimulated, the schema has been modified. The stimulus is never again experienced in quite the same way, nor is the response quite the same. Thus the schema is invoked to account for the modification of response, *and* for the alteration of perception in the course of learning. In other words, the organism experiences and reacts to the environment always in terms of an existing organization. All experiences of a particular kind are molded into the already present schema, and in turn alter it according to the reality conditions. Hence, experiences are not recorded as isolated stimulus-response connections, or engrams impressed on a passive brain field, but are integrated into a constantly changing structure.

For the dual aspects of learning, Piaget has used the terms *assimilation* and *accommodation*. He points out first that there exists a fundamental coordination or tuning of the organism to its environment. We have eyes and skin receptors preadapted for the photic and thermal radiation found on earth, ears for sensing rapid waves of pressure in earth's atmosphere, and so forth. There exists, moreover, a fundamental tendency of organisms to take in substances and stimulations for which there already exist the appropriate internal structures and organization. This taking in is called *assimilation*. At a biological level, it refers to the physical incorporation of suitable nutrients into organic structure. At a primitive psychological level, it refers to the incorporation of the sensory and motor components of a behavioral act into the reflex schema they have activated. At more complex levels, assimilation refers to the tendency of the mental apparatus to incorporate ideas into a complex system of thought schemata.

Parallel to assimilation is the function of *accommodation*, i.e., the process by which a schema *changes* so as to adapt better to the assimilated reality. At the biological level, accommodation refers to modification of the organism in response to stimulation, e.g., skin tanning in response to sunlight, or muscle growth in response to exercise. At the lowest psychological level, it refers to the gradual adaptation of the reflexes to new stimulus conditions—what others have called conditioning or stimulus generalization. At higher levels it refers to the coordination of thought patterns to one another and to external reality.

While assimilation and accommodation seem not too far from conventional learning theory, the concept of *aliment* is more unfamiliar. Whatever can be assimilated to a schema is aliment for that schema. Now the aliment is not the *object* which seems from the point of view of the observer to activate behavior, but rather those properties of the object which are assimilated and accommodated to. For example, a nursing bottle filled with milk may be organic aliment for the metabolism, sucking aliment for the reflex sucking schema, and visual aliment for the visual schema. And if the idea strikes you as bizarre that a reflex requires to be fed, as it were, by appropriate stimulation, consider Riesen's (1947) report on the degeneration of the visual apparatus in chimpanzees reared in the dark—or the more familiar degeneration of unstimulated muscles when polio destroys the motor pathways.

Why the careful distinction between an object and its properties? Because for the infant the object does not exist! The idea of an object grows gradually out of the coordination of several schemata—that which is perceived by several sensorial avenues *becomes* the object. At first, the infant has not even awareness of the boundaries of his own body. Objects in the perceptual field—including his own hands and feet—are responded to according to the infant's limited reflexive repertoire. He sucks in response to oral stimulation, grasps in response to palmar stimulation, but makes no attempt to grasp the nursing bottle which he competently sucks, or to follow visually the bottle he can clutch if placed in his hand. Only gradually, by a process called generalizing assimilation, do stimuli which were initially specific aliment for one schema become aliment for other schemata. In parallel accommodation, a schema becomes attuned to more complex inputs, and tends to become coordinated with other schemata which are simultaneously activated. When this happens, things previously known tactilely by being grasped can be recognized by sight alone. Similarly, grasping attempts of increasing accuracy can be directed toward sources of visual stimulation. In such a fashion does the baby come to populate the world with objects, one of which is his own body, which supplies him at once with visual, tactile and kinesthetic stimuli—and when he cries, with auditory ones.

However, the infant still does not attach the concept of permanence to objects. "Out of sight" is quite literally "out of mind." One of Piaget's most interesting experiments—and one which can be repeated by any parent of an infant—concerns the growth of the idea of permanent objects. If you catch a young baby's attention with a small toy, and then hide it, he will make little response. When somewhat older, he will show diffuse motor behavior. If now he once happens to touch it, he will gradually learn to search more efficiently where the object is hidden. However, if the object is hidden in a different place, in full sight of the baby, he will search not where he saw it hidden, but where previously he had touched it. It is an intellectual achievement of some magnitude when the very young child learns to coordinate the space of things seen with the space of things touched, and seeks to touch an object where hitherto he has only seen it.

We can conclude our rapid survey of Piaget's basic concepts with a brief reference to *equilibrium*. Bruner (1959), otherwise most sympathetic, regards the notion of equilibrium as excess baggage, contributing to Piaget a conforting sense of continuity with biology, but offering little else. Perhaps the idea of disequilibrium is more easily described. A schema is in disequilibrium if adaptation (i.e., assimilation and accommodation) to the stimulus is incomplete.

It seems to me that the ideas of equilibrium and disequilibrium constitute most of Piaget's theory of motivation, which is a rather underelaborated part of his psychological system. The organism has a basic need to continue contact with an object as long as adaptation to it is incomplete—or, as Piaget would say, as long as the corresponding schema is in disequilibrium. The need for commerce with an object persists until the child's behavior has been wholly adapted to whatever novelty it presents, that is to say, it persists until the child has acquired mastery. Once accommodation is complete and assimilation is total, the schema is said to be "in equilibrium," and there is no further adaptation. There is, in short, no learning without a problem.

Further, two *schemata* are in disequilibrium until they have mutually accommodated and assimilated, and thereby been integrated into a new superordinate mental structure. This tendency to integrate schemata into more and more complex wholes is assumed by Piaget to be a native propensity of the mind, and as fundamental as the tendency toward equilibrium in physical systems. To put the matter in less cosmic terms, the person strives continually for more and more comprehensive mastery of his world. At each *stage,* however, he is concerned with those things which lie just beyond his intellectual grasp—far enough away to present a novelty to be assimilated, but not so far but what accommodation is possible. Phenomena too simple—i.e., already in equilibrium—and phenomena too complex for present adaptation are ignored in favor of those in the critical range. Anyone who has ever watched the persistence, and resistance to satiation, of a baby intent on mastering a developmental task—for example, learning to walk—will agree with Piaget as to the strength of the motivation, whether or not he accepts Piaget's thermodynamic metaphor.

What then are the general *stages* of intellectual development, and how may they be characterized? Piaget's stages are one of the best known aspects of his work, but he has not been altogether consistent either in the number of them or in the names assigned. Moreover, the stages are linked to particular chronological ages only rather loosely, and Piaget has himself offered data to show that the age at which a particular stage is reached differs for different content domains. For example, conservation (i.e., invariance under transformation) of a plastic object, such as a lump of clay, is acquired first with respect to mass, a year or so later with respect to weight, and a couple of years after that with respect to volume. Moreover, the Geneva group are concerned to demonstrate the invariance of the *sequence* of stages, not the age at which a given stage is achieved. In Martinique the children are 4 years retarded compared to those in Montreal (Laurendeau & Pinard, 1963), and certain Brazilian Indians appear never to achieve the last stage—but the sequence is everywhere the same.

When Piaget visited Berkeley, he deplored the preoccupation of American psychologists with accelerating a child's progress through the successive stages, and commented on recent work of Gruber, who found that kittens achieve awareness of the permanence of objects in 3 months, the human baby only in 9 months; but the important fact is that the cat never acquires the power to think in terms of formal logic, and the human being may!

The more recent books from Geneva usually divide development into four stages: the sensorimotor, from birth to 2 or 3 years; the preoperational stage, from around 2 to around 7 years; the stage of concrete operations, from roughly 7 years to 11 or 12; and finally the stage of formal operations. Each stage in turn has substages—no less than six for the sensorimotor period alone—which we shall not have time to describe today.

The sensorimotor period as a whole (i.e., from birth up to age 2) carries the child from inborn reflexes to acquired behavior patterns. It leads the child from a body-centered (i.e., self-centered) world to an object-centered one. During this period the various sensory spaces, of vision, touch, and the rest, are coordinated into a single space and objects evolve from their separate sensory properties into *things* with multiple properties, permanence, and spatial relationships to other objects. Altogether this stage comprises a most important set of intellectual achievements.

The preoperational stage (2 years to around 7 years) covers the important period when language is acquired. This permits the child to deal symbolically with the world instead of directly through motor activity, though his problem solving tends to be "action ridden." The child is himself still the focus of his own world, and space and time are centered on him. Time is only "before now," "now," and "not yet"; and space moves as the child moves. When he is taken for an evening walk, the moon follows *him*. Traces of this attitude are present even in adults, who often locate places and things in terms of distance and direction from themselves, rather than in terms of objective spatial relationships. By a process of "decentering," the child during this stage learns gradually to conceive of a time scale and of a spatial world which exist independent of himself. In dealing with physical objects and quantities, the child pays attention to one aspect to the neglect of other aspects. He concludes, for example, that there is more water in a glass graduate than in a beaker—though he has just seen it poured from the one vessel into the other—because in the graduate the column of water is taller, and the child neglects the reduction in diameter.

The stage of concrete operations has its beginnings as early as age 6 or 7. Now the child grows less dependent upon his own perceptions and motor actions and shows a capacity for reasoning, though still at a very concrete level. Among his "logical" acquisitions are classifying, ordering in series, and numbering. Asked to put a handful of sticks in order by length, he need no longer make all the pair comparisons but can pick out the longest, then the longest one left, and so forth, until the series is complete. When shown that Stick A is longer than Stick B, and Stick B is longer than Stick C, he can infer without actual demonstration that A is longer than C.

Here at Berkeley, my students and I have been developing test materials based on Piaget experiments, and intended to measure the abilities of children in the primary grade; i.e., at the transition point from the perceptual attitude of the preoperational stage to the reasoning attitude of the stage of concrete operations. Thus far, fifteen tests have been developed and administered to more than 300 school children. Although we abandoned the *méthode clinique* for a strictly standardized psychometric approach, we have observed precisely the same types of behavior which Piaget had previously reported.

The last of Piaget's major stages of intellectual development begins usually somewhere around 11 or 12 years and matures a couple of years later. He calls it the stage of formal operations. Now the child can deal with abstract relationships instead of with things, with the form of an argument while ignoring its content. For the first time he can intellectually manipulate the merely hypothetical, and systematically evaluate a lengthy set of alternatives. He learns to handle the logical relationships of Identity (I), Negation (N), Reciprocity (R), and Correlation (C), which permit him to deal with problems of proportionality, probability, permutations, and combinations.

I have just referred to the INRC logical group whose acquisition marks the last stage of intellectual growth. In Piaget's writings over the years, the characteristics of each stage and the differences between them have increasingly been formulated in the notation of symbolic logic—a circumstance which does not increase the comprehensibility of his latest books for nonmathematicians.

Nevertheless, this transition to the language of formal logic is of profound importance for Piaget's theory because it provides a set of explicit, mathematical models for cognitive structure, and serves as a vehicle to describe in a unified way the findings of experiments very different in content. The unity and economy of the logical theory as contrasted with his earlier multiplicity of explanatory terms—egocentrism, syncretism, animism, realism, etc.—is obvious. However, Piaget's critics have sometimes found the mathematical formulation strained, and have accused Piaget of distorting intellectual development to force it into the categories of formal logic.

Piaget's point of view may have been misunderstood. As he phrases it (1957),

> The aim is . . . to study the application of logical techniques to the psychological facts themselves. . . . The question whether the structures and operations of logic correspond to anything in our actual thought, and whether the latter conforms to logical laws, is still an open one. . . . On the other hand, the algebra of logic can help us to specify psychological structures, and put into calculus form those operations and structures central to our thought processes. . . . The psychologist welcomes the qualitative character of logic since it facilitates the analyses of the actual structures underlying intellectual operations, as contrasted with the quantitative treatment of their behavioral outcome. Most "tests" of intelligence measure the latter, but our real problem is to discover the actual operational mechanisms which govern such behavior, and not simply to measure it [pp. xvii–xviii].

Many psychologists who acknowledge the brilliant originality of many of Piaget's experiments, and the enormous importance of his empirical contribution taken as a whole, continue nevertheless to reject the formal, mathematical theory which lies closest to Piaget's heart. Yet one of the most impressive parts of Piaget's discussions here in Berkeley concerned the isomorphism between his stages and the most basic structure of mathematics itself.

Piaget points out that if one considers not the content, but the architecture, as it were, of the various branches of mathematics, one discovers first a level where the prototype structure is the group and the type of reversibility is inversion or negation. Next comes a level where structures of order, such as the lattice, are typical, and reversibility is not inversion but reciprocity. Last comes the level of topology with key concepts of neighborhood, boundary, etc. Now the first of these three levels is the oldest, one part of it, Euclidean geometry, going back to the Greeks. The second level, typified by projective geometry, dates from the late seventeenth century; and the last, or topological, level is a product only of the nineteenth century. Taken in sequence, each level is more general, i.e., involves *fewer* axioms than the preceding, and the entire sequence might theoretically be expected to have developed in the opposite order. Now the curious part, is that the sequence of acquisition of mental operations by children follows not the historical sequence, but the theoretical sequence. Small children of 3 years of age, who for example are quite unable even to copy a simple geometrical figure such as a square, have no difficulty differentiating between a closed figure like a circle and an open one like a cross, and they can easily follow instructions in putting a second circle, however imperfectly drawn, inside, or outside, or even half in and half out of the experimenter's circle. Further evidence of young children's grasp of topological principles is seen in their sure knowledge of the forms into which a sphere, such as a balloon, can be deformed—i.e., sausagelike, flat sided, or dimpled figures, etc.—and those forms such as the torus or doughnut, which cannot be obtained by deformation of a sphere. Later, with the shift from the preoperational stage to the stage of concrete operations at age 6 or 7, the child learns to handle relations of order—seriation, transitivity, reciprocal relationships, and the rest to which I have already referred. Only with the approach of adolescence does he spontaneously utilize the propositional algebraic structures which are the oldest development in the history of mathematics.

What finally are the implications of Piaget's work for fields other than psychology and mathematics? Certainly they have a major bearing upon education.

If Piaget is correct—and much work now substantiates his empirical findings at least in broad outline—methods of education will be most effective when they are attuned to the patterns of thought which are natural to a child of the age concerned. It may not be true that you can teach a child *anything* if your approach is correct, but it does look as if you can teach him a great deal more than anyone might have guessed. Of course, teachers long before Piaget recognized intuitively that a child learned better when problems were approached at a concrete rather than at an abstract level. But there is more to it than that. Bruner, at Harvard, and others in this country are attempting to find ways to introduce children to some of the abstract ideas of mathematics—for example, the algebraic concept of squaring a number—by concrete, geometric models. They hope thus possibly to accelerate a child's progress—a goal which Piaget has his reservations about. Perhaps the most dramatic evidence of a revolution which owes a great deal of its impetus to Piaget is the new elementary school mathematics, in which children even in the lower grades are being taught, and learning, and actually enjoying learning basic arithmetical and geometrical ideas introduced via set theory, which most of their parents have never heard of.

I could not better conclude this appreciation of Piaget than by quoting from William James (1890) who wrote 75 years ago in his famous *Principles of Psychology* as follows: "To the infant, sounds, sights, touches and pains form probably one unanalyzed bloom of confusion [p. 496]." We can now go beyond the philosopher's speculations and describe in some detail how the unanalyzed "bloom of confusion" of the infant becomes the world of the child—in which not only objects, but time, space, causality and the rest acquire a coherent organization. And we owe this achievement in large measure to the analyses of Jean Piaget.

REFERENCES

BRUNER, J. S. Inhelder and Piaget's *The growth of logical thinking*. I. A psychologist's viewpoint. *British Journal of Psychology*, 1959, **50**, 363–370.

FLAVELL, J. H. Historical and bibliographic note. In W. Kessen & Clementina Kuhlman (Eds.), Thought in the young child. *Monographs of the Society for Research in Child Development*, 1962, **27**(2, Whole No. 83).

FLAVELL, J. H. *The developmental psychology of Jean Piaget*. Princeton, N.J.: Van Nostrand, 1963.

HUNT, J. McV. *Intelligence and experience*. New York: Ronald Press, 1961.

INHELDER, BARBEL. Some aspects of Piaget's genetic approach to cognition. In W. Kessen & Clementina Kuhlman (Eds.), Thought in the young child. *Monographs of the Society for Research in Child Development*, 1962, **27**(2, Whole No. 83).

JAMES, W. *The principles of psychology*. New York: Holt, 1890.

KOCH, S. (Ed.) *Psychology: A study of a science*. Vol. 3. *Formulations of the person and the social context*. New York: McGraw-Hill, 1959.

LAURENDEAU, MONIQUE, & PINARD, A. *Casual thinking in the child, a genetic and experimental approach*. New York: International Universities Press, 1963.

LOCKE, J. *An essay concerning human understanding*. London: Dent, 1947.

PIAGET, J. *The child's conception of the world*. New York: Harcourt, Brace, 1929.

PIAGET, J. Autobiography. In E. G. Boring (Ed.), *A history of psychology in autobiography*. Vol. 4. Worcester, Mass.: Clark Univer. Press, 1952. (a)

PIAGET, J. *The origins of intelligence in children.* (2nd ed.) New York: International Universities Press, 1952. (b)

PIAGET, J. *Logic and psychology.* New York: Basic Books, 1957.

RIESEN, A. H. The development of visual perception in man and chimpanzee. *Science,* 1947, **106,** 107–108.

RUSSELL, B. *A history of western philosophy.* New York: Simon & Schuster, 1945.

WOHLWILL, J. F. Developmental studies of perception. *Psychological Bulletin,* 1960, **57,** 249–288.

WOHLWILL, J. F. From perception to inference: A dimension of cognitive development. In W. Kessen and Clementina Kuhlman (Eds.), Thought in the young child. *Monographs of the Society for Research in Child Development,* 1962, **27**(2, Whole No. 83).

WOLFF, P. H. The developmental psychologies of Jean Piaget and psychoanalysis. *Psychological Issues,* 1960, **2**(1, Whole No. 5).

20
INTELLIGENCE—WHY IT GROWS*

JOHN L. HORN

ONE OF THE oldest and most thoroughly-studied concepts in psychology is the concept of intelligence. Yet the term "intelligence" still escapes precise definition. There are so many different kinds of behavior that are indicative of intelligence that identifying the essence of them all has seemed virtually impossible. However, some recent research indicates that much of the diversity seen in expressions of intelligence can be understood in terms of a relatively small number of concepts. What's more, this research has also given us insight into understanding where intelligence originates; how it develops; and why and when it increases or decreases.

Studies of the interrelationships among human abilities indicate that there are two basic types of intelligence: *fluid* intelligence and *crystallized* intelligence. Fluid intelligence is rather formless; it is relatively independent of education and experience; and it can "flow into" a wide variety of intellectual activities. Crystallized intelligence, on the other hand, is a precipitate out of experience. It results when fluid intelligence is "mixed" with what can be called "the intelligence of the culture." Crystallized intelligence increases with a person's experience, and with the education that provides new methods and perspectives for dealing with that experience.

These two major kinds of intelligence are composed of more elementary abilities, called "primary" mental abilities. The number of these primaries is small. Only about 30 can be accepted as really well-established. But with just these 30 primaries, we can explain much of the person-to-person variation commonly observed in reasoning, thinking, problem-solving, inventing, and understanding. Since several thousand tests have been devised to measure various aspects of intelligence, this system of primaries represents a very considerable achievement in parsimony. In much the same way that the chemical elements are organized according to the Periodic Law, these primary mental abilities fall into the patterns labeled fluid and crystallized intelligence.

Fluid Intelligence

What follows are some examples of the kinds of abilities that define fluid intelligence—and some of the tests that measure this kind of intelligence.

Induction is the ability to discover a general rule from several particular incidents and then apply this rule to cover a new incident.

For example, if a person observes the characteristics of a number of people who are members of a particular club or lodge, he might discover the rule by which membership is determined (even when this rule is highly secret information). He might then apply this rule to obtain an invitation to membership!

Among the tests that measure induction ability is the letter series. Given some letters in a series like

A C F J O —

the task is to provide the next letter. Of course, the test can be used only with people who know the alphabet, and this rules out illiterates and most children. We can't eliminate the influence of accumulated learning from even the purest examples of fluid intelligence.

Figural Relations refers to the ability to notice changes or differences in shapes and use this awareness to identify or produce one element missing from a pattern.

What figure fits into the lower right? (Answer: a square with two dots.)

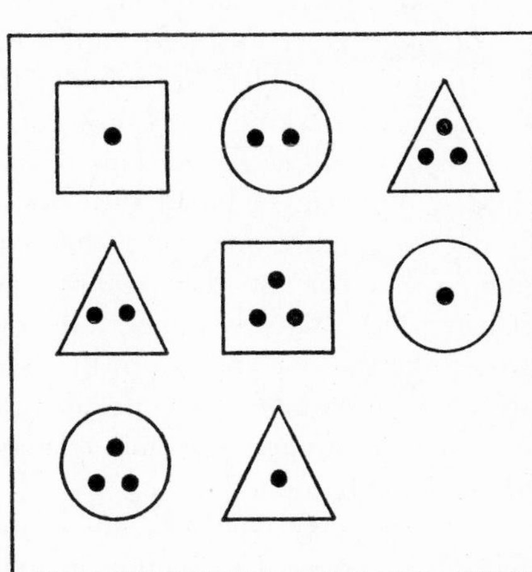

An everyday example of intelligence in figural relations is the ability to navigate cloverleaf and expressway turnoff patterns—an ability that may mean as much for adequate adjustment today as skill in finding one's way through a virgin forest had in the days of Daniel Boone. This ability also has ready application in interior decorating and in jobs where maps (or aerial views) must be compared a good deal—as by cartographers, navigators, pilots, meteorologists, and tourists.

Span of Apprehension is the ability to recognize and retain awareness of the immediate environment. A simple test is memory span: Several digits or other symbols are presented briefly, and the task is to reproduce them later, perhaps in reverse order. Without this ability, remembering a telephone number long enough to dial it would be impossible.

Other primary abilities that help define fluid intelligence include:

General Reasoning (example: estimating how long it would take to do several errands around town);

Semantic Relations (example: enjoying a pun on common words);

Deductive Reasoning, or the ability to reason from the general to the particular (example: noting that the wood of fallen trees rots and concluding that one should cover—for example, paint—wooden fence posts before inserting them into the ground);

Associative Memory, or the ability to aid memory by observing the relationships between separate items (example: remembering the way to grandmother's house by associating various landmarks en route, or remembering the traits of different people by association with their faces).

Crystallized Intelligence

Most of what we call intelligence—for example, the ability to make good use of language or to solve complex technical problems—is actually crystallized intelligence. Here are some of the primary abilities that demonstrate the nature of this kind of intelligence:

Verbal Comprehension. This could also be called general information, since it represents a broad slice of knowledge. Vocabulary tests, current-events tests, and reading-comprehension tests all measure verbal comprehension, as do other tests that require a person to recall information about his culture. The ability is rather fully exercised when one quickly reads an article like this one and grasps the essential ideas. Verbal comprehension is also called for when a person reads news items about foreign affairs, understands their implications, and relates them to one another and to their historical backgrounds.

Experiential Evaluation is often called "common sense" or "social intelligence." Experiential evaluation includes the ability to project oneself into situations, to feel as other people feel and thereby better understand interactions among people. Everyday examples include figuring out why a conscientious foreman is not getting good results from those under him, and why people disobey traffic laws more at some intersections than at others.

One test that measures experiential evaluation in married men is the following:

Your wife has just invested time, effort, and money in a new hairdo. But it doesn't help her appearance at all. She wants your opinion. You should:

1. try to pretend that the hairdo is great;
2. state your opinion bluntly;
3. compliment her on her hairdo, but add minor qualifications; or,
4. refuse to comment.

Answer 3 is considered correct—on the grounds that husbands can't get away with answers 1 and 4, and answer 2 is likely to provoke undue strife.

Formal Reasoning is reasoning in ways that have become more or less formalized in Western cultures. An example is the syllogism, like this one:

No Gox box when in purple socks.
Jocks is a Gox wearing purple socks.
Therefore: Jocks does not now box.

The task is to determine whether or not the conclusion is warranted. (It is.)

An everyday example of formal reasoning might be to produce a well-reasoned analysis of the pros and cons of an issue presented to the United Nations. Formal reasoning, to a much greater extent than experiential evaluation or verbal comprehension, depends upon dealing with abstractions and symbols in highly structured ways.

Number Facility, the primary ability to do numerical calculations, also helps define crystallized intelligence, since to a considerable extent it reflects the quality of a person's education. In a somewhat less direct way, this quality is also represented in the primary abilities called mechanical knowledge, judgment, and associational fluency.

Semantic Relations and *General Reasoning,* listed as primary aspects of fluid intelligence, are also—when carrying a burden of learning and culture —aspects of crystallized intelligence. This points up the fact that, although fluid and crystallized intelligence represent distinct patterns of abilities, there is some overlap. This is what is known as *alternative mechanisms* in intellectual performance. In other words, a given kind of problem can sometimes be solved by exercise of different abilities.

Consider the general-reasoning primary, for example. In this, typical problems have a slightly mathematical flavor:

There are 100 patients in a hospital. Some (an even number) are one-legged, but wearing shoes. One-half of the remainder are barefooted. How many shoes are being worn?

We may solve this by using a formal algebraic equation. Set x equal to the number of one-legged patients, with $100 - x$ then being the number of two-legged patients, and $x + \frac{1}{2}(100 - x)2$ being the number of shoes worn. We don't have to invent the algebraic techniques used here. They have been passed down to us over centuries. As Keith Hayes very nicely puts it, "The culture relieves us of much of the burden of creativity by giving us access to the products of creative acts scattered thinly through the history of the species." The use of such products is an important part of crystallized intelligence.

But this problem can also be solved by a young boy who has never heard of algebra! He may reason that, if half the two-legged people are without shoes, and all the rest (an even number) are one-legged, then the shoes must average one per person, and the answer must be 100. This response, too, represents learning—but is not so much a product of education, or of the accumulated wisdom passed from one generation to the next, as is the typical product of crystallized intelligence. Fluid intelligence is composed of such relatively untutored skills.

Thus the same problem can be solved by exercise of *either* fluid intelligence *or* crystallized intelligence. We can also see the operation of such alternative mechanisms in these two problems.

ZEUS—JUPITER: :ARTEMIS—?
Answer: Phidias Coria Diana

HERE—NOW: :THERE—?
Answer: Thus Sometimes Then

The first problem is no harder to solve than the second, *provided* you have acquired a rather sophisticated knowledge of mythology. The second problem requires learning too, but no more than simply learning the language—a fact that puts native-born whites and Negroes on a relatively equal footing in dealing with problems of this sort, but places Spanish-speaking Puerto Ricans or Mexican-Americans at a disadvantage. As measures of fluid intelligence, both items are about equally good. But the first involves, to a much greater extent, crystallized intelligence gleaned from formal education or leisure reading.

Because the use of alternative mechanisms is natural in the play of human intelligence, most intelligence tests provide mixed rather than pure measures of fluid or crystallized abilities. This only reflects the way in which we usually go about solving problems—by a combination of natural wit and acquired strategies. But tests can be devised in which one type of intelligence predominates. For example, efforts to devise "culture fair" intelligence tests that won't discriminate against people from deprived educational or cultural backgrounds usually focus on holding constant the effect of crystallized capabilities—so that fluid capabilities can be more fully represented.

Now that we have roughly defined what fluid and crystallized intelligence are, let us investigate how each of them develops over time.

The infant, whose reasoning powers extend little beyond the observation that a determined howl brings food, attention, or a dry diaper, becomes the man who can solve legal problems all day, execute complicated detours to avoid the five o'clock traffic on his way home, and deliver a rousing speech to his political club in the evening. But how? To understand the intertwined development of the fluid and crystallized abilities that such activities require, we need to consider three processes essential to the development of intelligence: *anlage function,* the *acquisition of aids,* and *concept formation.*

Anlage function, which includes the complex workings of the brain and other nervous tissue, provides the physical base for all of the infant's future mental growth. ("Anlage" is a German word meaning "rudiment.") The second two factors—the aids and concepts the child acquires as he grows up—represent the building blocks that, placed on the anlage base, form the structure of adult intelligence.

The anlage function depends crucially and directly upon physiology. Physiology, in turn, depends partly on heredity, but it can also be influenced by injury, disease, poisons, drugs, and severe shock. Such influences can occur very early in life—often even in the womb. Hence it is quite possible that an individual's anlage functioning may have only a remote relationship to his hereditary potential. All we can say for sure is that the anlage process is closely tied to a physiological base.

A good everyday measure of a person's anlage functioning is his memory span (provided we can rule out the effects of anxiety, fatigue, or mental disturbance). Given a series of letters or numbers, most adults can immediately reproduce only about six or seven of them in reverse order. Some people may be able to remember 11, others as few as four, but in no case is the capacity unlimited or even very great. Memory span increases through childhood—probably on account of the increasing size and complexity of the brain—but it is not much affected by learning. This is generally true of other examples of anlage functioning.

Short-cuts to Learning

Aids are techniques that enable us to go beyond the limitations imposed by anlage functioning. An aid can, for example, extend our memory span. For example, we break up a telephone or social-security number with dashes, transforming long numbers into short, more easily recalled sets, and this takes the strain off immediate memory.

Some aids, like the rules of algebra, are taught in school. But several psychologists (notably Jean Piaget) have demonstrated that infants and children also invent their own aids in their untutored explorations of the world. In development, this process probably continues for several years.

Concepts are categories we impose on the phenomena we experience. In forming concepts, we find that otherwise dissimilar things can be regarded as "the same" in some sense because they have common properties. For instance, children learn to distinguish the features associated with "bike"—two wheels, pedaling, riding outside, etc.—from those associated with "car." Very early in a child's development, these categories may be known and represented only in terms of his own internal symbols. In time, however, the child learns to associate his personal symbols with conventional signs—that is, he learns to use language to represent what he "knows" from direct experience. Also, increased proficiency in the use of language affords opportunities to see new relations and acquire *new* concepts.

The concepts we possess at any time are a residue of previous intellectual functioning. Tests that indicate the extent of this residue may, therefore, predict the level of a persons' future intellectual development. A large vocabulary indicates a large storehouse of previously acquired concepts, so verbal ability itself is often taken as a good indication of ability to conceptualize. Many well-known tests of intelligence, especially of crystallized intelligence, are based on this rationale.

However, language is really only an indirect measure of concept awareness. Thus verbally-oriented tests can be misleading. What about the child raised in an environment where language is seldom used, but which is otherwise rich in opportunity to perceive relationships and acquire concepts (the backwoods of Illinois, or by a pond in Massachusetts)? At the extreme, what about a person who never hears the spoken word or sees the written word? He does not necessarily lack the awareness that we so glibly represent in language. Nor does he necessarily lack intelligence: A child who doesn't know the spoken or written word "key" surely understands the concept if he can distinguish a key from other small objects and use it to open a lock.

What is true of conventional language is also true of conventional aids. Lack of facility or familiarity with aids does not mean that a child has failed to develop intellectually, even though it may make him *appear* mentally slow on standard intelligence tests. Just as verbally-oriented tests penalize the child who has not had the formal schooling or proper environment to develop a large vocabulary, many tests of so-called mathematical aptitude rely heavily on the use of conventional aids taught in school—on algebraic formulas, for example. Someone who has learned few of these conventional aids will generally do poorly on such tests, but this does not mean that he lacks intelligence.

We cannot overlook the fact that an intelligent woodsman may be just as intelligent, in one sense of this term, as an intelligent college professor. The particular combination of primary abilities needed to perform well may differ in the two cases, but the basic wherewithal of intellectual competence can be the same—adequate anlage functioning, plus an awareness of the concepts and a facility with the aids relevant to dealing with the environment at hand. Daniel Boone surely needed as much intelligence to chart the unexplored forests of the frontier as today's professor needs to thread his way through the groves of academe.

Education and Intelligence

It is obvious, then, that formal education is not essential to the development of important aspects of intelligence. Barring disruption of anlage functioning by accident or illness, the child will form concepts and devise aids to progressively expand his mental grasp as he grows up, and this will occur whether he goes to school or not.

Where formal instruction *is* significant is in making such development easier—and in passing along the concepts and aids that many people have deposited into the intelligence of a culture. The schools give children awareness of concepts that they may not have had the opportunity to gain from first-hand experience—the ability to recognize an Australian platypus, for example, without ever having seen one, or a knowledge of how the caste system works in India. Aids, too, are taught in school. A child well-armed with an array of mathematical formulas will likely be able to solve a problem faster and more accurately than one who must work it out completely on his own. Indeed, some problems simply cannot be solved without mathematical aids. Since the acquisition of both concepts and aids is cumulative, several years of formal education can put one child well ahead of another one, unschooled, who has roughly the same intellectual potential.

Education can thus play a powerful role in developing intelligence. Too often, however, it doesn't. Even in school, some children in perfectly good health and physical condition fail to develop, or develop slowly. Some even seem to be mentally stunted by their school experience. Why? What sorts of experiences can foster—or retard—the developmental processes of concept-formation and aid-formation in the school environment?

Even though we are only beginning to find answers in this area, it is already clear that learning can be speeded up, slowed down, or brought almost to a dead halt by a variety of school experiences. On the favorable side, abilities improve by *positive transfer*. Learning one skill makes it easier to learn a related one. A student who already knows Spanish, for example, will find it easier to learn Portuguese. And positive transfer also works in less obvious ways. There is even evidence to suggest that new learning is facilitated simply by having learned before—by a sort of learning how to learn.

But other factors too can affect the course of learning, and these factors are particularly prominent in the context of our formal educational system. For example, merely having the *opportunity* to learn may depend on both previous learning and previous opportunity to learn. Thus, even if his native potential and level of self-education are good, the person who has not had the opportunity to finish high school has a poor chance of going on to college.

Labeling operates in a similar way. If a person is labeled as lacking in ability, he may receive no further chance to develop. Kenneth B. Clark states this very well:

> If a child scores low on an intelligence test because he cannot read and then is not taught to read because he has a low score, then such a child is being imprisoned in an *iron circle* and becomes the victim of an educational self-fulfilling prophecy.

Avoidance-learning is similar. This is learning not to learn. Punishment in a learning situation—being humiliated in school, for example—may make a child "turn off." Problem-solving may become such a threat that he will avoid all suggestion of it. Since an active, inquiring curiosity is at the root of mental growth, avoidance-learning can very seriously retard intellectual development. Moreover, since a child typically expresses avoidance by aggression, lack of attention, sullenness, and other behavior unacceptable to educators and parents, they—being human—may react by shutting the child out of further learning situations, and thus create another kind of iron circle.

Labeling, lack of opportunity, and avoidance-learning affect the development of both fluid and crystallized intelligence. Both depend upon accultural influences—the various factors that provide, or block, chances for learning. And both depend upon anlage function and thus upon physiological influences as well. However, fluid intelligence depends more on physiological factors, and crystallized intelligence more on acculturational ones. It is the interplay of these factors throughout a child's development that produces the fact that fluid and crystallized intelligence can be separated in adult intellectual performances. But how does this separation arise?

A Climate for Growth

In many respects, the opportunities to maintain good physiological health are the same for all in our society. The climate, air pollution, water, the chances of injury, and other hazards in the physical environment do not vary greatly. Even the social environments are similar in many ways. We acquire similar language skills, go to schools that have similar curricula, have a similar choice of television programs, and so on. In this sense, the most advantaged and the most disadvantaged child have some of the same opportunities to develop anlage functioning, and to acquire concepts and aids.

Moreover, we should be careful about how we use the term "disadvantaged." We do not yet know what is superior in all respects, at every age level, for the development of all the abilities that go into intelligence. At one stage, what seems a "bad" home may give intelligence a greater impetus than an apparently "good" home. It may be, for instance, that in early childhood "lax" parents allow more scope for development. In later development, "stimulating" and "responsible" (but restrictive?) parents might be better. Some of the intellectual leaders of every period of history and of every culture have developed in environments that, according to many definitions, would have had to be classified as "disadvantaged."

It is clear, however, that favorable conditions for the development of intelligence are not the same for all. To avoid the iron circle, to gain opportunities to go on, children have to display the right abilities at the right times. To some extent, this depends on early and basic endowment. Intelligent parents may provide good heredity, good environmental conditions for learning, and good stimulation and encouragement. But the opportunities a child gets, and what he meets them with, can also be quite independent of his own characteristics. His opportunities depend on such haphazard factors as the neighborhood in which he lives, the kind of schooling available, his mother's interests and his father's income, the personality qualities of the teachers he happens to get, and the attitudes and actions of his playmates.

Thus, through a child's years of growth and education, societal influences can produce an effect that is largely independent of those produced by physiological influences. In an infant, cultural influences could not have accumulated independently of the physiological. But as children pass through preschool and school, their awareness of concepts and use of aids becomes more evident, and the influence of acculturation is felt and exhibited. The probable shape of future learning and opportunity becomes more clear. The child who has already moved ahead tends to be ready to move farther ahead, and to be accepted for such promotion. Crystallized intelligence feeds the growth of crystallized intelligence. By contrast, the child who has not moved ahead, for whatever reasons, tends to be less ready and to be viewed as such. His acquisition of the lore of the culture proceeds at a decelerating rate. This is how two children with roughly the same hereditary potential can grow apart in their acquisition of crystallized intelligence. Among adults, then, we should expect to find great variation in the crystallized pattern of abilities—and we do!

The cultural influences that can produce this kind of inequality operate almost independently of physiological factors, however. Thus, the child who fails to progress rapidly in learning the ever-more-abstruse concepts and aids of crystallized intelligence may still acquire many concepts and aids of a more common type. And if he is lucky in avoiding accidents and maintaining good health, this kind of development can be quite impressive. His intellectual growth may even surpass that of a seemingly more favored child who is slowed down by illness or injury. Thus, two children with about the same hereditary makeup can grow apart in fluid intelligence, too. The result is a wide range of variation in adult fluid intelligence—a range even wider than we would expect to be produced by differences in heredity alone.

21
FEEDBACK DELAY AND THE TEACHING MACHINE*

YVONNE BRACKBILL
JOHN E. WAGNER
and
DOROTHY WILSON

The operations of a teaching machine make simultaneous use of several learning principles that have been studied to varying extents as separate problems in the psychology of human learning. One such principle, a standard feature of teaching machines, is an active rather than passive mode of learning. The student's active participation is required when he learns via a teaching machine; he is not allowed such passive modes as unrelieved reading or listening to other students recite. Active participation is a condition of learning that has been studied extensively, and the conclusion that it is superior to passive learning holds for a wide variety of learning situations.

Another condition that is also a universal feature of teaching machines is immediate feedback. Under teaching machine instruction the student finds out immediately upon his making a response whether that response was correct or not. The more traditional instructional procedures are typified by delayed feedback, so that the student must wait a matter of seconds, minutes, or even days to know how he fared. In contrast to the principle of active participation, length of interval between response and feedback is a condition that has not been investigated extensively in human learning. Furthermore,

---

* From *Psychology in the Schools,* 1964, *1,* 148–156. Reprinted with permission from the authors and Psychology Press, Inc.

This investigation was supported in part by Research Grant M-5994 awarded by the National Institutes of Health to the first author.

The authors are very grateful for the cooperation and facilities provided by Rolland G. Walters, Helen Chancellor, and Dorothy W. Wills, Englewood Public Schools, Colorado.

until recently, the effect of feedback interval on *retention* has not been investigated at all. The current, widespread belief that immediate feedback improves the efficiency of human learning is a simple extension of results from rat studies. The extension is unwarranted, as we shall see. The further inference, that immediate feedback must be good for retention, if it's good for learning, is also incorrect.

Feedback, Reinforcement, and Knowledge of Results. Feedback interval can be defined as the length of time intervening between the subject's response to a learning or test time and the occurrence of an informative event that tells him whether his response was right, wrong, or somwhere in between.

The subject's response may relate to an item he is trying to learn or be an answer to a question on a test; it may come at the instigation of a real flesh-and-blood teacher or a mechanical teacher. In form, the response may be predominantly motor or verbal, and either overt, as in class recitation, or covert, as when the student formulates an answer to himself.

Similarly, the informative event or feedback may be classified according to a variety of physical and psychological attributes. Its one essential attribute is that it gives the student information about the correctness or incorrectness of his response. In the type of research that we are considering, the informative event has been called both reinforcement and knowledge of results. The term *reinforcement* is generally used when referring to the feedback of information plus a small, tangible reward—or the withholding of a reward when the response is incorrect. *Knowledge of results* is used when referring to the feedback of information only. In this paper, *feedback* is being used as equivalent to both reinforcement and knowledge of results.

It is important to note, before proceeding, that the traditional distinction between reinforcement and knowledge of results reflects an apparent difference rather than a real one, and hence, that the literature on reinforcement in human learning is just as applicable to our discussion and to classroom application as is the literature on knowledge of results. Traditionally, the choice of one term or the other has depended upon the motivational characteristics of the experimental subject—or more precisely, upon the amount of extrinsic motivation that must be supplied the subject in order to get him to learn the task at hand. If the learner comes to the learning situation with a "built-in" motivation to learn, the experimenter need supply him only with knowledge of results. Normal adults and older children are such self-rewarding or self-motivating subjects. If, on the other hand, the learner is not intrinsically motivated, the experimenter must supply some incentive along with knowledge of results. Otherwise, learning will proceed slowly or not at all. This is always the case for lower animals, and is generally the case for very young children. It is also likely to be the case for those older children who come from homes in which educational achievement is poorly esteemed.

The Effect of Feedback Delay during Learning on Learning Efficiency.

The problem of the amount of time intervening between response and feedback has a long history of research in the psychology of animal learning. In his review of the literature on this problem, Renner (in press) indicates that the first study was published in 1913. Throughout the intervening 50 years, the results of such research have demonstrated without question that in lower animals, learning efficiency decreases the longer the feedback delay. Under some conditions, with delays of only a few seconds, learning may not occur at all.

It is this finding, based largely on the performance of rats, that has been used to support the claim that teaching machines must incorporate immediate feedback in order to be maximally effective for human learning.

Rats and men have yielded surprisingly similar results in terms of a variety of simple responses to learning and conditioning situations. But there are other, more complex aspects of behavior for which it is foolhardy to expect parallel results across genera. It appears that the human's response to feedback delay involves just such complex aspects of behavior.

In the particular case we are considering, the complexity seems to arise from the human being's distinctive ability to use language in regulating his present behavior with respect to his remembrance of past events and his anticipation of future events. No lower animal has such an ability; neither, of course, does the infant or very young child.

Physiologically speaking, even the newborn human can "estimate" the length of a passage of time with astounding precision—a phenomenon that may have all manner of adaptive significance, but is psychologically of little value to him until the day it gains real cognitive significance through the mediation of language (Krachkovskaia, 1959). Even when he is a year or two old, he cannot be quieted when he is very hungry by explaining to him that his food will be ready in three mintues. Nor can he be effectively punished for a misdeed that occurred five minutes before its detection, for there is no way of getting him to associate the punishment with that particular behavior of five minutes past. Instead, any such punishment will have the (frequently unwanted) effect of modifying future occurrences of that response which immediately preceded the punishment. In short, for the organism without language proficiency, the informational and motivational effects of rewards and punishments are limited to the immediate present.

The situation changes once the child has acquired sufficient language facility to span time cognitively, to link meaningful but temporally nonconsecutive events, and to unlink meaningless but temporally consecutive events. From this point on, the time delays of ordinary life probably have little if any detrimental effect in the shaping of his behavior. The nine-year old may be clever enough, in the execution of a misdeed, to escape detection for several hours, but when he is found out and punished, there is, by virtue of the verbal exchange between him and his mother, no question in his mind about the reason for the punishment. He knows that the punishment is not contingent upon his immediately preceding behavior, but upon the earlier deed. Furthermore, there is good reason to suppose that, if the punishment is effective at all in changing his future behavior, it will be just as effective under these circumstances as it would have been if administered immediately following the crime.

As adults, our real life behavior is largely governed by a complex system of delayed reinforcements and delayed knowledge of results. However, this does not prevent our behaving effectively nor learning effectively even under long delays, for as normal adults our behavior, particularly with respect to the bridging of events over time, is verbally mediated and verbally regulated. This enables us to do the two things essential to effective learning under delayed feedback: to couple related events that are separated in time and to prevent the coupling of consecutive events that are unrelated. First, we can and do find out which responses were the crucial ones in bringing about reinforcement. (The bonus check was for supervision of a student teacher two months ago.) Second, we can and do ascertain the extent of the relationship (frequently zero) between the reinforcement and our behavior immediately preceding it. (Being paid a bonus by the school administration has no relation to asking the secretary for checks.)

In view of these common sense considerations, one might expect that humans in a laboratory learning situation would respond to delay more like humans in real life than like rats in a laboratory learning situation. And this does seem to be the case. Of the 13 experiments on human learning reviewed by Renner, roughly three out of four show that delay of reinforcement or delay in knowledge of results has no detrimental effect on learning—even with feedback interval as long as one week. To this count can be added seven experiments of our own, not included in Renner's review. Of the 14 learning-score comparisons between immediate—and delayed—feedback groups, 11 show no difference in learning efficiency, one shows a difference in favor of immediate feedback, and two show a difference in favor of delayed feedback.

It seems clear from present considerations that unqualified generalization from rats to humans on the effects of feedback delay is not warranted, that feedback delay is not a crucial variable in human learning efficiency, and that the ability of a teaching machine to give immediate knowledge of results is not a valid reason for preferring automated instruction to the old-fashioned garden or classroom variety.

The Effects of Feedback Delay during Learning on Retention of the Learned Material. Of the two processes that constitute the very core of education, retention must necessarily be considered more important than learning—for what is the sense of teaching anything if it is not remembered? The goal of education is not simply to teach students, but to teach them so they stay taught—so that they may apply educationally the solution of more acquired skills and knowledge directly to life's problems or may transfer them to advanced educational problems. Educators and laymen alike would consider ridiculous any proposal to use an instructional method known to maximize learning efficiency and to minimize retention.

Strangely enough, however—particularly in view of our knowledge that learning and retention are not always affected in the same way by the same variable—while learning has received an enormous amount of attention in both applied and laboratory research, retention has received very little. From the hundreds of studies and demonstrations concerning automated instruction, the reader is probably acquainted with many that bear on learning, but can he recall a single study showing what happens to retention following automated learning? Similarly, although the effects on learning of the single variable, feedback delay, has a research history of 60 years, the more practically important problem, the effects on retention of feedback delay during learning is, relatively speaking, in its infancy. The last five years have seen the publication of a few studies dealing with the retention of motor skills following feedback delay during learning (Lavery & Suddon, 1962; Suddon & Lavery, 1962), but the only systematic studies that have focussed upon the retention of verbal material have been those from our own laboratory (Brackbill, Bravos, & Starr, 1962; Brackbill, Isaacs, & Smelkinson, 1962; Brackbill & Kappy, 1962; and Brackbill, Boblitt, Davlin, & Wagner, 1963). All of these have been done with elementary school children as subjects.

From the first of these studies, there emerged an unexpected result: feedback delay during learning actually improved retention of the learned material, while immediate feedback during learning impaired retention. This experiment has been followed by 11 more; all of them verify the results obtained initially. The results have been shown to hold up for both meaningful and meaningless material, for kindergartners as well as third grade children, for difficult as well as easy tasks, and for learning situations free of distraction as well as those marked by distraction and interference.

In all our experiments, however, the learning material has been a sort that only distantly approximates that learned in the typical school room. The purpose of the experiment to be reported here was to extend the generalizability and usefulness to education of the previous findings by using learning material that is more nearly representative of elementary school curricula. The subjects' task in this experiment was to learn 18 French words via an apparatus simulating a teaching machine. One group of subjects learned them under a condition of immediate feedback, while the other group learned them under a condition of delayed feedback. The experiment was comparable to its predecessors in terms of basic experimental design, procedure, apparatus, and relevant characteristics of the subjects.

METHOD

Experimental design. Thirty-two subjects were randomly assigned to one of two learning conditions: immediate feedback vs. delayed feedback. After learning had been completed, the two groups were further subdivided: one-half of each group was tested for retention one day later, while the other half was tested one week later. Therefore, in the analysis of the learning data, there are four groups of eight subjects each.

Subjects. The subjects were third grade boys with a median age of 8.8 years, and a median I.Q. of 110, as determined by the California Mental Maturity Test. They spoke English as a native language; none had been exposed to French. The subjects were obtained from two elementary schools located in a middle class suburban area. They were seen in individual sessions in a private room in their school.

Experimental Material. The material for the learning task consisted of 18 English words and their French equivalents. In each case the French equivalents were exactly three letters in length, since pilot work had shown that longer unfamiliar words were somewhat too difficult for the subjects and circumstances of our experiment.

On each learning trial two stimulus cards were presented. One card contained the English word and its correct French equivalent; the other card contained the same English word and an incorrect "French equivalent." Thus, for example, two cards appeared as follows:

Street RUE	Street CAS

The goal was, of course, to learn the correct French translation of each of the 18 English words.

The "degree of incorrectness" of the incorrect word ranged from an entirely wrong word, as illustrated above, to an error of one letter, as *emi* for *ami.*

At the beginning of the experiment, the child was informed that one of the French words meant the same thing as the English word, and that one did not. Then, on each learning trial he was asked to pronounce the French word he thought correct and to press the lever adjacent to that stimulus card. (Lever pressing was for the purpose of activating delay timers and other automatic equipment.) Whenever the subject chose the correct French word, then, either immediately or after the 10 second delay interval, a pilot lamp above that stimulus card flashed on, a buzz was heard, and a marble dropped into a plastic box. Whenever he made an incorrect response, and after the appropriate time interval, a click sounded, and the lamp above the correct word flashed on. Therefore, the subject received knowledge of results whether he made a correct or incorrect response; but in the former event, he also received a small token reward. (The accumulated marbles could be exchanged at the end of the session for a 10-cent toy of the child's choice.) The items were presented in random orders, with a 20-second interval between presentations. The left-right position of the correct card was also randomized.

Two sessions, held on consecutive days, were devoted to learning. Relearning, our measure of retention, took place for one-half the subjects on the third consecutive day, i.e., one day following the second learning session. For the remaining subjects, retention was tested seven days following the second learning session. For both learning and relearning, in order to control differential overlearning of items, each item was withdrawn from subsequent presentation after it had been responded to correctly three consecutive times. (A detailed account of the apparatus and procedure is given in Brackbill & Kappy, 1962.)

RESULTS

Learning. Two measures of learning efficiency were used: the number of errors made and the number of trials taken to reach the criterion of learning, three consecutive correct responses to each item. The average or mean number of errors made by subjects learning under the immediate feedback condition was 24.06, while the mean number of errors made by subjects learning under a 10-second feedback delay was 25.56. The mean numbers of trials to criterion were 48.12 and 47.25 for the immediate and delay groups, respectively. Neither difference between groups is statistically significant, t being less than 1.00 in each case. It is apparent that feedback delay did not reduce learning efficiency. This confirms the general finding of our previous studies.

Retention. It will be recalled that the measure of retention, relearning, took place under identical conditions for all subjects, differences in test-retest interval aside. Thus, any significant differences between groups tested at the same time are attributable to the earlier, experimentally imposed differences in learning conditions.

Average relearning scores for the four experimental groups are shown in the upper half of Table 1. It is apparent that subjects who had learned under immediate feedback made more errors in relearning and took more trials to relearn the material than did the delay subjects. This is true for subjects tested one day after learning and also for those tested seven days after learning.

The lower half of Table 1 contains the average saving scores for the four experimental groups. These are defined as the number of learning errors minus the number of relearning errors, and the number of trials taken to reach learning criterion minus the number of trials taken to reach relearning criterion. The two sets of saving scores were calculated because they are influenced less than are relearning scores by individual differences in learning ability per se. Again, subjects who had learned under immediate reinforcement have lower saving scores (retained less) than did the delay subjects. There is clear agreement, then, among the results of all four measures: to learn material under immediate feedback is to impair its retention.

Learning, Retention, and Item Difficulty. As mentioned above, the type of error incorporated into the incorrect "French word" was varied systematically over the 18 items. Specifically, there were three samples of each of six types of errors: (1) reversal of two consecutive vowels, (2) substitution of an incorrect vowel for the correct one, (3) substitution of an incorrect consonant for the correct one, (4) reversal of vowel and consonant, (5) sequence reversal of two nonconsecutive consonants, and (6) substitution of an incorrect "word" for the correct one.

TABLE 1

Mean Retention Scores Obtained from the Four Experimental Groups (N = 8/Group)

	Interval between Learning and Relearning			
	1 Day		*7 Days*	
	Feedback Condition during Learning		*Feedback Condition during Learning*	
Measure of retention	*Immediate*	*Delayed*	*Immediate*	*Delayed*
Mean no. errors in relearning	23.50	14.12	18.50	8.25
Mean no. trials to relearn	33.00	19.25	26.12	11.25
Saving in errors: Learning errors Minus relearning errors	2.75	13.19	3.38	13.25
Saving in trials: Trials to learn minus trials to relearn	17.75	33.28	17.62	30.62

An analysis was made of the difficulty of learning each item according to the type of error it incorporated. This analysis showed that type of error did affect learning difficulty, but that this effect was equal in direction and amount for both the immediate and delayed feedback groups. The combined rank order of learning difficulty according to item type is shown in the paragraph above: items containing a reversal of two consecutive vowels were the most difficult to learn; items in which a whole new "word" was substituted were the least difficult to learn.

A similar analysis was made of the effect of item difficulty on relearning. It was found that for those subjects who had learned under immediate feedback, degree of item difficulty affected retention as much as it had affected learning. These subjects made 10.5 times as many errors in relearning the most difficult triad of items as they did in relearning the easiest three. However, for the subjects who had learned under delayed feedback, the results were quite different. For these subjects, the items that had been difficult to learn were retained just as well as the items that had been easy to learn. These results confirm previous findings (Brackbill, Bravos, & Starr, 1962), and indicate that, other things equal, the more difficult the learning material, the more important it is for its retention that the material be learned under delayed rather than immediate feedback.

CONCLUSION

The experiment just described has shown that delayed feedback is just as conducive to learning efficiency as is immediate feedback. It has also shown that delayed feedback is more effective than immediate feedback for retention—much more effective, in fact, for the retention of difficult material. These results confirm all essentials in those of the earlier studies of this series, in spite of learning-material differences among them.

The uniformity of these results suggests that two conclusions may be stated with a reasonable degree of certainty. First, if it is true that the acquisition of knowledge proceeds more efficiently under machine instruction than under traditional instructional procedures, then this superiority is *not* due to the fact that the teaching machine furnishes immediate knowledge of results, contrary to the usual allegation. (See, for example, Porter, 1958; Skinner, 1958.) Second, and more important, if the retention of machine-taught material is ever found to be superior to retention following traditional instructional methods, then this superiority will be *in spite of* the fact that teaching machines furnish immediate knowledge of results.

The question that intrudes itself most saliently at this point is why an erroneous conclusion favoring immediate feedback has been perpetuated through many hundreds of teaching machine studies. In part, the answer to this question is to be found in the first sentence of this article, in which it was stated that the operations of a teaching machine make *simultaneous* use of several learning conditions. Whenever two or more variables are allowed to operate simultaneously in any situation, the outcome of that situation cannot be pinpointed to the influence of any one of those variables, because their separate contributions to the outcome are inextricably confounded. The way to increase the efficiency of the teaching machine—or any other complex learning situation—is to study the separate contribution of each of its identifiable variables, one by one. Only by identifying and weeding out the ineffective or negatively contributing variables, such as immediate feedback, can the complex be improved. This has not yet been done in teaching machine research, but it must be done and certainly can be done.

Furthermore, such systematic work must be done on human subjects, in a learning situation that at least approximates that provided by teaching machines. To generalize to the case of machine instruction from research done on lower animals—or even from research done on human subjects under conditions obviously dissimilar from teaching machine conditions—is all too frequently inaccurate.

There is also a second question, touched on earlier, that should be considered again. Why has teaching machine research concentrated its attack on the study of the learning process and ignored the study of retention? Although most variables show the same direction of effect on both learning and retention, this is not uniformly true. For example, the use of intermittent rather than regular reinforcement generally has a negative effect upon learning and a positive effect on retention and resistance to extinction. And as we have seen, the use of immediate rather than delayed feedback has no effect on learning but a negative effect on retention. Furthermore, there is no evidence that the *amount* of the effect of any given variable is of equal magnitude for both learning and retention. That is to say, if we could rank order all the variables that affect learning according to their quantitative effects or relative importance for learning efficiency, we still would not know how well that same rank order would serve the interests of retention efficiency.

In short, it is not prudent to overlook the singular importance to education of the retention process, nor is it wise to assume that research on learning yields information about retention.

REFERENCES

Brackbill, Y., Boblitt, W. E., Davlin, D., & Wagner, J. E. Amplitude of response and the delay-retention effect. *J. exp. Psychol.*, 1963, *66*, 57–64.

Brackbill, Y., Bravos, A., & Starr, R. H. Delay-improved retention of a difficult task. *J. comp. physiol. Psychol.*, 1962, *55*, 947–952.

Brackbill, Y., Isaacs, R. B., & Smelkinson, N. Delay of reinforcement and the retention of unfamiliar, meaningless material. *Psychol. Rep.*, 1962, *11*, 553–554.

Brackbill, Y., & Kappy, M. S. Delay of reinforcement and retention. *J. comp. physiol. Psychol.*, 1962, *55*, 14–18.

Krachkovskaia, M. V. Reflex changes in the leukocyte count of newborn infants in relation to food intake. *Pavlov J. high. nerv. Act.*, 1959, *9*, 193–199.

Lavery, J. J., & Suddon, F. H. Retention of simple motor skills as a function of the number of trials by which KR is delayed. *Percept. mot. Skills*, 1962, *15*, 231–237.

Porter, D. Teaching machines. *Harvard Grad. Sch. Educ. Ass. Bull.*, 1958, *3*, No. 1.

Renner, K. E. Delay of Reinforcement. *Psychol. Bull.*, in press.

Skinner, B. F. Teaching machines. *Science*, 1958, *128*, 969–977.

Suddon, F. H., & Lavery, J. J. The effect of amount of training on retention of a simple motor skill with 0- and 5-trial delays of knowledge of results. *Canad. J. Psychol.*, 1962, *16*, 312–317.

22

EXPERIENCE AND THE DEVELOPMENT OF MOTIVATION: SOME REINTERPRETATIONS*

J. McV. HUNT

A RECENT ISSUE of the *Saturday Evening Post* carried a cartoon that some of you may nave noted. It depicts a boy entering his house, perhaps from school, where his father is sitting with his paper. The boy appears to be fixing his father with an accusing glare. The punch line reads, "Somebody goofed, I'm improperly motivated."

This cartoon depicts the vantage point from which I have been examining what we think we know about the relation between experience and motivation. When a child's behavior fails to fit the standards somebody in our society holds for him, it is pretty well agreed among us who are supposed to be experts on human nature that "somebody goofed." And that somebody is usually considered to be a parent.

The question is: what is the proper formula? If one examines the accruing evidence relevant to what has been the dominant conception of the experiential sources of motivation, one can hardly escape the conclusion that this conceptual scheme needs some revisions. If we based our child-rearing entirely on our dominant theory of motivational development, we would probably goof as often and as badly as run-of-the-mill parents.

Today I wish, first, to remind you of three of the most basic and general of the propositions in that theory of motivation which has been dominant for the past 30 to 40 years. These are propositions which, although stated in somewhat varied forms, have been shared by both psychoanalysts and academic behavior theorists. Secondly, I wish to cite evidence which calls these propositions into question, and thirdly, to suggest, tentatively, three new

---

* From *Child Development,* 1960, *31,* 489–504. Reprinted with permission from the author and the Society for Research in Child Development.

Earlier versions of this paper were read at the Eleventh Annual Institute in Psychiatry and Neurology of the Veterans Administration Hospital at North Little Rock, Arkansas, 27 February 1959, and at colloquia of the Department of Psychiatry at the Medical School of Colorado. The paper was prepared in connection with a survey of the implications of the work in behavioral science for childbearing which has been supported by the Russell Sage Foundation.

interpretative principles which appear to me to be congruent with a large number of facts and which have interesting implications.

Our conceptions of motivation have traditionally been concerned with three large questions: (*a*) Why does an organism or person become active? (*b*) Why does the organism or person act one way rather than another? and (*c*) How do you get the organism or person to change his behavior to something conceived to be more desirable or appropriate?

THE DOMINANT THEORY

Drive

According to our dominant theory, it is claimed, first of all, that "all behavior is motivated," and that the aim or function of every instinct, defense, action, or habit is to reduce or eliminate stimulation or excitation within the nervous system. It is not easy to state when this view was first presented. Signs of it appear in the seventh chapter of Freud's *Interpretation of Dreams* (*15*) in 1900, and the idea is full-blown in his paper entitled *Instincts and Their Vicissitudes* (*17*) in 1915. The idea also appears in Woodworth's *Dynamic Psychology* (*68*), published in 1918, where the term *drive* was first introduced into the glossary of American psychology. The idea was full-blown in Dashiell's *Fundamentals of Objective Psychology* (*11*) in 1928.

Although Freud (*17*) believed that the source of motivation lay outside the domain of psychology in physiology, American psychologists, untroubled by such limits to their domain, have gone on to answer the first question concerning what motivates organisms to become active by saying that they are *driven*. Organisms have been conceived to be driven, first by those so-called primary inner stimuli which arise from homeostatic imbalances or needs. With no shame whatsoever, psychologists have long cited the evidence from the work of such physiologists as Claude Bernard (*5*) and his successors, and especially of Walter B. Cannon (*10*), and also of the psychologist Curt Richter (*59*) to document this answer. Organisms are driven, second, by various forms of intense and painful external stimulation. It has been assumed that these two forms of stimulation arouse an inner state of excitement which has usually been called *drive*.

It is also assumed, as the proposition that "all behavior is motivated" implies, that the organism would be inactive unless driven by either inner or outer stimuli. Freud (*17*) has been highly explicit about this assumption, and the assumption lies implicitly behind the notion of conditioned or learned drive in behavior theory and behind the traumatic notion of anxiety in psychoanalysis. It is obvious, of course, that animals and people are sometimes active when it is hard to see how either homeostatic drive or painful external stimulation could be operative. It is then assumed that some of the weak, innocuous stimuli present must have been associated in the past with either painful stimuli or homeostatic needs. In such a way the weak stimuli which are present must have acquired the capacity to arouse the drive, often now called anxiety by psychologists as well as psychoanalysts, and it is such acquired or conditioned drive that is conceived to activate the organism.

Such conditioned drive or anxiety has been well demonstrated in the laboratory. Before World War II, Miller (*45, 46*) at Yale showed that rats which had been repeatedly shocked in a white box would, when later returned to the white box, make an effort to escape. Moreover, in the course of these efforts, they could be got to learn new skills such as that of turning a wheel to open a door. Rats which had not been shocked in the white box made no such efforts to escape. In another demonstration, Solomon and Wynne (*64*) have shown that dogs which have experienced a tone or a buzzer paired a few times with a subtetanizing shock will run away from that tone or buzzer for hundreds of trials, with the average reaction time of starting continuing to decrease through 600 such trials. In my own work (*31*) rats fed irregularly in infancy ate more than their littermate controls and sometimes (*32*) hoarded food in adulthood after a period without food. Here, as I conceived it, the cues of hunger were conditioned to intense hunger excitement during the infantile experience. In adulthood the conditioned hunger drive facilitated the rate of eating and, sometimes, hoarding.

Such work has demonstrated that this notion of conditioned drive or anxiety, which goes back to the work of Bechterev (*2*) and Watson and Raynor (*67*), has a solid basis in reality. But in what has been the dominant theory of motivation, as epitomized by Freud's (*18*) later traumatic theory of anxiety, and by the Hull (*30*) and Dollard-Miller (*13, 47*) theory of acquired drives, conditioning is conceived to be the only way in which an organism can become fearful of innocuous stimuli.

Habit

Habit has been the answer to the second question concerned with why an animal or person acts one way rather than another. The organism is controlled by the habits which have served to reduce drive in the past when that organism was in the presence of the inner and outer drive stimuli, and the cue stimuli impinging upon him at any given moment now. Under the term *habit,* I am including psychoanalytic modes, which have supposedly been fixated during infancy in the course of either too much gratification or too much frustration, and I am including also ego-defenses, or anxiety equivalents, and cathexes, as well as the instrumental responses and traits commonly investigated in psychological laboratories.

Changing behavior has been conceived to be a matter of motivating the organism with either punishment or homeostatic need to make the desired behavior which can then be reinforced by arranging for it to reduce the drive aroused by the punishment or the need. Although the conditions and conceptions of psychotherapy in the clinic differ considerably from the conditions and conceptions of the behavior theorist investigating learning in laboratory animals, in either case it is conceived that motivation is a necessity, and motivation means changing the emotional or drive conditions which are quite extrinsic to either the instrumental behavior or the cognitive, informational processes concerned.

This dominant theory has been a conceptual edifice of large dimensions and of considerable detail. It has provided a plausible account of both personality development and social motives. The experimental facts of homeostasis and of conditioned drive and fear are sound. Nevertheless, it has become more and more evident in the past 10 years that some of the basic assumptions of this dominant theoretical scheme and some of the explanatory extrapolations contradict facts and call for reinterpretation.

REINTERPRETATIONS

Is All Behavior Motivated?

The first of the assumptions to be called into question is the one that *all behavior is motivated* and that *organisms become inactive unless stimulated* by homeostatic need or painful stimulation or conditional stimuli for these. A large variety of observations contradict this assumption and imply spontaneous molar activity. Beach (*1*) has reviewed the observations of play in the young to show that playful activities are most likely to occur when either young animals or children are homeostatically satisfied and also comfortably warm. The very occurrence of either homeostatic need or strong external stimulation stops play and turns the young animal or child to activities calculated to relieve such stimulation. Berlyne (*3, 4*) has shown that well-fed and watered rats will explore areas new to them if given only the opportunity. Montgomery (*49*) moreover, has shown that hunger and thirst tend to limit the exploratory behavior of rats rather than facilitate it, and Montgomery and Monkman (*50*), as well as others, have shown that conditioned fear inhibits exploration. Harlow, Harlow, and Meyer (*23*) have demonstrated that well-fed monkeys will learn to unassemble a three-device puzzle with no other drive and "no other reward than the privilege of unassembling it." In another study Harlow (*20*) found two well-fed and well-watered monkeys worked repeatedly at unassembling a six-device puzzle for 10 continuous hours, and they were still showing what he characterized as enthusiasm for their work on the tenth hour of testing. From his observations of the human child, moreover, Piaget (*55*) remarks repeatedly on the enthusiastic and repeated performance of such emerging skills as the release of a toy, sitting up, standing, etc.

Such evidences of spontaneous behavior, which is unmotivated in the traditional sense, have led to the naming of such new motives as a curiosity drive by Berlyne (*4*), an exploratory drive by Montgomery (*48*), and exteroceptive and curiosity drives by Harlow (*21*). I would like to object that merely naming such drives explains nothing. If we continue, we shall be revisiting McDougall's (*44*) practice of postulating a separate drive for almost every variety of activity. Let us stop with noting that such observations do contradict our assumption that organisms will become inactive unless driven by homeostatic needs and painful stimuli, and give up this ancient Greek notion that living matter is inert substance to which motion must be imparted by extrinsic forces. We can then embrace the thermodynamic conception of living things as open systems of energy exchange which exhibit activity intrinsically and upon which stimuli have a modulating effect, but not an initiating effect.

This notion of activity being intrinsic in living tissue is receiving support from studies of organ systems as well as studies of molar organisms. The EEG, for example, shows that brain cells are continuously active (*33, 58*). In sleep the slow waves of large amplitude are taken to imply that large numbers of cells are firing synchronously, and the effect of waking and stimulation and exciting the brain-stem-reticular formation is to asynchronize this firing which shows in rapid waves of low magnitude (*42*).

Granit (*19*) points out that the spontaneous firing of retinal cells increases with dark adaptation and thereby functions to prevent the deafferentization of visual cortex with darkness. Twenty years ago, this spontaneous firing was considered, at worst, to be due to some failure of experimental control, or at best, noise in the channel of information. Recently, the Laceys (*36*) have found spontaneous fluctuations of sudomotor activity and cardiac activity which they also see as functioning in the control of the organism's relations with its environment. Especially intriguing is their notion that the carotid sinus mechanism functions as a feedback loop which participates in the directing of attention inward or outward by inhibiting or facilitating receptor inputs. But the point of mentioning these evidences of spontaneous activities of organ systems here is merely to help inter for good the notion that activity of living systems requires homeostatic need or painful external stimulation and to foster the idea that to live means to be active in some degree.

Reinforcement

This idea of activity being intrinsic in living organisms has implications for our conception of reinforcement. It makes it unnecessary to see all activity as a matter of either reducing or avoiding stimulation which is implied in the assumption that organisms become inactive unless stimulated. This is a second fundamental assumption of the dominant theory which has been shared by psychoanalysts and behavior theorists alike.

On the one hand, there is still a place for drive reduction. It is clear that under conditions of homeostatic need and painful stimulation, and perhaps under circumstances when the conditions of stimulation are changing with too great rapidity, both animals and persons learn techniques and strategies leading to gratification or reduction in external stimulation. The evidence that led Thorndike to formulate the "law of effect" is as convincing as ever. Moreover, in association with reductions of homeostatic need, animals and men may also learn cathexes or emotional attachments. The facts referred to are those highly familiar in secondary reinforcement (*30, 54*).

On the other hand, the facts implying that organisms show spontaneous molar activity also imply that, when animals and human beings have been living under conditions of low and unchanging stimulation for a time, increases of stimulation become reinforcing. Butler has shown that rhesus monkeys will learn quite complex discriminations with the only reward being a peek through a glass window (*7*) at the things in the next room or a few seconds of auditory experience (*8*). Berlyne (*3*) has shown that, the greater the variety of stimulation in an area which rats are permitted to explore, the longer they continue their explorations.

Especially important in this connection are the studies of human behavior under conditions of minimal variation in stimulation. I refer to the studies of perceptual isolation by Bexton, Heron, and Scott (*6*) at McGill and also the work of Lilly (*41*). At McGill, college students were paid 20 dollars a day to do nothing. They lay for 24 hours a day on a comfortable bed. The temperature was optimal and constant. Eyes, ears, and hands were shielded to minimize stimulus variation. Few subjects could endure more than two or three days of such conditions. They developed a desire for variation which was almost overwhelming.

While interpreting such facts in terms of a multiple set of drives for curiosity, exploration, or stimulation will get us only to a redescription of them, Hebb's (*26*) notion of an optimal level of activation—and, I would like to add, stimulus variation below which *increases* are reinforcing and above which *decreases* are reinforcing—is an integrative conception of fair magnitude. Morover, the drive-reduction principle of reinforcement may be seen to be but half of this more general curvilinear principle.

But this is probably not the whole story. It looks as if there were, natively, both positive and negative forms of exciting stimulation. Shefield, Roby, and Campbell (*61*) have argued that the reinforcing effect of eating is not a matter of reduction of the hunger drive but rather a matter of the positive value of the consummatory act of eating. Moreover, Sheffield, Wulff, and Backer (*62*) have shown that male rats will learn mazes to get to females in heat even when they are allowed only intromission but not allowed to continue coitus to the point of drive-reducing ejaculation. From the fact that Davis (*12*) and his collaborators at Indiana have shown that showing pictures of nude women to college males increases excitement as shown by increased palmar conductance and the arrest of EEG-alpha, it is clear that such stimulation is exciting rather than excitement-reducing. Young (*69*) has long emphasized the importance of the hedonic quality of experience for reinforcement, and he has shown that speed of running in rat subjects increases with the concentration of sucrose in the incentive drink.

The suggestion that the two forms of excitation, one positive and one negative, are built into organisms comes also from the work of Olds and Milner (*53*). Electrical stimulation of the septal area is positively reinforcing, but electrical stimulation of the brain-stem reticular formation is negatively reinforcing. Perhaps, it is not without significance that the septal area is part of the old olfactory brain which has been considered to have an especially important part in the mediation of sexual and consummatory behavior in mammals. At any rate, it looks as though certain types of stimulation may be positively reinforcing even though they be intense and exciting. This may mean that the curvilinear principle may be limited in its domain to strong stimulation via the exteroceptors when homeostatic needs are minimized.

The suggestion of innate, positive and negative exteroceptive stimulation comes secondly from recent work by Harlow (*22*). It has been customary to see an infant's cathexis or love for its mother developing as secondary reinforcement largely out of its feeding experiences. Freud (*16*), of course, contended that the pleasure from stimulation of the oral erogenous zone furnished the experiential basis for both pleasure-sucking and maternal attachment, a contention which contradicted his most definitive formulations of drive theory (*17*). The fact that an infant must suck for its nourishment, according to libido theory (*16,* p. 587), merely guaranteed discovery of the pleasures of oral stimulation. Behavior theorists have seen both sucking and love of mother as forms of secondary reinforcement deriving from the fact that the child satisfies its hunger by means of sucking the mother's breasts (*51,* pp. 137 ff.). Harlow (*22*), however, has recently compared the degree of attachment of young monkeys to a wire mother-surrogate on which they nursed at a bottle with attachment to a padded and cloth-covered mother-surrogate on which they received nothing but the feel of softness. In terms of the amount of time spent on each of the two mother-surrogates, the monkeys showed more than 10 times the attachment to the soft-padded surrogate as to the wire surrogate. When various fear-evoking stimuli were presented to the baby monkeys in their cages, it was to the padded and cloth-covered surrogate that the frightened infant monkey turned, not to the wire surrogate on which it had been nursed. Harlow argues from these findings that it is the sensory quality of softness which gives the reinforcement. His study suggests, moreover, that it is important to investigate the capacity for various kinds of stimuli for positive and negative reinforcement in the very young. Pratt (*57*) cites a monograph by Canestrini (*9*) on the sensory life of the newborn for an observation that certain stimuli are associated with decreases in the rate of the heart rate, and are therefore pleasant, while others are associated with increases in heart rate and are unpleasant. In view of the finding by Davis (*12*) and his collaborators that seeing a picture of a nude female results in reduction of the heart rate of male college students, it is possible that this physiological indicator may provide a technique for determining the direction of the reinforcing effect of stimuli in the newborn. At any rate, what is suggested is that McDougall's (*44*) old notion of natively positive and negative values for receptors inputs be reexamined.

Conditioned Fear and Anxiety

The third assumption that I wish to examine in the light of empirical evidence is the notion that fear and anxiety are *always* inculcated as a consequence of traumatic experiences of helplessness in the face of homeostatic need or painful external stimulation. Note that I am not denying that such conditioned fears do exist. I am only questioning the word *always* . . . are always inculcated as a consequence of traumatic experiences.

The first relevant studies go way back to the 1920s. Harold and Mary Cover Jones (*34*) attempted to test the claims of Watson (*66*) and Watson and Raynor (*67*) concerning conditioned fears. They exposed their subjects of various ages, ranging from early infancy to adult, to a large but sluggish and harmless bull-snake. Fear of the snake was exceedingly common among adults, teenagers, and latency-age children, but it was absent in children below three years of age. It began to appear among children older than 3 and was typical of children 6 and older. From the fact that the fear appeared at a younger age in those of higher intelligence than those of lower intelligence, the Joneses argued that fear of snakes is a response which comes automatically into the developing child's repertoire through maturation. This remains as an alternative hypothesis to that of conditioned fear.

A study by Frances Holmes (*29*), which is seldom cited, calls both of these interpretations into question. Holmes compared the fearfulness of the children of lower-class background who were attending a day nursery, with the fearfulness of children of upper-class background who were attending a private nursery school. She got her fear scores by indicating that the child could get some attractive toys with which to play by going into the dark room adjacent to the examining room, or by taking them off a chair situated beside that of a strange woman dressed in a large floppy black hat and a long gray coat, or by climbing along a plank some three feet off the floor. If the child started immediately for the toys, he got a score of one for that item. If he hesitated but ultimately went ahead on his own, he got a score of two. If he would go only if accompanied by the examiner, the score was three. If he refused to go at all, the score was four. There were seven such situations. The results show that the fear scores of the lower-class children averaged only about half the size of those for the upper-class children, and the fear scores for boys were lower than those for girls. Yet it would be the lower-class children who had experienced the more homeostatic need and painfully rough treatment than the upper-class children, and the boys had probably experienced more painful experiences than the little girls. That intelligence is not the factor is shown by the fact that the fear scores showed a correlation of only about +.2 with mental age, and the differences were still significant when intelligence was partialed out. Something besides either conditioned fear or the correlation between fear and intelligence is required to make these results comprehensible.

Recently, evidence even more contradictory to the notion of conditioned fears has been coming from the work of Seymour Levine. Levine, Chevalier, and Korchin (*40*) have compared the adult behavior of rats shocked and rats petted daily from birth to their 20th day with the adult behavior of rats left continuously in their nest with their mothers. When he started this work, Levine expected to find that the shocked animals would show traumatic effects of their shock experiences in heightened emotionality and damaged capacity to learn adaptive responses. On the contrary, the shocked animals, along with the handled animals gained weight faster than those left in the nest (*37, 38, 39, 40*). Byron Lindholm, working with the writer, has repeated and confirmed this finding. Moreover, Levine's shocked and handled animals both showed less emotionality than those left continuously in the nest with their mothers, i.e., less emotionality in the sense that they defecated and urinated less frequently when placed in a strange situation. Finally, the shocked and handled animals, which have appeared alike in all of these experiments, learned an avoidance response more rapidly and drank more readily after 18 hours without water than did the rats left in the nest with their mother.

Clearly these results on both human children and rats imply that fear and anxiety must sometimes have some other basis than that of being associated with painful stimulation. As many of you know, Hebb (*24, 25*) has formulated a radically different explanation of fear which may be termed either an incongruity or a dissonance theory.

The facts which suggested Hebb's conception came largely from observing chimpanzees being raised under controlled conditions at the Yerkes Laboratory. Fear, defined as withdrawal behavior in response to the appearance of some object, does not appear in young chimpanzees until they are approximately four months old. Then, the objects feared are familiar objects in unfamiliar guise. Fear of strangers is an example. This appears spontaneously to the first stranger seen, so it cannot be based on associating strangers with painful stimulation. Fear of strangers does not appear in chimpanzees—or in children, I might add—who have always been exposed to a large number of persons. While the avoidance response is unlearned, the familiar, expected aspects of objects must be learned. The young animal must have established as residues of his experience cortical firing patterns (or cognitive structures—whichever term you like) from which new receptor inputs can be incongruous. Consider the kinds of objects regularly feared. They are, for instance, the familiar keeper or experimenter in strange clothes, the experimenter in a Halloween mask, a plaster cast of a chimpanzee head (which lacks, of course, the familiarly attached body), an anesthetized chimpanzee infant (from which the familiar patterns of motion are absent). On the other hand, objects which have never entered into the young chimpanzee's life may be strange without evoking withdrawal. In other words, the feared object is one which excites receptors in a fashion which is incongruous with the central, sequential pattern of neural firing which has accrued as a residue of the chimpanzee or human infant's past experience. Until the central pattern has been learned, incongruous stimulation is impossible.

Such a conception can well account for Holmes' findings that lower-class children are less fearful than higher-class children and that boys are less fearful than girls even though both lower-class children and boys of nursery school age are likely to have had the wider experience with the sorts of situations used by Holmes to evoke fear. It may well be that being shocked and handled provides a variety of experience which leaves the rat pups which have been subjected to it less disturbed by such things as open fields and 18 hours without water, but these effects may ultimately be found to be a matter of still another mechanism. It is too early to say.

Taking seriously this incongruity-dissonance conception of the genesis of fear leads to interesting reinterpretations of a great many of the motivational phenomena of child development. Consider these few. In considering separation anxiety, the incongruity principle makes it necessary to puzzle about how the absence of mother could be the conditional stimulus for the traumatizing and helpless distress that has been supposed to have occurred in her absence. In considering fear of the dark, it also becomes unnecessary to puzzle about how the absence of light stimulation could so widely have been associated with painful stimulation. Multiple mothering need not be seen as a traumatizing experience in the light of this conception, but rather as an inoculation against social shyness and fear. The timidity of the overprotected child and the social shyness of the rural mountain people get an explanation which has been difficult in terms of the theory of conditioned fear.

MOTIVATION IN TERMS OF THE INCONGRUITY-DISSONANCE PRINCIPLE

This introduction of the incongruity-dissonance principle concludes the three reinterpretations I wish to present today, but I do wish to call your attention to the pervasive character of this incongruity-dissonance principle. It appears to have great explanation power which figures, in one guise or another, in several systematic theories besides that of Hebb, all of which have been characterized as nondynamic.

Hebb's (*25*) theorizing is physiological, at least in a verbal sense, in that he conceives the residues of past inputs to be stored in semiautonomous, reverberating cerebral circuits which he terms *cell assemblies*. These cell assemblies are the neural analogue of concepts, and they get sequentially integrated into what he calls *phase sequences*. The sequential organization in time provides for the subjective phenomenon of expectation. When markedly incongruous receptor inputs disrupt this sequential organization, behavior is changed and the process is felt as unpleasant emotion. Slight degrees of incongruity, which can readily be accommodated, lend interest and may provide attractive problems, but the larger ones are repelling and perhaps even devastating.

Piaget (*55, 56*) utilizes very much the same incongruity notion to account for the development of intelligence and concepts in human children. In his system, the child comes at birth with certain sensory-motor coordinations which he terms *schemata*. Variation in stimulus situations call for adaptive *accommodations* or changes in these schemata, which changes are *assimilated* or stored as residues. Piaget also finds limited incongruities between central schemata and receptor inputs to be interesting and facilitative of growth, but incongruities which extend beyond the child's capacity for accommodation instigate withdrawal or fear and even terror. In Piaget's theory the child's gestalt-like conceptions of reality (space, time, and number) are schemata which develop through a continuous process of accommodations and assimilations and become fixed or static only when the child's schemata come to correspond so well with reality that no further accommodations are required. Here agreement among people is dictated by reality.

Helson (*27, 28*) has called the residues of immediate past experience in the typical psychophysical experiment an *adaptation level*. Both he and McClelland (*43*) have seen affective arousal to be a matter of the size of the discrepancy between receptor inputs and the adaptation level. Small discrepancies may be attractively pleasant, large ones repellingly unpleasant. As an example, some of you will readily recall having experienced the affective startle that comes when you have been set to pick up what you thought was a full pail, only to find it empty.

Festinger (*14*) has recently written a book entitled *A Theory of Cognitive Dissonance* in which he shows that a discrepancy between belief about a situation and perception of that situation acts like a drive. The subject acts to reduce the *dissonance* by either withdrawing from the incredible situation or by changing his beliefs, and, not incidentally, he finds the dissonance highly unpleasant.

Rogers (*60*) has described the basis for anxiety as discrepancy between the "phenomenological field" and the perceived reality as represented by his two circles. Roger's phenomenological field, however, is not the perceptually-given phenomenal field of such German phenomenologists as Delthei and Husserl. It is rather the inferred storehouse of past experience and represented in the present by expectations, aspirations, self-concept, and the like. Thus, his conceptual scheme appears to fall within the domain of the incongruity-dissonance principle.

Kelly's (*35*) *Psychology of Personal Constructs* also makes central use of this principle. The term *personal constructs* refers to the ways in which individuals construe and anticipate events. These each person derives from the way in which he has experienced such events in the past. When a person's constructions fail to predict events, this is disturbing, even anxiety-producing, and it motivates some kind of change, but the change may take place in defenses against such change of constructs or in avoiding such events, or in the constructs themselves.

Perhaps, it is worth noting in closing that this incongruity-dissonance principle makes both motivation and reinforcement intrinsic to the organism's relations with its environment, intrinsic, if you will, to the organism's information-processing. It is as if the organism operated like an error-actuated, feedback system where the error is derived from discrepancy between receptor-inputs of the present and the residues of past experience which serve as the basis for anticipating the future. The dominant view of the past half century has seen both motivation and reinforcement as extrinsic to the information-processing. This has put a tremendous burden of responsibility for the management of affective motivation on parents, teachers, and all those in positions of authority and control. Visions of man completely controlled, as exemplified by George Orwell's *1984,* are conceivable only by assuming that the extrinsic motivating forces of homeostatic need and painful stimulation are completely dominant. In this light the terror of the baby chimp at seeing his keeper in a Halloween mask and the irritation of the believer when his beliefs are disconfirmed are perhaps symbols of hope. They may justify Abraham Lincoln's well-known dictum that "you can fool some of the people all the time, and all the people some of the time, but you cannot fool all the people all the time."

To return to the cartoon of the lad who was improperly motivated: Perhaps, the task of developing proper motivation is best seen, at least in nutshell form, as limiting the manipulation of extrinsic factors to that minimum of keeping homeostatic need and exteroceptive drive low, in favor of facilitating basic information-processing to maximize accurate anticipation of reality.

REFERENCES

1. Beach, F. A. Current concepts of play in animals. *Amer. Naturalist,* 1945, **79,** 523–541.
2. Bechterev, V. M. *La psychologie objective* (N. Kostyleff, Trans.). Paris: Alcan, 1913.
3. Berlyne, D. E. Novelty and curiosity as determinants of exploratory behavior. *Brit. J. Psychol.,* 1950, **41,** 68–80.

4. Berlyne, D. E. The arousal and satiation of perceptual curiosity in the rat. *J. comp. physiol. Psychol.*, 1955, **48**, 238–246.
5. Bernard, C. *Lecons sur les propriétés physiologiques et les alterations pathologiques des liquides de l'organisme.* Paris: Ballière, 1859. 2 vols.
6. Bexton, W. H., Heron, W., & Scott, T. H. Effects of decreased variation in the sensory environment. *Canad. J. Psychol.*, 1954, **8**, 70–76.
7. Butler, R. A. Discrimination learning by rhesus monkeys to visual-exploration motivation. *J. comp. physiol. Psychol.*, 1953, **46**, 95–98.
8. Butler, R. A. Discrimination learning by rhesus monkeys to auditory incentives. *J. comp. physiol. Psychol.*, 1957, **50**, 239–241.
9. Canestrini, S. Uber das Sinnesleben des Neugebornen. In Alzheimer, A., & Lewandowský, M. (Eds.), *Monogr. Gesamt. Neurol. Psychiat.* (Heft 5), Berlin: Springer, 1913.
10. Cannon, W. B. *Bodily changes in pain, hunger, fear, and rage.* New York: Appleton-Century, 1915.
11. Dashiell, J. *Fundamentals of objective psychology.* Boston: Houghton Mifflin, 1928.
12. Davis, R. C., & Buchwald, A. M. An exploration of somatic response patterns: stimulus and sex differences. *J. comp. physiol. Psychol.*, 1957, **50**, 44–52.
13. Dollard, J., & Miller, N. E. *Personality and psychotherapy.* New York: McGraw-Hill, 1950.
14. Festinger, L. *A theory of cognitive dissonance.* Evanston, Ill.: Row, Peterson, 1957.
15. Freud, S. The interpretation of dreams (1900). In *The basic writings of Sigmund Freud* (A. A. Brill Trans.). New York: Modern Library, 1938. Pp. 179–548.
16. Freud, S. Three contributions to the theory of sex (1905). In *The basic writings of Sigmund Freud.* (A. A. Brill, Trans.). New York: Modern Library, 1938. Pp. 553–629.
17. Freud, S. Instincts and their vicissitudes (1915). In *Collected papers.* Vol. IV. London: Hogarth, 1950. Pp. 60–83.
18. Freud, S. *Inhibition, symptom, and anxiety* (1926). (Translated by H. A. Bunker as *The Problem of Anxiety.*) New York: Norton, 1936.
19. Granit, R. *Receptors and sensory perception.* New Haven: Yale Univer. Press, 1955.
20. Harlow, H. F. Learning and satiation of response in intrinsically motivated complex puzzle performance by monkeys. *J. comp. physiol. Psychol.*, 1950, **43**, 289–294.
21. Harlow, H. F. Motivation as a factor in the acquisition of new responses. In *Current theory and research in motivation: a symposium.* Lincoln: Univer. of Nebraska Press, 1953. Pp. 24–49.
22. Harlow, H. F. The nature of love. *Amer. Psychologist,* 1958, **13,** 673–685.
23. Harlow, H. F., Harlow, M. K., & Meyer, D. R. Learning motivated by a manipulation Drive. *J. exp. Psychol.*, 1950, **40**, 228–234.
24. Hebb, D. O. On the nature of fear. *Psychol. Rev.*, 1946, **53,** 259–276.
25. Hebb, D. O. *The organization of behavior.* New York: Wiley, 1949.
26. Hebb, D. O. Drives and the CNS (conceptual nervous system). *Psychol. Rev.*, 1955, **62**, 243–254.

27. Helson, H. Adaptation-level as frame of reference for prediction of psychophysical data. *Amer. J. Psychol.*, 1947, **60**, 1–29.
28. Helson, H. Adaptation-level as a basis for a quantitative theory of frames of reference. *Psychol. Rev.*, 1948, **55**, 297–313.
29. Holmes, Frances B. An experimental study of the fears of young children. In A. T. Jersild & Frances B. Holmes. Children's fears. *Child Developm. Monogr.*, 1935, **20**, 167–296.
30. Hull, C. L. *Principles of behavior*. New York: Appleton-Century, 1943.
31. Hunt, J. McV. The effects of infant feeding-frustration upon adult hoarding in the albino rat. *J. abnorm. soc. Psychol.*, 1941, **36**, 338–360.
32. Hunt, J. McV., Schlosberg, H., Solomon, R. L., & Stellar, E. Studies on the effects of infantile experience on adult behavior in rats: I. Effects of infantile feeding frustration on adult hoarding. *J. comp. physiol. Psychol.*, 1947, **40**, 291–304.
33. Jasper, H. H. Electrical signs of cortical activity. *Psychol. Bull.*, 1937, **34**, 411–481.
34. Jones, H. E., & Jones, Mary C. A study of fear. *Child Educ.*, 1928, **5**, 136–143.
35. Kelly, G. A. *The psychology of personal constructs*. New York: Norton, 1955.
36. Lacey, J. I., & Lacey, Beatrice C. The relationship of resting autonomic activity to motor impulsivity. In *The brain and human behavior*. Baltimore: Williams & Wilkins, 1958. Pp. 144–209.
37. Levine, S. Infantile experience and consummatory behavior in adulthood. *J. comp. physiol. Psychol.*, 1957, **50**, 609–612.
38. Levine, S. Infantile experience and resistance to physical stress. *Science*, 1957, **126**, 405.
39. Levine, S. Noxious stimulation in infant and adult rats and consummatory behavior. *J. comp. physiol. Psychol.*, 1958, **51**, 230–233.
40. Levine, S., Chevalier, J. A., & Korchin, S. J. The effects of shock and handling in infancy on later avoidance learning. *J. Pers.*, 1956, **24**, 475–493.
41. Lilly, J. C. Mental effects of reduction of ordinary levels of physical stimuli on intact, healthy persons. *Psychiat. Res. Rep.* 1956 (5), 1–9.
42. Lindsley, D. B. Psychophysiology and motivation. In M. R. Jones (Ed.), *Nebraska symposium on motivation*. Lincoln: Univer. of Nebraska Press, 1957, Pp. 44–105.
43. McClelland, D. C., Atkinson, J. W., Clark, R. A., & Lowell, E. L. *The achievement motive*. New York: Appleton-Century-Crofts, 1953.
44. McDougall, W. *An introduction to social psychology*. Boston: Luce, 1915.
45. Miller, N. E. An experimental investigation of acquired drives. *Psychol. Bull.*, 1941, **38**, 534–535.
46. Miller, N. E. Studies of fear as an acquirable drive: I. Fear as motivation and fear-reduction as reinforcement in the learning of new responses. *J. exp. Psychol.*, 1948, **38**, 89–101.
47. Miller, N. E., & Dollard, J. *Social learning and imitation*. New Haven: Yale Univer. Press, 1941.
48. Montgomery, K. C. The relation between exploratory behavior and spontaneous alternation in the white rat. *J. comp. physiol. Psychol.*, 1951, **44**, 582–589.

49. Montgomery, K. C. The effect of the hunger and thirst drives upon exploratory behavior. *J. comp. physiol. Psychol.*, 1953, **46**, 315–319.
50. Montgomery, K. C., & Monkman, J. A. The relation between fear and exploratory behavior. *J. comp. physiol. Psychol.*, 1955, **48**, 132–136.
51. Mussen, P. H., & Conger, J. J. *Child development and personality.* New York: Harper, 1956.
52. Olds, J. Physiological mechanisms of reward. In M. R. Jones (Ed.), *Nebraska symposium on motivation.* Lincoln: Univer. of Nebraska Press, 1955. Pp. 73–139.
53. Olds, J., & Milner, P. Positive reinforcement produced by electrical stimulation of septal area and other regions of the rat brain. *J. comp. physiol. Psychol.*, 1954, **47**, 419–427.
54. Pavlov, I. P. *Conditioned reflexes.* (G. V. Anrep, Trans.) Oxford: Oxford Univer. Press, 1927.
55. Piaget, J. *The origins of intelligence in children.* New York: International Universities Press, 1952.
56. Piaget, J. *The construction of reality in the child.* (Margaret Cook, Trans.) New York: Basic Books, 1954.
57. Pratt, K. C. The neonate. In L. Carmichael (Ed.), *Manual of child psychology.* (2d. ed.) New York: Wiley, 1954. Pp. 215–291.
58. Prosser, C. L. Action potentials in the nervous system of the crayfish: I. Spontaneous impulses. *J. cell. comp. Physiol.*, 1934, **4**, 185–209.
59. Richter, C. P. Animal behavior and internal drives. *Quart. Rev. Biol.*, 1927, **2**, 307–343.
60. Rogers, C. R. *Client-centered therapy.* Boston: Houghton Mifflin, 1951.
61. Sheffield, F. D., Roby, T. B., & Campbell, B. A. Drive reduction versus consummatory behavior as determinants of reinforcement. *J. comp. physiol. Psychol.*, 1954, **47**, 349–355.
62. Sheffield, F. D., Wulff, J. J., & Backer, R. Reward value of copulation without sex drive reduction. *J. comp. physiol. Psychol.*, 1951, **44**, 3–8.
63. Solomon, R. L., & Brush, Elinor S. Experimentally derived conceptions of anxiety and aversion. In M. R. Jones (Ed.), *Nebraska symposium on motivation.* Lincoln: Univer. of Nebraska Press, 1956. Pp. 212–305.
64. Solomon, R. L., & Wynne, L. C. Traumatic avoidance learning: acquisition in normal dogs. *Psychol. Monogr.*, 1953, **67**, No. 4 (Whole No. 354).
65. Thorndike, E. L. *Educational psychology.* Vol. I, *The original nature of man;* Vol. II, *The psychology of learning.* New York: Teachers Coll., 1913.
66. Watson, J. B. *Psychological care of the infant and child.* New York: Norton, 1928.
67. Watson, J. B., & Raynor, Rosalie. Conditional reactions. *J. exp. Psychol.*, 1920, **3**, 1–4.
68. Woodworth, R. S. *Dynamic psychology.* New York: Columbia Univer. Press, 1918.
69. Young, P. T. The role of hedonic processes in motivation. In M. R. Jones (Ed.), *Nebraska symposium on motivation.* Lincoln: Univer. of Nebraska Press, 1955. Pp. 193–237.

23

THE ROLE OF SOCIAL CLASS IN LANGUAGE DEVELOPMENT AND COGNITION*

MARTIN DEUTSCH

IN A SENSE probably no child ever has had a maximally fostering environment, where within neuro-developmental limits on intellectual growth individuals have been appropriately stimulated so that they reach their developmental ceilings at each level. But the absence of such an environment and the presence of varying examples of the converse makes it possible to study the permutations in the interaction of environment with development.

The particular area of research on which we have been focusing at the Institute for Developmental Studies has as one of its objectives the delineation of the major dimensions through which environment is likely to operate in a manner inhibiting development. Another objective is to attempt to specify the cognitive and language areas that have been most influenced by unfavorable environmental circumstances. As we learn about the typology of cognitive and language deficiencies, we also learn something more about human learning and evolve methods that might be effective in facilitating development.

The delineation of the area of concern in this way reflects a basic thesis that human potential is not being nearly fully exploited by the available educational structures and that the possibilities for development are most especially being neglected with regard to what Harrington has termed "The Other America."

Simply obtaining relationships between social class or ethnic attributes and intelligence or other singular factors has been historically useful, but inadequate in telling us how the structure of experience as mediated through particular environments influences the patterning of cognitive processes.

---

* From the *American Journal of Orthopsychiatry,* 1965, *35,* 78–88. Reprinted with permission from the author and the American Orthopsychiatric Association.

Presented at the 1964 Annual Meeting of the American Orthopsychiatric Association, Chicago, Illinois.

I should like to express appreciation to those of the Institute for Developmental Studies staff who worked on the Verbal Survey, and especially to Vera John, Martin Whiteman, Bert Brown, Cynthia Deutsch, Estelle Cherry Peisach and Barry Karp.

Therefore, our attack on this problem has included an initial attempt to make a microanalysis of the environment. This encompasses such molar data as the traditional information on the social structure of the family, communication, economic circumstances, the educational histories of the family members, their child-rearing practices, dominance-passivity patterns, sex role determinations, and the like. The attempt also has been made to analyze the activity structure of the home, the quality of interaction between adults and children, and the whole matrix of behavioral expectations, in terms of both immediate behavior and long-range educational and general goal aspirations. What we are attempting to do in this series of studies is to identify patterns in the context of background variables at two developmental stages, and to relate these background patterns to specific cognitive and linguistic patterns. The purpose, thus, is not simply to demonstrate the existence of cognitive and learning disabilities in association with disadvantaged environments, but to define both anomalies and orderliness in perceptual, linguistic, and conceptual processes, so that eventual compensatory action on the areas of disability can be based on empirical evidence.

In the study to be discussed here, emphasis was placed on the evaluation of linguistic variables. This was not only because language is the primary avenue for communication, absorption, and interpretation of the environment, but because it also reflects highly acculturated styles of thought and ideational modes for solving and not solving problems. It seems reasonable to conclude that as we study the background influences on qualitative variables in language and language development, we also are studying the effects of the same influences on cognitive development and problem-solving styles and abilities. As Bruner puts it in his introduction to Vygotsky's book *Thought and Language* (1962):

> For it is the internalization of overt action that makes thought, and particularly the internalization of external dialogue that brings the powerful tool of language to bear on the stream of thought. Man, if you will, is shaped by the tools and instruments he comes to use, and neither the mind nor the hand alone can amount to much . . .

Strong evidence can be adduced to support the assumption that it is the active verbal engagement of people who surround him which is the operative influence in the child's language development. The structuring of these verbal engagements in terms of the family's conditions and style of life, and the further relationship between style of life and social class membership leads to the analysis of children's language skills and verbal behavior in terms of their families' socioeconomic status. In the cognitive style of the lower-class family, Bernstein (1960) points out, language is used in a convergent or restrictive fashion rather than a divergent, elaborative fashion. An explanation or an imperative or a partial sentence frequently replaces a complete sentence or an explanation: if a child asks for something, the response is too frequently "yes," "no," "go away," "later," or simply a nod.

The feedback is not such that it gives the child the articulated verbal parameters that allow him to start and fully develop normative labeling and identification of the environment. Family interaction data which we have gathered in both lower-class socially deprived and middle-class groups indicate that, as compared with the middle-class homes, there is a paucity of organized family activities in a large number of lower-class homes. As a result, there is less conversation, for example, at meals, as meals are less likely to be regularly scheduled family affairs. In a recent paper (Deutsch and Brown, 1964), we reported that children from fatherless homes have significantly lower IQ scores by the time they get to the fifth grade than do children who come from intact homes, and we hypothesized that this finding was a consequence not so much of the absence of the father, as it was of the diminution of organized family activity.

The data to be discussed in this paper come from a four-year study called the "Verbal Survey." The population studied included a core sample of 292 children and an extended population of about 2500 children of various racial and social class groupings. Negro and white, lower- and middle-class children were included in a relatively well-balanced sample.

In general, we have found that lower-class children, Negro and white, compared with middle-class children, are subject to what we've labeled a "cumulative deficit phenomenon," which takes place between the first and fifth grade years. Though there are significant socio-economic and race differences seen in measured variables at the first grade level, it is important to note that they become more marked as the child progresses through school. While we can accept that some of this cumulative deficiency is associated with inadequate early preparation because of corresponding environmental deficiencies, the adequacy of the school environment also must be questioned: in a model system, one should expect linearity in cognitive growth.

In a caste society it is very difficult to control for socio-economic status, and it is possible that some of the Negro child's measured increasing deficit stems artificially from this incomplete control. At the same time, inferior caste must imprint itself on the child at an early age and is a constant presence in the environment.

As indicated above, the data to be reported here were collected on a balanced sample of children at two age levels, and it is some of the analysis and interpretation of a portion of these data which will now be discussed. In the study, we assessed over 100 identifiable variables concerned with home background, language functioning, conceptual behavior, intelligence test performance, reading, general orientation, self-systems, various sub-components of language, and assorted related factors. This paper will make reference (by no means exhaustively) to only 52 of these variables concerned with a range of cognitive functions and a few demographic measures, but with language variables at the core.

The entire correlational matrices will not be reproduced here. Rather, the over-all patterning of results will be examined in terms of social class, race, and developmental levels as more-or-less independent variables. Only those correlations which are significant at the .01 level or better will be considered as significant. For the size of the current samples, this means including correlations of .21 or higher (Table 1). Definition of each of the variables is listed in Table 2.

On the first-grade level, lower social class status is associated with poorer performance on all the IQ scores: the Lorge-Thorndike, the WISC vocabulary test, and the Peabody Picture Vocabulary Test; the three scores on a Verbal Identification Test which have to do with a more abstract conceptualization of a visual stimulus; several rhyming, fluency, and verbal explanation scores on a Verbal Fluency and a Concept Sorting Test; scores on a Cloze Test; and a score reflecting general environmental orientation (Variables 8, 9, 10, 11, 12, 13, 18, 19, 20, 21, 22, 25, 35, 39, 40, 41, 43, 47, 50, 51, 52).

If for the first grade subjects we examine the variables which correlate significantly with both SES and race, there are only two in addition to those which correlated only with SES. These are one verbalization score on the Concept Formation Test and scores on the Wepman test of auditory discrimination (Variables 35, 47).

There are only six variables which relate to race but not SES. These are three enumeration scores on the Verbal Identification Test, two scores relating to the inclusiveness of grouping on the Concept Sorting Test, and a verbalization score on the Concept Formation Test (Variables 15, 16, 17, 23, 26, 27). The tasks on the Verbal Identification Test involved labeling and are measures highly reflective of experience and the specific availability of labels, whereas the Concept Sorting Test required a knowledge of categories including occupations, transportation, housing and animals.

It might be noted that all the significant relationships were between poorer performance and lower-class status. The race differences are present and are in the direction of poorer performance by Negro children, but they are reflected in *only* eight of the possible 43 comparisons for the first grade group.

It is important to note that the correlation with the Wepman auditory discrimination test is associated with both SES and race. What might be operative here is the presence of dialect variations in the Negro group, influencing and limiting the communication possibilities in school, and possibly having direct relevance to the three enumeration scores that are associated only with race, as there may be a general contamination here of comprehension.

On examining similar relationships for the fifth grade group, we find that all the IQ measures now no longer relate just to SES but also to race. Still relating only to SES are two gestalt scores involving abstract categorization of visual stimuli, and the scores on the Cloze Test, which are associated with the manipulation and syntactical control of language. Additional variables

TABLE 1

Comparisons between First and Fifth Grade Verbal Survey Samples: Significant Correlations with Race and SES*

	Correlations with Race†		*Correlations with SES*‡	
Variables	*First Grade* (N = 127)	*Fifth Grade* (N = 165)	*First Grade* (N = 127)	*Fifth Grade* (N = 165)
7—Age in months				−.21
8—L-T IQ Score		−.36	.42	.38
9—L-T subtest #1		−.34	.35	.25
10—L-T subtest #2		−.30	.26	.32
11—L-T subtest #3		−.30	.26	.38
12—L-T raw score		−.35	.34	.37
13—WISC Vocab. score		−.31	.22	.49
14—Gates score			(test not given)	.44
Verbal Identification:				
15—Noun enumer. score	−.25	−.28		
16—Action enumer. score	−.28	−.20		
17—Combined enumer. score	−.27	−.27		
18—Noun gestalt score			.33	.24
19—Action gestalt score			.24	
20—Combined gestalt score			.32	.27
21—PPVT raw score			.32	(test not given)
22—PPVTIQ			.33	(test not given)
Concept Sorting:				
23—# piles score	.21			
25—Verbal score			.23	
26—Verbal score/# piles (ratio)	−.21			.23
Concept Formation:				
29—Percept. similarities scores				.22
35—Verbaliz. score, class specificity	−.25	−.36	.26	.20
36—Verbaliz. score, class generaliz.		−.24		.21
37—Total verbaliz. score	−.24	−.32		.21
38—Word Knowledge score (Verbal Fluency)		−.24		
Verbal Fluency:				
39—All rhymes score		−.20	.24	.28
40—Meaningful rhymes		−.24	.28	.33
41—Sentence fluency		−.20	.25	
43—Orientation Scale		−.30	.36	.51
47—Wepman test of auditory discrimination§	.24		−.24	
Word Association:				
48—Form class score				.27
49—Latency score		.35		
Cloze Test:				
50—Grammatical score			.26	.33
51—Correct score			.25	.33
52—Popular score			.30	.37

* Only correlations significant at $p < .01$ are shown.
† For purposes of coding, white was coded as 1 and Negro as 2.
‡ Higher index numbers denote higher SES.
§ Error score.

TABLE 2

Brief Description of Verbal Survey Test Measures

Variable Number	*Identification*
7.	S's Age in Months at Time of Lorge-Thorndike Testing
8–12.	Lorge-Thorndike IQ Score (Subtests 1, 2, 3 and Raw Score)
13.	WISC Vocabulary Score
14.	Gates Reading Score
	VERBAL IDENTIFICATION TEST
	The child is shown 20 simple drawings one at a time and given a set to enumerate the objects in the pictures. The child is then shown the 20 pictures a second time and asked to give the one word that best describes each picture.
15.	*Noun Enumeration Score*—The number of items identified correctly on those stimulus cards best described by a noun, e.g., kitchen.
16.	*Action Enumeration Score*—The number of items identified correctly on those stimulus cards best described by a verb, e.g., saluting.
17.	*Combined Enumeration Score*—15 + 16—All the items identified correctly on the stimulus cards of the Verbal Identification test.
18.	*Noun Gestalt Score*—The measure of the child's ability to describe a scene with a single word when the scene is best described by a noun.
19.	*Action Gestalt Score*—The measure of the child's ability to describe a scene with a single word when the scene is best described by a verb.
20.	*Combined Gestalt Score*—18 + 19—The measure of the child's ability to describe the scenes of the Verbal Identification test with a single word.
21.	*Peabody Picture Vocabulary Test (PPVT) Raw Score*—The number of words tried minus the number incorrect.
22.	*PPVT IQ Score*—Obtained from the appropriate tables in the PPVT manual.
	CONCEPT SORTING TEST
	The child is presented 16 cards in random order (four each representing: modes of transportation, housing, occupations and animals) and asked to sort the cards into piles. He also is asked to explain his grouping.
23.	*Number of Piles Score*—The exact number of piles sorted. Four would be best. Usually anything above four indicates inadequacy at the task. This number has been primarily intended as a denominator for the other scores.
24.	*Sort Score*—This score reflects the implicit quality of the child's sorting, e.g., sorting by class generalization receives more credit than functional pairings. Generally, the higher the score the better the quality.
25.	*Verbalization Score*—For this score the child is asked to explain the basis of his sorting procedure. The basis of his sorting is evaluated and scored. Higher forms of classification, e.g., generalization vs. functional pairing get higher scores.
26.	25/23 = Verbal Score Ratio
27.	24/23 = Sort Score Ratio
	CONCEPT FORMATION TEST
	The child is presented with a booklet consisting of pictures representing concepts of identity, similarity, class specificity (persons or animals), and class generalization (living things). He is instructed to choose stimuli which belong together and to give a verbal explanation for the grouping.
28.	*Perceptual Identification Score*—The number of correctly matched items when the intended basis for matching is perceptual identity, e.g., the same dog.
29.	*Perceptual Similarity Score*—The number of correctly matched items when the intended basis for matching is perceptual similarity, e.g., a collie with terriers.
30.	*Class Specificity Score*—The number of items correctly matched when the intended basis for matching is that the items belong to the same class, e.g., a dog and a horse are both animals.

TABLE 2, continued

Brief Description of Verbal Survey Test Measures

Variable Number	*Identification*
31.	*Class Generality Score*—The number of items correctly matched when the items to be matched belong to different classes which are subclasses of a more general category, e.g., a dog and a rose are both living things.
32.	*Total Choice Score*—The total number of items matched correctly—28 + 29 + 30 + 31.
33.	*Verbalization Score, Perceptual Identification Items*—The Verbalization Score is the evaluation of the child's expressed reason for putting two items together, with higher levels of generalization getting higher scores. This is the verbalization score for those items where the basis for matching is perceptual identity.
34.	*Verbalization Score, Perceptual Similarity Items*—The evaluation of the child's expressed reason for putting together items when the basis of matching is perceptual similarity.
35.	*Verbalization Score, Class Specificity Items*—The evaluation of the child's expressed reason for matching items when the intended basis for matching is class specificity.
36.	*Verbalization Score, Class Generality Items*—The evaluation of the child's expressed reason for matching items when the intended basis for matching is class generality.
37.	*Total Verbalization Score*—33 + 34 + 35 + 36.
	VERBAL FLUENCY TEST
38.	*Word Knowledge Score*—The number of words the child can give in 45 seconds.
39.	*All Rhymes Score*—Total number of rhymes given (whether or not a response is a meaningful word) in response to specific stimuli.
40.	*Meaningful Rhymes Score*—Total number of *meaningful rhymes* given by child in response to specific stimuli.
41.	*Sentence Fluency Score*—The child is requested to make sentences using first one word, then the original word plus a second stimulus, and finally a sentence containing the first two stimuli plus a third. The sentences are evaluated for quality and organization.
42.	*Difference Score*—All rhymes minus meaningful rhymes (39–40).
43.	*Orientation Scale Test.* A measure of the child's general knowledge, e.g., what state does he live in?
	Word Distance Test. To the same stimuli presented in the Word Association Test, the child is requested to state whether or not ten specific words go with each stimulus. The specific words were previously ranked for distance from stimulus.
44.	*Distance Score*—The number (1–10) of the most distant association accepted as going with the stimulus word.
45.	*Association Score*—The number of associations accepted as going with the stimulus word.
46.	*Discrepancy Score*—44 — 45. The Most Distant Association minus the number of associations made.
47.	*Wepman Auditory Discrimination Test—Different Score*—This is an error score, and refers to errors made in identifying as different, pairs of words which have very similar sounds.
	WORD ASSOCIATION TEST
48.	*Form Class Score*—The number of first word responses which are of the same form class as the stimulus word.
49.	*Latency Score*—The time in seconds before first association to each stimulus is given.
	CLOZE TEST
50.	*Grammatical Score*—The number of fill-ins which are grammatically correct. These responses do not have to be contextually correct as well.
51.	*Correct Score*—The number of contextually correct fill-ins including popular responses.
52.	*Popular Score*—The number of responses which correspond to the most popular responses given most frequently by school teachers and medical students.

associated with SES for the fifth grade sample are a Form-Class score on the Word Association Test, also probably associated with syntax and logical sequence; a perceptual similarities score on a Concept Formation Test; and a score on a Concept Sorting Test which reflects the adequacy of categorizing visual stimuli (Variables 48, 29, 26). The final variable which relates to SES is the reading score (Variable 14)—a score which at the time of the Survey could not be obtained for the first grade group. We now are completing the standardization of a Reading Prognosis Test for kindergarten and first grade children, and are collecting data which will be parallel to those reported here for fifth grade children.

For the fifth grade sample, there are 12 variables which are related to both SES and race, as opposed to three variables for first graders. What happens in terms of specific measures is that the Wepman correlation drops, no doubt for developmental reasons; the other two measures—both verbalization scores—remain and are joined by 10 additional variables, none of which was associated with race for the first grade sample, but all of which were associated with SES. These 10 measures include all the IQ scores, two verbal fluency measures, and the general orientation score (Variables 8, 9, 10, 11, 12, 13, 39, 40, 43). What this seems to indicate is that the deficit associated with lower SES status on these measures is joined by a deficit associated with race. A more exact breakdown of these shifts is currently underway by means of partial correlations and analyses of variance.

The variables for the fifth grade sample associated with race but not SES include the same three enumeration scores as were found for the first graders, but do not include the two categorization scores found at the first grade level. However, a word knowledge and a sentence fluency score have been added to this category, and, very interestingly, a latency score has also been added (Variables 38, 41, 49). This last is consistent with some other data on expressive language behavior (Deutsch, Maliver et al., 1964), and might indicate a hesitation phenomenon among Negro children when handling language material. It also could reflect a different temporal expectation in verbal interchange, and this might be a fruitful hypothesis to investigate.

Over-all, of 42 measures for the first grade sample, six correlated significantly with race alone, 19 with SES alone, and two with both. Of 43 scores for the fifth grade sample, six correlated with race alone, 10 with SES alone, and 12 with both. This means that significant correlations with race were found in eight comparisons for the first graders, and in 18 for the fifth grade sample. The number of significant comparisons on SES for each group was 22. Also, for each group 15 measures were related to neither race nor SES. There was great overlap between the groups on these nondiscriminating measures, and they tended to be the more concrete ones. (First Grade: Variables 7, 24, 27, 28, 29, 30, 31, 32, 33, 34, 36, 38, 42, 48, 49. Fifth Grade: Variables 19, 23, 24, 25, 27, 28, 30, 31, 32, 33, 34, 42, 44, 45, 46, 47.)

If we now look for the functions underlying measures for which race is associated with poor performance, they are found in areas of abstraction, verbalization, and experientially dependent enumeration. It should be emphasized, however, that not all measures reflecting these functions related to race.

In a recent paper by John (1963) reporting on work done at the Institute, she suggests that the middle-class child has an advantage over the lower-class child in the amount of tutoring and help available to him in his home. She emphasizes that without such help it is very difficult for a child to acquire the more abstract and precise use of language. Indeed, in the data just discussed, what is found is a deficiency based on class and race in the measures which reflect abstract and categorical use of language, as opposed to denotative and labeling usage.

If the tri-partite language ordering that we have used in formulating measures for our research is applied, it is found that as the complexity of the levels increases, from labeling, through relating, to categorizing, the negative effects of social disadvantage are enhanced. It is also true, in looking at the enumeration scores, that as labeling requirements become more complex and related to more diverse and variegated experience, lower-class people with more restricted experience are going to have more difficulty in supplying the correct labels. In Hunt's terms (1961), there is an inappropriate "match" between the child's intrinsic development and the external requirements.

In the formulation of Bernstein, the cumulative deficiency in language functioning is the failure in development of an elaborated language system that has accurate grammatical order and logical modifiers, which is mediated through a grammatically complex sentence structure, which has frequent use of prepositions and impersonal pronouns, and a discriminative selection of adjectives and adverbs. These and other characteristics described by Bernstein are those which he feels give direction to the organization of thinking. The elaborated language code is differentiated from what he defines as the restricted language code, which is systematically used largely as the major speech form of the lower class. It is characterized by grammatically simple and often unfinished sentences, poor syntactical form, simple and repetitive use of conjunctions, the inability to hold a formal topic through speech sequences, a rigid and limited use of adjectives and adverbs, etc. In essence, he is describing a class-based language system that effectively denies the lower-class person the necessary verbal strategies to obtain vertical mobility. This is probably more true in England, where Bernstein works, with its rigid class-oriented school system, than it is here. But in our society it might be particularly cogent for rural to urban migrants marked by caste factors or by the highly delineated social class factors possessed, for example, by the Appalachian whites. In our society, if school is to be effective and these youngsters are not to be discharged into that very large group of unskilled unemployables, then mediating, expressive, and receptive language training should be a conscious part of curriculum organization. You just cannot become a computer technologist unless you can read the instructions and utilize the necessary mechanisms for symbolization and concept attainment. And for this you must have available an elaborated language system with appropriate mediators.

What makes the implications of the findings reported so significant is their apparent contribution to the cumulative deficit hypothesis. Also, they provide insight into the nature of the cumulative deficit. Essentially, it would appear that when one adds four years of a school experience to a poor environment, plus minority group status, what emerge are children who are apparently less capable of handling standard intellectual and linguistic tasks. One also might postulate that when the Negro child broadens his environmental contacts by going to school (and to and from school) he is made more aware of his inferior caste status, and this has the same depressing effect on his performance that his inferior class status had all along. The data indicate that being lower class, Negro or white, makes for lower language scores. Being Negro makes for lower scores. But being both lower class and Negro does not disproportionately make for lower language scores.

As indicated, these children have poorer capabilities in handling syntax. I would suggest that they are aware of their grammatical ineptness, and this leads to a reticence and a hesitancy to communicate across social class lines. This would mean that speech as Luria conceives of it (as a single complex leading to changes in the stimulus field) is not operative for these children in the school situation. If language cannot be used as an elaborating form of communication, school loses much of its socializing and teaching capabilities, regardless of the curriculum content. As a consequence, for a significant proportion of these children, functional motivation may not exist in terms of the learning strategies demanded by the school situation. As a result, the negative properties associated with lower-class and minority group status tend to become reinforced, and for these children, language becomes an effective tool only when it has adequate feedback properties in communicating with peers or others who share the particular subculture. In other words, it becomes intra-class contained. The breakdown in communication here is probably a major operative variable which leads for example to the high dropout rate: the student is no longer in communication with anything that is meaningful to him in the school. When teachers report they are frustrated with the learning attitudes and potentials of many of the disadvantaged children, they are responding objectively to a reality condition that, through their expectations, they have helped to produce.

It would seem that in the long run the most effective remedial and enrichment programming would have to follow developmental stages, and curriculum change should be introduced at the earliest possible time in the school experience in order to arrest the cumulative deficit, for as development goes on in the individual child, it probably is progressively more difficult to reverse the deficit, as there is more of it.

In a sense, we still know a minimum of what the school does and does not do to the child. The exciting aspect is that with more specific knowledge of developmental processes and of the influences of environmental factors and of special stimulating conditions on them, it should be possible to program stimulation in increasingly less amorphous ways and with methods that are appropriate to basic learning capabilities, so as to vitiate the effects of unfavorable environments.

REFERENCES

1. Bernstein, B. **1960.** Language and social class. *Brit. Jour. Sociol.* **11:** 271–276.
2. Dennis, W. **1960.** Causes of retardation among institutional children: *Iran. Jour. Genet. Psychol.* **96:** 47–59.
3. Deutsch, M. Some aspects of the relationship of language development and social experience. Paper read at Amer. Orthopsychiat. Assoc. Chicago, March, 1964.
4. Deutsch, M. and B. Brown. **1964.** Social influences in Negro-white intelligence differences. Paper read at meeting of Soc. Res. Child Developmt., Berkeley, Calif., April, 1963. Jour. Soc. Issues. **20**(2): 24–35.
5. Deutsch, M., A. Maliver, B. Brown, and E. Cherry. Communication of information in the elementary school classroom. Cooperative Research Project No. 908 of the Office of Education, U.S. Department of Health, Education and Welfare. April, 1964.
6. Fowler, W. **1962.** Cognitive learning in infancy and early childhood. *Psychol. Bull.* **59**(2): 116–152.
7. Harrington, M. **1962.** *The other America.* Macmillan. New York.
8. Hunt, J. McV. **1961.** *Intelligence and Experience.* Ronald Press, New York.
9. Jensen, A. R. **1963.** Learning ability in retarded, average and gifted children. *Merrill-Palmer Quarterly.* **9**(2): 123–140.
10. Jensen, A. R. **1963.** Learning in the preschool years. *J. nursery Educ.* **18**(2): 133–138.
11. John, V. P. **1963.** The intellectual development of slum children: some preliminary findings. *Amer. Jour. Orthopsychiat.* **33**(5): 813–822.
12. Kendler, T. S. **1963.** Development of mediating responses in children. In S. C. Wright and J. Kagan (Eds.), *Basic cognitive processes in children.* Soc. Res. Child Developm. Monogr. **28**(2): 33–48.
13. Kendler, T. S., H. H. Kendler, and B. Learnard. Mediated responses to size and brightness as a function of age. *Amer. Jour. Psychol.* **75**(4): 571–586.
14. Luria, A. R. **1961.** *The Role of Speech in Regulation of Normal and Abnormal Behavior.* Liveright, New York.
15. Luria, A. R. and F. Y. Yudovich. **1959.** *Speech and development of mental processes in children.* Staples Press, London.
16. Skodak, M. and H. M. Skeels. **1949.** A final follow-up study of one hundred adopted children. *Jour. Genet. Psychol.* **75:** 85–125.
17. Vygotsky, L. S. **1962.** *Thought and language.* M.I.T. Press, Boston.

24

A CROSS-CULTURAL SURVEY OF SOME SEX DIFFERENCES IN SOCIALIZATION*

HERBERT BARRY III
MARGARET K. BACON
and
IRVIN L. CHILD

In our society, certain differences may be observed between the typical personality characteristics of the two sexes. These sex differences in personality are generally believed to result in part from differences in the way boys and girls are reared. To the extent that personality differences between the sexes are thus of cultural rather than biological origin, they seem potentially susceptible to change. But how readily susceptible to change? In the differential rearing of the sexes does our society make an arbitrary imposition on an infinitely plastic biological base, or is this cultural imposition found uniformly in all societies as an adjustment to the real biological differences between the sexes? This paper reports one attempt to deal with this problem.

DATA AND PROCEDURES

The data used were ethnographic reports, available in the anthropological literature, about socialization practices of various cultures. One hundred and ten cultures, mostly nonliterate, were studied. They were selected primarily in terms of the existence of adequate ethnographic reports of socialization

* From the *Journal of Abnormal and Social Psychology*, 1957, *55*, 327–332. Reprinted with permission from the authors and the American Psychological Association.

This research is part of a project for which financial support was provided by the Social Science Research Council and the Ford Foundation. We are greatly indebted to G. P. Murdock for supplying us with certain data, as indicated below, and to him and Thomas W. Maretzki for suggestions that have been used in this paper.

practices and secondarily so as to obtain a wide and reasonably balanced geographical distribution. Various aspects of socialization of infants and children were rated on a 7-point scale by two judges (Mrs. Bacon and Mr. Barry). Where the ethnographic reports permitted, separate ratings were made for the socialization of boys and girls. Each rating was indicated as either confident or doubtful; with still greater uncertainty, or with complete lack of evidence, the particular rating was of course not made at all. We shall restrict the report of sex difference ratings to cases in which both judges made a confident rating. Also omitted is the one instance where the two judges reported a sex difference in opposite directions, as it demonstrates only unreliability of judgment. The number of cultures that meet these criteria is much smaller than the total of 110; for the several variables to be considered, the number varies from 31 to 84.

The aspects of socialization on which ratings were made included:

1. Several criteria of attention and indulgence toward infants.

2. Strength of socialization from age 4 to 5 years until shortly before puberty, with respect to five systems of behavior; strength of socialization was defined as the combination of positive pressure (rewards for the behavior) plus negative pressure (punishments for lack of the behavior). The variables were:

(*a*) Responsibility or dutifulness training. (The data were such that training in the performance of chores in the productive or domestic economy was necessarily the principal source of information here; however, training in the performance of other duties was also taken into account when information was available.)

(*b*) Nurturance training, i.e., training the child to be nurturant or helpful toward younger siblings and other dependent people.

(*c*) Obedience training.

(*d*) Self-reliance training.

(*e*) Achievement training, i.e., training the child to orient his behavior toward standards of excellence in performance, and to seek to achieve as excellent a performance as possible.

Where the term "no sex difference" is used here, it may mean any of three things: (*a*) the judge found separate evidence about the training of boys and girls on this particular variable, and judged it to be identical; (*b*) the judge found a difference between the training of boys and girls, but not great enough for the sexes to be rated a whole point apart on a 7-point scale; (*c*) the judge found evidence only about the training of "children" on this variable, the ethnographer not reporting separately about boys and girls.

SEX DIFFERENCES IN SOCIALIZATION

On the various aspects of attention and indulgence toward infants, the judges almost always agreed in finding no sex difference. Out of 96 cultures for which the ratings included the infancy period, 88 (92%) were rated with no sex difference by either judge for any of those variables. This result is consistent with the point sometimes made by anthropologists that "baby" generally is a single status undifferentiated by sex, even though "boy" and "girl" are distinct statuses.

On the variables of childhood socialization, on the other hand, a rating of no sex difference by both judges was much less common. This finding of no sex difference varied in frequency from 10% of the cultures for the achievement variable up to 62% of the cultures for the obedience variable, as shown in the last column of Table 1. Where a sex difference is reported, by either one or both judges, the difference tends strongly to be in a particular direction, as shown in the earlier columns of the same table. Pressure toward nurturance, obedience, and responsibility is most often stronger for girls,

TABLE 1

Ratings of Cultures for Sex Differences on Five Variables of Childhood Socialization Pressure

Variable	*Number of Cultures*	*Both Judges Agree in Rating the Variable Higher in*		*One Judge Rates No Difference, One Rates the Variable Higher in*		*Percentage of Cultures with Evidence of Sex Difference in Direction of*		
		Girls	*Boys*	*Girls*	*Boys*	*Girls*	*Boys*	*Neither*
Nurturance	33	17	0	10	0	82%	0%	18%
Obedience	69	6	0	18	2	35%	3%	62%
Responsibility	84	25	2	26	7	61%	11%	28%
Achievement	31	0	17	1	10	3%	87%	10%
Self-reliance	82	0	64	0	6	0%	85%	15%

whereas pressure toward achievement and self-reliance is most often stronger for boys.

For nurturance and for self-reliance, all the sex differences are in the same direction. For achievement there is only one exception to the usual direction of difference, and for obedience only two; but for responsibility there are nine. What do these exceptions mean? We have reexamined all these cases. In most of them, only one judge had rated the sexes as differently treated (sometimes one judge, sometimes the other), and in the majority of these cases both judges were now inclined to agree that there was no convincing evidence of a real difference. There were exceptions, however, especially in cases where a more formal or systematic training of boys seemed to imply greater pressure on them toward responsibility. The most convincing cases were the Masai and Swazi, where both judges had originally agreed in rating responsibility pressures greater in boys than in girls. In comparing the five aspects of socialization we may conclude that responsibility shows by far the strongest evidence of real variation in the direction of sex difference, and obedience much the most frequently shows evidence of no sex difference at all.

In subsequent discussion we shall be assuming that the obtained sex differences in the socialization ratings reflect true sex differences in the cultural practices. We should consider here two other possible sources of these rated differences.

1. The ethnographers could have been biased in favor of seeing the same pattern of sex differences as in our culture. However, most anthropologists readily perceive and eagerly report novel and startling cultural features, so we may expect them to have reported unusual sex differences where they existed. The distinction between matrilineal and patrilineal, and between matrilocal and patrilocal cultures, given prominence in many ethnographic reports, shows an awareness of possible variations in the significance of sex differences from culture to culture.

2. The two judges could have expected to find in other cultures the sex roles which are familiar in our culture and inferred them from the material on the cultures. However, we have reported only confident ratings, and such a bias seems less likely here than for doubtful ratings. It might be argued, moreover, that bias has more opportunity in the cases ambiguous enough so that only one judge reported a sex difference, and less opportunity in the cases where the evidence is so clear that both judges agree. Yet in general, as may be seen in Table 1, the deviant cases are somewhat more frequent among the cultures where only one judge reported a sex difference.

The observed differences in the socialization of boys and girls are consistent with certain universal tendencies in the differentiation of adult sex role. In the economic sphere, men are more frequently allotted tasks that involve leaving home and engaging in activities where a high level of skill yields important returns; hunting is a prime example. Emphasis on training in self-reliance and achievement for boys would function as preparation for such an economic role. Women, on the other hand, are more frequently allotted tasks at or near home that minister most immediately to the needs of others (such as cooking and water carrying); these activities have a nurturant character, and in their pursuit a responsible carrying out of established routines is likely to be more important than the development of an especially high order of skill. Thus training in nurturance, responsibility, and, less clearly, obedience, may contribute to preparation for this economic role. These consistencies with adult role go beyond the economic sphere, of course. Participation in warfare, as a male prerogative, calls for self-reliance and a high order of skill where survival or death is the immediate issue. The childbearing which is biologically assigned to women, and the child care which is socially assigned primarily to them, lead to nurturant behavior and often call for a more continuous responsibility than do the tasks carried out by men. Most of these distinctions in adult role are not inevitable, but the biological differences between the sexes strongly predispose the distinction of role, if made, to be in a uniform direction.

The relevant biological sex differences are conspicuous in adulthood but generally not in childhood. If each generation were left entirely to its own devices, therefore, without even an older generation to copy, sex differences in role would presumably be almost absent in childhood and would have to be developed after puberty at the expense of considerable relearning on the part of one or both sexes. Hence, a pattern of child training which foreshadows adult differences can serve the useful function of minimizing what Benedict termed "discontinuities in cultural conditioning" (see Chapter 5).

The differences in socialization between the sexes in our society, then, are no arbitrary custom of our society, but a very widespread adaptation of culture to the biological substratum of human life.

VARIATIONS IN DEGREE OF SEX DIFFERENTIATION

While demonstrating near-universal tendencies in direction of difference between the socialization of boys and girls, our data do not show perfect uniformity. A study of the variations in our data may allow us to see some of the conditions which are associated with, and perhaps give rise to, a greater or smaller degree of this difference. For this purpose, we classified cultures as having relatively large or small sex difference by two different methods, one more inclusive and the other more selective. In both methods the ratings were at first considered separately for each of the five variables. A sex difference rating was made only if both judges made a rating on this variable and at least one judge's rating was confident.

In the more inclusive method the ratings were dichotomized, separately for each variable, as close as possible to the median into those showing a large and those showing a small sex difference. Thus, for each society a large or a small sex difference was recorded for each of the five variables on which a sex difference rating was available. A society was given an over-all classification of large or small sex difference if it had a sex difference rating on at least three variables and if a majority of these ratings agreed in being large, or agreed in being small. This method permitted classification of a large number of cultures, but the grounds for classification were capricious in many cases, as a difference of only one point in the rating of a single variable might change the over-all classification of sex difference for a culture from large to small.

In the more selective method, we again began by dichotomizing each variable as close as possible to the median; but a society was now classified as having a large or small sex difference on the variable only if it was at least one step away from the scores immediately adjacent to the median. Thus only the more decisive ratings of sex difference were used. A culture was classified as having an over-all large or small sex difference only if it was given a sex difference rating which met this criterion on at least two variables, and only if all such ratings agreed in being large, or agreed in being small.

We then tested the relation of each of these dichotomies to 24 aspects of culture on which Murdock has categorized the customs of most of these societies and which seemed of possible significance for sex differentiation. The aspects of culture covered include type of economy, residence pattern, marriage and incest rules, political integration, and social organization. For each aspect of culture, we grouped Murdock's categories to make a dichotomous contrast (sometimes omitting certain categories as irrelevant to the contrast). In the case of some aspects of culture, two or more separate contrasts were made (e.g., under form of marriage we contrasted monogamy

TABLE 2

Culture Variables Correlated with Large Sex Difference in Socialization, Separately for Two Types of Sample

	More Selective Sample		*More Inclusive Sample*	
Variable	ϕ	N	ϕ	N
Large animals are hunted	.48*	(34)	.28*	(72)
Grain rather than root crops are grown	.82**	(20)	.62**	(43)
Large or milking animals rather than small animals are kept	.65*	(19)	.43*	(35)
Fishing unimportant or absent	.42*	(31)	.19	(69)
Nomadic rather than sedentary residence	.61**	(34)	.15	(71)
Polygyny rather than monogamy	.51*	(28)	.38**	(64)

* $p < .05$.
** $p < .01$.
Note.—The variables have been so phrased that all correlations are positive. The phi coefficient is shown, and in parentheses, the number of cases on which the comparison was based. Significance level was determined by χ^2, or Fisher's exact test where applicable, using in all cases a two-tailed test.

with polygyny, and also contrasted sororal with nonsororal polygyny). For each of 40 comparisons thus formed, we prepared a 2 x 2 frequency table to determine relation to each of our sex-difference dichotomies. A significant relation was found for six of these 40 aspects of culture with the more selective dichotomization of overall sex difference. In four of these comparisons, the relation to the more inclusive dichotomization was also significant. These relationships are all given in Table 2, in the form of phi coefficients, along with the outcome of testing significance by the use of χ^2 or Fisher's exact test. In trying to interpret these findings, we have also considered the nonsignificant correlations with other variables, looking for consistency and inconsistency with the general implications of the significant findings. We have arrived at the following formulation of results:

1. Large sex difference in socialization is associated with an economy that

places a high premium on the superior strength, and superior development of motor skills requiring strength, which characterize the male. Four of the correlations reported in Table 2 clearly point to this generalization: the correlations of large sex difference with the hunting of large animals, with grain rather than root crops, with the keeping of large rather than small domestic animals, and with nomadic rather than sedentary residence. The correlation with the unimportance of fishing may also be consistent with this generalization, but the argument is not clear. Other correlations consistent with the generalization, though not statistically significant, are with large game hunting rather than gathering, with the hunting of large game rather than small game, and with the general importance of all hunting and gathering.

2. Large sex difference in socialization appears to be correlated with customs that make for a large family group with high cooperative interaction. The only statistically significant correlation relevant here is that with polygyny rather than monogamy. This generalization is, however, supported by several substantial correlations that fall only a little short of being statistically significant. One of these is a correlation with sororal rather than nonsororal polygyny; Murdock and Whiting (2) have presented indirect evidence that co-wives generally show smoother cooperative interaction if they are sisters. Correlations are also found with the presence of either an extended or a polygynous family rather than the nuclear family only; with the presence of an extended family; and with the extreme contrast between maximal extension and no extension of the family. The generalization is also to some extent supported by small correlations with wide extension of incest taboos, if we may presume that an incest taboo makes for effective unthreatening cooperation within the extended family. The only possible exception to this generalization, among substantial correlations, is a near-significant correlation with an extended or polygynous family's occupying a cluster of dwellings rather than a single dwelling.

In seeking to understand this second generalization, we feel that the degree of social isolation of the nuclear family may perhaps be the crucial underlying variable. To the extent that the nuclear family must stand alone, the man must be prepared to take the woman's role when she is absent or incapacitated, and vice versa. Thus the sex differentiation cannot afford to be too great. But to the extent that the nuclear family is steadily interdependent with other nuclear families, the female role in the household economy can be temporarily taken over by another woman, or the male role by another man, so that sharp differentiation of sex role is no handicap.

The first generalization, which concerns the economy, cannot be viewed as dealing with material completely independent of the ratings of socialization. The training of children in their economic role was often an important part of the data used in rating socialization variables, and would naturally vary according to the general economy of the society. We would stress, however, that we were by no means using the identical data on the two sides of our comparison; we were on the one hand judging data on the socialization of children and on the other hand using Murdock's judgments on the economy of the adult culture. In the case of the second generalization, it seems to us that there was little opportunity for information on family and social structure to have influenced the judges in making the socialization ratings.

Both of these generalizations contribute to understanding the social background of the relatively small difference in socialization of boys and girls which we believe characterizes our society at the present time. Our mechanized economy is perhaps less dependent than any previous economy upon the superior average strength of the male. The nuclear family in our society is often so isolated that husband and wife must each be prepared at times to take over or help in the household tasks normally assigned to the other. It is also significant that the conditions favoring low sex differentiation appear to be more characteristic of the upper segments of our society, in socioeconomic and educational status, than of lower segments. This observation may be relevant to the tendency toward smaller sex differences in personality in higher status groups (cf. Terman and Miles, 5).

The increase in our society of conditions favoring small sex difference has led some people to advocate a virtual elimination of sex differences in socialization. This course seems likely to be dysfunctional even in our society. Parsons, Bales *et al.* (3) argue that a differentiation of role similar to the universal pattern of sex difference is an important and perhaps inevitable development in any social group, such as the nuclear family. If we add to their argument the point that biological differences between the sexes make most appropriate the usual division of those roles between the sexes, we have compelling reasons to expect that the decrease in differentiation of adult sex role will not continue to the vanishing point. In our training of children, there may now be less differentiation in sex role than characterizes adult life —so little, indeed, as to provide inadequate preparation for adulthood. This state of affairs is likely to be especially true of formal education, which is more subject to conscious influence by an ideology than is informal socialization at home. With child training being more oriented toward the male than the female role in adulthood, many of the adjustment problems of women in our society today may be partly traced to conflicts growing out of inadequate childhood preparation for their adult role. This argument is nicely supported in extreme form by Spiro's analysis of sex roles in an Israeli kibbutz (4). The ideology of the founders of the kibbutz included the objective of greatly reducing differences in sex role. But the economy of the kibbutz is a largely nonmechanized one in which the superior average strength of men is badly needed in many jobs. The result is that, despite the ideology and many attempts to implement it, women continue to be assigned primarily to traditional "women's work," and the incompatibility between upbringing or ideology and adult role is an important source of conflict for women.

Note on regional distribution. There is marked variation among regions of the world in typical size of sex difference in socialization. In our sample, societies in North America and Africa tend to have large sex difference, and societies in Oceania to have small sex difference. Less confidently, because of the smaller number of cases, we can report a tendency toward small sex differences in Asia and South America as well. Since most of the variables with which we find the sex difference to be significantly correlated have a similar regional distribution, the question arises whether the correlations might better be ascribed to some quite different source having to do with large regional similarities, rather than to the functional dependence we have suggested. As a partial check, we have tried to determine whether the correlations we report in Table 2 tend also to be found strictly within regions. For each of the three regions for which we have sizable samples (North America, Africa, and Oceania) we have separately plotted 2 x 2 tables corresponding to each of the 6 relationships reported in Table 2. (We did this only for the more inclusive sample, since for the more selective sample the number of cases within a region would have been extremely small.) Out of the 18 correlations thus determined, 11 are positive and only 3 are negative (the other 4 being exactly zero). This result clearly suggests a general tendency for these correlations to hold true within regions as well as between regions, and may lend further support to our functional interpretation.

SUMMARY

A survey of certain aspects of socialization in 110 cultures shows that differentiation of the sexes is unimportant in infancy, but that in childhood there is, as in our society, a widespread pattern of greater pressure toward nurturance, obedience, and responsibility in girls, and toward self-reliance and achievement striving in boys. There are a few reversals of sex difference, and many instances of no detectable sex difference; these facts tend to confirm the cultural rather than directly biological nature of the differences. Cultures vary in the degree to which these differentiations are made; correlational analysis suggests some of the social conditions influencing these variations, and helps in understanding why our society has relatively small sex differentiation.

REFERENCES

1. Murdock, G. P. Comparative data on the division of labor by sex. *Social Forces,* 1937, **15**, 551–553.

2. MURDOCK, G. P., & WHITING, J. W. M. Cultural determination of parental attitudes: The relationship between the social structure, particularly family structure and parental behavior. In M. J. E. Senn (Ed.), *Problems of infancy and childhood: Transactions of the Fourth Conference,* March 6–7, 1950. New York: Josiah Macy, Jr. Foundation, 1951. Pp. 13–34.
3. PARSONS, T., BALES, R. F. *et al. Family, socialization and interaction process.* Glencoe, Ill.: Free Press, 1955.
4. SPIRO, M. E. *Kibbutz: Venture in Utopia.* Cambridge: Harvard Univer. Press, 1956.
5. TERMAN, L. M., & MILES, CATHERINE C. *Sex and personality.* New York: McGraw-Hill, 1936.

25
ACQUIRING DEPENDENCE AND INDEPENDENCE: A THEORETICAL ORIENTATION*

GLEN HEATHERS

EVERYONE'S PERSONALITY develops in a social world and every aspect of personality reflects one's relationships and experiences with others. A central aspect of the process of becoming "socialized" is developing needs, perceptions, and response patterns having to do with dependence on others, or with independence. Currently, a major research program on the development of dependence-independence in preschool children is underway at the Fels Research Institute. This paper presents the general theoretical orientation basic to the research program. Its purposes are to define certain forms of dependence-independence and to indicate how they may be learned.

FORMS OF DEPENDENCE AND INDEPENDENCE

A person is dependent on others to the extent that he has needs which require that others respond in particular ways if these needs are to be satisfied. A person is independent of others to the extent that he can satisfy his needs without requiring that others respond to him in particular ways.

One way of depending on others is *instrumental dependence* which is present when a person seeks help in reaching goals. Thus, an infant depends on others for help in satisfying hunger and other bodily needs. When a child seeks help, as in getting food, help is the sub-goal in relation to the end-goal of food.

With emotional dependence, the responses of others are the end-goals rather than means of reaching them. Thus, the need for affection is an emotional-dependence need which is satisfied by others' affectionate responses. Three forms of emotional dependence may be distinguished—needs for reassurance, for affection, and for approval. The need for *reassurance* occurs in situations when a person anticipates undesired or feared outcomes

* From the *Journal of Genetic Psychology*, 1955, *87*, 277–291. Reprinted with permission from the author and The Journal Press.

In preparing this paper, I am indebted to L. W. Sontag, Vaughn Crandall, Judith Gruender, Anne Preston, and Edna Small of the Fels Staff for valuable suggestions.

—failure, rejection, injury, etc. Seeking reassurance is a matter of placing oneself in the care of another person as a way of avoiding such outcomes. Thus, a child who fears the dark desires someone he trusts to share the darkness with him, and a child who is anxious about failing a task wants to be told that he will make out all right. A person's need for *affection* is the need for others to respond with physical signs of affection such as caresses and kisses or with words and deeds which show that they care for him. A person's need for *approval* is the need for others to make positive responses toward him either on the basis of his performance or on the basis of status-giving characteristics such as his appearance, his possessions, or his social rôles.

Instrumental independence means conducting activities and coping with problems without seeking help. It is the obverse of instrumental dependence.

Emotional independence means, first, the absence of needs for reassurance, affection, or approval in particular situations. This aspect may be called "emotional self-reliance" and is the obverse of emotional dependence. In addition, emotional independence is defined to include "self-assertion" in the form of needs to master tasks, and to dominate others. It should be noted that emotional self-reliance does not assume any specific independence needs while self-assertion does. The need to master a task is assumed to be more than the need to complete it; it is the need for self-approval on the basis of one's performance. Similarly, the need to dominate is assumed to be a need for self-approval on the basis of one's assertive behavior. These definitions of self-reliance and self-assertion assume that the behavior expressing them is not used as a means of gaining approval. When approval is the goal, as when a person dominates in order to attract attention or praise, emotional dependence rather than independence is shown.

ASSUMPTIONS ABOUT THE LEARNING PROCESS

In offering an account of how dependence and independence are learned, it is assumed that learning takes place in relation to needs which a person tends to satisfy through making appropriate goal-directed responses. A person learns certain "meanings" of aspects of situations in relation to his needs and he learns "predispositions" to make or not to make certain goal-directed responses when a given need is active in a situation. His overt responses depend on which of his needs are active as he enters the situation, on what *need-relevancies* he perceives in the situation, and on his *expectancies* of satisfying or not satisfying his needs by responses directed toward goals in the situation.

The need-relevancies of a situation may be divided into three categories: (*a*) need-arousal—a situation may evoke needs as when a person perceives the threat of injury; (*b*) goals—a situation may provide opportunities for satisfying needs; and (*c*) goal-pathways—a situation may provide opportunities to make responses which lead to goals.

A person learns the need-relevancies of a situation through the simultaneous association of his perceptions of the situation, and of his responses in the situation, with positive or negative *reinforcement.* When perceptions of the situation and of his responses to it are associated with *positive* reinforcement (achieving goals) he learns to expect a positive outcome and acquires predispositions to make the goal-directed responses which led to positive reinforcement. Conversely, when perceptions of the situation and of his responses are associated with *negative* reinforcement (failure to achieve goals, punishment, injury) he learns to expect this sort of outcome and acquires predispositions not to make the responses which led to negative reinforcement.

A point which requires special emphasis is that the reinforcement value of a goal is not determined by the goal as such but by its relation to one's expectations. Thus a child who is seeking affection from his mother may perceive her hug as rejection because she doesn't take him on her lap and caress him as she usually has done. Another child may perceive a similar hug as rewarding because it equals or exceeds what he has learned to expect.

An important aspect of learning need-relevancies is that stimuli from a situation which are associated with reinforcement acquire reinforcement value. When this has occurred, these accompaniments or "signs" of reinforcement may function as goals in the absence of the previous reinforcement. Thus, if a child's mother smiles whenever she gratifies any of his needs, her smile will come to be a goal in its own right.

When substitute goals are learned, new needs are also acquired in the sense that a person tends to seek these substitute goals in the absence of the needs which were previously active. In this article, needs for reassurance, affection, approval, mastery, and domination are considered to be acquired needs. It is assumed that the reason one comes to need affection, approval, etc., is because of a general tendency to seek positive reinforcement. So, when a person perceives the opportunity for achieving a goal (such as affection or approval) he not only has the expectancy of achieving it but also the predisposition to achieve it.

INSTRUMENTAL DEPENDENCE

At birth, the infant is relatively helpless and is *passively* dependent on others to satisfy almost all his needs. He can breathe, and, if his supply of air is interrupted, his struggling may restore it. He can suck in and swallow liquid brought to his mouth and he can digest and eliminate. He reacts to annoying stimuli by general bodily activity which may remove the annoyance. However, beyond such reflexes and such general bodily responses, the very young infant can do nothing to satisfy his needs.

Despite his helplessness, it is wrong to say that the neonate is *actively* dependent on others, since he must first learn to associate others with the satisfaction of his needs. Neither instrumental nor emotional dependence are present until the child has learned to perceive others as related to achieving goals, and until he has learned to use certain responses as means of inducing others to attend to his needs. For example, the basis for learning to use crying as an expression of instrumental dependence is the fact that a child's mother responds to his crying by trying to discover and satisfy his needs. Learning principles predict that through this sort of experience the child comes to associate crying with his mother's responding to him, and with relieving his distress. When this learning has taken place, crying may be used as a device to express instrumental dependence.

In developing instrumental dependence on others, the child learns various devices for stimulating others to help him reach his goals. Crying is generally effective in alerting others to the fact that he wants something, and also is apt to disturb others enough to make them try to find out what he wants and "pacify" him. But crying isn't a good way of indicating *what* he wants. A child learns to indicate what he wants by looking toward it, pointing at it, naming it, etc. In this process of learning instrumental-dependence devices, each child is taught by his mother and others to use certain ways of asking for help which are acceptable to them, and to which they will respond by helping him. He is also taught not to use certain devices because these are ineffective in getting help. Thus a child may be taught to stop crying, to smile, or to say "please" as conditions for getting others to help him.

One form of instrumental dependence is imitation in which one depends on another for his cues as to where to go or what to do in order to reach his goals. Imitation has been analyzed in detail by Miller and Dollard (2) who showed that one child will learn to imitate another child if following the other leads to reward while not following him leads to nonreward. They showed also that imitation "generalizes" from one situation to another. That is, imitation becomes a general instrumental-dependence device which may be used in any appropriate situation as a means of reaching a goal.

It is essential that the person from whom instrumental aid is sought be motivated to give help. Very often this means that a child must "earn" the help he seeks by offering his prospective helper some inducement. Thus a mother who desires that her child show signs of "growing up" may require that he try first before she will help him. This give-and-take is obviously important in developing the socialized individual. Instead of passive, one-sided relationships it requires active, mutual relations with other people. Sears (3) offers a beginning toward the systematic analysis of this interaction process in his consideration of the "dyadic group."

EMOTIONAL DEPENDENCE

Acquiring Emotional Dependence Needs

In explaining how emotional dependence develops, the first question is how others' responses become the end-goals which are sought rather than means toward end-goals as with instrumental dependence. In the analysis which follows, this will be discussed in relation to acquiring needs for reassurance, affection, and approval.

a. Needs for Reassurance. Reassurance satisfies needs for emotional support in "anxiety" situations when a person anticipates injury, failure, or rejection. In order to anticipate unpleasant experiences in a situation, one must previously have had such experiences in situations having something in common with the present one. The need for reassurance in situations perceived as threatening develops if other people, by their presence or their responses, have given instrumental aid which prevented the threatening outcomes. In this way, other people become associated with avoiding or relieving anxiety in threatening situations. More generally, the presence and responses of others, including their verbal assurance, come to be associated with anxiety reduction in any situation. Thus a person comes to "trust" others and to count on them to prevent undesired outcomes. The need for reassurance, and responses of seeking it, thus develop as means of preventing or relieving anxiety.

Obviously a person does not learn to trust everybody since in his experiences some people have failed to protect him from harm and some have punished him through frustrating, rejecting, or injuring him. On the basis of these differential experiences, each person learns to direct his needs for reassurance toward certain people or categories of people and not toward others.

b. Needs for Affection. To explain how a child's needs for affection develop, it is necessary to show how affectionate responses by others become associated with the satisfaction of certain of the child's "basic" needs. The infant's earliest experiences of receiving affection have to do with being made comfortable and relaxed, and with being given pleasant sensual stimulation. One of the primary expressions of affection is when a mother holds her infant as she feeds him. Another is holding him in her arms and caressing him while rocking him to sleep. Each of these classical expressions of affection involves a comfortable posture, warmth, and mild stimulation tending to relax the child. Also each involves direct sensual stimulation to which the child responds with signs of pleasure. After a few weeks, the child experiences affection from his mother and others through being played with—being tumbled about, being surprised in games like peek-a-boo, being given toys to play with, being teased with funny faces or funny sounds, etc. On the basis of such experiences, the child comes to perceive its mother and others as sources of comfort and pleasure. Also it develops impulses toward being responded to in ways associated with such comfort and pleasure—it develops needs for affection.

While satisfying her child's needs in direct physical ways the mother also smiles at her child, talks gently to him, calls him pet names, and uses other verbal expressions of her affection. Since these responses are associated with the direct physical gratification of his needs, they come to have reward value in their own right so that needs which were satisfied originally by physical affection may now be satisfied (at least in part) by these symbolic expressions of affection.

c. Needs for Approval. When the child first learns to depend on others for instrumental aid, for reassurance, or for affection, nothing much is required of him beyond letting others know what his needs are. In other words, if his mother understands his capacities, she won't demand that he behave in any particular way as a condition for giving him help or reassurance or affection. However, after a time, she begins to require that he act in certain ways if he is to get her to coöperate in meeting his needs. The child's choice of response in a situation thus becomes a condition of his being rewarded, ignored, or punished by others.

When the child learns that his choice of response determines whether others will satisfy his needs, he develops the need to respond in ways which others approve. When they tell him "that's fine," "you're a big boy," "you did it by yourself," etc., at the same time they reward him in other ways, their verbal expressions of approval acquire reward value. Thereafter, when the need for approval is present, these signs of approval may satisfy the need.

On the other hand, signs of disapproval (frowning, yelling at the child, saying "don't" or "that's naughty") are associated with rejection or punishment and acquire negative reinforcement value. Disapproval thus becomes a basis for learning not to do certain things even when those acts are not discouraged in any other way. Also, since disapproval is often accompanied by punishment, it will tend to arouse anxiety about being punished. This anxiety will be relieved by getting others to respond positively.[1]

Developing Response Patterns for Expressing Dependence Needs

In analyzing any need, three aspects may be distinguished: (*a*) a state of *tension* or expectancy which may be experienced as dissatisfaction, anxiety, or pleasant anticipation; (*b*) *goals* (objects, circumstances, others' responses) which are ways of satisfying the need; and (*c*) *response patterns* which are means of achieving these goals. The analysis to this point has dealt mainly with the tensional and goal aspects of emotional dependence. This section considers how a person develops or selects particular response patterns (devices) for stimulating others to satisfy his dependence needs.

In seeking a dependence relationship with another person, one's overtures

[1] The present account of the development of instrumental and emotional dependence implies two basic steps in the socialization process. When the child has learned to depend on others for help, protection, reassurance, and affection, the first step—acquiring "infantile dependence"—has been made. When he learns to seek approval by conforming to others' requirements, he takes the second step which leads him out of infantile dependence toward what may be called "social maturity." Social maturity is primarily the readiness for mutual relations with others where one tries to satisfy others' needs as a condition for their satisfying his own.

should do three things—attract the other person's attention, indicate what is wanted, and motivate the other person to respond in the desired way. During the child's first year or so, crying is one of the most frequently used dependence devices. Crying usually induces the child's mother to approach, pick him up, and comfort him, thus satisfying needs for reassurance or for affection. One of the child's earliest learned dependence devices is turning or leaning toward his mother and reaching out his arms. This is a postural adjustment associated with being picked up; when it occurs in anticipation of being picked up it serves as a stimulus to the mother and is a dependence device. When the child is able to crawl or walk, he tends to approach his mother when seeking to satisfy dependent needs.

Language adds greatly to the child's ability to indicate what he wants and also give him further weapons for motivating others to comply with his wishes. When he learns to say "mama" and "dada" he can indicate which one he wishes to serve him. As his vocabulary grows, he can say specifically what his wishes are, or what he wants others to do: "I'm scared," "I'm tired," "come here," "carry me," "watch me," "look what I made." Each of these verbal expressions is taught the child in association with the situations or acts to which it applied, and in association with the satisfaction of the needs which were present at the same time.

Each child learns his own unique set of dependence devices according to which of his response patterns his parents and others rewarded. Thus it is not possible to present a list of dependence response patterns which applies to all children. However, there are common elements in every child's set of dependence devices which reflect the fact that each child's needs for reassurance, affection, and approval call for certain kinds of responses from others. Also, each child in a cultural group tends to be taught a set of dependence devices which reflect the values and norms of the group.

REACTIONS WHEN DEPENDENCE OVERTURES ARE REJECTED

Sontag (4) proposes that the frustration of dependent needs leads to "defenses" against further frustration of one's dependence-seeking overtures. Obviously the most radical defense against rejection is to stop trying to induce others to satisfy one's dependence needs. However, before a child adopts this sort of reaction to felt rejection, he may respond to rejection by changes in his dependence-seeking devices, or by shifting his overtures away from one person toward another. Thus, if a child's mother rejects his requests to sit on her lap but offers affection in other ways, the child will tend to modify his affection-seeking overtures correspondingly. If the child's mother almost always refuses to pick him up and play with him while his father usually does so, he will tend to turn to his father rather than to his mother for this sort of expression of affection.

Sontag (4) has indicated how over-conformity may be adopted as a general device for avoiding rejection of dependence overtures. As he points out, through being "good" a child lessens his chances of being disapproved or punished as well as increasing his chances of winning affection and approval from his parents or others. Being good, of course, means paying the price of catering to adults' standards of conduct as a way of inducing them to gratify his dependence needs.

In the cases described above, a child reacts to rejection by modifying his dependence-seeking overtures or by changing the person toward whom he directs such overtures. These types of adjustive reactions to rejection occur as the child perceives an alternative way of satisfying his dependence needs. However, if such alternative channels are not available to him, if he consistently meets rejection when he makes dependence-seeking overtures to the people around him, he may come to expect rejection generally. In such a case, expressing his emotional dependence needs becomes associated with punishing consequences (frustration) and the child tends to quit trying to induce others to satisfy these needs. Thus, constant rejection may produce a general withdrawal from seeking dependence relationships, although dependent needs may still be active. Experimental evidence in support of this point is offered by Carl (1) who showed that the frequency of dependence responses declines when the adult toward whom these responses are directed consistently fails to respond to them.

Where consistent rejection has produced strong withdrawal tendencies, one may find the child showing evidence of a conflict between the tendency to make dependence overtures and the tendency to hold back in ancitipation of being rejected. Hesitant, timorous overtures may result from these opposed impulses. The child who wants affection may start toward his mother, then stop half way and stand there. Or he may go over and stand at her side, touch her dress, then wait for an encouraging sign from her before making more definite indications of his wishes.

INSTRUMENTAL INDEPENDENCE

When a child initiates his own activities and copes with difficulties he encounters without asking for help, he shows instrumental independence. Suppose a child starts working out a cut-out puzzle with the goal of completing it. If the puzzle is hard for him he will take quite a while and make many mistakes before he reaches his goal. The extent to which he persists in the task without asking for help may be taken as a measure of his instrumental independence.

Whether a child shows instrumental independence in a situation depends on a number of factors. The hypotheses which follow specify five of these factors and predict their effects on a child's tendencies to seek help.

(*a*). *The more frustration a child encounters while performing an activity, the more will he tend to seek help.* This hypothesis simply assumes that children learn to seek help as one way of overcoming obstacles in their goal-directed behavior.

(*b*). *The more a child expects that help is available, the more will he tend to seek it.* If a child has learned through repeated experiences that others will help him under certain conditions, he will tend to resort to help when those conditions exist. If he usually has been refused help at such times, he will tend not to expect or seek it.

(*c*). *The more a child expects he can reach his goal unaided, the less will he tend to seek help.* If the child has previously completed the activity or similar activities without help, he has a basis for expecting to succeed on his own and for going ahead without asking for help.

(*d*). *The more reassurance a child receives while performing an activity, the less is he apt to seek help.* This factor of reassurance is illustrated when someone says, "You're doing fine," or "You can finish it." The hypothesis assumes that reassurance fosters instrumental independence by lessening anxiety in instances when the child is anticipating failure.

(*e*). *The more a child expects approval for reaching a goal unaided, the less will he tend to seek help.* This assumes the child has the need for approval and that this need provides a positive incentive for finishing an activity without help if he expects approval upon completing it.

The development of "frustration tolerance" is an aspect of acquiring instrumental independence. The critical factor in learning to cope with frustrations is whether the child actually persists until he reaches his goal. When a parent helps a child "over the rough spots" so that he continues at the task rather than giving up, he is helping his child learn to tolerate frustration. Also, if he makes the task easy at the outset and gradually steps up its difficulty as the child's expectation of success increases along with increasing frustration, the chances are good that more and more frustration will be tolerated. Finally, if the desirability of the goal is increased, the child is more apt to persist until reaching it and so to develop the expectation of overcoming obstacles on future occasions.

In analyzing how instrumental independence develops, the role of emotional dependence deserves special consideration. If a situation is one in which the child anticipates injury or rejection, he may require reassurance (emotional dependence) in order to face the situation and so be enabled to develop instrumental independence. Also, as discussed by Stendler (5), the child's need for approval may play a key role in motivating him to exhibit instrumental independence rather than quitting or asking for help when he encounters difficulties.

EMOTIONAL INDEPENDENCE

Emotional dependence and independence are relative terms. No one at any age is emotionally dependent in every situation. However, comparing children or adults of the same age, there are great differences in the types of situation, and in the proportion of all situations, where emotional dependence and independence are shown. As an individual grows older, the situations in which he shows emotional dependence and independence change. It is these differences which require explanation.

Developing Emotional Self-Reliance

A child may be called emotionally self-reliant (or self-confident) when he faces threats of injury or rejection without requiring emotional support. A lack of emotional self-reliance is shown by avoiding threat situations or by seeking emotional "props" which make one feel safer while coping with threats. These props may be means of reducing the actual threat in the situation, or "security symbols" such as the doll a child takes to bed with him, or reassurance from a trusted person.

In analyzing how emotional self-reliance is acquired, threats of injury and of rejection will be discussed separately.

a. Acquiring Self-Confidence in Physical Threat Situations. Initially, each child is fearless in many situations where his parents know he may injure himself. When a 12-month-old crawls off the porch and tumbles to the ground he need not be showing self-confidence. He may simply not know any better. Eventually, a child will fall enough times in one situation or another to learn the painful consequences and to anticipate them whenever he is at the point of falling again. When he has learned to associate a situation with the threat of hurting himself, the issue of emotional dependence or independence in that situation is relevant. In responding to the threats he perceives in a situation where he may hurt himself, a child shows emotional independence if he copes with the situation without requiring any protective devices or without leaning on another person for reassurance.

The question of how self-confidence is learned applies in particular to situations where a child has been frightened or hurt and reacts by showing fear or avoidance, or by requiring emotional support in order to face the situation. Methods of learning self-confidence may be illustrated by ways in which children overcome the fear of deep water. Assume a child who swims a little, but is afraid to be in water over his head. Six methods of overcoming his fear are described below.

(1). *Sink-or-Swim Method.* In this case, the child is forced to cope with the situation by being tossed into the water and left to fend for himself. If he gets to land under his own power a few times, he may perceive himself as capable of coping with the situation and lose his fear. This is a hazardous method of teaching self-confidence, since the child may panic and have to be rescued. Or the experience may intensify his fear of the water even though he makes it to land.

(2). *Distraction Method.* This method includes any means by which the child temporarily forgets or pushes aside his fear so that he jumps into the water and tries to swim. For example, if others say, "I dare you," or "coward," the child may be distracted from his fear long enough to plunge in. Swimming successfully under these conditions is a way for the child to replace his expectation of failure and injury with the expectation of success.

(3). *Threshold Method.* This is the method of starting out a stroke or two from land and going a bit farther out each time as confidence grows in one's ability to swim back. The success of this method depends on the threat in the situation increasing slowly enough that the child's anxiety or fear does not exceed the level which he will tolerate.

(4). *Over-Learning Method.* This method calls for practicing swimming under safe conditions to the point where one becomes so skillful and experienced that he becomes confident he can take care of himself in the deep water.

(5). *Crutch Method.* In this case the child uses water wings or a life belt which he relies on to keep him from sinking. With the protection this device gives him, he practices swimming until he has sufficient confidence in his ability that he will venture into water without a crutch.

(6). *Reassurance Method.* In this method the child depends on some person whom he trusts to protect him. The reassurance given him enables him to practice swimming and to discover that he can take care of himself.

Each of the six methods described applies to acquiring self-confidence in the great variety of physical threat situations—overcoming the fear of being alone in a room, the fear of animals, the fear of high places, the fear of fighting, etc. Acquiring self-confidence by any of these methods depends on coping with the feared situation successfully and on developing the expectation of being successful on one's own.

b. Acquiring "Rejection Tolerance." One form of emotional self-reliance is the capacity to tolerate rejection by others. Two bases for exhibiting rejection-tolerance are proposed. First, a person may be emotionally self-reliant following instances of being rejected if he has alternative ways of satisfying his needs for affection and approval when they arise. If he has usually been successful in satisfying these dependent needs he may expect to be able to satisfy them again and so will be secure against specific instances of being rejected. Second, a person while developing channels for expressing his emotional dependence needs, learns to discriminate the people who are important sources of gratification of these needs from others who are not. When this learning has occurred, he will be able to take rejection from people who "don't matter" as long as those whom he counts on are not rejecting.

Developing Self-Assertion

Self-assertion expresses needs to master tasks or to dominate other people. In satisfying these needs the relevant goals are feelings of adequacy or superiority: "I did it," "I'm smarter than you are," "I beat him," etc. In short, it is assumed that self-assertion needs are satisfied by self-approval.

a. Acquiring Mastery Needs and Behavior. A basis for explaining how mastery develops is the child's desire to win others' approval. On this basis, three aspects of the process of developing this form of self-assertion may be distinguished, as follows: (*a*) acquiring needs for approval, (*b*) learning to perform tasks with persistence, speed, or skill in order to win approval, and (*c*) "internalizing," i.e., adopting others' standards as to the sort of performance required to gain approval, and feeling self-approval when these standards are satisfied. The first two aspects fall under emotional dependence and have been discussed earlier in this paper. It is with the third aspect that emotional independence enters the picture since the child who has internalized his approval-seeking doesn't require approval from others to motivate his performance.

Internalization of approval may be explained as follows. After learning to do things which win others' approval, a child anticipates approval whenever he performs the acts which have been approved. It is assumed that anticipated approval is rewarding by itself, giving a feeling of security or pleasure. Since it is rewarding, it may function as a goal to reinforce the performance of the customarily approved behavior.

The degree to which a child develops mastery needs, and the activities and standards of performance he uses to express those needs, are determined by his individual learning experiences. A child will tend to express mastery needs in those activities in which he has been successful in getting approval. Getting approval, of course, depends on doing things which his parents and others value—going to the toilet, keeping clean, solving puzzles, catching a ball, reciting a rhyme, etc. Also a child learns to strive for the levels of accomplishment which others have set up as a basis for giving approval—speed, accuracy, grace, persistence, originality, etc.

b. Acquiring Dominance Needs and Behavior. Learning dominance needs and behavior may be accounted for on the basis of winning others' approval in the same way that learning mastery was explained above. Once others' approval has been internalized, self-approval (from anticipated approval) serves as reinforcement for dominant behavior. The great differences in dominative behavior among children of the same age may be explained as due in part to differences in the amount of approval or disapproval others have given them for being dominant in particular ways in various situations.

A child does not have to win in order to satisfy dominance needs if approval has been given him for daring, for doing his best, or for making a good showing. However, other things being equal, the more often a child is defeated in tests for dominance, the less apt he will be to express dominative behavior. Since dominating others often has instrumental value in obtaining goals other than approval (as when two children want the same toy), being successful in competing for such goals reinforces one's tendencies toward expressing domination, while being unsuccessful sets up expectations of failure and tends to weaken those tendencies.

SUMMARY

This paper defines certain dependence-independence aspects of personality and outlines how they may be learned. In this analysis, the distinction is made between instrumental dependence (needs for help) and emotional dependence (needs for reassurance, affection or approval). Similarly, instrumental independence is distinguished from emotional independence. Emotional independence is defined to include self-assertive needs to master tasks and to dominate other people.

An important link between dependence and independence is offered by the need for approval, which is not only a dependence need but also a basis for learning both instrumental and emotional independence.

Dependence and independence needs are discussed as acquired or "secondary" needs. Also, this article discusses the acquisition of expectancies of satisfying or not satisfying these needs by making goal-directed responses in particular situations. It is assumed that such expectancies are associated with predispositions to make, or not to make, particular goal-directed responses, dependent on the outcomes which are anticipated.

In the analysis of instrumental and emotional dependence, this article stresses the fact that dependence needs require interaction with others since these needs can be satisfied only when others respond in certain ways. Since others must be motivated to satisfy one's dependence needs, and since others set up certain requirements the dependent person must meet before they will gratify his needs, it is evident that dependence needs play a central role in shaping one's personality to meet social expectations.

REFERENCES

1. Carl, L. J. An experimental study of the effect of nurturance on preschool children. Unpub. Ph.D. Dissertation, State Univ. Iowa, 1949.
2. Miller, N. E., & Dollard, J. *Social Learning and Imitation.* New Haven: Yale Univ. Press, 1941.
3. Sears, R. R. A theoretical framework for personality and social behavior. *Am. Psychol.,* 1951, **6,** 476–483.
4. Sontag, L. W. Dynamics of personality formation. *Personality,* 1951, **6,** 119–130.
5. Stendler, C. B. Critical periods in socialization and over-dependency. *Child Devel.,* 1952, **23,** 3–12.

26
EARLY PRESSURES IN CHILD DEVELOPMENT*

WILLARD W. HARTUP

WHAT TO demand of a child? How much to demand of him? When to demand it? The problem of early pressures is a core concern within the field of practical child psychology. Also, much of the scientific work currently being conducted in the areas of learning, motivation, cognitive processes, and personality development in children has implications for this problem. More and more frequently, responsible educators are endorsing the concept of early pressures in child development. Francis Keppel, the U.S. Commissioner of Education, added his support by suggesting that we have been wasting enormous creative powers by beginning education too late, by assuming that there is some magical, fixed age at which learning takes place, and by adhering slavishly to the notion of predetermined developmental levels.

As a consequence of changing educational views, present-day parents and teachers are caught in a bind. "Should I help my four-year-old pick out words in 'Cat in the Hat'? I hear the first-grade teacher doesn't like parents to do this." "Should reading, or prereading experiences, be part of every nursery school and kindergarten curriculum?" "How far should I go in urging my three-year-old to fight back when the neighbor kids have pre-empted his toys?"

Descending to us, on the one hand, is a tradition which suggests that those responsible for the socialization of children exercise their responsibility best by helping children do what they are free or ready to do without trying to force them into particular channels of expression. The idea that children develop optimally in a benign, hot-house type of environment is identified, albeit mistakenly, with the tradition in pedagogy known as "progressive education" and with the psychological theories of the psychodynamic schools. Such terms as *permissiveness* and *liberalism* are closely associated with these

---

* Reprinted with permission from the author and *Young Children*. Vol. *20,* No. 5, May, 1965, 270–283. 1834 Connecticut Avenue, N.W., Washington, D.C. 20009.

Address presented at the National Association for the Education of Young Children, Miami Beach, Florida, October 29, 1964.

child-rearing approaches, and few words in the lexicon of social psychology have been so overworked or badly misused.

Running counter to educational doctrine based on concepts of readiness and free expression is the doctrine of early pressures. Those who hold this view argue that there should be early and persistent demands for conformity to accepted standards of moral and social conduct, as well as early demands for excellence in cognitive performance and self-motivated achievement. Further, these demands should be buttressed by "old-fashioned" discipline stemming from strong, watchful, authoritative parents, teachers, preachers, and law-enforcement officials. Advocacy of early pressures in the educational development of the child has a long-standing tradition, but it has been particularly strong since the advent of the space age. Emphasis on early pressures for characterological development has been particularly intense since the advent of the "new conservatism" in American politics.

The philosophical conflict experienced by those who live and work with children is intense. I regard this conflict with the utmost seriousness. Occasionally, the conflict between opposing child-rearing ideologies can be resolved by rational methods. A teacher can say to himself, coolly and objectively, "Let's look at the evidence concerning the results of structured language experiences for children of preschool age. To be sure, the evidence is not very good and more research should be done, but the choice can be a rational one."

Unfortunately, the problem is complicated by feelings or, as Leon Festinger (1957) has termed it, *cognitive dissonance*. Acceptance of a permissive philosophy of child-rearing is, after all, to act in opposition to an old and strong cultural tradition that endorses the necessity for pressure. A certain amount of discomfort or dissonance inevitably follows for the individual who deliberately chooses the permissive view. Further, because rearing children is extremely serious business, the amount of dissonance evoked by the necessity for choosing an educational philosophy is likely to be great rather than minimal. It is the rare parent who, when his child has successfully gotten away with something, can dismiss this without a feeling of "maybe I should have been tougher on him." For example, in our hourse, we have a 22-month-old named Barry who misbehaves by opening the oven door on the kitchen stove, climbing up, and nonchalantly lighting the burners. (One Playskool toy and at least two pans have been permanently scorched as a consequence of Barry's actions.) Our reaction to Barry's behavior has been a kind of disorganized attempt to evoke verbal mediational processes in our son. I experienced enormous dissonance one day when a very child-centered, liberal-minded colleague informed me that she had instantly stopped similar behavior in her child. She simply said, "Hot, hot, Benjy," and then deliberately burned him! The dissonance experienced by people responsible for the rearing of children ranges from that evoked by simple, specific instances such as the one just described to conflict evoked by whole philosophies. For example, the most dedicated, psychodynamically-oriented preschool teacher seldom has personal defenses of sufficient strength, or the "tunnel vision" needed, to escape dissonance evoked by the rising popularity of the Montessori schools—and, vice versa.

The antecedents of the child-rearing traditions being discussed here are pertinent. After some historical remarks, selected research evidence supporting an eclectic philosophy of child-rearing will be presented. The point of view to be expressed is based on social learning principles. It will be argued that pressures of certain kinds should, indeed, be brought to bear on the young child. It will be argued, however, that these pressures should be exerted within a context of nurturance and permissiveness. No admixture of liberal and conservative philosophies of child rearing stressing that the adult should keep an iron hand concealed in a velvet glove will be proposed here. Rather, it will be argued that, when the child's early years include encouragement of dependence and trust in adults, early pressures for independence and achievement, for appropriate identifications, for motivation to learn, and for competence in certain areas of intellective functioning are not only appropriate but desirable. It should be emphasized that this is not a simple middle-of-the-road philosophy.

The doctrine that children accomplish best what they are ready to do in the absence of pressure for accomplishment is the culmination of two ideologies concerning the nature of the child. First, this doctrine is based on a belief in the innate capacity for goodness in children. The name of Jean Jacques Rousseau is usually identified with the point of view that, if the child is permitted to express his natural impulses and to develop without restriction the abilities given him by nature, he will show little of the depravity characteristic of adults and his capacity for constructive social good will be maximized.

A second influence on present-day liberal education has been the hypothesis of "critical periods." The notion of critical periods is comprised of two interrelated hypotheses. First, it is assumed that both the physical and behavioral development of children proceed according to more or less orderly sequences. For most children, turning over, creeping, walking, running, and jumping proceed in an orderly sequence. We have thoroughly adequate norms concerning both the average ages at which these events occur and the amount of variability across groups of children in the timing of each of these events. Probably the most famous critical periods postulated in all child psychology are Freud's psychosexual stages; others who have recognized critical periods in behavioral development are Erik Erikson, who has described regularities in psychosocial development, and Piaget, who has argued that intellectual development takes place according to a patterned sequence.

Implicit also in the critical-periods principle is the notion that "there is a time to plant and a time to pluck up that which is planted." That is, it appears that interference with certain developmental phenomena seems to be of greater significance for the later development of the child when the interference occurs at some points in the life history rather than at others. This component of the critical-periods hypothesis is supported by developmental observations at many different levels. Students of human embryology report that there are clear-cut periods in the morphogenesis of the embryo during which neural tissue, visceral tissue, and other parts of the physical structure of the organism are sensitive to extrinsic stimulation, but beyond these periods the embryo is fairly resistant to such influences. Similarly, McGraw (1935) found that attempts to speed learning of certain motor skills were ineffectual when introduced at an inappropriate time. Students of personality development have argued that attachment to a love object during the first months of a child's life is prerequisite to successful subsequent socialization. Piaget and other students of cognitive development have suggested similar critical periods in intellectual functioning.

Virtually all students of developmental processes have acknowledged that the timing of developmental events is, to some extent, unique for each individual child. The time schedule or stages formulated for various aspects of behavioral development are not rigid but apply within fairly broad limits. Nevertheless, the critical-periods notion is the reason why eight out of ten textbooks in child psychology are organized in terms of chronological age and why children are not taught to read until they are six.

Descriptive norms relating to the behavioral development of children are, and will continue to be, very useful in constructing educational programs for masses of children. "Best guesses" about the capacities of children at various ages, when based on adequate normative research, facilitate many a sound educational decision. But norms are seductive. For example, they do not by themselves furnish a parent or teacher with an adequate basis for a philosophy of child rearing. "Slavish attention to developmental levels" (to use Mr. Keppel's phrase) draws attention away from a more basic issue in child development—the processes which bring behavioral changes about. The question that educators, as well as research psychologists, should persistently seek to answer is *why* development occurs rather than *when* development occurs.

Educational emphasis on the concept of early pressures does not stem from a clearly identifiable group of principles within developmental psychology. The notion of early pressures is reminiscent, in some ways, of the prescientific view that children are smaller, weaker, more stupid versions of adults, or the Calvinist view of childhood as the crucial period for containing and eliminating the evil in man's nature. But the doctrine of early pressures has picked up support from more modern quarters. Espousal of the belief that man is "infinitely perfectible," or general endorsement of the belief that nurture has much power over maturation, supports the concept of early pressures. Such sharply differing theorists as John B. Watson and Maria Montessori have enunciated views consonant with the early-pressures notion. Further, those applied psychologists who have argued for cultural enrichment, or that good nursery school experience increases the child's competence in intellectual functioning and social adjustment, imply an endorsement of the early pressures concept.

To be sure, some of these viewpoints emphasize appropriate *experiences* for the young child, rather than appropriate early *pressures*. The distinction between experiences and pressures, however, is not clear-cut. The simple act of sending a child to nursery school is a form of pressure; the simplest limits for social conformity are pressureful; the simplest curriculum activity involves pressure, too. Only the condition of laissez faire does not imply pressure. But laissez faire is an abstraction and is not a philosophy of education; it is, rather, the absence of education and need not concern us further here.

Educators of young children have accepted many of the ramifications of the critical-periods hypothesis, but they have also recognized the child's early capacity for relatively complex forms of learning. The "right pressures at the right times" has been the educational touchstone of many nursery school teachers. But child psychology is a young and tentative science. Continuing questions have been formulated concerning the developmental stages. Would intellectual competence be enhanced by introducing achievement demands earlier than we do now? Are the developmental stages we have abstracted from our studies of children immutable? Even if these stages accurately represent the facts of development for most children, are there necessarily harmful consequences for the individual child when social-learning demands are introduced earlier than usual (or, for that matter, later than usual)? These are the problems, traced in historical perspective, that we now face. The dissonant position in which teachers and parents now find themselves stems from the convergence of long-standing beliefs concerning the nature of child development.

Selected research that bears on these problems is now relevant. But first, a word about independence and achievement and some of the determinants of these aspects of child behavior.

To begin with, I am familiar with no evidence that suggests an optimal age for beginning either training for independence or attempts to motivate the child toward achievement. The evidence we have, however, suggests that the preschool years, as a whole, are crucial in developing both of these qualities.

Independence, for the young child, involves taking initiative, overcoming obstacles, persistence in activity, just wanting to do things, and wanting to do things by oneself. Research by Beller (1955) has shown that independence and dependence are only *partially* separable components of social behavior. Preschool children are neither independent nor dependent, at one end or the other of a single continuum. Instead, young children are a mixture of two quite distinct clusters of traits—self-reliant striving for mastery, on the one hand, and dependency, on the other. The preschool child is learning simultaneously to depend on others and to be independent of others, paradoxical as this sounds. The child is learning new ways for *being helped* at the same time that he is learning to *help himself*.

Virtually all theories of socialization consider early learning to rely on other people as a necessary vehicle for later social learning. Therefore it would not seem sensible to set about teaching a preschool child to *inhibit* his dependent behavior in order to establish self-reliance. On the contrary, support and reinforcement for dependence need to be forthcoming during the early preschool years, rather than systematic inhibitory influences. Some evidence suggests that early, strong, inhibitory socialization in the area of dependence has undesirable consequences. Cross-cultural studies, for example, (Whiting and Child, 1953) suggest that severe handling of dependence in early childhood is associated with adult anxiety about social relationships and personal insecurity. Also, the folklore of cultures that inhibit dependence in children at early ages frequently contains aggressive and hostile themes. Finally, the work of other investigators (e.g., Sears, Whiting, Nowlis & Sears, 1953; Gewirtz, 1954) suggests that early deprivation of dependency gratifications serves in many instances to motivate the child to redouble his efforts to gain attention and approval from adults. I conclude that independence training should not begin by abrupt, premature attempts to decrease dependency behavior.

At the same time, early direct training and encouragement of self-reliance and assertiveness seems to increase such efforts by the child. This statement does not contradict the foregoing thesis that reinforcements for dependency should not be pervasively withdrawn from young children. Studies with preschool children indicate that independence is increased both by reinforcement of independent effort and by providing the child with experiences that increase his proficiency in the task at hand. For example, Fales (1944) trained nursery school children to take off their wraps; she also praised some of the children for their endeavors. Later observations showed that the trained *and* reinforced group refused assistance far more frequently than did the untrained and unreinforced groups. In another, quite different investigation, Winterbottom (1958) studied the child-rearing antecedents of independent and achievement-oriented behavior in elementary school boys. This study will be mentioned again further on in this paper. Suffice it to say here that information was obtained concerning the demands made by the mothers of the subjects for independent accomplishment, the rewards given for fulfillment of these accomplishments, and the restrictions placed on autonomous performance. The nine-year-old subjects in this investigation showed more signs of independent accomplishment when their mothers reported themselves as placing fewer early restrictions on independent activity and furnishing more early rewards for autonomous behavior.

Thus far, I have postulated that two conditions are requisite for optimal development of independence in the child: (1) dependence should not be broadly inhibited; and (2) independent activity should be rewarded frequently and early. In addition to these child-training components I would add a third. As independent, self-reliant behavior emerges and becomes a stable part of the child's hierarchy of social responses, *inappropriate* forms of dependent behavior can be weakened. But weakening of inappropriate dependency should stem from withdrawal of reinforcement, rather than the application of criticism or punishment. Recent work in the area of behavior modification conducted in the Laboratory of Developmental Psychology at the University of Washington suggests that careful withdrawal of reinforcement for inappropriate behavior is a necessary component in the execution of early pressures for more desirable activity (Harris, Wolf, & Baer, 1964).

It should be made clear that effective early pressures for independence do not involve withdrawal of reinforcement for all, or even most, manifestations of dependency. As mentioned earlier, socialization cannot proceed (conscience development is impeded, for example) in the absence of motivations for reliance on people. Dependency is a kind of social glue; culture, social institutions, the family, existence as we know it, could not be maintained in the absence of emotional interdependence among people. Dependency, however, is a form of social behavior that is "change-worthy." Rather than being pressured to give up social attachments, young children need to be pushed in the direction of altering the *objects* from whom they seek gratification. Children of two and three years of age certainly require ready access to the affection and attention of teachers, parents, and other adults. On the other hand, Heathers (1955) has shown, in his very interesting observational studies, that a shift to peers as objects for dependency occurs during the later preschool years. Active encouragement of this shift would seem desirable; the teacher of four-year-olds should gradually withdraw some of her reinforcement for dependence on adults, at the same time stepping up rewards for seeking attention from, and seeking contact with, peers.

Pressure can also be brought to bear on young children concerning the *methods* used for obtaining dependency gratifications. Whereas regular reinforcement for clinging and affection-seeking may be appropriate for three-year-olds, reinforcements for these components of dependence should be given under more selective circumstances in the case of the four- and five-year-olds. Older children may be appropriately pressured to seek approval for completing tasks well and to seek praise for accomplishing things. In our society, seeking approval is a "mature" form of dependence. By instituting early pressures for approval-seeking, teachers not only facilitate maturity in the ways children seek social gratification; such early pressures also set in motion strivings for excellence and achievement.

Achievement behavior refers to attempts to perform well—to perform efficiently or quickly, or to produce something of quality. McClelland, Atkinson, Clark, & Lowell (1953) have emphasized two major factors leading to the development of achievement motivation. First, the child must have opportunity to associate feelings of satisfaction produced by simple changes in the environment with his own striving or effort. That is, children need the opportunity to exert themselves in an independent and effortful way and to observe satisfying environmental changes as a consequence of their actions.

Second, early achievement efforts are enhanced by attempts of parents and teachers to structure performance standards and by adult demands for striving and excellence. This means that children must know or be informed as to what worthwhile effort is. Put in another way, the child must be helped to discriminate between a good try and a poor try. He must learn to differentiate between a good product and a poor product. Further, he must understand that the important people in his environment hope and desire that he will produce effective tries rather than lackadaisical efforts and good products rather than poor ones. This point of view implies that parents and teachers should not praise indiscriminately every intellectual, creative, or athletic effort made by young children. It is easy (and probably comforting to children) to respond to every painting or every high jump with, "Oh, that's nice," or with the noncommittal "Umhum." To be sure, at certain stages major interest may lie in simply getting the child involved in activities —in getting *any* response at the easel or *any* move on the climbing apparatus. At such times, wholesale reinforcement of the child's efforts may be defensible. But excellence in subsequent endeavor is, by definition, not possible unless the child has some idea as to what excellence is. Both parents and teachers frequently underestimate the capacity of young children for making such discriminations. It is my belief that at least rudimentary concepts of excellence can be conveyed to most children of preschool age with respect to such diverse activities as singing, physical movement, the graphic arts, and verbal communication.

It follows from the preceding discussion that the teacher's own esthetic values—her own evaluations of grace and elegance in movement and dance and her own judgments concerning excellence in verbal functioning—are key contributors to the acquisition of behavioral standards by the child. Children cannot be pressured to acquire definitions of excellence if those doing the pressuring do not have valid conceptions of excellence. But the process of structuring standards for young children is not simply a matter of transmitting the teacher's own values to the children. The idiosyncratic potentialities of the individual child and his family are pertinent to this problem. Further, the value structure of the cultural milieu in which the teacher finds herself with the child should supplement, and not work at cross purposes, with the school's efforts to teach the young child what excellence means.

The late Vaughn Crandall (1963) and his associates have also studied the early childhood determinants of achievement. This group has argued that the emergence of autonomous achievement-striving depends on direct approval and reinforcement of the child's early efforts at mastery. Of particular significance is reinforcement of early achievement efforts by means of attention, approval, and affection from adults. Earlier in this presentation I endorsed the hypothesis that the first meaningful step toward independent striving for excellence consists of learning to use performance as an avenue through which one can acquire dependency gratifications. Perhaps the point should be made once again. It is important that the young child learn to seek approval for things he does. This is important not only because seeking approval happens to be a mature, socially acceptable way for expressing dependency needs, but because this kind of social learning is a prerequisite for later stages in development wherein autonomous, self-sustaining, prideful, self-approving efforts to achieve will be required of the child.

Early reinforcement for achievement is probably only one determinant of motivation for learning in children. For example, I doubt if social approval for achievement-striving could ever produce the autonomous determination necessary for the consistent "A" report card, the contributions of a great scientist, or the world's record in the 10,000 meter run. Intrinsic rewards stemming from within acts of learning or mastery are themselves obviously important. The efforts of the infant to roll over, to reach for objects, and to orient toward complex stimuli are primitive demonstrations that intrinsic motivation contributes significantly to strivings for excellence. It is for this reason that I have always been gratified by those nursery school teachers who feel pressured themselves to provide young children with a broad array of rich, intrinsically rewarding experiences. A simple occurrence, such as watching what happens when blue and yellow paint are mixed together, is probably rewarding to the young child for intrinsic perceptual reasons. Early social reinforcement for skillful paint-mixing probably contributes far less than these intrinsic perceptual gratifications to the child's motivation for excellence in the large, molar process of painting. But the point is made, I am sure. Early reinforcement for achievement-striving appears to be related to the strength of the child's later achievement efforts. Other factors, such as early opportunities to experience intrinsic motivation, also contribute to the strength of achievement efforts. Social reinforcement for achievement cannot, in all likelihood, do the job alone; at the same time, it is doubtful that strong achievement efforts seldom emerge when this kind of early reinforcement is absent.

Research evidence supporting the assertions contained in the preceding paragraphs stems from several different sources. For example, data are beginning to emerge from projects studying the effects of nursery-school experience on the achievement behavior of culturally deprived children. The experimental nursery schools involved in these projects usually provide frequent positive reinforcement for the child's autonomous efforts at mastery. Consequently, findings showing increases in IQ or elementary school achievement among children who have attended experimental nursery schools suggest that reinforcement facilitates the development of an achievement orientation. But the experimental effort to offset the effects of cultural deprivation also involves frequent opportunity for the child to experience intrinsic gratifications from cognitive and social experiences. At best, then, the evidence emerging from these projects is only suggestive concerning the role of early reinforcement for achievement behavior in increasing autonomous achievement-striving in the child.

Other evidence is to be found in studies of child-rearing practices. In a study mentioned previously Winterbottom (1958) reported that nine-year-old boys evincing strong motivation for achievement had mothers who expected self-reliant behavior relatively early, who provided more frequent and larger rewards when their sons succeeded in performing independently and well, and who placed fewer restrictions on their sons' spontaneous independent behavior. Another investigator (Feld, 1959) studied these same boys after they had reached adolescence. The mother's behavior with respect to her son's early autonomous efforts continued to be related to the strength of achievement motivation in adolescence. This is a particularly interesting finding since the mother's tendency to reinforce independence *after* her son reached adolescence was actually negatively related to strength of achievement motivation. Tentative as these data are, they suggest that early pressures for achievement are more effective than late ones.

A quasi-experimental study by Rosen and D'Andrade (1959) involved elementary school boys, their fathers, and their mothers. It was found that parents of boys with strong motivation for achievement had higher aspirations, set higher standards, and expected better performance than parents of boys with lower levels of achievement motivation. Mothers, in particular, gave more approval for successful achievement efforts and were quicker to criticize unsuccessful efforts in the case of high achievement-oriented boys than the mothers of low achievement-oriented boys. Crandall, Preston, & Ralson (1960) also report a positive relation between maternal reinforcement of achievement behaviors and the frequency of achievement efforts on the part of nursery school children. And finally, longitudinal data from the Fels Institute (Moss & Kagan, 1958) indicate that children of pushing, achievement-oriented mothers scored higher on IQ tests early in the preschool years and increased their scores on IQ tests during the elementary school years more than children of nonaccelerating mothers. Taken together, the few studies mentioned here point clearly to early reinforcement of achievement behavior as a major determinant of efforts at mastery in later childhood.

In her forthcoming review, Mrs. Crandall concludes that "our education for excellence is accompanied by certain psychological costs." While achievement-oriented preschoolers seem to enjoy relatively good social and personal adjustment, some evidence suggests that older children and adolescents with high achievement motivation suffer disruptions in their social relationships, manifest higher levels of anxiety, and the like. More information is needed than is currently available concerning the correlates of achievement motivation in children. It is possible, however, that the extant results do not tell the whole story. For example, research on level of aspiration in children suggests that striving and aspiring to excellence have at least two motivational roots. Some children, boys in particular, seem to be intrinsically motivated toward competence and task-mastery; one might say these children wish to do well for the sake of doing well. Others, girls somewhat more often than boys, seem to strive because of strong fears of failure. Relatively little is known concerning the child-rearing antecedents of these two forms of motivation for high aspiration and achievement.

To recapitulate: there is reason to believe that early positive pressures for achievement are beneficial to the young child. Early, successful achievement efforts need to be vigorously supported. Next, the young child needs to be helped to discriminate between successful and unsuccessful effort. Finally, the consequences of early failure probably should not include withdrawal of adult esteem, strong criticism and punishment, since these pressures may enhance achievement striving at the cost of strong fears of failure.

Finally, I should like to touch on conflict, frustration, and anxiety as these motivational forces act on the child. Most of the literature (both scientific and popular) concerning conflict in child development emphasizes the dangerous and debilitating consequences of the so-called negative emotions. Thousands of pages in hundreds of volumes, as well as parent meetings too numerous to estimate, have focused on the relation of conflict to hostility, to disrupted social relationships, to defensive processes, and to learning inhibitions. There is little question that frustration and conflict are key determinants of many disturbances in the personality and intellectual development of young children. Until recent years, however, very little has been said concerning the constructive role in human development played by the negative emotions. One recent plea for recognition of the positive consequences of conflict was heard at the Philadelphia meetings of NANE. The paper, "Conflict and Controversy in Child Development," by Meyer Sonis (1963), included the following statement: ". . . the potential for good or bad, constructive or destructive, resides in conflict *but conflict itself is not good or bad.*" I urge you to reread Dr. Sonis's address.

Constructive consequences of conflict, frustration, and anxiety can be found in many aspects of behavioral development in children. Consider, for example, the development of identificatory behavior. Conflict is a key construct in virtually every modern theory of identification. The Oedipal conflict was emphasized by Freud. To be sure, Freud regarded the Oedipus complex as an antecedent of neurosis, but he also argued that "the superego is the heir to the Oedipus complex." That is, Freud recognized conflict as an important antecedent of appropriate sex-typing, self-control, and resistance to temptation—conscience, in a word. Consider also the theory which suggests that identification stems from the conflict over loss of love. Consider, too, the sociological theories which suggest that children identify with powerful figures or with people perceived as prestigeful, or privileged, or in possession of important gratifications.

Conflict motivates much cognitive learning. Would children learn to read if no conflict were present? I do not mean that conflict produced by telling a child, "You'd better learn to read, or else!" Rather, being aware of what it means to be able to read and realizing that one *cannot* read is a form of conflict which probably helps greatly in motivating the child to acquire reading skills.

Conflict also contributes significantly to social behavior. The cohesiveness of children's groups and the frequency of constructive social activity are, in many instances, enhanced by frustration and conflict. Wright (1940) for example, found that preschoolers who were best friends actually became more socially outgoing and cooperative under frustrating circumstances than under satiation conditions. Further, the frustration used in the Wright experiment (the Lewin barrier, which prevented the children from reaching attractive toys) reduced the interchild hostility characteristic of ordinary play. Instead, the frustrated children pointed their aggression in a highly appropriate direction—toward the experimenter! And in still another area, my own recent studies of peer reinforcement (Hartup, 1964) have demonstrated that preschool children worked more vigorously and sustained higher levels of performance on simple tasks when they received praise and approval from another child who was *not* liked than when reinforcement was forthcoming from a child whom the subject regarded as a good friend. Even elementary school children, we find, work harder at simple tasks when reinforced by unpopular children than when praised by children regarded as popular.

All the foregoing illustrations of constructive responses to conflict have one element in common, namely, that conflict was attached to an *appropriate, socially-desirable response*. Thus, conflict and frustration are powerful, effective forces for socialization, but only when conflict-reduction reinforces appropriate behavior. Those instances in which conflict-reduction is associated with undesirable responses are, of course, to be eschewed; still, this does not mean that children need to be protected from all contact with conflict and frustration.

There are certain heretical elements in this philosophy concerning the role of conflict and frustration in child behavior. In one sense, these comments furnish a modern rationale for the old "spare the rod" approach to child rearing. These comments also suggest that the ends justify the means in the process of bringing up children. Most certainly, these implications *are* present in the position here put forward. Unquestionably, however, limits must be placed on the deliberate use of conflict and frustration in child rearing. Even though the behaviors to be acquired on the basis of conflict may be socially appropriate, high and sustained levels of pressure are probably harmful. For one thing, in many instances, the arousal of particularly strong emotions interferes with learning instead of facilitating it. Also, some sort of balance between frustration and more positive inducements for learning is surely needed. Other motivational bases are available for learning; several have been mentioned (e.g., desire for mastery and intrinsic motivation). But my major thesis must not be obscured nor made to sound like the arguments of the devil's advocate. Everyone engaged in child rearing needs to recognize the fact that conflict carries constructive possibilities; to deny this is probably to deny that children can be educated.

To conclude: This has been a social-learning approach to the problem of early pressures in child development. The emphasis has been on reinforcement, withdrawal of reinforcement, and conflict-reduction. All these factors are known to produce desirable modifications in behavior and they can all be brought to bear on the young child. Social-learning theory remains, in 1964, a set of principles derived mostly from studies of simple behavioral phenomena. Thus, in using this theoretical framework to explain and predict complex patterns of behavior (such as those dealt with in this paper) simplifications are bound to occur. That is, the principles on which this discussion is based may not be entirely adequate, by themselves, to account for all of the variability involved in complex patterns of behavior such as independence and achievement-striving. I am confident, however, that these principles have wide applicability in child rearing and in education. If the theory fails at certain points to account for all the complexities contained in child development, please understand that this does not mean that the theory is wrong. It simply needs improvement. In the meantime, I submit that a social-learning approach has many immediate, applicable, constructive implications for every one of us who lives and works with children and for every one of us who is concerned about early pressures in child development.

REFERENCES

Beller, E. K. Dependency and independence in young children. *J. genet. Psychol.,* 1955, 87, 23–25.

Crandall, V. Achievement. In H. W. Stevenson (Ed.), *Child psychology.* Sixty-second Yearbook of the National Society for the Study of Education, Part I. Chicago: Univer. Chicago Press, 1963.

Crandall, Virginia. Achievement behavior in young children. *Young Children,* 1964, 20, 76–90.

Crandall, V., Preston, Anne, & Ralson, Alice. Maternal reactions and the development of independence and achievement behavior in young children. *Child Develpm.,* 1960, 31, 243–251.

Fales, E. Genesis of level of aspiration in children from one and one-half to three years of age. Reported in Lewin, K. *et al.* Level of aspiration. In J. McV.

Hunt (Ed.), *Personality and the behavior disorders.* Vol. I. New York: Ronald, 1944, 333–378.

Feld, Sheila. Need achievement and test anxiety in children and maternal attitudes and behaviors toward independent accomplishments: a longitudinal study. Paper read at convention of American Psychological Association, Cincinnati, 1959.

Festinger, L. *A theory of cognitive dissonance.* Stanford: Stanford Univ. Press, 1957.

Gewirtz, J. L. Three determinants of attention-seeking in young children. *Monogr. soc. Research in child Develpm.,* 1954, 19, No. 2 (Serial No. 59).

Harris, Florence R., Wolf, M. M., and Baer, D. M. Effects of adult social reinforcement on child behavior. *Young Children,* 1964, 20, 8–17.

Hartup, W. W. Friendship status and the effectiveness of peers as reinforcing agents. *J. exp. child Psychol.,* 1964, 1, 154–162.

Heathers, G. Emotional dependence and independence in nursery-school play. *J. genet. Psychol.,* 1955, 87, 37–58.

McClelland, D., Atkinson, J., Clark, R., and Lowell, E. *The achievement motive.* New York: Appleton, Century, Crofts, 1953.

McGraw, Myrtle B. *Growth: a study of Johnny and Jimmy.* New York: Appleton Century, 1935.

Moss, H. A., and Kagan, J. Maternal influences on early IQ scores. *Psychol. Rep.,* 1958, 4, 655–661.

Rosen, B., and D'Andrade, R. The psychosocial origins of achievement motivation. *Sociometry,* 1959, 22, 185–218.

Sears, R. R., Whiting, J. W. M., Nowlis, V., and Sears, Pauline S. Some child-rearing antecedents of dependency and aggression in young children. *Genet. Psychol. Monogr.,* 1953, 47, 135–234.

Sonis, M. Controversy and conflict in child development. *J. nursery Ed.,* 1963, 18, 160–167.

Whiting, J. W. M. and Child, I. *Child training and personality.* New Haven: Yale Univer. Press, 1953.

Winterbottom, Marian. The relation of need for achievement learning experiences in independence and mastery. In J. Atkinson (Ed.), *Motives in fantasy, action, and society.* Princeton: D. Van Nostrand, 1958, 453–478.

Wright, M. E. The influence of frustration upon the social relationships of young children. Ph.D. dissertation. State Univ. of Iowa, 1940.

Moral Development

27

LEARNING THEORY AND THE ACQUISITION OF VALUES*

WINFRED F. HILL

THE PROCESSES by which a child acquires the values of his culture and his various overlapping subcultures is, as a recent review of the subject points out (Dukes, 1955), still rather obscure. This obscurity is certainly not due to lack of interest in the topic. Psychologists, psychiatrists, anthropologists, sociologists, pediatricians, and educators have all given attention to the question of how children come to share the attitudes, ideals, and ethical standards of those around them. Nor is this interest undeserved, for few topics are of greater practical importance.

Perhaps this very convergence of interest from many directions is partly responsible for the difficulties involved in studying the topic. This area of research has become a battleground for conflicting terminologies, with one term often having a multiplicity of half-distinct meanings, and with what appears to be the same meaning often bearing different labels. Although many terms contribute to this confusion, three are of particular interest here: *identification, introjection,* and *internalization*. All involve some relation between an individual, hereinafter designated the subject (*S*), and another person or personalized entity, the model or *M*, such that *S*'s behavior is in some way patterned after *M*'s. However, these terms may refer either to a state of affairs or to the process which brought it about (Lazowick, 1955); the *M* may be a person, a group, or an idea (Glaser, 1958); and the relation may involve specific responses, broad meanings, or emotional reactions.

---

* From *Psychological Review,* 1960, *67,* 317–331. Reprinted with permission of the author and the American Psychological Association, Inc.

The research for this article was supported by a grant from the Carnegie Corporation to the Department of Psychology and the School of Education at Northwestern University. The author wishes to express his appreciation to Donald Campbell, Robert Winch, and the members of their seminar in social psychology for their many contributions to his thinking on this topic.

Some of the confusion as to the meaning of the term identification may be seen in the following uses. Lazowick (1955) distinguishes three main uses of the term identification in the literature: pseudoidentity, imitation, and personality change. He suggests that the term should be used only with regard to broad meanings, with imitation being the corresponding term for specific acts. Freud (1950) contrasts a boy's identification with his father, which forms the basis of his ego ideal, and his identification with his mother as an abandoned object cathexis. Davis and Havighurst (1947) maintain that a child will identify with his parents only if he loves them, but Anna Freud (1946) emphasizes identification with the aggressor. Lynn (1959) contrasts sex-role identification, which is "reserved to refer to the actual incorporation of the role of a given sex, and to the unconscious reactions characteristic of that role" (p. 127), with sex-role preference and sex-role adoption. He regards figure drawing as a measure of identification and choice of dolls for play as a measure of preference. Sears, Maccoby, and Levin (1957), however, use children's choices of dolls as a measure of identification. Sanford (1955), discouraged by such confusions of meaning, considers the possibility of abandoning the term identification altogether, but decides to retain it to describe a defense mechanism involving extreme adoption of *M*'s behavior by *S*, a mechanism which is not important in normal personality development. Finally, this collection of meanings, diverse as it is, still omits those cases where identification is used as a synonym for loyalty or for empathy.

There is similar confusion concerning the meaning of introjection and internalization. Both carry the implication of values being incorporated into the personality. Hence, particularly with introjection, there is the suggestion of some relation with orality (Freud, 1950). However, Freud in the same discussion also uses introjection synonymously with identification. Parsons (1955), on the other hand, treats identification and internalization as synonyms.

The many discussions of these three terms in the literature seem to indicate that there are several processes involved but no generally accepted conventions for labeling them. A number of writers, including several already cited, have expressed discouragement at this state of affairs, but the usual result of such discouragement seems to be a redefinition of terms, which may clarify the particular exposition but which only serves further to confuse the field as a whole. Whereas Lynn (1959) believes that a term as widespread as identification must have potential usefulness, the present writer believes that clarity would be served by abolishing not only identification but also introjection and internalization from the technical vocabulary of personality development.

What, then, should be substituted? The topics to which the above terms have been applied certainly deserve discussion, and if the redefinition of the old terms is unsatisfactory, the introduction of new terms would be even worse. An answer may be found, however, in a sort of reductionism.

Since the processes involved are learning processes, the existing vocabulary of learning is the obvious candidate for the job of describing them. It is quite possible, of course, that the existing vocabulary of learning theory will be inadequate for the complexities of value acquisition. However, if its use is carried as far as possible, the successes of this application should clarify our thinking about personality development, while any gaps which result should point to possible extensions of learning theory.

This approach involves treating human learning in a sociocultural environment in the same terms, at least for a first approximation, as animal learning in the environment of laboratory apparatus. For this purpose, the social rewards and punishments applied to humans may be treated as equivalent to the food pellets and electric shocks used with rats. Similarly, social roles are the equivalents of mazes which must be learned in order to obtain the rewards and avoid the punishments. Human beings of course constitute a far more variable environment than laboratory hardware, and one on which *S* can exercise greater influence. However, since most of the theory in this area is concerned with the adaptation of *S* to a relatively constant human environment (whether it be called culture, social system, or the personalities of the parents), this should not prove a serious stumbling block. There is ample precedent for such an approach in the writings of Dollard and Miller (1950), Mowrer (1950), Whiting and Child (1953), and others.

In addition, this approach treats values as nothing more than inferences from overt behavior. In principle this assumption should cause no difficulty. Few behavioral scientists would regard values (in the empirical, not the transcendental sense) as fundamentally different from such behavioristic constructs as Hull's (1943) habit strength or Tolman's (1949) equivalence beliefs. In practice, however, some theorists might take issue with this view on at least two bases.

For one thing, the measurement of values (including attitudes, ideals, and ethical standards) is commonly by verbal methods (see the review by Dukes, 1955). This leads to the suspicion that any measurement of values by nonverbal means must be inadequate, that only verbal measures can get at the significance of an act for an individual. However, verbal responses are part of the total behavior of the human organism and may be studied like other responses. The processes of unconscious motivation, semiconscious hypocrisy, and deliberate concealment all indicate that it would be unwise to treat verbal and nonverbal measures of values as equivalent. Rather than treat either verbal or nonverbal behavior as the true indicator of values and the other as a side issue, it seems more useful to study both and to ascertain empirically to what extent they lead to the same generalizations about a given *S*.

Another possible objection involves the distinction between specific acts and broad meanings, as in Lazowick's (1955) contrasting definitions of imitation and identification, noted above. This distinction between specific acts and broad meanings may refer either to the presence of mediating responses (see Osgood, 1953) or to the generality of the stimuli and responses involved. Neither of these distinctions, however, is dichotomous. Hull (1952) has indicated how a mediator, the fractional antedating goal response, may function in animal behavior, and Russell and Storms (1955) have demonstrated mediational processes in rote learning. Thus the mediation mechanism is by no means restricted to the "higher mental processes" of humans. As for the generality of the behavior and of the stimuli which guide it, this presumably represents a continuum from the most specific to the most inclusive categories. If, for example, washing the hands before meals is an example of imitation and cleanliness, an example of identification, where would wearing clean clothes be classified? So, although the distinction between specific acts and broad meanings is a legitimate one, there are no sharp breaks on the continuum and there is no reason to assume that basically different laws are involved.

In view of the above considerations, an attempt to study the acquisition of values as a branch of learning theory appears justified.

KINDS OF REINFORCEMENT

The concept of reinforcement is basic to learning theory. While theorists are by no means unanimously agreed on the value of reinforcement terminology, there is little question that an empirical law of effect holds, that the consequences of an act influence its subsequent occurrence. A classification of kinds of reinforcers will be used here as the basis for analyzing the learning of values.

Primary Reinforcement

For the present purpose, three kinds of reinforcement may be distinguished: *"primary," secondary,* and *vicarious*. Placing "primary" in quotes indicates that it refers to the effects not only of innate physiological reinforcers but also of those social reinforcers which play a primary role in human motivation. Presumably the positively reinforcing effects of attention and praise and the negatively reinforcing effects of criticism, ridicule, and rejection are at least partly learned, but the nature of the learning process is obscure, and at the present level of analysis it seems preferable to treat praise for a human as comparable to food for a rat. The distinction between "primary" and secondary reinforcement is thus one of convenience between that which we take as given and that for which we can find a specific learned basis. Though arbitrary, this distinction is perhaps no more so than the decision as to whether food in the mouth should be considered a primary or a secondary reinforcer.

One particular kind of learning by "primary" reinforcement is the acquisition of a generalized tendency to imitate others. Miller and Dollard (1941) have indicated how a generalized tendency to imitate the behavior of others may be learned in the same way as any other class of responses. Although their demonstrations of imitation involved *S*'s patterning his behavior after a leader who was present, Church (1957) has shown that rats can also learn to respond appropriately to the same cues to which the leader rat is responding. In spite of some negative animal evidence (Solomon & Coles, 1954), there is little doubt that humans can learn to pattern their behavior after that of other people, not only when the *M* is present, but also in *M*'s absence by utilizing the appropriate environmental cues. As the child is repeatedly rewarded for imitative behavior in a variety of otherwise different situations, and as his capacity for abstraction increases, it seems plausable that a generalized imitative tendency would develop. It would be desirable, however, if the widespread anecdotal support for this deduction could be bolstered by experimental data.

The same process presumably applies to verbal instructions. The child is typically reinforced (though with some striking exceptions) for doing what others tell him to do. Hence (common parental impressions to the contrary notwithstanding), a generalized tendency toward conformity to verbal instructions may be expected to develop. With increasing intellectual development, this tendency should come to include conformity to fictional examples or to abstract ethical exhortations.

Secondary Reinforcement

Although no basic distinction is made here between primary and secondary reinforcement, there is one case frequently discussed in the literature where the acquisition of reinforcing properites by certain stimuli may be analyzed in detail. These stimuli are those which are connected with care of the child by adults, i.e., the nonessential aspects of nurturance. These include patterns of speech, facial expressions, gestures, and the like. Since these occur with those nurturant behaviors which are primary reinforcers, such as feeding and cuddling, they may become secondary reinforcers. By stimulus generalization, these behaviors should also be rewarding to the child (although less so) when produced by himself. As the child grows older and the parents expect him to take greater care of his own needs, he is more and more forced to provide not only his own primary reinforcers, but his own secondary reinforcers as well. Hence he may be expected to show some of the same mannerisms as his parents showed when caring for him.

This kind of learning appears to be one of those processes which Freud (1950) includes under the heading of identification or introjection, that in which abandoned object cathexes become incorporated into the ego. However, in the view presented here, the coincidence of abandonment and incorporation into the ego refers only to performance, not to learning. The secondary reinforcing value of the parental mannerisms is built up during the period of nurturance, but becomes evident in the child's behavior as nurturance begins to be withdrawn. This learning process has been discussed by Mowrer (1950, Ch. 24) in connection with the learning of language, and by Lindemann (1944) as a reaction to the death of a loved one. Although this process appears better adapted to the learning of rather trivial mannerisms, it is capable at least in principle of being adapted to more general and significant values as well.

Vicarious Reinforcement

Vicarious reinforcement does not have the same dignified status in learning theory as do primary and secondary reinforcement, but some such process appears necessary in order to explain some important human learning. Vicarious reinforcement involves the generalization of reinforcing effects from others to oneself, hence learning from the reinforcers which others receive. A given act is reinforced for *S* as a result of the act being performed by *M,* followed by reinforcement to *M*. For example, if *S* observes *M* trying to solve a problem by certain techniques and succeeding, *S* is more likely to use the same techniques when faced by a similar problem than if *M* had failed to solve the problem. Although most of the evidence for such learning is anecdotal, Lewis and Duncan (1958) have provided some evidence of it in a human gambling situation, and Darby and Riopelle (1959) have demonstrated it in discrimination learning by monkeys.

Although vicarious reinforcement involves selective imitation, it differs from the selectivity of imitation, described by Miller and Dollard (1941), in which *S* imitates some *M*s and not others because of differential reinforcement received by *S* for imitating the two *M*s. Vicarious reinforcement does not involve any reinforcers delivered directly to *S;* the discrimination of *M*s to be imitated or not is made entirely on the basis of *S*'s observation of *M*'s experience. This distinction is emphasized by Campbell (in press). In Hullian terms, vicarious reinforcement involves the acquisition of *K* by observation.

This type of learning need not be restricted to the effect of particular reinforcers administered to *M* under specific conditions. Stimulus generalization should occur not only from *M*'s behavior to *S*'s but also from one act of *M*'s to another. As a result, if *M* is frequently reinforced, *S* should find it rewarding to resemble *M* in general, including imitation of some of *M*'s behaviors which *S* has never seen rewarded. Thus a beginning salesman (*S*) might treat a customer with extreme politeness because he had observed another salesman (*M*) making a large sale while using such behavior, and he might also smoke a cigar because he had observed his highly successful salesmanager (*M*) doing so. In the former case *M*'s behavior (politeness) and *M*'s reinforcement (a large sale) were paired, whereas in the latter case the reinforcement (business success) was a perennial experience of *M*, but not paired with the particular behavior (smoking cigars) in question. Both, however, are examples of vicarious reinforcement.

Vicarious reinforcement corresponds to identification as defined by Masserman (1946) and to that aspect of identification referred to by Kagan (1958) as "the motivation to command or experience desired goal states of a model" (p. 298). Freud's (1946) identification with the aggressor also fits under this heading if successful aggression is assumed to be reinforcing to the aggressor. Sanford's (1955) concept of identification also involves the adoption as *M* of someone perceived by *S* as successful.

Conflicting Sources of Reinforcement

Traditionally the terms identification, introjection, and internalization might be applied to any or all of the learning processes described above or to their end product, similarity between *S* and some *M*. Since for the most part these processes involve learning by imitation, require some kind of reinforcement, and result in similarity between *S* and *M*, it may be asked why detailed analysis of the rather subtle differences among them is called for.

The answer is apparent when the possibility of conflict is considered. Conditions for a given *S* may be such that one of these processes tends to produce one kind of behavior while another tends to produce quite different or even opposite behavior. Such a conflictful situation might be expected in a child reared by a nurturant mother, whose mannerisms would become secondarily reinforcing, and a domineering father, who would be perceived as successful in mastering the environment. Freud (1950) recognized the frequent occurrence of just such a conflict, but did not consider it necessary to use different words for the two learning processes. Another common conflict is between the tendency to imitate *M*s whom *S* is directly reinforced for imitating (e.g., well behaved children) and the tendency to imitate *M*s whom *S* perceives as successful (e.g., tough kids). Such conflict is inevitable to a certain extent in children, since they are not permitted to imitate their (presumably more successful) elders in all respects, but it is particularly prominent in members of low-status social categories (e.g., Negroes), who are often conspicuously not reinforced for imitating high-status *M*s. In the broadest sense, any situation where there is discrepancy among what *S* is told to do, what he is rewarded for doing, and what he sees others doing is a potential conflict situation, and one in which the use of any single inclusive term such as "identification" obscures the relevant variables.

The occurrence of conflict among the various reinforcement processes makes possible a finer analysis of the acquisition of values than could be made otherwise. If there is perfect agreement among what *S* is told to do, what those who nurture him do, what those around him conspicuously master the environment by doing, and what he himself is directly rewarded for doing, there is little basis for judging how much each of these factors contributed to *S*'s adoption of the values of those around him. By observing situations in which they conflict, greater knowledge of the efficacy of each kind of reinforcement may be obtained. Research in conflict situations might answer such theoretically and practically important questions as: "Does dominance or nurturance on *M*'s part do more to make *M* effective in modifying *S*'s values?"; "Do words and examples completely lose their efficacy if the appropriate behaviors, when elicited, are not reinforced?"; and "To what extent is behavior influenced by *M*s presented verbally (e.g., in literature)?"

There is of course no special merit to the classificatory scheme presented here. Except for the concept of vicarious reinforcement, the writer has avoided attaching distinctive labels to the learning processes described. The purpose of this discussion was to show how the terminology of learning theory can be applied to processes of value acquisition which have been described by personality theorists. This not only serves as a step toward the integration of these two areas of study, but also suggests the probable usefulness of employing such independent variables as number, percentage, magnitude and delay of reinforcement, distribution of practice, and discriminability of stimuli in the study of value acquisition. As both learning theory and personality theory develop further, it is to be expected that any schema developed now will be at least partially replaced by newer concepts. Rather than developing in further detail the ideas suggested above, the remainder of this discussion will therefore concentrate on the application of this kind of thinking to a narrower area, the development of conscience.

CONSCIENCE

Negative values, or conscience, have received much more attention than positive values. Educators seeking to improve children's characters, psychoanalysts concerned with the tyranny of the superego, anthropologists trying to distinguish between shame and guilt cultures, and experimental psychologists noting the persistence of avoidance responses have shared this emphasis on values of the "Thou shalt not" variety. Because of this widespread interest in conscience, it is a particularly appropriate topic with which to illustrate the possibilities of the learning theory approach to the study of values. Sears, Maccoby, and Levin (1957), in their challenging book *Patterns of Child Rearing,* devote a chapter to the development of conscience in preschool children. Their treatment of the topic will serve as a starting point for the present analysis.

Criteria for Conscience

Sears, Maccoby, and Levin give three criteria for recognizing the operation of conscience in young children: *resistance to temptation, self-instruc-*

tions to obey the rules, and *evidence of guilt* when transgression occurs. These three criteria are treated jointly as defining conscience, and no attempt is made to analyze their separate developments. Although the authors mention that the aspects of conscience do not necessarily all appear at once, they regard conscience as representing an internalization of control which is fundamentally different from external control, whether by force, fear of punishment, or hope of material reward. This treatment of conscience as essentially a single variable seems premature in our present state of knowledge; certainly the learning theory approach to personality advocated here would involve separate analyses of these diverse response patterns.

The first criterion, *resistance to temptation,* may be viewed simply as avoidance learning. Although this kind of learning is still a focus of theoretical controversy, much experimental data are available concerning it (Solomon & Brush, 1956). Sidman's (1953) studies of avoidance behavior without a warning signal and Dinsmoor's (1954) analysis of punishment show how feedback from an individual's own acts can become a cue for avoidance, and how persistent such avoidance may be. Although children can presumably learn to respond to more abstract characteristics of cues than can animals, there is no reason to regard a child's learning to avoid certain behaviors as fundamentally different from a rat's learning to do so. The fact that the child avoids the forbidden acts even in the absence of the parents is presumably due to the parents' having in the past discovered and punished (in the broadest sense of that word) transgressions committed in their absence.

This relating of conscience to avoidance learning suggests that independent variables known to be effective in animal avoidance learning would be among the most appropriate ones for study in connection with the development of conscience in children. Within certain limits, the greater the intensity of the punishments (Brush, 1957; Miller, 1951) and the shorter the delay between transgression and punishment (Mowrer & Ullman, 1945; Solomon & Brush, 1956), the greater should be the resulting inhibition. Though the data are somewhat ambiguous, greater certainty of punishment might be expected to produce inhibition which would be more complete in the short run but also less persistent once punishment was permanently withdrawn (Grant, Schipper, & Ross, 1952; Jenkins & Stanley, 1950; Reynolds, 1958). This prediction suggests that even this one criterion of conscience may not be unitary, that different laws may apply depending on whether one asks how completely the child obeys the prohibitions or how long he continues to obey them after leaving the parental home. If partial reinforcement should turn out to be a crucial variable in the human situation, these two criteria might even be inversely related. The prediction also suggests that the question, "Is inconsistent discipline bad?" is far too simple; one must at least ask, "Bad for what?"

It must also be kept in mind that punishment is not restricted to physical chastisement or even to noxious stimuli in general, including scolding and ridicule. Withdrawal of positive reinforcers may be very effective as a punishment, a fact which complicates the analysis. As this is a much discussed topic in personality theory, it will be considered below.

Sears, Maccoby, and Levin's second criterion of conscience, *self-instruction,* obviously makes the human case different from the animal case, but it does not introduce any new motivational principle. One of the advantages of membership in the human species is the possibility of using verbal symbolization in dealing with one's problems. It is natural that a person learning an avoidance, like a person learning any other difficult response pattern, should give himself verbal instructions, especially since verbal coaching by others is so important in the learning of social prohibitions. Moreover, such self-instruction is an imitative act which might be learned according to any of the reinforcement paradigms discussed above. Presumably the learning of prohibitions proceeds differently in verbal and nonverbal organisms, but observations of the relation between moral statements and moral behavior (Hurlock, 1956, pp. 406, 411–412) argue against the assumption that there is a high correlation between verbal and other criteria of conscience, except as both are influenced by the values represented in the social environment.

The third criterion of conscience, *guilt* at violations of the prohibitions, is itself complex, with many verbal, autonomic, and gross behavioral aspects. However, the striking paradox about guilt, which has seemed to some students to set it apart from the ordinary laws of learning, is that it often involves the seeking of punishment. The person who has transgressed, rather than trying to avoid punishment, or even waiting passively for it to come, actively seeks out the authorities, confesses, and receives his punishment with apparent relief. He may also, or instead, go to great lengths to make restitution. Were it not for these phenomena of punishment-seeking and self-sacrificing restitution, it would be easy to dismiss guilt as merely the kind of fear associated with anticipation of certain sorts of punishment. As it is, the existence of guilt serves as an argument for regarding conscience as something more than the sum of all those avoidances which have moral significance in one's culture.

However, the attempt to distinguish between guilt-controlled and other behaviors has not been very successful. Though the distinction between guilt cultures and shame cultures has had a considerable vogue in anthropology (e.g., Benedict, 1946; Havighurst & Neugarten, 1955; Mead, 1950), the inadequacies of the distinction have been pointed out by Ausubel (1955) and by Singer (1953). Moreover, the relation between conformity to a standard and guilt when the standard has been violated is open to question. Shaw (1948) suggests that confession may even be so satisfying to some people that it constitutes a reinforcement for sinning. So, although the phenomena of guilt may raise difficulties for learning theory, these difficulties probably cannot be solved by using guilt to define a distinctive kind of learning.

The above considerations should suffice to indicate that conscience cannot be assumed a priori to be unitary. The extent to which short-run conformity, long-run conformity, self-instructions to conform, certain kinds of distress at having failed to conform, and voluntary confession of nonconformity are intercorrelated is a matter to be empirically determined. Moreover, even if high positive intercorrelations are found, it is possible that they may reflect correlations in the environment rather than any fundamental unity of process. If environmental pressures toward conformity vary markedly, artificially high correlations among the criteria of conscience are to be expected. However, even when this artifact is removed, an analysis of separate learning processes for different behaviors may still lead to the prediction of high correlations among the behaviors. Such an analysis is presented below.

Learning of Conscience

Sears, Maccoby, and Levin found that the development of conscience, as defined jointly by their three criteria, was greater in those children whose parents used love-oriented forms of discipline (praise, isolation, and withdrawal of love) than in those whose parents used "materialistic" forms of discipline (material rewards, deprivation of privileges, and physical punishment). A similar finding, though not highly reliable statistically, is reported by Whiting and Child (1953, Ch. 11) in a cross-cultural study of guilt as measured by attitudes toward illness. This is consistent with the widely held view that the acquisition of parental values occurs most fully in an atmosphere of love (e.g., Ausubel, 1955; Davis & Havighurst, 1947). It is possible, however, that this finding may be due, not to love-oriented discipline as such, but to other characteristics of discipline which are correlated with it. The effect of this kind of discipline may be to accentuate the learning of several different responses, all of which contribute to the overall diagnosis of high conscience.

The various kinds of punishments commonly applied to children probably differ markedly in the temporal relations and the reinforcement contingencies involved. Physical punishment is likely to occur all at once and be over quickly, while punishment by deprivation of objects or privileges is likely to be either for a fixed period of time or for as long as the disciplinarian finds convenient. Discipline by withdrawal of love, on the other hand, probably much more often lasts until the child makes some symbolic renunciation of his wrongdoing, as by apologizing, making restitution, or promising not to do it again. The child is deprived of his parents' love (or, the parents would claim, of the outward manifestations of it!) for as much or as little time as is necessary to get him to make such a symbolic renunciation. When he has made it, he is restored to his parents' favor. If the normal relation between the parents and child is one of warmth, such discipline strongly motivates the child to make the renunciation quickly. On repeated occasions of transgression, punishment by withdrawal of love, and symbolic renunciation, the child may be expected not only to learn the renunciation response as an escape from parental disfavor but eventually to use it as an avoidance rather than merely an escape response. Thus if the wrongdoing is not immediately discovered, the child may anticipate his parents' impending disfavor by confessing in advance and making the symbolic renunciation.

The result of this hypothesized sequence of events is that the child makes a verbal response which is in effect an instruction to himself not to repeat his wrongdoing. The next time temptation comes, he is more likely to make this verbal response before transgressing. Although this does not guarantee that he will not transgress, it is likely to reduce the probability. If he succumbs to temptation, he is more likely to confess before being caught and thereby avoid the temporary loss of his parents' love. Thus if the above reasoning is correct, all three criteria of conscience should be present to a greater degree in the child who has been disciplined in this fashion than in other children. According to the present hypothesis, however, this will be due to the fact that punishment continues until the child makes a symbolic renunciation, rather than to the fact that the punishment involves withdrawal of love. If physical chastisement or loss of privileges are used in the same way, the same outcome is predicted.

A possible weakness of this hypothesis is that children might learn a discrimination between the symbolic and the actual avoidances, so that they would develop a pattern of violating parental standards, immediately confessing and apologizing, and then transgressing again at the next hint of temptation. If forgiveness is offered freely and uncritically enough, such a pattern presumably does develop. In this case the correlation among the criteria of conscience would be expected to drop, actual avoidance of wrongdoing no longer being associated with the other criteria. (For this reason, Sears, Maccoby, and Levin might have found smaller relations if they had studied older children.) However, if the parents' discrimination keeps up with the child's so that the child cannot count on removing all the parents' disfavor with a perfunctory apology, the efficacy of this kind of discipline should be at least partially maintained.

If this explanation of greater conscience in children disciplined by withdrawal of love is correct, why was greater conscience also found with the other kinds of love-oriented control? Since these were all found to be intercorrelated, and since their relations to the degree of conscience were uniformly low, interpretations either of separate techniques or of love orientation as a general trait are necessarily somewhat dubious. As an example of the difficulties involved, it may be noted that reasoning with the child is counted as a love-oriented technique solely on the grounds of its correlation with the other such techniques. Nevertheless, it shows a higher relation to conscience than do two of the three clearly love-oriented techniques. In view of such complexities, it seems legitimate to suggest that the crucial factor in those techniques associated with conscience may not be love orientation as such, but something else correlated with it.

To test this hypothesis, it would be necessary to have further detailed information of the sort that Sears, Maccoby, and Levin used, so that disciplinary methods could be classified according to the time relations discussed above. It is predicted that the parents' tendency to make termination of punishment contingent on symbolic renunciation would be correlated with love-oriented discipline. However, if each were varied with the other held constant, conscience should be more closely related to response contingency than to love orientation.

Along with this overall analysis of conscience, more detailed analyses could be made of the various components of conscience. According to the present view, intercorrelations among these criteria would be moderate for the entire sample and low when method of discipline was held constant.

The learning sequence discussed above is only one of several possible explanations of the Sears, Maccoby, and Levin finding. By suggesting that the crucial causal factor is not the distinction between materialistic orientation and love orientation, but another distinction correlated with it, the present hypothesis gains an advantage in objectivity and in practical applicability. Whether it also has the advantage of correctness must be empirically determined. The chief purpose of the present example is to point to the availability of such reductionist hypotheses in the study of values and to argue that they deserve priority in the schedule of scientific investigation.

Permanence of Conscience

It would be particularly desirable to have a follow-up study to compare evidences of conscience in kindergarten with those of the same people later in life, when they were no longer primarily under the direct influence of their parents. Such a follow-up would help to clarify the relation between short-run and long-run conformity discussed above. Is the child who thoroughly obeys all his parents' prohibitions also the one who sticks to these standards when his parents are no longer around and his new associates have different standards? Anecdotal evidence can be cited on both sides, though the bulk is probably in the affirmative. To the extent that current and later conformity are independent, what variables influence one more than the other?

Predictions from learning theory on this topic are by no means unambiguous. Nevertheless, two lines of reasoning may be suggested concerning the type of discipline likely to result in the most persistent avoidances. (Persistence here refers, not to absolute level of avoidance, but to relative lack of decrement in the strength of avoidance with time.)

The first line of reasoning is from the differences in the slopes of *generalization gradients* for different kinds of learning (Dollard & Miller, 1950). In most cases the contrast in slope is between approach (or excitatory) and avoidance (or inhibitory) tendencies. It appears, however, that the basic distinction is between response tendencies activated by innate and by learned (generally fear) drives (Miller & Murray, 1952). When stimulus conditions change, the resultant removal of cues for fear produces a greater weakening of response tendencies based on fear than of response tendencies based on other drives. Hence, the generalization gradient of responses and inhibitions based on fear is steeper than that of other responses and inhibitions. This implies to that complex continuum along which an individual makes the transi-discipline based on rewards as distance from the disciplinarian or any other change in conditions increases. Since this difference in slope is found on continua both of distance (Miller, 1944) and of similarity (Miller & Kraeling, 1952; Murray & Miller, 1952), it seems reasonable to predict that it also applies to that complex continuum along which an individual makes the transition away from parental apron strings. It would follow from this analysis that of two inhibitions learned in childhood, equal in age and original strength, one learned from the threat of losing rewards would be more effective later in life than one learned from the fear-provoking threat of punishment.

In this analysis, the advantages of discipline by manipulation (including withdrawal) of reward would apply to any kind of reward, material or social, not merely to parental love. However, the desire to continue receiving love from the parents may persist after the child has outgrown the need for other parental rewards, such as gifts and privileges. Discipline by withdrawal of love, in an atmosphere of warmth, might therefore be even more effective than other forms of discipline by denial of reward in producing persistent avoidances.

The other line of reasoning, involving the *partial reinforcement effect,* argues for the persistence of conscience learned by the process outlined above, in which a symbolic renunciation of wrongdoing terminates punishment. Although the greater resistance to extinction of responses which have received less than 100% reinforcement has been demonstrated primarily with positive reinforcement, it applies to negative as well (Humphreys, 1939, 1940; Grant, Schipper, & Ross, 1952). Partial reinforcement is of course present with all kinds of discipline, since punishment depends on the parents' moods and on the social situation, as well as on the child's being caught. However, the above analysis of the kind of punishment which terminates when the child makes a symbolic renunciation of wrongdoing suggests that such discipline may involve an additional source of partial reinforcement. As was indicated above, the child may learn that he can avoid punishment by confessing and apologizing. When this happens, the avoidance starts to extinguish. However, the discerning parent then learns not to accept the apology, and the child is punished anyway. The child must then make a more vigorous and convincing symbolic renunciation than before in order to terminate the punishment. In addition, the discrimination he has made between the symbolic renunciation and the actual avoidance is broken down; punishment can only be prevented by actual avoidance of wrongdoing. If, however, after a period of obedience he once more transgresses and then confesses, he is likely again not to be punished. This starts the cycle of extinction and reconditoning of the avoidance response going again, thus continuing to provide a reinforcement schedule in which only part of the child's transgressions are punished.

To predict that such partial reinforcement will retard extinction is admittedly problematic, both because of the complexity of the avoidance paradigm and because the unpunished transgressions are assumed to occur in blocks rather than randomly. Nevertheless, the hypothesis deserves consideration, not only as a prediction from learning principles to personality, but also as a case where the needs of personality theory might guide research in learning.

Although these two lines of reasoning agree in predicting maximally persistent conformity to parental prohibitions by children reared in an atmosphere of parental warmth and disciplined by withdrawal of love, they differ in their other predictions. To test these various hypotheses separately would require both short-run and long-run analyses of the effects of a variety of parental discipline patterns. The following hypotheses might be tested: (*a*) that discipline by deprivations (whether of things, privileges, or love) has more persistent effects than discipline by noxious stimulation (whether physical or social); (*b*) that where the child is taught to confess and apologize for his transgressions, avoidance behavior will go through cycles of extinction and reconditioning; and (*c*) that punishing only part of a child's transgressions results in more persistent obedience than does punishing all of them.

SUMMARY

It is suggested that the terms identification, introjection, and internalization be replaced by detailed analyses in learning-theory terms of the acquisition of values. A reinforcement framework for such analyses is outlined, and examples are presented dealing with the concept of conscience and the factors influencing its development. It is argued that this would simplify terminology, encourage more precise study, and further the integration of learning and personality theories.

This analysis, like all attempts to integrate the harder-headed and the softer-hearted portions of behavioral science, is open to attack from both sides. On the one hand it may be objected that the present treatment is too cavalier with the interpersonal and intrapsychic complexities of personality development, that the internalization of values and the identification of one person with another cannot be treated as though they were nothing but the simple learning of a rat in a maze. The answer to this objection is that no "nothing but-ism" is intended; it is an empirical matter both to determine how far the principles of learning (not necessarily simple) can go in explaining personality development and to decide how much the additional principles suggested by some writers actually contribute to our understanding of the phenomena in question. The attempt to catch too much complexity at a single stroke may retard rather than advance our understanding.

On the other hand it may be objected that the interpretations given here are untestable, that the variables involve such diverse and subtle behaviors over such long periods of time as to defy adequate measurement. Admittedly the questionnaire, interview, and brief-observation techniques used in this area leave much to be desired. However, as long as applied behavioral scientists are called upon to deal with questions of personality development, poor data to guide their decisions are better than none. Study of learning of values by humans, guided by the principles of learning based on both animal and human studies, has the potential to make vital contributions to many theoretical and applied areas of knowledge. It is hoped that the present discussion may contribute something to that goal.

REFERENCES

Ausubel, D. P. Relationships between shame and guilt in the socializing process. *Psychol. Rev.,* 1955, **62,** 378–390.

Benedict, Ruth. *The chrysanthemum and the sword.* Boston: Houghton Mifflin, 1946.

Brush, F. R. The effects of shock intensity on the acquisition and extinction of an avoidance response in dogs. *J. comp. physiol. Psychol.,* 1957, **50,** 547–552.

Campbell, D. T. Social attitudes and other acquired behavioral dispositions. In S. Koch (Ed.), *Psychology: A study of a science.* Vol. 6. *Investigations of man as socius: Their place in psychology and the social sciences.* New York: McGraw-Hill, in press.

Church, R. M. Transmission of learned behavior between rats. *J. abnorm. soc. Psychol.,* 1957, **54,** 163–165.

Darby, C. L., & Riopelle, A. J. Observational learning in the rhesus monkey. *J. comp. physiol. Psychol.,* 1959, **52,** 94–98.

Davis, W. A., & Havighurst, R. J. *Father of the man.* Boston: Houghton Mifflin, 1947.

Dinsmoor, J. A. Punishment: I. The avoidance hypothesis. *Psychol. Rev.,* 1954, **61,** 34–46.

Dollard, J., & Miller, N. E. *Personality and psychotherapy.* New York: McGraw-Hill, 1950.

Dukes, W. F. The psychological study of values. *Psychol. Bull.,* 1955, **52,** 24–50.

Freud, Anna. *The ego and the mechanisms of defense.* New York: Int. Univer. Press, 1946.

Freud, S. *The ego and the id.* London: Hogarth, 1950.

Glaser, D. Dynamics of ethnic identification. *Amer. sociol. Rev.,* 1958, **23,** 31–40.

Grant, D. A., Schipper, L. M., & Ross, B. M. Effect of intertrial interval during acquisition on extinction of the conditioned eyelid response following partial reinforcement. *J. exp. Psychol.,* 1952, **44,** 203–210.

Havinghurst, R. J., & Neugarten, Bernice L. *American Indian and white children.* Chicago: Univer. Chicago Press, 1955.

Hull, C. L. *Principles of behavior.* New York: Appleton-Century, 1943.

Hull, C. L. *A behavior system.* New Haven: Yale Univer. Press, 1952.

Humphreys, L. G. The effect of random alternation of reinforcement on the acquisition and extinction of conditioned eyelid reactions. *J. exp. Psychol.,* 1939, **25,** 141–158.

Humphreys, L. G. Psychogalvanic responses following two conditions of reinforcement. *J. exp. Psychol.,* 1940, **27,** 71–75.

Hurlock, Elizabeth B. *Child development.* (3d ed.) New York: McGraw-Hill, 1956.

Jenkins, W. O., & Stanley, J. C. Partial reinforcement: A review and critique. *Psychol. Bull.,* 1950, **47,** 193–234.

Kagan, J. The concept of identification. *Psychol. Rev.,* 1958, **65,** 296–305.

Lazowick, L. On the nature of identification. *J. abnorm. soc. Psychol.,* 1955, **51,** 175–183.

Lewis, D. J., & Duncan, C. P. Vicarious experience and partial reinforcement. *J. abnorm. soc. Psychol.,* 1958, **57,** 321–326.

Lindemann, E. Symptomatology and management of acute grief. *Amer. J. Psychiat.,* 1944, **101,** 141–148.

Lynn, D. B. A note on sex differences in the development of masculine and feminine identification. *Psychol. Rev.,* 1959, **66,** 126–135.

Masserman, J. H. *Principles of dynamic psychiatry.* Philadelphia: Saunders, 1946.

Mead, Margaret. Some anthropological considerations concerning guilt. In M. L. Reymert (Ed.), *Feelings and emotions: The Mooseheart symposium.* New York: McGraw-Hall, 1950.

Miller, N. E. Experimental studies of conflict. In J. McV. Hunt (Ed.), *Personality and the behavior disorders.* New York: Ronald, 1944. Pp. 431–465.

Miller, N. E. Learnable drives and rewards. In S. S. Stevens (Ed.), *Handbook of experimental psychology.* New York: Wiley, 1951. Pp. 435–472.

Miller, N. E., & Dollard, J. *Social learning and imitation.* New Haven: Yale Univer. Press, 1941.

Miller, N. E., & Kraeling, Doris. Displacement: Greater generalization of approach than avoidance in a generalized approach-avoidance conflict. *J. exp. Psychol.,* 1952, **43,** 217–221.

Miller, N. E. & Murray, E. J. Displacement and conflict: Learnable drive as a basis for the steeper gradient of avoidance than of approach. *J. exp. Psychol.,* 1952, **43,** 227–231.

Mowrer, O. H. *Learning theory and personality dynamics.* New York: Ronald, 1950.

Mowrer, O. H., & Ullman, A. D. Time as a determinant in integrative learning. *Psychol. Rev.,* 1945, **52,** 61–90.

Murray, E. J., & Miller, N. E. Displacement: Steeper gradient of generalization of avoidance than of approach with age of habit controlled. *J. exp. Psychol.,* 1952, **43,** 222–226.

Osgood, C. E. *Method and theory in experimental psychology.* New York: Oxford Univer. Press, 1953.

Parsons, T. Family structure and the socialization of the child. In T. Parsons & R. F. Bales (Eds.), *Family, socialization and interaction process.* Glencoe: Free Press, 1955.

Reynolds, W. F. Acquisition and extinction of the conditioned eyelid response following partial and continuous reinforcement. *J. exp. Psychol.,* 1958, **55,** 335–341.

Russell, W. A., & Storms, L. H. Implicit verbal chaining in paired-associate learning. *J. exp. Psychol.,* 1955, **49,** 287–293.

Sanford, N. The dynamics of identification. *Psychol. Rev.,* 1955, **62,** 106–118.

Sears, R. R., Maccoby, Eleanor E., & Levin, H. *Patterns of child rearing.* Evanston, Ill.: Row, Peterson, 1957.

Shaw, G. B. Preface to "Androcles and the Lion." In *Nine Plays.* New York: Dodd, Mead, 1948.

Sidman, M. Two temporal parameters of the maintenance of avoidance behavior by the white rat. *J. comp. physiol. Psychol.,* 1953, **46,** 253–261.

Singer, M. B. Shame cultures and guilt cultures. In G. Piers & M. B. Singer (Eds.) *Shame and guilt.* Springfield, Ill.: Charles C Thomas, 1953.

Solomon, R. L., & Brush, Eleanor, S. Experimentally derived conceptions of anxiety and aversion. In *Nebraska symposium on motivation IV.* Lincoln: Univer. Nebraska Press, 1956.

Solomon, R. L., & Coles, M. R. A case of failure of generalization of imitation across drives and across situations. *J. abnorm. soc. Psychol.,* 1954, **49,** 7–13.

Tolman, E. C. There is more than one kind of learning. *Psychol. Rev.,* 1949, **56,** 144–155.

Whiting, J. W. M., & Child, I. L. *Child training and personality.* New Haven: Yale Univer. Press, 1953.

28

INFLUENCE OF SOCIAL REINFORCEMENT AND THE BEHAVIOR OF MODELS IN SHAPING CHILDREN'S MORAL JUDGMENTS*

ALBERT BANDURA
and
FREDERICK J. McDONALD

MOST OF THE literature and theorizing in the area of developmental psychology has been guided by various forms of stage theories (Erikson, 1950; Freud, 1949; Gesell & Ilg, 1943; Piaget, 1948, 1954; Sullivan, 1953). Although there appears to be relatively little agreement among these theories concerning the number and the content of stages considered to be necessary to account for the course of personality development, they all share in common the assumption that social behavior can be categorized in terms of a predetermined sequence of stages with varying degrees of continuity or discontinuity between successive developmental periods. Typically, the emergence of these presumably age-specific modes of behavior is attributed to ontogenetic factors rather than to specific social stimulus events which are likely to be favored in a social learning theory of the developmental process.

The stage and social learning approaches differ not only in the relative emphasis placed upon time schedules or reinforcement schedules in explaining the occurrence of change in social behavior, but also in the assumptions made concerning the regularity and invariance of response sequences, and the nature of response variability. Stage theories, for example, generally stress

* From the *Journal of Abnormal and Social Psychology,* 1963, *67,* 274–282. Reprinted with permission of the authors and the American Psychological Association, Inc.

This investigation was supported in part by Research Grant M-5162 from the National Institutes of Health, United States Public Health Service.

The authors wish to express their appreciation to Florence Mote, Charles Carver, and Nathan Kroman for their aid in arranging the research facilities, and to Peter Gumpert for his assistance with the statistical analyses. We also wish to express our gratitude to the many students who served as experimenters and as models in this project.

intraindividual variability over time, and minimize interindividual variability in behavior due to sex, intellectual, socioeconomic, ethnic, and cultural differences. To the extent that children representing such diverse backgrounds experience differential contingencies and schedules of reinforcement, as well as exposure to social models who differ widely in the behavior they exhibit, considerable interindividual behavioral variability would be expected. Similarly, the sequence of developmental changes is considered in social learning theory to be primarily a function of changes in reinforcement contingencies and other learning variables rather than an unfolding of genetically programed response predispositions.

Despite the considerable attention devoted to theoretical analyses of the learning process, a comprehensive theory of *social learning* has been relatively slow in developing. By and large, current principles of learning have been based upon investigations involving simple fractional responses which are neither social nor developmental in nature, and often use animals as subjects. Although recent years have witnessed a widespread application of learning principles to developmental psychology, the experimentation has been primarily confined to operant or instrumental conditioning of responses that are modeled on the fractional responses elicited in experimentation with infrahuman organisms (for example, manipulating plungers, pressing bars, levers, buttons, etc.). Moreover, a good deal of this research has been designed to compare complex social learning to available simple learning principles, rather than to extend the range of principles and procedures in order to account more adequately for complex social phenomena.

It is generally assumed that social responses are acquired through the method of successive approximations by means of differential reinforcement (Skinner, 1953). The effectiveness of reinforcement procedures in shaping and maintaining behavior in both animals and humans is well documented by research. It is doubtful, however, if many social responses would ever be acquired if social training proceeded solely by this method. This is particularly true of behavior for which there is no reliable eliciting stimulus apart from the cues provided by others as they performed the behavior. If a child had no occasion to hear speech, for example, or in the case of a deaf-blind person (Keller, 1927), no opportunity to match laryngeal muscular responses of a verbalizing model, it would probably be exceedingly difficult or impossible to teach a person appropriate linguistic responses.

Even in cases where some stimulus is known to be capable of eliciting an approximation to the desired behavior, the process of learning can be considerably shortened by the provision of social models (Bandura & Huston, 1961; Bandura, Ross, & Ross, 1961, 1963). Thus, in both instances, imitation of modeling behavior is an essential aspect of social learning.

In the experiment reported in this paper a social learning theory combining the principles of instrumental conditioning and imitation was applied to a developmental problem that has been approached from a stage point of view.

According to Piaget (1948), one can distinguish two clear-cut stages of moral judgment demarcated from each other at approximately 7 years of age. In the first stage, defined as *objective responsibility,* children judge the gravity of a deviant act in terms of the amount of material damages, and disregard the intentionality of the action. By contrast, during the second or *subjective responsibility* stage, children judge conduct in terms of its intent rather than its material consequences. While these stages are predetermined (for example, Piaget reports that young children are relatively incapable of adopting a subjective orientation and he was unable to find a single case of objective morality in older children), the factors responsible for the transition from one stage to the other are not entirely clear. Presumably, the principal antecedent of objective judgmental behavior is the "natural spontaneous and unconscious egocentrism" of child thought reinforced to some extent by adult authoritarianism, which produces submissiveness and preoccupation with external consequences. As the child matures, however, he gains increasing autonomy, his relationships become based upon mutual reciprocity and cooperation, giving rise to the emergence of subjective morality.

The purpose of the present investigation was to demonstrate that moral judgment responses are less age-specific than implied by Piaget, and that children's moral orientations can be altered and even reversed by the manipulation of response-reinforcement contingencies and by the provision of appropriate social models.

In this experiment children who exhibited predominantly objective and subjective moral orientations were assigned at random to one of three experimental conditions. One group of children observed adult models who expressed moral judgments counter to the group's orientation and the children were positively reinforced for adopting the models' evaluative responses. A second group observed the models but the children received no reinforcement for matching the models' behavior. The third group had no exposure to the models but each child was reinforced whenever he expressed moral judgments that ran counter to his dominant evaluative tendencies. Thus the experimental design permitted a test of the relative efficacy of social reinforcement, the behavior of models, and these two factors combined in shaping children's moral judgments.

It was predicted, for reasons given in the preceding sections, that the combined use of models and social reinforcement would be the most powerful condition for altering the children's behavior and that the provision of models alone would be of intermediate effectiveness. Since the presence of a strong dominant response limits the opportunity for reinforcement of an alternative response which is clearly subordinate, it was expected that social reinforcement alone would be the least effective of the three treatment methods.

METHOD

Subjects

A total of 78 boys and 87 girls ranging in age from 5 to 11 years served as subjects in various phases of the study. They were drawn from two sources, a Jewish religious school and an elementary public school serving predominantly middle-class communities. The research was conducted on week ends in the religious school and on weekdays in the public school facility. Female students from Stanford University served in the roles of experimenters and models.

Stimulus Items

Following the procedure employed by Piaget (1948), the children were presented with pairs of stories each of which described a well-intentioned act which resulted in considerable material damage, contrasted with a selfishly or maliciously motivated act producing minor consequences. The children were asked to judge, "Who did the naughtier thing?" and to provide a reason for their choice. An illustrative stimulus item, taken from Piaget, is given below:

1. John was in his room when his mother called him to dinner. John goes down, and opens the door to the dining room. But behind the door was a chair, and on the chair was a tray with fifteen cups on it. John did not know the cups were behind the door. He opens the door, the door hits the tray, bang go the fifteen cups, and they all get broken.
2. One day when Henry's mother was out, Henry tried to get some cookies out of the cupboard. He climbed up on a chair, but the cookie jar was still too high, and he couldn't reach it. But while he was trying to get the cookie jar, he knocked over a cup. The cup fell down and broke.

Six of the story items employed in the present experiment were identical with those developed by Piaget except for minor modifications in wording or content to make the story situations more appropriate for American children. In addition, a set of 36 new paired items was devised to provide a sufficient number of stories so as to obtain a fairly reliable estimate of children's moral judgments at three different phases of the experiment, i.e., base operant test, experimental treatment, and posttest. In each of these story situations which were modeled after Piaget's items, intentionality was contrasted with serious consequences. These items were carefully pretested on a sample of 30 children in order to clarify any ambiguities, to gauge the children's interpretations of the seriousness of the depicted consequences, and to remove any irrelevant cues which might lead the children to judge the depicted actions in terms other than intentions or consequences.

Except for the assignment of the six Piaget items to both the operant test and the posttest set, for reasons which will be explained later, the remaining stories were distributed randomly into three different groups.

Design and Procedure

A summary of the overall experimental design is presented in Table 1.

Operant level of objective and subjective responses. In the first phase of the experiment, the children were individually administered 12 pairs of stories to furnish measures of the operant levels of objective and subjective moral judgments at the various age levels. These data provided both a check

TABLE 1

Summary of the Experimental Design

Experimental Groups	Step 1 *Assessment of Operant Level of Objective and Subjective Moral Responses*	Step 2 *Experimental Treatments*	Step 3 *Posttreatment Measurement of Subjective and Objective Moral Responses with Models and Reinforcement Absent*
Subjective moral orientation:			
I ($N = 16$)	Step 1	Model emits objective responses and positively reinforced; child reinforced for objective responses.	Step 3
II ($N = 16$)	Step 1	Model emits objective responses and positively reinforced; child not reinforced for objective responses.	Step 3
III ($N = 16$)	Step 1	No model present; child reinforced for objective responses.	Step 3
Objective moral orientation:			
IV ($N = 12$)	Step 1	Model emits subjective responses and positively reinforced; child reinforced for subjective responses.	Step 3
V ($N = 12$)	Step 1	Model emits subjective responses and positively reinforced; child not reinforced for subjective responses.	Step 3
VI ($N = 12$)	Step 1	No model present; child reinforced for subjective responses.	Step 3

on Piaget's normative findings and the base for forming the experimental treatment groups.

Experimental treatments. On the basis of operant test performances, 48 children who were decidedly subjective in their moral orientation (Mean percentage of subjective responses = 80), and 36 who gave high base rates of objective responses (Mean percentage of objective responses = 83) were selected from the total sample to participate in the second and third phases of the experiment. The children in each of the two classes of moral orientation were equally divided between boys and girls. They were also further categorized into younger and older children and then assigned at random to one of three experimental treatment conditions. Thus the experimental groups were balanced with respect to age and sex of child.

In the *model and child reinforced condition,* both the model and the child were administered alternately 12 different sets of story items with the model receiving the first story, the child the second one, and so on. To each of the 12 items, the model consistently expressed judgmental responses in opposition to the child's moral orientation (for example, objective responses with subjective children and vice versa), and the experimenter reinforced the model's behavior with verbal approval responses such as "Very good," "That's fine," and "That's good." The child was similarly reinforced whenever he adapted the model's class of moral judgments in response to his own set of items. To control for any intermodel variability in length or content of evaluative responses, the subjective and objective answers for the models' test items were prepared in advance.

The procedure for children in the *model reinforced, child not reinforced condition,* was identical with the treatment described above with the exception that the children received no reinforcement for matching the moral judgment responses of their respective models.

In the *model absent, child reinforced condition,* no model was present; the experimenter simply administered the 24 story items to the child and reinforced him with verbal approval whenever he produced an evaluative response that ran counter to his dominant orientation.

The time elapsing between the operant testing and the experimental phase of the study ranged from 1 to 3 weeks with the majority of the children receiving the experimental treatment after a 2-week period.

A total of nine experimenter-model pairs participated in the treatment phase of the experiment. To control for possible differences in experimenter or model influences across conditions or sex groups, each pair was assigned groups of subjects in triplets, i.e., boys and girls taken from each of the three treatment conditions.

Students who served as the experimenters' assistants brought the children individually from their classrooms to the experimental session and introduced them to their experimenters. The experimenter explained that she would like to have the child judge a second set of stories similar to the ones he had completed on a previous occasion. In the conditions involving the presence of models, the experimenter further explained that she was collecting normative data on a large sample of people, including both children and adults, and to expedite matters she invited the adult subjects to appear at the school so that the items could be administered to both groups simultaneously. To add to the credibility of the situation, the experimenter read to the model the same instructions the child had received in the operant test session, as though the model was a naive subject. The experimenter then read the story situations to the model and the child, who were seated facing the experimenter, delivered the soical reinforcement whenever appropriate, and recorded the responses.

It was found in the preliminary pretesting of the stories that they were sufficiently structured with respect to the intentionality-consequences dichotomy so that children's identification of the naughtier story character was virtually a perfect predictor that the children would provide the corresponding subjective for objective reasons or their choices. Since there is some evidence that reinforcement given immediately is considerably more effective than when delayed (Mahrer, 1956), the reinforcement value of the experimenter's approval would have been considerably reduced if administered following the children's explanations, not only because of the delay involved but also because many responses, some relevant others irrelevant, occur during the intervening period, thus making it difficult to specify the behavior being reinforced. For this reason, the experimenters reinforced the children immediately following correct choice responses, and again after they gave the appropriate explanations.

The measure of learning was the percentage of objective judgmental response produced by the subjective children and the percentage of subjective responses performed by the objectively oriented subjects.

Posttest. Following the completion of the treatment procedure, the child reported to another room in the building. Here a second experimenter presented the child with 12 additional stories to obtain further information about the generality and stability of changes in judgmental responses when models and social reinforcement were absent. The experimenter simply read the stories to the child and recorded his verbal responses without comment.

In view of Piaget's contention that moral judgments are age-specific and considerably resistant to out-of-phase changes, it was decided to repeat, in the posttest, the Piaget items included in the set of operant test stories. If the interpolated social influence experience succeeded in altering children's evaluative responses, such findings would throw considerable doubt on the validity of a developmental stage theory of morality.

Different sets of experimenters conducted each of the three phases of the study, with a total of 10 experimenters participating in the posttesting. The utilization of different rooms and different sets of experimenters provided a more stringent test of generalization effects than if the same experimenters had been used throughout the investigation.

The experiment was concluded with a brief interview designed to assess the child's awareness of the behavior exhibited by the model, the social reinforcers administered by the experimenter, and the response-reinforcement contingency in the experimental situation.

RESULTS

Since the data disclosed no significant differences in operant levels or in responsivity to the social influence procedures for children drawn from the two different school settings, the data were combined in the statistical analyses.

Judgmental Responses as a Function of Age

The normative data based on the present sample of children show that subjectivity is positively associated with age ($F = 4.84$, $p < .01$), but unrelated to sex differences at any age level. It is evident from these findings, however, that objective and subjective judgments exist together rather than as successive developmental stages. Most young children were capable of exercising subjective judgments, and a large majority of the older children exhibited varying degrees of objective morality.

Influence of Reinforcement and Modeling Cues

Figure 1 presents the curves for the acquisition and the generalization of objective moral judgment responses by subjective children in each of the three experimental conditions.

Results of the analysis of variance performed on these data are summarized in Table 2. The main effects of experimental conditions and phases, as well as their interaction effects, are highly significant sources of variance. Further comparisons of pairs of means by the *t* test reveal that subjective children who were exposed to objective models, and those who were positively reinforced for matching their model's moral judgments, not only modified their moral orientations toward objectivity, but also remained objectively oriented in their post-experimental judgmental behavior (Table 3).

The provision of models alone, however, was as effective in altering the children's moral judgments as was the experimental condition combining modeling cues with social reinforcement. As predicted, the experimental conditions utilizing modeling procedures proved to be considerably more powerful than was operant conditioning alone, which produced a slight

FIGURE 1

Mean Percentage of Objective Moral Judgment Responses Produced by Subjective Children at Each of the Three Test Periods for Each of Three Experimental Conditions

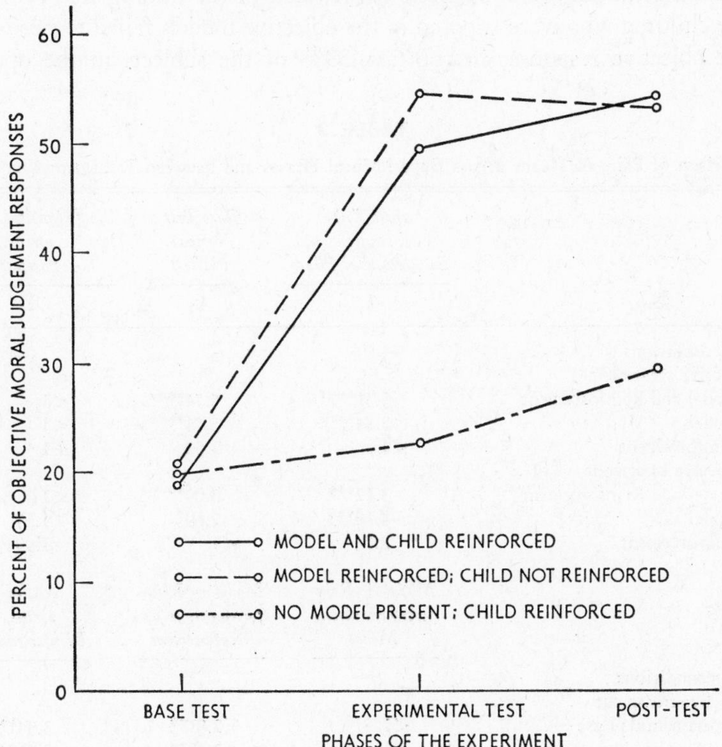

TABLE 2

Analysis of Variance of Objective Moral Judgment Responses Produced by Subjective Children

Source	df	MS	F
Conditions (C)	2	5,226.2	3.24*
Sex (S)	1	1,344.4	<1
C × S	2	3,671.4	2.28
Error (b)	42	1,612.1	
Phases (P)	2	9,505.8	35.46**
P × C	4	1,430.3	5.34**
P × S	2	203.8	<1
P × C × S	4	747.6	2.79*
Error (w)	84	268.1	

* $p < .05$.
** $p < .001$.

increase in objective judgmental responses but not of statistically significant magnitude (Table 3).

Some additional evidence for the efficacy of the behavior of models in accelerating the acquisition process is provided in the finding that only 9% of the children who were exposed to the objective models failed to produce a single objective response; in contrast, 38% of the subjects in the operant conditioning group did not emit a single objective response despite obtaining twice as many acquisition trials.

TABLE 3

Comparison of Pairs of Means across Experimental Phases and between Treatment Conditions

Scores	*Base Test versus Experimental Phase* t	*Base Test versus Posttest* t	*Experimental Phase versus Posttest* t
Within conditions			
Objective treatment			
Model and Reinforcement	5.31****	5.74****	<1
Model	5.84****	5.74****	<1
Reinforcement	<1	1.52	<1
Subjective treatment			
Model and Reinforcement	3.12***	3.09**	<1
Model	4.10***	2.69*	1.87
Reinforcement	2.04	<1	1.99
	Model + Reinforcement versus Model	*Model + Reinforcement versus Reinforcement*	*Model versus Reinforcement*
Between conditions			
Objective treatment			
Experimental phase	<1	2.81**	3.34***
Posttest	<1	2.68**	2.61**
Subjective treatment			
Experimental phase	<1	1.11	1.13
Posttest	<1	2.81**	2.15*

* $p < .05$.
** $p < .02$.
*** $p < .01$.
**** $p < .001$.

The significant triple interaction effect shows that modeling combined with reinforcement exerted a greater influence on girls than on boys whereas, relative to girls, boys were more responsive to modeling cues when reinforcement was absent.

The acquisition and generalization data for objective children treated subjectively are presented graphically in Figure 2.

Analysis of variance of this set of scores reveals that the experimental

FIGURE 2

Mean Percentage of Subjective Moral Judgment Responses Produced by Objective Children on Each of Three Test Periods for Each of Three Experimental Conditions

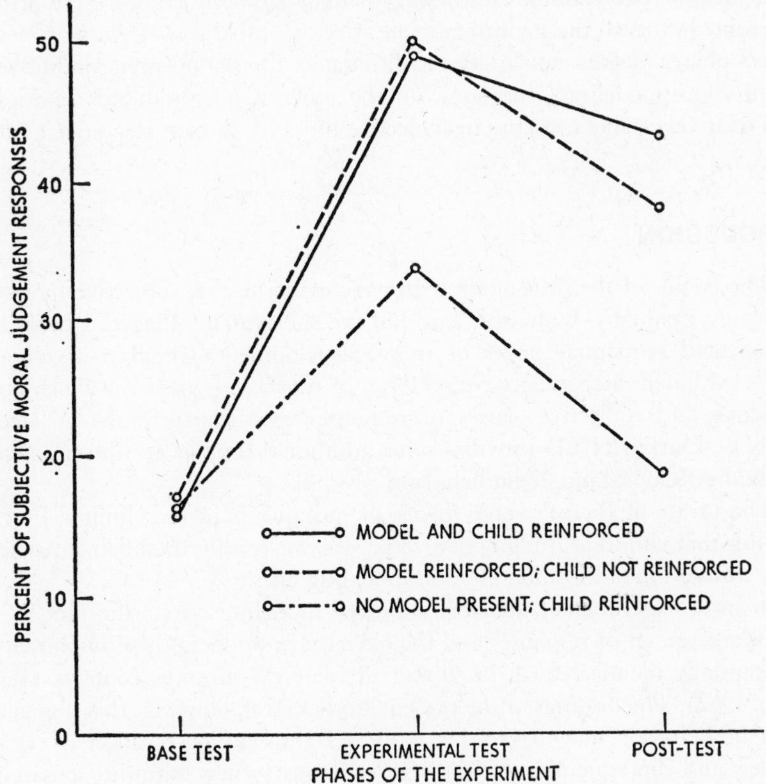

TABLE 4

Analysis of Variance of Subjective Moral Judgment Responses Produced by Objective Children

Source	df	MS	F
Conditions (C)	2	1,869.2	1.76
Sex (S)	1	2,821.3	2.66
C × S	2	208.6	<1
Error (b)	30	1,059.9	
Experimental phases (P)	2	7,057.5	16.38**
P × C	4	422.1	<1
P × S	2	99.4	<1
P × C × S	4	132.9	<1
Error (w)	60	430.9	

** $p < .001$.

treatments were highly influential in modifying the children's orientations from objective to subjective morality (Table 4). Although the differences between the three experimental groups did not reach statistical significance, evidently the two conditions utilizing modeling procedures were the principal contributors to the main treatment effect. Comparison of pairs of means across phases yielded no significant differences for the operant conditioning group. The modeling conditions, on the other hand, produced significant and relatively stable increases in subjective moral judgment responses (Table 3).

DISCUSSION

The results of the present study provide evidence that subjective morality increases gradually with age, but fail to substantiate Piaget's theory of demarcated sequential stages of moral development. Children at all age levels exhibited discriminative repertories of moral judgments in which both objective and subjective classes of responses exist concurrently. A recent study by Durkin (1961) provides some additional support for the specificity of children's moral judgment behavior.

The utility of Piaget's stage theory of morality is further limited by the finding that children's judgmental responses are readily modifiable, particularly through the utilization of adult modeling cues.

In most experimental demonstrations of modeling effects the model exhibits a given set of responses and the observer reproduces these responses in substantially identical form in similar or identical stimulus contexts (Bandura, 1962). The findings of the present study reveal, however, that a general class of behavior may be readily acquired through observation of social models and consequently, the observer responds to new stimulus sensations in a manner consistent with the model's predisposition, even though the subject had never observed the model respond to the same stimuli. These results illustrate the potency of modeling cues for shaping generalized patterns of social behavior.

The failure of operant conditioning procedures alone in altering moral judgment behavior is not at all surprising considering that the desired responses were much weaker than the competing dominant class of moral judgments. In many cases, particularly in the objective treatment condition, the subordinate responses occurred relatively infrequently; consequently there was little opportunity to influence them through reinforcement. In fact, the absence of a statistically significant conditions effect for children who experienced the subjective treatment largely resulted from several of the subjects in the operant conditioning group who happened to emit subjective responses on early trials and increased this behavior under reinforcement.

It is apparent, however, from both sets of data that operant conditioning procedures are particularly inefficient when there are strong dominant response tendencies and the desired alternative responses are only weakly developed or absent. In such cases, the provision of models who exhibit the desired behavior is an exceedingly effective procedure for eliciting from others appropriate matching responses early in the learning sequence and thus accelerating the acquisition process.

The results of the present study fail to confirm the hypothesis that a combination of reinforcement and modeling procedures constitutes a more powerful learning condition than modeling alone. Several factors might have accounted for the lack of differences between these two treatment conditions. In some cases the mere exposure to modeling cues produced rapid and complete changes in moral orientations and consequently the addition of reinforcement could not contribute any performance increments. This interpretation, however, does not fully account for the data since the majority of children were not performing at or near the ceiling level. Results from a series of experiments of social learning by means of imitation provide an alternative explanation (Bandura, 1962). These studies suggest that the process of response acquisition is based upon contiguity of sensory events and that reinforcement may function primarily as a performance related variable. In the present investigation the models' responses were highly consistent and sufficiently distinctive to insure observation and imitative learning. The experimenters' positive evaluative statements, however, may have served as relatively weak reinforcers. Had more highly desired incentives been employed as reinforcing agents, it is very likely that the addition of reinforcement would have significantly enhanced the children's reproduction of the modeled judgmental orientations.

REFERENCES

Bandura, A. Social learning through imitation. In M. R. Jones (Ed.), *Nebraska symposium on motivation: 1962.* Lincoln: Univer. Nebraska Press, 1962. Pp. 211–269.

Bandura, A., & Huston, Aletha C. Identification as a process of incidental learning. *J. abnorm. soc. Psychol.,* 1961, **63,** 311–318.

Bandura, A., Ross, Dorothea, & Ross, Sheila A. Transmission of aggression through imitation of aggressive models. *J. abnorm. soc. Psychol.,* 1961, **63,** 575–582.

Bandura, A., Ross, Dorothea, & Ross, Sheila A. Imitation of film-mediated aggressive models. *J. abnorm. soc. Psychol.,* 1963, **66,** 3–11.

Durkin, Dolores. The specificity of children's moral judgments. *J. genet. Psychol.,* 1961, **98,** 3–13.

Erikson, E. H. *Childhood and society.* New York: Norton, 1950.

Freud, S. *An outline of psychoanalysis.* New York: Norton, 1949.

Gesell, A., & Ilg, F. L. *Infant and child in the culture of today.* New York: Harper, 1943.

KELLER, HELEN. *The story of my life*. New York: Doubleday, 1927.
MAHRER, A. R. The role of expectancy in delayed reinforcement. *J. exp. Psychol.*, 1956, 52, 101–106.
PIAGET, J. *The moral judgment of the child*. Glencoe, Ill.: Free Press, 1948.
PIAGET, J. *The construction of reality in the child*. New York: Basic Books, 1954.
SKINNER, B. F. *Science and human behavior*. New York: Macmillan, 1953.
SULLIVAN, H. S. *The interpersonal theory of psychiatry*. New York: Norton, 1953.

29

SOVIET METHODS OF CHARACTER EDUCATION: SOME IMPLICATIONS FOR RESEARCH*

URIE BRONFENBRENNER

Every society faces the problem of the moral training of its youth. This is no less true of Communist society than of our own. Indeed, Communist authorities view as the primary objective of education not the learning of subject matter but the development of what they call "socialist morality." It is instructive for us in the West to examine the nature of this "socialist morality" and the manner in which it is inculcated, for to do so brings to light important differences in the ends and means of character education in the two cultures. For research workers in the field of personality development, such an examination is especially valuable, since it lays bare unrecognized assumptions and variations in approach. Accordingly, it is the purpose of this paper to provide a much-condensed account of Soviet methods of character education and to examine some of the provocative research questions that emerge from the contrast between the Soviet approach and our own.

THE WORK AND IDEAS OF A. S. MAKARENKO

To examine Soviet methods of character training is to become acquainted with the thinking and technology developed primarily by one man—Anton Semyonovich Makarenko. Makarenko's name is virtually a household word in the Soviet Union. His popularity and influence are roughly comparable to those of Dr. Spock in the United States, but his primary concern is not with the child's physical health but with his moral upbringing. Makarenko's influence extends far beyond his own voluminous writings since there is scarcely a manual for the guidance of Communist parents, teachers, or youth workers that does not draw heavily on his methods and ideas. His works have been translated into many languages and are apparently widely read not only in the Soviet Union but throughout the Communist bloc countries,

* From the *American Psychologist,* 1962, *17,* 550–564. Reprinted with permission of the author and the American Psychological Association.

Reprinted from: *Relig. Educ.,* 1962, **57**(4, Res. Suppl.), S45–S61.

notably East Germany and Communist China. Excellent English translations of a number of his works have been published in Moscow (1949, 1953, 1959) but they are not readily available in this country.

Makarenko developed his ideas and methods over the course of a lifetime of practical work with young people. In the early 1920's, as a young school teacher and devout Communist, Makarenko was handed the assignment of setting up a rehabilitation program for some of the hundreds of homeless children who were roaming the Soviet Union after the civil wars. The first group of such children assigned to Makarenko's school, a ramshackle building far out of town, turned out to be a group of boys about 18 years of age with extensive court records of housebreaking, armed robbery, and manslaughter. For the first few months, Makarenko's school served simply as the headquarters for the band of highwaymen who were his legal wards. But gradually, through the development of his group-orientated discipline techniques, and through what can only be called the compelling power of his own moral convictions, Makarenko was able to develop a sense of group responsibility and commitment to the work program and code of conduct that he had laid out for the collective. In the end, the Gorky Commune became known throughout the Soviet Union for its high morale, discipline, and for the productivity of its fields, farms, and shops. Indeed, Makarenko's methods proved so successful that he was selected to head a new commune set up by the Ministry of Internal Affairs (then the Cheka, later to become the GPU and NKVD). In the years which followed, Makarenko's theories and techniques became widely adopted throughout the USSR and now constitute the central core of Soviet educational practice.

To turn to the ideas themselves, we may begin with an excerpt from what is possibly the most widely read of Makarenko's works, *A Book for Parents* (1959).

> But our [Soviet] family is not an accidental combination of members of society. The family is a natural collective body and, like everything natural, healthy, and normal, it can only blossom forth in socialist society, freed of those very curses from which both mankind as a whole and the individual are freeing themselves.
>
> The family becomes the natural primary cell of society, the place where the delight of human life is realized, where the triumphant forces of man are refreshed, where children—the chief joy of life—live and grow.
>
> Our parents are not without authority either, but this authority is only the reflection of societal authority. The duty of a father in our country towards his children is a particular form of his duty towards society. It is as if our society says to parents:
>
> You have joined together in good will and love, rejoice in your children and expect to go on rejoicing in them. That is your personal affair and concerns your own personal happiness. Within the course of this happy process you have given birth to new human beings. A time will come when these beings will cease to be solely the instruments of your happiness, and will step forth as independent members of society. For society, it is by no means a matter of indifference what

kind of people they will become. In delegating to you a certain measure of societal authority the Soviet State demands from you the correct upbringing of its future citizens. Particularly it relies on you to provide certain conditions arising naturally out of your union; namely, your parental love.

If you wish to give birth to a citizen while dispensing with parental love, then be so kind as to warn society that you intend to do such a rotten thing. Human beings who are brought up without parental love are often deformed human beings (Makarenko, 1959, p. 29).

Characteristic of Makarenko's thought is the view that the parent's authority over the child is delegated to him by the state and that duty to one's children is merely a particular instance of one's broader duty towards society. A little later in his book for parents, the author makes this point even more emphatically. After telling the story of a boy who ran away from home after some differences with his mother, he concludes by affirming: "I am a great admirer of optimism and I like very much young lads who have so much faith in Soviet State that they are carried away and will not trust even their own mothers" (Makarenko, 1959, p. 37–38). In other words, when the needs and values of the family conflict with those of society, there is no question about who gets priority. And society receives its concrete manifestation and embodiment in the *collective,* which is an organized group engaged in some socially useful enterprise.

This brings us to Makarenko's basic thesis that optimal personality development can occur only through productive activity in a social collective. The first collective is the family, but this must be supplemented early in life by other collectives specially organized in schools, neighborhoods, and other community settings. The primary function of the collective is to develop socialist morality. This aim is accomplished through an explicit regimen of activity mediated by group criticism, self-criticism, and group-oriented punishments and rewards.

Makarenko's ideas are elaborated at length in his semibiographical, semifictional accounts of life in the collective (1949, 1953). It is in these works that he describes the principles and procedures to be employed for building the collective and using it as an instrument of character education. More relevant to our purposes, however, is the manner in which these methods are applied in school settings, for it is in this form that they have become most systematized and widely used.

SOCIALIZATION IN THE SCHOOL COLLECTIVE

The account which follows is taken from a manual (Novika, 1959) for the training and guidance of "school directors, supervisors, teachers, and Young Pioneer leaders." The manual was written by staff members of the Institute on the Theory and History of Pedagogy at the Academy of Pedagogical Sciences and is typical of several others prepared under the same auspices and widely distributed throughout the USSR.

This particular volume carries the instructive title: *Socialist Competition in the Schools*. The same theme is echoed in the titles of individual chapters: "Competition in the Classroom," "Competition between Classrooms," "Competition between Schools," and so on. It is not difficult to see how Russians arrive at the notion, with which they have made us so familiar, of competition between nations and between social systems. Moreover, in the chapter titles we see already reflected the influence of dialectical materialism: Conflict at one level is resolved through synthesis at the next higher level, always in the service of the Communist collective.

Let us examine the process of collective socialization as it is initiated in the very first grade. Conveniently enough, the manual starts us off on the first day of school with the teacher standing before the newly assembled class. What should her first words be? Our text tells us:

> It is not difficult to see that a direct approach to the class with the command "All sit straight" often doesn't bring the desired effect since a demand in this form does not reach the sensibilities of the pupils and does not activate them.

How does one "reach the sensibilities of the pupils" and "activate them"? According to the manual, here is what the teacher should say: "Let's see which row can sit the straightest." This approach, we are told, has certain important psychological advantages. In response,

> The children not only try to do everything as well as possible themselves, but also take an evaluative attitude toward those who are undermining the achievement of the row. If similar measures arousing the spirit of competition in the children are systematically applied by experienced teachers in the primary classes, then gradually the children themselves begin to monitor the behavior of their comrades and remind those of them who forget about the rules set by the teacher, who forget what needs to be done and what should not be done. The teacher soon has helpers.

The manual then goes on to describe how records are kept for each row from day to day for different types of tasks so that the young children can develop a concept of group excellence over time and over a variety of activities, including personal cleanliness, condition of notebooks, conduct in passing from one room to the other, quality of recitations in each subject matter, and so on. In these activities considerable emphasis is placed on the externals of behavior in dress, manner, and speech. There must be no spots on shirt or collar, shoes must be shined, pupils must never pass by a teacher without stopping to give greeting, there must be no talking without permission, and the like. Great charts are kept in all the schools showing the performance of each row unit in every type of activity together with their total overall standing. "Who is best?" the charts ask, but the entries are not individuals but social units—rows, and later the "cells" of the Communist youth organization which reaches down to the primary grades.

At first it is the teacher who sets the standards. But soon, still in the first grade, a new wrinkle is introduced: Responsible monitors are designated in each row for each activity. In the beginning their job is only to keep track of the merits and demerits assigned each row by the teacher. Different children act as monitors for different activities and, if one is to believe what the manual says, the monitors become very involved in the progress of their row. Then, too, group achievement is not without its rewards. From time to time the winning row gets to be photographed "in parade uniforms" (all Soviet children must wear uniforms in school), and this photograph is published in that pervasive Soviet institution, the wall newspaper. The significance of the achievements is still further enhanced, however, by the introduction of competition between *classes* so that the winning class and the winning row are visited by delegates from other classrooms in order to learn how to attain the same standard of excellence.

Now let us look more closely at this teacher-mediated monitoring process. In the beginning, we are told, the teacher attempts to focus the attention of children on the achievements of the group; that is, in our familiar phrase, she accentuates the positive. But gradually, "it becomes necessary to take account of negative facts which interfere with the activity of the class." As an example we are given the instance of a child who despite warnings continues to enter the classroom a few minutes after the bell has rung. The teacher decides that the time has come to evoke the group process in correcting such behavior. Accordingly, the next time that Serezha is late, the teacher stops him at the door and turns to the class with this question: "Children, is it helpful or not helpful to us to have Serezha come in late?" The answers are quick in coming. "It interferes, one shouldn't be late, he ought to come on time." "Well," says the teacher, "How can we help Serezha with this problem?" There are many suggestions: get together to buy him a watch, exile him from the classroom, send him to the director's office, or even to exile him from the school. But apparently these suggestions are either not appropriate or too extreme. The teacher, our text tells us, "helps the children find the right answer." She asks for a volunteer to stop by and pick Serezha up on the way to school. Many children offer to help in this mission.

But tragedy stalks. The next day it turns out that not only Serezha is late, but also the boy who promised to pick him up. Since they are both from the same group, their unit receives two sets of demerits and falls to lowest place. Group members are keenly disappointed. "Serezha especially suffered much and felt himself responsible, but equal blame was felt by his companion who had forgotten to stop in for him."

In this way, both through concrete action and explanation, the teacher seeks to forge a spirit of group unity and responsibility. From time to time, she explains to the children the significance of what they are doing, the fact "that they have to learn to live together as one friendly family, since they will have to be learning together for all of the next ten years, and that for this reason one must learn how to help one's companions and to treat them decently."

By the time the children are in the second grade, the responsibilities expected of them are increased in complexity. For example, instead of simply recording the evaluations made by the teacher, the monitors are taught how to make the evaluations themselves. Since this is rather difficult, especially in judging homework assignments, in the beginning two monitors are assigned to every task. In this way, our text tells us, they can help each other in doing a good job of evaluation.

. . .

In the third grade still another innovation is introduced. The monitors are taught not only to evaluate but to state their criticisms publicly.

> Here is a typical picture. It is the beginning of the lesson. In the first row the link leader reports basing his comments on information submitted by the sanitarian and other responsible monitors: "Today Valadya did the wrong problem. Masha didn't write neatly and forgot to underline the right words in her lesson, Alyoshi had a dirty shirt collar."
>
> The other link leaders make similar reports (the Pioneers are sitting by rows).
>
> The youngsters are not offended by this procedure: they understand that the link leaders are not just tattle-telling but simply fulfilling their duty. It doesn't even occur to the monitors and sanitarians to conceal the shortcomings of their comrades. They feel that they are doing their job well precisely when they notice one or another defect.

Also in the third grade, the teacher introduces still another procedure. She now proposes that the children enter into competition with the monitors, and see if they can beat the monitor at his own game by criticizing themselves. "The results were spectacular: if the monitor was able to talk only about four or five members of the row, there would be supplementary reports about their own shortcomings from as many as eight or ten pupils."

To what extent is this picture overdrawn? Although I have no direct evidence, the accounts I heard from participants in the process lend credence to the descriptions in the manual. For example, I recall a conversation with three elementary school teachers, all men, whom I had met by chance in a restaurant. They were curious about discipline techniques used in American schools. After I had given several examples, I was interrupted: "But how do you use the collective?" When I replied that we really did not use the classroom group in any systematic way, my three companions were puzzled. "But how do you keep discipline?"

Now it was my turn to ask for examples. "All right," came the answer. "Let us suppose that 10-year-old Vanya is pulling Anya's curls. If he doesn't stop the first time I speak to him, all I need do is mention it again in the group's presence; then I can be reasonably sure that before the class meets again the boy will be talked to by the officers of his Pioneer link. They will remind him that his behavior reflects on the reputation of the link."

"And what if he persists?"

"Then he may have to appear before his link—or even the entire collective—who will explain his misbehavior to him and determine his punishment."

"What punishment?"

"Various measures. He may just be censured, or if his conduct is regarded as serious, he may be expelled from membership. Very often he himself will acknowledge his faults before the group."

Nor does the process of social criticism and control stop with the school. Our manual tells us, for example, that parents submit periodic reports to the school collective on the behavior of the child at home. One may wonder how parents can be depended on to turn in truthful accounts. Part of the answer was supplied to me in a conversation with a Soviet agricultural expert. In response to my questions, he explained that, no matter what a person's job, the collective at his place of work always took an active interest in his family life. Thus a representative would come to the worker's home to observe and talk with his wife and children. And if any undesirable features were noted, these would be reported back to the collective.

I asked for an example.

"Well, suppose the representative were to notice that my wife and I quarreled in front of the children [my companion shook his head]. That would be bad. They would speak to me about it and remind me of my responsibilities for training my children to be good citizens."

I pointed out how different the situation was in America where a man's home was considered a private sanctuary so that, for example, psychologists like myself often had a great deal of difficulty in getting into homes to talk with parents or to observe children.

"Yes," my companion responded. "That's one of the strange things about your system in the West. The family is separated from the rest of society. That's not good. It's bad for the family and bad for society." He paused for a moment, lost in thought. "I suppose," he went on, "if my wife didn't want to let the representative in, she could ask him to leave. But then at work, I should feel ashamed." (He hung his head to emphasize the point.) "Ivanov," they would say, "has an uncultured wife."

But it would be a mistake to conclude that Soviet methods of character education and social control are based primarily on negative criticism. On the contrary, in their approach there is as much of the carrot as the stick. But the carrot is given not merely as a reward for individual performance but explicitly for the child's contribution to group achievement. The great charts emblazoned "Who IS Best?" which bedeck the halls and walls of every classroom have as entries the names not of individual pupils but of rows and links (the link is the smallest unit of Communist youth organization, which of course reaches into every classroom, from the first grade on). It is the winning unit that gets rewarded by a pennant, a special privilege, or by having their picture taken in "parade uniforms." And when praise is given, as it frequently is, to an individual child, the group referent is always there: "Today Peter helped Kate and as a result his unit did not get behind the rest."

Helping other members of one's collective and appreciating their contributions—themes that are much stressed in Soviet character training—become matters of enlightened self-interest, since the grade that each person receives depends on the overall performance of his unit. Thus the good student finds it to his advantage to help the poor one. The same principle is carried over to the group level with champion rows and classes being made responsible for the performance of poorer ones.

Here, then, are the procedures employed in Soviet character education. As a result of Khrushchev's educational reforms, they may be expected to receive even wider application in the years to come, for, in connection with these reforms, several new types of educational institutions are to be developed on a massive scale. The most important of these is the "internat," or boarding school, in which youngsters are to be entered as early as three months of age with parents visiting only on weekends. The internat is described in the theses announcing the reforms as the kind of school which "creates the most favorable conditions for the education and communist upbringing of the rising generation" (Communist Party of Soviet Russia, 1958). The number of boarding schools in the USSR is to be increased during the current seven-year plan from a 1958 level of 180,000 to 2,500,000 In 1965 (figures cited in *Pravda,* November 18, 1958), and according to I. A. Kairov, head of the Academy of Pedagogical Sciences, "No one can doubt that, as material conditions are created, the usual general educational school will be supplanted by the boarding school" (Kairov, 1960).

If this prophecy is fulfilled, we may expect that in the years to come the great majority of Soviet children (and children in some other countries of the Communist bloc as well) will from the first year of life onward be spending their formative period in collective settings and will be exposed daily to the techniques of collective socialization we have been describing. It is therefore a matter of considerable practical and scientific interest to identify the salient features of these techniques and subject them to research study, in so far as this becomes possible within the framework of our own society.

GUIDING PRINCIPLES OF THE SOVIET APPROACH TO CHARACTER TRAINING

As a first approximation, we may list the following as distinguishing characteristics or guiding principles of communist methods of character education.

1. The peer collective (under adult leadership) rivals and early surpasses the family as the principal agent of socialization.

2. Competition between groups is utilized as the principal mechanism for motivating achievement of behavior norms.

3. The behavior of the individual is evaluated primarily in terms of its relevance to the goals and achievements of the collective.

4. Rewards and punishments are frequently given on a group basis; that is to say, the entire group benefits or suffers as a consequence of the conduct of individual members.

5. As soon as possible, the tasks of evaluating the behavior of individuals and of dispensing rewards and sanctions is delegated to the members of the collective.

6. The principal methods of social control are public recognition and public criticism, with explicit training and practice being given in these activities. Specifically, each member of the collective is encouraged to observe deviant behavior by his fellows and is given opportunity to report his observations to the group. Reporting on one's peers is esteemed and rewarded as a civic duty.

7. Group criticism becomes the vehicle for training in self-criticism in the presence of one's peers. Such public self-criticism is regarded as a powerful mechanism for maintaining and enhancing commitment to approved standards of behavior, as well as the method of choice for bringing deviants back into line.

There are of course many other important features of the Soviet approach to socialization, but the seven listed above are those which present the greatest contrast to the patterns we employ in the West. It is for this reason that they are selected for special consideration here. We shall now proceed to examine each feature in greater detail with particular attention to the research ideas which it may generate.

THE FAMILY VERSUS THE COLLECTIVE

American theory and research on moral development have given almost exclusive emphasis to the family as the principal context and agent of socialization. The Soviet pattern, with its predominant emphasis on the collective, therefore raises the question of how these two socializing agents may differ in the nature and effect of the techniques they employ. To put the problem in another way: What types of socialization process and character structure emerge under the predominant influence of one or the other agent, or a combination of the two?

Stated in this form, the question seems an obvious and important one. Yet, to the writer's knowledge, research to date has little to offer in reply. True, there have been studies of personality development in several diverse types of children's groups who, for one reason or another, have grown up outside the context of the nuclear family. But for several reasons these studies do not shed much light on the problem at hand. The limitation springs in part from the highly specialized character of the groups investigated: youngsters removed to residential nurseries during war time (Burlingham & A. Freud, 1944), children rescued from Nazi concentration camps (A. Freud & Dann, 1954), delinquent gangs (Cohen, 1955; Cohen & Short, 1958; W. Miller, 1958; Thrasher, 1936; Whyte, 1943), and kibbutz children (Caplan, 1953; Faigin, 1958; Irvine, 1952; Rabin, 1958; Spiro, 1958).

Second, by and large these investigations take the form of clinical or case studies focusing on the particular problem at hand; they lack the structured design and comparative frame of reference which enhance the possibility of recognizing important differences, distinguishing characteristics, functional relationships. The advantages of these strategic devices are evidenced in the researches which employ them. Thus in a comparative ethnographic study, Eisenstadt (1956) demonstrated that peer collectives are most likely to develop in a society when there is marked discontinuity between values and role allocations in the family and in the adult world. Exploiting another kind of naturalistic experiment, two investigations (Haire & Morrison, 1957; Rosen, 1955) have studied situations in which parental values conflict with those of the peer group, and have found in each instance that although both sources are influential, the peer group tends to outweigh the parent in the age range studied (12 to 18). The research bearing most directly on the problem at hand is Boehm's comparative study (1957) of conscience development in Swiss and American children. She finds that the latter transfer parent dependence to peer dependence at an earlier age, and that

> One result of this earlier transferring appears to be that the American child's conscience becomes less egocentric and interiorizes earlier than does that of the Swiss child. There is, however, some indication that the content of conscience differs in these two types of societies. Whereas the American child's conscience is turned, primarily, toward social adjustment, the Swiss child's is geared toward character improvement (1957, pp. 91–92).

The principal shortcoming of all these studies for the issue at hand, however, is their failure to examine and analyze their data from the point of view of the group processes of socialization that may be occurring in the collective setting outside the family. To the extent that socialization is dealt with at all in these investigations, it is treated in conventional fashion with attention accorded primarily to the behavior of a parent or a parent surrogate toward the child. Such a restricted focus is of course understandable, given the traditional emphasis in Western culture, reflected in scientific work, on the centrality of the parent-child relationship in the process of upbringing. It is this circumscribed conception which probably accounts for the fact that Western personality theory and research, highly developed as they are in comparison with their Russian counterparts (Bronfenbrenner, 1961c), offer little basis for ready-made hypotheses bearing on processes and effects of socialization in collective settings.

Nevertheless, despite their limitations, the existing researches have considerable potential value. To begin with, many of them, especially the clinical and case studies, contain excellent descriptive data that could be re-examined from our new perspective to discover whether they might not shed some light on phenomena of collective socialization. Second, the more structured investigations suggest research designs that might profitably be employed in future work. The first research paradigm, exemplified by both the Eisenstadt and Boehm studies, makes use of groups with contrasting degrees of exposure to socialization in family versus collective settings. Such contrasts are understandably found most readily in different cultures, but under these circumstances interpretation is complicated by the presence of other factors associated with each culture that might account for the observed differences in character development. Eisenstadt endeavors to circumvent this difficulty by using data from a large number of societies in which other factors besides those under immediate investigation may be expected to vary widely. While highly useful, particularly in the exploratory stages of research, this approach has its serious limitations. Either one must make do with only partially adequate data gathered by other investigators with other objectives in mind, or one must carry out new specially designed cross-cultural studies in a substantial number of different settings.

But there is an alternative strategy which, to the writer's knowledge, has hardly been exploited to date. It involves finding groups exposed to different agents of socialization within the same or closely comparable cultural contexts. Such comparable groups may be difficult to discover, but once identified they offer rich opportunities for research on differential processes and outcomes of character training in familial versus peer-group settings. The ideal contrast in this regard would be two groups of children from the same social milieu, one group having attended boarding school from an early age, the other raised at home with minimal and relatively late exposure to group influences in school or peer group. Obviously this ideal would be almost impossible to achieve but it can certainly be approximated, especially in such countries as England, Switzerland, or, should the opportunity arise, the Soviet Union, where boarding schools are relatively common; or in Israel, with a focus on the comparison between children raised in the kibbutz, where the young are reared primarily outside the family in collective settings, and the moshav, where adult life is collectively organized but children are brought up in the nuclear family. The last contrast should be particularly instructive since collective ideology would be present in both settings but the principal agent of socialization would differ.

Another research opportunity found more easily outside the United States is that provided by families living in relative geographic isolation. An extreme example in a modern Western country occurs in Norway, where some families live in mountainous areas that remain isolated during a large part of the year. A current study of this group by Aubert, Tiller, and their associates at the Oslo Institute for Social Research should shed light on the character development of children raised in a nuclear family under conditions of minimal contact with others outside the home.

The American scene is of course not without its possibilities for research along the same lines, even if over a somewhat more restricted range. Thus we, too, have our boarding schools, and although their enrollment tends to be limited to children who are highly selected on socio-economic, religious, or psychological characteristics, an appropriately matched sample of controls not attending boarding school can usually be found. Indeed, to minimize differences in family values and background one could make use of those private schools which enroll both boarding and say pupils. Similarly, instances of families living in geographic isolation can still be found especially in the receding remnants of the American frontier in mountains, deserts, and north country; moreover, with the occasional influx of skilled technicians to such areas, the possibility arises of studying families who are living in an isolation which is primarily physical and not cultural as well. Finally, among the run-of-the-mill families in any American community there is likely to be an appreciable range of variation in the amount of socialization children experience outside the nuclear family. Some youngsters participate from an early age in nursery schools, camps, clubs, gangs, and other peer-group settings both with and without adult supervision. Others remain relatively isolated from peers until they enter kindergarten or first grade and, even thereafter extrafamilial associations may be minimal. A study of differences in character development in children exposed to varying degrees of familial versus extrafamilial socialization could be illuminating.

The last proposal highlights a difficulty plaguing all of the research designs outlined above. It is obvious that families in which contact with peers is postponed and minimized are likely to exhibit different value systems and techniques of socialization from those in which children are permitted or encouraged to have early associations outside the home. Such differences will be found also even in the "cleanest" and most closely matched comparisons. Thus day and boarding pupils in the same school will still differ in family background, values, and child-rearing practices. The fact that particular values and techniques may be functionally linked to the setting in which they occur does not remove the necessity of identifying them and taking them into account in the interpretation of results and in the design of subsequent studies.

Comparing groups with differing socialization experience is not the only strategy available for studying the differential influences of the family versus the peer collective. The researches of Rosen and Haire mentioned above suggest still another gambit, that of comparing the relative effects of both types of influence on the same children. The strategy here involves finding instances in which familial and peer-group standards conflict in varying degrees and to observe which influence prevails under what circumstances.

The last strategy focuses even more sharply the question of what dependent variables should be investigated in studies of this kind. Quite naturally one thinks first of the variables that have been emphasized in American studies of moral development; namely, projective measures of conscience and guilt of the type employed by Allinsmith (1957, 1960), Aronfreed (1959, 1960), Hoffman (1961), and D. R. Miller and Swanson (1960), or the behavioral measures of similar variables growing out of the work of Whiting and Sears and their colleagues at the Harvard Laboratory of Human Development (Sears, Maccoby, & Levin, 1957; Whiting, 1954; Whiting & Child, 1953) and implemented most recently in a study of antecedents of resistance to temptation conducted by Burton, Maccoby, and Allinsmith (undated).

It would clearly be a matter of considerable theoretical and practical interest whether children experiencing different ratios of exposure to socialization within the family versus within the peer group exhibit differences in types and degrees of self-blame, tendency to blame others, resistance to temptation or in any of the other patterns of moral judgment commonly examined in current research on this topic. The psychoanalytic theories on which most of these instruments are based would lead one to expect stronger internalization and self-blame among children raised primarily within the nuclear family, and this prediction receives at least indirect support from the one study we have found (Boehm, 1957) that comes near to dealing with the problem. But much depends on the particular socialization processes employed in one or another collective setting. In the absence of adequate data or theory dealing directly with this issue, we can only resort to speculation on the basis of what knowledge we do have about socialization processes in general. And since this knowledge is based almost entirely on studies of the family, we are forced into the risk expedient of arguing by analogy. Accordingly, in order to try to become aware both of the possibilities and pitfalls of this approach, we shall begin by assuming isomorphism and then call the assumption into question.

What are the principal generalizations, then, to be drawn from existing studies of factors in the nuclear family affecting the moral development of the child? A growing number of independent researches (Bronfenbrenner, 1961a, 1961b, 1961d; Hoffman, 1961; D. R. Miller & Swanson, 1958, 1960; Sears *et al.*, 1957) point to the conclusion that the internalization of moral standards is a function of the degree and ratio of parental affection and discipline. Specifically, internalization appears to be maximized when both affection and discipline are high. When parents rely primarily on the assertion of power in a relatively nonaffectionate context, the child is likely to be responsive only to external controls (i.e., fear of punishment). When both affection and discipline are low, or when the former appreciably outweighs the latter, moral standards tend to be weak or ineffective and the child resorts to distortive mechanisms such as denial or displacement (for example, unjustly blaming others). But internalization can also take non-adaptive forms characterized by inflexibility or excessive self-blame. Such rigid or self-deprecatory standards are especially likely to arise when parents are generally affectionate but rely on discipline techniques which "involve ego attack and depreciation of the child" (Hoffman, 1961, p. 5). In contrast, parents of children whose moral standards are more realistic and responsive to extenuating circumstances tend to "appeal more to approach motives." Hoffman, in the most recent and extensive study of this problem, elaborates on the differences between the two groups of parents as follows:

> The two groups are similar in that their parental discipline relies primarily on the frequent use of inductive techniques within an affectionate context, and the infrequent use of power assertion. What mainly characterizes and differentiates [that adaptive group] is that they report their parents as more frequently using techniques that communicate disappointment in the child for not living up to the parent's expectations and less frequently as using ego attack and love withdrawal techniques. It seems to us that the expression of disappointment, while it indicates that the parent has in a sense hurt the child, also conveys the feeling that the child is capable of living up to an ideal (Hoffman, 1961, pp. 37–38).

Pursuing our argument by analogy and shifting the context from the family to the school collective, we may ask whether any of these patterns of socialization apply to the Soviet case and, if so, what kinds of consequences in moral development we might expect. With due regard to the tentative and largely impressionistic character of this initial comparison, it is nevertheless striking to note the correspondence between the techniques recommended in our Soviet manual and Hoffman's description of the pattern of socialization most likely to lead to the internalization of realistic and appropriately flexible moral standards. Both situations involve high levels of discipline and support with the primary emphasis on an appeal to motives of approach rather than of avoidance. (e.g., "How can we help Serezha with his problem?") Also in both instances, there is infrequent use of power assertion. Finally, the many examples of group criticism appearing in the Soviet manual are surely more appropriately described in Hoffman's terminology not as an "ego attack and depreciation of the child" but precisely as statements "that communicate disappointment in the child for not living up to expectations," which "convey the feeling that the child is capable of living up to an ideal."

If the analogy is a valid one, and *if* the Russians actually practice what they preach, we should therefore expect that the pattern of socialization in the peer collective would lead to the development of the same quality of moral standards achieved by an optimal balance of support and control in the American nuclear family. The two "if's," however, can hardly be allowed to stand unquestioned. To consider the purely empirical question first, it seems likely that, as in every society, actual practice in Soviet society falls somewhat short of the ideal, or at least deviates from it. The nature of this deviation must await the results of systematic objective observations in Soviet schoolrooms. And it may be some time before such data are made available by either Soviet or Western behavioral scientists. In the meanwhile, however, there is nothing to prevent American workers from initiating a systematic program of research on group atmospheres in the classroom or other peer-collective settings and observing, through naturalistic or contrived experiments, the differential effects of various ratios of support and control on the development of moral standards and behavior. Indeed, the prototype of such research already exists in the classic experiment of Lewin, Lippitt, and White (1939), and it is both regrettable and surprising that this study has not been followed up by others in a systematic program of research on socialization processes in peer-group settings. Perhaps White and Lippitt's (1960) recently published reanalysis of their data will help stimulate a renewed interest in this neglected area.

Our second "if" gives rise to even more questions and complexities. It seems hardly likely that generalizations derived from studies of the American family could be applied directly to the analysis of socialization processes in the classroom, and a Soviet classroom at that. To begin with, such an analogy assumes that the teacher and the classroom group have re-enforcement power equivalent to that of the parent. This assumption can be challenged from both directions. On the one hand psychoanalytic theory, and probably common belief as well, discounts the possibility that any other social group could approach the family in the strength of its affectional and controlling influences. Yet, a growing body of research stemming from the work of Asch (1956) demonstrates that the group is capable of exerting tremendously powerful forces toward conformity, even to the extent of inducing distortions in reality perception. The question of the relative potential of the family and the peer group as agents of socialization therefore remains an open one resolvable only through empirical research.

The issue is complicated further by the fact that, to a greater or lesser degree, the child is usually exposed to some measure of socialization within the family before he enters the collective. In fact the responsiveness of the child to socialization in a group setting may even depend on prior experience in the family. It is noteworthy in this connection that, up until now, most of the children who have been exposed to Soviet methods of character education in school have spent the first seven years of their lives in the bosom of the family. Should the preceding speculation be valid, the Russians may experience some difficulty with their methods once they begin, as they propose, to place children in collectives during the first year of life.

Apart from questions about the relative socializing power of the family and the collective, there are of course important differences in the social structure of the two systems. Yet, while influential theorists like S. Freud

(1948) and Parsons and Bales (1955) have stressed the analogy between parent and children on the one hand and group leader and group members on the other, to this writer's knowledge little attention has been given to the theoretical implications for the process of socialization of such obvious differences as group size, range of role differentiation, specificity of function, duration through time, and their psychological consequences in degree of ego involvement. At the same time, so far as Soviet society is concerned, we must take note of the two-way theme constantly reiterated in Russian writings on character education that the family must become a collective and the collective must take on the characteristics of a family. As a result, it is conceivable that over time the differences between these two types of social structure in Soviet society will become attenuated and the similarities maximized. This possibility highlights the value of comparative longitudinal studies of the changing character of Western and Communist family and peer-group structures. Such studies would of course have special significance as necessary background for research on character development.

The preceding consideration points directly to the most important difference between American and Soviet socialization practice, whether in the family or out. This is the matter of ideological content and the special procedures which this content inspires. It is this content and procedure which are the burden of the remaining six of the guiding principles we have listed earlier.

GROUP INCENTIVES

Principles 2–4 emphasize the importance of the collective over the individual as the frame of reference for evaluating behavior and distributing punishments and rewards. As the principles indicate, there are three elements to the pattern: Desired behavior is motivated through competition between groups rather than between individuals; behavior is judged in terms of its implication for the achievement and reputation of the group; and rewards and punishments are given on a group basis so that all members of the group stand to gain or lose from the actions of each individual.

The arousal of motivation through competition between groups is certainly not an unfamiliar phenomenon in American society or in the American schoolroom. But even without the support of systematic evidence, one could confidently assert that this motivating device used to be employed far more frequently three or more decades ago than it is today. This same trend is dramatically reflected in the character of research studies being carried out in the late twenties and thirties as compared with the present time. Thus Murphy, Murphy, and Newcomb in the 1937 revision of their *Experimental Social Psychology* (pp. 476–493) tabulate as many as 25 studies dealing with competition in children's groups, many of them focusing directly on the issue of group versus individual incentive. In contrast, a contemporary survey of group research (Thibaut & Kelley, 1959) scarcely mentions the topic. Even though the earlier studies of group incentives focus almost entirely on motor and intellectual tasks rather than attitude formation, the results are instructive. Group competition generally increases output but is less effective as an incentive than self-oriented or individual competition. As Murphy, Murphy, and Newcomb properly caution, however, "Any discussion of . . . studies of the effects of incentives must be seen in relation to the cultural background which has set so much store by individual achievement, and has nourished this movement to find ways of stimulating the greatest achievement in the individual" (1937, p. 501).

This caveat carries implications for a potentially fruitful research design in which children with contrasting individualistic versus collectivistic backgrounds would be exposed to both types of competitive situations and their performance observed. Although one's first impulse is to discount such a proposal on the practical ground that it would be virtually impossible to find children with such diverse backgrounds in the same culture, further consideration suggests that good research opportunities do exist. The most obvious example is Israel, where both types of orientation are common even within the same ethnic and socio-economic subgroups. Furthermore, the contrast can be approximated in our own society, since many private schools differ widely precisely along this continuum. For example, many progressive schools are ultra-individualistic in their philosophy and practice whereas others would probably be shocked to learn that their emphasis on subgroup solidarity and competition is properly described as collectivistic.

But in view of the dearth of research studies of the phenomenon over the last 25 years, there would be much to learn from research on the effects of group incentives even with children coming from the predominantly individualistic background characteristic of American society. On the independent side, these researches should give attention to such specific variables as the motivating power of intergroup versus interindividual competition, evaluation of individual behavior in terms of its contribution to the status of the group as a whole, and the giving of punishments and rewards on a group basis. On the dependent side, the spectrum of variables should be broadened beyond problem solving to include personality measures such as the indices of moral standards employed in much current research as well as other relevant social attitudes and behaviors. These important additions are more appropriately discussed after we have completed examination of the last three of the distinguishing characteristics of Soviet methods of character education—these having to do with group criticism and self-criticism.

GROUP CRITICISM AND SELF-CRITICISM

The feature of Soviet socialization practices which clashes most sharply with the American pattern is the Russians' widespread resort to the procedure of criticizing others and one's self in public. The practice is common throughout all levels of Soviet society from school, farm, and factory to the highest echelons of the party. Thus by being taught these techniques in early childhood, Soviet youth are being prepared in patterns of response that will be expected and even required of them throughout their life span. Since such practices are uncommon in American society, it is not surprising that they have not been subjected to research study in any direct way. As already noted, however, the work of Asch and others (Asch, 1956; Berenda, 1950) testifies to the power of an overwhelming majority forcing the deviant individual to conform. In these rigged experiments members of the majority do not engage in criticism but simply give responses which conflict with the reality perceptions of the experimental subject. The effect on the subject is to lead him, in an appreciable number of instances, to change his own response in the direction of the majority. In a sense, such alteration represents a confession of his own previous "error." Obviously, the experiments cannot be said to reproduce explicit features of Soviet group criticism and self-criticism, but the fit could be made much closer by instructing confederates to engage in criticism and by asking the subject to admit that his previous responses had not been correct. Such variations would of course make even more salient questions of scientific ethics that invariably arise when experiments of this kind are viewed from the perspective of the Western Judeo-Christian moral tradition. (It is doubtful, incidentally, that such questions would ever be raised in a Communist society.) Still ways can probably be found to conduct experiments on the processes of group criticism and self-criticism without doing serious violence to our own ethical traditions.

The fact remains, however, that such socialization procedures as group criticism and self-criticism have moral implications and hence may be expected to have moral consequences; that is to say, they are likely to influence the moral attitudes, actions, and character structure of the individuals on whom they are employed. Moreover, it is doubtful whether such consequences are fully or even adequately reflected by the measures of conscience and guilt currently employed in research on moral development. Certainly it would be important to know about the nature of conscience and guilt in the "new Soviet men" who have been exposed to a lifetime of experience in group criticism and self-criticism. But in building "socialist morality" Soviet educators are less concerned with such questions as whether the individual tends to blame others or himself than with his sense of commitment to the collective, especially in the face of competing individualistic values and preferences.

Accordingly, perhaps the most important research implication to be drawn from our examination of Soviet methods of character education is the necessity of expanding the spectrum of what we conceive as moral development beyond the characteristically Judeo-Christian concern with personal responsibility and guilt to a consideration of the broader moral issues inherent in the relation of man to man and of the individual to his society.

We have tried to take some beginning steps in this direction in the research on character development being conducted at Cornell by Bronfenbrenner, Devereux, and Suci. Specifically, as a point of departure we have distinguished five hypothetical extreme types of character structure representing the presumed products of five divergent patterns of socialization and moral development in children and adolescents. These five are tentatively designated as self-oriented, adult-oriented, peer-oriented, collective-oriented, and objectively-principled character structures.

The self-oriented child is motivated primarily by impulses of self-gratification without regard to the desires or expectations of others or to internalized standards. Such an asocial and amoral orientation is presumed to arise when the child's parents are so permissive, indifferent, inconsistent, or indulgent that immediate self-indulgence becomes the practicable and, in the long run, most rewarding course of action for the child. The development of this personality type is further facilitated by participation in peer groups which encourage self-indulgence and exact neither loyalty nor discipline from their members.

The adult-oriented child is one who accepts parental strictures and values as final and immutable. He is completely submissive to parental authority and the moral standards imposed by the parent. This orientation generalizes to adult authority outside the home in school and community. In other words, here is the oversocialized "good child," already a little adult, who causes no trouble but is relatively incapable of initiative and leadership. He is presumed to be the product of intensive socialization within the nuclear family but with minimal experience outside the home.

In contrast, the peer-oriented child is an adaptive conformist who goes along with the group and readily accepts every shift in group opinion or conduct. This is the "outer-directed" character type of Riesman's (1950) typology or the future "organization man" described by Whyte (1956). His values and preferences reflect the momentary sentiments of his social set. The optimal circumstances for the development of this personality type involve a combination of parents who are either permissive or actively encourage conformity to group norms, accompanied by early and extensive participation in peer groups requiring such conformity as the price of acceptance. The norms of such groups, however, are ephemeral in character and imply no consistent standards or goals.

The prototype of the collective-oriented personality is of course the "new Soviet man"—a person committed to a firm and enduring set of values centering around the achievement of enduring group standards and goals. These group values take precedence over individual desires or obligations of particular interpersonal relationships. Such an orientation presumably springs from a developmental history in which from the very outset the parents place the needs and demands of the collective above those of the child or of particular family members. Affection and discipline are bestowed in the name and interests of the social group and the child spends most of his formative years in collective settings under the guidance of adults and leaders who train him in the skills and values of collective living.

Finally, the behavior of the objectively-principled child is guided by values which, although learned through experience in the family and in peer groups, do not bind him to undeviating conformity to the standards of the one or the other. This is the "inner-directed" personality of Riesman's (1950) typology. On one occasion he may act in accordance with the standards of his parents, on another with the mores of the peer group, or in still a third instance he may take a path which deviates from the preferences of both parents and peers. There is, however, a consistency in pattern of response from one situation to the next which reflects the child's own now autonomous standards of conduct. The developmental history posited for this type of character structure assumes a strong, differentiated family organization with high levels of affection and discipline but at the same time considerable opportunity granted to the child to participate in selected but varied peer-group experiences both with and without adult supervision. These peer groups, in turn, are also characterized by high levels of affectional involvement and their own particular disciplinary codes. The hypothesis implicit in this developmental sequence is that an autonomous set of moral standards is developed from having to cope with different types of discipline in a variety of basically accepting social contexts, so that the child is forced to compare and come to terms with different codes of behavior imposed by different persons or groups each of whom is supportive and wins his liking and respect. This hypothesis, though highly speculative, derives in part from some of our research results (Bronfenbrenner, 1961a, 1961b, 1961d) which suggested that children who are rated by teachers and peers as high in social responsibility and initiative tend to come from families where parental affection and discipline are relatively strong, parental roles are moderately differentiated (e.g., one parent tends to exercise authority slightly more than the other), but the child also participates in many group activities outside the home. Unfortunately, in these initial studies very little information was obtained about the child's experiences in peer-group settings.

We are currently in the process of devising instruments for measuring the five types of character structure outlined above as these are manifested both in attitudes and behavior. Several of our instruments have yielded promising results in pilot studies but have also brought to light shortcomings in theory and method. The principal value of the approach in its present stage of development is its capacity to generate fruitful hypotheses and research designs for the investigation of character development as a social process.

The last consideration brings us back to the main objective of this paper. Its primary purpose is not to argue for a particular theoretical orientation or methodology; the sole and central aim is to encourage and assist behavioral scientists and educators to give careful attention to the problems and processes implicit in collective methods of character education such as those employed in the Soviet Union and elsewhere in the Communist bloc. We have tried to show that these problems and processses have considerable social relevance and theoretical importance far beyond their immediate social context. We have also attempted to demonstrate that they can be made amenable to empirical investigation. This paper will have served its purpose if it contributes to a renewal of research interest in the study of extrafamilial groups as socializing agents, for such scientific study should do much to enhance our understanding of intriguing social processes through which human character is formed.

REFERENCES

ALLINSMITH, W. Conscience and conflict: The moral force in personality. *Child Develpm.,* 1957, **28,** 469–476.

ALLINSMITH, W. The learning of moral standards. In D. R. Miller & G. E. Swanson, *Inner conflict and defense.* New York: Holt, 1960. Pp. 141–176.

ARONFREED, J. Internal and external orientation in the moral behavior of children. Paper read at the American Psychological Association, Cincinnati, September 1959.

ARONFREED, J. Moral behavior and sex identity. In D. R. Miller & G. E. Swanson, *Inner conflict and defense.* New York: Holt, 1960. Pp. 177–193.

ASCH, S. E. Studies of independence and conformity: A minority of one against a unanimous majority. *Psychol. Monogr.,* 1956, **70**(9, Whole No. 416).

BERENDA, R. W. *The influence of the group on the judgments of children.* New York: King's Crown Press, 1950.

BOEHM, L. The development of independence: A comparative study. *Child Develpm.,* 1957, **28,** 85–92.

BRONFENBRENNER, U. The changing American child. In E. Ginsberg (Ed.), *Values and ideals of American youth.* (Also in *Merrill-Palmer Quart.,* 1961, **7,** 73–84.) New York: Columbia Univer. Press, 1961. Pp. 71–84. (a)

BRONFENBRENNER, U. Some familial antecedents of responsibility and leadership in adolescents. In L. Petrullo & B. M. Bass (Eds.), *Leadership and interpersonal behavior.* New York: Holt, Rinehart, & Winston, 1961. Pp. 239–272. (b)

BRONFENBRENNER, U. Soviet studies in personality development and socialization. Ithaca, N.Y.: Cornell University, Department of Child Development and Family Relationships, 1961. (c) (Ditto)

BRONFENBRENNER, U. Toward a theoretical model for the analysis of parent-child relationships in a social context. In J. C. Glidewell (Ed.), *Parental attitudes and child behavior.* Springfield, Ill.: Charles C Thomas, 1961. Pp. 90–109. (d)

BURLINGHAM, D., & FREUD, A. *Infants without families.* London: George Allen & Unwin, 1944.

BURTON, R. V., MACCOBY, E. E., & ALLINSMITH, W. Antecedents of resistance to temptation. Washington, D.C.: National Institute of Mental Health, United States Department of Health, Education, and Welfare, undated. (Mimeo)

CAPLAN, G. Clinical observations on the emotional life of children in the communal settlements in Israel. In M. J. Senn (Ed.), *Transactions of the*

Seventh Conference on Problems of Infancy and Childhood. New York: Josiah Macy, Jr., Foundation, 1953.

Cohen, A. K. *Delinquent boys—The culture of the gang.* Glencoe, Ill.: Free Press, 1955.

Cohen, A. K., & Short, J. F., Jr. Research in delinquent subcultures. *J. soc. Issues,* 1958, **14,** 23–37.

Communist Party of the Soviet Union. *Ob ukreplenii svyazi shkoli s zhiznyu i o dalneishem razvitii sistemi naraodnogo obrazovaniya b strane* [On the strengthening of ties between school and life and the further development of the system of public education in the country]. (Theses of the Central Committee of the Communist Party of the Soviet Union) Moscow: Gospolitizdat, 1958.

Eisenstadt, S. N. *From generation to generation.* Glencoe, Ill.: Free Press, 1956.

Faigin, H. Case report: Social behavior of young children in the kibbutz. *J. abnorm. soc. Psychol.,* 1958, **56,** 117–129.

Freud, A., & Dann, S. An experiment in group upbringing. In W. E. Martin & C. B. Stendler (Eds.), *Readings in child development.* New York: Harcourt Brace, 1954.

Freud, S. *Group psychology and the analysis of the ego.* London: Hogarth Press, 1948.

Haire, M., & Morrison, F. School children's perceptions of labor and management. *J. soc. Psychol.,* 1957, **46,** 179–197.

Hoffman, M. L. Techniques and processes in moral development. Detroit: Merrill-Palmer Institute, 1961. (Mimeo)

Irvine, E. E. Observations on the aims and methods of child-rearing in communal settlements in Israel. *Hum. Relat.,* 1952, **5,** 247–275.

Kairov, I. A. [Long range plans for the development of pedagogical sciences and coordination of the work of the Academy and Chairs of Pedagogy of Pedagogical Institutes, USSR.] (Translation of an article in *Sovetsk. Pedag.,* 1960, 24(2), 16–44.) New York: United States Joint Publications Research Service, 1960.

Lewin, K., Lippitt, R., & White, R. K. Patterns of aggressive behavior in experimentally created "social climates." *J. soc. Psychol.,* 1939, **10,** 271–299.

Makarenko, A. *Pedagogicheskaya poema* [A pedagogical poem.] (Available in English under the title *The road to life,* translated by Ivy and Tatiana Litvinov. Moscow: Foreign Languages Publishing House, 1951.) Leningrad: Leningradskoye gazetno-zhurnalnoye i knizhnoye izdatelstvo [Leningrad Newspaper-Periodical and Book Publishing House], 1949.

Makarenko, A. S. *Learning to live.* Moscow: Foreign Languages Publishing House, 1953.

Makarenko, A. S. *Knigda dlya roditelei* [A Book for Parents]. (Available in English. Moscow: Foreign Languages Publish House, undated.) Petrozavodsk: Gosudarstvennoye Izadatelstvo Karel'skoi ASSR [State Publishing House of the Karelian Autonomous Soviet Socialist Republic], 1959.

Miller, D. R., & Swanson, G. E. *The changing American child.* New York: Wiley, 1958.

Miller, D. R., & Swanson, G. E. *Inner conflict and defense.* New York: Holt, 1960.

Miller, W. Lower class culture as a generating milieu of gang delinquency. *J. soc. Issues,* 1958, **24,** 5–19.

Murphy, G., Murphy, L. B., & Newcomb, T. M. *Experimental social psychology.* (Rev. ed.) New York: Harper, 1937.

Novikova, L. E. (Ed.). *Sotsialisticheskoye sorevnovaniye b shkole* [Socialist competition in the school]. Moscow: Uchpedgiz, 1950.

Parsons, T., & Bales, R. F. *Family, socialization and interaction process.* Glencoe, Ill.: Free Press, 1955.

Rabin, A. I. Kibbutz children—research findings to date. *Children,* 1958, **5,** 179–184.

Riesman, D. (with N. Glazer & R. Denney). *The lonely crowd: A study of the changing American character.* New Haven: Yale Univer. Press, 1950.

Rosen, B. C. Conflicting group membership: A study of parent-peer group cross pressures. *Amer. sociol. Rev.,* 1955, **20,** 155–161.

Sears, R. R., Maccoby, E. E., & Levin, H. *Patterns of child rearing.* Evanston, Ill.: Row, Peterson, 1957.

Spiro, M. E. *Children of the kibbutz.* Cambridge, Mass.: Harvard Univer. Press, 1958.

Thibaut, J. W., & Kelley H. H. *The social psychology of groups.* New York: Wiley, 1959.

Thrasher, F. M. *The gang.* Chicago: Univer. Chicago Press, 1936.

White, R. K., & Lippitt, R. O. *Autocracy and democracy.* New York: Harper, 1960.

Whiting, J. W. M. Fourth presentation. In J. M. Tanner & B. Inhelder (Eds.), *Discussions on child development.* Vol. 2. London: Tavistock Publications, 1954.

Whiting, J. W. M., & Child, I. L. *Child training and personality.* New Haven: Yale Univer. Press, 1953.

Whyte, W. F. *Street corner society.* Chicago: Univer. Chicago Press, 1943.

Whyte, W. H. *The organization man.* New York: Doubleday, 1956.

PART V

Adolescence

INTRODUCTION

THE TERM "adolescent" is generally used to refer, roughly, to a person in his teens; that is, one in the period between childhood and adulthood. The period is defined at its inception by physiological changes, termed puberty, and at its termination by sociological changes, namely full adult status. As with all the stages of development, however, these end points are not very well defined. For example, the physiology of puberty is a complex set of phenomena (Schock, 1944), including rapid body growth, bone ossification, hormonal changes, sudden development of the primary and secondary sex characteristics as well as the psychological reactions to body image changes and the onset of sexuality (Frazier & Lisonbee, 1950; Jones & Bayley, 1950). Not all of these physiological changes are highly correlated, nor are the psychological reactions equally intense for all individuals.

Just as the onset of adolescence is difficult to define, so is its termination. Generally a person is considered an adult when the adult community allows him the privileges and expects from him the responsibilities of an adult. But once again, this definition is ambiguous. For instance, most legal contracts in the United States recognize the adult status of an individual who is over 21 years old; yet other laws vary with respect to the age at which an individual begins to be treated as an adult. Each of the following, for example, has its own specific age requirement: driver's licenses, marriage licenses, freedom to buy and consume alcoholic beverages, voting rights, and the right to work. In some cases the minimum age even varies from state to state.

Some societies clarify the distinction between childhood and adulthood by initiations and puberty rites (Brown, 1963; Bettelheim, 1962). Such a dramatic debut has the effect of clarifying the discontinuity in the developmental cycle. In some cultures, as we have seen (Chapter 5) there is less discontinuity in cultural conditioning than in others, but among those cultures where such discontinuity exists, there is a great deal of variation in how adequately the change in status is clarified. While "rites of passage" (VanGennep, 1960) serve this function in many societies, the American counterparts in such ceremonies as graduations and debuts and such religious observances as confirmations and bar mitzvahs are not universal enough to provide this clarification of status.

In some respects the period of adolescence belies exact definition. In as much as it is a transitional stage between childhood and the full maturity of adulthood, it relies on the definition of those periods for its own clarification. And in this very difficulty with definition we encounter one of the main characteristics of this period, namely, the lack of clarification of one's own position within the community. Kurt Lewin (1939) has made this point very nicely in a paper on the development of adolescence, wherein he refers to the adolescent as a marginal man. The term "marginal man" comes from sociology where it is used to refer to a person whose membership in a group is no longer firm and clear. A member of a minority group, for example, who shares the values and goals of the majority and obtains some of his social reinforcement therefrom, becomes a marginal man in his own minority group. An immigrant with two languages and two cultures and often two conflicting sets of values gains acceptance into the culture of his immigration often only at the risk of becoming "marginal" to the culture of his birth. In effect, he never belongs to either group completely, but to both groups incompletely and in a way which lacks clarity.

It is not hard to see why Lewin thought this situation described the plight of the adolescent well, caught as he is between the cultures of childhood and adulthood. Emotional instability and sensitivity, two psychological characteristics of the marginal man, might aptly be applied to the adolescent as well. Literature abounds with examples of adolescents whose lives seem to provide excellent descriptions of the marginal man. In fact, one wonders to what extent the authors of such works are describing adolescence, or rather an overly psychologized view of adolescence gleaned from reading the latest psychoanalytic treatment of the subject. However, the study of personality through literature is not new. For the student interested in a cautious assessment of the validity of this approach, Allport (1942) is an excellant reference. Two recent examples of collections of fiction about the adolescent are *The Rite of Becoming* (Waldhorn & Waldhorn, 1966) and *The Adolescent Through Fiction* (Kiell, 1965).

Carson McCullers (1946) has written such a literary description of adolescent marginality in *The Member of the Wedding*. She begins that novel by introducing the heroine: "It happened that green and crazy summer when Frankie was twelve years old. This was the summer when for a long time she had not been a member. She belonged to no club and was a member of nothing in the world. Frankie had become an unjoined person who hung around in doorways, and she was afraid." (McCullers, 1946, p. 1).

The separation experienced during adolescence has many sources. First there is a separation from one's own previous experience. Sudden changes in body size and shape, new urges related to the unsure area of sexuality, and the resulting changes in status and role expectations create a situation in which the adolescent may well imagine that he is not the same person as before. The term "identity crisis" has been used by Erik Erikson (1963) to describe this situation.

Another and related form of separation occurs between the individual and his companions who are all developing at slightly different rates, with each becoming self-consciously aware of differences among them. One result of these separations is the self-conscious examination of those characteristics which make one separate—that is, different—from others. The individual as a subject confronts himself as an object. This "I am me" experience has been described by Spiegelberg (1964). The individuation between subject and object is something which has gone on since infancy, but only assumes dramatic proportions in adolescence because of the suddenness of the onset of puberty. Each stage of development has its own specific resolution of this separateness between the self and outer world. In infancy after the child has learned to walk and to recognize distinctions among people, and between himself and others, he develops a set of concepts and later a language with which he bridges the gap between himself and others. Another form of communication in adolescence fulfills the same purpose, namely, the development of what one psychoanalyst, Sullivan (1953), has called "full-blown, psychiatrically defined love." In his book, *The Art of Loving,* Erich Fromm (1956) distinguishes between two sorts of love: the love of an object, that is being loved, and the love of a subject, that is "the overcoming of separateness."

Sullivan (1953) distinguishes between two dynamisms which develop during the adolescent period—the intimacy dynamism and the lust dynamism. He defines intimacy in the following way: "Intimacy is that type of situation involving two people which permits validation of all components of personal worth. Validation of personal worth requires a type of relationship which I call collaboration, by which I mean clearly formulated adjustments of one's behavior to the express needs of the other person in the pursuit of increasingly identical—that is, more and more nearly mutual—satisfactions, and in the maintenance of increasingly similar security operations." (Sullivan, 1953, p. 246). According to Sullivan, the intimacy dynamism develops in preadolescence, usually with a member of the same sex before it does with a member of the opposite sex. He considers this "isolphilic" relationship a necessary precursor to healthy adult heterophilic relations. This is not unlike the so-called "homosexual" phase in psychoanalytic theory. Once again, literature is replete with examples of this sort of relationship. *Anne Frank:*

The Diary of a Young Girl (Frank, 1952) describes such a situation as do Freud's *A Young Girl's Diary* (1961) and John Knowles' *A Separate Peace* (1959).

The lust dynamism is defined by Sullivan as the development of genital sexuality with all its interpersonal implications. Lust is the last of the integrating dynamisms to develop in Sullivan's scheme and ushers in the actual beginning of adolescence. The importance of these two dynamisms in Sullivan's theory lies in their becoming integrated in the development of an interpersonal system which amounts to the resolution of the earlier isolation, of the feelings of separateness.

For the student interested in exploring more fully other theoretical treatments of the period of adolescence, Muuss (1968) is an excellent reference.

PHYSICAL DEVELOPMENT

One of the main physical attributes of adolescence is the well known preadolescent "growth spurt." A relatively sudden increase in height and weight occurs roughly between the ages of eleven and thirteen for girls and between the ages of thirteen and fifteen for boys (Tanner, 1955). This sex difference is characteristic of the other aspects of physical growth during this period as well. Girls tend to be earlier with ossification of bones, an excellent index of skeletal maturation (Todd, 1937). They are also earlier than boys in their dental development (Cattell, 1928), and in the development of primary and secondary sex characteristics (Kinsey, Pomeroy, & Martin, 1948; Kinsey, Pomeroy *et al.,* 1953).

Important correlates of physical growth in adolescence are the psychological reactions and body image changes which young people experience. Frazier and Lisonbee (1950) present the concerns about physical appearance which a group of 580 ninth graders reported. Girls expressed more concern about their being heavy (over 50% expressing such concern) while boys were primarily concerned about slow development (40%) and being short (39%). With respect to facial appearance, over 50% of the boys and 82% of the girls expressed concern with blackheads and pimples. It appears that in this age group physical appearance is of major concern.

Several interesting investigations have been conducted which deal with the rate of maturation during puberty and adolescence (Jones & Bayley, 1950; Jones & Mussen, 1958; Mussen & Jones, 1958; Shipman, 1964; Jones, 1957). Many of the studies have been conducted with a group of adolescents from the Oakland Growth Study in which maturation rate was defined by skeletal age and psychological correlates of maturation were measured in terms of teacher and peer ratings, personality inventories, and projective techniques.

Two studies of this group are reprinted in the unit on adolescence. Chapter 30, by Mussen and Jones, is an example of a comparison of the projective data gathered on a group of early and late maturing boys. The data support the hypothesis that there is a psychological advantage to early maturing during the adolescent years. In her article (Chapter 31) Professor Jones of the University of California extends these findings and reports that the same pattern continues into adulthood. The final article (Chapter 32) by Professors Broverman, Broverman, Vogel, Palmer and Klaiber, concerns the relationship between preadolescent and postadolescent body dimensions. The authors report that preadolescent body dimensions contribute more to postadolescent body dimensions than does the amount of growth during adolescence.

PARENT-CHILD RELATIONS

The social relations of adolescents often appear strained and difficult. G. Stanley Hall (1904), one of the first to make a major psychological study of adolescence, referred to adolescence as a period of "Sturm und Drang," or storm and stress. Hall proposed a biogenetic view of adolescence and related this period to the other stages of growth in terms of his "recapitulation" theory of human development. Briefly, the recapitulation notion stated that the developing individual goes through stages which recapitulate, or repeat, the various stages in the development of the species. Thus, for example, the prenatal period was seen to recapitulate that epoch in man's evolutionary history when he was an aquatic animal. The reflexes of infancy, such as involuntary grasping, mimic man's simian ancestry. Similarly, the stages of ontogenetic development were said to be ordered as the stages of phylogenetic development had been. In this setting, Hall compares adolescence to the "Sturm und Drang" period of 18th-century German literature. Some of the characteristics of this period of romanticism were passion, intensity, and a commitment to a goal.

Whether the period of adolescence is really such a time of stress and trial is a debatable issue. Douvan and Adelson (1966) in a major study of American teenagers conclude that the period is not as marked by rebellion as it is popularly believed to be. In one sense, however, it is true that the opposing behavioral patterns of rebellion and conformity may have a similar base (Goodman, 1960), namely, the need to establish one's own identity whether positively, by acting like others, or negatively, by deviant behavior.

To the extent that the period of adolescence is a stormy one, it is necessary to attribute that condition more to cultural than to genetic influences. Hall had thought this stress was simply part and parcel of the biological maturing process and Freud had added the idea that the onset of new sexual urges during this period was biologically determined and would of necessity be upsetting. But a serious blow to this position came from the work of cultural anthropologists. Margaret Mead (1961) discovered that Samoan adolescence was not a disturbing period. The changing of relations with parents up until adolescence had been gradual, and freedom of sexual expression was the rule throughout development. In other words, there was less discontinuity of conditioning, to use the term of Ruth Benedict, the other main cultural anthropologist whose works cast doubt on a strictly biologically oriented view of adolescence (Benedict, 1964).

In any event, whether or not one accepts the view of adolescence as a period of intense stress, it is safe to say that in American society, at least, the ushering in of this period of independence is accompanied by certain strains with those upon whom the child has been dependent. Because the dependence-independence struggle is mainly a parent-child struggle, it is usually in his relation with parents that the adolescent encounters the most trouble.

It has been suggested that one of the dramatic changes in the social relations which takes place during adolescence is the shift from a parental reference group to a reference group of peers. While values during middle childhood were based largely on parental standards, the values of the peer culture take on increased meaning during adolescence. Despite this fact, there is evidence that the choices which adolescents make are not solely dependent on the values of peers. In Chapter 33, Professor Brittain presents evidence that the reference group for adolescents' decisions is dependent on the nature of the content of the decision itself. In some cases the most competent guides are considered one's peers; for example, in matters of taste and dress. In other cases, for example those decisions of more permanent consequence, parents are still considered the better guides.

In addition, it is clear that earlier parental practices continue to exert their influence in the decision making of adolescents. For example, Kagan and Freeman (Chapter 34) report that the importance that adolescent boys assign to intellectual mastery is related to both their mother's justification of criticism and acceleration attempts when the boys were children. Conformity in adolescence is found to be related in boys to acceptance and overaffection in childhood and in girls to be negatively correlated with acceleration but positively correlated with restrictiveness. The authors summarize this result by saying that, "Thus, restriction of autonomy predicts later conformity in daughters; excessive nurturance predicts later conformity for boys" (Kagan & Freeman, Chapter 34, p. 517–518).

In Chapter 35, Professor Heilbrun deals with the antecedents of behavioral consistency in adolescents. Once again, the findings point to the importance of the type of model that the parents have provided in determining behavioral attributes in adolescence.

IDENTITY AND PERSONALITY

Erik Erikson has elaborated a theory of personality development which perhaps more than any other gives central importance to the period of adolescence. His main thesis (Erikson, 1963) is that the adolescent period is a time of searching for identity. In an important chapter of his well known work, *Childhood and Society,* Erikson describes the "eight stages of man." The resolution of "identity v. role confusion" is the main task of the age of adolescence. Because of the discontinuity with previous experience, based on sudden body growth and sexual awareness, the adolescent strives for a sense of sameness with his earlier years. Erikson sums up the task by saying, "The growing and developing youths, faced with this physiological revolution within them, are now primarily concerned with what they appear to be in the eyes of others as compared with what they feel they are, and with the question of how to connect the roles and skills cultivated earlier with the occupational prototypes of the day." (p. 261) In language reminiscent of the other two modern psychoanalysts we have discussed—Sullivan and Fromm—Erikson alludes to a subject-object conflict. The self-conscious concern with how one perceives himself and with how others perceive him is the essence of the separateness described by Fromm. This theme is more fully elaborated in *The Psychological Issues Monograph,* "Identity and the Life Cycle," (1959) and in Erikson's recent volume, *Identity: Youth and Crisis* (1968).

In Chapter 36, Sister M. Howard Dignan of Clarke College, examines the role that maternal identification plays in the development of this ego identity in late adolescent girls. In one of the few studies based on Erikson's theory, Sister Dignan provides data to support the importance of early identification with the mother in establishing strong ego-identity, and demonstrates again the general continuity of personality development, despite the behavioral discontinuities which are also characteristic of adolescence.

Chapter 37 by Professors Kagan and Moss, and Chapter 38 by Professor Carlson deal with different aspects of this continuity of development. Kagan and Moss analyze data gathered at the Fels Research Institute in a longitudinal study of human development. They point to the "long term stability of passive and dependent behavior from childhood through adulthood" (Kagan & Moss, 1960, p. 590). Carlson's study demonstrates the stability of another aspect of personality, namely self-image. Two independent aspects of self-image, namely self-esteem and social-personal orientation, showed differentially characteristic growth changes dependent on the sex of the subjects. Carlson ends the paper by warning that ". . . the meaning of a personality dimension is dependent upon the developmental level of the individual and . . . sex differences must be considered in conceptualizing the development and dynamic of the self-image" (Chapter 38, p. 568).

That warning of Carlson's receives additional support in the study by McKinney presented in Chapter 39. The study indicates that children's choices of favorite objects and behaviors become more stable with age and that, at every age studied, girls choices tend to be more stable than those of boys. Once again, if the stability of personality develops with age (Bloom, 1964) and varies with sex, one must be careful to take these two factors into account in making statements about personality characteristics.

REFERENCES

Allport, G. W. The use of personal documents in Psychological science. *Bulletin 49, Social Science Research Council,* New York, 1942.

BENEDICT, R. Continuities and discontinuities in cultural conditioning. In P. Mullhay (Ed.). *A study of interpersonal relations.* Hermitage Press, Inc., 1949.

BENEDICT, R. *Patterns of culture.* Boston: Houghton Mifflin Company, 1964.

BETTELHEIM, R. *Symbolic Wounds: Puberty rites and the envious male.* 2d ed. New York: Collier Books, 1962.

BLOOM, B. *Stability and change in human characteristics.* New York: Wiley, 1964.

BROWN, J. Adolescent initiation rites among preliterate peoples. In R. E. Grinder (Ed.). *Studies in adolescence.* New York: Macmillan, 1963, pp. 75–85.

CATTELL, P. Dentition as a measure of maturity. *Harvard Monographs in Education,* No. 9. Cambridge, Harvard University Press, 1928.

DOUVAN, E., & ADELSON, J. *The adolescent experience.* New York: Wiley, 1966.

ERIKSON, E. *Childhood and society.* 2d ed. New York: W. W. Norton, 1963.

ERIKSON, E. Identity and the life cycle. *Psychological Issues,* 1959, *1* (monograph No. 1).

ERIKSON, E. *Identity, youth and crisis.* New York: W. W. Norton, 1968.

FRANK, A. *Anne Frank: the diary of a young girl.* New York: Doubleday, 1952.

FRAZIER, A., & LISONBEE, L. Adolescent concerns with physique. *School Review,* 1950, *58,* 397–405.

FREUD, S. *A young girl's diary.* New York: Barnes & Noble, 1961.

FROMM, E. *The art of loving.* New York: Harper & Row, 1956.

GOODMAN, P. *Growing up absurd.* New York: Random House, 1960.

HALL, G. S. *Adolescence.* New York: Appleton, 1904.

JONES, M. C. The later careers of boys who were early or late-maturing. *Child Development,* 1957, *28,* 113–128.

JONES, M. C., & BAYLEY, N. Physical maturing among boys as related to behavior. *J. educ. Psychol.,* 1950, *41,* 129–148.

JONES, M. C., & MUSSEN, P. H. Self conceptions, motivations, and interpersonal attitudes of early and late maturing girls. *Child Development,* 1958, *29,* 491–504.

KIELL, N. *The adolescent through fiction.* New York: International Universities Press, 1965.

KINSEY, A. C., POMEROY, W. B. *et al. Sexual behavior in the human female.* Philadelphia: Saunders, 1953.

KINSEY, A. C., POMEROY, W. B., & MARTIN, C. E. *Sexual behavior in the human male.* Philadelphia: Saunders, 1948.

KNOWLES, J. *A separate peace.* New York: Houghton Mifflin, 1946.

LEWIN, K. Field theory and experiment in social psychology concepts and methods. *American Journal of Sociology,* 1939, *44,* 868–897.

MCCULLERS, C. *The member of the wedding.* New York: Houghton Mifflin, 1946.

MEAD, M. *Coming of age in Samoa.* New York: Morrow, 1961.

MUSSEN, P. H., & JONES, M. C. Self-conceptions, motivations, and interpersonal attitudes of late- and early-maturing boys. *Child Development,* 1957, *28,* 243–256.

MUUSS, R. E. *Theories of adolescence.* 2d ed. New York: Random House, 1968.

SCHOCK, N. W. Physiological changes in adolescence. *Adolescence, 43d Yearbook of the NSSE.* Chicago: University of Chicago Press, 1944.

Shipman, W. G. Age of menarche and adult personality. *Archives of general Psychiatry,* 1964, *10,* 155–159.

Spiegelberg, H. On the 'I-Am-Me' experience in childhood and adolescence. *Review of Existential Psychology and Psychiatry,* 1964, *4,* 3–21.

Sullivan, H. S. *The interpersonal theory of psychiatry.* New York: W. W. Norton, 1953.

Tanner, J. S. *Growth at adolescence.* Springfield, Ill.: C. CC. Thomas, 1955.

Todd, T. W. *Atlas of skeletal maturation (Hand).* St. Louis: Mosby, 1937.

VanGennep, A. *The rites of passage.* Chicago: University of Chicago Press, 1960.

Waldhorn, A., & Waldhorn, H. (Eds.). *The rite of becoming: Stories and studies of adolescence.* Cleveland: World Publishing Company, 1966.

Physical Development

30

SELF-CONCEPTIONS, MOTIVATIONS, AND INTERPERSONAL ATTITUDES OF LATE- AND EARLY-MATURING BOYS*

PAUL HENRY MUSSEN
and
MARY COVER JONES

WHILE MANY intensive case studies show that personal and social adjustment during adolescence may be profoundly influenced by rate of physical maturation, there is a scarcity of systematic data on the relationship between the adolescent's physical status and his underlying motivations, self-conceptions and interpersonal attitudes. There is, however, a small body of evidence which demonstrates that greater physical maturity is associated with greater maturity of interest among girls (10) and that early-maturing boys differ from their late-maturing peers in both overt behavior and reputational status. In one study (8) in which a staff of trained observers assessed a large group of adolescents on a number of personality variables, boys who were consistently retarded in physical development were rated lower than those who were consistently accelerated, in physical attractiveness, grooming, and matter-of-factness; and higher in sociability, social initiative (often of a childish, attention-getting sort), and eagerness. Reputation Test (11) data indicated that classmates regarded the late-maturing boys as more attention-getting, more restless, more bossy, less grown-up and less good-looking than those who were physically accelerated.

* From *Child Development,* 1957, *28,* 243–256. Reprinted with permission of the authors and the Society for Research in Child Development.

The TAT data for this study were obtained by Harold E. Jones in connection with a test program at the Institute of Child Welfare.

On the basis of these findings, it may be inferred that adult and peer attitudes toward the adolescent, as well as their treatment and acceptance of him, are related to his physical status. This means that the sociopsychological environment to which late-maturers are subjected—and consequently the social learning situations they encounter—may be significantly different from that of their early-maturing peers. As a consequence, according to the ratings summarized above, they acquire different patterns of overt social behavior. It seems reasonable to hypothesize that groups differing in physical status will also differ in more covert aspects of behavior and personality.

Indirect evidence relevant to this hypothesis comes from an investigation of the long-term consequences of physical acceleration or retardation during adolescence. Jones (6) found that group differences in physique had practically disappeared by the time her early- and late-maturing subjects reached their early thirties. Nevertheless, young adults who had been physically retarded adolescents differed from those who had been accelerated in several important psychological characteristics. In general, it appeared that the adult subjects could be described much as they had been during adolescence. Thus, those who had been early-maturers scored higher on the good impression, socialization, dominance, self-control (low score on impulsivity), and responsibility scales of the California Personality Inventory, while those who had been slow in maturing scored higher on the flexibility scale. On the Edwards Personal Preference Schedule, early-maturers scored significantly higher on the dominance scale, while the late-maturing were high in succorance. Jones concludes that the early-maturing "present a consistently favorable personality picture with regard to . . . important social variables" (6). Moreover, there was some evidence that these men had attained more stable vocational adjustments than those who had been late in maturing. These group differences in later adjustments suggest that the sociopsychological atmosphere in which the adolescent lives may have profound immediate and enduring effects on his personality structure as well as on his overt behavior.

The present study was designed to investigate the relationship between maturational status and certain important, covert aspects of personality during late adolescence. Personality structure was assessed by means of the Thematic Apperception Test (TAT) which seems to be the most appropriate and sensitive instrument for this purpose. More specifically, on the basis of the literature reviewed above and other general works on the psychology of adolescence (1, 4, 5), we formulated and tested a series of propositions relating to differences between the physically retarded and the accelerated in self-conceptions, underlying motivations, and basic interpersonal attitudes. These variables were translated into TAT categories—needs (*n*), press (*p*), and descriptions (defined briefly in Table 1)—and the scores of early- and late-maturers in each of these categories were compared. The propositions and the rationale underlying them, together with the TAT variables involved, follow.

1. In view of their obvious physical retardation, relatively unfavorable reputations and disadvantageous competitive position in many activities, the late-maturing boys are more likely to have feelings of inadequacy. Hence, more boys in this group than in the early-maturing group are likely to have negative self-conceptions (TAT category: *negative characteristics*).

2. The adolescent in our culture generally desires some independence and adult status. This may be the source of a major problem for the late-maturer, however, since he is often regarded and treated as a small boy by adults and peers and is not likely to be granted independence as early as physically accelerated boys. Therefore, it may be anticipated that more late- than early-maturers regard adults, particularly their parents, as dominating, forcing them to do things they don't want to or preventing them from doing things they want to do (high scores in *p Dominance*). Moreover, the parental treatment these boys experience and parental refusal to grant them independent status may be interpreted as personal rejection. Hence, we predicted that more late-maturing boys would score high in *p Rejection*.

3. These feelings of being dominated and rejected may result in attitudes of rebellion against the family and in feelings of hostility. We therefore expected that more of the late-maturing group would reveal strong aggressive needs (high scores in *n Aggression*) and desires to escape from (*n Autonomy—leaving parents*), or to defy, the family (*n Autonomy—defying parents*).

4. On the basis of the data indicating that slow-maturers showed a great deal of social interest (although often of an immature kind), we hypothesized that more members of this, than of the early-maturing group would reveal strong interests in friendly, intimate interpersonal relationships (high scores in *n Affiliation*).

5. Assuming that, as Jones and Bayley (8) suggest, the social initiative and attention-getting devices of the late-maturers are of a compensatory nature, we would expect this group to be basically dependent and to have strong needs for support from others. These should be manifest by higher scores in TAT *n Succorance* and *p Nurturance*. The latter may be considered a more indirect measure of dependence, a kind of wish-fulfilling view of the world as helpful and friendly.

6. The early-maturer, being regarded and treated as more adult, is more likely to become self-confident, and to acquire high status goals. For these reasons, we predicted that more of the physically accelerated would give evidence of high achievement goals (high scores in *n Achievement*) and concern with personal recognition (high scores in *n Recognition*).

7. Late-maturing boys in our culture probably face more problems of personal adjustment than do their early-maturing peers. As a result of this, they may become more aware of their problems, and, as the high degree of flexibility of young adults who had been retarded in maturing suggests, more

insightful. Hence we predicted that they would be more willing and able than early-maturers to face their own feelings and emotions (low scores in the TAT variable *denial of feeling*).

In summary, we attempted to test seven propositions related to differences in the personalities of early- and late-maturing boys. It was hypothesized that more late-maturers would score high in variables relating to negative self-conceptions, dependence, aggression, affiliation, rebelliousness, and feelings of being dominated and rejected. More early-maturers, on the other hand, were expected to reveal strong achievement and recognition needs, feelings of personal success, and tendencies toward denial of feelings.

PROCEDURE

The 33 seventeen-year-old male subjects of this investigation were members of the Adolescent Growth Study which included a normal sample of boys in an urban public school system (3). The subjects of the present investigation represented two contrasting groups, selected on the basis of their physical maturity status: 16 of them had been among the most consistently accelerated throughout the adolescent period; the other 17 had been among the most consistently retarded. All of them took the Thematic Apperception Test, which provides the basic data of this study, at age 17.

The TAT consisted of 18 pictures: nine from the Murray set which is now standard (cards 1, 5, 6, 7BM, 10, 11, 14, 15, 17); five pictures from the set generally used in 1938 when these data were collected (a man and woman seated on a park bench; a bearded old man writing in an open book; a thin, sullen, young man standing behind a well-dressed older man; a tea table and two chairs; an abstract drawing of two bearded men); and four designed especially for this investigation (the nave of a large church; a madonna and child; a dramatic view of mountains; a boy gazing at a cross which is wreathed in clouds).

The tests were administered individually. Each card was projected on a screen while the subject told a story which was recorded verbatim. Standard instructions were given for the Murray cards, and subjects were asked to describe the feelings elicited by the other four pictures. Most of the stories were brief, consisting of only one or two sentences.

As we noted earlier, each of the personality variables involved in the seven propositions was translated into a TAT scoring category. The scoring scheme involved counting the relevant needs, press, and descriptions of the heroes of the stories, the assumption being that the storyteller has identified with the hero: the hero's needs are the same as the boy's; the press that impinge upon the hero are the ones that affect the boy telling the story. A total of 20 needs, press, and descriptive categories, each defined as specifically as possible, was developed in the analysis of the protocols. A score for each

TABLE 1

Number of Early- and Late-Maturers Scoring High in TAT Variables

TAT Variable	*Definition of Variable*	*High Early-Maturers*	*High Late-Maturers*	*Chi Square Value*	*p*
Proposition 1					
Negative Characteristics	H is described in negative terms (e.g., imbecile, weakling, fanatic)	5	13	6.80	<.01
Proposition 2					
p Dominance 1	H forced by parents to do something he doesn't want to	4	8	1.73	.09
p Dominance 2	H prevented by parents from doing something he wants to	6	8	.31	>.30
p Dominance 3	Total instances of H's being forced by parents to do something and/or prevented from doing something	7	11	1.46	.11
p Rejection	H rejected, scorned, or disapproved of by parents or authorities	5	11	3.69	.03
Proposition 3					
n Aggression 1	H is aggressive in physical, asocial way	8	3	3.88	.02
n Aggression 2	H is mad at someone, argues	7	4	1.52	.10
n Aggression 3	Total of all H's aggressive actions	11	8	1.26	.10
n Autonomy 1	H leaves home	7	10	.75	.20
n Autonomy 2	H disobeys or defies parents	7	11	1.46	.11
n Autonomy 3	Total of instances in which hero leaves and/or defies his parents	3	9	4.16	.02
Proposition 4					
n Affiliation 1	H establishes good relations with his parents	8	8	.00	>.50
n Affiliation 2	H falls in love, has a romance, marries	9	14	2.66	.05
n Affiliation 3	Total instances in which H establishes and/or maintains friendly relations	8	12	1.46	.11
Proposition 5					
n Succorance	H feels helpless, seeks aid or sympathy	7	12	2.43	.06
p Nurturance 1	H is helped, encouraged, or given something by parents	5	8	.93	.18
p Nurturance 2	H is helped, encouraged, or given something by someone else (not parents)	8	14	3.88	.02
Proposition 6					
n Achievement	H attempts to attain a high goal or to do something creditable	9	10	.02	>.50
n Recognition	H seeks fame and/or high prestige status	9	8	.28	>.30
Proposition 7					
Denial of Feeling	S states that picture elicits no thoughts or feelings	9	5	2.43	.06

subject for each TAT category was derived by counting the number of stories in which it appeared. A list of the categories used, together with brief descriptions of them, is found in Table 1.

To test the reliability of this analysis, one of the authors (PM) and another psychologist[1] independently scored 15 complete protocols (300 stories). The percentage of interrater agreement was 90, computed by the usual formula (number of agreements divided by number of agreements plus number of disagreements).

In order to eliminate bias, the scoring used in the present study was done "blind," that is, independently of knowledge of the subject's maturational status.

RESULTS

Frequency distributions of the scores of all subjects were made for all the TAT variables. Each distribution was then dichotomized at the point which most nearly enabled the placing of half of the 33 subjects above, and half of them below, the dividing point. Subjects having scores above this point were considered high in this particular variable; those with scores below this point were considered low in this variable. Chi square tests were used to test the seven propositions, i.e., to ascertain whether or not high scores in certain TAT variables were in fact more characteristic of one group (late- or early-maturers) than of the other.

Table 1 lists the TAT variables, the number of late- and early-maturers with high scores in the variable, the chi square value obtained and the level of significance. It should be noted that the hypotheses tested were one-sided hypotheses, while the chi square value is in terms of a two-sided hypothesis. When Chi square has only one degree of freedom, the square root of chi square has a distribution which is the right hand half of a normal distribution. In order to test a one-sided hypothesis, the chi square test must be converted into the equivalent value in terms of a unit normal deviate (2). The levels of significance reported in Table 1 were evaluated in these terms.

Table 1 shows that, as had been predicted, more late-maturing than early-maturing boys revealed feelings of inadequacy and negative self-concepts, i.e., scored high in the TAT variable *negative characteristics*. Hence proposition 1 was confirmed. This finding is consistent with the frequently made clinical observation that retardation in physical maturation may be an important source of personal maladjustment and attitudes of inferiority.

Proposition 2 stated that more late-maturers regard their parents as highly dominating and rejecting. The evidence summarized in Table 1 substantially supported this proposition. While the difference was not statistically significant, more late- than early-maturers scored high in *p Dominance by parents*

---

[1] We are indebted to Dr. Virginia B. Ware for her participation in this aspect of the study.

(total). There was a marked difference between the groups in the variable which involves parental domination by forcing the child to do something he does not want to do (*p Dominance by parents, forcing*). However, examination of the data with respect to the variable *p Dominance by parents* (*prevention*) makes it necessary to reject that part of the proposition which maintains that late-maturers are more likely to view their parents as highly restrictive of their activities.

That aspect of proposition 2 which deals with feelings of rejection was confirmed by our data. Compared with the early-maturing group, a significantly greater proportion of the late-maturers told stories in which the hero was rejected by parents or authority figures. These feelings of rejection may stem from different sources. In some cases, the parents' behavior may make it clear that they are disappointed in their physically retarded son whom they regard as immature. The boy, perceiving this attitude, may interpret it as rejection. In other cases, parental reluctance to allow the late-maturing boy to establish his independence may lead to considerable tension in the family and the boy's feelings of rejection may simply reflect the ongoing parent-child conflict.

It is possible that earlier in their teens, soon after the physical changes of adolescence became apparent, many of the early-maturing boys also experienced conflicts with their parents, arising from difficulties in establishing their independence or in handling emerging heterosexual interests. At that time they too may have felt dominated or rejected. However, by the age of 17, when these data were collected, these boys were ordinarily treated as adults and granted more freedom. Hence, they were more likely to have resolved many of their conflicts with their parents and to feel accepted and independent.

The hypothesis (part of proposition 3) of that more late-maturers would be highly aggressive was rejected on the basis of the evidence given in Table 1. In fact, the differences between the two groups on all the TAT aggression variables were in the opposite direction from the prediction. High scores in the variables relating to aggression of the most overt and violent type were significantly more frequent among the early-maturers, and more members of this group also scored high in measures of milder (verbal) aggression and of total aggression. While late-maturers may experience more problems of adjustment and greater frustrations than their early-maturing peers, they apparently do not manifest greater aggressive motivation. It may be that their own feelings of inadequacy or fears of retaliation and punishment for aggression inhibit their expression of hostile feelings, even in fantasy. On the other hand, the early-maturers who feel more secure personally, and recognize their own relatively advantageous physical and social status, may feel freer to express their aggresssive needs. Since aggression is a culturally stereotyped masculine trait, it seems possible that the physically accelerated, being accepted as mature and identifying readily with adult males, are more likely to acquire this characteristic. In any case, the finding that early-maturers express higher aggressive motivation during late adolescence seems consistent with Jones' finding that, as young adults, they score high on the dominance scale of the Edwards Personal Preference test (6). Perhaps the relatively strong aggressive motivation of the early-maturer, or the mature sex-role identification it may imply, serves as a basis for the development of later qualities of leadership and persuasiveness (7).

As Table 1 indicates, the other aspect of proposition 3 was confirmed: a significantly greater proportion of late- than of early-maturers displayed strong motivations to escape from, or defy, their parents. These may be essentially aggressive reactions, stemming from feelings of parental domination and rejection, or they may reflect the late-maturers' awareness of their strife with their parents whom they perceive as blocking their drives for independence. These strong needs for escape and defiance may also be considered evidence of a generally immature way of handling parent-child conflicts. Perhaps, by the age of 17, the early-maturers have already resolved many of their conflicts with their families and/or have learned to handle these in less rebellious and in more direct and mature ways.

Proposition 4 stated that, compared with their early-maturing peers, more late-maturers would manifest strong needs for establishing close social contacts with others. While there was some confirmatory evidence, the results were not clear-cut. When all affiliative needs were considered together (score for *n Affiliation—total*), the group differences were in the predicted direction, but not statistically significant. Examination of the protocols revealed that almost all instances of affiliation concerned either parents or the opposite sex; there were very few stories involving close, friendly associations between like-sexed peers. The two major types of affiliation were scored separately. As Table 1 shows, late-maturers did not differ from early-maturers with respect to need for affiliation with parents, but a significantly greater proportion of the former group displayed strong motivation for heterosexual affiliation.

In view of the late-maturers' strong feelings of inadequacy and dependent needs (see below), it is surpring that a greater proportion of this group did not exhibit strong needs to establish and maintain close bonds with their parents. This may be due to the late-maturers' more intense conflicts with their parents at this age (17 years), their fears of being rejected and dominated by them, and their generally defiant attitudes which prevent them from admitting, even in fantasy, their strong underlying needs to form close contacts with them.

The significant difference between the groups in *n Affiliation* (*love, romance, marriage*) is subject to several possible interpretations. For one thing, this category may refer to general needs to establish close relations with others (with peers or adults other than parents) and not merely to desire for contact with the opposite sex. The set of stimulus cards may not have been adequate to elicit responses indicative of more general affiliative needs; hence, these were expressed through responses in the heterosexual affiliation category. If this is true, proposition 4 was confirmed, and the late-maturers' high scores in this variable indicate their greater general interest in establishing and maintaining friendly relationships.

It is also possible that the late-maturers' strong affiliative needs are actually directed only toward members of the opposite sex, i.e., that *n Affiliation (love, romance, marriage)* measures specifically heterosexual interests. Assuming that this is true, there is another plausible explanation for the discovered difference. As we saw earlier, the late-maturer may be afraid to admit that he desires close associations with his parents. He may also feel that his immaturity and poor reputational status prevent him from establishing successful social relationships with like-sexed peers. Hence, he may "displace" his affiliative needs to members of the opposite sex, who, in his fantasies, may seem more responsive.

A third possible explanation of the difference is based on Jones and Bayley's findings that the late-maturers show less overt interest in girls and are regarded as less good-looking (8). From these data, it may be inferred that the physically retarded probably do not have successful and rewarding experiences with girls. Hence their heightened need for affiliation with the opposite sex, expressed in the TAT, may reflect their attempts to satisfy in fantasy needs which they cannot satisfy adequately in reality.

The data were generally supportive of proposition 5, which stated that late-maturers are likely to have strong underlying dependent needs. A higher proportion of this group than of their early-maturing peers scored high in *n Succorance,* the difference between the two groups approaching statistical significance ($p = .06$). Furthermore, high scores in the category involving receiving help and support from others (not including parents) (*p Nurturance—non-parents*)—an indirect measure of dependent needs—were significantly more characteristic of the physically retarded than of the physically accelerated. In view of the late-maturers' attitudes toward their parents, discussed above, it is not surprising to find that perceptions of parents as kindly and supportive (high scores in *p Nurturance-parents*) were not significantly more common in this group than in the early-maturing group.

On the basis of the data involving the TAT variables *n Achievement* and *n Recognition,* we rejected proposition 6, which stated that more early-maturers would be self-confident and have high needs for achievement and personal recognition. In our culture there is strong pressure to develop needs for achievement and personal recognition, and, according to our results, these needs and feelings may become intense regardless of—or perhaps in spite of —the child's maturational status, feelings of personal adequacy, dependency, and adjustment to parents.

Two interesting incidental findings from the TAT data seem to be consistent with the proposition that more early- than late-maturers are likely to be self-confident. Seven boys in this sample of 33 adolescents told stories in which the hero was helpful or kind to someone else (*n Nurturance*). Of this group, six were early-maturers, while only one was a late maturer ($\chi^2 = 2.09$, $p = .07$). Insofar as *n Nurturance* may be a measure of the storyteller's own feelings that he can accept an active, mature role, more of the accelerated group feel self-assured with respect to having attained mature status.

The other incidental finding which seems to support proposition 6 is based on responses only to card 1 of the Murray series which depicts a young boy contemplating a violin which rests on a table in front of him. Eight of the subjects spoke of the boy (the hero) as a prodigy or a genius. Of these, seven were early-maturers; only one was physically retarded ($\chi^2 = 5.25$, $p = .01$). If the attribution of this prestige status and accomplishment to the hero reflects the subject's own feeling that he has been an achiever, it follows that more of the physically accelerated have positive self-concepts. In view of the small number of cases involved, both of these findings must be considered tentative, but they do offer some evidence in support of proposition 6.

Proposition 7, which stated that relatively few of the physically retarded boys are unwilling or unable to face their own feelings and emotions, received some support from the TAT data summarized in Table 1. A smaller proportion of the members of this group than of the physically accelerated group specifically denied that the pictures evoked any feelings or emotions (e.g., "It doesn't make me think of anything"). While this variable may not adequately measure *denial of feeling* as a major defense mechanism, this result seems to indicate that late-maturers are more sensitive to their own feelings and more ready to admit and face them openly. Since these qualities are basic to the development of psychological insight, it may be inferred that late-maturers, as a group, are more likely to become insightful individuals.

DISCUSSION

The results of the study support the general hypothesis that, in our culture, the boy whose physical development is retarded is exposed to a sociopsychological environment which may have adverse effects on his personality development. Apparently, being in a disadvantageous competitive position in athletic activities, as well as being regarded and treated as immature by others, may lead to negative self-conceptions, heightened feelings of rejection by others, prolonged dependent needs, and rebellious attitudes toward parents. Hence, the physically retarded boy is more likely than his early-maturing peer to be personally and socially maladjusted during late adolescence. Moreover, some of his attitudes are likely to interfere with the process of identification with his parents, which is generally based on perceptions of them as warm and accepting (9). This, in turn, may inhibit or delay the acquisition of mature characteristics and attitudes which are ordinarily established through identification with parents. Fortunately for the late-maturers' subsequent adjustments, they seem more willing and able to face their feelings and emotions. This may be a result of their awareness of others' attitudes toward their immaturity or their feelings of personal inadequacy and dependency.

The physically accelerated boys, on the other hand, are likely to experience environmental circumstances which are much more conducive to good psychological adjustment. Hence, their psychological picture, as reflected in their TAT stories, is much more favorable. By the time they were 17, relatively few early-maturers harbored strong feelings of inadequacy, perceived themselves as rejected or dominated by parents or authorities, or felt rebellious toward their families. As a group, they appeared to have acquired more self-confidence and had probably made stronger identifications with mature adults. Hence, they perceived themselves as more mature individuals, less dependent and in need of help, and more capable of playing an adult male role in interpersonal relationships.

These findings assume additional, probably greater, importance when they are considered in the light of Jones' findings on the early adult (age 33) adjustments of boys who had been retarded or accelerated in physical maturing (6). It should be recalled that by this age physical differences between the two groups had practically disappeared. Certain important psychological differences were noted, however, and these were consistent with the differences at age 17, reported in the present study. For example, the responses of the early-maturing group to two paper-and-pencil tests revealed that, as young adults, they were more dominant, more able to make a good impression and more likely to be turned to for advice and reassurance; more self-controlled; and more willing and able to carry social responsibility. In short, they present a general picture of psychological maturity. Moreover, more of the early-maturers seemed to have made successful vocational adjustments. In contrast to this, when the late-maturers became adults, they tended to be highly dependent individuals who could be described, on the basis of their test responses, as tending to be rebellious, touchy, impulsive, self-indulgent, and insightful. Most of these characteristics are indicative of poor adjustment and psychological immaturity. Fewer members of this group had made good vocational adjustments.

The striking correspondence between the two descriptions of the groups, derived from different kinds of tests and collected at widely separated periods of time, lends further support to Jones' conclusion that "the adolescent handicaps and advantages associated with late- or early-maturing appear to carry over into adulthood to some extent" (6). It seems clear that many attributes of adolescent personality (patterns of motivation, self-conceptions, and attitudes toward others) characteristic of late- and early-maturing boys are relatively stable and durable rather than situational and transitory. This may be attributable to the fact that in our culture adolescence is generally a critical and difficult period of adjustment. Within a relatively brief interval of time, the child must work out numerous complex and vitally important personal problems—e.g., adaptation to his changed biological and social status, establishment of independence, vocational adjustment. In dealing with these problems, he may acquire new behaviors and personality attributes which have broad ramifications, not only on his current adjustment, but also on his subsequent development. If the adolescent can cope with his problems without too much inner stress and turmoil, his self-esteem, feelings of adequacy, and consequently his subsequent adjustment, are likely to be enhanced. On the other hand, if his problems induce great tension and anxiety, he is likely to feel frustrated and inadequate, and, if these feelings are maintained, to adjust less satisfactorily as an adult.

Obviously, the adolescent's success or failure, as well as ease or tension, in handling his problems will be determined to a large degree by the sociopsychological forces to which he is subjected during this time, and these, as we have seen, may be significantly related to his rate of maturation. Thus, physical status during adolescence—mediated through the sociopsychological environment—may exert profound and lasting influences on personality. For this reason, many aspects of the adult's behavior and personality seem consistent with his adolescent adjustments, attitudes and motivations.

Insofar as our results permit generalization, they suggest that some important aspects of motivation, such as needs for achievement and personal recognition, are not significantly affected by maturational status. It may be that among subjects whose achievements are strongly encouraged and rewarded from very early childhood, the need to achieve becomes powerful and resistant to change even in the face of feelings of helplessness and inadequacy. The latter may inhibit the achievement-oriented overt behavior of some late-maturers, but the underlying motivation to achieve seems as strong in this group as it is among the physically accelerated.

In conclusion, it should be noted that, although rate of maturing and associated factors may affect personality development, the relationship between physical status and psychological characteristics is by no means simple. A vast number of complex, interacting factors, including rate of maturation, determine each adolescent's unique personality structure. Hence, in any specific instance, the *group* findings of the present study may not be directly applicable, for other physical, psychological, or social factors may attenuate the effects of late- or early-maturing. For example, an adolescent boy who is fundamentally secure and has warm, accepting parents and generally rewarding social relationships may not develop strong feelings of inadequacy even if he matures slowly. Analogously, the early-maturing boy who has deep feelings of insecurity, for whatever reasons, will probably not gain self-confidence simply because he matures early. In summary, in understanding any individual case, generalizations based on the data of the present study must be particularized in the light of the individual's past history and present circumstances.

SUMMARY

The present investigation was designed to test seven propositions concerning the relationship between rate of physical maturation and important aspects of personality structure, specifically, self-conceptions, underlying motivations, and basic interpersonal attitudes. The TAT protocols of 33 seventeen-year-old boys—16 who had been consistently physically accelerated throughout adolescence and 17 who had been consistently retarded—were analyzed according to a scoring schema involving 20 needs, press, and descriptive categories. The scores of early- and late-maturers in each of the categories were compared.

An earlier study (8) demonstrated that late-maturing boys are more likely than their early-maturing peers to encounter a generally unfavorable sociopsychological environment. Analysis of the data of the present study indicates that this situation may have adverse effects on the personalities of the physically retarded. These boys are more likely to have negative self-conceptions, feelings of inadequacy, strong feelings of being rejected and dominated, prolonged dependency needs, and rebellious attitudes toward parents. In contrast, the early-maturing boys present a much more favorable psychological picture during adolescence. Relatively few of them felt inadequate, rejected, dominated, or rebellious toward their families. More of them appeared to be self-confident, independent, and capable of playing an adult role in interpersonal relationships. Early- and late-maturing groups did not differ significantly from each other in needs for achievement or personal recognition.

These findings make it clear that rate of physical maturing may affect personality development in crucially important ways. However, it is important to note that in any particular case the effects of early- or late-maturing may be significantly modified by the individual's psychological history and present circumstances.

REFERENCES

1. FARNHAM, M. L. *The adolescent.* New York: Harper, 1951.
2. FISHER, R. A. *Statistical methods for research workers.* (7th Ed.) Edinburgh: Oliver & Boyd, 1938.
3. JONES, H. E. Observational methods in the study of individual development. *J. consult. Psychol.,* 1940, *4,* 234–238.
4. JONES, H. E. *Development in adolescence.* New York: Appleton-Century, 1943.
5. JONES, H. E. Adolescence in our society. In *The family in a democratic society, Anniversary papers of The Community Service Society of New York.* New York: Columbia Univer. Press, 1949. Pp. 70–82.

6. Jones, Mary C. The later careers of boys who were early- or late-maturing. *Child Develpm.*, 1957, *28*, 113–128.
7. Jones, Mary C. A study of socialization at the high school level. In preparation.
8. Jones, Mary C., & Bayley, Nancy. Physical maturing among boys as related to behavior. *J. educ. Psychol.*, 1950, *41*, 129–148.
9. Payne, D. E., & Mussen, P. H. Parent-child relations and father identification among adolescent boys. *J. abnorm. soc. Psychol.*, 1956, *52*, 358–362.
10. Stone, C. P., & Barker, R. G. The attitudes and interests of premenarcheal and postmenarcheal girls. *J. genet. Psychol.*, 1939, *54*, 27–71.
11. Tryon, Caroline M. Evaluation of adolescent personality by adolescents. *Monogr. Soc. Res. Child Develpm.*, 1939, *4*, No. 4.

31

PSYCHOLOGICAL CORRELATES OF SOMATIC DEVELOPMENT*

MARY COVER JONES

This study continues a series that has dealt with the relationship between some aspects of rate of physical maturing in adolescent boys and certain behavioral and personality characteristics. Since the 1950 report on physical maturing among boys as related to behavior (M. C. Jones & Bayley, 1950), there have been more than a dozen publications that use the Oakland Growth Study sample and deal with some psychological concomitants of rate of maturing as defined by skeletal age. The published studies were reviewed in 1963 (Eichorn).

THE SAMPLE

Members of this longitudinal study (H. E. Jones, 1938) are now in their early 40's. They were observed, measured, and tested as school children and studied again at intervals in adulthood (H. E. Jones, Macfarlane, & Eichorn, 1960). Evaluation of the adult sample as compared to the original has shown that although death, distance, and disinclination have attentuated the sample of 150 who were with the study at high-school graduation to 99 in the 1958–60 follow-up, there has been no consistent bias that would seem to account for dropouts (M. C. Jones, 1957).

The adult study members did not differ from the original sample in (*a*) general intelligence as measured by the Terman Group Test of Mental Ability, (*b*) socioeconomic status (Edwards, 1933), (*c*) childhood family size, and (*d*) some selected adolescent personality variables (Haan, 1962; Stewart, 1962).

* From *Child Development,* 1965, *36,* 899–916. Reprinted with permission from the author and the Society for Research in Child Development.

This article is based on a Presidential Address to Division 7 at the American Psychological Association, Los Angeles, Calif., August, 1964. The author wishes to express appreciation to Herbert R. Stolz and Lois Meek Stolz for their help in providing data and encouragement for this research. Author's address: Institute of Human Development, University of California, Berkeley 94270.

THE PROCEDURE

The purpose of this report is threefold: first, to consider the value of using age measures of maturing other than consistent skeletal age for comparisons on personality measures; second, to specify the contributions of certain physical characteristics associated with pubescence, such as stature, strength, and sexual development to behavior; third, to report on recently available psychological measures from an intensive follow-up when the groups were in their late 30's.

Psychological Comparisons Based on Age Measures

To examine age measures of maturity other than consistent skeletal age, the following were used:

1. The Stolzes' (1951) Analysis of the Physical Characteristics of This Same Sample. The assessments used by the Stolzes began at around the eleventh year. (Skeletal-age measures were not available until age 14.) A comparison of extreme groups using the Stolzes' indexes of chronological age at the onset, at the apex, and at the end of puberal growth in height enabled a comparison at stages within the puberal-growth cycle to determine whether some periods were more predictive than others of certain psychological behaviors. There are, of course, overlapping cases in all of these extreme group samples. (Comparisons were also made between early or late-maturing boys and those who matured at an average rate. The relationships were not as pronounced nor as consistent as those that emerged from comparing extreme groups.)

2. Chronological Age at Reaching 90 Percent Mature Height. Nicolson and Hanley's (1953) factor-analytic study of 11 indicators of adolescent-maturation rate found this to be the best single measure of the general factor, which was sufficient to account for all reliable covariations. Correlational procedures were used with this measure and included the entire sample of 88 boys.

For all of these comparisons using age indexes, only two psychological measures will be reported. These are observational ratings of individuals in small, like-sexed groups in a free-play setting in adolescence (Newman & H. E. Jones, 1946) and the California Personality Inventory (CPI) scale (Gough, 1960) scores at age 33.

Free-Play Ratings in Adolescence. Free-play ratings were compared at yearly intervals (ages 13 through 16) for three groups of individuals who are contrasted in rate of maturing at the onset (average age for the total group 12½ years), at the apex (average age 14), and at the end (average age 15½) of the growth period for height.

One-tenth of the cases considered here in the early maturing category appear in all three distributions; 16 per cent appear at two levels each.

Among the late developers the overlap is greater, the corresponding percentages being 24 in all three categories, 61 per cent in the onset and end group, 52 per cent common to the apex and end categories. The number of cases in each group varied from 12 to 22.

Those who represent opposite extremes of the maturity distribution at the onset of puberty show the most strikingly differentiated patterns, and these are most marked near the end of their high-school years. These individuals were conspicuously disparate at the beginning of the race toward maturity,

TABLE 1

Free-Play Ratings—Comparison of Three Maturity Measures

	Puberal-Height Index				*Skeletal*		*r*
	Age				*Age*		
High Ratings	13	14	15	16	14	16	*(90% Mature Height)*
Early maturers rate high:							
Good physique		*	***	***	***	**	—*
Masculine physique		*	***	***	*	***	—*
Physical efficiency		*	**	**	**	***	—*
Sex appeal			*	**	**	***	...
Matter of fact				**	...	**	...
Relaxed				***	...	***	...
Late maturers rate high:							
Talkative	...	...	...	**	...	...	...
Active	...	...	...	**	**	*	...
Peppy	...	...	...	**	...	...	*
Busy	...	...	...	*	...	...	**
Eager	*	**	...	***	**	**	**
Social	...	...	...	**	...	...	...
Submissive	...	...	**	...	...	...	...
Carefree	...	**	...	...	...	...	...
Good natured	...	**[a]	...	...	...	***[b]	...
Unaffected	...	*[a]	...	...	...	**[b]	...

[a] Late.
[b] Early.
* Significant at the .10 level.
** Significant at the .05 level.
*** Significant at the .01 level.

and some continued in this relative position throughout adolescence. The reinforcing effect of this continued variation in development might be expected to reveal pronounced behavioral concomitants. In this respect they resemble those who were consistently deviate in skeletal maturity. Table 1 presents the significance of the difference in standard scores on the free-play ratings for the index of puberal height, for the consistently early or late in skeletal maturity, and for correlations with the total sample of 88 boys at the age of reaching 90 per cent mature height.

The over-all pattern that emerges is consistent with that described in the first published report in 1950. The early maturing are rated as having superior physique and physical abilities. "Good physique" is representative of 14 items in these categories. Differences first appear in contrasting groups at age 14 and are significant at later ages for all three groups (those whose growth in height was early at the onset, the apex, or the end of their puberal period). By the end of high school, these boys are also rated as more "poised," "relaxed," "good natured," and "unaffected." The late-maturing boys are expressive, dynamic, and buoyant. However, they are also rated as more "tense" and "affected" in their high-school years.

Peskin (1963), with rather similar findings based on interview data for boys in the Guidance Study (Macfarlane, 1938), considers the activity and

TABLE 2

CPI Scale Scores Comparison of Three Maturity Measures

	Puberal-Height Index			*Consistent Skeletal Age*			*r*
	Early	*Late*	*Significance*	*Early*	*Late*	*Significance*	*(90% Mature Height)*
No. of cases	13	12		12	15		58
Early are high:							
Dominance	33	27	*	33	26	*	***
Capacity for status	22	21	...	23	21	**	...
Sociability	27	23	**	28	25	*	**
Well being	41	38	*	41	39	...	**
Responsibility	34	30	**	33	30	*	*
Socialization	41	34	***	40	34	**	***
Self-control	33	28	...	34	29	**	...
Good impression	23	16	***	24	17	***	***
Achievement via conformity	31	27	...	32	28	**	**
Late are high:							
Psychologically minded	12	15	**	13	14	...	...
Flexible	10	14	*	10	15	**	...
Psychoneurotic	4	8	**	5	8	**	***

* Significant at the .10 level.
** Significant at the .05 level.
*** Significant at the .01 level.

zestfulness of the late maturer to be evidence of his freedom to experiment and resist confining social rules which would circumscribe his behavior.

The description of the late maturer in the Oakland Growth Study sample likewise could be interpreted to indicate that he is more exploratory and tolerant of impulse, especially in the light of the CPI scale scores in adulthood (Table 2).

CPI Measures in Adulthood

The *California Personality Inventory Manual* (Gough, 1960) groups the first six scales under the heading "Measures of Poise, Ascendancy, and

Self-Assurance." All of these scales show higher scores for those who matured early by one or another of the three criteria. The second series of six scales are labeled "Measures of Socialization, Maturity, and Responsibility." Again the early maturers earn higher scores. The third CPI scale score group —"Measures of Achievement Potential and Intellectual Efficiency"—is meaningful chiefly in indicating that early maturers achieve via conformity.

Scores are slightly higher for the late maturers on the scale "Achievement via Independence." (We have found no significant differences in tested mental ability for the late as contrasted with the early maturers.) The implication is that difference in rate of maturing may be related to different modes of expressing intellectual competencies. This is further suggested in the late maturers' higher scores on psychological mindedness and flexibility.

The most clear-cut differentiation occurs on the psychoneurotic scale developed by Jack Block (1961a). Since the late developers score near the average, this means that the accelerated mark fewer diagnostic items on this scale. The early maturers' denial of negative feelings is in keeping with their tendency to mark items positively, which give them high scores on the good-impression scale.

The CPI scale scores at age 33 for the various maturity groups reflect the greatest differentiation for those who were consistently early or late to mature by the skeletal age criterion, the measure used in the earliest publications. There are more significant differences here than reported earlier, due to the fact that three additional cases in each extreme group came in late for study and were added to the sample for this report. Also, some changes and additions have been made in the CPI scales.

Psychological Comparisons Based on Physical Indexes Related to Maturity Status

What were some of the external signs of maturity that served to alert these growing individuals to their developmental progress? A question in the follow-up interview when the subjects were in their late 30's was: "Do you think you developed earlier, at about the same time as, or later than the boys of your age?"

Most individuals answered correctly in terms of our corroborating data. This is evident from their retrospective memories concerning size, strength, weight, growth of pubic hair and of sex organs.

Some of the somatic characteristics associated with maturing as suggested by these comments were examined to determine what part they play in producing the psychological picture that emerges in the contrasting groups. The extreme groups compared here were:

1. The Stolz sample of those who were tallest as contrasted with those who were shortest at the onset and at the end of the puberal period.

2. Boys with a fat period as contrasted with those who had no fat period —a group selected by the Stolzes for this report.
3. Those with a puberal period of short duration as contrasted with those with a long puberal period.
4. Those who were contrasted in pubic-hair rating near the onset of puberty and also half way through the puberal cycle at age 15 when ratings were most disparate.
5. Those whose onset and cessation of growth of the glans penis was early or late.
6. The H. E. Jones (1949) sample of those consistently strong or weak during adolescence.

Again, free-play ratings and CPI scores were used for the comparisons.

Free-Play Ratings. The behavioral characteristics associated with strength are very similar to those for early maturity. Shortness yields ratings comparable to those for late maturity. Boys with a fat period are seen as more phlegmatic and feminine than those with whom they are compared. Pubic-hair ratings for this sample are less differentiating than would have been predicted, since they are frequently used as a measure of maturity status. Most productive was the correlation of free-play ratings with the assessment of the pubic-hair index near the onset of puberty. Early growth of the glans penis is associated with many favorable ratings of behavior and personality (Table 3).

CPI Measures. The data on groups contrasted in physical characteristics for the CPI scores conform to that for the maturity groups, though the differences are fewer. The tall and strong resemble the early maturing in their scores, the weak tend to earn scores similar to those of the late maturing. The other categories yield only tentative findings in line with expectations.

Measures of Adult Interviews

Of all the criteria examined in this effort to relate somatic variation to psychological characteristics, both in adolescence and in adulthood, our first selection, that of being a consistently early or late developer by skeletal-age criteria, still seemed as satisfactory as any other. Therefore, it was the classification used to examine measures available from the follow-up study when the members were approximately 38 years old.

Impressions in the form of ratings have been recorded for these individuals as they related their life histories in interviews and as they retrospectively described themselves as adolescents. Four separate rating schemes have been used by the institute staff.

First to be examined were ratings of retrospective memories (in 17 categories) made by the interviewer and another psychologist, neither of whom had had previous contact with the subject. The material was provided by the study members as they answered questions pertaining to their adolescent social behavior, relation to parents, school experiences, and self concepts.

Differences between the two maturity groups (those consistently accelerated or retarded in skeletal age) appear, with the early developers remembering enjoyment of social activities, of being early to develop, and of having a

TABLE 3

Comparison of Free-Play Ratings for Extreme Groups on Five Physical Variables

	Tall	*Short*	*Strong*	*Weak*	*Not Fat*	*Fat*	*Pubic-Hair Ratings (r)*	*Early Onset Growth Glans Penis*
No. of Cases:	18	13	10	10	28	22	88	12
Eager	...	**	...	...	**	...	—**	*
Good natured	...	*	*	...	**	...	...	**
Social	...	**	...	...	***	...	—*	*
Popular	...	**	**	...	*	...	...	**
Enjoys games	...	*	...	...	**	...	—*	...
Leader	...	...	...	...	...	...	...	***
Effect on group	...	...	*	...	...	...	—*	**
Confident	...	...	...	...	...	...	...	***
Uninhibited	...	...	...	...	...	...	—**	*
Assured	...	...	...	...	...	...	...	***
Matter of fact	...	...	...	...	...	...	**	...
Relaxed	...	...	***	...	...	...	...	**
Cheerful	...	...	...	...	...	...	...	**
Carefree	...	**	**	...	...	...	...	**
Laughing	...	...	...	...	...	...	**	...
Good physique	...	...	**	...	...	...	*	***
Good grooming	...	...	*	...	...	**	*	**
Masculine physique	...	...	***	...	**	...	...	***
Sex appeal	...	...	***	...	...	...	*	***
Physical efficiency	...	...	**	...	...	...	...	***

* Significant at the .10 level.
** Significant at the .05 level.
*** Significant at the .01 level.

pleasant affect in regard to being physically mature at an early age (Table 4).

The late maturing are rated as having reported a significantly greater number of memories concerning their heterosexual or social-sex development. But examination of protocols indicates that, without exception, this greater verbalization was laden with concern about peer rejection, shyness and ineptness.

A second source of data from the interviews is the Kroeber-Haan ratings of ego mechanisms (Haan, 1963). Few significant differences can be re-

TABLE 4

Ratings of Interview Protocols at Age 38: Consistently Early or Late Skeletal-Age: Ratings of Retrospective Adolescent Memories

	Scores		
	Early	*Late*	*Significance*
No. of cases	9	8	...
Developed early	4.5	2.9	*
Positive effect for developmental status	4.3	2.6	*
Enjoyed social life	5.0	3.6	*
Social-sex development	3.0	4.8	*

* Significant at the .05 level.

ported, but the analysis suggests that with the 20 alternative coping and defense mechanisms rated, the late maturing are seen as more often using the coping devices: "tolerance of ambiguity," "selective awareness," "playfulness in the service of the ego," and "egalitarian attitudes." This supports the evidence from the CPI scores showing greater perceptiveness and insight for the late maturing.

Justification for continuing the examination for the remaining two rating schedules cannot be made on statistical grounds because of the paucity of the relationships. But the few findings to be reported are clearly in line with what would have been predicted.

From Block's *Q* sorts (1961b), composed of 100 items, those contrasts that do emerge are consistent with the descriptions from other measures. The early maturing boy is more often represented in adulthood (*a*) as priding himself on being objective and rational and (*b*) as judging himself to be conventional. These two items can be related to the CPI scale for achievement via conformity, on which the early developers scored higher. The early maturer is rated as "power oriented," as "condescending," and as "satisfied with his appearance." The CPI scales indicating dominance and ascendance and the ability to make a good impression are suggested by these variables.

Those who developed late are rated as "initiating humor,"—clearly allied to early adolescent ratings of emotional buoyancy, to the Playfulness (Haan, 1961) and Flexibility scales on the CPI, and to the ego-mechanism rating of playfulness in the service of the ego. His "vulnerability to threat" recalls the frequent appearance of differences between extreme groups in various somatic categories on the psychoneurotic scale.

Reichard's (1961) extensive system of ratings of dynamic- and cognitive-personality variables yielded several plausible relationships. The early maturers are rated as more "moralistic," reflecting the responsible, socialized, conventional syndrome reported for CPI responses.

The "conscious negative identification with mother" of the late developers recalls their adolescent TAT stories of rejection by parents (Mussen & M. C. Jones, 1957). It reflects, also, the lower scores on the CPI Socialization and Social-Control scales on which the late maturing less often checked items pertaining to a happy family life. Finally, the following two differences on the Reichard scale rewarded this search through some 70 items: the early developers are rated as having "premature identity formation," late developers as having "delayed identity formation." This suggests support for the theoretical formulation that accelerated developers escape prematurely into adulthood while the retarded take more time in which to integrate their impulses and capacities.

Discussion of Interview Ratings

The extreme maturity groups are less differentiated by the ratings of intensive interview material from the late 30's than by the observational ratings in adolescence or the self-report inventory scores when the subjects were 33.

These are possible explanations: First, the sample is further attenuated by the lapse of an additional 5 years. Although the shrinking sample seems not to have been qualitatively altered, there are fewer cases for comparison at each extreme. A second possibility is that the additional 5 years of time have erased some of the differences that had persisted from adolescence to the thirty-third year of life when the CPI was administered. One would not expect this to be a major factor in view of the greater stability of life patterns over the 5-year space in the 30's as contrasted with the numerous changes involving war service, occupational choices, and the beginning of family life between the end of high school and the early 30's. A third possibility is that the rating of interviews represents a different methodology than that employed in observational ratings or self-report techniques (Radke-Yarrow, 1963). The explicit purpose of the follow-up interviews was to plumb areas of deeper and more dynamic import than had been possible in the earlier explorations of personality in adolescence. Perhaps in these more theoretically oriented classifications of personality, physical maturity variations have less import, or their influence is less readily discernable through indirect assessment of interview material.

DISCUSSION OF GROUP FINDINGS

What has this study contributed to information or understanding concerning the psychological correlates of maturity status? For the early maturing boys, conclusions do not require an alteration of earlier findings. As a group, early maturing boys have assets that are valued by the peer culture.

The picture continues in adulthood (Jones, 1958; Ames, 1957). Men who matured early describe themselves on the CPI as able to make a good impression, as poised, responsible, achieving in conformity with society's expectations, and as relatively free from neurotic symptoms. They may be somewhat rigid in cognitive processes and in attitudes as contrasted with the average and with the late maturing in this sample.

The boys whose pubescence came late cling to a little-boy type of activity which may be salutary in respect to impulse expression. It is accompanied by more tense and attention-getting behavior in the high-school years.

The CPI measures support the earlier findings (M. C. Jones, 1957) for the late maturers by adding significant differences for some somatic categories on related scales. In addition, the interview ratings suggest that the late maturer has the ability to cope—with humor, with tolerance of ambiguity and of individual idiosyncrasies, with perceptiveness, and with playfulness in the service of the ego. However this adaptability is accompanied by a certain fearfulness and vulnerability to threat.

When growth timing within the adolescent period is considered, differences in maturity at the onset phase are most productive of psychological relationships. However, these behavior differences may not be evident concomitantly with the growth phase but may become increasingly significant and tend to be most pronounced in the later high-school years. A consistently extreme maturity status in adolescence is most promising of predictive value for adult measures.

This is a predominantly urban, middle-class, Western sample. It is not possible to generalize to other classes, times, or climes. The number of cases compared in our extreme groups is small, and there is some overlapping in the various categories. Correlational procedures with the total sample have confirmed the results for extreme groups. But the tentative findings await verification from other populations.

INDIVIDUAL DIFFERENCES

We have been discussing group trends to which not all cases conform. This is obvious when we look at the distribution of scores that contribute to the statistical average.

Late developers score higher on the CPI Psychoneurotic Scale, but the group average for late maturers is very near the average for the total sample. It is the early maturers who show exceptionally low scores. The highest psychoneurotic score is earned by a professor, as is the lowest score among the late developers. These two men are at occupational levels far above their fathers'. The second highest and the second lowest scores of the late maturers belong to men with drinking problems who are among the most downward mobile of our group. How do we generalize from these facts?

More in line with expectations are the scores on the Good Impression Scale. The two highest scores on the Psychoneurotic Scale were made by the same late developers who have the lowest score on the Good Impression

Scale, and vice versa; the lowest psychoneurotic score belongs to the business executive with the highest score on the Good Impression Scale.

Ego-mechanism ratings at age 38 were obtained for tolerance of ambiguity. The highest score was earned by a late maturer, but the next highest belong one each to an early and a late maturer. A professor is one of these. And the business executive with the lowest score, who presumably can make the best impression and has the lowest psychoneurotic score, is rated as the least able to tolerate ambiguity.

To explain scores as different as these we need to consider the complexity of human growth and the multiplicity of factors, cultural and psychological as well as physical, that produce the individual adjustment patterns of late- and early-maturing boys.

REFERENCES

Ames, R. Physical maturing among boys as related to adult social behavior. *Calif. J. educ. Res.*, 1957, **8**, 67–75.

Block, J. A psychoneurotic scale. California personality inventory. Berkeley: Univer. of Calif. Institute of Human Development, 1961. (a)

Block, J. *The Q sort method in personality assessment and psychiatric research.* Springfield, Ill.: Charles C Thomas, 1961. (b)

Edwards, A. A social and economic grouping of the gainful workers of the United States. *J. Amer. statist. Ass.*, 1933, **28**, 377–387.

Eichorn, Dorothy. Biological correlates of behavior. In H. Stevenson (Ed.), *Yearb. nat. Soc. Stud. Educ.*, 1963, Part I, 4–61.

Gough, H. G. *California personality inventory manual.* Palo Alto, Calif.: Consulting Psychologists Pr., 1960.

Haan, Norma. A playfulness scale. California personality inventory. Unpublished manuscript. Berkeley: Institute of Human Development, Univer. of Calif., 1961.

Haan, Norma. Some comparisons of various Oakland growth study sub-samples on selected variables. Unpublished manuscript. Berkeley: Institute of Human Development, Univer. of Calif., 1962.

Haan, Norma. Proposed model of ego functioning: coping and defense mechanisms in relationship to IQ change. *Psychol. Monogr.*, 1963, **77**; No. 8 (Whole No. 571).

Jones, H. E. The California adolescent growth study. *J. educ. Res.*, 1938, **31**, 561–567.

Jones, H. E. *Motor performance and growth.* Berkeley: Univer. of Calif. Pr., 1949.

Jones, H. E., Macfarlane, Jean W., & Eichorn, Dorothy H. A progress report on growth studies at the University of California. *Vita Humana,* 1960, **3**, 17–31.

Jones, Mary C. The later careers of boys who were early- or late-maturing. *Child Develpm.*, 1957, **28**, 113–128.

Jones, Mary C. A study of socialization patterns at the high school level. *J. genet. Psychol.*, 1958, **93**, 87–111.

JONES, MARY C., & BAYLEY, NANCY. Physical maturing among boys as related to behavior. *J. educ. Psychol.,* 1950, **41,** 129–148.

MACFARLANE, JEAN W. Studies in child guidance. I. Methodology of data collection and organization. *Monogr. Soc. Res. Child Develpm.,* 1938, **3,** 254.

MUSSEN, P. H., & JONES, MARY C. Self-conceptions, motivations, and interpersonal attitudes of late- and early-maturing boys. *Child Develpm.,* 1957, **28,** 243–265.

NEWMAN, FRANCES B., & JONES, H. E. The adolescent in social groups. *Appl. Psychol. Monogr.,* 1946, **9,** 94.

NICOLSON, ARLINE B., & HANLEY, C. Indices of physiological maturity: derivation and interrelationships. *Child Develpm.,* 1953, **24,** 3–28.

PESKIN, H. Possible relations of growth and maturity to early psychic experiences. In *Biological Time,* Sympos., Soc. Res. Child Develpm. mtgs., Berkeley, Calif., 1963.

RADKE-YARROW, MARIAN. The elusive evidence. Presidential address given at Amer. Psychol. Ass., Philadelphia, Pa., September, 1963.

REICHARD, SUZANNE. Dynamic and cognitive personality variables. Oakland growth study. Unpublished manuscript. Berkeley: Institute of Human Development, Univer. of Calif., 1961.

STEWART, L. Social and emotional adjustment during adolescence as related to the development of psychosomatic illness in adulthood. *Genet. Psychol. Monogr.,* 1962, **65,** Part I, 175–215.

STOLZ, H. R., & STOLZ, LOIS M. *Somatic development of adolescent boys.* New York: Macmillan Co., 1951.

32
PHYSIQUE AND GROWTH IN ADOLESCENCE*

DONALD M. BROVERMAN
INGE K. BROVERMAN
WILLIAM VOGEL
ROBERT D. PALMER
and
EDWARD L. KLAIBER

The relations between body build and temporal aspects of adolescent development, such as age at onset and termination of puberty, have a long history of investigation. Several investigators (2, 4, 12, 16) have reported that linear, ectomorphic individuals tend to mature later and grow more slowly during adolescence than mesomorphs. Results differing with this consensus, however, have been reported by Livson and McNeill (9) who report no difference between ectomorphs and mesomorphs in rate of adolescent development, and by Reynolds and Wines (11) who found a tendency for ectomorphs to mature sexually earlier than mesomorphs.

A possible reason for this inconclusive state of affairs may lie in the fact that whereas researchers have examined the relation of preadolescent and postadolescent body builds to temporal indices of adolescent growth, they have not typically treated adolescent growth, itself, as a variable to be related to the temporal indices of development. It is possible that the amount and pattern of adolescent growth have different relations to the temporal indices of development than have either pre- or postadolescent body builds. In this case some of the disparity in results noted above might be due to a failure to control for the variable of adolescent growth.

Hence, the goals of the present paper are to examine the interrelations of pre- and postadolescent body dimensions, amount and pattern of growth during adolescence, and temporal aspects of adolescent growth.

---

* From *Child Development*, 1964, *35*, 857–870. Reprinted with permission of the authors and the Society for Research in Child Development.

This study was supported by research grants M-5773 and M-6369 from the National Institute of Mental Health, United States Public Health Service. This work was done in part at the Massachusetts Institute of Technology Computation Center, Cambridge, Massachusetts.

METHOD

Subjects

Ss employed in this study were the 67 males for whom Stolz and Stolz (15) report complete longitudinal growth data. These data have been previously analyzed from other points of view by Bayley (1, 2), Jones and Bayley (6), Jones (5), Livson and McNeill (9), as well as, of course, Stolz and Stolz (15).

Body Dimensions, Growth Scores, and Temporal Indices of Development

Measurements for each *S* on nine body dimensions were taken from the data published by Stolz and Stolz. The nine variables are (*a*) height, (*b*) stem length, (*c*) leg length, (*d*) shoulder breadth, (*e*) hip width, (*f*) subcutaneous tissue, (*g*) thigh circumference, (*h*) weight, and (*i*) strength (dynamometer). Two measurements for each *S* on each of these variables were taken from Stolz and Stolz; one at the onset and one at the end of the puberal growth period for height (Stolz and Stolz's *b* and *d* measurements, respectively). The puberal growth period for height seems to be a good index of the period of adolescent growth in general. Stolz and Stolz (15) have shown that the correlations between the age at the beginning of the adolescent growth period in height and the age at onset of growth in the penis and the testes, which also indicate the onset of puberty, are .87 and .86, respectively. The correlations between the age at the end of the growth period in height and the age at termination of puberal growth in the penis and testes are both .89.

The indices of body growth employed in this study are the differences between the onset (preadolescent) and end (postadolescent) measurements of each of the nine dimensions.

Finally, three temporal indices of development in adolescence were taken from Stolz and Stolz (15): (*a*) age at beginning of puberal growth in height, (*b*) age at end of puberal growth in height, and (*c*) duration in years of the period of puberal growth in height.

Statistical Procedures

The various distributions of data, i.e., the nine preadolescent and the nine postadolescent body dimensions, the nine distributions of growth scores, and the three distributions of temporal indices of development were each transformed into distributions of McCall *T* scores with a mean of 50 and a sigma of 10. This was done (*a*) to normalize all distributions before intercorrelating, and (*b*) to make the various body dimensions additive. Additivity of the body dimensions is required to derive ipsative, or self-reference body dimension scores as discussed below.

Ipsative body dimension scores reflect the relative size of the different parts of the body independent of the absolute size of the body in general. For instance, a generally small individual whose legs tend to be long for his body size would have a large positive ipsative leg length score, while a generally large individual whose legs are short for his body size, would have a large negative ipsative leg length score.

Ipsative scores for the preadolescent body dimensions were obtained by summing the nine body dimension *T* scores for each *S* and dividing by nine to produce the individual's mean body dimension *T* score. The differences between each individual's mean preadolescent body dimension *T* score and each of his nine preadolescent body dimension scores are ipsative scores, i.e., scores reflecting the extent to which a given body dimension deviates from the individual's average body dimension.

Both normative and ipsative correlations (Broverman, 3) were calculated for the various body dimension relations. Normative correlations, i.e., the correlations between the various *T* scores, reflect between-individual relations of body dimensions relative to the group mean.

Ipsative correlations reflect intraindividual relations between body dimensions relative to the individual's mean or general body size. Ipsative correlations seem well suited to the investigation of body build since the concept of body build is, itself, an ipsative concept insofar as it refers to relations between different parts of the body of a given person. These two methods of correlation, normative and ipsative, are supplementary since relations both between and within individuals are being sought in this paper.

RESULTS

Relations between Pre- and Postadolescent Body Dimensions

Each of the nine preadolescent body dimensions was correlated, both normatively and ipsatively, with the corresponding postadolescent body dimension. As may be seen in Table 1, the normative correlations between pre- and postadolescent body dimensions are uniformly high, ranging from .69 to .87 with a mean correlation of .77. Similarly, the ipsative correlations range from .64 to .88 with a mean correlation of .79. Preadolescent body dimensions are highly related then, both normatively and ipsatively, to postadolescent body dimensions.

Relations of Amounts and Pattern of Growth of the Body during Adolescent to Postadolescent Body Dimensions

Correlations were computed, both normatively and ipsatively, between the body growth scores and the postadolescent body dimensions. As shown in

TABLE 1

Relations between Pre- and Postadolescent Body Dimensions

	Normative Correlation	*Ipsative Correlation*
Height	.80***	.77***
Stem length	.73***	.77***
Leg length	.86***	.88***
Shoulder breadth	.81***	.85***
Hip width	.87***	.84***
Subcutaneous tissue	.70***	.74***
Thigh circumference	.77***	.81***
Weight	.73***	.64***
Strength	.69***	.81***

*** $p < .001$.

Table 2, the normative correlations between growth and postadolescent body dimensions are, with one exception, statistically significant and range from .16 to .81 with a mean correlation of .41. The ipsative correlations between growth and postadolescent body dimensions tend to be similar, ranging from .34 to .65 with a mean of .50.

Adolescent growth, then, is significantly related to the postadolescent body dimensions although to a much lesser extent than are the preadolescent body dimensions.

Relations between Preadolescent Body Dimensions and Growth during Adolescence

Interpretation of the relations reported above between the pre- and postadolescent body dimensions, and of the relations reported above between

TABLE 2

Relations between Adolescent Growth and Postadolescent Body Dimensions

	Normative Correlation	*Ipsative Correlation*
Height	.37**	.45***
Stem length	.48***	.47***
Leg length	.32**	.43***
Shoulder breadth	.40**	.34**
Hip width	.28*	.65***
Subcutaneous tissue	.39**	.48***
Thigh circumference	.16	.36**
Weight	.48***	.63***
Strength	.81***	.67***

* $p < .05$.
** $p < .01$.
*** $p < .001$.

adolescent growth and the postadolescent body dimensions, depends upon the relations existing between preadolescent body dimensions and growth. Strong interrelations between preadolescent body dimensions and amount of growth during adolescence would indicate that these two phenomena are different aspects of a single underlying factor determining postadolescent body shape. On the other hand, a lack of strong relations between preadolescent body dimensions and growth would indicate that the two phenomena contribute independently to postadolescent body shape.

The nine normative and the nine ipsative distributions of preadolescent body dimension scores were correlated with the corresponding nine normative and ipsative growth scores.

TABLE 3

Relations between Preadolescent Body Dimensions and Adolescent Growth

	Normative Correlation	*Ipsative Correlation*
Height	−.16	.03
Stem length	−.20	−.06
Leg length	−.16	.04
Shoulder breadth	−.14	−.06
Hip width	−.18	.34**
Subcutaneous tissue	−.39**	−.19
Thigh circumference	−.43***	−.10
Weight	−.19	.02
Strength	.16	.28*

* $p < .05$.
** $p < .01$.
*** $p < .001$.

As shown in Table 3, the normative intercorrelations are, with two exceptions, not statistically significant.

The ipsative correlations between growth and preadolescent body dimensions are also, with two exceptions, not statistically significant.

With but a few exceptions, then, the preadolescent body dimensions are unrelated to amount and pattern of adolescent growth. Hence, it does not seem possible, in general, to predict the amount or pattern of adolescent growth from preadolescent body dimensions.

More important for the purposes of this paper is the fact that preadolescent body dimensions and adolescent growth seem to be two independent variables which summate to produce the postadolescent body dimensions. Accordingly, the relations of each of these variables to temporal aspects of development in adolescence will now be examined.

Relations between Preadolescent Body Dimensions and Temporal Aspects of Development

The nine preadolescent body dimensions were related, both normatively and ipsatively, to the three temporal aspects of development: age at onset of puberal growth in height, age at end of puberal growth in height, and duration of puberal growth in height.

Table 4 indicates a number of significant correlations, both normative and ipsative, between the preadolescent body dimensions and the indices of temporal development.

TABLE 4

Relations between Preadolescent Body Dimensions and Temporal Aspects of Development

	Normative Correlations			*Ipsative Correlations*		
	Age at Onset of Puberty	*Age at End of Puberty*	*Duration of Puberty*	*Age at Onset of Puberty*	*Age at End of Puberty*	*Duration of Puberty*
Height	.13	.10	−.04	.15	.25*	.17
Stem length	−.05	−.13	−.11	−.14	−.13	.06
Leg length	.25*	.18	−.14	.31*	.34**	.01
Shoulder breadth	−.06	−.11	−.10	−.13	−.10	.06
Hip width	.02	−.09	−.16	−.03	−.10	−.03
Subcutaneous tissue	−.21	−.25*	−.05	−.27*	−.23	.11
Thigh circumference	−.10	−.22	−.21	−.19	−.26*	−.10
Weight	.00	−.14	−.23	−.09	−.23	−.20
Strength	.34**	.26*	−.25*	.37**	.37**	−.13

* $p < .05$.
** $p < .01$.

The significant normative correlations indicate that strong, long-legged preadolescents start their puberal growth relatively late; and that strong preadolescents end their puberal growth period late and have a short duration of puberal growth. On the other hand, preadolescents with a large amount of subcutaneous tissue tend to finish their puberal growth relatively early. A similar situation is indicated by the ipsative correlations which show that relatively tall, long-legged individuals with small thighs end their puberty relatively late.

The general pattern suggested by both the normative and ipsative correlations, then, is that linear (that is, relatively tall, long-legged) preadolescents, who presumably are ectomorphic individuals, tend to start and finish their puberal growth period later than nonlinear (that is, relative short, heavily built) individuals. Bayley (2) has reported similar relations in her analysis of these data. This finding is also consistent with the observations of those investigators (4, 12, and 16) who report that ectomorphic individuals tend to be late maturers. The amount of variance accounted for by these relations, however, is rather meager.

Relations between Growth in Adolescence and Temporal Aspects of Development

The nine growth scores were related, both normatively and ipsatively, to the three indices of temporal development in adolescence.

The normative correlations in Table 5 indicate that growth in all body dimensions except subcutaneous tissue are strongly related to duration of the puberal growth period, i.e., the longer an individual's adolescent growth

TABLE 5

Relations between Growth in Adolescence and Temporal Aspects of Development

	Normative Correlations			*Ipsative Correlations*		
	Age at Onset of Puberty	*Age at End of Puberty*	*Duration of Puberty*	*Age at Onset of Puberty*	*Age at End of Puberty*	*Duration of Puberty*
Height	−.48***	−.09	.81***	−.47***	−.27*	.45***
Stem length	−.30*	.03	.71***	−.08	−.02	.20
Leg length	−.59***	−.22	.76***	−.54***	−.42***	.27*
Shoulder breadth	−.43***	−.10	.70***	−.33**	−.27*	.18
Hip width	−.32**	.02	.68***	−.13	−.03	.15
Subcutaneous tissue	.04	.15	.16	.28*	.10	−.42***
Thigh circumference	−.01	.23	.44***	.33**	.26*	−.21
Weight	−.25*	.10	.71***	.00	.14	.28*
Strength	.09	.26*	.37**	.45***	.29*	−.30*

* $p < .05$.
** $p < .01$.
*** $p < .001$.

period the greater his absolute growth during that period. The normative correlations also indicate that the earlier an individual starts his adolescent growth period, the more he grows. On the other hand, there is little relation between amount of adolescent growth and when an individual stops his adolescent growth period. This pattern of relations indicates that while the amount of growth is predominantly a function of the duration of the adolescent period, the age at onset of the puberal growth period is far more important to amount of growth than is the age at termination.

The normative correlations between growth and the temporal indices of development reflect the relations of the increase of each body dimension separately to the temporal indices. The ipsative correlations, on the other hand, reflect the relations of the relative amounts of growth of the various body dimensions to the temporal indices of development. The large number of statistically significant ipsative correlations shown in Table 5 indicate that individuals who grow predominantly in height, leg length, and shoulder breadth tend to start their development early, end their growth period early, and have long puberal growth periods. On the other hand, individuals who grow predominantly in strength, circumference of the thigh, and in subcutaneous tissue tend to start late, finish late, and have short puberal growth periods.

The intraindividual patterns of adolescent growth, then, are strongly related to temporal aspects of development. The general pattern seems to be that individuals who grow predominantly in tissue and muscle during adolescence start puberal growth relatively *late,* whereas individuals whose adolescence is characterized by a predominance of skeletal growth start puberal growth *early*. This pattern of relations, however, tends to oppose the relations existing between preadolescent body dimensions and temporal aspects of development, e.g., long-legged, linear preadolescents tend to start and end their puberal growth period *late*. Thus, whereas preadolescent linearity is associated with late development, a predominance of linear growth during adolescence is associated with early development.

Relations between Postadolescent Body Dimensions and Temporal Aspects of Development

As indicated in the previous section, the preadolescent body dimensions and adolescent growth tend to have opposing relations to the temporal indices of development. The postadolescent body dimensions, however, are determined entirely by the preadolescent body dimensions and adolescent growth. It seems reasonable to argue, therefore, that the correlation between a given postadolescent body dimension and a given temporal index of development is necessarily a compromise resultant of two opposing variables and, as such, must be somewhat less than the larger correlation obtained by either of the two component variables. Inspection of the correlations in Table 6 shows that, in general, this is indeed so. The normative correlations, with the exception of strength, are obviously modal relations between the preadolescent and adolescent growth relations to the temporal indices.

The ipsative correlations in Table 6, again with the exception of strength, fail to produce significant relations. Here, as with the normative correlations, it is obvious that this lack of significant relations is a function of the opposing relations between the preadolescent relations to the temporal indices (which are largely negative) and the growth relations to the temporal indices (which are largely positive).

The correlations between postadolescent body dimensions and the temporal indices of development, then, suggest that the use of the postadolescent body dimensions as criterion variables in investigations of the relations between physical and temporal aspects of development is often undesirable

TABLE 6

Relations between Postadolescent Body Dimensions and Temporal Aspects of Development

	Normative Correlations			*Ipsative Correlations*		
	Age at Onset of Puberty	*Age at End of Puberty*	*Duration of Puberty*	*Age at Onset of Puberty*	*Age at End of Puberty*	*Duration of Puberty*
Height	−.15	.00	.33***	−.07	.02	.20
Stem length	−.27*	−.10	.37***	−.22	−.12	.23
Leg length	−.03	.10	.26*	.10	.15	.08
Shoulder breadth	−.27*	−.14	.27*	−.22	−.17	.08
Hip width	−.12	−.09	.10	−.02	−.12	−.16
Subcutaneous tissue	−.18	−.14	.08	−.07	−.12	−.13
Thigh circumference	−.08	−.04	.11	.04	−.03	−.13
Weight	−.15	−.05	.23	−.09	−.08	.04
Strength	.28*	.35*	.11	.46***	.42***	−.11

* $p < .05$.
*** $p < .001$.

since this practice may conceal otherwise significant and meaningful correlations existing between the two components of postadolescent body dimensions (preadolescent body dimensions and adolescent growth) and temporal aspects of development.

DISCUSSION

The conflicting results in the literature concerning the relation of body build to the temporal indices of development may be a function of the fact that preadolescent body build and growth during adolescence have opposite patterns of relations to the temporal indices of development.

The preadolescent body dimensions were found to be much more consistently related to the postadolescent body dimensions than were the indices of adolescent growth. That preadolescent body dimensions contribute heavily to adult or postadolescent body dimensions in absolute terms as well as correlatively is reflected by the following percentages: The means of preadolescent height, stem length, shoulder breadth, and hip width (five skeletal measures) range from 86 to 89 percent of the respective postadolescent measures. The mean of postadolescent subcutaneous tissue is 91 percent of that preadolescent measure (a net loss of subcutaneous tissue occurs during adolescence); and the mean preadolescent thigh circumference is 89 percent of the mean postadolescent thigh circumference. The means for preadolescent weight and strength are 69 and 60 percent of the respective postadolescent measures. These percentages indicate, with the notable exceptions of weight and strength, that the postadolescent body dimensions are predominantly a function of the preadolescent body dimensions. The above percentages also indicate that the adolescent growth spurt contributes, in absolute terms, relatively little to the postadolescent skeletal dimensions, and only moderately to weight and strength. While the relation of preadolescent to postadolescent body dimensions has previously been noted (McNeill and Livson, 10; Tanner, 16) the amount which preadolescent body dimensions contribute to postadolescent body dimensions does not seem to have been emphasized.

That preadolescent body build should be the main component of postadolescent body build with the adolescent growth spurt contributing less strongly to postadolescent body build is not too surprising when the relative lengths in time of these two processes are considered: preadolescence lasts from 11 to 15 years; the adolescent growth spurt lasts 2 to 4 years.

This study indicates, however, that preadolescent body build, the main component of postadolescent body build, is but weakly related to the temporal indices of development; whereas adolescent growth, a relatively minor component of postadolescent build, is strongly related to the temporal indices of development.

The preadolescent body dimensions and adolescent growth, however, have opposing relations to the temporal indices of development, e.g., whereas linear preadolescents start their puberal growth *late,* individuals who grow predominantly in a linear manner during adolescence start their adolescent growth *early*. Since the preadolescent body dimensions and adolescent growth are summated to produce the postadolescent body dimensions, these opposing relations tend to cancel each other when the postadolescent body dimensions are related to the temporal indices of development. In view of this, it is easy to imagine how variations in the contribution of these two factors to postadolescent body dimensions in different samples could induce unstable relations of postadolescent body build to temporal aspects of development.

The findings reported in this study may also be understood in terms of the biological events which occur prior to and during adolescence. Physical maturity can be assessed in terms of skeletal age, i.e., the degree to which bone epiphyses are calcified or united. As long as the bone epiphyses remain uncalcified, or open, a potential for future bone growth exists. Conversely, when the bone epiphyses are fully calcified or closed, no further potential for bone growth remains and skeletal maturity is said to have been reached. Calcification or closure of the bone epiphyses is thought to be a function of the various bone growth inducing hormones, i.e., pituitary growth hormone, thyroid, estrogens, and androgens. Pituitary growth hormone and thyroid are primarily responsible for bone growth and skeletal aging in childhood since androgens and estrogens are not produced in quantity until the onset of adolescence. Androgens and estrogens, on the other hand, are thought to be primarily responsible for the increased rate of bone growth and epiphyseal closure during adolescence. In general, then, bone growth over time in normal individuals is associated with increased skeletal age.

The finding that persons who start adolescent growth early show a large amount of skeletal growth in adolescence may be interpreted within this concept of bone growth. Since skeletal age tends to advance throughout the preadolescent years, the earlier an individual begins his adolescence the less should his skeletal age tend to be at that time, and, therefore, the greater should his potential for future bone growth be. We would expect, then, as the data indicate, that individuals who mature early should grow more skeletally in adolescence than late maturers.

The discussion to this point suggests that a relation should exist between the amount of preadolescent bone growth in normal individuals, and bone growth during adolescence (i.e., the greater the preadolescent bone growth, the more advanced should the individual's skeletal age be, and, therefore, the less potential for future bone growth in adolescence should there be). The results of this study, however, show an absence of significant correlations between preadolescent body dimensions and adolescent growth. This difficulty may be due to the following considerations. Although certain of the preadolescent body dimensions are significantly related, statistically, to the duration of childhood growth (as measured by onset of puberty, Table 4) the amount of variance accounted for by the significant correlations is small (approximately 10 percent on the average). Obviously, the rate and pattern of growth in childhood are powerfully influenced by factors other than duration of growth.

Two factors, then, should affect an individual's skeletal age at the time of onset of adolescence, and, therefore, bone growth in adolescence: (*a*) the amount of bone growth completed prior to adolescence due to differing rates of bone growth, and (*b*) the age at which puberty begins. In this case, it is possible that one factor is obscuring the other when these relations are assessed by simple correlational techniques. A more appropriate method of testing for the effects of these two factors on bone growth during adolescence would be to compare long-boned early maturers to short-boned early maturers, and long-boned late maturers to short-boned late maturers, etc., in an analysis of variance design. The results of such an analysis on length of the leg are reported in Table 7. As may be seen, a large statistically significant effect ($p < .001$), occurs between the age at which puberty begins and the amount of adolescent leg-bone growth (early maturers grow more than late maturers). This phenomenon was previously observed in the correlational analysis. Table 7 indicates, however, as theoretically expected, that a significant relation also exists between preadolescent leg length and the amount of leg growth during adolescence. Long-legged preadolescents grow less during adolescence than short-legged preadolescents. This effect becomes discernable, however, only after the much more powerful influence of age at onset of puberty is controlled. Thus, the results shown in Table 7 are consistent with the expectations derived from the biological understanding of bone growth. Stolz and Stolz (15) reached a similar conclusion by observing a —.34 correlation between preadolescent leg length and gain in adolescence expressed as a percentage of preadolescent leg length.

TABLE 7

Analysis of Variance for Growth of the Leg in Adolescence

Source of Variation	*df*	*Mean Square*	*F*	*p*
Late v. early matures (A)	1	9455.63	26.67	<.001
Long-legged v. short-legged preadolescents (B)	1	1500.63	4.23	<.05
Interaction: A × B	1	5.62	.02	
Pooled individuals	36	354.51		
Total	39			

	Mean (mm.)
Late maturers (N = 20)	84.75
Early maturers (N = 20)	115.50
Long-legged preadolescents (N = 20)	94.00
Short-legged preadolescents (N = 20)	106.25
Late-maturing, long-legged preadolescents (N = 10)	79.00
Late-maturing, short-legged preadolescents (N = 10)	90.50
Early-maturing, long-legged preadolescents (N = 10)	109.00
Early-maturing, short-legged preadolescents (N = 10)	122.00

NOTE.—N = 40. Subjects were dichotomized into late v. early maturers and long- v. short-legged preadolescents. Since preadolescent leg length is significantly related to age at onset of puberty (see Table 4), only ten subjects could be classified as long-legged, early maturers. The need for proportionality between cells (Lindquist, 5) required that no more than ten subjects be in the remaining three cells. Subjects closest to the cutting points of the two variables were eliminated in the three cells with surplus subjects.

It might be noted that the key point of the above discussion with respect to the temporal aspects of skeletal growth is the *beginning* rather than the *end* of the adolescent spurt. It is the beginning of adolescence which determines how much bone growth potential remains when the individual starts his adolescent growth spurt. This same emphasis is indicated by the statistical results: Table 5 indicates that the earlier the onset of puberty the more skeletal growth takes place, but no relation exists between the end of puberty and skeletal growth.

It should also be noted that five of the six significant (positive) normative correlations between amount of growth and the age at onset of puberty are bone or skeletal measures. The age at onset of puberal growth in height is apparently not associated with extent of growth of subcutaneous fat, thigh circumference, or muscle (strength). This is interesting since while late adolescence implies reduced bone growth potential, it does not imply reduced muscle or tissue growth potential. Hence, normatively, there is no relation between age at onset of adolescence and muscle growth. Ipsatively, however, a relation does occur. This is reasonable, since if bone growth is reduced, but not muscle or tissue, a predominance of muscle and tissue growth would occur with late adolescence.

Finally, the findings of this paper have major implications for investigations of relations between body dimensions and personality traits. For instance, considerable effort has gone into attempts to relate postadolescent body dimensions to personality variables (Sheldon, 13; Kretschmer, 7). This study suggests, however, that the main component of the postadolescent body dimensions are the preadolescent body dimensions. Accordingly, the above studies would seem to bear mainly on phenomena which are preadolescent in origin. It is not unreasonable, however, to suspect that the pattern of adolescent growth may also be associated with personality functions. Effects on personality of androgens, the hormones primarily responsible for the adolescent growth spurt, have been described by Simpson (14). Hence, adolescent growth, independent of body build, might prove a worthwhile phenomenon to relate to behavioral variables.

REFERENCES

1. Bayley, N. Skeletal maturing in adolescence as a basis for determining percentage of completed growth. *Child Develpm.,* 1943, 14, 1–46.
2. Bayley, N. Size and body build of adolescents in relation to rate of skeletal maturing. *Child Develpm.,* 1943, 14, 47–90.
3. Broverman, D. M. Normative and ipsative measurement in psychology. *Psychol. Rev.,* 1962, 69, 295–305.
4. Dupertuis, C. W., & Michael, N. B. Comparison of growth in height and weight between ectomorphic and mesomorphic boys. *Child Develpm.,* 1953, 31, 203–214.
5. Jones, M. C. The later careers of boys who were early or late maturing. *Child Develpm.,* 1957, 28, 113–128.
6. Jones, M. C., & Bayley, N. Physical maturing among boys as related to behavior. *J. educ. Psychol.,* 1950, 41, 129–148.
7. Kretschmer, E. *Physique and character.* London: Kegan, Paul, Trench, Tubner, 1925.
8. Lindquist, E. F. *Design and analysis of experiments.* Houghton Mifflin, 1953.
9. Livson, N., & McNeill, D. Physique and maturation rate in male adolescents. *Child Develpm.,* 1962, 33, 145–152.
10. McNeill, D., & Livson, N. Maturation rate and body build in women. *Child Develpm.,* 1963, 34, 25–32.
11. Reynolds, E. L., & Wines, J. V. Physical changes associated with adolescence in boys. *Amer. J. Dis. Child.,* 1951, 82, 529–597.
12. Richey, H. G. The relation of accelerated, normal, and retarded puberty to the height and weight of school children. *Monogr. Soc. Res. Child Develpm.,* 1937, 2, No. 1 (Serial No. 8).
13. Sheldon, W. H. *The varieties of human physique.* Harper, 1940.
14. Simpson, S. L. Hormones and behavior patterns. *British med. J.,* 1957, 2, 839–843.
15. Stolz, H. R., & Stolz, L. M. *Somatic development of adolescent boys. A study of the growth of boys during the second decade of life.* Macmillan, 1951.
16. Tanner, J. M. *Growth in adolescence.* Thomas, 1955.

33

ADOLESCENT CHOICES AND PARENT-PEER CROSS-PRESSURES*

CLAY V. BRITTAIN

As THEY are commonly portrayed, adolescents confronted with parent-peer cross-pressures tend to opt in favor of the peer-group. But to what extent and under what circumstances does this image square with reality?[1] Does the tendency toward peer-conformity vary as a function of the type of choice to be made by the adolescent?

The concept of reference group is useful in attacking this problem. Following Shibutani's[2] formulation that a reference group is one whose perspective constitutes the frame of reference of the actor, both peers and parents might be thought of as reference groups; i.e., as groups each provides perspectives in terms of which adolescents make choices. Does the extent to which adolescents tend to adopt these different perspectives vary systematically across situations? We hypothesized that in making certain kinds of choices, adolescents are inclined to follow peers rather than parents; in making certain other types of choices, the opposite is true.

PROCEDURE

Situations involving conflict between parent-peer expectations were described to the subjects—girls in grades 9 through 11. Each situation was

* From *American Sociological Review,* 1963, *28,* 385–391. Reprinted with permission from the author and the American Sociological Association.

The writer gratefully acknowledges the guidance of Professors Robert D. Hess, Jacob W. Getzels, and Robert J. Havighurst.

[1] There is controversy about the legitimacy of this image. For contrasting views see Frederick Elkin and William A. Westley, "The Myth of the Adolescent Peer Culture," *American Sociological Review,* 20 (December, 1955) pp. 680–684; and James S. Coleman, *The Adolescent Society,* New York: The Free Press, 1961, Ch. 1.

[2] Tamotsu Shibutani, "Reference Groups as Perspectives," *American Journal of Sociology,* 60 (May, 1955), pp. 562–569.

structured around an adolescent girl who was trying to choose between two alternatives, one of which was favored by her parents and the other by her friends. The following item illustrates the procedure:

A large glass in the front door of the high school was broken. Jim broke the glass. But both he and Bill were seen at the school the afternoon the glass was broken and both are suspected. Bill and Jim are friends and they agree to deny that they know anything about the broken glass. As a result, the principal pins the blame on both of them. Nell is the only other person who knows who broke the glass. She was working in the typing room that afternoon. She didn't actually see the glass broken, but she heard the noise and saw Jim walking away from the door a few moments later. Nell is very much undecided what to do. The three girls she goes around with most of the time don't think Nell should tell the principal. These girls hate to see an innocent person punished. But they point out to Nell that this is a matter between Jim and Bill and between Jim and his conscience. Nell talks the matter over with her mother and father. They felt that Jim is unfairly using Bill in order to lighten his own punishment. Her parents think Nell should tell the principal who broke the glass.

Can you guess what Nell did when the principal asked her if she saw who broke the glass?

She told him that she didn't see it broken.

She told him who broke the glass.[3]

Two versions of 12 items each were constructed to make up two forms (A and B) of the present instrument, which will be called the Cross-Pressures Test, or CPT. The two forms were identical in all respects except for the opinions and preferences attributed to parents and friends. These were reversed from one form to the other. The parent-favored alternatives on Form A were the peer-favored alternatives on Form B, and vice versa.[4] The instructions accompanying the CPT were:

The following stories are about young people like your friends and the people you know. These people are in situations where they are not sure what to do. We would like to have you read each story carefully and tell us which one of the two things the person in the story is more likely to do. Do *not* tell us what the person should do, but what she is *likely* to really do. We hope you will enjoy doing this.

The CPT was administered to an experimental group and a small control group. The experimental group responded to one form and then to the

---

[3] Item number 4 on the instrument used in the study.

[4] The alternate version of the item given above read as follows: "The three girls she goes around with most of the time feel that Jim is unfairly using Bill in order to lighten his own punishment. They think that Nell should tell the principal who broke the glass. Nell talks the matter over with her mother and father. They don't think Nell should tell the principal. Nell's parents hate to see an innocent person punished. But her father points out to Nell that this is a matter between Jim and Bill and between Jim and his conscience." There are obviously many situations for which this type of reversal would not be plausible.

other; the control responded twice to the same form. Both were divided into subgroups and tested as follows:

	First Testing	*Second Testing*
Experimental Group:		
Group AB..........	Form A	Form B
Group BA..........	Form B	Form A
Control group:		
Group A...........	Form A	Form A
Group B...........	Form B	Form B

One to two weeks intervened between the testing dates. The subjects were not told that they were to be tested a second time.

As can be seen from the specimen item, the dilemmas described on the CPT were double-barrelled (as well as double-horned). There is the dilemma embodied in the content of the alternatives (e.g., telling who broke the glass in the door of the high school versus not telling; or going steady with a boy having certain personal qualities versus going steady with a boy having other personal qualities), and, on top of this, the dilemma posed by the cross-pressures from parents and friends. The subjects could respond to either dilemma or to both. We anticipated that they would respond to both; i.e., the tendency to choose the parent-favored or the peer-favored alternative would depend upon what the dilemma was about. Hence, there would be marked inter-item variation in the frequency of parent-conforming and peer-conforming choices.

The experimental group data were analyzed for differential preferences for the parent-favored and peer-favored alternatives. In response to each item there were three possibilities: (1) The subject, responding to the content of the dilemma, chooses the same content alternative on both forms of the CPT. (2) The peer-favored alternative is selected on both forms. (3) The parent-favored alternative is selected on both forms. In event of 2 or 3, the choice of content alternative shifts from the first testing to the second. The data, then, were analyzed for shifts in choice of content alternatives from one form of the CPT to the other.[5] The control group was used to help establish that the shifts in the experimental group were due to differences in the forms of the test and not simply to the tendency to respond randomly.

Items on which peer-conforming response shifts were more frequent and those on which parent-conforming shifts were more frequent were identified. From the content of these items inferences were drawn about the bases of preferences for peer-favored and parent-favored alternatives.

Following the second testing, 42 girls in grades 9 and 10 were individually

[5] Biases toward parent-favored or peer-favored alternatives showed up also as differences in first test responses between experimental subgroups AB and BA. A comparison of these groups, not reported here, reveals substantially the same trends as shown in the present analysis.

interviewed.[6] The interview data help to clarify the above analysis of responses to the CPT.[7]

SUBJECTS

The subjects were girls[8] from high schools in Alabama and Georgia. The 280 girls in the experimental group came from an urban high school, a high school in a small city, and three small rural high schools. Analysis of the data did not reveal any rural-urban differences. The 58 control respondents were from a high school in a small town and a rural high school.

RESULTS

Comparison of the experimental and control groups indicates that the findings reported below were not due to the tendency to respond randomly, but that changes in form did elicit changes in choice of content alternatives. The data are given in Table 1. On item one, for example, 23 per cent of the

TABLE 1

Proportion of Control Group and Experimental Group Shifting Responses

Item	*Experimental Group* $N = 280$	*Control Group* $N = 58$	*Difference* $P_E - P_C$	*Chi Square*†
1. Which course to take in school	.52	.23	.29	15.60**
2. Which boy to go steady with	.50	.28	.22	12.71**
3. How to get selected for a school honor	.33	.28	.05	.94
4. Whether to report boy who damaged school property	.35	.14	.21	13.57**
5. Whether to enter beauty contest or be cheerleader	.44	.16	.28	22.52**
6. How to dress for football game and party	.51	.19	.32	26.42**
7. Whether to be beauty contestant or appear on TV program	.39	.14	.25	18.56**
8. Which dress to buy	.58	.19	.39	39.39**
9. Which one of two boys to date	.49	.16	.33	29.00**
10. Which part-time job to take	.34	.16	.18	10.66*
11. Whether to report adult who damaged public property	.38	.19	.19	10.23*
12. How to let boy know she is willing to date him	.36	.21	.15	6.66*

† Chi square computed from frequencies. df = 1, * $p < .1$ ** $p < .001$.

[6] Both the interviewing and the testing were done by the writer.

[7] Sociometric data were collected in one of the schools included in the study, but only brief reference is made to them in this study.

[8] This imposes an important qualification in generalizing the findings. If a sample of adolescent boys were studied in similar manner, the findings would undoubtedly diverge at some points from those presented here.

control subjects, who responded twice to the same form, shifted content alternatives from the first testing to the second as compared to 52 per cent in the experimental group. On each of the 12 items, shifts in choice of content alternative occur more frequently in the experimental group. On 11 of the items the experimental-control differences were significant at the .01 level or better.

An analysis of the experimental group data is given in Table 2. The

TABLE 2

Frequency of Shifts in Choice of Content Alternatives from One Form to the Other

Item	*Not Shifting Content Alternatives (NS)*	*Shifting Content Alternatives* Total (S)	*Alternative Selected* Parent(P)	Peer(F)	*Chi Square†*
1. Which course to take in school	135	145	48	97	16.56***
2. Which boy to go steady with	141	139	70	69	.01
3. How to get selected for a school honor	187	93	63	30	11.70***
4. Whether to report boy who damaged school property	182	98	58	40	3.30
5. Whether to enter beauty contest or be cheerleader	156	124	93	31	28.26***
6. How to dress for football game and party	138	142	47	95	16.22***
7. Whether to be beauty contestant or appear on TV program	170	110	83	27	31.00***
8. Which dress to buy	118	162	59	103	11.92***
9. Which one of two boys to date	143	137	81	56	4.56*
10. Which part-time job to take	184	96	69	27	18.37***
11. Whether to report adult who damaged public property	174	106	73	33	15.09***
12. How to let boy know she is willing to date him	180	100	64	36	(7.84)**
Column totals	1908	1452	808	644	—

† Chi square for differences between columns P and F computed on the basis of 50/50 assumption. df = 1. * $p < .05$; ** $p < .01$; *** $p < .001$.

responses to each item were first broken down in terms of the following two categories: (1) The choice of content alternatives did not shift from one form to the other. (2) The content choice did shift; i.e., the peer-favored or parent-favored alternative was consistently chosen. (See colums NS and S.) The second category was then broken down into peer-conforming and parent-conforming choices. (See columns P and F.) As can be seen from this break-down, items 1, 6, and 8 tended more strongly to elicit peer-conforming choices; items 3, 4, 5, 7, 9, 11, and 12 tended to elicit parent-conforming choices. All of these differences except that for item 4 are significant at the

.05 level or better. Parent-conforming and peer-conforming choices were distributed equally on item 2.

Before interpreting these findings, note the following observations. They suggest the results were not dictated simply by the method.

(1) The subjects responded naively. Of the 42 girls individually interviewed soon after the second testing, only two were able to tell how the two forms of the CPT differed.

(2) Responding to the CPT seemed to be accompanied by anxiety. In informal group discussions immediately following the second testing there were expressions of irritability at having to make the choices called for. This suggests that the subjects did tend to become emotionally involved in the hypothetical situations themselves.

(3) Groups of subjects differentiated on the basis of their responses to the CPT were also differentiated on the basis of sociometric data. For example, subjects who most frequently chose peer-favored alternatives tended not to be well accepted by their peers.

(4) At least some of the response trends were consistent with what informal observation of adolescent behavior would lead one to expect. For example, choices relating to dress were especially likely to be peer-conforming.

DISCUSSION

The findings, as reported in Table 2, are consistent with the hypothesis that responses of adolescents to parent-peer cross-pressures are a function of the content of the alternatives and that peer-conformity in adolescence, rather than being diffuse, tends to vary systematically across situations. The response variation across items supports the hypothesis.

More specific interpretations of the response trends are now in order. Why were the peer-favored alternatives more commonly selected in response to some of the hypothetical situations and parent-favored alternatives in response to others? This question relates to the more general problem of understanding the processes involved in coming to terms with conflicting pressures, which, as Merton[9] has pointed out, is salient for reference group theory.

From the content of the hypothetical dilemmas, viewed against the response trends shown in Table 2, the following hypotheses are offered:

1. The responses reflect the adolescent's perception of peers and parents as competent guides in different areas of judgment.

The general social orientation of adolescents is of a dual character. Choices tend to derive meaning from either of two general reference groups, or both: the peer society in which many status and identity needs are

---

[9] Robert K. Merton, *Social Theory and Social Structure*. Revised and Enlarged Edition, New York: The Free Press, 1957, p. 244.

gratified, and the larger society in which the status positions which one can aspire to as an adult are found. When choices pertain to the latter, parents are perceived as the more competent guides. In response to the hypothetical situation involving choice of part-time jobs (item 10), for example, preferences commonly were for the parent-favored rather than the peer-favored alternatives.

2. The responses reflect concern to avoid being noticeably different from peers. Two of the items to which responses showed clearcut peer-conforming trends involved a choice of dress; i.e., item 6—how to dress for a football game and party, and item 8—which one of two dresses to buy.

3. The responses reflect concern about separation from friends. Peer-conforming choices were predominant in response to item 1—which one of two courses to take in school, where the consequence of a peer-defying choice would have been some degree of separation from friends.[10]

4. A fourth hypothesis overlapping but different from those above is that the choices reflect perceived similarities and differences between self and peers and self and parents. Adolescents, for example, perceiving themselves to be more like peers in regard to tastes in clothes and in regard to feelings about school, find peer-favored alternatives in these areas psychologically closer and more acceptable. But in other areas the greater perceived similarity is between self and parents. For example, with respect to values involved in the difficult choice whether to report a person who has destroyed property (items 4 and 11), the parent-favored alternatives are closer and more acceptable.[11]

The interviews referred to above provided a source for further inferences. According to one hypothesis derived from the interview data, responses to the CPT were a function of the perceived difficulty of the content choices. Parent-conformity was more prevalent in response to dilemmas posing what were perceived to be the more difficult choices. The 42 subjects interviewed soon after the second testing were asked to rank the content choices according to difficulty. The items from the CPT, with the parent-versus-peer aspect deleted, were typed on small cards; the subjects were asked to select from among them, first the situation in which the girl would have the greatest difficulty making up her mind, then the situation in which she would have the least difficulty. This was repeated until the choices were ordered from most to least difficult. Median ranks were computed. The items eliciting predominantly peer-conforming trends fell at the least difficult end of the resulting rank order. Hence, the tendency toward parent-conformity was directly related to the perceived difficulty of the choice.

A second inference was suggested by a discrepancy between the interview

---

[10] An example identical on both forms concerned which one of two high schools to attend. Responses to it were predominantly peer-conforming.

[11] This hypothesis holds, in effect, that there is a close interrelationship between what Merton refers to as normative type and comparison type reference groups, Merton, op. cit., p. 283.

data and CPT responses. Interviewees were asked to select from among the content dilemmas, as presented on the cards, the two about which a girl would most likely talk to her friends rather than her parents. Neither of the two items most frequently selected had elicited predominantly peer-conforming CPT response shifts. Choices in response to one of them (item 9—which one of two boys to date) were more frequently parent-conforming; while in response to the other (item 2—which one of two boys to go steady with) parent-conforming and peer-conforming choices were equally frequent. No such discrepancy was found when the girls were asked to select the two dilemmas about which a girl was most likely to talk to her parents rather than her friends. The three items most commonly selected (i.e., 4, 10, and 11) had all elicited predominantly parent-conforming response shifts.

This divergence of interview and test data may indicate that the latter lead to an overestimate of parent-conformity. But it also suggests a device used by adolescents in coping with parent-peer cross-pressures, namely, avoiding communication with parents. This would be likely to occur in areas in which parent-peer conflict is most acute. If this is the case, such discrepancies as those reported here could be used to identify points at which adolescents tend to be most disturbed by cross-pressures from parents and peers.

Let me note one other aspect of the data. Despite the greater overall incidence of parent-conformity, there was greater convergence relative to peer-conforming choices. As shown in Table 2, a majority of the items elicited a preponderance of parent-conforming over peer-conforming choices. On each of the items where there was a reversal of this trend (i.e., items 1, 6, and 8) there were, however, more peer-conforming choices than parent-conforming choices on any single item. This suggests the following possibility: Analogous trends in the social behavior of adolescents create the impression that peer-conformity in adolescence is more diffuse than actually is the case. Lack of parent-adolescent communication about certain types of choices contributes to this impression.

SUMMARY AND FURTHER APPLICATIONS

The study explored the hypothesis, suggested by reference-group theory, that adolescent choices in response to parent-peer cross-pressures are dependent upon the character of the content alternatives presented. Hypothetical dilemmas were described to adolescent girls. In each dilemma a girl was confronted with a complex choice where one course of action was favored by parents and another by peers. The respondents were asked in each case to indicate what the girl would probably do. With the situations remaining otherwise unchanged, peer-favored and parent-favored alternatives were interchanged and the hypothetical dilemmas again presented to the respondents. Comparison of responses to the two forms of the test revealed that peer-conforming choices were more prevalent in response to certain of the dilemmas and parent-conforming choices in response to others. These results were taken to support the hypothesis.

The content of the items suggested additional specific hypotheses as partial explanations of the trends toward peer-conforming and parent-conforming responses: (1) The responses reflect the adolescent's perception of peer and parents as competent guides in different areas of judgement. (2) The responses reflect a concern to avoid being noticeably different from peers. (3) The responses reflect concern about separation from peers. (4) The choices reflect perceived similarities and differences between self and peers and self and parents.

Additional data were collected by interviewing a number of the respondents. From the interview data and from discrepancies between test and interview it was hypothesized that: (1) The tendency toward parent-conformity is directly related to the perceived difficulty of the choices. (2) Adolescents attempt to come to terms with parent-peer cross-pressures by simply not communicating with parents.

The present study argues the value of the approch exemplified here in exploring an important facet of adolescence. What considerations predispose adolescents toward peer-conformity in situations where they are confronted with parent-peer cross-pressures? What are the persisting cognitive schemata against which choices in such situations are made? We believe that through applications of the present method or adaptations of it, hypotheses relating to these questions could be investigated. For example:

1. Stability of social values: Adolescents are more strongly given to peer-conformity in making choices in areas in which social values are changing rapidly, than making choices in areas in which social values are relatively stable.

2. Time perspective: Adolescents are more strongly disposed toward peer-conformity in making choices where immediate consequences are anticipated than in making choices where the emphasis is on long term effects.

In addition, the present procedure might be used to assess individual differences in predispositions toward peer-versus parent-conformity. Although the study did not deal with the problem, the subjects were found to differ from one another in their tendencies to make parent-conforming or peer-conforming choices. At the extremes four groups were identified: (1) subjects manifesting relatively strong tendencies toward parent-conformity; (2) subjects manifesting relatively strong tendencies toward peer-conformity; (3) a mixed-conformity group composed of subjects making parent-conforming choices and peer-conforming choices with relatively great and about equal frequency; and (4) subjects making very few responses of either type; i.e., subjects whose responses were mostly consistent by content. The stability of these response biases and their possible correlates remain a problem for further study.

34

RELATION OF CHILDHOOD INTELLIGENCE, MATERNAL BEHAVIORS, AND SOCIAL CLASS TO BEHAVIOR DURING ADOLESCENCE*

JEROME KAGAN
and
MARION FREEMAN

A CHILD'S SCORE on the Stanford-Binet Intelligence Test, especially when it falls within the range 85 to 130, is moderately correlated with the educational level of his parents and is a moderately good predictor of degree of future involvement in intellectual mastery (3, 4, 6, 7). Since the IQ score is the result of a representative sampling of the culture's definition of mental skills, we might expect it to be moderately predictive of degree of future mastery of intellectual tasks.

In an earlier investigation (7) it was found that the degree of involvement in intellectual mastery during childhood (ages 3 to 10) was correlated with degree of involvement during adolescence and adulthood. Moreover, the behavioral correlates of intellectual mastery were different for boys and girls. More specifically, high mastery girls showed a greater rejection of traditional sex typed interests than high mastery boys, and these high mastery girls had mothers who were highly critical of them during early childhood.

The present paper presents some additional data on an independent group of 30 males and 20 females that support the findings of this earlier and more extensive investigation. In brief, this report summarizes the relations among four sets of variables: (*a*) child's IQ at 3½, 5½, and 9 years of age, (*b*) parental educational level, (*c*) maternal childrearing practices during ages 2 through 7, and (*d*) selected aspects of child's personality during adolescence.

* From *Child Development,* 1963, *34,* 899–911. Reprinted with permission from the authors and the Society for Research in Child Development.

This research was supported, in part, by research grants M-4464 and M-1260 from the National Institute of Mental Health, United States Public Health Service.

METHOD

Subjects

The subjects were 30 boys and 20 girls from the Fels Research Institute's longitudinal population. Their ages at the time of the study ranged from 13–0 to 18–3 with a median age of 15–0.

Procedure

Adolescent Interview. Each *S* was interviewed by one of us (MF). The interview was tape recorded with the *S*'s knowledge and followed a standard question schedule. Following the interview, which lasted about an hour, the interviewer rated the child on a series of variables (7-point scale). The variables to be discussed in this report follow:

1. Importance of intellectual mastery
2. Masculine interests and activities
3. Feminine interests and activities
4. Dependence upon mother
5. Dependence upon father
6. Withdrawal from task mastery
7. Withdrawal from social contact
8. Withdrawal to attack by others
9. Conformity to adult demands
10. Popularity with same sex peers
11. Heterosexual activity (erotic behavior)

Detailed definitions of these variables have been presented in an earlier report (7). A student[1] listened to the tape recordings of each interview and made an independent set of ratings for the above 11 variables. The average reliability coefficient was .85, and the coefficients ranged from .70 to .93, indicating that these variables have an acceptable degree of interrater reliability.

Adolescent Self-Rating Scale. Following the interview, each child was asked to fill out a 110-item self-rating scale (scale points 1 to 4) describing his traits and attitudes. A complete description of the scale and its predictive validity appear in an earlier report (7). The inventory contained eight subscales that are relevant to this report. These eight scales have been labeled: aggressive behavior, admission of hostile feelings, dependency, anxiety over sexuality, affiliative needs, compulsivity, status strivings, and anxiety over physical harm.

---

[1] The authors express their gratitude to Miriam Young for the independent ratings of the adolescent interviews.

Maternal Childrearing Practices. The mothers of these children had been observed in their homes by a social worker or psychologist when the children were between 2 and 7 years of age, and the Fels Parent Behavior Ratings were made following the visit to the home. Typically each mother was observed twice a year and each visit lasted 3 to 4 hours. The span from 2 to 7 was divided into two age periods—age 2–0 through 4–0 and 4–1 through 7–0—and the ratings made during each of these two periods were averaged for each of 10 maternal variables. The maternal behavior rating variables used were: restrictiveness, severity of discipline, justification of discipline, coerciveness, acceleration, babying, protectiveness, criticism, acceptance, and affection. The interrater reliabilities for these variables are also in the eighties, and interested readers can consult several publications for detailed descriptions of these variables (1, 2, 5). These parent behavior ratings were unknown to the interviewer at the time of the adolescent interview.

TABLE 1

Distribution of Educational Level of Parents of Children (numbers refer to per cent of group)

	Boys		*Girls*	
Educational Level	*Mother*	*Father*	*Mother*	*Father*
Part high school	.0	13.3	5.0	15.0
High school graduate	20.0	13.3	25.0	10.0
Part college	40.0	16.7	30.0	30.0
College graduate	33.3	53.4	40.0	35.0
Post graduate	6.7	3.3	.0	10.0

Parental Education. The formal educational level of each parent was assigned a discrete value (1 to 6) depending on years of formal schooling. The scale points were: 8 years or less, part high school, high school graduate, part college, college graduate, and post graduate training. Table 1 presents the distribution of educational levels for the parents of these children.

The distribution of educational levels indicates that about 25 per cent of the children had parents who did not attend college, whereas the majority of the group had parents with some college training. This sample, therefore, is predominantly middle class. There were no significant sex differences for either range or mean educational attainment.

Child's IQ Scores. Each *S* had been administered the Stanford-Binet Scale (Form L or Form M) by the same female examiner[2] at ages 3½, 5½, and 9. These children had also received the Binet at age 4½, 7, and 8, but we arbitrarily selected scores at these three ages for analysis. The IQ scores ranged from 89 to 158, with mean IQ scores of 125 and 119 for boys and girls

[2] Dr. Virginia L. Nelson administered the IQ tests.

at age 3½; 121 and 116 at age 5½; and 125 and 112 at 9 years of age. The standard deviations averaged 13 points for boys and 12 points for girls. The interviewer was unaware of the childhood or adolescent IQ scores at the time of the adolescent interview.

Statistical Analysis. We were concerned primarily with five sets of relations: (*a*) childhood IQ and adolescent behavior, (*b*) childhood IQ and maternal practices, (*c*) educational level of parents and mother's childrearing practices, (*d*) parental education and the child's behavior during adolescence, and (*e*) maternal childrearing practices and adolescent behavior. All correlations are product-moment except for those involving the interview variables *feminine interests, withdrawal to attack,* and *heterosexual erotic activity* which are point biserial correlations.

The sample sizes were 30 for boys and 20 for girls except for the following variables for which data were incomplete. For boys, the sample size was 29 for the eight self-rating variables and for each of the 10 maternal variables during the period 4–1 through 7–0 years of age. For girls, the sample size was 16 for the self-rating variables, 19 for the 10 maternal variables during the period 2–0 through 4–0, and 15 for the maternal variables during the period 4–1 through 7–0 years of age.

The means and standard deviations for each variable were examined for sex differences. *There were no significant sex differences in variability for any of the variables.* Significant sex differences in mean score were found on the following variables: Boys received higher interview ratings on masculine interests and higher scores on self-rated aggression. Boys had lower scores than girls on the interview ratings of feminine interests and task withdrawal and lower self-rating scores on affiliative needs and physical harm anxiety ($p < .05$; two tails for each difference). These sex differences in self-rated aggression, affiliation, and anxiety over physical harm are consistent with adult scores on this scale (7).

On the maternal variables, sons were protected more than daughters during age 2 to 4; restricted more during 4 to 7 years of age; and punished less severely during 2 to 4 years of age ($p < .05$ for each difference).

RESULTS

Table 2 gives the relation between each of the three IQ scores (age 3½, 5½, and 9) and the parental education scores, on the one hand, and the maternal practices and adolescent variables on the other. These relations are presented for the sexes separately.

Social Class and Maternal Practices

The mother's educational level was, in selected instances, highly related to her childrearing practices. The greater the education of the mother the more

TABLE 2

Correlations between Childhood IQ and Parental Education with Other Variables—Males

Variable	*IQ* 3½	*IQ* 5½	*IQ* 9	*Education Mother*	*Education Father*
1. Education mother	.46***	.46***	.34*	..	.60***
2. Education father	.32*	.39**	.06	.60***	..
Maternal Variables					
3. Restrictiveness (2–4)	−.32*	−.40**	−.36**	−.32*	−.15
4. Restrictiveness (4–7)	−.19	−.24	−.25	−.41**	−.27
5. Severity (2–4)	−.26	−.41**	−.13	−.32*	−.45**
6. Severity (4–7)	−.36**	−.25	−.09	−.15	−.04
7. Justification (2–4)	.10	.19	.20	.57***	.48***
8. Justification (4–7)	.50***	.63***	.51***	.62***	.33*
9. Coerciveness (2–4)	−.45**	−.46***	−.26	−.54***	−.22
10. Coerciveness (4–7)	−.41**	−.40**	−.30*	−.16	.01
11. Acceleration (2–4)	.23	.20	.26	.48***	.26
12. Acceleration (4–7)	.05	.22	.00	.55***	.61***
13. Babying (2–4)	−.08	−.08	−.05	−.23	−.03
14. Babying (4–7)	−.19	−.10	−.08	−.05	−.19
15. Protectiveness (2–4)	.11	.02	−.01	−.01	−.05
16. Protectiveness (4–7)	−.07	.02	−.03	.05	−.04
17. Criticism (2–4)	−.15	.09	−.20	.17	.07
18. Criticism (4–7)	−.10	.08	.14	.00	−.19
19. Acceptance (2–4)	−.22	−.17	−.16	.07	−.10
20. Acceptance (4–7)	−.28	−.23	.08	.05	−.27
21. Affection (2–4)	−.19	−.22	−.17	−.14	−.25
22. Affection (4–7)	−.16	−.11	.13	.00	−.21
Interview Variables					
23. Importance intellectual mastery	.43**	.50***	.32*	.62***	.51***
24. Masculine interests	.10	−.03	−.07	−.29	.11
25. Feminine interests	−.14	.05	.02	.20	.14
26. Popularity	.27	.13	.14	−.06	.23
27. Dependence on mother	−.25	−.18	−.10	.04	−.05
28. Dependence on father	.09	−.04	.04	.10	.08
29. Task withdrawal	−.09	−.19	−.24	−.28	−.34*
30. Social withdrawal	−.10	−.23	−.03	−.15	−.32*
31. Withdrawal to attack	.17	.13	.16	.40**	.29
32. Conformity	−.06	−.10	.04	.23	.08
33. Erotic activity	.28	.33	.17	.16	.23
Self-Rating Variables					
34. Aggression	.00	−.03	.19	−.09	−.05
35. Hostile feelings	−.08	.05	.13	.10	−.09
36. Dependency	.00	.08	−.16	−.27	−.07
37. Sex Anxiety	−.27	−.26	−.06	−.25	−.24
38. Afflliative needs	−.06	−.06	.15	−.13	−.11
39. Compulsivity	−.18	−.03	.06	.11	−.17
40. Status striving	−.04	.19	.05	−.08	.16
41. Physical harm anxiety	−.06	−.14	−.27	.08	.10

* = .10 level of confidence for two tails.
** = .05 level of confidence for two tails.
*** = .01 level of confidence for two tails.

TABLE 2 (*continued*)

Correlations between Childhood IQ and Parental Education with Other Variables—Females

Variable	*IQ* 3½	*IQ* 5½	*IQ* 9	*Education Mother*	*Education Father*
1. Education mother	.17	.45**	.42*	..	.86***
2. Education father	.28	.35	.41*	.86***	..
Maternal Variables					
3. Restrictiveness (2–4)	−.51**	−.48**	−.38*	−.53**	−.53**
4. Restrictiveness (4–7)	−.16	−.41	−.36	−.39	−.13
5. Severity (2–4)	−.50**	−.42*	−.37	−.27	−.35
6. Severity (4–7)	−.38	−.29	−.35	−.34	−.22
7. Justification (2–4)	.42*	.53**	.26	.54**	.56***
8. Justification (4–7)	.60**	.64***	.69***	.57**	.69***
9. Coerciveness (2–4)	−.41*	−.47*	−.37	−.53**	−.53**
10. Coerciveness (4–7)	−.33	−.40	−.35	−.16	.06
11. Acceleration (2–4)	−.22	.21	−.16	.29	.10
12. Acceleration (4–7)	.42	.64***	.35	.12	.06
13. Babying (2–4)	.00	−.10	.02	−.27	−.39*
14. Babying (4–7)	−.28	−.40	−.37	−.10	−.16
15. Protectiveness (2–4)	.27	.03	.26	−.32	−.11
16. Protectiveness (4–7)	−.21	−.26	−.26	−.22	−.11
17. Criticism (2–4)	.47**	.46**	.43*	.04	.10
18. Criticism (4–7)	.24	.07	.64***	.41	.49*
19. Acceptance (2–4)	.49**	.32	.31	−.26	−.15
20. Acceptance (4–7)	−.08	−.21	.19	.21	.27
21. Affection (2–4)	.08	.02	.30	−.02	.01
22. Affection (4–7)	−.18	−.29	.28	.07	.09
Interview Variables					
23. Importance intellectual mastery	.66***	.68***	.27	.44**	.45**
24. Masculine interests	−.09	.11	.20	.51**	.54**
25. Feminine interests	−.38	−.05	−.42*	.07	−.10
26. Popularity	.44**	.41*	.28	.56***	.60***
27. Dependence on mother	.18	.09	−.03	−.17	−.20
28. Dependence on father	.26	.09	−.02	−.03	.23
29. Task withdrawal	−.15	−.47**	.00	−.35	−.30
30. Social withdrawal	−.27	−.23	−.05	−.20	−.23
31. Withdrawal to attack	−.13	−.13	−.31	−.05	.13
32. Conformity	.30	.09	.05	−.23	−.12
33. Erotic activity	−.45**	−.50**	−.65***	−.27	−.37
Self-Rating Variables					
34. Aggression	.58**	.60**	.54**	.40	.24
35. Hostile feelings	.06	−.03	.35	.20	−.06
36. Dependency	.20	−.05	−.09	−.37	−.29
37. Sex anxiety	.45*	.37	.43*	.42*	.41*
38. Affiliative needs	−.06	−.28	−.38	−.15	−.11
39. Compulsivity	.04	−.13	−.28	−.38	−.10
40. Status striving	.28	.17	−.15	.18	−.01
41. Physical harm anxiety	.13	−.14	−.69***	−.15	−.11

* = .10 level of confidence for two tails.
** = .05 level of confidence for two tails.
*** = .01 level of confidence for two tails.

likely she was to justify her discipline and accelerate her son and the less likely she was to be restrictive or coercive during the preschool years. It is interesting to note that maternal acceptance and affection were relatively independent of maternal education and, by implication, of social class standing. These data are in agreement with those of Bayley and Schaefer (4) who reported a negative relation between maternal education and mother's restrictiveness and a nonsignificant relation between maternal education and maternal expression of affection during the school years. These data are also congruent with those derived from other samples of mother-child pairs in the Fels population (7).

The strong positive relation between maternal education and acceleration of sons and the suggestive relation with criticism of daughters ($r = .41$; $p = .12$) were also found in the earlier study (7). This replication strengthens the possibility that well educated mothers are more critical of shortcomings in their daughters and more accelerative of their sons during the ages 4 through 7 than less well educated mothers. Social class membership is associated not only with different childrearing practices, but also with differential behavior toward sons and daughters.

IQ and Maternal Practices

Early maternal restrictiveness and coerciveness (age 2 through 4) were associated with lower IQ scores, whereas maternal justification of discipline during ages 4 through 7 was related to higher IQ scores for both boys and girls. Maternal criticism was related to higher IQ scores, only for girls. However, restrictiveness, coerciveness, and justification were associated with mother's educational level, and the latter variable was almost as effective a predictor of intelligence as the maternal behavior variables. This set of coefficients neatly illustrates the danger of glibly assigning causality to correlational data. It is potentially fallacious to conclude that maternal restriction leads to lower IQ scores for there well may be unknown experiences, associated with social class standing, that obstruct the attainment of high scores on intelligence tests. In order to assess the magnitude of the relation between the maternal practices and childhood intelligence with the influence of maternal social class controlled (as assessed by level of maternal education), we computed partial correlation coefficients between the maternal variables and IQ score with maternal education controlled. Partial coefficients were computed for those maternal variables that were related consistently to the child's intelligence (i.e., restrictiveness, justification, coerciveness, acceleration, and criticism). Since the sample sizes were small, these data should be viewed with some caution. These partial correlations appear in Table 3.

It appears that the magnitude of the negative relation between restrictiveness or coerciveness and IQ drops to nonsignificant levels when maternal

TABLE 3

Partial Correlations between IQ Score and Maternal Variables with Maternal Education Controlled

	IQ at 3½ years		*IQ at 5½ years*		*IQ at 9 years*	
Maternal Variables	*Boys*	*Girls*	*Boys*	*Girls*	*Boys*	*Girls*
Restrictiveness (2–4).....	−.19	−.57**	−.29	−.32	−.28	−.21
Restrictiveness (4–7).....	.00	−.10	−.06	−.27	−.13	−.23
Justification (2–4).......	−.20	.43	−.09	.41	.01	.04
Justification (4–7).......	.31	.76***	.56***	.60**	.44**	.75***
Coerciveness (2–4).......	−.27	−.42	−.28	−.31	−.10	−.19
Coerciveness (4–7).......	−.38**	−.32	−.30	−.37	−.27	−.31
Acceleration (2–4).......	.01	−.30	−.02	.09	.12	−.30
Acceleration (4–7).......	−.24	.44	−.04	.78***	−.23	.32
Criticism (2–4).........	−.24	.52**	.01	.51**	−.27	.46
Criticism (4–7)..........	−.10	.19	.08	−.12	.14	.67**

** $p < .05$, two tails.
*** $p < .01$, two tails.

education is controlled. For ages 5½ and 9 there was no significant relation between these two maternal practices and the intelligence of the child.

Maternal justification of discipline during ages 4 through 7, however, continued to be associated with higher IQ scores for both boys and girls, even when mothers' education was controlled. Moreover, for girls, early criticism was positively associated with IQ at age 3½ ($r = .52$), 5½ ($r = .51$) and 9 ($r = .46$), with maternal education held constant.

Justification and criticism appear to have a special relation to the child's level of mental development. It is possible to generate several *post hoc* interpretations of the intriguing association involving justification and IQ. One of the more appealing explanations is that a mother who stops to reason verbally with her disobedient child—in contrast to arbitrary physical punishment or deprivation—is doing several significant things simultaneously. First, she is using adult language to the child and stimulating his own language development. Second, a mother who attempts to reason with her 4-year-old probably has greater respect for the conceptual capacity of her child than one who punishes arbitrarily. For she would not invest the energy in explaining her punishments if she did not believe (or want to believe) that the child would comprehend the reason for the disciplinary action. Such a mother probably communicates this faith in her child's *ability to comprehend* in other ways, and one might assume that this kind of mother would create conditions conducive to confidence in attempting mastery of intellectual tasks. Finally, it is not unlikely that mothers who pause to justify punishments create less anxiety, less frustration, and less hostility in the child than those who are more arbitrary. Current theory and existing data—albeit not definitive—suggest that intense anxiety over adult reprisals and hostility to adults interfere with effective performance on problem tasks. This interpretation is but one of several that might fit the data. Future work in our laboratory is directed at a better understanding of this relation.

The positive relation between early maternal criticism followed by acceleration and IQ scores in girls—with education controlled—matches closely results from our earlier investigation (7). Our interpretation of this finding rests on the assumption that mothers who set high mastery standards for their children will be critical of them during the early years of life before the child's mastery efforts have been realized. The critical mother is impatient and finds fault with the child's slow rate of development. When the child reaches school age, she accelerates and encourages mastery of culturally approved skills. Since daughters are more likely than sons to adopt mothers' values—as a result of identification—we would expect this set of maternal practices to lead to stronger attempts at mastery of intellectual skills among girls than among boys and, therefore, to higher IQ scores.

The lack of a relation between maternal criticism or acceleration and IQ score among boys suggests that the antecedents of intellectual mastery are different for the sexes. Since there were no significant sex differences in variability on these variables, these differences in correlation patterns can not be the result of excessively restricted ranges for the boys.

Achievement Behavior and Childhood IQ

There were important sex differences in the pattern of relations between childhood intelligence and adolescent behavior. For boys, the only consistent correlate of high IQ in childhood was involvement in intellectual mastery during adolescence. The other interview and self-rating variables were essentially unrelated to childhood intelligence scores.

For girls, however, IQ predicted not only concern with intellectual competence, but also popularity with peers, avoidance of heterosexual erotic activity, rejection of traditional feminine interests, self-rated aggression, and self-rated sex anxiety. Girls with high IQ scores during ages 3½ to 9 (which we interpret as a reflection, in part, of strong motivation to master intellectual skills) grew to be adolescents who tended to reject a traditional feminine sex role identification (i.e., not involved in domestic activities; willing to describe the self as aggressive, avoided dating and heterosexual interactions). This relation was also found in our earlier investigation (7). Since the interview rating of degree of involvement in feminine interests was unrelated to parental education, it appears that degree of adoption or rejection of traditionally sex typed traits among girls is one potentially significant correlate of degree of intellectual mastery. Traditional sex typing among girls often calls for rejection of intense involvement in intellectual activities —especially a competitive attitude to intellectual effort in school. The girl who shows early signs of such involvement is prone to reject traditional feminine role models.

Knowledge of degree of involvement in intellectual mastery for a girl allows one to predict several salient behaviors in domains outside of intellectual mastery. For males, however, high IQ is relatively independent of sex typing and is not as clearly associated with aspects of aggression or sexuality as it is for girls.

Maternal Practices and Adolescent Behavior

The correlations between each of the 10 maternal variables (for ages 2 through 4 and 4 through 7) and the 11 adolescent interview variables were computed to see if any consistent patterns emerged. Study of this set of 440 coefficients revealed that six of the adolescent interview variables displayed a cluster of theoretically meaningful associations with the selected maternal variables. In the interest of space and readability we will only present the relations between maternal practice and adolescent behavior for those six variables that yielded coefficients significant at the .05 level or better for two tails. The interested reader can write the authors for the complete set of correlations. Table 4 presents these relationships.

The positive relation, for boys, between both maternal justification and acceleration, on the one hand, and adolescent intellectual mastery on the other is not too surprising. Both the maternal and adolescent variables are positively associated with parental education, and presumably other social experiences that would promote intellectual mastery. As might be expected from the relation to intellectual mastery, task withdrawal was negatively associated with maternal justification and acceleration. This set of relations is reasonable, for mastery and task withdrawal are negatively related to each other ($r = -.60$).

The associations between maternal practices and adolescent conformity and dependence upon parents are of more interest because these adolescent behaviors were not highly related to parental educational level. The data suggest important sex differences in the set of maternal practices associated with these adolescent response dispositions.

For boys, maternal overprotection and affection during ages 4 through 7 (i.e., excessive nurturance) predicted conformity to adult demands. For girls, excessive severity of discipline and restrictiveness during ages 4 through 7 were the best predictors of adolescent conformity. Similarly, dependence upon mother was linked to maternal affection and acceptance for boys, but to severity of discipline for girls. Since restrictiveness and severity of discipline were associated with social class, while babying and protection were not, it might appear that social class variables were more relevant for prediction of conformity among females than among males. This position is not supported by the partial correlation of .65 ($p < .05$) between maternal restriction (ages 4 through 7) and adolescent conformity among the girls, with maternal education controlled. Thus, restriction of autonomy predicts

TABLE 4

Relation between Selected Adolescent Interview Variables and Selected Maternal Childrearing Practices

Maternal Variable (Males)	r	Maternal Variable (Females)	r
Adolescent Variable: Intellectual Mastery			
Acceleration (4–7)	.51		
Justification (2–4)	.51		
Justification (4–7)	.54		
Adolescent Variable: Conformity			
Babying (4–7)	.45	Acceleration (2–4)	−.66
Protection (4–7)	.44	Protection (2–4)	.52
Acceptance (4–7)	.52	Restrictiveness (4–7)	.60
Affection (4–7)	.59	Severity (4–7)	.50
Criticism (4–7)	.47		
Adolescent Variable: Dependence Mother			
Affection (2–4)	.43	Acceleration (2–4)	−.52
Acceptance (2–4)	.48	Severity (4–7)	.52
Adolescent Variable: Dependence Father			
		Protection (2–4)	.50
		Restrictiveness (4–7)	.73
		Severity (4–7)	.58
		Coerciveness (4–7)	.77
Adolescent Variable: Task Withdrawal			
Justification (2–4)	−.44	Acceleration (4–7)	−.50
Acceleration (2–4)	−.37	Acceptance (4–7)	.54
Acceleration (4–7)	−.41	Affection (4–7)	.68
Adolescent Variable: Social Withdrawal			
Criticism (4–7)	.42		
Affection (4–7)	.38		

later conformity in daughters; excessive nurturance predicts later conformity for boys.

It is of interest to note that maternal practices during age 4 through 7 were generally more predictive of adolescent behavior than similar practices displayed during ages 2 through 4. This was particularly true of the discipline variables (severity and restrictiveness). Affection, acceptance, and acceleration during ages 2 through 4 did display some associations with the adolescent variables. One implication of this pattern of coefficients is that the ultimate effect of individual differences among mothers in the disciplinary variables may be most sensitive when the child has reached school age and has begun to test parental authority with more consistency and intensity.

DISCUSSION AND SUMMARY

The results of this study are generally congruent with earlier work and support the following conclusions.

1. Childhood intelligence scores, which were positively associated with educational level of the family and degree of maternal justification of discipline, predicted degree of involvement in mastery of intellectual tasks during late adolescence. The most reasonable interpretation of the association with social class is that children born to parents who value intellectual mastery, in contrast to those who are less concerned with this domain, will more frequently reward academic competence and proficiency at intellective skills. They will also be more effective identification models for this sector of behavior. That is, the child typically strives to increase behavioral similarity between himself and his parent as part of the identification process. The parent who is himself actively involved in intellectual pursuits will, therefore, foster a more intense adoption of such responses in his child than a parent who may preach academic competence but not practice such behavior. The relation between maternal justification of discipline and both IQ and later mastery has intriguing implications. It was suggested that the mother who adopts such a tactic not only verbally stimulates the child but also communicates a faith in his conceptual capacity.

2. Maternal restrictiveness was inversely related to maternal educational level and to child's intelligence test scores. The relation between restrictiveness and social class agrees with other research. The relation between restriction and child's IQ appears to be an indirect effect of the association between restrictiveness and social class, for it was of decreased magnitude when maternal education was held constant.

3. Daughters with higher IQ scores had mothers who were both more acceleratory during ages 4 through 7 and more critical during ages 2 through 4 than mothers of daughters with low IQ scores—even when mothers' level of education was controlled statistically. Moreover, acceleration and criticism during these years were not highly related to maternal social class. It appears that a combination of fault finding during the preschool years and acceleration during the early school years facilitates intelligence test performance among girls but not among boys. This pattern also appeared in an earlier investigation in which early maternal criticism of the daughter (during the first 3 years of life) followed by acceleration during the school years was

associated with intellectual mastery in early adulthood (7). As in the present study, early criticism of boys was independent of later intellectual mastery in males.

4. Girls who reject traditional feminine sex role behaviors have slightly higher IQ scores than girls who adopt traditional sex typed traits. This relationship is absent for boys. This association was also present in our earlier analysis and suggests that the motivation for intellectual mastery is more closely linked to sex role identification among females than among males. In effect, intellectual mastery for girls is tied to a series of other sex typed traits such as independence, aggression, and rejection of traditional heterosexual relations during adolescence. Intellectual mastery for boys, on the other hand, is more independent of these sex typed classes of behavior. One important implication of this finding is that the antecedent processes for intellectual mastery may be different for the sexes.

5. Adolescent conformity to adult demands and dependence upon mother were associated with different early maternal practices for boys and girls. Acceptance, affection, and protection during the early school years predicted conformity and dependence for boys; severe discipline and restrictiveness during ages 4 through 7 were predictive for girls.

In sum, these data affirm results and conclusions discussed in an earlier and more extensive study (7). The strong relation between disciplinary practices and mothers' social class makes it somewhat dangerous to attribute a causal relation between these maternal practices and a specific set of child responses, be it intelligence or more complex behavioral variables. It is likely that other unknown experiences, associated with social class membership, are critical antecedents of the dependent variable in question.

REFERENCES

1. Baldwin, A. L., Kalhorn, J., & Breese, F. H. Patterns of parent behavior. *Psychol. Monogr.,* 1945, 58, No. 3.
2. Baldwin, A. L., Kalhorn, J., & Breese, F. H. The appraisal of parent behavior. *Psychol. Monogr.,* 1949, 63, No. 4.
3. Bayley, N. Some increasing parent-child similarities during the growth of children. *J. educ. Psychol.,* 1954, 45, 1–21.
4. Bayley, N., & Schaefer, E. S. Relationships between socioeconomic variables and the behavior of mothers toward young children. *J. genet. Psychol.,* 1960, 96, 61–77.
5. Crandall, V. J., & Preston, A. Patterns and levels of maternal behavior. *Child Develpm.,* 1955, 26, 267–277.
6. Kagan, J., & Moss, H. A. Parental correlates of child's IQ and height: a cross-validation of the Berkeley Growth Study results. *Child Develpm.,* 1959, 30, 325–332.
7. Kagan, J., & Moss, H. A. *Birth to maturity: a study in psychological development.* Wiley, 1962.

35

PARENTAL MODEL ATTRIBUTES, NURTURANT REINFORCEMENT, AND CONSISTENCY OF BEHAVIOR IN ADOLESCENTS*

ALFRED B. HEILBRUN, JR.

THE IMPORTANCE of behavioral consistency over time and over interpersonal situations has been accorded an important role in the theoretical treatment of adolescent maladjustment. Erikson (15) considers the sense of identity to be crucial to successful psychological development of the adolescent and suggests that the three requisites of identity are that the person perceives himself as essentially the same over time, that people in his social environment perceive the essential similarity, and that the person gains confidence in his perception through social validation. Benedict (4) attributes to cultural discontinuities between child and adult roles a major role in adolescent confusion. She points out that, along such dimensions as dominance-submission, the transition from childhood to adult status not only requires the learning of a new role but also the unlearning of an old, well-established role. Adolescence should be marked by behavioral inconsistency to the extent that role transition is incomplete.

There are two lines of research evidence that provide support for the hypothesized relation between behavior consistency and adjustment in adolescents. Cartwright (9, 10) demonstrated that mixed adolescent-adult groups from a college counseling center perceive themselves as being less consistent in their mode of relating to a series of other individuals than normals; further, consistency increased as a function of psychotherapy. Whereas Cartwright used Q-sort procedures to estimate role consistency, Block (7) employed a rank ordering technique for self-descriptive adjectives and came to the same conclusion. The less the role consistency of college adolescents, the greater the maladjustment.

---

* From *Child Development,* 1964, *35,* 151–167. Reprinted with permission from the author and the Society for Research in Child Development.

Sincere appreciation is extended to Dr. John D. Black and his staff at the Counseling and Testing Center, Stanford University, whose cooperation and support in the summer, 1962, made possible the scoring and analysis of the data in this study.

Role consistency (RC), investigated by Cartwright and by Block, reflects the similarity in manifest behaviors over social situations. A second type of consistency variable has been considered in a series of studies from the Iowa laboratories, that is, the consistency between the value imposed upon a given social behavior and its tendency to be manifested socially. Two studies (18, 21) found social value-social behavior (SV-SB) consistency to be positively related to adjustment in college adolescents. A third study (11) showed disturbed adult schizophrenics to have lower SV-SB consistency than better adjusted schizophrenics or hospitalized normal adults with respect to behaviors requiring initiative in social interaction. Although both the RC and SV-SB variables have shown the same relation to level of adjustment, their relation to each other has not as yet been empirically established.

Since it seems reasonably certain that behavioral consistency is a correlate of adolescent adjustment, the investigation of the developmental antecedents of inconsistency may contribute to our still sketchy notions of the origins of psychopathology. The two variables investigated in the present study seemed to hold some a priori, theoretical relevance to behavior consistency.

The first of these variables is the nature of the social models which the parents present to the child during his formative years. Bandura and his students (1, 3) and other investigators (6, 28) have accrued clear evidence that children will readily imitate the behavior of adult models, and Bandura *et al.* (3) further demonstrated that imitative behaviors will generalize to a situation in which the model is absent. The relation between the model attributes of parents and behavior consistency should, in turn, be influenced by the correspondence between the attributes and the sex-typical behaviors which are socially reinforced. Thus, if a boy imitates a masculine father model, the imitated behavior will also tend to be reinforced by his social environment; the consistency of these behaviors should be enhanced. However, if a boy imitates a more feminine father model, the influence of social reinforcement should tend to deter the occurrence of the imitated behavior and behavioral inconsistency should result.

The second variable considered relevant to behavior consistency is degree of parental nurturance. Just as imitation of model attributes may mediate the *form* of the child's social behavior, model nurturance may act as a *reinforcer* to instigate the initial imitation of his behaviors and to strengthen their subsequent response strength, whatever the form. Bandura and Huston (1) report that a helpful, attentive, and warm adult model was more readily imitated than a nonnurturant model. They presented this finding as consistent with a secondary reinforcement theory of identification (26) where the child comes to derive reinforcement from imitating the behavior of an adult who has been the source of need gratification. Social power theory would also predict that degree of nurturance would affect the amount of social influence a parental model would exert upon the behaviors of a child. French and Raven (16) list "reward power" as one of five major bases of influence, and they define this construct in terms of perceived control over need satisfying resources. Perceived parental nurturance would appear to meet the operational requirements of such a definition. Bandura and Ross (2) have provided empirical support for social power as a factor in identificatory learning.

Hypotheses

Although the RC and SV-SB variables are both concerned with forms of behavioral consistency and relate similarly to adolescent maladjustment, it is proposed that important differences exist. RC refers to the similarities in manifest social behaviors over occasions and, by definition, to their habit strength. The form of these behaviors should be influenced by the manifest behaviors presented by the parental model which are accessible for imitation. In addition, since these patterns of behavior in the child are open to public observation, they may serve as cues to positive or negative reinforcement from both the parents of the child and his social environment. Thus, both the reinforcing properties of parental nurturance and social pressures to conform to sex-typical behaviors should also directly influence the strength of these manifest social behaviors and their tendency to reoccur over occasions.

SV-SB consistency, on the other hand, refers to the congruence between an internal (and nonobservable) system of values as to how the child feels he should behave and his actual manifest social behaviors. A value is defined here as the perceived social reward or punishment which the individual anticipates as a consequence of a response in a given social situation. Accordingly, the greater the SV-SB inconsistency, the more the individual anticipates punishment or loss of reward as a function of his behavior; the greater the SV-SB consistency, the more he anticipates reward or avoidance of punishment as a function of his behavior. The evidence from two studies in which lower SV-SB consistency was related to higher anxiety (18) and greater social withdrawal (11, 18) is consistent with such an interpretation of the SV-SB variable. Since the relation between the anticipatory response and social behavior is not open to direct social reinforcement, it is more difficult to specify how SV-SB consistency should relate to model attributes, parental nurturance or pressures toward sex-role conformity.

METHOD

Measures

The four variables investigated in this study were all psychometrically measured from the responses of late adolescent college students who acted as *S*s.

Model Attributes. Model scores for the parents were based upon a series of ratings in which *S* was asked to judge whether various sets of behaviors were more characteristic of his (her) mother or father. These descriptions were taken from Edwards (12) and represent types of behaviors which define the traits measured by his personality inventory. Nine of the 15 traits tend to be parentally sex-typed by college adolescents[1] (19). The number of times out of these nine ratings an *S* judged the behaviors to be more or less characteristic of the same-sexed parent in line with masculine or feminine stereotype provided the model score. Thus, the higher the model score, the more masculine the model behaviors of the father for a male *S* or the more feminine the model behaviors of the mother for a female *S*. It should be noted that masculinity-femininity is a relative factor (i.e., father compared to mother) in this method of measurement.

Degree of Nurturance. The Parent-Child Interaction Rating Scales were especially developed for the present study. Rather than attempting to select a restricted number of modes by which parental nurturance can be expressed, it was decided to develop an omnibus nurturance measure which would include eight nurturant modes; thus, some conceptual overlap was preferred to the omission of important aspects of nurturance. The eight modes were defined for *S* and included: (*a*) affection I (degree of affection felt for *S*), (*b*) affection II (degree of affection physically expressed toward *S*), (*c*) approval of *S* and his behavior, (*d*) sharing of personal feelings and experiences, (*e*) concrete giving (e.g., gifts, money, etc.) to *S*, (*f*) encouragement of *S* in meeting responsibilities and pursuing personal interests, (*g*) trust placed in *S*, and (*h*) sense of security felt by *S* in relations with parents.

Each mode was presented with a five-point rating scale, each point being anchored by a descriptive phrase. Five always represented the highest degree of perceived nurturance, although the direction of scoring was alternated from one page to the next to counteract position rating sets. Both the father and mother were rated for each nurturant mode by *S*.

Prior to its inclusion in this study, the Interaction Rating Scales were revised in line with the comments of several colleagues regarding clarity and inconsistencies. A pilot study was also run with 20 male and 20 female college *S*s to determine whether greater dispersion of ratings would be obtained under self-identifying or anonymous testing conditions. This was considered a special problem since public descriptions of intimate details of parental behavior might be expected to restrict the range of ratings to the favorable end of the scales. As it turned out, anonymity led to the greater restriction of ratings so the Interaction Rating Scales were administered under self-identifying conditions in the study, as were all other measures.

The mother and the father nurturance scores derived from the Interaction

---

[1] Achievement, autonomy, dominance, and endurance were rated as more characteristic of fathers and deference, affiliation, succorance, abasement, and nurturance as more characteristic of mothers by 400 male and female *S*s.

Rating Scales represented the cumulative rating total over the eight modes. Cumulative scoring was used to be consistent with the omnibus measurement approach with no special weights being assigned to any specific mode.

Role Consistency. The RC measure was identical to that employed by Block (7). Twenty self-descriptive adjectives (e.g., relaxed, independent, witty, unselfish, responsive) were presented in a set order to *S*, and he was requested to rank them from most to least descriptive in eight interpersonal situations involving: (*a*) "Someone in whom you are sexually interested," (*b*) "An acquaintance you don't care much about," (*c*) "Your employer or someone with equivalent status," (*d*) "A child," (*e*) "Your mother (or a mother figure)," (*f*) "Your father (or a father figure)," (*g*) "A close male friend (for male *S*s)" or "A close female friend (for female *S*s)," and (*h*) "An acquaintance whom you would like to know better."

The RC score was calculated by the Kendall coefficient of concordance *W* (29), a method which provides the degree of association between several rankings of *N* objects. *W* coefficients range from .00 to 1.00 with higher scores indicating greater similarity in self-descriptions over interpersonal situations and greater RC.

SV-SB Consistency. The SV-SB consistency score was derived from two measures. *S* was administered the Edwards Personal Preference Schedule (EPPS) (12) under standard conditions. In this personality test, items include two types of behavior, and *S* is required to select the one which is more self-descriptive. Following the administration of the personality tests, *S* was given all of the behavioral statements included in the EPPS and asked to rate each on a nine-point scale from highly socially undesirable to highly socially desirable. The self-descriptions on the EPPS were then scored for the percentage of times that *S* had endorsed the statement in each item pair having the higher social desirability for him.

The SV-SB consistency scores, which can range from 0 to 100 percent, have two attributes which are noteworthy. One, the social values (i.e., anticipations of social reinforcement) employed to derive the SV-SB score for each *S* are uniquely his own. Second, although social desirability ratings involve value judgments about social behaviors in others, these have been shown to be highly correlated ($r = .90$) with ratings of the same behaviors in oneself (17) and thus to have high personal relevance to *S*'s own value system.

It should be further noted that the magnitude of the SV-SB consistency score has no necessary implications regarding the nature (e.g., social acceptability) of the values or behaviors in any given case.

Subjects

Samples of 61 male and 63 female volunteers were obtained from a large undergraduate class in psychology at the University of Iowa. They were tested in small groups in three separate one-hour sessions. The five measures included in the present study (other tests were also included in the total battery) were administered in a set order with the EPPS given during the first session, the social desirability and model ratings obtained during the second, and the RC measure and Parent-Child Interaction Rating Scales given during the third.

The mean age and educational levels for the males were 21.0 and 14.2 years, respectively; these figures for the females were 20.3 and 14.2 years, respectively.

RESULTS

Nurturance

Since no evidence had accrued regarding the validity of the Parent-Child Interaction Rating Scales, evidence relevant to its usefulness as a measure of parental nurturance was sought. Several studies (8, 13, 14, 22) have found that mothers provide greater nurturance to their children than do their fathers. In the present study the number of times that the mother was attributed a higher total nurturance score than the father by all *S*s (omitting ties) was 87, whereas the reverse was true for only 17 *S*s. These figures differ reliably from a 50 per cent split ($\chi^2 = 25.07$ for 1 *df*; $p < .001$, one-tailed) and in the direction predicted from prior evidence.

Freud observed that mothers usually manifest most affection and preference for their sons, while fathers are partial to their daughters (27). If so, the difference between the nurturance scores attributed to the mother and the father should be greater for males than for females. The mean difference score for males (mean $= 4.5$; SD $= 5.3$) and for females (mean $= 2.3$; SD $= 4.3$) did differ significantly ($t = 2.56$ for 116 *df*; $p < .01$, one-tailed) and in the direction consistent with Freud's observations.

A third check on the validity of scores for the Interaction Rating Scales is provided by the relation between these scores and the model scores. Since the studies cited above (i.e., 8, etc.) and a later study by Heilbrun (19) indicate that nurturance is sex-typically a feminine trait, it would be expected that fathers who are perceived by *S* as more masculine models should be relatively less nurturant than fathers who are less masculine models; conversely, mothers who are perceived as more feminine models should be more nurturant than mothers who are less feminine models. The mother and father model score distributions were split near their respective medians to test whether these expectancies were met. More masculine fathers (model scores 7 through 9) were perceived as less nurturant than more feminine fathers (6 or less) by the combined male and female *S*s. Their respective mean nurturance scores were 27.2 (SD $= 6.3$; $N = 56$) and 29.7 (SD $= 6.2$; $N = 60$), the difference being in the predicted direction and significance

($t = 2.24$ for 114 *df*; $p < .05$, one-tailed). However, the mean nurturance score of more feminine mothers (model scores 7 through 9) was almost identical to that of more masculine mothers (6 or less). These means were 31.8 (SD $= 4.2$; $N = 58$) and 31.9 (SD $= 4.5$; $N = 60$), respectively.

The correlation between the mother and father nurturance scores provided by each *S* has no necessary bearing upon their validity but does have important implications for methodology and inference. Whenever an analysis is made of a relation between a characteristic of one parent and some behavior in a child, as was done in this study, it is necessary to remember that the remaining parent remains an uncontrolled and unmeasured source of variance. For example, if father nurturance alone is related to RC in the son, mother nurturance is ignored. The correlations between father and mother nurturance for male *S*s ($r = .68$) and female *S*s ($r = .41$) indicate a moderate degree of correspondence between the nurturance attributed to both parents. The assumption is made in the present study that some degree of generalization is possible to the marriage partner when a significant relation involving the nurturance variable is found for the other. However, it is further assumed that primacy can be accorded to the relation found to be significant for the one. The latter assumption appears legitimate in light of the fact that no nurturance relation found to be significant for one parent was ever significant when tested for the opposite-sex parent of the same *S*s, although the direction of the relation was usually the same.

Relations between Consistency Measures

The mean RC score (*W* coefficient) was .44 for males ($N = 59$) and .50 for females ($N = 62$). The mean SV-SB consistency score for males was .67 ($N = 60$) and .71 for females ($N = 62$).

Product-moment correlations between the consistency measures were $r = .24$ for males ($N = 59$; $p < .06$) and $r = .26$ for females ($N = 62$; $p < .05$). The combined $r = .25$ ($N = 121$) was highly significant ($p < .01$).

Relations between RC and Nurturance

The 29 males who attributed a relatively high degree of nurturance to their fathers (greater than 26) showed significantly higher RC (mean $= .49$; SD $= .09$) than did the 26 males who perceived their fathers as less nurturant (mean $= .40$; SD $= .12$). The t value of the difference was 3.29 for 53 *df* ($p < .001$).

When female RC was related to nurturance of the mother in similar fashion, no relation was obtained. For the 31 *S*s with more highly nurturing mothers (greater than 33) the mean RC score was .50 (SD $= .12$), whereas this value for the 31 *S*s attributing lower nurturance to their mothers was .49 (SD = .13). The t value of .28 for 60 df was clearly nonsignificant ($p > .70$). However, inspection of the RC score distribution by nurturance level suggested a curvilinear relation. Accordingly, female RC was determined for three levels of maternal nurturance, high (greater than 35), moderate (32 to 35), and low (less than 32). RC under the condition of moderate maternal nurturance (mean = .55; SD = .07; $N = 72$) was significantly higher than RC under the condition of high nurturance (mean = .47; SD = .14; $N = 18$) or low nurturance (mean = .46; SD = .13; $N = 21$). The t values were 2.29 ($p < .05$) and 2.18 ($p < .05$), respectively.

Relations between SV-SB Consistency and Nurturance

No relations were found between SV-SB consistency and nurturance for the males when high v. low nurturance groups were compared and the median used for the cut. The same analysis for females showed the girls with

TABLE 1

SV-SB Consistency Scores Relative to Degree of Father Nurturance for Males and Degree of Mother Nurturance for Females

*Degree of Nurturance for Same-Sexed Parent**	*SV-SB Consistency—Males*			*SV-SB Consistency—Females*		
	N	*Mean*	*SD*	*N*	*Mean*	*SD*
High	29	.68	.11	31	.73	.06
Low	27	.66	.10	31	.68	.08
		t = .72†			t = 2.50†	

* For fathers, high nurturance >26; for mothers, high nurturance >33.
† $t = .79$, $p > .40$; $t = 2.50$, $p < .05$.

more nurturant mothers to be reliably higher in SV-SB consistency than those with less nurturant mothers. The data are given in Table 1.

Relations between RC and Model Attributes

When RC was analyzed by masculinity-femininity of same-sex parental model, no differences were found in either the male or female samples. Males ($N = 28$) with more masculine father models (greater than 6) had a mean RC score of .43 (SD = .12) compared with a mean of .46 (SD = .15) for the 26 males whose fathers presented a less masculine model. The t value of the difference was .84 for 52 df ($p > .40$).

The 27 female *S*s who perceived their mothers as most feminine (greater than 6) provided a mean of .48 (SD = .10) whereas the 33 females with less feminine mothers had a mean RC score of .50 (SD = .14) ($t = .22$ for 58 df; $p > .80$).

Relations between SV-SB Consistency and Model Attributes

The male SV-SB scores showed no relation to father model attributes when analyzed by a high (greater than 6) v. low grouping procedure; however, females whose mothers were more feminine (greater than 6) showed higher SV-SB consistency than those with more masculine mothers. Results of these analyses are provided in the top section of Table 2.

Inspection of the distribution of male SV-SB scores suggested curvilinear-

TABLE 2

Relations between SV-SB Consistency and Parental Model Scores of Same-Sex Parents for Male and Female Subjects

	SV-SB Consistency—Males			*SV-SB Consistency—Females*		
Model Scores	*N*	*Mean*	*SD*	*N*	*Mean*	*SD*
High (>6)	28	.66	.10	27	.73	.06
Low (<7)	26	.68	.11	33	.69	.08
		$t = .69$			$t = 2.17$*	
High (>7)	22	.66	.11			
Moderate (6–7)	16	.71	.08			
Low (<6)	18	.66	.11			
Replication						
High (>7)	20	.64	.14	36†	.70	.09
Moderate (6–7)	33	.74	.10			
Low (<6)	29	.71	.13	43	.67	.09
Combined‡						
High (>7)	42	.65	.13	63	.71	.08
Moderate (6–7)	49	.73	.10			
Low (<6)	47	.69	.12	76	.68	.09
					$t = 2.00$*	

* Significant at .05 level.
† Model cutting score for female replication sample was high >6.
‡ The t values of the mean differences for combined male groups are: t (high v. moderate) = 3.25 for 89 *df* ($p < .001$); t (high v. low) = 1.39 for 87 *df* ($p < .20$); and t (moderate v. low) = 1.77 for 94 *df* ($p < .10$).

ity in relation to father model scores, and, when model scores were considered by low, moderate, and high masculinity, the highest SV-SB was associated with moderate masculinity of the father. These data are given in the second section of Table 2. Replication of the male and female results was possible using data collected for a previous study (18), and these are presented in the third section of Table 2. It can be seen that the replication analysis provided similar findings for both males and females.

The fourth section, Table 2, presents statistical analyses for the present and replication samples combined. The males whose fathers presented moderately masculine models had the highest SV-SB consistency, whereas lowest consistency was associated with high masculinity of the father. The low masculine father model condition resulted in an intermediate degree of SV-SB consistency. The combined female results in section four, Table 2, showed *S*s with more feminine mothers to have significantly higher SV-SB scores than females with more masculine mothers.

Relations between RC, Nurturance, and Model Attributes

Table 3 provides the relations between RC, nurturance of the same-sex model, and model attributes. There was no interaction between these three variables for males (t for interaction = .99 for 50 df; $p > .30$) or females (t for interaction = .05 for 57 df; $p > .90$). That is, the differences in RC as a function of parent model attributes did not differ from one level of model nurturance to the other for either sex.

TABLE 3

Role Consistency as a Function of Nurturance and Model Attributes of the Same-Sex Parent for Male and Female Adolescents

	Males						*Females*					
	High Masculine Model			*Low Masculine Model*			*High Feminine Model*			*Low Feminine Model*		
Degree of Nurturance for Same-Sex Parent	N	*Mean*	*SD*	N	*Mean*	*SD*	N	*Mean*	*SD*	N	*Mean*	*SD*
High	16	.51	.15	12	.45	.09	15	.49	.09	15	.50	.14
Low	14	.39	.11	12	.40	.13	13	.48	.10	18	.50	.14

NOTE.—Cutting scores for the various groupings for males are: high nurturance >26, high masculine model >5 for high nurturance and >7 for low nurturance groups. Cutting scores for females are: high nurturance >33, high feminine model >6.

Since nurturance tends to be sex-typically feminine, it remained a possibility that the RC × nurturance × model analyses might have been influenced by the manner in which the model groupings were made. For example, father nurturance might vary curvilinearly as a function of masculinity-femininity. This, in fact, turned out to be true. When father models were separated into three groups definable as high masculine (model scores 8 to 9), moderate masculine (6 to 7), and low masculine (less than 6), their respective mean nurturance scores were 26.4, 24.0, and 30.1. Accordingly, the preceding RC × nurturance × model analysis was repeated for males using these three model groupings rather than two, and the results are given in Table 4. There were significant nurturance × model interactions when the low masculine model group was compared with both the moderate (t for interaction = 2.76 for 31 df; $p < .01$) and the high (t for interaction = 2.00 for 33 df; $p < .05$) masculine groups. Thus, when the father presented a low masculine model for the male *S*s, greater nurturance was associated with

TABLE 4

Further Data on Role Consistency as a Function of Nurturance and Model Attributes of the Father for Male Adolescents

Degree of Paternal Nurturance	High Masculine Model (8–9)			Moderate Masculine Model (6–7)			Low Masculine Model (<6)		
	N	Mean	SD	N	Mean	SD	N	Mean	SD
High	11	.45	.08	9	.57	.17	8	.42	.10
Low	9	.38	.11	9	.38	.14	9	.48	.08

NOTE.—Cutting scores for the three groups were: high masculine model, high nurturance >25; moderate masculine model, high nurturance >26; low masculine model, high nurturance >28.

lower RC. When the father provided either a moderately masculine or a high masculine model, greater nurturance was related to higher RC.

There were no indications of nurturance × model interactions for the females when three model groupings were used.

Relations between SV-SB Consistency, Nurturance, and Model Attributes

Data relevant to the contingency of SV-SB consistency upon nurturance and model attributes are found in Table 5. The interaction between nurturance and model was significant for the male *Ss* (t for interaction = 3.16 for 51 *df*; $p < .005$). If the father is more masculine, greater nurturance is associated with higher SV-SB consistency. If the father is less masculine, greater nurturance is associated with lower SV-SB consistency.

TABLE 5

SV-SB Consistency as a Function of Nurturance and Model Attributes of the Same-Sex Parent for Male and Female Adolescents

Degree of Nurturance for Same-Sex Parent	Males						Females					
	High Masculine Model			Low Masculine Model			High Feminine Model			Low Feminine Model		
	N	Mean	SD	N	Mean	SD	N	Mean	SD	N	Mean	SD
High	16	.72	.08	12	.63	.12	15	.75	.05	15	.71	.07
Low	14	.62	.12	13	.71	.07	13	.70	.06	18	.67	.08

NOTE.—Cutting scores for the males were: high nurturance >26 with high masculine model >5; low nurturance <27 with high masculine model >7. Cutting scores for females were: high nurturance >33, high feminine model >6.

There was no indication of a nurturance × model interaction for females (t for interaction = .53 for 57 *df*; $p > .50$); those with more feminine mother models displayed higher SV-SB consistency whether the model was more or less nurturant.

DISCUSSION

The relation between the consistency of manifest role behaviors and the consistency between manifest behaviors and their anticipated consequences was positive, as expected from their common relation to psychological adjustment, but low enough to allow for a wide divergence in their psychological meanings. As it turned out, the two consistency measures did vary considerably in the nature of their relations to the parental variables investigated.

RC was hypothesized to be an associative variable reflecting the strength of interpersonal habits and influenced by the attributes of the imitated parental model, degree of reinforcement obtained from the model, and more generalized pressures to conform to sex-typical behaviors. Partial support for this hypothesis in the case of male adolescents is obtained from the finding that higher RC occurs when fathers are perceived as relatively more nurturant and thus a superior source of secondary reinforcement for imitative acts. No simple relation was obtained between RC and the masculinity-femininity of the parental model which on the surface fails to be consistent with hypothesis. However, it was also found that, given either a moderately or highly masculine father model, greater nurturance is associated with higher RC, whereas, in contrast with the overall effect of nurturance, low masculinity of model and greater nurturance mediate lower RC in male adolescents. Thus, when the father presents a relatively feminine model and yet provides greater reinforcement for imitation, the behavior learned through imitation tends to run counter to socially reinforced stereotype. Negative reinforcement of the manifest social behaviors would tend to weaken their habit strength and lower RC would result. On the other hand, nurturant reinforcement for imitation of more masculine behaviors would elicit responses receiving positive social reinforcement, which, in turn, would increase their habit strength and heighten RC.

The present results for males are viewed as supporting the RC hypothesis with respect to nurturant reinforcement by the paternal model and with respect to sex-typicality of the parental model.

It is not surprising that the RC findings for females were somewhat at variance with those obtained with males, since there is a plethora of studies which suggest that the contemporary female adolescent is exposed to a changing and often contradictory array of expectancies regarding female sex-typical behavior (5, 23, 24, 25, 30). Accordingly, less consistent social reinforcement for sex-typical behavior in the female might introduce a different set of relations of RC to the model and nurturance variables.

The only significant RC result obtained for females was a curvilinear relation between the role variable and maternal nurturance. Moderate mother nurturance provided higher RC than either high or low nurturance. In line with the inconsistent social rewards associated with feminine sex-typed behavior, it might be inferred that lower RC for girls with high nurturant mothers evolves from the highly reinforced character of their feminine behaviors which have failed to receive adequate social reinforcement. On the other hand, low maternal nurturance might mediate lower RC because there has been insufficient imitative learning of the behavior of the mother model.

SV-SB consistency was considered to be an index of intrapersonal agreement between the anticipated social reinforcement to be elicited by one's social behaviors and the actual manifest social behaviors themselves. Although the latter category of behaviors (SB) was measured differently from RC, it simply represents another way of talking about the strength of interpersonal habits. It is considered as genotypically the same as RC and governed by the same relations with model attributes and nurturance as were inferred for RC. However, the fact that the relation between SV and SB has not been rigorously formulated in terms of its functional relations with other developmental variables makes the task of interpreting the present results a difficult one.

It was established that, when the adolescent has a more masculine father model, paternal nurturance is positively related to SV-SB consistency; when the father presents a less masculine model to his son, paternal nurturance is negatively related to SV-SB consistency. This finding is reminiscent of the RC $\times$ model $\times$ nurturance interaction in which greater nurturance in moderate and high masculine fathers resulted in higher RC, whereas the greater nurturance of low masculine fathers was associated with lower RC in their sons. Thus, the more firmly established the imitated behaviors, the stronger the SB component when the social behaviors satisfy the requisites of masculine sex-typing. When the model's behaviors are more feminine and these behaviors are more highly reinforced by the model, the result should be a failure to satisfy social stereotype, negative social reinforcement, and a weaker SB component. Strength or weakness of social habits should, in turn, affect the variability in social behaviors of the male adolescent and increase or decrease the consistency between his social anticipations and social behaviors.

It is acknowledged that such an interpretation fails to consider alterations in the SV component. Future research is necessary to test the possible alternative hypotheses which might be offered and which place greater emphasis upon SV modification.

One additional SV-SB finding for males demands explanation since the interpretation offered fails to adequately take it into account. Sons with moderately masculine father models displayed higher SV-SB consistency than those with low or *high* masculine models. The findings for the low masculine model group is not surprising and has been treated above, but lower SV-SB consistency as a function of high masculinity of the father appears paradoxical. However, reference to Table 4 will recall that paternal nurturance had its greatest differential effect upon RC for moderately masculine fathers, whereas this effect was considerably less apparent although in the same direction for high masculine fathers. This suggests that highly masculine behaviors as well as more feminine behaviors receive less social reinforcement than behaviors which are only moderately masculine. Further evidence for such an hypothesis will be discussed later in this section.

The SV-SB results for females suggest the positive importance of femininity of the maternal model and model nurturance. Since there was no indication of a model × nurturance interaction, it must be inferred that these two variables impose their effects upon SV-SB consistency in the daughter independently of each other. That is, daughters are more consistent if their mothers are more feminine no matter how nurturant their mothers are; also, daughters are more consistent if their mothers are more nurturant no matter what type of model she presents. It follows though that the combined effects of model femininity and nurturance should produce the highest SV-SB consistency, the concomitant effects of model masculinity and low nurturance should provide the lowest, and a mixture of model femininity—low nurturance or model masculinity—high nurturance intermediate values. Evidence for this hierarchy is found in Table 5 and suggests that, despite inconsistent expectations for girls, more feminine (although not necessarily highly feminine) social behaviors are accorded greater social reinforcement than less feminine behaviors. Some currently unpublished data collected by the writer provide support for this. The incidence of college girls presenting personal adjustment problems and who have more masculine mother models (46 per cent) is higher than that for girls who do not present such problems (36 per cent). The other implication of the SV-SB relations for girls, in line with the males, is that parent model nurturance is a requisite for developing strong imitative behavioral patterns in the child which allow for consistency between anticipated social consequences and manifest behaviors.

One further attribute of mothers suggested by this study which distinguishes them from fathers is that degree of nurturance does not vary as a function of their masculinity-femininity. Apparently, the stereotype of the mother in our culture is so well imbued that mothers provide nurturant relations for their children whether their psychological orientation is in other respects sex-typical or not. This distinction between mothers and fathers may very well account for some of the sex differences in relations obtained in the present study.

To this point no mention has been made of the possible antecedents of the anticipatory social reinforcement responses (SV component). It might be supposed that such anticipations would be learned in part by systematic schedules of parental reinforcement for various classes of behavior. For example, if aggressive behaviors were always punished, the child should have no difficulty in learning that aggression elicits an unfavorable social response and in establishing a negative value for this class of behaviors. Needless to say, numerous factors can interfere with the establishment of a clear value system including inconsistent reinforcement from one or both parents for the same class of behaviors, differences between parental reinforcement and peer reinforcement, adolescent rebellion against parental values, and the inability of the child to identify the class behaviors in himself (e.g., the various modes of aggression). It is also likely that values may be learned observationally. Simply because a reinforcing model behaves in a certain way or verbalizes that such behavior is commendable may be sufficient for anticipatory responses to be learned without any systematic rewards or punishments being imposed upon the child's own overt acts.

Although identification has not been introduced into the discussion of results, it is quite possible that the model and nurturant reinforcement

TABLE 6

SV-SB Consistency Scores as a Function of Degree of Identification with Same-Sex Parent at Three Levels of Sex-Typicality of Model Attributes for Male and Female Adolescents

	Males						*Females*					
	Identified			*Nonidentified*			*Identified*			*Nonidentified*		
*Level of Sex Typicality**	N	*Mean*	*SD*	N	*Mean*	*SD*	N	*Mean*	*SD*	N	*Mean*	*SD*
High	11	.61	.16	9	.67	.10	15	.68	.07	13	.69	.10
Moderate	16	.76	.10	17	.72	.09	12	.68	.11	10	.72	.08
Low	14	.69	.12	15	.72	.13	18	.67	.08	11	.68	.11

* High = model score 8–9; moderate = 6–7; low <6.

variables would prove sufficient to account for much of the parent-child similarity which is mediated by identification; identification, in turn, might prove to be a useful explanatory concept as far as behavioral consistency is concerned. The present data do not allow for a test of these possibilities and, in fact, some negative evidence was provided by a previous study (20). No relation was found between identification and SV-SB consistency for male or female college *S*s, whereas SV-SB scores did relate to the model and nurturance measures in the present study. However, the method used to measure identification, which employed a model concept, did not anticipate the curvilinear relation between father model attributes and SV-SB consistency in the case of males.

A reanalysis of the SV-SB consistency—identification data for both sexes from the earlier study in such a way as to allow for curvilinearity was performed, and the results are given in Table 6. The SV-SB scores for identified males showed the same pattern as was found in the present study.

If the father was highly masculine, SV-SB consistency was very low; if the father was moderately masculine, SV-SB consistency was very high, the difference being significant ($t = 2.71$ for 25 *df*; $p < .05$). Identification with a low masculine model resulted in an intermediate SV-SB mean. The SV-SB consistency mean for identified males with moderately masculine fathers also differed from the combined mean (.66) for the high and low groups ($t = 2.27$ for 39 *df*; $p < .05$). None of the mean differences for nonidentified male groups at the three model levels differed reliably nor did any of the female comparisons. Although the statistical analysis is far from conclusive (i.e., none of the identification by model level interactions for males was significant), there is at least a suggestion here of an increased effect of masculinity-femininity of paternal attributes upon SV-SB consistency when the son identifies with the father. Since the measure of identification was based upon behavioral similarity to the same-sex parent, the males who identify with highly masculine fathers were, by definition, highly masculine in their own behavior. Since college males tend to be more feminine in their interests patterns than their noncollege counterparts, lower SV-SB consistency could follow from less social reinforcement for highly masculine behavior, a conclusion rendered earlier in this section. If so, the question still remains whether SV-SB consistency is affected primarily through alterations in the value system of the boy, the manifest behavior, or both.

REFERENCES

1. Bandura, A., & Huston, A. C. Identification as a process of incidental learning. *J. abnorm. soc. Psychol.,* 1961, 63, 311–318.
2. Bandura, A., & Ross, D. An experimental test of the status envy, social power, and secondary reinforcement theories of identificatory learning. Reported in Bandura, A. Social learning through imitation. In M. R. Jones (Ed.), *Nebraska symposium on motivation,* 1962.
3. Bandura, A., Ross, D., & Ross, S. A. Transmission of aggression through imitation of aggressive models. *J. abnorm. soc. Psychol.,* 1961, 63, 575–582.
4. Benedict, R. Continuities and discontinuities in cultural conditioning. In J. M. Seidman, *The adolescent—a book of readings.* Holt, Winston, & Rinehart, 1960.
5. Binger, C. A. L. Emotional disturbance among college women. In G. B. Blaine, Jr. & C. C. McArthur (Eds.), *Emotional problems of the student.* Appleton-Century-Crofts, 1961.
6. Blake, R. R. The other person in the situation. In R. Tagiuri & L. Petrullo (Eds.), *Person perception and interpersonal behavior.* Stanford Univer. Press, 1958.
7. Block, J. Ego identity, role variability, and adjustment. *J. consult. Psychol.,* 1961, 25, 392–397.
8. Burchinal, L. G. Mothers' and fathers' differences in parental acceptance of children for controlled comparisons based on parental and family characteristics. *J. genet. Psychol.,* 1958, 92, 103–110.

9. Cartwright, R. D. Effects of psychotherapy on self-consistency. *J. counsel. Psychol.,* 1957, 21, 15–22.
10. Cartwright, R. D. The effects of psychotherapy on self-consistency: a replication and extension. *J. consult. Psychol.,* 1961, 25, 376–382.
11. Day, C. W. Social value—social behavior consistency and adjustment in normal and schizophrenic groups. Unpublished master's thesis, State Univer. of Iowa, 1962.
12. Edwards, A. L. *Manual for the Edwards Personal Preference Schedule.* Psychological Corp., 1959.
13. Emmerich, W. Parental identification in young children. *Genet. psychol. Monogr.,* 1959, 60, 257–308.
14. Emmerich, W. Young children's discrimination of parent and child roles. *Child Develpm.,* 1959, 30, 403–419.
15. Erickson, E. H. *Childhood and society.* Norton, 1950.
16. French, J. R. P., & Raven, B. The bases of power. In D. Cartwright (Ed.), *Studies in social power.* Ann Arbor, Mich.: Inst. Soc. Res., 1959.
17. Goodstein, L. D., & Heilbrun, A. B. Relationships between personal and social desirability sets and performance on the Edwards Personal Preference Schedule. *J. consult. Psychol.,* 1959, 43, 302–305.
18. Heilbrun, A. B. Social value—social behavior inconsistency and early signs of psychopathology in adolescence. *Child Develpm.,* 1963, 34, 187–194.
19. Heilbrun, A. B. Perceived maternal attitudes, masculinity-femininity of the maternal model and identification as related to incipient psychopathology in adolescent girls. *J. gen. Psychol.,* in press.
20. Heilbrun, A. B. Social value—social behavior consistency, parental identification, and aggression. *J. genet. Psychol.,* in press.
21. Heilbrun, A. B., & Goodstein, L. D. The consistency between social desirability ratings and item endorsement as a function of psychopathology. *Psychol. Rep.,* 1961, 8, 69–70.
22. Kagan, J., & Lemkin, J. The child's differential perception of parental attributes. *J. abnorm. soc. Psychol.,* 1960, 61, 440–447.
23. Komarovsky, M. Cultural contradictions and sex roles. *Amer. J. Sociol.,* 1946, 52, 184–189.
24. Lynn, D. B. A note on sex differences in the development of masculine and feminine identification. *Psychol. Rev.,* 1959, 66, 126–135.
25. McKee, J. B., & Sherrifs, A. C. Men's and women's beliefs, ideals, and self-concepts. In J. M. Seidman (Ed.), *The adolescent—a book of readings.* Holt, Winston, & Rinehart, 1960.
26. Mowrer, O. H. *Learning theory and personality dynamics.* Ronald, 1950.
27. Mullahy, P. *Oedipus—myth and complex.* Hermitage, 1948.
28. Rosenblith, J. F. Learning by imitation in kindergarten children. *Child Develpm.,* 1959, 30, 69–80.
29. Siegel, S. *Nonparametric statistics for the behavioral sciences.* McGraw-Hill, 1956.
30. Wallin, P. Cultural contradictions and sex roles: a repeat study. In J. M. Seidman (Ed.), *The adolescent—a book of readings.* Holt, Winston, & Rinehart, 1960.

36

EGO IDENTITY AND MATERNAL IDENTIFICATION*

SISTER M. HOWARD DIGNAN

CENTRAL TO Erikson's (1950) comprehensive theory of the epigenesis of the ego is the construct of ego identity, the usefulness of which has been widely acknowledged. While it has enriched clinical practice and has begun to demonstrate heuristic value as theory, doubts have been expressed that its measurement could be achieved (Ruesch, 1961). In the present research, a new instrument designed to measure ego identity was used to test the hypothesis that ego identity and maternal identification in women are related.

The study is confined to the adolescent period, the stage at which the conflict of identity versus role diffusion becomes intensified. In the throes of this phase-specific conflict, many adolescents, experiencing a keen sense of futility and aimlessness, lose themselves in "the crowd" to reduce the anxiety of what Erikson (1956) has called the "identity crisis." In many of these students, clinical experience reveals poor mother-daughter relationships, which, in turn, suggest that faulty maternal identification is related to the syndrome of identity diffusion just described.

Theoretical Framework

Erikson's (1956) psychosocial theory of ego development encompasses the life span of eight stages, from the oral period, to adolescence, and eventually to maturity. Each stage involving as it does a decisive encounter with the environment, embodies a conflict that must be resolved for continued devel-

* From the *Journal of Personality and Social Psychology,* 1965, *1,* 476–483. Reprinted with permission of the author and the American Psychological Association.

Based on a doctoral dissertation at Fordham University. The author wishes to express her appreciation to Joseph F. Kubis for his advice and guidance.

opment of the individual. The conflicts are not necessarily restricted to any one stage, but tend to predominate at particular periods.

Identity has been described by Erikson, although not clearly defined in his treatment. His description stresses the psychosocial nature of ego identity, with the focus, not on conflicts between psychic structures, but rather on a conflict within the ego itself, namely, of identity versus role diffusion. Emphasis has shifted to the ego and the way it is affected by society. Ego identity can therefore be defined as the complex of self-referent images which evolves through social interactions, thereby delineating the self.

Identity formation encompasses both continuity of self and identification with something beyond self. This means the individual must live up to his own expectations as well as those of the society of his time. He is constantly striving to maintain a sameness of meaning for himself and to assure himself that this constancy is recognized by others.

Identifications with significant persons of his past contribute to an individual's ego-identity formation. At the time of adolescence, childhood identifications are reintegrated into the matrix of self-images which then gradually assimilates new social and occupational roles. Among the single early identifications, that with the mother is most important. As the ego resynthesizes all childhood identifications, including maternal identification, with recent libidinal changes, emergent aptitudes, and current social and vocational roles, a unique configuration emerges. In the process, the ego works toward self-continuity, as well as constancy and sameness of meaning for himself and others. Erikson calls this sense of continuity and sameness which embraces early identification, ego identity.

Research in Ego Identity

While the concept of ego identity has appeared increasingly in the literature, research has been limited. In one of the first attempts to verify the construct operationally, G. W. Bronson (1959) demonstrated the existence of "identity diffusion" as a dimension of identity structure. His study would seem to imply that adequate ego identity is characterized by a self-concept evolved gradually from roots in earlier identifications and experienced as continuity in the personality.

Using younger subjects, Howard (1960) found that girls with more identity diffusion experience a greater sense of isolation from one or both parents. No differences in identity diffusion were found among subgroups differing in age, religion, or locale.

Rassmussen (1961) studied ego identity in relation to character disorders, where psychosocial functioning is disturbed. He found that ego-identity scores differentiated the best adjusted group from the poorly adjusted men and from those with character disorders. Age was not significantly related to ego identity within the three groups.

Identification

In Freudian theory, identification plays a fundamental role in personality development (Fenichel, 1953). Osgood, Suci, and Tannenbaum (1957) have related this view of identification to recent developments in learning theory by postulating that the process of modeling in identification takes place through meanings, as subsets of behavior which the child learns. Lazowick (1955) emphasized the distinction between imitation, which refers to the learning of behavior, and identification, which refers to the learning of meanings. The extent of the relationship between meanings of parent and meanings of child indicates the degree to which identification has taken place. Wanda Bronson (1959) calls this relationship "ego identification," implying a striving *to be like* the model in such a way that a blending of self with the qualities of the model brings about a real likeness but not an identity.

Several studies have defined identification operationally as the assumed or real similarity between parent and child (Beier & Ratzeburg, 1953; Gray, 1959; Helper, 1955; Sopchak, 1952). Multiple administrations of the Minnesota Multiphasic Personality Inventory (MMPI), rating scales, and the semantic differential were employed to determine similarity. A consistent finding was that female patterns of identification with the mother or father were not as well defined as male patterns of parental identification.

Erikson (1956) has explained how overidentification with parents cuts off a "budding identity" from its milieu, thus stifling the ego and restricting its emergent identity. In other words, such overidentification can only result in poor ego identity. Some investigators (Helper, 1955; Sopchak, 1952) have suggested that even strong identification with the mother may be detrimental to the daughter's adjustment.

On the other hand, Erikson indicates that where adequate feminine and masculine identification take place, the personality develops into a healthy and harmonious blend of feminine and masculine qualities. Ordinarily these identifications are acquired through the mother and father. If, however, one of the identifications is suppressed, it remains unsynthesized by the ego, thus weakening the identity structure. Thus, where sex identity, central to one's being (Snygg & Combs, 1959), is denied its appropriate place in the complex of self-referent ideation, it is inevitable that identity formation will be unsatisfactory. Implicit in the theory is the expectation that girls with inadequate maternal identification will have poor ego identity.

It is expected, then, that ego identity is weak with poor maternal identification, strong with good maternal identification, and poor again with overidentification which borders on the pathological. In a normal group of girls, however, where such excessive overidentification may be minimal, one would generally anticipate a positive relationship between ego identity and maternal identification. This hypothesis underlies the present research inasmuch as the sample selected, college freshmen and sophomores, represents a normal group of girls in which excessive overidentification with the mother was a relatively rare occurrence.

PROCEDURE

Subjects

College students and their mothers were asked to participate in the study. Included in the sample were 130 freshmen and 115 sophomores, who ranged in age from 17 to 20 years. All were of middle-class socioeconomic background, whose parents were living at home. The students were in residence on the campus of a Catholic women's college in the Midwest.

Of the 329 mothers who were invited by mail to participate in the study, mothers of 143 freshmen and 131 sophomores returned their ratings on the semantic differential. Of this group, responses from 99 freshman and 83 sophomore mothers were included in the sample. The remainder were excluded either because their daughters were not participating, because their own responses were incomplete, or because of clerical coding errors.

Measuring Instruments

Three test instruments were used: an Ego Identity Scale, a semantic differential, and a Rating Scale for Identity Traits. In addition, scores from the Scholastic Aptitude Test (SAT) of the College Entrance Examination Board (CEEB) were obtained from the college records.

Ego Identity Scale. Since no personality inventory available at the time appeared to be suitable for the measurement of ego identity, an Ego Identity Scale was constructed (Dignan, 1963). Its rationale was based on Erikson's (1947, 1955) description of ego identity, and on several other discussions of identity (Academy of Religion and Mental Health, 1960; G. W. Bronson, 1959; Lynd, 1958; Rassmussen, 1961; Rubins, 1961; Ruesch, 1961; Strauss, 1959; Symonds, 1951; Wheelis, 1958; White, 1952). After analyzing these reports on ego identity, the author derived several components of ego identity implicit in the various descriptions of the construct: Sense of Self, Uniqueness, Self-Acceptance, Role Expectations, Stability, Goal-Directedness, and Interpersonal Relations (Dignan, 1963). Examining the implications of these components of identity, the author then constructed 161 statements representative of them.

After a pilot study, some items were eliminated, many were reworded to avoid ambiguity, and a few more were added. Content validity was determined by submitting a final pool of 163 items to five judges who evaluated and selected items relevant to ego identity. One of the five was a woman, a clinical psychologist, and Dean of Women at a coeducational university. Of the four male judges, two were psychologists, working mainly with adolescents, and two were psychiatrists. Fifty of the 163 items were considered indicative of aspects of ego identity in the judgment of 80–100% of the judges. These 50 items constituted the Ego Identity Scale, yielding a maximum score of 50.

As indicated above, the construction of items was based on a description of ego identity found in the writings of Erikson and others who have critically examined and developed the construct. The several components which emerged as consistent descriptive indicators of ego identity are presented here in succinct form with illustrative items from the Ego Identity Scale.

Sense of Self—an abiding and intimate experience of self, an interior knowledge of what one is, a self-image central to one's being (Academy of Religion and Mental Health, 1960; Erikson, 1956; Ruesch, 1961).
At times I think I am a mystery even to myself.
What I am now is pretty much what I am going to be.

Uniqueness—a recognition of one's separate identity, distinctness from others, independence (Academy of Religion and Mental Health, 1960; G. W. Bronson, 1959; Erikson, 1950; Symonds, 1951; White, 1952).
People seldom mistake me for another girl.
I feel swallowed up by the crowd here at college.

Self-Acceptance—self-knowledge, self-appraisal, and subsequent self-acceptance or rejection of these self-images (G. W. Bronson, 1959; Rassmussen, 1961; Strauss, 1959; White, 1952).
I like to picture myself as someone else.
I know I'm not perfect but I prefer to be as I am.

Role Expectations—responsiveness to expectations of "important others" in the achievement of adequate sex identity, appropriate social roles, and satisfactory vocational roles (Erikson, 1950; Gesell & Ilg, 1946; Snygg & Combs, 1959; Symonds, 1951; White, 1952).
I believe I see myself pretty much as others see me.
It seems to me that most of the things girls do are very dull.

Stability—preservation of the same meaning for oneself and for others; implies a "rootedness," an enduring "I," consistency (G. W. Bronson, 1959; Erikson, 1947; Rubins, 1961; Ruesch, 1961; White, 1952).
First I try to be like one person I know, then another.
I don't seem to be changing as much in college as I did in high school.

Goal-Directness—awareness of what one stands for, where he is going, and self-assertion to achieve goals (Academy of Religion and Mental Health, 1960; Erikson, 1950; Symonds, 1951; Wheelis, 1958; White, 1952).
I feel a deep need to live up to my ideals.
My problem is that I don't really know what I would like to become.

Interpersonal Relations—sufficient delineation of self to permit involvement with others; intimacy, competition, love (Erikson, 1955; Lynd, 1958).
Meeting new people is fun for me.
It is easier to lay aside my principles than to fight for them against opposition.

The distributions of freshman and sophomore ego-identity scores were basically normal. The means and standard deviations for the Ego Identity Scale were 34.58 and 5.55 for 130 freshmen; 37.42 and 4.73 for 115 sophomores. The difference between these means was significant well beyond the .01 level.

The reliability of the Ego Identity Scale was determined in two ways. The odd-even correlation coefficient, corrected by the Spearman-Brown Formula, was .74 for 130 freshmen and .64 for 115 sophomores. The test-retest coefficients for a 1-week interval were .72 and .78 for smaller groups of 83 freshmen and 96 sophomores, respectively.

One estimate of validity of the Ego Identity Scale was obtained by correlating ego-identity scores with self-ratings on the Rating Scale for Identity Traits, administered to the same smaller group of 83 freshmen and 96 sophomores. The correlation coefficient for 83 freshmen was .34, for 96 sophomores, .60, both significant beyond the .01 level. It was recognized, however, that part of the variance in these coefficients may be due to a response set inasmuch as both measures were obtained from self-report inventories.

Data from the present study and from the investigations of two other researchers who used the Ego Identity Scale contribute some beginnings toward construct validity. As expected, the difference between freshman and sophomore ego-identity scores was significant and in the predicted direction. Working with a similar age group, ranging from 17 to 22 years, Thompson (1963) also reported that ego identity is a positively increasing function of age. Results of both studies are construed as a verification of White's (1952) observation that the sense of identity becomes more pronounced with age. Corroborative evidence for Erikson's (1947) statement that "In a general way it is plain that everything that makes for a strong ego contributes to its identity [p. 379]" comes from Thompson (1963) and Cleare (1963), who, although utilizing different tests of ego strength, found significant positive correlations with ego identity. Implicit in all discussions of deficient ego identity are the associated feelings of malaise, bewilderment, and dissatisfaction. The anticipated negative relation between ego identity and anxiety was confirmed for both freshmen and sophomores (Dignan, 1963). The alleged importance of one's commitment to goals and values in determining ego identity was substantiated by Thompson when she found that modification of an individual's value system entails some disintegrating effects upon ego identity. However, with subsequent assimilation of a newly embraced value system, one's sense of self is restored, and his ego-identity score increases.

The Ego Identity Scale proved independent of intellectual performance. The correlation between the scale and CEEB scores for freshmen was .10, for sophomores, .01, neither of which reached the .05 level of significance. This finding confirms a similar one by G. W. Bronson (1959) who studied identity diffusion in 46 collegians.

Semantic Differential. This instrument, devised by Osgood (1952) as a generalized technique for the measurement of meaning, was adopted by Lazowick (1955) to measure identification. In the present study, the same form, consisting of 10 concepts and 9 scales of bipolar adjectives employed by Lazowick, was given to both students and mothers. The semantic differential yielded two scores, measuring Assumed Similarity and Real Similarity between mothers and daughters. The difference between a student's ratings and her mother's ratings on the 10 concepts yielded a comparable measure of Real Similarity to mother. The difference between the scale positions for each of 10 concepts as rated by the student herself and then as she "thinks mother would do it" provided a basis for measuring Assumed Similarity to mother. The difference between a student's ratings and her mother's ratings on the 10 concepts yielded a comparable measure of Real Similarity to mother. In both cases, the root of the summed squared differences was used as the measure of similarity. To facilitate the interpretation of the similarity scores, this difference statistic was scaled on the negative real line. With this scaling, a low score means low maternal identification, a high score, high identification. Both Assumed and Real Similarity have been reported in the literature as measures of maternal identification and were used in the present study.

Rating Scale for Identity Traits. This scale, employed for purposes of validation, consists of 17 paired traits, each rated on a 6-point scale (Dignan, 1963). The traits were evaluated by the same five clinicians who provided content validity for the Ego Identity Scale.

Administration

A procedure was employed to insure anonymity for all subjects. The students were tested in two sessions held a week apart. During the first, the Ego Identity Scale and the semantic differential were administered. The semantic differential was completed twice; initially the students rated the concepts according to standard instructions; next they were instructed to rate the same 10 concepts as they believed their mothers would do it. During the second session, the Ego Identity Scale was readministered, and students also rated themselves on the Rating Scale for Identity Traits.

The semantic differential was also mailed to 329 mothers of freshmen and sophomores, with a covering letter, soliciting their cooperation, and providing instructions for returning the ratings by mail.

RESULTS

The hypothesis that ego identity would vary with maternal identification was tested in a two-way analysis of variance design. One criterion of classification was level or degree of identification (low, medium, and high), the other was class designation (freshman, sophomore). The high, medium, and low levels of maternal identification consisted of the upper, middle, and lower 20% of the identification scores. The analysis utilized both measures of maternal identification, namely, Assumed and Real Similarity to mother.

Assumed Similarity to Mother

Table 1 presents the means and standard deviations for ego-identity scores at three levels of maternal identification, that is, as measured by assumed similarity. Since heterogeneity of variance was not indicated, an analysis of variance of the ego-identity scores was completed, the results of which may

TABLE 1

Means and Standard Deviations of Ego Identity Scores at Three Levels of Maternal Identification (Assumed Similarity to Mother)

Level of Identification*	Ego Identity			
	M		*SD*	
	Freshman	*Sophomore*	*Freshman*	*Sophomore*
Low	33.80	36.65	5.21	4.98
Medium	34.10	37.55	3.90	4.46
High	37.60	39.35	3.61	3.15

* Twenty scores randomly selected at each level for each class.

be found in Table 2. There is significant variation (.01 level) among the three levels of maternal identification. For both freshmen and sophomores, ego-identity scores increase from levels of low to high maternal identification. Table 2 also reveals significant class differences in ego-identity scores. Sophomores obtained significantly higher ego-identity scores than freshmen. The Level × Class interaction is nonsignificant.

The relationship between ego identity and maternal identification is positive, as hypothesized; students who show high identification with their

TABLE 2

Analysis of Variance of Ego Identity Scores for Three Levels of Maternal Identification (Assumed Similarity to Mother)

Source	*SS*	*df*	*MS*	*F*
Level of identification	239.27	2	119.64	6.20*
Class	216.02	1	216.02	11.19*
Interaction	14.86	2	7.43	.39
Error	2,199.85	114	19.30	
Total	2,670.00	119		

* $p \leq .01$.

mothers obtained high ego-identity scores, and girls with low maternal identification were found to have low ego-identity scores.

Real Similarity to Mother

The means and standard deviations for ego-identity scores at three levels of maternal identification, as measured by Real Similarity to mother, are shown in Table 3. The data are based on a sample of 99 freshmen and 83 sophomores, whose mothers completed and returned the semantic differential. It is evident from Table 3 that for freshmen, the positive trend for

TABLE 3

Means and Standard Deviations of Ego Identity Scores at Three Levels of Maternal Identification (Real Similarity to Mother)

Level of Identification*	*Ego Identity*			
	M		*SD*	
	Freshman	*Sophomore*	*Freshman*	*Sophomore*
Low	31.80	36.60	5.89	4.53
Medium	33.87	38.60	3.93	4.19
High	35.53	38.00	4.49	2.88

* Fifteen scores selected randomly at each level for each class.

ego-identity scores and maternal identification (real similarity) corresponds to that found for ego identity and assumed similarity. For sophomores, the trend is disrupted by a maximum ego-identity score at mid-level of maternal identification.

However, the analysis of variance revealed that differences in ego-identity scores among the three levels of identification were not significant, as indicated in Table 4. Nevertheless, class differences, as expected, are significant.

In comparing the degree of Assumed and Real Similarity demonstrated

TABLE 4

Analysis of Variance of Ego Identity Scores for Three Levels of Maternal Identification (Real Similarity to Mother)

Source	*SS*	*df*	*MS*	*F*
Level of identification	110.06	2	55.03	2.64
Class	360.00	1	360.00	17.29**
Interaction	26.47	2	13.24	.64
Error	1,749.07	84	20.82	
Total	2,245.60	89		

** $p \leq .001$.

by students, it was found that 81 of 99 freshmen showed greater Real than Assumed Similarity to their mothers, and 77 of 83 sophomores manifested a similar pattern. A chi-square analysis indicated that results for both classes are significant beyond the .001 level.

DISCUSSION

As predicted, low identification (Assumed Similarity) with the mother was related to low ego identity, while high maternal identification was associated with strong ego identity. This is interpreted to mean that shared meanings between mother and daughter, indicative of maternal identification, contribute to stabilization of the daughter's identity formation. A common fund of meanings may reflect the daughter's interiorization of the maternal image, which brings about a feeling of closeness to her mother. This identification, reaching back to childhood, safeguards the sense of self-continuity during adolescence when many new and transient role identifications disturb the continuity and sameness of meaning for self and others.

Moreover, since maternal identification is one of the important identifications resynthesized by the ego with other elements of personality at adolescence, it provides a long-standing identification with the feminine role. Perhaps it is this sex-role identification, established through the mother, which contributes another stabilizing element of personality during the period of role diffusion in adolescence. Anchored in her feminine role, as she has come to see it, the young girl can experiment more freely with other roles, and at some point make the initial social and vocational commitments that begin to stabilize her identity formation. Such initial role commitments do not prevent students from embracing other roles later on; they simply mean that current stabilization of ego identity is facilitated by clarity of sex role.

It is, of course, recognized that the group studied is a special one in several respects. The students are college girls, in a small woman's college, living away from home, girls whose parents' marriage is still intact. These circumstances do not afford the same opportunities for experimentation with the wider variety of roles as those to which a working girl might have access, or those available to a student living at home and perhaps working to support her college education. Undoubtedly other populations of girls in late adolescence would provide fruitful areas for evaluating the impact of such critical environmental variables on ego identity formation in young women.

The better ego identity achieved by sophomores illustrates, in part, the resolution of the "identity crisis" described by Erikson (1956). During adolescence, stabilization of ego identity occurs gradually as the individual resynthesizes newly acquired social and vocational roles with other elements of personality. Several factors contribute to the more successful resolution of the identity crisis by sophomores. First, they have experienced continuity of place to a greater extent than freshmen, an important factor in identity formation, according to Ruesch (1961). They feel at home in the college milieu. Second, they have identified with the social roles of young woman and college student longer than freshmen who are still experimenting with varied social roles and expectations in collegiate life. In the third place, while freshmen continue to weigh vocational possibilities, sophomores usually have already committed themselves to major fields of study and fairly definite vocational goals.

Research relevant to ego identity and maternal identification is sparse. Howard (1960) reported that among high-school girls those with poorer identity were more isolated from one or both parents. This report did not specify results for the same-sex or cross-sexed parent. A similar finding emerged in the present investigation; that is, when maternal identification, implying an emotional closeness to the mother, is low, so also is ego identity.

In the present study, both Assumed and Real Similarity to mother were employed as measures of maternal identification. A consistent trend for ego-identity scores to increase with levels of maternal identification was found with both measures, although with the Real Similarity measure differences in ego-identity scores were not significant. These findings suggest that identity formation is more closely related to the girl's subjective experience of mother-daughter similarity than to any objective likeness of thought between them.

Contrary to Lazowick's (1955) findings that college women showed greater Assumed than Real Similarity to mother, the present study indicates that by far the greater majority of students manifest more Real than Assumed Similarity to mother. Thus the present findings fail to confirm the "masculine protest" reported by Lazowick. Differences in methodology and sampling may account for the contradictory results. Although both studies used the same technique to assess Real Similarity, Lazowick measured Assumed Similarity by students' ratings on only 2 concepts, "Myself" and "Mother," whereas, in the present investigation, all 10 concepts were rated by the students *twice,* once as they evaluated them and again as they thought their mothers would do so. The two samples also differ in size and background. Lazowick's 30 subjects included male and female students in a coeducational university, hence the size of the female sample was small. However, the present investigation used a sample of 245 students in a women's college. Furthermore, scores for two college classes were analyzed separately and found to yield consistent results. Not only does the present study fail, then, to corroborate Lazowick's hypothesized "masculine protest" in college women; it indicates that girls who identify well with their mothers manifest better ego identity.

REFERENCES

Academy of Religion and Mental Health. *Religion in the developing personality.* New York: New York Univer. Press, 1960.

Beier, E. G., & Ratzeburg, F. The parental identification of male and female college students. *Journal of Abnormal and Social Psychology*, 1953, **48**, 569–572.

Bronson, G. W. Identity diffusion in late adolescence. *Journal of Abnormal and Social Psychology*, 1959, **59**, 414–417.

Bronson, Wanda. Dimensions of ego and infantile identification. *Journal of Personality*, 1959, **27**, 532–545.

Cleare, William Maria, Sr. The relationship between value systems and personality integration. Unpublished master's thesis, Fordham University, 1963.

Dignan, M. Howard, Sr. Ego identity, maternal identification, and adjustment in college women. Unpublished doctoral dissertation, Fordham University, 1963.

Erikson, E. H. Ego development and historical change. In Anna Freud, H. Hartman, & E. Kris (Eds.), *Psychoanalytic study of the child*. Vol. 2. New York: International Univer. Press, 1947. Pp. 359–396.

Erikson, E. H. *Childhood and society*. New York: Norton, 1950.

Erikson, E. H. Growth and crises of the "healthy personality." In C. Kluckhohn & H. A. Murray (Eds.), *Personality in nature, society, and culture* (2d ed.) New York: Knopf, 1955. Pp. 185–225.

Erikson, E. H. The problem of ego identity. *Journal of the American Psychoanalytic Association*, 1956, **4**, 56–119.

Fenichel, O. Identification. In Hanna Fenichel & D. Rapaport (Eds.), *The collected papers of Otto Fenichel*. New York: Norton, 1953. Pp. 97–113.

Gesell, A., & Ilg, Frances. *The child from five to ten*. New York: Harper, 1946.

Gray, Susan. Perceived similarity to parents and adjustment. *Child Development*, 1959, **30**, 91–107.

Helper, M. M. Learning theory and the self concept. *Journal of Abnormal and Social Psychology*, 1955, **51**, 184–194.

Howard, Linda. Identity conflicts in adolescent girls. *Smith College Studies in Social Work*, 1960, **31**, 1–21.

Lazowick, L. M. On the nature of identification. *Journal of Abnormal and Social Psychology*, 1955, **51**, 175–183.

Lynd, Helen. *On shame and the search for identity*. New York: Harcourt, Brace, 1958.

Osgood, C. E. The nature and measurement of meaning. *Psychological Bulletin*, 1952, **49**, 197–237.

Osgood, C. E., Suci, G. J., & Tannenbaum, P. *The measurement of meaning*. Urbana: Univer. Illinois Press, 1957.

Rassmussen, J. E. An experimental approach to the concept of ego identity as related to character disorders. Unpublished doctoral dissertation, American University, 1961.

Rubins, J. L. The self concept, identity and alienation from self. *American Journal of Psychoanalysis*, 1961, **21**, 135–141.

Reusch, J. *Therapeutic communication*. New York: Norton, 1961.

Snygg, D., & Combs, A. *Individual behavior*. (Rev. ed.) New York: Harper, 1959.

Sopchak, A. Parental "identification" and "tendency toward disorder" as measured by the MMPI. *Journal of Abnormal and Social Psychology*, 1952, **47**, 159–165.

Strauss, A. L. *Mirrors and masks: A search for identity.* New York: Free Press of Glencoe, 1959.

Symonds, P. M. *The ego and the self.* New York: Appleton-Century-Crofts, 1951.

Thompson, M. St. George, Sr. Modifications in identity: A study of the socialization process during a sister formation program. Unpublished doctoral dissertation, University of Chicago, 1963.

Wheelis, A. *In quest of identity.* New York: Norton, 1958.

White, R. W. *Lives in progress.* New York: Dryden Press, 1952.

37

THE STABILITY OF PASSIVE AND DEPENDENT BEHAVIOR FROM CHILDHOOD THROUGH ADULTHOOD*

JEROME KAGAN
and
HOWARD A. MOSS

A BASIC ASSUMPTION of developmental theory is that adult behaviors are often established in early childhood. Although retrospective reports obtained from the verbal protocols of adults support this assumption, it has been difficult to produce a more objective demonstration of the long term stability of childhood behavior patterns. This unhappy state of affairs is a consequence of the expense and difficulty associated with collecting long term longitudinal information on a large sample of children. Only extensive, longitudinal research programs, as exemplified by the Berkeley Growth Study or the Fels Research Institute, can furnish the answers to this developmental problem.

This paper presents one set of results which have emerged from a recent study of a group of "normal" adults from the Fels longitudinal research population for whom extensive information was available from birth through adolescence. The findings deal specifically with the long term stability of passive and dependent behavior in the face of situations which are frustrating and/or demand problem solving activity. This particular behavioral variable was chosen for initial analysis because theoretical essays on personality development emphasize that the early dependence of the child on the parent is of the utmost importance in shaping his future personality. That is, the development of a variety of adult motives and behaviors are based on the quality and intensity of the dependent relationship with the mother and mother-substitute figures. Further, psychological symptoms are

* From *Child Development,* 1960, 31, 577–594. Reprinted with permission from the authors and the Society for Research in Child Development.

This research was supported, in part, by research grant M-1260 from the National Institute of Mental Health, United States Public Health Service. Parts of this paper were presented at the annual meeting of the Midwestern Psychological Association in Chicago, May 1959.

theoretically attributed to inconsistency in the gratification of the child's dependent overtures and/or to denial or inhibition of dependent motives or behavior.

In addition to the longitudinal material, each subject was recently assessed during early adulthood by means of both interview and test procedures. The adult assessment was focused on the behavioral variables of dependency, aggression, achievement, and sexuality and on the degree of conflict and type of defensive responses associated with behavioral strivings in these areas. It was anticipated that there might be important sex differences with respect to occurrence of these behaviors, and the assessment procedures were designed to detect these potential sex differences.

METHOD

The Sample

The subjects (*Ss*) in this analysis were 27 male and 27 female Caucasian adults born between 1930 and 1939 who had recently been through a comprehensive assessment program which included an average of five hours of tape recorded interview and a variety of test procedures. The *Ss* were between 20 and 29 years of age at the time of the assessment. In addition, these *Ss* had fairly complete longitudinal records from 3 to 10 years of age. The *Ss* were predominantly middle class but came from a variety of vocational backgrounds including agricultural, skilled labor, tradesmen, and professional groups. The religious affiliations of the group included 43 Protestants, 10 Catholics and 1 Jewish subject. The mean Wechsler-Bellevue IQ of the group was 120 with an IQ range of 97 to 142.

Interview Variables: Adult Assessment

Each *S* was interviewed by the senior author for approximately five hours over two to three sessions. *The interviewer had absolutely no knowledge of any of the longitudinal information on the* Ss. Since these *Ss* had been studied by psychologists for over 20 years, rapport was usually excellent, and defensive and evasive answers were infrequent. Following the interviews, each *S* was rated (7-point scale) on 59 variables. Six of these adult interview variables dealt specifically with passive and dependent behavior; abridged definitions of these variables follow:

Degree to which dependent gratifications were sought in choice of vocation. This variable assessed the degree to which security was an important aspect of job choice, the degree to which the subject looked to his employer for gratification of his dependent needs, reluctance to shift jobs because of temporary loss of security. For nonworking women, emphasis was placed on her attitudes about the importance of security in her husband's job.

Degree of dependent behavior toward a love object. This variable assessed the degree to which the subject sought advice and emotional support from a love object (sweetheart, husband, wife), degree to which the subject looked for stability and wisdom in a love object, degree to which responsibility for decision making was given to love object.

Degree of dependent behavior with parents. This variable assessed the degree to which the subject looked for advice, support, emotional encouragement, and nurturance from one or both parents.

Degree of dependent behavior toward nonparental figures. This variable assessed the degree to which the subject sought advice, emotional support, and nurturance from nonparental figures who were not love objects, e.g., friends, relatives, and teachers.

Tendency to display behavioral withdrawal in the face of anticipated failure. This variable assessed the frequency and consistency with which *S* tended to withdraw from tasks and situations which he thought were difficult to master and in which failure was anticipated.

Degree of conflict over dependent behavior. This variable assessed the degree to which the subject avoided placing himself in dependent positions, his derogation of dependent behavior in self and others, and his emphasis on the value and importance of independent behavior.

A random sample of 32 taped interviews were independently studied and rated. The interrater reliabilities for the six dependency variables ranged from .63 to .82 with an average coefficient of .74.

Procedure for Evaluation of Childhood Behavior

The junior author, who had no knowledge of the adult psychological status of the *S*s, evaluated narrative reports based on direct observation of the child in a variety of situations. Summaries of interviews with the child and the mothers were also available. The observation reports were based on (*a*) semiannual visits to the home in which a staff member observed the child interact with mother and siblings for a two to four hour period, (*b*) semiannual or annual observations of the child in the Fels experimental nursery school and day camp settings, (*c*) interviews with the child, and (*d*) observations of the child in the classroom. After studying this material, the psychologist rated each child for a comprehensive set of variables (7-point scale). The rater studied the material for each *S* for ages 3 to 6 and made his ratings. Following a period of interpolated work, he then studied all the material for each *S* for ages 6 to 10 and again made the ratings. A period of approximately six months intervened between the evaluation of the material for any one child for ages 3 to 6 and 6 to 10. The rater felt that retroactive inhibition was sufficiently intense to mask any halo effect of the preschool ratings upon the later ratings made for 6 to 10 years of age. That is, the amount of material studied and the large number of variables rated militated against the recall of specific ratings over such a long period of time. In addition, the high degree of interrater reliability for these ratings supports the above statement. Independent ratings of the four childhood dependency variables by a second psychologist produced satisfactory interrater reliabilities. The product-moment correlations for each variable were all in the .80's with an average reliability of .86. The four childhood variables which involved passive and dependent behavior were defined as follows:

Tendency to behave in a passive manner when faced with environmental obstacles or stress (rated for ages 3 to 6 and 6 to 10). This variable assessed the degree to which the child was behaviorally passive in the face of external frustrations and failed to make any active mastery attempts to obtain desired goal objects following frustration. The rating of a passive behavioral reaction emphasized withdrawal from the frustration but included whining, crying, and soliciting help.

Tendency to seek support, nurturance, and assistance from female adults when under stress: general dependence (rated for age 3 to 6). This variable assessed the *S*'s behavioral tendency to obtain assistance, nurturance, or affection from mother and other female adults when confronted with a threat to his well-being, a problem, or loss of a desired goal object. Dependent behavior included seeking out adults when faced with a problem or personal injury, reluctance to start a task without help or encouragement, seeking assistance of others, seeking affection from and close contact with female adults.

Tendency to seek affection and emotional support from female adults (rated for ages 6 to 10). This variable assessed the degree to which the child sought affection or emotional encouragement from mother or mother substitute figures. Evidence included kissing, holding hands, clinging, seeking encouragement or proximity to female adults.

Tendency to seek instrumental assistance from female adults (rated for ages 6 to 10). This variable assessed the degree to which the child sought instrumental help with specific problems from mother, teachers, or other female authority figures. Instrumental dependent acts included seeking help with tasks, seeking help when physically threatened.

As mentioned above the average interrater reliability for these four variables was + .86.

The distributions for both the childhood and interview variables were normal. Product-moment correlations were computed between each of the childhood variables and the six interview based dependency variables obtained in adulthood with separate analyses for males and females.

Tachistoscopic Perception

After the interviews and interview ratings were completed, each adult *S* was seen for a variety of test procedures, one of which was a tachistoscopic perception task. A series of 14 scenes were drawn to suggest action in the areas of dependency, aggression, sexuality, and physical danger. Three motivationally neutral, control pictures were also included. For nine of the 14 pictures, separate pairs of illustrations were made for males and females so that the sex of the central figure was the same as the sex of the subject. The pictures were black and white line drawings with minimal background details. A brief description of the three dependency pictures follows:

1. A young adult in the foreground (male for male *S*s and female for female *S*s) is on his knees clutching to the waist of a figure of the same age but of opposite sex who is standing and looking forward. The figure on the floor is looking up at the face of the standing figure.
2. A young adult in the foreground (male for male *S*s and female for female *S*s) has his arms extended in an imploring gesture toward an adult of the same sex who is standing in the background with his back to the figure in the foreground.
3. A young adult (male for male *S*s and female for female *S*s) is seated on a chair with head buried in the abdomen of an adult of the opposite sex who is standing and comforting the seated figure.

The 14 pictures were presented seven times at seven different exposure speeds and in six different orders. The seven speeds ranged from .01 to 1.0 seconds. The pictures were shown initially at the fastest exposure (.01 second), and each succeeding series was presented at a slower exposure speed. All exposures were above threshold and all *S*s reported seeing something at each exposure. The *S* sat in a light proof room, 22 in. from a flash-opal milk glass screen. The image was projected from the back of the screen, and the field was constantly illuminated by a 35 mm. projector (30 ft.-candles at the screen). The subject was told to state for each picture (*a*) the sex of each figure, (*b*) the approximate ages of each figure, and (*c*) what each figure on the picture was doing. The *S* was given three practice pictures to adapt him to the task and its requirements, and the entire protocol was electrically recorded and transcribed verbatim.

The protocols were scored for recognition threshold for each picture. Recognition threshold was defined as the first series at which the picture was described accurately and all succeeding trials were accurately described. The distribution of recognition thresholds differed among the 14 pictures and were markedly skewed either to the low or high end of the scale. Thus, the distribution of recognition thresholds for each picture was divided at the median into early and late recognition groups for statistical operations.

RESULTS

Stability of Dependent Behavior

Table 1 presents the product-moment correlations between the childhood and adult ratings of passive and dependent behavior.

TABLE 1

Correlations between Passive-Dependent Behavior in Childhood and Adulthood

Childhood Variables	Dependency in Vocation		Dependency on Love Object		Dependency on Parents		Dependency on Others		Withdrawal to Failure		Dependency Conflict	
	M	F	M	F	M	F	M	F	M	F	M	F
Passivity (ages 3 to 6)	−.07	.24	.10	.23	−.28	.25	.04	.19	.06	.26	.03	.01
Passivity (ages 6 to 10)	.11	.73**	.25	.36*	−.20	.54**	.04	.06	.21	.52**	−.26	−.63**
General dependence (ages 3 to 6)	−.06	.21	.13	.20	−.07	.07	.11	−.06	.12	.00	.05	.26
Emotional dependence (ages 6 to 10)	.21	.08	.18	.37*	.02	.51**	−.02	.06	.35*	.37*	−.12	−.31
Instrumental dependence (ages 6 to 10)	.19	.39*	.06	.58**	.14	.32	.37*	.01	.09	.39*	−.04	−.17

Adult Dependency Variables

* $p < .05$, one tail.
** $p < .01$, one tail.

The major result is that passive and dependent behaviors were fairly stable for females but not for males. For girls the ratings of passivity during ages 6 to 10 correlated significantly with the adult ratings of a dependent orientation in vocational choice, dependency on love object, dependency on parents, and withdrawal to failure. Childhood passivity was inversely correlated with adult conflict over dependent behavior. That is, females who were passive as children were apt to accept their dependent behavior in adulthood and show minimal anxiety over their dependent motives. Only dependent behavior toward nonparental figures failed to show a significant, positive correlation with the childhood ratings of passivity. Similarly, the childhood ratings of both instrumental and emotional dependency on female adults, for girls aged 6–10, predicted adult ratings of dependency on love object, dependency on parents, and withdrawal to anticipated failure situations.

For the men there were only two significant correlations between the childhood dependency ratings and those based on the adult interview. Boys who were high on instrumental dependency for ages 6 to 10 were high on dependent behavior towards nonparental figures in adulthood. Second, emotional dependence during ages 6 to 10 was positively correlated with adult withdrawal to failure.

Of the 18 correlations between each of the three childhood variables for ages 6 to 10 and the six adult variables, 60 per cent were significant in the expected direction for females, while only 9 per cent were significant for the men.

Tables 2 and 3 present the intercorrelations among the childhood and adult interview variables, respectively.

The correlations among the passive and dependency variables between

TABLE 2

Intercorrelations among Childhood Dependency Variables

	Passivity (6 to 10)		*Gen. Dep.* (3 to 6)		*Emot. Dep.* (6 to 10)		*Instr. Dep.* (6 to 10)	
	M	*F*	*M*	*F*	*M*	*F*	*M*	*F*
Passivity (3 to 6)	.82**	.76**	.74**	.83**	.26	.80**	.38	.79**
Passivity (6 to 10)	..	..	.40*	.63**	.43*	.65**	.53**	.61**
General dependence (3 to 6)	..	..	..	..	.37	.61**	.38*	.63**
Emotional dependence (6 to 10)	..	..	..	..	..	..	.60**	.79**
Instrumental dependence (6 to 10)	..	..	..	..	..	..	..	..

* $p < .05$, two tails.
** $p < .01$, two tails.

ages 3 to 6 and 6 to 10 were generally more consistent for girls than for boys. That is, for girls the correlations among passivity and general dependence for ages 3 to 6 and the three variables for ages 6 to 10 were all consistently high. For boys the stability of the passivity rating for ages 3 to 6 and 6 to 10 was quite high. However, the relationships between passivity for 3 to 6 and the two dependency behaviors for 6 to 10 were not as high as they were for girls. This finding suggests that overt seeking of affection and/or instrumental aid in school age boys begins to be dissociated from a passive withdrawal reaction to problem situations.

The intercorrelations among the adult dependency variables were generally positive for both sexes. Dependency on parents and dependency on love objects were each associated with withdrawal to failure and negatively related to conflict over dependency. It is interesting to note that women who are dependent on their parents tended to be dependent on their love object

TABLE 3

Intercorrelations among Adult Dependency Variables

	Dependence Love Object		*Dependence Parents*		*Dependence Others*		*Withdrawal*		*Dependence Conflict*	
	M	*F*	*M*	*F*	*M*	*F*	*M*	*F*	*M*	*F*
Dep. vocation	.61**	.42*	.53**	.49**	.12	−.10	.41*	.50**	−.61**	−.56**
Dep. love object	..	..	.24	.54**	.48**	.16	.49**	.54**	−.66**	−.50**
Dep. parents	..	..	..	..	.39*	.03	.44**	.57**	−.59**	−.71**
Dep. others	..	..	..	..	..	..	.38*	−.15	−.46**	.15
Withdrawal	..	..	..	..	..	..	..	..	−.57**	−.70**
Dep. conflict	..	..	..	..	..	..	..	..	..	..

* $p < .05$, two tails.
** $p < .01$, two tails.

but not on friends or authority figures. Men, on the other hand, who were dependent on their parents tended to be dependent on friends and authority figures rather than on a love object. Dependency on parents and friends usually involves instrumental aid with problems, while dependency on a love object more often included the soliciting of emotional support and affection. It will be recalled that one of the two significant correlations for males between childhood and adult dependency involved instrumental dependency for ages 6 to 10 with adult dependency on nonparental authority figures. Emotional dependency for boys age 6 to 10 showed no correlations with the adult dependency variables. Thus, male dependent behavior is apt to emphasize the seeking of instrumental assistance with problems, while females are likely to seek affection and emotional support in addition to instrumental aid.

It is important to note that passive and dependent behavior for ages 6 to 10 showed a better relation to adult dependent behavior than the ratings for 3 to 6 years of age. This finding indicates that important age changes occur between ages 3 and 10 and that behavior displayed during the first few years of school is a better index of adult functioning than the earlier preschool behavior patterns.

Tachistoscopic Perception of Dependent Pictures

There were significant sex differences in recognition threshold for the three dependency pictures with the females recognizing all three pictures earlier than the males. The scene that depicted a person imploring a same sexed adult (picture 2) yielded the most significant sex difference ($p < .001$, two tails). The picture of the adult on his knees clutching on to an opposite sexed adult (picture 1) and that of the seated adult holding on to an opposite sexed adult (picture 3) yielded sex differences significant at the .005 and .08 levels, respectively, for two tails. The aggressive pictures, on the other hand, produced opposite results, for the females recognized two of the four aggression pictures significantly later than the men ($p < .01$, two tails). There were no significant sex differences for the sex, physical danger, or three neutral scenes.

There was not a highly consistent relationship between recognition threshold for the dependent scenes and the interview ratings of dependency conflict. Only recognition of the scene that illustrated a man on his knees in front of a woman (picture 1) showed a relation to dependency conflict, and this held only for males. The males who were above the median in recognition threshold for this scene (late recognition) were rated as more conflicted over dependent behavior than males who recognized this picture early ($p = .07$, two tails). For the females, recognition threshold for the dependency pictures showed no significant relation to ratings of dependency conflict.

DISCUSSION

The results support a basic hypothesis of developmental theory which states that the acquisition of certain adult response patterns begins in early childhood. The differential stability of passive-dependent behavior for men and women is probably the result of several factors. However, one set of processes which may contribute to this phenomenon is derived from the commonly accepted hypothesis that passive and dependent behavior is less punished in females than in males. Further, females are often encouraged to be passive while men are expected to be independent and autonomous in the face of frustration. Parental and peer group punishment for passive and dependent behavior should result in some inhibition of this behavior in males. Thus, we would not expect this class of behavior to be as stable for men as for women. Studies of both overt behavior and fantasy (2, 3, 4, 6, 7) all indicate that dependent responses are more frequent for girls than for boys. Further, the sex stereotypes presented by communication media fit this description. The analysis of children's books by Child, Potter, and Levine (1) indicated that girls are portrayed as passive while boys are presented as independent and heroic. Finally, a study of the likes and dislikes of 10-year-old children (5) confirms the belief that girls accept passive behavior as more appropriate for their sex role than do boys.

The present tachistoscopic threshold data support the notion that men are more conflicted over dependent behavior than women. It will be recalled that the women recognized all three scenes depicting dependent behavior much earlier than the men. This finding suggests that the tendency to perceive dependent behavior in adults is much weaker in men than it is in women. One possible cause of this "weaker perceptual hypothesis" is that dependent action is less acceptable to men, i.e., that men are more conflicted over dependent behavior. This conclusion finds support in the correlation, for men, between late recognition of dependency (picture 1) and the interview rating of dependency conflict.

Detailed analysis of the 54 cases indicates that there was a greater proportion of men, than women, who shifted from high dependency during childhood to independent behavior as adults. The women tended to be either dependent or independent for both childhood and adulthood. For example, in comparing emotional dependence for ages 6 to 10 with adult dependency on parents, not one female showed a major shift from high dependency in childhood to low dependency in adulthood. For the men, however, 20 per cent were rated very dependent during the ages 6 to 10 and very independent in adulthood.

The authors do not suggest that passive and dependent behavior in girls is rigidly fixed at school age and that change is a rare or unusual phenomenon. It must be kept in mind that the social milieu of these particular subjects remained rather constant throughout their lives. Their familial and extrafamilial environments were not disrupted to any marked degree. The parents and peers of these *S*s retained their same values, their reference groups remained constant, and, in most cases, their geographical travel was limited. Thus, the degree of behavioral stability obtained for these females might not hold for populations that are more mobile or transient, for different ethnic or class samples, or for people subjected to major traumata during adolescence and early adulthood.

Implicit in these results is a strategy for certain research problems in developmental psychology. It would appear that a select group of theoretically relevant behaviors become clearly established as preferential response tendencies as early as 6 to 10 years of age. This means that one can study the child longitudinally without having to wait 15 to 20 years before asking important questions of the data. Since the current philosophy of financial support for research allows an investigator to chart a 5 to 10 year program, it is now feasible for one investigator to see the products of a longitudinally oriented project in a reasonable length of time.

. . . .

SUMMARY

This paper summarized some results from a larger investigation of the stability of behavior in a group of subjects who were part of the Fels Research Institute's longitudinal population. This report dealt specifically with the long term stability of passive and dependent behavior from childhood through adulthood.

The *S*s were 27 males and 27 females for whom extensive longitudinal information was available from birth through adolescence. One psychologist studied narrative reports based on observations of the child in various settings and rated each child on four variables describing types of passive and dependent behavior for ages 3 to 6 and ages 6 to 10. A second psychologist, who had no knowledge of the childhood data, interviewed each *S* in adulthood and rated each *S* on six variables related to aspects of adult passive and dependent behavior. In addition, each adult *S* was administered a tachistoscopic perception task in which scenes illustrating dependent activity were presented at seven different exposure speeds.

The results revealed that passive and dependent behaviors were quite stable for women, but minimally stable for men. Over 60 per cent of the correlations between the childhood (ages 6 to 10) and adult ratings of dependency were statistically significant for females, while only 9 per cent were significant for men. For example, the correlation between passive withdrawal from problem situations for ages 6 to 10 and adulthood was .52 ($p < .01$) for women and .21 for men. Similarly, the correlation between emotional dependence for ages 6 to 10 and adult dependency on parents was

.51 ($p < .01$) for women and .02 for men. The correlations between the ratings for ages 3 to 6 and adulthood were considerably lower and not statistically significant.

It was suggested that environmental disapproval and punishment of dependent behavior in young males led to inhibition of and conflict over dependency in the growing boy. The social acceptance of passive and dependent behavior in females would be expected to result in greater stability for this class of responses for women than for men. The fact that females recognized the tachistoscopically presented dependency scenes earlier than the men was interpreted as support for this explanation.

REFERENCES

1. Child, I. L., Potter, E. H., & Levine, Estelle M. Children's textbooks and personality development: an exploration in the social psychology of education. *Psychol. Monogr.,* 1946, 60, No. 279.
2. Hattwick, Bertha. Sex differences in behavior of nursery school children. *Child Develpm.,* 1937, 8, 323–355.
3. Kagan, J. The stability of TAT fantasy and stimulus ambiguity. *J. consult. Psychol.,* 1959, 23, 266–271.
4. Sanford, R. N., Adkins, M. M., Miller, R. B., & Cobb, E. N. Physique, personality and scholarship: a comprehensive study of school children. *Monogr. Soc. Res. Child Develpm.,* 1943, 8, No. 1.
5. Tyler, Leona E. The development of vocational interests. I. The organization of likes and dislikes in ten year old children. *J. genet. Psychol.,* 1955, 86, 33–44.
6. Watson, R. I. *Psychology of the child.* New York: Wiley, 1959.
7. Whitehouse, Elizabeth. Norms for certain aspects of the Thematic Apperception Test on a group of nine and ten year old children. *J. Pers.,* 1949, 1, 12–15.

38

STABILITY AND CHANGE IN THE ADOLESCENT'S SELF-IMAGE*

RAE CARLSON

CURRENT PERSONALITY theory defines as a central problem of adolescence the task of achieving a sense of personal identity. While the psychological processes involved in consolidating a sense of identity cannot, as yet, be fully specified, one reflection of the basic personality change might be found by observing continuities and changes in the self concept during this developmental period.

Surprisingly little is known about stability and change in the self concept during adolescence. The basic problem would seem to require longitudinal study of the structure of the self concept over a period of adolescent development. Such longitudinal studies are rare, however, and at present the major empirical work is represented by Engel's (1959) study. Engel found a relatively high degree of stability in adolescents' *Q*-sort self-descriptions over a 2-year period and found indicators of self concept related to adjustment but independent of age, sex, and intelligence within her sample. The implications of Engel's findings—that the self concept remains stable through adolescence and is unrelated to sex role—are limited by certain problems of method. The developmental period encompassed only a 2-year span, and the conceptualization of "self concept" was apparently limited to a dimension of self-esteem. A further problem derives from her self-concept measure, built upon the adolescent's ordering of clearly favorable or unfavorable self-descriptive statements. Thus some of the stability observed may represent the *S*s response in terms of fairly transparent social desirability of the items.

The present paper reports a longitudinal study that attempts a more-differentiated conception of stability and change in the self concept of the adolescent. Basically, the study examines the "fate" of two independent dimensions of the self-image—social versus personal orientation and self-esteem—over a 6-year period of adolescent development and seeks evidence bearing upon the construct validity of these concepts.

* From *Child Development*, 1965, *36*, 659–666. Reprinted with permission from the author and the Society for Research in Child Development.

In a previous study of preadolescents (Carlson, 1963), social-personal orientation and self-esteem, conceptually independent dimensions of the self-image, were shown to be related to the quality of the preadolescent's parental identification and to his sociometric status. Social orientation refers to the salience of interpersonal experiences in the individual's conceptions of himself and implies a degree of vulnerability to social appraisals, while personal orientation refers to conceptions of self which are independent of concern with social experiences. Self-esteem here refers to the correspondence between one's present concept of self and his self-ideals. A major expectation of the present study is that these two dimensions of self develop in different ways during the adolescent years.

Current personality theory and research would suggest that social-personal orientation is linked to sex-role differentiation during this period. Important differences in definitions of social sex roles center upon the emphasis upon autonomy, activity, and independence in males and the emphasis upon social sensitivity, passivity, and conformity in females. In terms of the present research variables, the stereotype of the masculine role implies a personal orientation; the stereotype of the feminine role implies a social orientation. Evidence supporting this expectation of sex differences comes from studies (Hovland & Janis, 1959) that suggest that, among adults, men are relatively autonomous and independent, while women tend to be more conforming, persuasible, and field-dependent. At the adolescent level, Douvan (1960) found ego integration among adolescent boys related to the development of personal, independent standards, while ego integration in girls was linked to interpersonal skill and sensitivity. However, in research with younger children, Carlson (1963) found the majority of preadolescent subjects personally oriented, with no evidence for sex differences in social-personal orientation. Apparently, then, it is during adolescence that sex differentiation on this dimension occurs. This reasoning led to Hypothesis 1: over a 6-year period of adolescent development girls show an increase in social orientation and boys show an increase in personal orientation.

In contrast to social-personal orientation, the second major variable, self-esteem, is conceptualized as independent of sex role. While males and females may be expected to differ in the content of their self-perceptions and self-ideals, the degree of congruence between self-perceptions and self-ideals should be comparable for the sexes. Hypothesis 2 predicted that the level of self-esteem and the stability of self-esteem over a 6-year period would be independent of sex.

Two hypotheses were concerned with the relationship of social-personal orientation to other aspects of personality. From assumptions about the developmental tasks of preadolescents, as compared with those of adolescents, one would expect the correlates of social-personal orientation to differ at the two developmental levels. For the preadolescent, as yet relatively unconcerned with assuming adult sex-role expectations, a major task is the development of competence and autonomy. Here a socially oriented self concept would imply an overreliance upon social experiences in defining the self and thus a potential instability of self-esteem. The adolescent, on the other hand, is establishing an identity consonant with culturally defined masculine and feminine adult roles. Here the sex of the individual would be expected to mediate the relationship between social-personal orientation and stability of self-esteem. Specifically, social orientation in adolescent girls would not connote instability of self-esteem, since a social orientation is thought to be a component of the feminine role. For the boy, however, a socially oriented self-image implies a degree of "failure" in his developmental task of achieving the independence and autonomy of the masculine role and thus should be associated with devalued self-esteem. Hypothesis 3 predicted that social orientation in the preadolescent is associated with a drop in the level of self-esteem over a 6-year period among both boys and girls and that social orientation in adolescence is associated with devalued self-esteem in boys, but not in girls.

A further correlate of social orientation is expected in the adolescent's perceptions of other people. Presumably, the socially oriented individual is relatively sensitive to "interpersonal" qualities of those around him, while the personally oriented individual is more likely to perceive others in terms of objective characteristics or "individual" qualities. Hypothesis 4 predicted that socially oriented adolescents more frequently use "interpersonal" constructs in their perceptions of others than do personally oriented adolescents.

Individual differences in the level of self-esteem are assumed to influence the quality of the individual's relationships with others. The adolescent who is low in self-esteem is expected to be relatively anxious, self-conscious, and more ready to interpret interpersonal experiences in an "egocentric" fashion. Two specific predictions explored this aspect of self-esteem. Hypothesis 5 predicted that adolescents low in self-esteem should more frequently show "egocentric" perceptions of other people. Hypothesis 6 predicted that low self-esteem *S*s should more often disclose their identities in responding to an anonymous questionnaire.

METHOD

Subjects

The preadolescent study was based upon the population of five sixth-grade classrooms drawn from middle-class neighborhoods of Seattle. In the initial testing only those pupils who were absent at one or the other of two group testing situations were excluded, in addition to those few who were known to have severe reading disabilities or foreign-language home backgrounds. Of this original group of 150 preadolescents, the 87 *S*s listed in the telephone directory at the same home address 6 years later were asked to participate in the follow-up study. A letter explaining the study and copies of the questionnaires were mailed during the summer vacation period. An imbalance in the sex distribution of the original population was successively increased by a slight, but consistent tendency for girls to respond more than boys. *S*s who returned incomplete questionnaires were discarded, and the final sample included 33 girls and 16 boys.

The biases in the sample are obvious: The research group is based upon volunteer *S*s and excluded children from socially and geographically mobile families. While there is no reason to expect any systematic bias in the results related to these factors, several steps were taken to detect and evaluate possible bias. The research sample was found to be comparable to the group lost on the follow-up in their initial (preadolescent) scores on social-personal orientation and self-esteem. To control for effects of possible interaction of sex differences and volunteer bias, separate analyses of sex differences on the major research variables were made for (*a*) the total sample of boys versus girls and (*b*) a subsample including the group of boys versus a special sample of girls matched with the boys on their initial (preadolescent) scores. Since the results of analyses based on the subsample were entirely comparable to results obtained on the total sample, no evidence of bias based upon interaction of sex and volunteering was observed. Therefore, only the data based upon the total sample of 49 are reported here.

Measures

Parallel forms of a self-descriptive questionnaire were given to provide self and ideal-self descriptions at the preadolescent and adolescent levels. The basic instrument was designed to control several response sets: Elevation and dispersion sets were controlled by using a multiple-choice, forced-choice format; a favorability set was controlled by equating the social desirability of response alternatives; and response in terms of sex-role stereotypes was minimized by eliminating obviously sex-typed content. Half of the self-descriptive statements were designed to reflect orientation to social experiences, and half of the items were concerned with individual characteristics having no direct implication of concern with social experiences. Judges' ratings were used to determine the social desirability of items and in coding social versus personal orientation on both the preadolescent and adolescent forms.

There were 95 items in the preadolescent form and 105 items in the adolescent form of the questionnaire. Approximately half of the content was replicated; on the follow-up form items were dropped which referred specifically to the life situation of the younger child, and new items were added to reflect more fully the increased complexity of interests and social experiences of the adolescent. The self-descriptive sentences of the questionnaire were arranged into clusters of five items each, and *S*s chose one "most" and one "least" characteristic item from each cluster. Items within clusters were approximately equal in social desirability but varied in terms of social-personal orientation, as shown in the following sample clusters from the preadolescent form. Letters in parentheses illustrate scoring of the social-personal orientation measure described below.

I like to play in team games against other schools. (S)
I can usually get kids to stop arguing and make up. (S)
I'd rather figure things out for myself before asking for help. (P)
I'm practically never sick. (P)
My friends spend a lot of time at my house. (S)

and from the adolescent form of the questionnaire:

I usually get along very well with my teachers. (S)
My friends spend a lot of time at my house. (S)
I prefer difficult tasks to easy ones. (P)
People think I have a good sense of humor. (S)
I enjoy many different kinds of recreation. (P)

Two measures were derived from the basic questionnaire: (1) social-personal orientation scores were derived from the content of the self-descriptions. *S* was classified as "socially oriented" if his choices of social items exceeded the number of personal items chosen; *S* was classified as personally oriented if personal items equaled or exceeded social items in his self-description. (2) Self-esteem scores were based upon the congruence between self and ideal-self descriptions. *S*'s score consisted of the number of agreements minus the number of contradictions. The possible range of self-esteem scores extended from —38 to +38 (preadolescent) and from —42 to +42 (adolescent). Actual ranges of self-esteem scores were from —2 to +26 and from —3 to +39, respectively. Stability of self-esteem was measured by classifying as "unstable" the one third of the group who had shifted 10 points or more on the follow-up testing.

The second instrument used in the follow-up study consisted of a modified form Kelly's Role Construct Repertory Test (RCRT) (Kelly, 1955) adapted for mail administration. *Ss* nominated individuals for nine roles (self, mother, father, same-sexed friend, opposite-sexed friend, respected person, pitied person, rejecting person, disliked person). Twelve triads were selected for comparison, and personal constructs were obtained from each of the 12 comparisons. Responses to the RCRT provided three measures: (1) Interpersonal scores were coded from references to relationships between persons or to qualities which imply an interpersonal orientation ("friendly and thoughtful," "push others around"). (2) Egocentric perception of others was inferred from the presence of either derogatory statements ("Selfish, narrow-minded, insane," "both are cheapskates"), or personal references ("I feel inferior to both of them"; "both used to be my boy friends"). (3) Self-disclosure was scored in instances in which *S* disregarded instructions to remove a slip of paper on which he had written his own name and those of other nominees, thus violating the request for anonymity.

In testing major hypotheses, frequency comparisons of *Ss* scoring above and below the medians on the several research variables were evaluated with χ^2 tests. Since the hypotheses involved directional predictions, one-tailed tests were used.

RESULTS

Developmental sex differences in social-personal orientation, predicted by the hypothesis 1, were clearly supported. Where there were no sex differences at the preadolescent level, 6 years later the girls were significantly more socially oriented than the boys ($\chi^2 = 6.24$, $p < .02$). However, directional changes within each sex group were also predicted. The proportions of boys (44 per cent) and girls (46 per cent) showing a change on this measure were equivalent, but the shifts occurred in opposite directions, as predicted. Where 9 girls were socially oriented and 24 personally oriented at preadolescence, 18 were socially oriented and 14 personally oriented 6 years later ($\chi^2 = 4.26$, $p < .05$). The increase in personal orientation among boys (from 7 socially oriented and 9 personally oriented in preadolescence to 2 socially oriented and 14 personally oriented in adolescence) fell just short of statistical significance (binomial test, $p < .07$).

Hypothesis 2 was also supported. There were no sex differences in either the level or the stability of self-esteem; median self-esteem scores for boys and girls were identical at both preadolescent and adolescent levels.

Hypothesis 3 predicted that social orientation at the preadolescent level would foreshadow a drop in self-esteem 6 years later. This was confirmed for girls ($\chi^2 = 4.41$, $p < .05$), but no trends were evident in the boys' data. The corollary that adolescent social orientation would not be related to devalued self-esteem in girls was also supported; with only two socially oriented boys, no test could be made on the male group.

Hypothesis 4—that socially oriented adolescents would use more interpersonal constructs—was not supported. The results showed a mean difference in the predicted direction, but fell considerably short of a reliable difference.

Adolescents low in self-esteem more often indicated egocentric perception of others on the RCRT ($\chi^2 = 4.77$, $p < .05$), confirming Hypothesis 5. The final prediction—that low self-esteem subjects would more often disclose their identities on an anonymous questionnaire—was confirmed for girls ($zU = 2.73$, $p < .004$), but this relationship did not hold up among boys.

DISCUSSION

While these findings, based upon preliminary measures and a restricted sample, do not allow broad generalizations, they would seem to have important implications for research on the basic problem. Based on a longitudinal study, the findings captured something of the process of change in the self-image which goes with adolescent development and add support to generalizations that have previously rested upon cross-sectional data. Self-esteem and social-personal orientation emerge as independent dimensions of the self-image which enter into different kinds of functional relationships with other aspects of personality.

Despite the differences in method, the present findings with regard to self-esteem are consistent with Engel's earlier data, suggesting that self-esteem is a relatively stable dimension of the self, and one which is independent of sex role. Social-personal orientation, on the other hand, appears to mirror the divergent processes of masculine and feminine character development among adolescents in our culture. The results also offer further warnings that the meaning of a personality dimension is dependent upon the developmental level of the individual and that sex differences must be considered in conceptualizing the development and dynamics of the self-image.

REFERENCES

Carlson, Rae. Identification and personality structure in preadolescents. *J. abnorm. soc. Psychol.,* 1963, **67,** 566–573.

Douvan, Elizabeth. Sex difference in adolescent character processes. *Merrill-Palmer Quart.,* 1960, **6,** 203–211.

Engel, Mary. The stability of the self-concept in adolescence. *J. abnorm. soc. Psychol.,* 1959, **58,** 211–215.

Hovland, C. I., & Janis, I. L. (Eds.). *Personality and persuasibility.* New Haven: Yale Univer. Press, 1959.

Kelly, G. A. *Psychology of personal constructs.* New York: Norton, 1955.

39
THE DEVELOPMENT OF CHOICE STABILITY IN CHILDREN AND ADOLESCENTS*

JOHN PAUL McKINNEY

A NUMBER OF studies have demonstrated that friendship stability in childhood and adolescence increases with age. This finding has been reported with rural children (3), urban children (6), preadolescents (2), and college students (5). A recent study comparing retarded and normal children (4) indicates that this increased stability is related to mental level.

The subjects in these earlier studies listed their three best friends in the order of preference, and two weeks later listed them again. The amount of change over the two-week period was the index of friendship fluctuation.

The fact that friendship fluctuations decrease with age has been interpreted as an indication of increased social and mental maturity. The question asked in the present study is whether the stability of other choices might also show the same developmental trend. It is predicted that the decrease in friendship fluctuation is a special case of a general pattern of increasing stability of choices with age. Such a prediction does not contradict the earlier interpretation based on social and mental maturity, but suggests a more general dimension of choice stability underlying the specific example of friendship stability.

METHOD

Subjects

The subjects were 156 boys and girls in Grades 2, 4, 6, 8, 10, and 12, enrolled in a parochial elementary school and high school.

---

* From *Journal of Genetic Psychology,* 1968, *113,* 79–83. Reprinted with permission from the author and the Journal Press.

I am indebted to Barbara Carroll, who collected the data for this study, and to Charles Hanley, Lauren Harris, and Ellen Strommen, who provided constructive criticism, and especially to the children at St. Mary's School, Northampton, Mass., who served as subjects.

Procedure

All of the *S*s were tested in their home classrooms with their teachers present. Each child answered a questionnaire which asked his name, age, sex, and grade, and the following nine questions:

1. What are your favorite colors?
2. What are your favorite television programs?
3. What are your favorite desserts?
4. What are our favorite animals?
5. Who are your favorite friends?
6. What are your favorite games?
7. What are your favorite subjects in school?
8. What things do you like to do when there's nothing else to do?
9. What profession or occupation would you like to have when you are thirty years old?

Three spaces were open at the end of each question for the *S*s to write their answers in the preferential order of first, second, and third choice. The *S*s were instructed to give each question careful consideration; and the younger *S*s (second graders) were helped individually, as needed, with instructions, spelling, etc.

Two weeks later the *S*s answered the same questionnaire under identical conditions. They were told that their choices may or may not be the same as their earlier choices, but that they should write their favorite current choices, regardless. In addition they were asked to estimate how long it had been since a first questionnaire.

A fluctuation score for each item was computed for each child by using the procedure described by Horrocks and Thompson (3). For any item, if the choices were the same and were given the same rank order on both occasions, the fluctuation score was zero. If the choices on the second occasion were identical to those given on the first occasion but differed in preferential order, a numerical value of 1 was given for each rank by which any choice had changed. If *S* gave new choices on the second testing, the following numerical values were assigned to the new choices: 2 for a new choice in third place, 3 for a new choice in second place, and 4 for a new choice in first place. The scores for each item for each child were then totaled.

RESULTS

Means and standard deviations were obtained for each item for the males and females in each grade. The combined means are presented in Figure 1.

FIGURE 1

Mean Choice Fluctuation Scores at Each Grade Level.
(numbers in parentheses refer to the number of subjects in each grade)

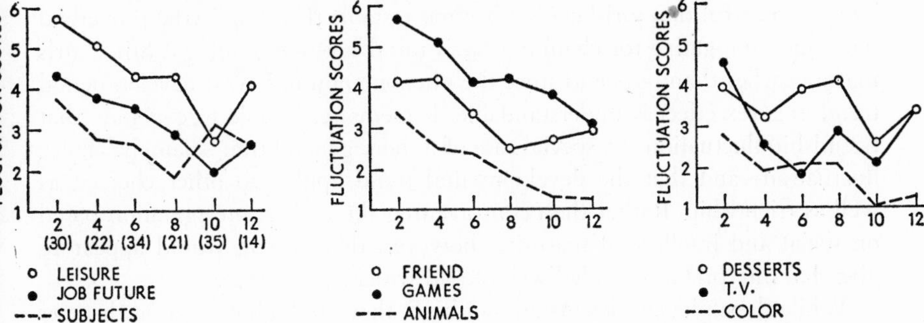

Table 1 gives the results of analyses of variance of log unit transformations of these scores. The major variables in these analyses were grade level and sex of the child. For six of the nine items and for the total score there were significant differences between the grade levels. There were significant differences between the boys and the girls for three items and the total score, indicating greater fluctuation for males than for females. Finally, for the list of nine items reliability coefficients were computed. Since there were too few items to compute an odd-even correlation, Cronbach's alpha (1) was used: The alpha for each grade was as follows: = .41, grade two; = .15, grade four; = .53, grade 6; = .70, grade 8; = —.06, grade 10; = .60, grade 12.

TABLE 1

F Ratios on Choice Fluctuation Scores for Each Item for the Main Effects of Grade Level (df = 5, 144) and Sex (df = 1, 144)

Item	*Grade level*[a]	*Sex*[b]
1. Color	2.52*	.01
2. TV program	1.33	5.13*
3. Dessert	3.28**	1.39
4. Animal	2.16	10.66**
5. Friend	1.16	1.89
6. Game	4.35**	.70
7. School subject	2.96*	1.96
8. Leisure activity	6.24**	7.34**
9. Occupation	2.31*	2.01
10. Total of items 1 thru 9	8.83**	12.68**

[a] Fluctuation *decreases* with grade level (see Figure 1).
[b] For each item, the mean fluctuation score was higher for males than for females.
* $p < .05$.
** $p < .01$.

CONCLUSIONS

These results substantiate the view that choice stability increases with age. They also reveal that girls' choices are more stable than boys' (the proverbial feminine prerogative for changing one's mind notwithstanding). Since girls mature earlier than boys and since the phenomenon follows a developmental trend, this sex effect is understandable. It seems reasonable to conclude that friendship fluctuation is a special case of a more general trait—namely, choice fluctuation—and that the developmental trend applies to other choices, as well as friendship. Rather than contravening the earlier interpretation based on social and intellectual maturity, however, this finding would appear to give that interpretation added weight and wider significance.

While the alpha coefficients are not high, they are high enough at three of the upper grade levels to be suggestive of an underlying dimension of choice stability. The simplicity of the technique for measuring such a potential dimension would argue for lengthening the questionnaire and attempting to rule out other interpretations. For example, the dimension might be largely a memory factor, although this was guarded against in the present study by telling the subjects that their second choices may or may not be identical to their earlier choices. If such alternate interpretations could be ruled out, and a choice stability dimension could be measured reliably, one might look for correlates other than age, mental maturity, and sex. What antecedent conditions give rise to permanence of choice? Is this one aspect of a construct of commitment which may also include intensity of choice? Does environmental stability, including such things as changes in the family structure, frequent changes in geographic location, etc. affect the permanence with which a child will state a preference?

SUMMARY

One hundred fifty-six boys and girls in Grades 2, 4, 6, 8, 10, and 12 were asked to respond to a questionnaire asking them to name their three favorite friends, games, animals, leisure activities, occupations, school subjects, TV programs, colors, and desserts. Two weeks later they were asked to complete an identical questionnaire. Results indicate a significant decrease in choice fluctuation with age and a significant sex difference, girls showing greater choice stability than boys. Moderate correlations (alpha) at three of the upper grade levels are suggestive of an underlying dimension of choice stability.

REFERENCES

1. Cronbach, L. J. Coefficient alpha and the internal structure of tests. *Psychometrika,* 1951, **16**, 297–334.

2. Horrocks, J. E., & Buker, M. E. A study of friendship fluctuations of preadolescents. *J. Genet. Psychol.,* 1951, **78,** 131–144.
3. Horrocks, J. E., & Thompson, G. G. A study of the friendship fluctuations of rural boys and girls. *J. Genet. Psychol.,* 1946, **69,** 189–198.
4. Kay, C. L., & McKinney, J. P. Friendship fluctuation in normal and retarded children. *J. Genet. Psychol.,* 1967, **110,** 233–241.
5. Skorepa, C. A., Horrocks, J. E., & Thompson, G. G. A study of friendship fluctuations of college students. *J. Genet. Psychol.,* 1963, **102,** 151–157.
6. Thompson, G. G., & Horrocks, J. E. A study of friendship fluctuations of urban boys and girls. *J. Genet. Psychol.,* 1947, **70,** 53–63.

Indexes

AUTHOR INDEX

K

L

M

N

O

P

T

SUBJECT INDEX

R

S

This book has been set in 11 and 10 point Granjon, leaded 1 point. Part and chapter numbers are in Helvetica Medium; part and chapter titles are in Granjon. The size of the type page is 27 by 45½ picas.